Resolving Disputes

ASPEN PUBLISHERS

Resolving Disputes
Theory, Practice, and Law

Second Edition

Jay Folberg

Professor and Former Dean
University of San Francisco Law School

Dwight Golann

Professor
Suffolk University Law School

Thomas J. Stipanowich

Academic Director, Straus Institute for Dispute Resolution and Professor
Pepperdine University School of Law

Lisa A Kloppenberg

Professor and Dean
University of Dayton School of Law

 Wolters Kluwer
Law & Business

AUSTIN   BOSTON   CHICAGO   NEW YORK   THE NETHERLANDS

To contact Customer Care, e-mail *customer.care@aspenpublishers.com*,
call 1-800-234-1660, fax 1-800-901-9075, or mail correspondence to:

Aspen Publishers
Attn: Order Department
PO Box 990
Frederick, MD 21705

Printed in the United States of America.

2 3 4 5 6 7 8 9 0

ISBN 978-0-7355-8901-8

Library of Congress Cataloging-in-Publication Data

Resolving disputes : theory, practice, and law / Jay Folberg . . . [et al.]. — 2nd ed.
   p. cm.
  ISBN 978-0-7355-8901-8
  1. Dispute resolution (Law) — United States. 2. Compromise (Law) — United States. I.
Folberg, Jay, 1941-
  KF9084.R475 2010
  347.73'9 — dc22

2009053341

About Wolters Kluwer Law & Business

Wolters Kluwer Law & Business is a leading provider of research information and workflow solutions in key specialty areas. The strengths of the individual brands of Aspen Publishers, CCH, Kluwer Law International and Loislaw are aligned within Wolters Kluwer Law & Business to provide comprehensive, in-depth solutions and expert-authored content for the legal, professional and education markets.

CCH was founded in 1913 and has served more than four generations of business professionals and their clients. The CCH products in the Wolters Kluwer Law & Business group are highly regarded electronic and print resources for legal, securities, antitrust and trade regulation, government contracting, banking, pension, payroll, employment and labor, and healthcare reimbursement and compliance professionals.

Aspen Publishers is a leading information provider for attorneys, business professionals and law students. Written by preeminent authorities, Aspen products offer analytical and practical information in a range of specialty practice areas from securities law and intellectual property to mergers and acquisitions and pension/benefits. Aspen's trusted legal education resources provide professors and students with high-quality, up-to-date and effective resources for successful instruction and study in all areas of the law.

Kluwer Law International supplies the global business community with comprehensive English-language international legal information. Legal practitioners, corporate counsel and business executives around the world rely on the Kluwer Law International journals, loose-leafs, books and electronic products for authoritative information in many areas of international legal practice.

Loislaw is a premier provider of digitized legal content to small law firm practitioners of various specializations. Loislaw provides attorneys with the ability to quickly and efficiently find the necessary legal information they need, when and where they need it, by facilitating access to primary law as well as state-specific law, records, forms and treatises.

Wolters Kluwer Law & Business, a unit of Wolters Kluwer, is headquartered in New York and Riverwoods, Illinois. Wolters Kluwer is a leading multinational publisher and information services company.

SUMMARY OF CONTENTS

CONTENTS

CHAPTER 6
GENDER, CULTURE, AND RACE   173

CHAPTER 10
A DEEPER LOOK INTO THE PROCESS   299

CHAPTER 13
SPECIFIC APPLICATIONS   407

PART III

ARBITRATION 535

CHAPTER 16
ARBITRATION—THE BIG PICTURE 537

CHAPTER 17
ARBITRATION AGREEMENTS, PROCEDURES, AND AWARDS   **561**

CHAPTER 18
THE LEGAL FRAMEWORK SUPPORTING ARBITRATION

CHAPTER 19
FAIRNESS IN ARBITRATION:
DEVELOPMENTS IN EMPLOYMENT, CONSUMER,
AND "ADHESION" CONTEXTS   691

PREFACE

The title of this book, *Resolving Disputes*, reflects the active role of lawyers in representing clients who retain us to conclude their disputes favorably. This text is based on three key assumptions: First, in order to represent clients effectively and craft successful outcomes, the next generation of lawyers must be able to use the full spectrum of dispute resolution options and match the appropriate process to the dispute. Second, new lawyers are much more likely to encounter dispute resolution processes as advocates or advisors to clients than as professional neutrals. Finally, a text on dispute resolution should be interesting to read and should bring together the latest and best writing on the use and limits of alternative dispute resolution (ADR).

Our book, therefore, has a different emphasis from most other ADR texts. It is written from the perspective of a lawyer representing clients, rather than for someone negotiating for themselves or serving as a neutral. The text is practical, while grounded in theory. The material is lawyer focused, but enriched by interdisciplinary knowledge. The readings are current yet do not neglect the historical roots of ADR.

Real-life disputes and literary examples are provided to illustrate vividly the readings and pique interest. Ample questions are asked and problems posed to provoke critical thinking about the readings and stimulate class discussion. Accompanying exercises and role-plays allow students to apply the readings and bring the material to life. Most of the exercises and role-plays are based on the types of disputes in which lawyers are most likely to find themselves— significant legal disputes.

We begin the book with an overview of the disputing universe, including the "vanishing trial" and the importance of counseling clients to help them match their dispute to the appropriate resolution process. After an orientation to the full spectrum of dispute resolution and its context for lawyers, we study the lawyer's role in the four categories of alternatives to trial—negotiation, mediation, arbitration, and stepped or hybrid processes. In each section we cover theory, techniques, policy issues, ethics, and law.

The negotiation section starts with the nature of conflict, the role of perceptions and psychological factors. We analyze both competitive and cooperative approaches, with a step-by-step explanation and comparison. The negotiation process and outcome-enhancing skills are covered in detail from preparation to writing the agreement. Students are guided to explore issues of style, gender, culture and race. A rich selection of readings is provided, and additional notes enhance the negotiation coverage, including decision analysis and the use of computer software.

An inside look at the mediation of a prominent student death case and the Microsoft litigation introduces the mediation section. Readings and exercises highlight how lawyers can shape the mediation process to their clients' advantage. We focus on caucus-based mediation because that is the format most students will encounter in law practice, but also discuss alternative approaches such as no-caucus and transformative mediation. In doing so we emphasize the law-yer's role representing clients and ways in which attorneys can take advantage of the mediator's presence to advance their clients' interests. The application of mediation to several important categories of disputes and situations involving lawyers is examined, including family, employment, environmental, intellectual property, victim-offender and business deals. Court-connected mediation and concerns about fairness are also covered.

In the arbitration materials we depart from the traditional emphasis on case decisions, while covering comprehensively the basics of arbitration for lawyers. We provide hands-on exercises that involve scenarios often encountered by new lawyers and narratives on what a lawyer needs to know to maximize clients' interests when drafting an agreement to arbitrate and advocating on their behalf. Concerns about the fairness of mandatory arbitration and other recent developments are also considered. The most important aspect of this second edition is the inclusion of additional discussion problems, procedural practicali-ties, innovations and updates.

The book concludes with a synthesis of conflict management approaches. We review popular court-annexed options as well as corporate and governmental programs using hybrid combinations of negotiation, mediation, and/or arbitra-tion. We preview emerging issues in conflict resolution, including systems design work, online dispute resolution and collaborative law. Finally, we present evolving opportunities for lawyers to become problem solvers for their clients and communities, calling on leaders from Abraham Lincoln to modern judges to inspire readers.

This new edition builds on the First Edition and benefits from the comments of many professors who have adopted it. This edition is updated with the most recent writings on ADR so teachers will not need to prepare supplements in order to assign entirely up-to-date material. Readings have been carefully selected and edited to keep the material interesting and lively. We also take advantage of technology, and of students' increasing preference for electronic and video formats. Items that have traditionally gone into a paper appendix now appear on the book's web site, including a bibliography. This makes this book lighter and easier to carry without sacrificing depth. An accompanying "Teaching DVD," which is available to adopting professors, shows different styles of negotiation and mediation, techniques ranging from empathic listen-ing to evaluation, as well as other examples coordinated with student role-plays.

A note about form: In order to focus discussion and conserve space, we have substantially edited the readings and have deleted most footnotes, references, and case citations. Excerpts from other publications are referenced only with the beginning page of the original source. Deletions of material are shown by three dots, but omitted footnotes and other references are not indicated.

This book is the culmination of our combined decades of teaching, practic-ing, and shaping dispute resolution in legal contexts. Although our acknowl-edgments follow, we are grateful to the many students and lawyers we have had the pleasure of teaching and from whom we have learned much about what they want in a dispute resolution text. We are also thankful to the professors who have suggested corrections and improvements for this new edition.

January 2010   J.F.
                                                                          D.G.
                                                                          T.S.
                                                                          L.K.

ACKNOWLEDGMENTS

This book, like ADR, has many mothers and fathers, as well as a supportive family too large to thank by name. We are most grateful to our past students who have inspired us and guided what we have selected here to present to the next generation of students. We are indebted to the many authors and publishers who have granted their permission for us to include and edit parts of their publications. We are thankful for the support and assistance we have received from the staffs of our respective institutions. Special thanks go to the anonymous reviewers, whose comments were incisive and extremely helpful in refining both the original text and this Second Edition.

The genesis of the book was a fellowship from the Rockefeller Foundation that allowed then Dean Folberg to spend a month at the Foundation's Bellagio Center completing an outline of the contents and writing a publishing proposal. Aspen Acquisition Editor Lynn Churchill was ever helpful and has continued to provide encouragement. Managing Editor Eric Holt has guided us along the way, and our editor of this Second Edition, Christie Rears, has kept us on track and tried to make us look good.

Jay Folberg thanks the management, neutrals, and staff of JAMS, who have provided the model of ADR success and inspiration that demonstrate what professional ADR can accomplish. Jay is particularly grateful to Jay Welsh and David Brandon for their collegial support and good cheer.

Dwight Golann would like to recognize Suffolk University Law School for supporting his work in a myriad of ways, Frank Sander, whose encouragement and example brought him into the field of ADR, and the many lawyers and parties who, by submitting their disputes to a peaceful process, tested and helped the authors to develop the theories and advice set forth in this book.

Tom Stipanowich thanks his family for their inspiration and continuing patience. He also thanks his colleagues at Pepperdine University School of Law and the Straus Institute for Dispute Resolution for their help in enriching these materials—and providing a laboratory for the development of new practical exercises. He is also grateful for the research assistance of law librarian Gina McCoy and law students Aly Challoner, Li Meng and Catie Royal.

Lisa Kloppenberg expresses her thanks to her family—Mark, Kelly, Tim, and Nick Zunich—who supported this work with great patience, love, and generosity. She is grateful to her colleagues at the University of Dayton who understood the importance of this project. Finally, Dean Kloppenberg is indebted to the excellent effort of her assistant, Kathleen Duell, and student research assistants who helped with this edition: Kelly Diggins, Michael Eshelman, Cara (Ziegelgruber) Hurak, Adam Petty, David Simmons, and Megan Thomas.

Again, we thank the professors who have suggested corrections and improvements for this Second Edition.

We are grateful to the following sources for permission to publish excerpts of their work:

Aaron, Marjorie, and David Hoffer, on Decision Analysis in Dwight Golann, Mediating Legal Disputes. Copyright © 1996 by Dwight Golann. Reprinted with permission.

Abramson, Harold, Mediation Representation: Advocating in a Problem-Solving Process. Copyright © 2004 by the National Institute for Trial Advocacy (NITA). Reprinted with permission from the National Institute for Trial Advocacy. Further reproduction is prohibited.

Adler, Robert S., and Elliot M. Silverstein, "When David Meets Goliath: Dealing with Power Differentials in Negotiations," 5 Harvard Negotiation Law Review 1. Copyright © 2000. Reprinted with permission.

Ambrose, Stephen, Undaunted Courage: Meriwether Lewis, Thomas Jefferson and the Opening of the American West. Abridged by permission of Simon & Schuster, Inc. Copyright © 1996 by Ambrose & Ambrose, Inc.

Arnold, Thomas, "Client Preparation for Mediation," 15 Corporate Counsel Quarterly 2:52 (April 1999). Copyright © 1999 by Tom Arnold, Esq. Reprinted with permission.

Arnold, Tom, "20 Common Errors in Mediation Advocacy," 13 Alternatives 69 (1995). Copyright © 1995. Reprinted with permission of John Wiley & Sons, Inc.

Bahadoran, Sina, "A Red Flag: Mediator Cultural Bias in Divorce Mediation," 18 Massachusetts Family Law Journal No. 3, 69. Copyright © 2000. Reprinted with permission of the author.

Bazerman, Max H., and Malhorta, Deepax, "Negotiation Genius: How to Overcome Obstacles and Achieve Brilliant Results at the Bargaining Table and Beyond." From Negotiation Genius: How to Overcome Obstacles and Achieve Brilliant Results at the Bargaining Table and Beyond Copyright © 2007 by Deepak Malhotra and Max H. Bazerman. Used by permission of Bantam Books, a division of Random House, Inc.

Binder, David A., Bergman, Paul, Price, Susan, "Lawyers as Counselors: A Client Centered Approach" Second Edition, Copyright © 2004 by The West Group. Reprinted with permission.

Birke, Richard, "Decision Trees — Made Easy" Copyright © 2004 by Richard Birke. Reprinted with permission.

Bowling, Daniel, and David Hoffman, "Bringing Peace into the Room: The Personal Qualities of the Mediator and Their Impact on the Mediation," 16 Negotiation Journal 5. Copyright © 2000 by Blackwell Publishers Ltd. Reprinted with permission.

Brazil, Wayne, "ADR in A Civil Action: What Could Have Been," Dispute Resolution, 13:4, p. 25 Copyright © 2007 by the American Bar Association. Reprinted with permission.

Brazil, Wayne D., "Why Should Courts Offer Non-Binding ADR Services?" 16 Alternatives 65 (May 1998). Copyright ß 1998. Reprinted with permission of John Wiley & Sons, Inc.

Bryant, Ken, and Dana Curtis, Reframing. Reprinted with permission of the authors.

Kolb, Deborah M., and Judith Williams, "Introduction: Recognizing the Shadow Negotiation." Reprinted with permission of Simon & Schuster Adult Publishing Group. From The Shadow Negotiation: How Women Can Master the Hidden Agendas That Determine Bargaining Success by Deborah M. Kolb, Ph.D., and Judith Williams, Ph.D. Copyright © 2000 by Deborah M. Kolb, Ph.D., and Judith Williams, Ph.D.

Korobkin, Russell, "A Positive Theory of Legal Negotiation," 88 Georgetown Law Review 1789. Copyright © 2000. Reprinted with permission.

Korobkin, Russell, Michael Moffit, and Nancy Welsh, "The Law of Bargaining," 87 Marquette Law Review 4, 839-842 (2004). Reprinted with permission.

Kritzer, Herbert M., "Fee Arrangements and Negotiation," 21 Law & Society Review. Copyright © 1987. Reprinted with permission.

Laflin, James, and Robert Werth, "Unfinished Business: Another Look at the Microsoft Mediation," 12 California Tort Reporter No. 3, 88 (April 2001). Reprinted with permission.

Lax, David A., and James K. Sebenius. "The Manager as Negotiator: Bargaining For Cooperation and Competitive Gain," Copyright © 1986 by David A. Lax and James K. Sebenius. All rights reserved.

Levin cartoon, © The New Yorker Collection 1982 from cartoonbank.com. All Rights Reserved.

Longan, Patrick, "Ethics in Settlement Negotiations: Foreword," 52 Mercer Law Review 810-816. Copyright © 2001. Reprinted with permission.

Lela Love, "The Top Ten Reasons Why Mediators Should Not Evalutate," 24 FL. ST. U. L. REV. Copyright © 1997. Reprinted with permission from Florida State University Law Review.

McGuire, James E., "Certification: An Idea Whose Time Has Come," Dispute Resolution, 10: 4, p. 22. Copyright © 2004 by the American Bar Association. Reprinted with permission.

McGuire, James E., and Frank E.A. Sander, "Some Questions About 'The Vanishing Trial," Dispute Resolution, 9:2, p. 17-18. Copyright © 2004 by the American Bar Association. Reprinted with permission.

Mcllwrath, Michael, "Can Mediation Evolve into a Global Profession?" Mediate.com. Copyright © 2009 by Michael Mcllwrath. Reprinted with permission.

Miller, Lee E., and Jessica Miller, "A Woman's Guide to Successful Negotiating," pp. 66-73 (2002). Reproduced with permission of the McGraw-Hill Companies.

Milne, Ann L., "Mediation and Domestic Abuse," in Folberg et al., Divorce and Family Mediation. Copyright © 2004 by Guilford Press. Reprinted with permission of the Guilford Press.

Mnookin, Robert H., Scott R. Peppet, and Andrew S. Tulumello. Reprinted by permission of the publisher from Beyond Winning: Negotiation to Create Value in Deals and Disputes by Robert H. Mnookin, Scott R. Peppet, and Andrew S. Tulumello, pp. 37-42, 282-286, Cambridge, MA: The Belknap Press of Harvard University Press. Copyright © 2000 by the President and Fellows of Harvard College.

Nelken, Melissa. Reprinted from Understanding Negotiation with permission. Copyright © 2007 Matthew Bender & Company, Inc., a member of the LexisNexis Group. All rights reserved.

O'Connor, Theron, "Planning and Executing an Effective Concession Strategy." Reprinted with permission of the author.

Peppet, Scott R., "Mindfulness in the Law and ADR: Can Saints Negotiate?" 7 Harvard Negotiation Law Review 83. Copyright © 2002. Reprinted with permission.

Phillips, Peter, "A Suitability Screen for Arbitration" Copyright © 2004 CPR Institute for Dispute Resolution, 366 Madison Avenue, New York, NY 10017-3122; (212) 949-6490, www.cpradr.org. This excerpt from A Suitability Screen for Arbitration reprinted with permission of CPR Institute. The CPR Institute is a nonprofit initiative of 500 general counsel of major corporations, leading law firms and prominent legal academics whose mission is to install alternative dispute resolution (ADR) into the mainstream of legal practice.

Phillips, Peter, ed., How Companies Manage Employment Disputes. Copyright © 2003 CPR Institute for Dispute Resolution, 366 Madison Avenue, New York, NY 10017-3122; (212) 949-6490, www.cpradr.org. This excerpt from How Companies Manage Employment Disputes reprinted with permission of CPR Institute. The CPR Institute is a nonprofit initiative of 500 general counsel of major corporations, leading law firms and prominent legal academics whose mission is to install alternative dispute resolution (ADR) into the mainstream of legal practice.

Picker, Bennet G., Navigating Relationships: The Invisible Barriers to Resolution. .2 Amer. J. of Mediation 41. Copyright © 2008 CRP Institute for Dispute Resolution. Reprinted with permission of the author.

Poswall, John M., The Lawyers: Class of '69. Reprinted with permission.

Price, Marty, "Personalizing Crime: Mediation Produces Restorative Justice for Victims and Offenders," Dispute Resolution, 7:1, p. 8-11. Copyright © 2000 by the American Bar Association. Reprinted by permission.

Reno, Janet. This excerpt from "The Federal Government and Appropriate Dispute Resolution: Promoting Problem Solving and Peacemaking as Enduring Values in Our Society" is reprinted from Into the 21st Century: Thought Pieces on Lawyering, Problem Solving and ADR, 19 Alternatives (CPR Institute January 2001).

Riskin, Leonard, "Retiring and Replacing the Grid of Mediator Orientations," 21 Alternatives to the High Costs of Litigation, No. 4, 69 (April 2003). Copyright © 2003. Reprinted with permission of John Wiley & Sons, Inc.

Rosenberg, Joshua D., "Interpersonal Dynamics Helping Lawyers Learn the Skills, and the Importance of Human Relationships in the Practice of Law," 55 University of Miami Law Review. Copyright © 2004 by the University of Miami Law Review. Reprinted with permission.

Rubin, Jeffrey Z., "Some Wise and Mistaken Assumptions About Conflict and Negotiation," in William Breslin and Jeffrey Rubin, eds, Negotiation

Theory and Practice, pp. 3-10, Copyright © 1991. 27 American Behavior Scientist (November/December 1983). Reprinted with permission of the author and the Journal of Dispute Resolution, University of Missouri-Columbia, Center for the Study of Dispute Resolution, 206 Hulston Hall, Columbia, MO 65211.

Rule, Colin, Online Dispute Resolution for Business: B2B, Ecommerce, Consumer, Employment, Insurance, and Other Commercial Conflicts. Copyright © 2002. Reprinted with permission of John Wiley & Sons, Inc.

Salacuse, Jeswald, "Mediation in International Business." Copyright © Jacob Bercovitch. From Mediation in International Relations: Multiple Approaches to Conflict Management by Jacob Bercovitch. Reprinted with permission of Palgrave Macmillan.

Salem, Richard, "The Benefits of Empathic Listening" (2003). Reprinted from beyondintractability.org with permission of the Conflict Research Consortium, University of Colorado.

Saperstein, Guy T., Civil Warrior: Memoirs of a Civil Rights Attorney. Copyright © 2003 by Guy T. Saperstein. Reprinted by permission of Berkeley Hills Books.

Sebenius, James K., "Caveats for Cross-Border Negotiations," Negotiation. Journal 18, 122-123, 126-131. Copyright © 2002 by Blackwell Publishers Ltd. Reprinted with permission.

Shell, G. Richard, "The Second Foundation: Your Goals and Expectations," from Bargaining for Advantage by G. Richard Shell, Copyright © 1999, 2006. Used by permission of Viking Penguin, a division of Penguin Group (USA) Inc.

Shell, G. Richard, "Step Four: Closing and Gaining Commitment," from Bargaining for Advantage, by G. Richard Shell. Copyright © 1999, 2006 by G. Richard Shell. Used by permission of Viking Penguin, a division of Penguin Group (USA) Inc.

Singer, Linda R. This excerpt from "The Lawyer as Neutral" is reprinted from Into the 21st Century: Thought Pieces on Lawyering, Problem Solving and ADR, 19 Alternatives (CPR Institute January 2001).

Smith, Robert M., "Advocacy in Mediation: A Dozen Suggestions," 26 San Francisco Attorney 14 (June/July 2000). Copyright © 2000 by the Bar Association of San Francisco. Reprinted with permission.

Stipanowich, Thomas J., "ADR and the Vanishing Trial: The Growth and Impact of 'Alternative Dispute Resolution,'" 10:4, pp. 7-10. Dispute Resolution. Copyright © 2004 by the American Bar Association. Reprinted with permission. 1 J. Empirical Legal Res. (2004). Reprinted by permission.

Stipanowich, Thomas J., "ADR and the Vanishing Trial: What We Know – and What We Don't," Dispute Resolution, 10:4, pp. 7-10. Copyright © 2004 by the American Bar Association. Reprinted with Permission.

Townsend, John, "Drafting Arbitration Clauses: Avoiding the 7 Deadly Sins," From 2003 Dispute Resolution Journal 58:1. Copyright © 2003 by the American Bar Association. Reprinted with Permission.

Technology Mediation Services, "Benefits of Mediating High Technology Disputes," www.technologymediation.com/hightech.htm. Copyright © 2004 by Technology Mediation Services. Reprinted with permission.

Uelmen, Gerald F., "Playing 'Godfather'" in Settlement Negotiations: The Ethics of Using Threats, California Litigation, pp. 3-8 (Fall 1990). Reprinted with permission.

Ukishima, Allyson, "Women and Legal Negotiation: Moving Beyond Gender Stereotypes and Adopting a 'Yin and Yang' Paradigm," University of San Francisco (Spring 2003). Reprinted with permission of the author.

Welsh, Nancy, and Barbara McAdoo, "Alternative Dispute Resolution in Minnesota—An Update on Rule 114," in Edward J. Bergman and John C. Bickerman, eds., Court-Annexed Mediation: Critical Perspectives on State and Federal Programs 203 (1998). Printed by permission of Pike & Fischer, Inc.

Wetlaufer, Gerald, "The Limits of Integrative Bargaining," 85 Georgetown Law Journal 369. Copyright © 1996. Reprinted with permission.

White, James J., "Pros and Cons of 'Getting to Yes'; Roger Fisher, Comments on White's Review," 34 Journal of Legal Education. Copyright © 1984. Reprinted with permission.

Williams, Gerald R., and Carver, Charles, "Legal Negotiation." Copyright © 2007 by The West Group. Reprinted with permission.

Wissler, Roselle, "To Evaluate or Facilitate? Parties' Perceptions of Mediation Affected by Mediator Style," 2001, Dispute Resolution, 7:2, p. 35. Copyright © 2001 by the American Bar Association. Reprinted with permission.

Wittenberg, Carol A., Susan T. Mackenzie, and Margaret L. Shaw, "Employment Disputes," in Dwight Golann, Mediating Legal Disputes. Copyright © 1996. Reprinted with permission of the author.

Zitrin, Richard A., and Carol M. Langford, "The Moral Compass of the American Lawyer." From The Moral Compass of the American Lawyer, Copyright © 1999 by Richard Zitrin and Carol M. Langford. Used by permission of Ballantine Books, a division of Random House, Inc.

Resolving Disputes

CHAPTER
1

Dispute Resolution — What It's All About

"I found the old format much more exciting . . . "

It is a popular legend that the use of lawyers for dispute resolution evolved from the hiring of gladiators to fight the battles of those who retained them. Referring to lawyers as "modern-day gladiators" is, however, a misnomer. It is the parties who now bear most of the costs, risks, and injuries of legal combat. There have evolved multiple formats to resolve legal disputes, so today's lawyer when advising and representing clients must be familiar with available alternatives for dispute resolution and skillful in their use.

The purpose of this course and this book is to provide you with the knowledge to counsel clients about the most appropriate process to resolve their dispute and to enhance your ability to represent them in the process chosen. The story about a carpenter with only a hammer and nails who has but one way to fix things is analogous to the limitations of a lawyer who only knows how to resolve disputes in court or a gladiator who only knows how to fight.

A.   The Landscape of Disputes

The landscape of disputes that you will encounter in practice will depend on the path you choose. If you become a transactional lawyer, you will help clients to evaluate and structure potential deals, and then will be called upon to negotiate terms that give them the greatest advantages and least possible risk. Clients will respect you for your ability to keep them out of disputes. They will value you most highly for your skill in bringing disparate parties together into productive agreements. Your ability to bargain well and be a problem solver will be crucial to your success as a deal maker.

If you become an inside counsel to a corporation or nonprofit organization, you will negotiate regularly as well, both with your counterparts in other entities and with colleagues in your own office. You may be surprised to learn that experienced corporate counsel often describe themselves not only as experienced negotiators, but also as "Mediators with a small 'm'." What this means is that many inside counsel find that a major aspect of their work is to resolve disagreements and disputes between people within their company. Inside lawyers often find that they in fact have multiple "clients" in the form of different personalities and constituencies in their organization. Unless their constituencies can agree on a common course of action, it is very difficult for the attorney to produce a coherent legal policy or negotiate effectively with outsiders. Corporate counsel thus often find themselves playing the role of "honest broker," using mediative skills to forge a consensus among their multidimensional client.

If you become a civil litigator, the disputing landscape you encounter will bear little resemblance to the public perception of lawyers in courtroom dramas. The birth of civil disputes and the role of lawyers in resolving them, which is the focus of this book, can be understood by imagining a fat triangle with the bottom base composed of a vast array of human interactions. The reason the triangle narrows from its broad base is that most interaction, whether social, work related, commercial, or recreational, does not result in economic loss or harm that we perceive as due to the actions or inactions of others. As we move up the triangle, even if we experience harm and think someone is at fault, we tend to absorb the harm, particularly if minor.

So what pushes some people to pursue redress and give birth to disputes for which they might engage a lawyer? A helpful response to this question comes in an article by Felstiner, Abel, and Sarat (1981). The authors describe the process by which harms become disputes through a sequence of "naming, blaming, and claiming." Naming means that people must recognize they have been harmed and want to do something about it. The distinguishing factor is not awareness of the harm, but rather the victims' subjective reactions to it. Rather than accepting the harm as fate or one of the risks of life and moving on, they feel this particular harm is too great, or is one harm too many.

In the next step, blaming, the person harmed assigns fault for the injury; he identifies a wrongdoer and holds that person or institution responsible for the harm. This, however, doesn't ripen into a dispute until the aggrieved party decides to assert himself by making a claim against the perceived wrongdoer and asking that the wrong be remedied. This is called claiming. But, there is no dispute yet unless the claim is rejected or the response is not satisfactory.

Some claims that are denied go no further because they are abandoned for reasons unique to that claimant or the situation. Other claims are pursued through informal mechanisms, like better business bureaus, complaint hotlines, trade association mechanisms, and government agencies, without the help of lawyers. A very small percentage of unmet claims are brought by clients to lawyers in the form of disputes to be resolved.

Many of the disputes that clients bring to litigators never become court cases. Good lawyers perform an important screening function, measuring their client's grievances against the requirements of the law and, perhaps even more critically, the client's larger interests.

Is there a viable legal theory on which to base a case? Will discovery produce factual evidence that supports a claim? Will the client be willing to persevere after his initial anger and frustration have died down, and does he have the resources to do so? Is it in the client's best long-term interest to be involved in litigation? Is a court likely to side with him, and even if it does, will the potential defendant be able to satisfy a judgment? Just as very few screenplays ever become movies, the large majority of potential legal cases fall by the wayside long before they reach a courtroom.

Assertion of the claim by a lawyer may result in providing the relief requested or negotiation of a mutually satisfactory outcome. If not, further cost-benefit analysis may result in a decision to drop the matter. If the claim is formalized by the lawyer in to a lawsuit, there are usually further negotiations. Some lawsuits are not contested and go by default. If contested, mediation, arbitration, or other alternative dispute resolution (ADR) mechanisms may resolve the case without the need for a trial. Motions and summary proceedings may also end the case without a trial. Between 1 and 3 percent of civil cases filed in court are actually tried. (See Bureau of Justice Statistics, 2009.) This is the point of the triangle. In simplified form, the triangle might look like this:

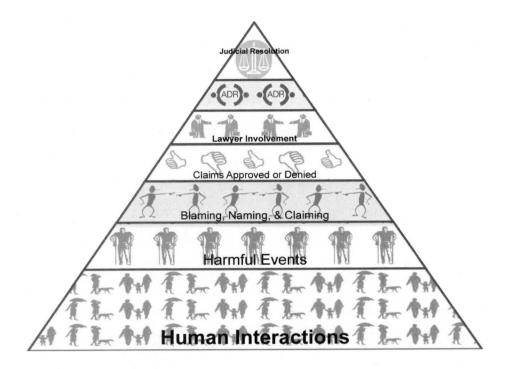

One important qualification needs to be noted when considering the relatively small number of cases going to trial. The possibility of going to trial has an impact on the dispute resolution landscape out of proportion to the actual frequency of trials. A major factor motivating parties to choose settlement is their wish to avoid the risks of trial. In other words, we bargain in the "shadow of the law." Decisions about whether, and on what terms, to settle a dispute are heavily influenced by predictions and concerns about what a court will do if an agreement is not reached (see Mnookin and Kornhauser, 1979).

Questions

1. Have you experienced a personal injury or an economic loss attributable to someone against whom you did not pursue a claim? If so, why did you not assert a claim?
2. What are other reasons why someone may forgo or "lump" a valid legal claim for damages?
3. Have friends or family asked you, as a law student, if they should pursue a claim for an injury or a wrong? What did you advise them and why?
4. Are those with higher education and higher income more or less likely to pursue claims related to products they buy?

B. Dispute Resolution Alternatives — The Spectrum

As a practicing lawyer, you will have a wide variety of options to resolve your clients' disputes. They fall along a spectrum. At one end is direct negotiation; at the other end is a trial in court. Negotiation and trial are polar opposites. Parties who opt for trial have relatively little control over either the process or the outcome: The proceeding is a formal and public one, conducted under detailed procedural and evidentiary rules, with a judge in control. A third party — either a judge or jury — decides the outcome, and in doing so is bound to follow established legal principles. By contrast, negotiation gives parties maximum control over both the process and its outcome. Direct bargaining is an informal process, generally conducted in private and without set rules. Parties are free to agree to whatever outcomes they wish, subject to limits of contract law and public policy in enforcing their agreement.

In between direct negotiation and trial is a continuum of ADR processes, or what is often referred to as appropriate dispute resolution. The continuum moves from processes that have characteristics very similar to negotiation to ones that closely resemble a trial. The key characteristic that distinguishes negotiation-like processes from trial-like methods is whether a neutral party has the ability to impose a binding outcome on the participants. Proceedings in which the neutral can decide the result are all forms of adjudication. Processes that authorize the neutral to facilitate, persuade, even pressure parties — but not to impose a result on them — are all forms of assisted negotiation.

Mediators assist negotiators in reaching a settlement, but do not have the power to require disputants to reach agreement or impose a decision. For that reason, mediation and all of its variants are on the non-binding, assisted-negotiation side of the spectrum. By contrast, in traditional arbitration the neutral does have the power to decide the outcome, so arbitration falls on the binding, adjudicative side of the spectrum. However, the terminology can be misleading. One example we will examine is a process known as advisory or judicial arbitration, which does not necessarily result in a binding decision. This is why we present dispute resolution processes as a spectrum of procedural shadings, with the central dividing characteristic or line being whether a neutral has authority to impose a binding outcome on the parties.

As we have noted, whenever a dispute involves a legal claim, the plaintiff can, at least in theory, obtain a binding decision from a court. The elephant in the closet of non-binding settlement efforts is the likely outcome if the dispute proceeds to trial. For this reason a "shadow of adjudication" extends across the non-binding side of the spectrum. Similarly, disputants can halt even a binding procedure by reaching agreement. Settlement negotiations, in effect, lurk in the closet of adjudication: We refer to this as the "shadow of settlement." A graphic presentation of the Dispute Resolution Spectrum is shown below.

The process possibilities on the non-binding side of the spectrum are infinite, limited only by what the parties can create, agree upon, and afford. The spectrum displays the settlement processes and methods that are most often discussed in the literature and commonly used, now or in the recent past. They are arranged in descending order of process and outcome control, moving from free-flowing negotiation on the left toward processes that are more structured and judgmental. The processes are explained in more depth in the chapters that follow.

The variations of arbitration shown on the spectrum are discussed in the arbitration chapters of the book. A key element of arbitration, as compared with trial, is that it is a private process, defined by contract: The parties themselves can, within broad bounds, shape the process and set its rules. Parties can, for example, agree on maximum and minimum amounts that an

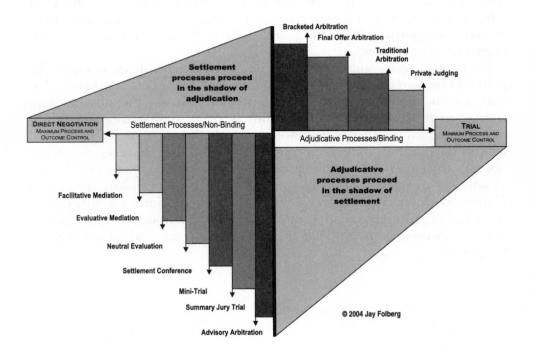

Dispute Resolution Spectrum

arbitrator can award, known as "bracketed" arbitration. Alternatively, they can agree that the arbitrator must enter as her award either the terms proposed by the plaintiff or those submitted by the defendant, but cannot "split the difference" between them; this is known as "final offer" or "baseball" arbitration. Although parties can set the process rules and standards for the arbitrator's decision by contract, once they have agreed on a binding process, they are bound by their choices.

C.   The Evolution of Dispute Resolution

Access to courts to remedy wrongs and enforce legal rights is central to American democracy. We have fashioned a system of rules of procedure and evidence to ensure fair trials. We pride ourselves on having an independent judiciary composed of experienced and respected judges. The Constitution preserves the right to jury trials on common law claims. The judicial system provides for appellate review to ensure that the law is applied correctly and procedural rules are properly followed. It is a complex and finely tuned system of public justice.

However, litigation with all of its procedural protections is slow, costly, and relatively inflexible. The process is also centered on lawyers, restricting the roles and expression of the disputing parties. The remedies available through adjudication are limited to what a court can enforce. Most commonly, a court judgment to resolve a dispute consists of ordering one party to pay money to another.

In part because of these limitations, alternatives to adjudication have long existed. Private negotiation of disputes and transactions has probably gone on literally since the beginning of human society, and third parties have helped people informally resolve conflicts since there were three people on earth. The early Quakers in the United States used mediation and arbitration as the principal means to resolve trade disputes and marital disagreements, and arbitration was used by merchants in pre-Revolutionary New York. Immigrants brought informal dispute resolution systems with them to the New World. Chinese immigrants, for example, set up Chinese Benevolent Associations to decide disputes between community and family members, and the American Jewish community reestablished its own dispute resolution forum, the Jewish Conciliation Board, in New York City (see Folberg, 1983).

Beginning in the 1960s the United States saw a flowering of interest in alternative forms of dispute resolution. The period was characterized by strife, conflict, and discontent on many fronts. The Vietnam War, civil rights struggles, student unrest, growing consumer awareness, challenges to gender roles, and protests against racial discrimination all produced distrust of the status quo and more demand for court redress. Legislation created many new causes of action, reflecting society's lower tolerance for perceived wrongs. Conflicts that in the past might have been resolved by deference, avoidance, or resignation were directed to the courts. Increased prosecution of drug-related crimes, which have a constitutionally based priority to speedy trial, also increased the demands on the courts. Court resources were not increased proportionately, and civil case dockets became more back-logged.

Domestic relations case filings also soared. With the adoption of no-fault divorce and the general increase in the divorce rate, court-connected family mediation services proliferated, partly to conserve judicial resources and partly to provide better outcomes for children. Parents more readily accepted a custody and visitation plan that they created with the help of a court mediator than one imposed by a judge and filed fewer post-divorce motions following mediation. This served as an example of how courts could be more proactive in managing their increasing caseload by providing settlement services (see Folberg, 2003).

At the same time community-based mediation programs grew up outside the courts to resolve neighborhood disputes. Some legal service programs began experimenting with mediating and arbitrating cases in which neither party could afford lawyers. Business people, who could afford lawyers but could not afford to wait for a court trial, increased their use of private arbitration, particularly for time-sensitive cases such as disputes involving ongoing construction projects. As all types of civil suits became more complex and expensive to prepare for trial, through extensive motion practice and use of experts, interest in alternative forms of dispute resolution increased.

Judges, motivated by a wish to relieve civil caseloads and reduce delay, convened bench-bar committees to recommend alternative methods to resolve cases. Local experimentation led to successes that were replicated and refined in other jurisdictions. A rich array of court-connected ADR processes developed. Traditional settlement conferences conducted by judges were augmented and sometimes replaced by more innovative dispute resolution options. Informal "settlement weeks" and case evaluation panels, both using volunteer lawyers, led to institutionalized programs, often imposed by statutes and court rules that required litigants to engage in ADR.

Mediation, often conducted for the court by lawyers in their own offices, became the most popular form of court-directed ADR. Some courts hired full-time staff to direct and manage cases in ADR programs. The Alternative Dispute Resolution Act of 1998 requires all federal district courts to establish an ADR program. Participation in some ADR processes, including early neutral evaluation and mediation, can be compelled in federal courts, as in many state courts.

Although court ADR processes vary greatly, they share some common elements. Court ADR is intended to:

- relieve each attorney from being the one to initiate settlement discussions

- provide a stimulus or requirement for attorneys to explore settlement early
- promote or require involvement of key decision makers
- use attorneys as neutrals to augment judicial resources
- provide more flexibility than formal adjudication
- avoid involving the judge who will preside at trial if there is no settlement

One perhaps unintended consequence of mandatory court-connected ADR programs, particularly mediation, has been to educate attorneys and business executives about the potential of non-binding forms of ADR. Even though most cases entered the court programs involuntarily, satisfaction rates were generally high. Occasional complaints about the quality of volunteer neutrals or bureaucratic restrictions could be remedied by having mutually respected neutrals serve for a fee privately outside the court. Corporate and insurance clients faced with long waits in court and increased litigation expenses pushed for more use of private ADR. Plaintiffs' lawyers, reluctant at first, became more supportive of non-binding, voluntary forms of ADR when they realized that these could speed the collection of damages for clients in need and payment of their contingent fees. Greater efficiency, lower costs, more control, less risk, and improved outcomes were the driving forces for increased use of both court-based and private ADR. The seeds were planted for what would later become a change in the legal culture regarding how disputes are resolved.

Existing private organizations providing ADR services had a growth spurt. The American Arbitration Association, which was arbitrating tens of thousands of cases in the 1980s, expanded and promoted the use of commercial mediation. The Center for Public Resources, now the CPR International Institute for Conflict Prevention & Resolution (CPR Institute), supported primarily by corporate counsel and law firms to promote the use of appropriate dispute resolution, collected pledges from hundreds of major corporations and then law firms promising to use ADR to resolve disputes, rather than pursue litigation against one another. The largest private ADR provider organization founded in 1979 as Judicial Arbitration and Mediation Services, now JAMS, has grown to 23 centers nationwide and has international affiliates. Local and regional groups of attorneys, as well as individual lawyers, retired judges, and others, offer professional ADR services in every legal market. Listings of ADR neutral providers can be found in most telephone directories, and their advertisements are a mainstay of legal newspapers and magazines. Some law firms advertise their expertise in representing clients in ADR proceedings.

Most state bar associations now have active dispute resolution sections. The Dispute Resolution Section of the American Bar Association is one of the largest sections, attracting more than 1,000 participants to its annual meeting and sponsoring numerous publications. Dispute resolution courses, like the one you are taking, are a regular part of law school curriculums.

Some law schools offer LL.M. and certification programs in ADR. Dispute resolution seems to be a growth industry.

Whether due to the ADR movement or other factors, civil filings in some state courts have declined, as ADR has been much more widely used. In California, for instance, civil filings in all state trial courts between 1998 and 2007 decreased over 14 percent, from 1,700,445 to 1,461,111 (Judicial Council of Calif., 2008). As previously noted, there has been a dramatic decrease in both the percentage and actual number of cases going to trial in federal and state courts. In the federal courts, the percentage of civil cases reaching trial fell between 1962 and 2002 from 11 percent to 1.8 percent. Over a 25-year period, the number of jury trials in 22 states shows an absolute decline of more than 25 percent (Galanter, 2004). More recently, civil jury trials in California Superior Courts from 1998 to 2007 decreased over 59 percent, from 1,902 to 767 (Judicial Council of Calif., 2008). The relationship between the decrease in the percentage of filed cases being tried and the increased use of ADR in courts and privately is not clear, but many have pointed to alternative processes as a cause for the change.

The retirement of some judges to become well-paid private mediators and arbitrators, as well as other public policy concerns about the impact of ADR, resulted in the Chief Justice of the California Supreme Court appointing a task force to study the effects of ADR on the quality of justice. The task force found that the opportunity to serve as private ADR neutrals was only one of several possible causes of why judges might be retiring earlier. It also concluded that ADR, whether private, community, or court related, offered litigants and the public the benefit of greater choice, speed, savings, and satisfaction (see Judicial Council of Calif., 1999, ADR Task Force Report, J. Folberg, Chair). The task force recommended several measures to educate the bench, the bar, and the public about the availability of ADR and to gather more information on its effects. As a result, plaintiffs and defendants in all California civil cases now receive ADR information and are provided a form they may use to stipulate to the use of an ADR process (Calif. Rules of Court 3.221). Also, based on a recommendation of the task force, California passed legislation creating court pilot programs to increase the use of early mediation and examine the results. The reading that follows reviews some of the data from the California pilot projects and examines the increased use of ADR by businesses and corporations.

❖ **Thomas J. Stipanowich,** *ADR AND "THE VANISHING TRIAL":
WHAT WE KNOW — AND WHAT WE DON'T*

7-10, Disp. Resol. Mag. (Summer 2004)

Did a quarter-century of proliferating and widely disparate efforts to change the culture of conflict resolution — encompassing thousands of federal and state court, community, business and administrative agency initiatives promoting mediation, arbitration or other strategies; the spawning of new professional fields; and reforms in the education and training of lawyers and law students — transform the litigation experience of disputants, attorneys, and judges? . . . Here is a look at what we know — and don't know — about the relationship between ADR and litigation. . . .

ADR and the Courts

A 2004 report published by the Judicial Council of California appears to have broken new ground in this regard, providing what may be the most enlightening examination of court-connected mediation ever conducted. The study produced a host of findings, including positive impacts on settlements and trial rate, disposition time, satisfaction and costs. Some salient points:

- In the San Diego and Los Angeles programs, the incidence of trial was 24 to 30 percent lower among cases in the mediation program group than those in the control group.
- All five pilot programs appeared to have resulted in reduced "disposition time" for cases and enhanced attorney perceptions of the services provided by the court and/or the litigation process.
- Additionally, four of the five pilot programs appear to have resulted in reduced numbers of motions or other pretrial court events.
- The data evidence significant reductions in litigant costs and attorney time resulting from the pilot programs: attorney estimates indicate that during 2000 and 2001, the programs may have saved in excess of $49 million in litigant costs and more than a quarter of a million attorney hours.

Within the 370+ pages of the report are important indicators of how program characteristics, the actions of courts, and local legal culture can cause wide variations in results. For example, whether a court-connected mediation program is officially "voluntary" or "mandatory," experiences, perceptions and results will vary considerably depending on the degree of judicial pressure to mediate, and the discretion judges show in determining which matters may be appropriately mediated. California's landmark study strongly supports the notion that court-connected mediation programs are capable of producing important benefits for courts, litigants and lawyers; it also reinforces the notion that much depends on the specific characteristics of a program, and the context within which it is established. The California data comes not a moment too soon; at least one of the court administrative centers connected to the pilot programs has already shut down for lack of funds.

Business and Conflict Management

The rapid growth of federal and state court-connected ADR programs affected, and was paralleled by, initiatives to promote mediation and other alternatives to litigation in the world of business. Although there has been extensive research regarding ADR in some commercial sectors, such as the construction industry, empirical data on business experience has been relatively hard to find.

In 1997, a study of ADR use among Fortune 1,000 corporations was conducted by Cornell University. Based on responses from more than six hundred companies, the study concluded "that ADR processes are well established in corporate America, widespread in all industries and for nearly all types of disputes . . . [and] ADR practice is not haphazard or incidental but rather seems to be integral to a systematic, long-term change in the way corporations resolve disputes." A full 87% of responding companies reported some of use of mediation in the prior three years, and 80% reported using arbitration during the same period. Other forms of ADR, such as in-house grievance procedures, mini-trial, fact-finding, and ombudsman, were also used by some companies. Mediation was far and away the preferred ADR process, based on perceptions that it offers potential cost and time savings, enables parties to retain control over issue resolution, and is generally more satisfying both in term of process and outcomes. . . .

A more current look at corporate approaches to conflict management, albeit from a much more selective sample, is provided by a 2002 survey of corporate counsel conducted by The CPR Institute for Dispute Resolution. The survey collected responses from forty-three large companies regarding their use of mediation, arbitration and other approaches in different transactional and dispute settings, as well as other strategies and tools. Most of these companies have implemented procedures to provide an early assessment of the suitability of disputes for settlement, and conduct post-dispute review of dispute resolution with affected business units. . . . For many responding companies, the use of mediation, arbitration and other "ADR" approaches are facets of more extensive programs aimed at constructively managing conflict, including the appointment of an "ADR counsel" within the legal department; the use of standardized internal analyses to develop strategies for dispute resolution; written policies respecting settlement for inside or outside counsel, including expectations regarding the use of ADR in retainer agreements with outside counsel; making early settlement or mediation presumptive processes and requiring attorneys to justify proceeding to trial, informing business executives of ADR options; and charge-back of dispute resolution costs to responsible corporate departments. . . .

Where We Are Now

The many-faceted "Quiet Revolution" in conflict management has resulted in many changes in the environment of court litigation, including the evolution of a wide range of process tools aimed at managing conflict. Although the evidence that court mediation programs reduce trial rates is mixed, there is substantial evidence that mediation often results in greater levels of satisfaction, reduced dispute resolution costs, shorter disposition times, and other benefits.

The great majority of corporations have some experience with ADR, with a number establishing programs aimed at resolving various kinds of disputes early, including multi-step systems addressing employee disputes.

As for litigation, while it has far from disappeared from the corporate world, it has changed shape. If fewer litigators are plying their trade in the courthouse, more seem to be finding employment in business and other arbitration — and in mediated negotiation.

The increased use of ADR and the decrease in trials, although generally viewed positively, have raised policy questions. Public trials and appeals have the dual purposes of deciding the immediate dispute and providing standards for conduct and responsibility in similar circumstances. Trials and resulting appeals are the basis by which legal norms are articulated and one way the rule of law is maintained. The reading that follows states concerns about the future of our public judicial values and the rule of law in light of the increased use of alternatives.

❖ **Deborah R. Hensler,** *Our Courts, Ourselves: How the Alternative Dispute Resolution Movement Is Reshaping Our Legal System*

108 Penn. St. L. Rev. 165 (2003)

... Looking backwards, we may well come to view the dispute resolution movement as contributing to — if not creating — a profound change in our view of the justice system. With increasing barriers to litigating, fewer citizens will find their own way into court (although they may be brought there to answer criminal charges). Those who are not barred from using the courts by contractual agreement will increasingly find themselves shepherded outside the courthouse to confidential conferences presided over by private neutrals in private venues. With little experience of public adjudication and little information available about the process or outcomes of dispute resolution, citizens' abilities to use the justice system effectively to achieve social change will diminish markedly. Surrounded by a culture that celebrates social harmony and self-realization and disparages social conflict — whatever its causes or aims — citizens' tendencies to turn to the court as a vehicle for social transformation will diminish as well. Over the long run, all of the doors of the multi-door courthouse may swing outward.

Why should we care? If disputes are resolved efficiently in private, by private individuals and organizations, if conflict is avoided and citizens learn to seek compromise when disputes do arise, won't society be better off? Leaving aside the still unanswered question about whether private dispute resolution is, in fact, more efficient than public dispute resolution, and the considerable evidence that in most circumstances people already avoid conflict by compromising or "learning to live with" life's misfortunes and unfairness, I think the answer is "no." Owen Fiss, Judith Resnik, and others have written about the importance of public adjudication for the articulation of legal norms. I think there are also important political values that derive from widespread access to, and use of, the public justice system.

The public spectacle of civil litigation gives life to the "rule of law." To demonstrate that the law's authority can be mobilized by the least powerful as well as the most powerful in society, we need to observe employees and consumers successfully suing large corporations and government agencies, minority group members successfully suing majority group members, and persons engaged in unpopular activities establishing their legal rights to continue those activities.

Dispute resolution behind closed doors precludes such observation. In a democracy where many people are shut out of legislative power either because they are too few in number, or too dispersed to elect representatives, or because they do not have the financial resources to influence legislators, collective litigation in class or other mass form provides an alternative strategy for group action. Private individualized dispute resolution extinguishes the possibility of such collective litigation. Conciliation has much to recommend it. But the visible presence of institutionalized and legitimized conflict, channeled productively, teaches citizens that it is not always better to compromise and accept the status quo because, sometimes, great gains are to be had by peaceful contest.

Notes and Questions

5.   Professor Hensler refers to "increasing barriers to litigating," and points to contractual agreements that bar lawsuits and require the arbitration of disputes arising under the contract. These contract provisions are used between businesses and, as she notes in her article, are increasingly imposed on consumers and employees. The rules of many courts also require parties to participate in non-binding ADR process as a precondition to getting a trial date. But ADR programs cannot bar citizens from access to court, a right guaranteed by virtually every state constitution. Are the concerns expressed by Professor Hensler about ADR diminishing citizens' abilities to use the justice system effectively to achieve social change limited to consumer and employee access to courts and the use of class actions? Do you share her concerns?

6.   Lawyers are increasingly directing their clients to mediation and customized forms of arbitration. Efficiency and cost savings are only part of the motivation to choose ADR. Shaping the process by which disputes are resolved and, in non-binding processes, retaining control of the end result also appeals to clients. The courts are limited in the remedies that can be imposed following a trial, but parties

can be expansive and creative in fashioning a settlement in mediation or setting the framework for arbitration. However, endorsement of ADR is not unanimous. What are the downsides/risks of ADR to individual clients and lawyers?

7. There are many explanations of why the rate and number of trials is decreasing. We do not completely know the causes, but the success of ADR is, no doubt, a contributing factor. When parties in a dispute choose an alternative to trial or otherwise settle their case after initiating or responding to a lawsuit, are they defeating the purposes of our civil justice system? Does settlement sometimes thwart good public policy? Should we discourage settlements in certain cases to sustain the adjudication system and maintain a flow of trials?

8. Some liken new ADR processes to the proverbial "better mousetrap." If too many disputants are choosing ADR over traditional litigation, they say, the solution is to improve adjudication, not discourage ADR. In Massachusetts, for example, state judges became concerned that the courts were losing "good civil cases" (that is, ones presenting sophisticated issues, litigated by leading lawyers) to ADR. In response, the state courts instituted a special "business litigation" session, limited to complex commercial cases. A single judge, known for expertise in complex business matters, presided over the session, which featured more predictable decisions that were delivered on an expedited basis. The session has been a great success. Does this suggest that the answer to Professor Hensler's concerns is to improve the traditional justice system?

These questions are among those being pondered by lawyers, judges, and policymakers regarding the increased use of ADR and what is referred to as "the vanishing trial." They are part of what you must consider in deciding whether society should endorse the extensive use of the alternative processes that you will encounter in this course. As you read about other ways to resolve disputes, ponder why the change is occurring, who might resist, and who gains and who loses. Keep in mind the following players in the ADR evolution and their interests:

- *Judges:* Judicial budgets have not generally kept pace with the increased number of criminal cases or the increased complexity of civil cases. Reporting requirements in most jurisdictions track the number and the length of time that civil cases have been on a judge's docket. Are these reporting requirements and increasing case management responsibilities likely to influence a judge's view of ADR?

- *Lawyers:* The gatekeepers who influence which disputes are filed as lawsuits and the method of their disposition are lawyers. Lawyers, in addition to their concerns about their client's interests, are also concerned about their own economic well-being, their careers, and their work satisfaction. Some lawyers in private practice are paid by the hour, and some work on a fee per case or a contingency fee basis. They all compete for clients and cases. How might these factors influence a lawyer's view of ADR?

- *Clients:* The clients of our civil justice system and of ADR services are the parties who have a claim or defense to assert or other difference to resolve. Clients have multiple interests, including the need to be heard, the need to control their own fate, an efficient and economical way to reach resolution, and an outcome they perceive as fair. Does ADR serve or frustrate these client interests?

- *ADR professionals:* There are a growing number of professionals who derive satisfaction and income working as mediators, arbitrators, and ADR trainers. Many are lawyers, some are not. Although virtuous in their dedication to providing a better way to resolve disputes, this ADR "community" can be seen as a special interest group that has a stake in promoting the increased use of ADR services. Much of the ADR literature, research, and analysis comes from this community, as well as others vested in the status quo. Is there a balanced assessment of the alternatives to litigation, and are you comfortable with the sources?

D. Matching the Process to the Dispute and Client-Centered Counseling

1. Fit the Forum to the Fuss

Setting forth a spectrum, or menu, of dispute resolution possibilities does not in itself indicate which, if any, is most appropriate for a specific client in a particular dispute. If you understand the available process choices and how to match them with your clients' needs, or as Professor Sander states, "fit the forum to the fuss," you can provide a value-added service (Sander, 1994). Each process fills a need. A courtroom may be the best forum for resolving some cases. A private office where the parties have come voluntarily to conclude their dispute may be better in other cases. Litigation culminating in a trial is still the forum of choice when it is important to know what happened and who was wrong and who was right. The availability in litigation of evidentiary discovery and depositions, as well as the examination of witnesses at trial, is designed to find historical truth. Publicly exposing wrongdoing and gaining the satisfaction of vindication is also best achieved through a public trial. A court judgment is the surest path to state enforcement of a financial obligation, and courts can compel specific performance in appropriate cases. Courts can provide provisional or interim relief while a lawsuit is pending, which more benign forms of ADR cannot. As discussed above, adjudication can, on appeal, establish precedent and shape rules of responsibility and future conduct, which might be important to some clients. Litigation can assist in organizing and rallying groups of people behind a principle or cause and in joining reluctant parties. The litigation process can also be used strategically in negotiations, and the prospect of a trial often compels settlement. Of course, the irony of all these advantages of litigation is that it can be a two-way street, where each reason for your client pursuing litigation can also be the reason the opposing side is doing so. The litigation curse is having a case in which your client and the other side both absolutely know they are right!

An alternative to adjudication is a more appropriate choice when potential litigation costs are high relative to the amount in controversy or where the dispute is time sensitive. Negotiation or mediation is likely to be appealing when standard adjudication remedies do not meet your client's real needs and interests. For example, sometimes the best resolution of an existing dispute is to make a deal that looks to the future. If your client is entrepreneurial and creative, he might want more of a voice in shaping the final outcome, which he can better do outside a trial. Similarly, if your client wishes to limit her risk or qualify the decision, she will want to pursue an alternative to trial. If it is more important to your client that he have an active role in the process, rather than totally depend on you as his lawyer, mediation will be more satisfying than arbitration or litigation. If it is in the interests of your client not to air her dispute in public, then the privacy afforded by ADR will be more desirable than a public trial. If the parties wish to preserve, or at least not worsen, their relationship, an alternative more gentle than a trial or arbitration will be a better choice. Disputes over matters requiring special expertise may be better resolved by being able to choose the arbitrator or mediator with the necessary expertise.

2.   *Client-Centered Dispute Resolution Counseling*

To effectively counsel and represent clients in resolving their disputes, you must know and understand their interests and goals. Only then can you match their needs to the most appropriate dispute resolution process. Client-centered interviewing and counseling are important skills that shape the attorney-client relationship and are the first steps in helping clients resolve their dispute. Your questions during the initial interview must allow you to discover what the client wishes to achieve and why. Then you can intelligently explore the process of resolution most likely to fulfill your client's interests and goals within the time and resources available. The following reading provides the basics about client-centered counseling from a problem-solving perspective.

❖ David A. Binder, et al., *Lawyers as Counselors:*
A Client-Centered Approach
───────────────────────────────
West Publishing, 2 (2nd ed., 2004)

Clients come to lawyers seeking help in solving problems. . . . [T]he range of people and problems that you are likely to encounter as a lawyer is enormous. The array embraces differences in size, complexity, emotional content and legal status. Some problems involve disputes over past events and others focus on planning for the future. Nonetheless, all of the problems have something in common — the clients hope that satisfactory solutions can be achieved with the aid of your lawyerly knowledge, skills and judgment.

Thus, no matter who your client, what the substantive legal issues or whether a situation involves litigation or planning, your principal role as a lawyer will almost always be the same — to help clients achieve satisfactory and effective solutions to problems. . . .

The client-centered conception has its source in a perspective that legal problems typically raise both legal and non-legal concerns for clients, that collaboration between attorneys and clients is likely to enhance the effectiveness of problem-solving, and that clients ordinarily are in the best position to make important decisions. . . .

Clients Are Autonomous "Owners" of Their Problems

Underlying client-centeredness is the philosophy that clients are autonomous and therefore deserving of making important decisions that lead to resolution of their legal problems. Whether a client is a labor organization involved in negotiations for a new contract, a parent with an abusive spouse, a young couple who want an estate plan that will protect their young children or a developer seeking permission to demolish an existing building, clients do not give up the right to shape their destinies simply because they seek the help of lawyers. . . . After all, clients, and not lawyers, live with decisions' consequences. For example, if a plaintiff in a wrongful termination matter decides to accept a sum of money in settlement rather than pursue reinstatement through trial, it is the plaintiff and not the lawyer whose future life the decision helps to shape. . . .

Clients Are Generally in a Better Position Than Lawyers to Identify and Assess the Importance of Solutions' Non-Legal Consequences

Clients consult lawyers rather than other helping professionals when they recognize that problems have important legal dimensions. . . . However, . . . the satisfactoriness of solutions often depends on how well they respond to clients' concerns about non-legal consequences. Significant non-legal ramifications are typically embedded in solutions to legal problems. . . .

[C]lients are almost always in a better position than you to identify non-legal consequences. This is especially likely to be true because clients with similar legal problems may have very different non-legal concerns. That is, two clients' matters may concern the same legal *issues,* but their legal *problems* may be very different because of differences in the clients' circumstances, personalities and values. . . .

Moreover, clients are typically in a better position than lawyers to assess the importance of the potential non-legal consequences of proposed solutions. For instance, the business executive faced with the decision to fire an employee will undoubtedly be in a better position than you to assess the importance of the harm to company morale and the effect of that harm on the company's operations when it comes time to decide whether to actually fire the employee.

In sum, clients are typically in the best position to identity non-legal consequences and assess their importance. . . . [I]t makes sense for clients to play an active role in developing and analyzing potential solutions and to have the final say in deciding what course(s) of action to choose when trying to resolve legal problems. . . .

Clients Are Normally in a Better Position Than Lawyers to Determine What Risks Are Worth Taking

A third primary justification for client-centered counseling emanates from the fact that decisions in legal matters (as in most other aspects of life) are almost always made under conditions of uncertainty. . . . For example, neither you nor clients can know for certain whether a client who settles a lawsuit will suffer "buyer's remorse," what the costs of complying with environmental requirements will be, or the extent to which firing a popular employee will harm employee morale.

However, as a few minutes observing the action at a Las Vegas blackjack table will verify, people vary enormously in their willingness to take risks. Some people are by dint of their personalities more willing to take risks than are other people. Moreover, risk-taking is often situational; people may take risks in some situations that they would be unwilling to take in others. For example, clients' readiness to take risks may be influenced by the importance they attach to the gains they foresee if their predictions are correct or to the losses they fear will ensue if their predictions are wrong. . . .

Clients Are Capable of and Interested in Participating in the Counseling Process and Making Important Decisions

Other justifications for client-centeredness would mean little if clients typically were incapable of making important decisions or rarely were willing to participate in the counseling process. However, quite the opposite is likely to be true. That is, most clients are quite capable of actively participating in the effort to resolve important problems. Moreover, clients typically want to participate in counseling, though of course their level of interest is likely to vary according to such factors as the relative importance of decisions and the time available to decide. . . .

Seek Out Potential Non-Legal Consequences

Helping clients develop satisfactory solutions requires you not only to uncover information that is relevant to legal *issues,* but also to help clients identify non-legal ramifications that are embedded in solutions to their legal *problems.* Hence, one hallmark of your counseling conversations is to actively encourage clients to identify potential non-legal consequences. With potential non-legal consequences on the table, you can assist clients in evaluating their likely impact on potential solutions. Actively encouraging clients to talk about non-legal concerns is often necessary because clients may not on their own identify and evaluate the non-legal ramifications that may legitimately bear on the problem-solving process. . . .

With experience, you will no doubt anticipate possible non-legal ramifications that tend to accompany particular types of legal problems. You may certainly raise such non-legal possibilities in the course of counseling conversations. At the same time, you will also need to encourage clients to identify non-legal concerns that may not be on your "radar screen" because no amount of experience and legal expertise can enable you to fully recognize or evaluate all the non-legal consequences that may attend a given client's situation.

Ask Clients to Suggest Potential Solutions

Clients reasonably expect you to develop potential solutions to their legal problems. . . . However, a second hallmark of client-centered counseling is that you encourage clients to identify potential solutions as well. Clients' backgrounds and experiences may lead them to suggest sensible options that you might have overlooked. At the very least, clients' suggested solutions may suggest concerns that you can account for in solutions that you devise. . . .

By way of illustration, consider a situation in which you represent a building contractor who has been sued by a residents' association for alleged construction defects in a large apartment complex. The residents contend among other things that a basement laundry facility floods as a result of the contractor's failure to properly seal the foundation walls. The contractor is probably more likely than you to identify a solution that includes a repair process that will cure the flooding. Thus, asking the contractor to suggest possible solutions promotes the likelihood that the contractor is satisfied with the eventual outcome.

Encourage Clients to Make Important Decisions

A third hallmark of client-centered counseling is that you encourage clients to make important decisions. The strategies and techniques that constitute a client-centered approach put clients in a position to make knowledgeable decisions by facilitating identification of possible outcomes and their likely consequences. At the end of the day, however, the factors described above, such as the inevitable non-legal ramifications and variations in values and risk-aversion, suggest that important decisions are for clients to make. . . .

This book on dispute resolution cannot provide all you need to know about client interviewing and counseling, although we do include readings on listening, questioning, and managing information, as well as on the role of perceptions and psychological factors. Separate courses in interviewing, counseling, and personal skills are offered at many law schools, and most have clinics that provide opportunities to interview and work with clients. This course will provide the knowledge of dispute resolution that will enable you to help counsel clients in choosing the most appropriate process, once you have learned their underlying needs, and to then represent them skillfully. Given the shrinking number of trials and changes in the legal culture supporting increased use of ADR, you are more likely in many jurisdictions to represent clients in mediation, or possibly arbitration, than in court. However, what lawyers do most often for clients is negotiate. So we start our study of dispute resolution processes in Part I with negotiation. Then, moving east along the ADR continuum, we take up mediation in Part II. Arbitration, which is growing in use, is next in our book's sequence and the subject of Part III. We conclude in Part IV with a look at how to mix, match, and layer dispute resolution alternatives to more fully serve the needs of your clients, as well as new developments in ADR.

PART
I

Negotiation

CHAPTER
2

Negotiation and Conflict — The Big Picture

A. Introduction to Negotiation

Negotiation is the process of communication used to get something we want when another person has control over whether or how we can get it. If we could have everything we wanted, materially and emotionally, without the concurrence of anyone else, there would be no need to negotiate. Because of our interdependence, the need to negotiate is pervasive.

Everyone negotiates as part of modern life. However, because lawyers are paid to negotiate for others, we are considered professionals. A law student reading only casebooks might not know that the vast majority of disputes in which lawyers are involved are negotiated to a settlement without trial. Many major transactions are also the result of lawyer-negotiated agreements. Negotiation is at the core of what lawyers do in representing clients.

Most lawyers think they are skilled negotiators because they negotiate frequently. Negotiating frequently does not necessarily result in negotiating effectively. Unlike trial practice, negotiation is usually done in private without the opportunity to compare results or benefit from a critique. Those with whom you negotiate rarely give an honest assessment of how you did, and it is most often in their interest for you to believe you did well. Regardless of our intuitive ability, negotiation skills and results can be improved with analysis and understanding, as well as practice.

Lawyer negotiation takes place within the dynamics of settling a dispute or shaping a deal. It is not always a tidy process that tracks a textbook diagram. In this book we use a seven-stage model of negotiation, recognizing that all negotiations do not follow the same lineal staging and each stage will not necessarily be completed. The negotiation dance can be improvised to fit the situation. For example, we list initial interactions and offers as part of Stage 2 before exchanging information; however, the initial offer or demand may often follow an exchange of information. The seven stages are:

1. Preparation and Setting Goals
2. Initial Interaction and Offers

3. Exchanging and Refining Information
4. Bargaining
5. Moving Toward Closure
6. Reaching Impasse or Agreement
7. Finalizing the Agreement

Negotiation occurs because there are differences between what parties want or how they perceive a situation. As a professional negotiator, you have an edge if you understand the nature of the conflict to be resolved, the psychology of negotiation, and contrasting styles of bargaining. So, we begin with the nature of conflict and the role of perceptions, as well as emotional dimensions and psychological traps. Next we look at the advantages and disadvantages of using a more competitive or cooperative bargaining style. We then examine the stages of negotiation and the activities associated with each step. Subsequent chapters look at gender and culture, ethics, and the role of law in negotiations.

B.   Conflict Is What We Make It

Although conflict can cause distress and is usually viewed negatively, it can function in positive ways. Conflict may motivate you to take action and change your situation in ways that improve your life and better fulfill your self-interests. Conflict can, however, also create a crisis mentality that becomes destructive. Lawyers can help create more constructive outcomes from conflicts or they can make a difficult situation worse. The ability to help clients better understand the conflict, reframe the issues, and realistically analyze their interests and how they can be negotiated is an important lawyering skill.

Conflict is divided into two categories: interpersonal (differences that arise between individuals or groups) and intrapersonal (conflicts within ourselves). Interpersonal conflict is a situation in which the parties each want something that they perceive as incompatible with what the other wants. Because the parties in an interpersonal conflict cannot both have all that they want, their interests or goals are divergent. Lawyers are retained to help resolve interpersonal conflicts between our clients and others. A client may also be conflicted internally about what it is they really want from an opponent. For example, does your client really want to return to the job from which she was fired, or does she want only to restore her self-respect and get compensation? Does the father you represent in a divorce really want custody of the children, or is he internally conflicted about the decision to divorce and trying to hold onto the marital relationship? Recognizing these two different types of conflict can be critical in achieving client goals.

Another distinction that can be useful in negotiation and mediation is between the manifest conflict, which is overt or expressed, and the underlying conflict, which is hidden or denied. Lawyers most often deal with manifest conflicts, which we refer to as disputes. As we saw in the previous chapter, a conflict may not become a dispute if it is not communicated in the form of a complaint or claim. However, what is communicated may be only a part of or symbol of the underlying conflict. The dispute between brothers over control of a family business seems safer to contest than the underlying conflict of who was the favored son or a better child. Indian tribes may actively dispute government fishing quotas, while the underlying conflict involves the more fundamental issue of outside control and alteration of Native American traditions. Residential development disputes may focus in court on specific environmental regulations or traffic issues, but the underlying conflict is about the changing character of the community. This dichotomy between the overt dispute and the hidden conflict can be viewed for purposes of negotiation as the presenting problem and the hidden agenda.

If the agreements reached in negotiation resolve only the presenting problems, they are less likely to last unless legally enforced. Surfacing the underlying conflict can clarify issues, focus objectives, generate new possibilities for settlement, and ultimately improve relationships. Dealing with the underlying conflicts, however, may be emotionally difficult for clients and can stimulate internal conflict. Many lawyers are not comfortable with opening emotional issues and may not have the capacity to address them. We will look more into the emotional aspects of conflict and settlements shortly.

Professor Rubin, in the excerpt that follows, emphasizes "building relationships in negotiations," and explains the concepts of "enlightened self-interest" and "ripeness."

❖ **Jeffrey Z. Rubin,** *Some Wise and Mistaken Assumptions About Conflict and Negotiation*

Negotiation Theory and Practice 3, Program on Negotiation Books (J.Z. Rubin and W. Breslin eds., 1991)

For many years the attention of conflict researchers and theorists was directed to the laudable objective of conflict resolution. This term denotes as an outcome a state of attitude change that effectively brings an end to the conflict in question. In contrast, conflict settlement denotes outcomes in which the overt conflict has been brought to an end, even though the underlying bases may or may not have been addressed. . . . The gradual shift over the last years from a focus on resolution to a focus on settlement has had an important implication for the conflict field: It has increased the importance of understanding negotiation — which, after all, is a method of settling conflict rather than resolving it. The focus of negotiation is not attitude change per se, but an agreement to change behavior in ways that make settlement possible. Two people with underlying differences of beliefs or values (for example, over the issue of a woman's right to abortion or the existence of a higher deity) may come to change their views through discussion and an exchange of views, but it would be inappropriate and inaccurate to describe such an exchange as "negotiation." . . .

Cooperation, Competition, and Enlightened Self-Interest

Required for effective conflict settlement is neither cooperation nor competition, but what may be referred to as "enlightened self interest." By this I simply mean a variation on what several conflict theorists have previously described as an "individualistic orientation" — an outlook in which the disputant is simply interested in doing well for himself or herself, without regard for anyone else, out neither to help nor hinder the other's efforts to obtain his or her goal. The added word "enlightened" refers to the acknowledgment by each side that the other is also likely to be pursuing a path of self interest — and that it may be possible for both to do well in the exchange. If there are ways in which I can move toward my objective in negotiation, while at the same time making it possible for you to approach your goal, then why not behave in ways that make both possible?

Notice that what I am describing here is neither pure individualism (where one side does not care at all about how the other is doing) nor pure cooperation (where each side cares deeply about helping the other to do well, likes and values the other side, etc.) — but an amalgam of the two. . . . I do not have to like or trust you in order to negotiate wisely with you. Nor do I have to be driven by the passion of a competitive desire to beat you. All that is necessary is for me to find some way of getting what I want — perhaps even more than I considered possible — by leaving the door open for you too to do well. "Trust" and "trustworthiness," concepts central to the development of cooperation, are no longer necessary — only the understanding of what the other person may want or need.

A number of anecdotes have emerged to make this point . . . Jack Sprat and his wife — one preferring lean, the other fat — can lick the platter clean if they understand their respective interests. The interesting thing about this conjugal pair is that, married though they may be, when it comes to dining preferences they are hardly interdependent at all. For Jack and his wife to "lick the platter clean" requires neither that the two love each other nor care about helping each other in every way possible; nor does it require that each be determined to get more of the platter's contents than the other. Instead, it is enlightened self interest that makes possible an optimal solution to the problem of resource distribution. . . .

The Importance of "Relationship" in Negotiation

Much of the negotiation analysis that has taken place over the last 25 years has focused on the "bottom line": who gets how much once an agreement has been reached. The emphasis has thus largely been an economic one, and this emphasis has been strengthened by the significant role of game theory and other mathematical or economic formulations.

This economic focus is being supplanted by a richer, and more accurate, portrayal of negotiation in terms not only of economic, but also of relational, considerations. As any visitor to the Turkish Bazaar in Istanbul will tell you, the purchase of an oriental carpet involves a great deal more than the exchange of money for an old rug. The emerging relationship between shopkeeper and customer is far more significant, weaving ever so naturally into the economic aspects of the transaction. . . .

Psychologists, sociologists, and anthropologists have long understood the importance of "relationship" in any interpersonal transaction, but only recently have conflict analysts begun to take this as seriously as it deserves. Although it seems convenient to distinguish negotiation in one time only exchanges (ones where you have no history of contact with the other party, come together for a "quickie," and then expect never to see the other again) from negotiation in ongoing relationships, this distinction is more illusory than real. Rarely does one negotiate in the absence of future consequences. Even if you and I meet once and once only, our reputations have a way of surviving the exchange, coloring the expectations that others will have of us in the future. . . .

The Role of "Ripeness"

Although it is comforting to assume people can start negotiating any time they want, such is not the case. First of all, just as it takes two hands to clap, it takes two to negotiate. You may be ready to come to the table for serious discussion, but your counterpart may not. Unless you are both at the table (or connected by a telephone line or cable link), no agreement is possible.

Second, even if both of you are present at the same place, at the same time, one or both of you may not be sufficiently motivated to take the conflict seriously. It is tempting to sit back, do nothing, and hope that the mere passage of time will turn events to your advantage. People typically do not sit down to negotiate unless and until they have reached a point of "stalemate," where each no longer believes it possible to obtain what he or she wants through efforts at domination or coercion. It is only at this point, when the two sides grudgingly acknowledge the need for joint work if any agreement is to be reached, that negotiation can take place.

By "ripeness," then, I mean a stage of conflict in which all parties are ready to take their conflict seriously, and are willing to do whatever may be necessary to bring the conflict to a close. To pluck fruit from a tree before it is ripe is as problematic as waiting too long. There is a right time to negotiate, and the wise negotiator will attempt to seek out this point.

It is also possible, of course, to help "create" such a right time. One way of doing so entails the use of threat and coercion, as the two sides (either with or without the assistance of an outside intervenor) walk (or are led) to the edge of "lover's leap," stare into the abyss below, and contemplate the consequences of failing to reach agreement. The farther the drop — that is, the more terrible the consequences of failing to settle — the greater the pressure on each side to take the conflict seriously. There are at least two serious problems with such "coercive" means of creating a ripe conflict: First, as can be seen in the history of the arms race between the United States and the Soviet Union, it encourages further conflict escalation, as each side tries to "motivate" the other to settle by upping the ante a little bit at a time. Second, such escalatory moves invite a game of "chicken," in which each hopes that the other will be the first to succumb to coercion.

There is a second — and far better — way to create a situation that is ripe for settlement: namely, through the introduction of new opportunities for joint gain. If each side can be persuaded that there is more to gain than to lose through collaboration — that by working jointly, rewards can be harvested that stand to advance each side's respective agenda — then a basis for agreement can be established. . . .

Notes and Questions

1. Morton Deutsch, who pioneered the modern study of conflict resolution, distinguished manifest conflict from underlying conflict, as summarized in our introductory comments (see Deutsch, 1973). Rubin, a former student of Deutsch, separates settlement of the manifest conflict behaviors from the attitude changes necessary to bring an end to the underlying base of conflict. We noted a similar distinction between the presenting problem and the hidden agenda. Do you agree that settlement only of the manifest problem is unlikely to last? Why or why not? Is litigation limited only to the manifest or presenting issues? Is Rubin correct in indicating that negotiation is only a method of settling conflict rather than resolving it?

2. Professor Rubin in his excerpt introduces the concept of "enlightened self-interest," which is related to the "utility" theory that began with Jeremy Bentham in the late 1700s and underlies much of the current analysis of negotiation. How does enlightened self-interest, or utility theory, explain Rubin's conclusion that Mr. and Mrs. Sprat could reach an "optimal solution" and "lick the platter clean?" Is he correct in indicating that "trust" and "trustworthiness" are not relevant to reaching optimal solutions? Why or why not?

3. Just as it takes two or more people to have a conflict, so it takes two or more people to reach agreement. Ripeness of the conflict is critical for those involved to begin serious negotiation toward resolution. What do you think Rubin means when he suggests that new opportunities for joint gain create ripeness? How might this concept help lawyers get disputes resolved?
4. How do lawyers most often create "ripeness" to seriously negotiate and settle disputes?

C. The Triangle of Conflict and Negotiation

Rubin discusses bottom-line negotiation and the limits of focusing only on the economic aspects of a conflict. There is increasing recognition that to negotiate a satisfactory resolution of a conflict, there must be an understanding of and attention to the emotional and relationship components, or what Rubin refers to as the underlying bases of the conflict. Even though the dominant focus in most lawyer negotiations is on the trade-offs involving legal claims or economic considerations measured in money damages, neglecting the two nonmonetary components resulting from conflicts can lead to an impasse or a settlement that does not hold.

The three sets of factors at work in most conflicts can be thought of as the three "Es": economic, emotional, and environmental. These form the three sides of the negotiation triangle, which relate to needs and interests that are discussed in Chapter 4.

Legal issues and rights are what often bring lawyers to the negotiation table to bargain over economic damages. Once there, the other two sides of the conflict triangle that impact clients enclose and influence the negotiation process and outcome. The emotional component refers to the internal pushes and pulls on parties created by the conflict that affect how they feel about themselves. The environmental elements are the setting and social considerations, including how others will view what is going on and how the resolution will appear to third parties. "Face saving" is frequently referred to; it is a social factor that also has an emotional impact. The three sides of the triangle are interrelated and have an impact on one another.

The mix of what matters for purposes of resolving a conflict will vary depending on the subject and the sensitivities and history between the parties, as well as their attorneys. A purely commercial case will most heavily involve economic considerations. However, all three elements are involved to some extent in every type of dispute. A business person sued for breach of

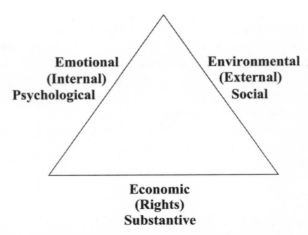

Three Components of Conflict and Satisfactory Settlements

contract has feelings about accusations from a longtime supplier and concerns about his reputation in the business community. A divorce or employment dispute, although focused on substantive rights and money, will invoke more emotional and environmental factors. For example, in a divorce, what will children, grandparents, and neighbors think about new parenting arrangements? In a wrongful termination case, how will acceptance of the economic offer appear to co-workers who remain friends with the terminated worker? Attention to the non-economic factors can help prevent or end a negotiation impasse and move the matter to resolution.

It can be difficult to quantify the emotional and environmental factors, but there might be ways to satisfy the internal-emotional and external-social factors in a manner that both settles the case and helps resolve the conflict. As you read the following fact situation and resulting lawsuit, settled a year and a half after the incident, consider what role both emotional and social factors might have played in negotiating a settlement agreement.

Problem

On December 25, 2007, Tatiana, a 250-pound Siberian tiger in the San Francisco Zoo, leapt out of her enclosure, killed 17-year-old Carlos Sousa, Jr., and injured two of his friends, brothers Amritpal Dhaliwal, then 19, and Kulbir Dhaliwal, then 23. The tiger was shot dead by police. The media coverage was extensive. Zoo spokesman Sam Singer, hired by the zoo for damage control, seemed to blame the brothers for the incident, suggesting that they taunted the tiger. Animal rights advocates protested the shooting of the tiger. Zoo attendance and donations dropped.

A claim for the death of Carlos Sousa, Jr. was settled. The Dhaliwal brothers sued the San Francisco Zoological Society, the City of San Francisco, and Sam Singer. Their federal lawsuit alleged that the zoo was negligent in maintaining a tiger enclosure several feet below recommended standards, claimed their civil rights were violated because their car was improperly seized, and accused Singer of libel and slander for comments he made to media implying that they might have been taunting the tiger. They also alleged that police officials had ordered officers to issue warrants for their arrest, accusing them of manslaughter in the death of their deceased friend, Carlos Sousa, Jr., even though an investigation could not substantiate any basis for bringing charges against them. Substantial damages were sought by the brothers, well beyond the relatively modest amounts for physical injuries and medical expenses.

1.   If you were advising the zoo, would you recommend that it negotiate a settlement? Is there any downside for the zoo in negotiating? Would your answers be different if you were representing the Dhaliwal brothers?
2.   What are the non-economic factors in this conflict, and how might they be addressed in negotiation?
3.   What might the Dhaliwal brothers obtain in a negotiated settlement that they could not win at trial?

The emotional side of the triangle of conflict might be the most difficult for you to deal with if you are not trained in psychology. You might negotiate what you think is a great resolution of a dispute, only to have it rejected by your client, who must agree before a settlement or deal is finalized. Understanding the emotional stages experienced by a client in a conflict can help you better represent your client in negotiations. Professor Gerald Williams identifies the emotional stages a client might follow to move out of a conflict and get on with his life or business. The last phase of renewal or transformation may be more an inspirational hope than a realized reality.

❖ **Gerald R. Williams,** *Negotiation as a Healing Process*

J. Disp. Resol. 1, 42 (1996)

The Five Steps for Recovering from Conflict

. . . Just as researchers have found that getting *into* a conflict is a multi-step process that typically involves naming, blaming, claiming, rejection, and a decision to go public, even so, the task of getting *out of* a conflict requires the disputants to work their way through a multistage process.

A. Denial

As a preliminary model of the process of recovering from conflict, the first stage is typically a condition of *denial*. As James Hall explains, there is in each of us "a deep-seated human desire *not* to be the one at fault, *not* to be the one who must change." This resistance to being the one at fault, to being the one who must change, is part of what makes conflict so painful and its resolution so difficult. Most conflicts are a story of two parties, both of whom contributed to the problem, and neither of whom wants to admit his or her role in it. In the literature on grieving we gain a broader sense of what is meant by the term *denial* and some of the risks it poses to the parties and others: "The person will strongly deny the reality of what has happened, or search for reasons why it has happened, and take revenge on themselves and others." . . . From this perspective, we might even say that, in most instances, conflicts are meaningful; they have a purpose. Their purpose is to hold up a mirror so disputants may see themselves in a new light, an experience as painful as it is valuable. . . .

Properly understood, then, conflicts serve as such a mirror. They expose the disputants' weaknesses; the areas in which they have been too much the victim, or too much the exploiter; their complexes, their unresolved angers, and their feelings of specialness and entitlement. Because it is so painful for disputants to see these parts of themselves exposed by their own involvement in the conflict, they need the protection and reinforcement, the containment and channeling, that the lawyer-client relationship provides, and they need the benefit of the full play of the negotiation process to help them gradually face what they see in the mirror and to come to terms with it. . . .

B. Acceptance

The next step is *acceptance*. It may take time, but at some point the parties need to move beyond denial and to *accept the possibility that they themselves are part of the problem.* They do not yet need to *do* anything about it, just to accept the possibility that the problem does not begin and end with the other side, that they themselves may have some complicity in the problem. In some cases, however, it may be that one side actually is wholly innocent and the other wholly to blame for the problem. But even when parties are wholly innocent, they still need to accept the possibility there is *something they could do now to move the situation in the direction of an appropriate resolution.* Again, they don't need to actually take action, they simply need to register a change in attitude that opens them to the possibility of movement in the direction of an appropriate solution.

C. Sacrifice

Assuming the parties have accepted the possibility they are part of the problem, or the possibility there is something they could do now to move in the direction of a resolution, the next step is to consider what they might be willing to do about it. In its starkest form, the principle is that, for the conflict to be resolved, the parties must be willing to make a sacrifice. From a judge's point of view, the minimum sacrifice required for a valid settlement agreement is a *compromise* by each side, meaning that both parties must make some concession, must move from their original position. But as a general matter, mere concessions or compromises do not require a change of heart. It has been observed that people usually are not willing to make a sacrifice until they have been brought to a more humble attitude. . . . Assuming that sacrifices need to be made, what should they be? This is an extremely delicate question. We know, for example, that some people have a history of being *too compliant*, of giving away too much, whether motivated by a need for affection and approval, by fear of reprisals, or for some other reason. For those who are too compliant, the sacrifice called for would probably *not* be to make more concessions to their antagonist, but rather to forebear from giving, to reverse themselves, to give up the part of themselves that always wants to please others. For other people, the problem may be just the opposite. They may be exploiters who are too good at looking out for themselves at others' expense. For them, the sacrifice may be to recognize their exploitive patterns and become more conscious of the interests and needs of other people. There are many other possibilities. The answer will depend on the personalities involved and the particularities of their situations. In some situations, parties may need to sacrifice — to let go of — such things as a desire for a total victory, or an impulse for revenge, a mistaken belief that they themselves are faultless and the other side totally to blame, their pride, their unwillingness to acknowledge or appreciate another's point of view, or their unwillingness to forgive another for his or her mistake. In other situations, parties may need to give up the belief that they can get away with exploiting others, their belief that they are better or more deserving than others, or their excessive opinions of their own abilities, worth, privileged status, etc. There may be situations in which parties need to give up their hope of obtaining a windfall or other unearned benefit, or give up their envy or spite or jealousy with respect to possessions, luck, and social position.

Before proceeding to the fourth step, there is one final consideration. Is it mandatory that parties make a sacrifice? The answer is a firm "no." There can be no *requirement* that the client have a change of heart. It is fundamental that, as lawyers, we implicitly and explicitly declare to our clients that they can stay just the way they are, and so long as they do not expect us to do that which is illegal or unethical, we will stand by them. Our willingness to represent our clients should not depend upon their willingness to change, much less to move in directions *we* think right. As Shaffer and Elkins remind us, "the client has to be free to be wrong." The negotiation process, then, is not intended for lawyers to impose our values upon our clients, but for us to help contain and channel our clients' energies in appropriate ways until they have had enough time to see their own situations more clearly and to discover for themselves what steps they may be willing to make.

D. Leap of Faith

The fourth stage refers to action or movement, what might be called the *leap of faith*. It is a leap of faith, for example, to admit to the other side that you might be *willing* to make a sacrifice to resolve the case. Practicing lawyers recognize it as the moment when their client looks them in the eye and asks, "If I do this, can you guarantee it will work?" And the lawyer has to reply, "No, I can't guarantee that, because I don't know that. But the trial is coming up really soon, and we haven't thought of anything better to do, but you decide." And the client must decide. . . .

E. Renewal or Healing from Conflict

If the process works well enough, and both parties are willing to move by incremental leaps of faith in the direction of agreement, and if they seek in the process to fathom the underlying problems and address them along the way, the effect can be two-fold: they may reach a mutually acceptable solution and, in the best of circumstances, they may also experience a change of heart, be reconciled to one another and healed and feel renewed as human beings. This is the transformation objective; it is the goal or purpose of all ritual processes, whether it be theater or court trial or graduation exercise or religious rite or negotiated settlement. Rituals are to help prepare the participants, those on whose behalf the ceremony is enacted, to move forward in a new condition, to a new phase of life. *Renewal* or transformation in this context means not simply they are as good as they were before the conflict, but they are better — they are more whole, or more compassionate, or less greedy, or otherwise changed in an important way from their attitude or condition before the crisis began. Certainly, when people experience such a fundamental change through the process of conflict resolution, they will be far less likely to find themselves in a similar conflict again. On the other hand, if they fail at this process, then to the extent the conflict was a product of their own developmental shortcomings, it is likely they will find themselves in similar conflicts in the future, returning again and again until the party acknowledges and addresses the underlying developmental need. . . .

Notes and Questions

5. Elizabeth Kubler-Ross, in her 1969 book *On Death and Dying*, introduced a model known as the five stages of grief, by which people deal with grief and tragedy, specifically when diagnosed with a terminal illness. Kubler-Ross's five stages are denial, anger, bargaining, depression, and acceptance. This five-stage model, or some variation, has since been applied by authors to every type of personal loss, including divorce and bankruptcy. How does Professor Williams's five-stage model differ from Kubler-Ross's five stages of dealing with death? Do you agree with Williams's five-stage analysis as applied to conflict?

6.   Many people have a negative view of conflict and try to avoid it. Do you? Was conflict viewed as negative in your family? During your childhood, how did your family deal with conflict? Will you try to model the same conflict process for your children?

7.   As a lawyer, will you welcome representing clients who seek your help to resolve their conflicts? Why or why not?

CHAPTER
3

Perception, Fairness, Psychological Traps, and Emotions

A. The Role of Perceptions

The key to understanding and mastering negotiation is to be aware that those in conflict and who want something from one another see the situation differently. It is these differences that give root to conflict and to the need to negotiate, as well as to the possibility of agreement. We assess conflict and evaluate a case or the worth of an item differently because of differing perceptions. Our individual perceptions determine how we view ourselves, others, and the world. No two views are exactly the same. For example, we may selectively perceive or differ in our perceptions of the following:

• facts	• abilities
• people	• available resources
• interests	• scarcity
• history	• timing
• fairness	• costs
• priorities	• applicable law or rules
• relative power	• likely outcomes

Our view of each of these elements, as well as our perceptions of other variables, shape how we see the world and how we form differences. It is because of such differences in perceptions that people bet on horse races, wage war, and pursue lawsuits.

A classic Japanese story, on which the film *Rashomon* is based, illustrates the role of perceptions and how the truth through one person's eyes may be very different from another's, as seen through the prism of the individuals' own perceptions. Through divergent narratives, the story and the film explore how perceptions distort or enhance different people's memories of a single event, in this case, the death of a Samurai warrior. Each tells the "truth" but perceives it very differently. The film, like the story, is unsettling because, as in much of life, no single truth emerges.

A popular book and film, *The War of the Roses*, by Warren Adler, and its 2004 sequel, *The Children of the Roses*, capture different truths as perceived by divorcing couples. Early in the original story, Oliver and Barbara Rose reveal to their separate lawyers their perspectives on the marriage and how their family home should be divided. Each sees the marriage relationship and what's fair differently, as filtered through his or her own experience, values, and selective vision. Is there any doubt, based on such different perceptions, that the war between the Roses would follow?

❖ Warren Adler, *The War of the Roses*
Stonehouse Press, 51 (1981)

[**Oliver Rose's perception:**] "She just upped and said, 'No more marriage.' Like her whole persona had been transformed. Maybe it's something chemical that happens as forty gets closer."

He had . . . been a good and loving husband. He had nearly offered "faithful" to complete the triad but that would have discounted his two episodes with hookers during conventions in San Francisco and Las Vegas when the children were small. My God, she had everything she could possibly want. . . .

What confused him most was that he had not been warned. Not a sign. He hated to be taken by surprise.

"And the house?" Goldstein asked.

"I don't know. Say half the value. After all, we did it together. Half of everything is okay with me. . . ."

[**Barbara Rose's perception:**] "He's like some kind of animal. Almost invisible. He leaves early, before we get up, and comes home late, long after we've gone to bed. He doesn't take his meals at home. . . ."

"You think it's fair for me to have devoted nearly twenty years to his career, his needs, his wants, his desires, his security. I gave up my schooling for him. I had his children. And I devoted a hell of a lot more time to that house than he did. Besides, the house is all I have to show for it. I can't match his earning power. Hell, in a few years he'll be able to replace its value. I'll just have cash. Well, that's not good enough. I want the house. I want all of it. It's not only a house. It's a symbol of a life-style. And I intend to keep it that way. That's fair. . . ."

"It's my house. I worked my ass off for it," she said.

The following reading further develops the theme that conflict is subjective and flows from different perceptions in people's minds. Rummel's "subjectivity principle" may help to explain the *War of the Roses* and many other conflicts that would otherwise defy understanding and resolution.

❖ **R.J. Rummel,** *The Conflict Helix*

Transaction Publishers, 13 (1991)

The Subjectivity Principle

Perceived reality is your painting. You are the artist. You mix the colors, draw the lines, fix the focus, achieve the artistic balance. Reality disciplines your painting; it is your starting point. As the artist, you add here, leave out there; substitute color, simplify; and provide this reality with a point, a theme, a center of interest. You produce a thousand such paintings every moment. With unconscious artistry. Each a personal statement. Individualistic.

Now, most people realize that their perception of things can be wrong, that they may be mistaken. No doubt you have had disagreements with others on what you all saw or heard. And probably you have heard of eyewitnesses who widely disagree over the facts of a crime or accident. Some teachers who wish to dramatically illustrate such disagreement have staged mock fights or holdups in a classroom. A masked man rushes in, pointing some weapon at the teacher; demands his wallet; and with it hastily exits, leaving the class stunned. Then each member of the class is asked to write down what he saw and heard. Their versions usually differ widely.

But, of course, such are rapidly changing situations in which careful observation is difficult. Surely, you might think, if there were time to study a situation or event you would perceive it as others do. This is easy enough to test. Ask two people to describe in writing a furnished room, say your living room, or a car you may own. Then compare. You will find many similarities, but you should also find some important and interesting differences. Sometimes such differences result from error, inattentiveness. However, there is something more fundamental. Even attentive observers often will see things differently. And each can be correct.

There are a number of reasons for this. First, people may have different vantage points and their visual perspectives thus will differ. A round, flat object viewed from above will appear round, from an angle it will appear an ellipse, from the side a rectangle. This problem of perspective is acute in active, contact sports such as football or basketball. From the referee's line of sight there is no foul, but many spectators (especially the television audiences who see multiple angles and instant replays) know they saw an obvious violation.

But people can compare or change perspectives. Were this all, perception would not be a basic problem. The second reason for different perceptions is more fundamental. You endow what you sense with meaning. The outside world is an amorphous blend of a multitude of interwoven colors, lights, sounds, smells, tastes and material. You make sense of this complex by carving it into different concepts, such as table, chair, or boy. Learning a language is part of learning to perceive the world.

You also endow this reality with value. Thus what you perceive becomes good or bad, repulsive or attractive, dangerous or safe. You see a man running toward you with a knife as dangerous; a calm lake as peaceful; a child murderer as bad; a contribution to charity as good. And so on.

Cultures are systems of meanings laid onto reality; to become acculturated is to learn the language through which a culture gives the world unique shape and evaluation. A clear example of this is a cross, which to a Christian signifies the death of Jesus for mankind as well as the whole complex of values and beliefs bound up in the religion. Yet, to non–Christian cultures a cross may be meaningless: simply two pieces of wood connected at right angles. . . .

Besides varying perspectives and meanings, a third reason for different perceptions is that people have unique experiences and learning capacities, even when they share the same culture. Each person has his own background. No two people learn alike. Moreover, people have different occupations, and each occupation emphasizes and ignores different aspects of reality. Simply by virtue of their separate occupational interests, the world will be perceived dissimilarly by a philosopher, priest, engineer, union worker, or lawyer.

Two people may perceive the same thing from the same perspective, therefore, but each through their diverse languages, evaluations, experience, and occupations, may perceive it differently and endow it with personal meaning. Dissimilar perspective, meaning, and experience together explain why your perception will often differ radically from others.

There is yet an even more basic reason: what you sense is unconsciously transformed within your mental field in order to maintain a psychological balance. This mental process is familiar to you. People often perceive what they want to perceive, what they ardently hope to see. Their minds go to great pains to extract from the world that which they put there. People tend to see things consistent with their beliefs. If you believe businesspeople, politicians, or bureaucrats are bad, you will tend to see their failings. If you like a person, you tend to see the good; hate him and you tend to see the worst. Some people are optimists, usually seeing a bottle half full; others are pessimists, seeing the same bottle half empty.

Your perception is thus the result of a complex transformation of amorphous sensory stimuli. At various stages your personal experience, beliefs, and character affect what you perceive. . . . Independent of the outside world's powers to force your perception, you have power to impose a perception on reality. You can hallucinate. You can magnify some things to fill your perception in spite of what else is happening. Think of the whisper of one's name.

What you perceive in reality is a balance between these two sets of powers: the outside world's powers to make you perceive specific things and your powers to impose a certain perception on the world. This is the most basic opposition, the most basic conflict. Its outcome is what you perceive reality to be. . . . The elements of The Subjectivity Principle are perception, mental field, and balance: your perception is a balance between the powers of your mental field and the outside world. It is a balance between the perception you tend to impose on the outside world and the strength of what is out there to force its own reality on you. It is a balance between what you unconsciously want to perceive and what you cannot help but perceive. . . .

This balance that envelopes your mental field changes with your interest and concentration. Its shape and extension will depend on your personality and experience. And, of course, your culture. No wonder, then, that you are likely to perceive things differently from others. Your perception is subjective and personal. Reality does not draw its picture on a clean slate — your mind. Nor is your mind a passive movie screen on which sensory stimuli impact, to create a moving picture of the world. Rather, your mind is an active agent of perception, creating and transforming reality, while at the same time being disciplined and sometimes dominated by it. . . .

You and I may perceive reality differently and we both may be right. We are simply viewing the same thing from different perspectives and each emphasizing a deferent aspect. Blind men feeling different parts of an elephant may each believe they are correct and the others wrong about their perception. Yet, all can be correct; all can have a different part of the truth.

Notes and Questions

Rummel's subjectivity principle explains how we process the information and stimuli around us through the filters of our experience, needs, and biases. The complexity of our environment and our minds prevents us from taking it all in whole, so we focus selectively on some stimuli and ignore others. We develop shortcuts in our perceptual systems that allow us to function and process information more quickly and make timely decisions. These shortcuts, known as heuristics, can serve us well. However, mental shortcuts create the risk that our selectivity will distort reality as seen by others. The different ways we process information can lead to conflict based on our different realities.

A key concept in understanding the cause of disputes is *selective perception*. Jeffrey Rubin describes this phenomenon and its offspring, *self-fulfilling prophecies*:

> Let us begin with selective perception. . . . In an escalating conflict, we tend to see what we want to see and to distort information to support our expectations. One way we do this is by selectively testing hypotheses. We form a hypothesis about the adversary such as, this person is nasty. Then we gather information to confirm our hypothesis and ignore information that does not support it. In selective perception we have only dealt with perceptions. When behavior is introduced, we have self-fulfilling prophecy, which connects attitudes and behaviors. I have an expectation of you that leads me to behave in a way that produces a response in you that confirms my expectation. My prophecy about the kind of person that you are is fulfilled. (Rubin, 1993)

1. Is the subjectivity principle, as explained by Rummel, the same concept as selective perception and self-fulfilling prophecies, as described by Rubin?
2. Can you recall a conflict you have experienced that might be better understood in light of the subjectivity principle?
3. John Milton, in *Paradise Lost,* poetically stated: "The mind is its own place, and in itself can make a heaven of Hell, a hell of Heaven" (Milton, 1909). In explaining his subjectivity principle, is Rummel just restating Milton?
4. If a conflict between people is the result of different perceptions, what might be of help in resolving the conflict?
5. Is there a connection between Rummel's subjectivity principle and the distinction made in Chapter 2 between the manifest conflict and the underlying conflict? Can you articulate an explanation of manifest conflict or underlying conflict based on Rummel's subjectivity principle?
6. Is the conflict between Barbara and Oliver Rose really over their house, or something else? If the division or ownership of the house is the manifest or presenting conflict, what is the underlying conflict or "hidden agenda?" Can lawyers negotiate what may be the underlying conflict regarding gender roles? Can they do something about each Rose's need for recognition of his or her contribution to the house and the marriage?

B. The Impact of Fairness

Our list of selective perceptions at the beginning of this chapter included "fairness." Differing views of fairness are at the heart of many litigated conflicts and failed negotiations. Fairness, like other perceptions, is in the mind of the beholder. A client may hire you to negotiate on her behalf because she feels she has been treated unfairly and that you, as a lawyer, can help her obtain what is fair. Fairness, as perceived by clients, can also become central in assessing whether to accept or reject a negotiated settlement or deal.

An outcome that appears fair can be more important than winning or losing. Fairness may define for some whether they won or lost. Offers may be rejected even though they are economically advantageous because in the client's mind the result is not fair.

Classroom experiments with "ultimatum games" illustrate the importance of perceived fairness in negotiation. In these games, Player 1 is given a fixed sum of money or chips (for example, $100) as a windfall that she might have found on the street and is asked to propose a division of that sum with Player 2 (e.g., $75 to Player 1 and $25 to Player 2). Player 1 has complete discretion to divide the money as she wishes; Player 2 can choose only whether to accept or reject Player 1's proposal. If Player 2 accepts the offer, both players will keep the money as allocated. If Player 2 rejects the offer, neither player will receive anything.

Economic theory dictates that Player 1 should offer only a little more than zero to Player 2, and that Player 2 should accept this amount as better than nothing. In fact, in classroom experiments Player 1 generally offers 30 to 50 percent of the sum to Player 2, and when less than 50 percent is offered, many recipients will reject the offer, preferring to walk away with nothing rather than accept what they perceive to be an unfair result. The results of this game reflect the importance of our innate value of being treated fairly (see Brams and Taylor, 1996). Ultimatum games are not restricted to the classroom. Consider the following real-life example.

THE HOME-RUN BALL CATCH

More than 40,000 fans were at the ballpark to see the San Francisco Giants' last game of the 2001 season. Most had come to see Barry Bonds add another home run to his already record-breaking total of 72. Alex Popov and Patrick Hayashi were two fans in the right field arcade standing-room section, hoping to catch a Bonds home-run ball. Sure enough, Bonds's 73rd home-run ball came sailing over the right field bleachers into Popov's outstretched glove. Within seconds, Popov fell to the ground as a rush of people converged on him and the ball. Madness followed before security officers arrived. When Popov was pulled from the pile of fans, the ball was no longer in his glove. Patrick Hayashi emerged with the ball in hand.

Both men claimed ownership of the valuable home-run ball, temporarily in Hayashi's possession. Both thought the ball was worth more than $1 million, based on the sale of Mark McGwire's 70th home-run ball in 1998 for more than $3 million. Each man offered the other less than $100,000 to relinquish any claim on the ball. Each expressed strong public views that he was entitled to complete ownership and was making a generous offer to the other. Both Popov and Hayashi cited principles of fairness and baseball fan culture entitling them to the ball. Popov argued that first possession controls, and Hayashi believed the fan who ended up in possession owned the ball. They insulted one another as liars and thieves. They both hired lawyers and filed suit in the California superior court.

Newspaper editorials, letters, talk show hosts, Barry Bonds, and several mediators all suggested that the ball be sold and the proceeds be split by the men or that the money be given to charity. Neither Popov nor Hayashi thought that evenly splitting what they were individually entitled to was fair, nor did they feel that they could concede anything in light of the insults cast on them by the other. Following 18 months of public bickering and litigation about what was fair, the judge ordered that the ball be sold and the proceeds evenly split. On June 25, 2003, the ball, seated on black velvet and encased in glass, was sold at auction to a comic book impresario for a final bid of $450,000. Popov and Hayashi each received $225,000, minus auction expenses, and each incurred attorneys' fees exceeding that amount. Popov was sued by his attorney for fees and expenses of $473,530, and also for $19,000 by a law professor who served as an expert witness. (The whole sorry story and background is captured in the 2004 film *Up for Grabs*.)

Perceptions of fairness consist of two components. Distributional fairness is a quantitative notion of material outcome — what you get as the result of a negotiation. Procedural fairness relates to the process used to reach the outcome — how you were treated during the negotiation. Both of these components shape people's willingness to accept settlements and their feelings of how well attorneys represented them in the negotiation process.

Fairness perceptions also are significant in understanding negotiation behaviors of opponents. Because perceptions of fairness are so important in attorney-conducted negotiations, we consider this element separately from the other factors that influence negotiations. The following reading examines the criteria that people use to judge fairness and the variables that determine perceptions of fairness.

❖ **Nancy A. Welsh,** *Perceptions of Fairness in Negotiation*

87 Marq. L. Rev. 753 (2004)

Distributive Fairness Perceptions

The concept of distributive fairness focuses on the criteria that lead people to feel that they have received their fair share of available benefits — i.e., that the outcome of a negotiation or other decision making process is fair. People often disagree, however, regarding the criteria that should be applied in order to determine whether an outcome is fair. As is obvious from reading judicial opinions in appellate cases, even impartial and educated people can review the identical record and reach widely disparate yet equally principled conclusions regarding what constitutes a fair outcome. The definition of distributive fairness is, therefore, inevitably subjective. This realization leads to the following questions: What criteria do people — including negotiators — use to guide their judgments regarding distributive fairness? What variables influence people's selection among different criteria, and why do people find it difficult to reach agreement even when they share a commitment to achieving an equitable outcome?

A. Competing Criteria for Judging Distributive Fairness

The various criteria for judging outcomes' fairness can be distilled into four basic, competing principles or rules — equality, need, generosity, and equity. The equality principle provides that everyone in a group should share its benefits equally. According to the need principle, "those who need more of a benefit should get more than those who need it less." The generosity principle decrees that one person's outcome should not exceed the outcomes achieved by others. Finally, the equity principle ties the distribution of benefits to people's relative contribution. Those who have - contributed more should receive more than those who have contributed less. The closer that the actual outcome of a negotiation is to the outcome a negotiator anticipated based on the application of one of these principles, the greater the likelihood that the negotiator will perceive the outcome as fair.

Imagine the application of the four principles described supra to a negotiation between two individuals who are establishing a joint venture and negotiating the distribution of income. The first negotiator, who has little capital, is contributing the idea and the time and energy to implement the idea. The other negotiator is supplying the needed funds for the development and marketing of the idea. If these individuals are guided by the equality principle, they will distribute the income from the joint venture equally. If they use the need principle, the poorer negotiator who is contributing "sweat equity" will receive a greater share of the income. Under the generosity principle, neither negotiator would want his income to exceed the income of the other. Last, and perhaps most difficult, is the application of the equity principle. Both contributions are needed. Whose is more valuable? . . .

B. Variables Affecting Negotiators' Selection Among Competing Fair Allocation Principles

Research has shown that several variables influence negotiators' selections among the various fair allocation principles that could apply to a particular negotiation. These variables include self-interest, social relationships, and the interaction between cultural norms and situational needs.

1.   The Influence of Self-Interest and Relationships Between Negotiators

If no relationship exists between negotiators, self-interest will guide their choice of the appropriate allocation principle to use in negotiation. A negotiator who does not expect future interactions with the other person will use whatever principle — need, generosity, equality, or equity — produces the better result for her. When a negotiator has a negative relationship with the other person, she will aim to gain more than the other negotiator, even if this requires undertaking a risky strategy. She certainly will not worry about achieving an outcome that is fair for that other, despised negotiator. Thus, "[n]egative affect within the context of potential relationships can remove fairness barriers."

On the other hand, the existence of a positive relationship with another negotiator makes the attainment of a fair outcome relevant. Further, positive social relationships influence negotiators' selection of the particular fair allocation principle that will anchor their negotiations. If a negotiator is dividing a resource with someone else and expects future, positive interactions with that person, the negotiator tends to use the equality principle to define distributive fairness. . . . Relationships obviously matter in negotiators' definitions of fair outcomes.

2.   The Influence of Situational Needs and Cultural Norms

As commerce has become increasingly global, cross-cultural negotiation has also become more commonplace. Some cultures are known for placing greater emphasis upon maintaining social relationships than attaining individual objectives. Many believe, therefore, that the cultural dimension of collectivism-individualism should have great salience in the negotiation context. Simply, "individualism refers to a tendency to put a stronger emphasis on one's personal interest and goals, whereas collectivism refers to a stronger emphasis on the interests and goals of one's in-group members." Collectivist negotiators ought to be more likely than individualists to choose harmony-enhancing principles for the distribution of benefits (e.g., equality, need, or generosity principles).

Research indicates, however, that negotiators' choices among the various allocation principles are not so predictable. First, and consistent with the importance of relationships noted above, it is only when collectivists are negotiating with other in-group members that they are more likely to use a harmony-enhancing principle. If they are not closely related to the other negotiators, collectivists behave like individualists and tie fair allocation to contribution, thus leading to their use of the equitable principle. Second, collectivists' choice among allocation principles depends upon the extent to which they anticipate receiving some portion of the benefits being allocated. If a collectivist will not be a recipient (e.g., a supervisor allocating rewards to employees), the collectivist is less likely to be concerned about fostering harmony and more likely to use the equitable principle that will enhance value creation (e.g., productivity). . . .

Procedural Fairness Perceptions

Definition and Effects of Procedural Fairness

Procedural fairness is concerned with people's perceptions of the fairness of the procedures or processes used to arrive at outcomes. Researchers have found that people's perceptions of procedural justice have profound effects. First, people who believe that they have been treated in a procedurally fair manner are more likely to conclude that the resulting outcome is substantively fair. In effect, a person's perception of procedural fairness anchors general fairness impressions or serves as a fairness heuristic. Second, people who believe that they were treated fairly in a dispute resolution or decision-making procedure are more likely to comply with the outcome of the procedure. This effect will occur even if the outcomes are not favorable or produce unhappiness . . .

Conclusion

Lawyers and clients rely upon their assessments of fairness to make all sorts of decisions during negotiation: What offer shall we make? How should we respond to the other side's demand? Should we settle or make a counter-offer? Is the other side being so ridiculous that it is time to call an impasse?

Each one of these questions requires consideration of fairness, and it should now be quite clear that fairness is largely a matter of perception. Perhaps what is most interesting about the research that has been done regarding fairness perceptions is the extent to which it undermines the iconic image of two rational negotiators locked in a battle of logic, economics, and will. Rather, the research reveals that negotiators' aspirations and moves will be significantly influenced by the culture and context within which they are negotiating, their own self-interest, and most intriguing of all, their sense of connection to each other. Ironically, as negotiations become increasingly global and virtual, it is the development of those old-fashioned relationships that may matter most.

Questions

7. In the home-run ball case, neither Popov or Hayashi appeared to be guided by rational self-interest in making decisions about how to maximize their ultimate economic outcome. What do you think got in the way? Might the negotiation result have been different if they had been friends or at least had not have publicly insulted one another?

8. After reading the article by Professor Welsh, can you explain why both men might not have attributed their contact with the home-run ball to luck, and why they were not happy to evenly divide the economic windfall?

9. Did the fact that the entire home-run ball melee was televised and that both men made boastful and insulting public statements influence the negotiation? How might you explain this in terms of the conflict/settlement triangle presented in Chapter 2?

10. If you were representing Popov, how might you have approached the negotiation in terms of the fairness issues? Did both men suffer from the litigation curse of being in a lawsuit in which they were absolutely convinced fairness was on their side?

C. Psychological Traps and Professional Objectivity

Studying the perceptions and distortions of reasoning that immerse people in conflict helps us better understand clients' disputes. Although lawyers advocate and negotiate on behalf of clients, we are less subject to the partisan perspectives that can skew our client's perceptions. This is because although we, as lawyers, may be professional adversaries, we do not have a direct stake in the outcomes, so we can think more clearly and rationally. This is the common wisdom, but is it true?

We can often recognize our clients' partisan perceptions, but we are easily fooled by our own biases and distortions. By definition, what we believe, even if selective, is our reality. The longer we work with a client on a case or a deal, the more we share the same reality — distorted or not. We might be no more able than our clients to objectively analyze the weaknesses of their case or the strengths of the other side's arguments. It can be very helpful for you to understand some of the psychological factors likely to affect not only your client's thinking, but also your own assessment of case value and the attractiveness of offers to settle. Psychological traps and biases often lead us into disputes and influence how we negotiate.

Much of what we know about the hidden forces that create conflict and shape our decisions is attributable to work done in the 1970s and 1980s by cognitive psychologists Amos Tversky and Daniel Kahneman, whose work was recognized with a Nobel Prize in 2002 (See Tversky and Kahneman, 1981; Kahneman, Slovic, and Tversky, 1982). They found that there are consistent biases in perceptions and decision making that can be traced to mental shortcuts, or what they labeled *heuristics*. More recently, experiments have been conducted with law students and lawyers that confirm that these cognitive traps apply to our bargaining decisions and advice.

> Problem
>
> Students at your school who had expected to attend a required lecture without charge are told after they arrive that they will each have to pay $20 to cover unexpected expenses. They can, however, spin a roulette wheel with four chances in five of paying nothing and one chance of having to pay $100. Which will most choose and why? (Hint: The answer is within the list below.)

Top Ten Psychological Traps

The following is an alphabetical list of the top ten common mental traps that can create disputes or make them more difficult to resolve. Some are interrelated. We return to these cognitive shortcuts and expand the list later when we examine why negotiations fail. They also come into play in the next section on how mediators can move negotiations through an impasse to settlement.

- *Anchoring:* A dispute over the value of an item often arises because we form an estimate of an unsure value by comparing it to something we know or to a number to which we are exposed that is then planted in our brain. The number you are exposed to as a value anchors your calculation and influences your thinking. When a client is burnt by hot soup at a restaurant, she may think the restaurant is to blame and her claim is worth millions because she heard about a multimillion-dollar verdict against McDonald's for coffee that was served too hot. You, as a sophisticated lawyer, understand that this case is distinguishable from the McDonald's case, which was reduced on appeal as excessive, and that this client's case is much weaker and worth less than that one, so you adjust from the McDonald's verdict downward. The question is whether you adjust far enough. Research suggests that you will not adjust sufficiently because of the anchoring effect, which could also distort your analysis and expectation.

- *Confirmation bias:* We tend to give credit to information that is consistent with our preexisting beliefs and wishes rather than information that challenges or contradicts them. This can dig us deeper into conflict when dealing with those who have different beliefs or values. We read and believe articles that confirm dark chocolate and red wine are good for us, and skim past articles that question the studies.

- *Consensus error (Projection):* We tend to falsely believe that others think the way we do or have values similar to ours. We also believe that others like what we like and want what we want. Those who enjoy loud music presume everyone wants to hear their amplified radio selections. Conflict can be created when we find out we were wrong.

- *Framing:* Our thinking about an issue and our answer to a question are affected by how the question is presented. Asking a priest if you can smoke while you pray is likely to result in a different answer than asking if you can pray while you smoke.

- *Loss aversion (Status quo bias):* Losses tend to be felt more painfully than equivalent gains are relished, so that a dollar loss is felt greater than a dollar gain. We don't value equal trades from a neutral perspective. We tend to overvalue what we have to give up relative to what we get, making us often regret what we have done. Also, negotiating parties are more likely to view their own concessions (losses) as more valuable than equivalent concessions they get from the other side (gains).

- *Naive realism:* We tend to think that the way we see the world is the way it really is and anyone seeing it differently is naive. This bias is in play when your idea or offer is rejected with the preface that in the "real world" things are different.

- *Overconfidence:* We tend to rate our abilities, chance of being right, and good luck more highly than is warranted. Because we can't always be right, disputes happen. We are also overconfident about our ability to assess uncertain data and tend to give more weight to what we know than what we don't know. As a matter of fact, we are overconfident about ourselves in general. As examples, surveys have found that 70 percent of all drivers believe that they are more competent than the average driver, and 80 percent of lawyers think that they are more ethical than the average attorney (Fox and Birke, 2000). In negotiation, overconfidence can be compounded by positive illusions we have about the relative righteousness of our case or cause.

- *Reactive devaluation:* Whatever proposal comes from the other side cannot be good for us. Anything done or suggested by them is suspect. For example, if Democrats propose legislation, Republicans are likely to reject it, and vice versa. Also any information or offer received is perceived as less valuable than what might be withheld. This tends to escalate conflict.

- *Selective perception:* Whenever we encounter a new situation, we must interpret a universe of unfamiliar, often conflicting data that is more than we can process. We respond by instinctively forming a hypothesis about the situation in the time available, then organizing what we see and hear with the help of that premise. Our hypothesis also operates as a filter, by automatically screening out what doesn't support it — which in turn reinforces the belief that our initial view was correct. Henry David Thoreau was probably thinking about this when he said, "We see only the world we look for." Selective perception is also the basis of self-fulfilling prophesies and stereotyping. For example, if you are negotiating with a lawyer you believe is hostile and not to be trusted, you may dismiss his initial friendly greeting as manipulative and selectively see him scrutinizing you with suspicion. Your stilted behavior toward him will likely result in him seeing you as antagonistic. Mutually reinforced surly behavior will be selectively observed and remembered to the exclusion of overtures of civility. You will feel that your own insight and keen ability to "read" others is confirmed, and your self-fulfilling prophecy will be realized.

- *Self-serving biases:* We are our own best friend in justifying our actions while seeing the same behavior in someone else as a shortcoming. We know that we are personally responsible for our successes, but our failures are the result of bad luck or circumstances beyond our control. When we are late it is for good reason; others keep us waiting because of their bad planning and insensitivity. Our miscalculation or misstatement is a simple mistake, but our opponent's similar error is the result of deception.

Some of the psychological factors and biases described above may work against one another when making tactical decisions driving a negotiation. For example, as will be discussed later, there are differing views about the advantages and disadvantages of making the first offer in a negotiation. Making the first offer, particularly if the values involved are uncertain or without ready comparisons, could take advantage of the anchoring bias set by your offer. However, reactive devaluation, which may be at a peak near the beginning of negotiations, could cause the other side to radically discount your first offer because of their suspicion.

> Questions
>
> 11.   Does knowing about the potential of these perceptual biases and cognitive errors result in not being affected by them? How can you best guard against them or overcome your own cognitive errors?
> 12.   What is your role if you are aware of your client's perception biases and cognitive distortions? Must you agree to a desired goal or an outcome acceptable to your client if you are aware that the goal or acceptance is the result of a misperception or cognitive error?
> 13.   How might you counter cognitive error and perceptual distortion that may result in your negotiating opponent rejecting a settlement that is otherwise acceptable? For example, how would you handle the anchoring problem, where your opponent is fixed on what you regard as an unrealistic outcome in another case, or the tendency of your opponent to reject your truly generous offer because of suspicion of any offer coming from you?

D.   The Role of Emotions and Emotional Intelligence

Many of us are attracted to the study of law because we value a rational approach to issues rather than emotional responses that seem to get in the way of logic and problem solving. The conventional wisdom is that lawyers should leave their emotions behind in their professional roles, including negotiating. This is easier said than done, and might not always be wise.

None of us are automatons, even when we try to appear so. Nor are those with whom we negotiate without emotional content that helps shape their conduct. We all have emotional needs and reactions that contribute to the creation of conflicts and are part of how we interact and deal with others. Recognizing and mastering these emotions is usually more helpful than denying and ignoring them.

More important, our clients have emotional needs that they might not readily express to us. As you learned from the readings in Chapter 2, emotional concerns, as well as substantive needs, may be critical factors that have to be satisfied to reach a settlement. Learning to recognize emotions as part of disputes and understanding their role can be an important key to negotiation success.

Negotiation effectiveness depends on interpersonal competency and a type of emotional intelligence. Emotional intelligence is the capacity to monitor our feelings and read the feelings of those whom we encounter as a guide to our actions and responses. Research (see Mayer, 2001) has helped isolate three primary components of emotional intelligence:

- emotional perception,
- emotional understanding, and
- emotional management.

An emotionally intelligent negotiator has an advantage in controlling her own emotions and understanding the emotions of an opponent to better control the negotiating process. Emotional intelligence may contribute to successful negotiator behavior (see Barry, Fulmer, and Van Kleef, 2004).

The theme of emotional intelligence and its role in success was brought to public attention by Daniel Goleman in his popular book, *Emotional Intelligence* (1995). Goleman identified 20 emotional intelligence competencies, which he thought "twice as important in contributing to excellence as . . . pure intellect and expertise." He clustered these emotional competencies in four related groups:

Self-Awareness	**Social Awareness**
Emotional self-awareness	Empathy
Accurate self-assessment	Organizational awareness
Self-confidence	Service orientation
Self-Management	**Social Skills**
Self-control	Developing others
Trustworthiness	Leadership
Conscientiousness	Influence
Adaptability	Communication
Achievement orientation	Change catalyst
Initiative	Conflict management
	Building bonds
	Teamwork and collaboration

Although there is a benefit in mastering any of these competencies, they complement one another. Mastering all 20 emotional competencies would be a tremendous advantage in negotiation and in life.

Joshua Rosenberg, a law professor and a psychologist, weaves together our previous readings on perception and self-fulfilling prophecies with emotional intelligence.

❖ **Joshua D. Rosenberg,** *Interpersonal Dynamics: Helping Lawyers Learn the Skills, and the Importance, of Human Relationships in the Practice of Law*

55 U. of Miami L. Rev. 1225 (2004)

Basically, most lawyers and academics vastly overestimate the importance of reason and logic. We tend to view them as both the primary motivator of our own behavior and the primary tool to change the thinking and behavior of others. Although they are important, they are only one part of the puzzle. There are important differences between the kind of dispassionate reasoning and analysis in which lawyers and law students engage while sitting at desks at home, in the office, or in the library, and the kind of activities in which we engage when we are dealing in real time with real people. Real time, real life interactions implicate emotions, learned patterns of behavior, habituated perspectives and frames of reference, and other human, but not reasoned, responses.

The reactions to emotions occur whether or not the person is aware of either the reaction or the emotion, and they significantly impact the outcome of most negotiations and most other interpersonal interactions. People who become anxious may tend to over-accommodate the other by inappropriately giving in on the substance of the discussion, or may tend to talk too much (or too little) in an unconscious effort to forestall that anxiety. People who become irritated may tend to become slightly belligerent or withdrawn in ways that can harm their interactions. Any feelings are likely to trigger unconscious patterns of thought and behavior that will inevitably influence an interaction. . . .

It is not just how we think about what we perceive that is tainted by our feelings. Our very perceptions themselves are determined, in part, by our feelings (and thoughts). As an initial matter, emotions precipitate changes in the autonomic nervous system. These changes include increasing the heart rate, changing breathing patterns, skin changes such as perspiration or blushing, and redirecting blood flow (anger has been found to direct blood to the hands, presumably for combat; fear has been shown to redirect blood to the legs, presumably for running). At a micro level, these changes in the autonomic nervous system change not only our ability to think, but also our ability to act and perceive. Along with our thoughts, our blood flow, and our energy, the focus of our attention and our ability to take in data are significantly changed by our emotional state. Not only our behavior, but also our perceptions become both differently focused and less accurate. . . .

The Result: Interacting Systems and Self-Fulfilling Prophecies

Basically, our thoughts, feelings, behaviors and perceptions influence each other. We react to our perceptions of the world around us while our own behavior impacts on the world. Of course, the patterns of our behavior, thoughts, perceptions and feelings are far from random. We tend to learn patterns of thought, feeling, and behavioral reactions in childhood. In adulthood we tend to engage in those patterns we learned as children, often resulting in "self- fulfilling prophecies" that tend to reinforce those same old patterns. Basically, because of our particular frame of reference (thoughts, feelings, etc.), we expect people to act in certain ways, and we act toward them in ways that tend to precipitate the behaviors we expect. When people do act in the ways we expected, we interpret that behavior in line with our expectations, and we react in certain predictable ways (which tend to confirm to us the validity of our earlier expectations).

Negotiation experts are aware of the significant impact of self-fulfilling prophecies on negotiations, but the actual impact of these patterns extends well beyond "negotiations," to encompass most of our interactions in life. . . . [S]elf-fulfilling prophecies and other generally unconscious learned responses significantly impact the outcome of most negotiations and most other interpersonal interactions.

Human Communication: Colliding Systems

As all of the above suggests, despite our typical estimation to the contrary, we are often unaware of the actual causes (and unintentional consequences) of our own behavior, thinking, emotions, and perceptions. We are not sufficiently self-aware to realize how many of our patterns of acting and thinking are ingrained, unconscious or triggered by our autonomic nervous system rather than by reason. Communication, of course, is a two way street, and much of the time we are even more misguided about what is headed toward us than we are about where we ourselves are going. Just as we incorrectly believe that we understand our own behavior better than we do, we also (and to a much greater degree) wrongly believe that we understand others much better than we actually do. . . .

As an initial matter, researchers have concluded that the single greatest weakness of most negotiators is that they too often fail to even consider the thinking and emotions of others. Perhaps even more significantly, when we do attempt to consider the thinking and feelings of others, we usually get it wrong. We often attribute to them moods, goals or motivations that simply are not there, or we exaggerate the significance of one of many reactions they may be having and forget that, like our own, their reactions might be both dynamic and complex.

While we tend to be accepting of situational factors that impact our own behavior, we tend to be unaware of, and inattentive to, the impact of such situational factors on others. As a result, we tend to think of ourselves as more sympathetic, as having a better case, or as being a better person than the one with whom we are dealing. In turn, this often leads us to devalue the other's case and proposals, and to fail to reach agreements that are available and would have been in our client's (or our own, as the case may be) best interest.

Basically, we tend to assume, too often inaccurately, that the message we take from the other is actually the message they intended to send. We vastly underestimate not only the impact of our own perspectives, feelings and thinking on the message we take in, but also the role of simple miscommunication.

Compounding the problem of our misperceptions of others is the fact that we are basically unaware that the problem even exists. Research clearly shows that more than 98% of us are unable to tell when others are lying or telling the truth. We are essentially equally likely to believe those who are lying as we are to believe those who are telling the truth, and we are equally likely to disbelieve those who are actually telling the truth as we are to disbelieve those who are actually lying. Interestingly, and typically, I have never met a person who believes that she is a part of that 98% majority.

All of this obviously makes for significant misunderstandings and unnecessary conflict. Even worse, it is often self-perpetuating. Because we believe that we already understand others, we rarely take the time to try to understand them better. If they do not act as we want or hope, we tend to attribute their "failure" to act "properly" to some personality defect on their part. Rather than seek to learn more about them, we tend to dismiss them or negatively characterize them. We will in turn likely act in ways that may ultimately alienate them, and they will likely react in ways that will confirm, in our minds, our initial understanding. Human communication is then the interaction of two individuals, each of whom believes that she alone understands both herself and the other, while in fact neither really understands either herself or the other, and neither seeks to gain understanding (because each thinks she already has it). Perhaps more surprising than the amount of miscommunication and conflict in the world is the fact that, at least occasionally, accurate communication does take place. . . .

Questions

14.   Do you agree that we vastly overestimate the importance of reason and logic?
15.   How would you describe the connection between emotional intelligence and successful negotiation?
16.   Can emotional intelligence be taught?

CHAPTER
4

Negotiator Styles

A. Competitive and Cooperative Negotiation

We each have our own approach of how to get what we want. So it is with negotiation. Our negotiation approach or style is rooted in our values, assumptions, experiences, goals, and the situation. Even though you may have a general style, you may change your approach to a negotiation based on the specifics and the needs of your client. Many terms are used to describe different negotiating styles in a range from hard to soft. For purposes of introducing the approaches and distinguishing them, we use here two basic categories: competitive and cooperative.

Consider the following example of two different approaches applied to an intellectual property claim at different stages in the dispute.

MICROSOFT v. STAC

Stac Electronics was an engineering company founded in 1983 by seven friends at Caltech. The company developed its "Stacker" disc compression software in 1990. Bill Gates, CEO of Microsoft, wanted Stac's data compression technology and met personally with Stac's president, Gary Clow, to discuss licensing of Stac's software. The negotiations were turned over to other Microsoft executives and lawyers to negotiate. Although willing to pay Stac a modest gross license fee, Microsoft refused to pay Stac any per-user royalty for its patented compression technology. Microsoft took a hard line, saying that it could have other sources develop reliable data compression technology that could be incorporated into the MS-DOS operating system, which would have an immediate and adverse effect on the viability of Stacker and threaten Stac's continued economic viability. Microsoft had a reputation of using its huge market share and resources to negotiate in a hard fashion and favorably license software that it incorporated into its products. Negotiations broke off, and in 1993, Microsoft released MS-DOS 6.0, which included a disk compression program called Double Space. Stac was outraged, as Microsoft had previously examined the Stacker code as part of the due diligence process in their earlier negotiations and Stac believed that Microsoft infringed its patent.

Microsoft would not budge on Stac's claim, and Stac filed a patent infringement suit against Microsoft. Microsoft counterclaimed that Stac had misappropriatedthe Microsoft trade secret of a preloading feature that was included in Stacker 3.1. In 1994, a federal court jury in California awarded Stac $120 million in compensatory damages, coming to about $5.50 per copy of MS-DOS 6.0 that had beensold. The jury also concluded that Stac misappropriated Microsoft's trade secret and simultaneously awarded Microsoft $13.6 million on the counterclaim.

Feelings on both sides were negative and intense. Mr. Clow appeared on CBS's *Eye to Eye with Connie Chung* and described his negotiations against Microsoft Chairman Bill Gates as "like a knife fight." Bill Gates, the subject of a profile on the show, walked out of an interview when Ms. Chung asked him about Mr. Clow's charges.

A new round of negotiations commenced in the changed circumstances of the jury verdict. Both sides had the option of legal appeals over the jury verdicts. Instead, their lawyers negotiated in a more cooperative manner and created a deal that caught Wall Street off guard, favorably affecting the share price of both companies. Each side agreed to drop its claims in exchange for cross-licensing all of their existing patents, as well as future ones over the next five years. The pact called for Microsoft to pay Stac license royalties totaling $43 million over 43 months, while also investing $39.9 million for a 15-percent equity stake in Stac. The total $82.9 million outlay represented a gain for Microsoft, which had already charged off $120 million for the jury award in its fiscal third quarter and now was able to credit much of the difference in the current period. Stac also came out ahead, by getting a significant cash infusion without a long appeals process to collect money from Microsoft. Mr. Clow said that $82.9 million being turned over by Microsoft represented more than Stac would have gotten had the $120 million been paid, because income taxes and Stac's own $13.6-million penalty would have whittled the final amount to about $64 million. In addition, Stac formed an alliance with the most powerful player in the software industry. Mr. Clow stated that, "this is not personal. This makes good business sense going forward. . . . This demonstrates it is possible to do win-win deals." Microsoft's executives concurred. "This is a lot more fun than disagreeing," said Michael Brown, Microsoft's vice president of finance, referring to the more cooperative final round of negotiation.

Bill Gates became the richest man in the world by being smart, diligent, and keenly competitive. As a negotiator, he was known for being aggressive and competitive, although there are accounts of him using his considerable creative skills to negotiate value-added cooperative outcomes. In the above example, Gates played hardball when he first negotiated with Stac's Clow because he thought it was to the advantage of Microsoft. That competitive approach, which in the past had served Microsoft's interest, backfired. Gates then changed his approach, having his lawyers negotiate a more cooperative deal going forward. Although the competitive and cooperative approaches are treated as seperate negotiation models, a skilled negotiator may at times employ one or the other, depending on assessment of the circumstances and goals. As we will see, your choice may also be a matter of your personal comfort zone.

The *competitive* approach assumes that the purpose of bargaining is to obtain the best possible economic result for your client, usually at the expense of the other side. A competitive bargainer is likely to think that negotiation involves a limited resource or fund that must be distributed between competing parties — in effect, a fixed economic "pie." In a competitive approach, the parties' relationships and other intangibles are not of primary importance. The competitive bargainer's goal is to pay as little as possible (if a buyer or defendant) or obtain as much as possible (if a seller or plaintiff), as a dollar more for your opponent is necessarily a dollar less for you. A competitive bargainer, in other words, sees negotiation much as a litigator sees a trial: Someone must win and someone must lose, and her central mission is to win. This approach is also known as "distributive" or "zero sum" bargaining, because the negotiators see their task as distributing a fixed, limited resource between them.

A simple example of where competitive bargaining is likely to occur is when a lawyer negotiates with an insurance adjuster in a distant city to settle a client's claim for property damage to a car caused by a falling tree limb. The client, we will assume, has since changed insurance companies, and the lawyer does not expect to do business with this adjuster again, so neither sees any interest in nurturing a relationship. In this situation both sides have a limited joint interest in conducting the bargaining process efficiently. Both the lawyer and the adjuster are likely to see their sole goal as agreeing on a dollar amount that the company will pay the insured to give up his claim, and to assume that a better settlement for one will necessarily be worse for the other.

In this negotiation, each side may posture about the dimensions of the issue or conflict, initiate a demand or offer (a specific proposal for resolving the dispute), and bargain over that proposal or present a counterproposal. A competitive negotiator will attempt to change the other side's perception to persuade them that their case is weaker and worth less than they thought and that her case is stronger and more valuable than her opponent previously recognized. Incremental concessions are usually made that narrow the bargaining range. Finally, a compromise settlement may be agreed upon. This approach to negotiation centers on predetermined positions and maximizing individual gain.

A *cooperative* bargainer, by contrast, does not view negotiation "pies" as fixed. Cooperative bargainers work to identify interests and examine differences in how the parties value items. They then search jointly with the other negotiator — viewed more as a partner rather than an opponent — for options and a solution that will best satisfy both parties' interests. Cooperative negotiation is marked by an effort to understand one another's perceptions and reexamine them together to arrive at a shared picture or a mutually acceptable valuation. This cooperative approach is frequently called "integrative" bargaining, because it emphasizes integrating the parties' needs to find the best joint solution. It is also referred to as "interest-based" negotiation because it sees the goal of bargaining as satisfying people's underlying interests.

Rather than moving from positions, to counter-positions, to a compromise settlement, cooperative negotiators search for a variety of alternatives that optimize the interests that they have prioritized. The parties can then create an outcome from a combination of generated options so that a joint decision, with more benefits to all, can be achieved. This more collaborative approach does not necessarily produce a simple compromise between competing positions. It seeks a creative settlement not bound by predetermined positions.

A classic situation that calls for cooperative bargaining is an effort by two businesses to form a joint venture. Cooperative bargainers would first ask what special resources and capabilities each partner could bring to the deal (for example, does Partner A have special expertise in marketing, whereas Partner B has more strength in design? Does one have good access to financing, whereas the other has open office space?). The negotiators would also ask whether either partner had particular needs, for example, one for an assured stream of income and the other for cutting-edge technology. Cooperative bargainers would focus on finding terms that best exploit each partner's abilities and minimize weaknesses, creating the strongest possible future partnership.

Cooperative and competitive bargaining are not mutually exclusive. Working to "bake" the biggest possible "pie" does not, in itself, say anything about how the final pie will be divided. Savvy competitive negotiators, for example, will look earnestly for ways to "expand the pie." Competitors, however, are likely to see expanding the pie as less important than getting the largest possible piece for their clients. Cooperative bargainers must also face the pie-dividing problem, but tend to give it less significance than competitors. In the joint venture example described above, cooperatives would emphasize creating the best possible deal. They would then look for a principle for dividing the benefits (that is, the "pie") that both partners saw as fair, rather than trying to outfox their partner to get the lion's share.

In practice, cooperative and competitive approaches may be mixed or sequenced, depending on the setting, subject matter, and personalities of the negotiators. However, descriptions of cooperative and competitive styles, as well as distinctions between these two approaches, provide a paradigm for understanding the dynamics of negotiation.

There are styles of negotiating that go beyond either cooperative or competitive, which might be seen as more intense versions of each approach. Those competitive negotiators that we label *adversarial* bargainers view negotiation as a kind of war and believe that all is fair in winning it. Extreme adversarial bargainers may be willing to renege on tentative agreements, misrepresent their authority, make empty threats, and distort facts that cannot easily be checked or challenged, if such tactics seem likely to win them a better outcome.

By contrast, *problem-solving* bargainers employ intensely cooperative, interest-based tactics. Problem solvers focus almost exclusively on finding solutions that will maximize the value of the deal for both parties. Problem solvers are extremely reluctant to obtain a better outcome for their client at the expense of their counterpart and insist on using genuinely neutral principles to accomplish the task of allocating benefits.

For simplicity, we follow the convention of generally referring to bargaining styles in terms of *competitive* and *cooperative*, but we also separately discuss adversarial and problem-solving techniques. The distinctions between adversarial and competitive styles (often used interchangeably), on the one hand, and cooperative and problem-solving styles (also used interchangeably), on the other hand, are not always clear. We will examine the underpinnings of the contrasting negotiation approaches and some of the strategies and tactics associated with each.

1. Competitive/Adversarial Approach

❖ Gary Goodpaster, *A Primer on Competitive Bargaining*
J. Disp. Resol. 325 (1996)

One cannot understand negotiation without understanding competitive behavior in negotiation. It is not that competing is a good way to negotiate; it may or may not be, depending on the circumstances. Understanding competition in negotiation is important simply because many people do compete when they negotiate, either by choice or happenstance. . . .

Competitive Negotiation Strategy

In competitive negotiation or distributive bargaining, the parties' actual or perceived respective aims or goals conflict. In this context, the negotiator's aim is to maximize the realization of its goals. Since the goals conflict, either in fact or supposition, one party's gains are the other party's losses. Therefore, a negotiator's goal is to win by gaining as much value as possible from the other party. . . . Not only is the competitive negotiator out to gain as much as he or she can, but he or she will take risks, even the risk of non-agreement, to secure a significant gain.

The competitive negotiator adopts a risky strategy which involves the taking of firm, almost extreme positions, making few and small concessions, and withholding information that may be useful to the other party. The intention, and hoped-for effect, behind this basic strategy is to persuade the other party that it must make concessions if it is to get an agreement. In addition to this basic strategy, competitive negotiators may also use various ploys or tactics aimed at pressuring, unsettling, unbalancing or even misleading the other party to secure an agreement with its demands.

In an important sense, the competitive negotiator plays negotiation as an information game. In this game, the object is to get as much information from the other party as possible while disclosing as little information as possible. Alternatively, a competitive negotiator sometimes provides the other party with misleading clues, bluffs, and ambiguous assertions with multiple meanings, which are not actually false, but nevertheless mislead the other party into drawing incorrect conclusions that are beneficial to the competitor.

The information the competitive negotiator seeks is the other party's bottom line. How much he will maximally give or minimally accept to make a deal. On the other hand, the competitive negotiator wants to persuade the other side about the firmness of the negotiator's own asserted bottom line. The competitive negotiator works to convince the other party that it will settle only at some point that is higher (or lower, as the case may be) than its actual and unrevealed bottom line.

In skillful hands the bargaining position performs a double function. It conceals, and it reveals. The bargaining position is used to indicate — to unfold gradually, step by step — the maximum expectation of the negotiator, while at the same time concealing, for as long as necessary, his minimum expectation.

By indirect means, such as the manner and timing of the changes in your bargaining position, you, as a negotiator, try to convince the other side that your maximum expectation is really your minimum breaking-off point. . . . Since you have taken an appropriate bargaining position at the start of negotiations, each change in your position should give ever-clearer indications of your maximum expectation. Also, each change should be designed to encourage or pressure the other side to reciprocate with at least as much information as you give them, if not more.

Taking a firm position and conceding little will incline the other party to think the competitor has little to give. Thus, if there is to be a deal, then the other party must give or concede more.

1. **Pure Bargaining, Haggling, and Just Trading Figures**

When the parties are apart and have no reason, other than their mutual choice, to settle at any particular point between them, they are in a "pure bargaining" situation. It is easy to see how the simple negotiation game . . . can degenerate into a contest of haggling or just trading figures. The parties' positions — the particular dollar figures they are offering — are not connected to any reason or rationale. Basically, both buyer and seller are seeking to maximize gains. Each attempts to accomplish this by seeing how far the other party can be pushed.

Often this happens in competitive bargaining, particularly with unsophisticated competitive bargainers and usually in the late and ending stages of a negotiation. When it occurs, the "take as much as you can" grab is transparent and signals that the parties, or at least one party, is bargaining just to win as much as possible. Automobile dealers' sales practices exemplify this phenomenon. A new car dealer usually pegs an asking price to a manufacturer's suggested retail sticker price and to items the dealer adds to the car. Once those starting prices are left behind, the dealer and buyer usually just trade dollar figures until they reach one they are both comfortable with. Similarly, travelers who visit native markets or bazaars, or those who visit flea markets or garage sales in this country, sometimes experience much the same kind of trading. Offers and counteroffers are thrown back and forth, each party testing the other party's resolve to stick with a figure by refusing to budge further or threatening to walk away. In essence, bargaining in this fashion is really nothing but a contest of firmness or a game of chicken.

2.   Focal Points or Mutually Prominent Alternatives

It is revealing to analyze a pure bargaining situation where two equally competitive negotiators bargain with each other. Once the bargaining parties have assured their bottom lines or reservation values and have staked out their respective positions on the bargaining range, nothing inherently seems to impel settlement at any particular point between the positions, except each party's expectations regarding what the other side in fact will accept. This is problematic, however, for with each guided by expectations and knowing that the other is too, expectations become compounded. A bargain is struck when somebody makes a final, sufficient concession. Why does he concede? Because he thinks the other will not. "I must concede because he won't. He won't because he thinks I will. He thinks I will because he thinks I think he thinks so. . . . " There is some range of alternative outcomes in which any point is better for both sides than no agreement at all. To insist on any such point is pure bargaining, since one always would take less rather than reach no agreement at all, and since one always can recede if retreat proves necessary to agreement. Yet if both parties are aware of the limits to this range, any outcome is a point from which at least one party would have been willing to retreat and the other knows it! . . .

Because people bargain competitively for various reasons, negotiators and mediators need to understand competition in negotiation in order to respond appropriately. Some people bargain competitively without giving much conscious attention to the matter. Others compete in response to the other party's competitive behavior. In this response, they follow the common pattern that a particular kind of behavior elicits a similar behavior in response. In other words, one party frames the negotiation as a contest, and the other party picks up the competitive cues and behaves accordingly. Further, people naturally incline to competitive bargaining when they are non-trusting. In such situations, in order to avoid putting themselves at risk, non-trusting people act guardedly and adopt elements of the competitive strategy, for example, withholding information or misrepresenting a position. Finally, one can readily imagine ambiguous bargaining situations, in which at least one party is non-trusting, quickly devolving into a competitive negotiation between both parties. The non-trusting party acts defensively, and the other party senses this as competitive behavior and, therefore, acts in a similar fashion.

Negotiators, however, can also consciously adopt a competitive strategy. Negotiators are most likely to compete purposefully when:

- the parties have an adversarial relationship;
- a negotiator has a bargaining power advantage and can dominate the situation;
- a negotiator perceives an opportunity for gain at the expense of the other party;

- the other party appears susceptible to competitive tactics;
- the negotiator is defending against competitive moves; or
- there is no concern for the future relationship between the parties.

This list suggests that competitive bargaining most likely occurs in situations such as labor and lawsuit negotiations, insurance and similar claims type settlements, and in one-time transactions between a relatively experienced party and a relatively inexperienced party. One would, for example, expect to see it in sales transactions where the parties will probably not see each other again.

Representative bargaining or bargaining for a constituency may also prompt competitive bargaining even when there will be future negotiations between equally sophisticated parties. The negotiator's accountability may override relationship concerns and reasons for cooperation. The concerned audience, consisting of a client, constituency, coalition partner, or other phantom party at the table, is, in effect, looking over the negotiator's shoulder. The negotiator, therefore, takes positions and makes moves she believes her client either expects or would approve. International negotiations between countries, union-management, lawsuit negotiations, and negotiations between different parties in interest-group coalition negotiations sometimes evidence this pattern.

Aside from circumstantial or situational pressures, there are some parties who bargain competitively because they believe that is the way to conduct business. There are also parties who are simply predisposed to bargain competitively and will incline to do so opportunistically in any bargaining situation if possible.

Finally, it is important to note that one can bargain competitively in a negotiation on some issues and cooperatively on others. In other words, a negotiator can selectively use competitive strategy or tactics on particular issues, while using a cooperative or problem-solving strategy on other issues. In such a case, extracting gain competitively may not greatly endanger future relationships. . . .

Obviously, competitive bargaining covers a continuum of behaviors from the simplest, unreflective adversarial actions to highly conscious and virtually scripted contests. As such, competitive bargaining moves are natural responses in some negotiation situations and advantageous or profitable actions in others. . . .

Questions

1. What are the advantages of adopting a competitive approach to bargaining?
2. What are the downsides of competitive bargaining?
3. Have you experienced competitive negotiation? What were the circumstances?

We turn now to a more aggressive form of competitive negotiation, which we refer to as *adversarial*. There is no shortage of advice about how to be a tough bargainer and how to get what you want in a negotiation. Check the self-help and business advice sections of large booksellers for an array of titles on this subject, including *Guerrilla Negotiating* (1999). Although adversarial negotiation may at times be advantageous, many of these guides appear to assume that the opposing side is ignorant or gullible and will have no future opportunity to retaliate. Other books and articles catalog "hardball'" tactics to warn you of what you might encounter. These writings are premised on the theory that to be "forewarned is forearmed." Roger Dawson, the author of *Secrets of Power Negotiating* (2001), challenges the myth of cooperative "win-win" negotiation before sharing his adversarial secrets and what you need to watch out for so you do not become the victim of others' hardball tactics. His list of power negotiating gambits includes the following:

- *Ask for more than you expect to get:* You can get away with an outrageous opening position if you imply some flexibility.
- *Never say yes to the first offer:* Saying yes triggers two thoughts in the other person's mind: "I could have done better," and "something must be wrong."
- *Flinch at proposals:* The other side may not expect to get what is asked for; however, if you do not show surprise you're communicating that it is a possibility.
- *Always play reluctant seller:* This is a great way to squeeze the other side's negotiating range before the negotiation even starts.
- *Use the vise technique:* "You'll have to do better than that."
- *Don't let the other side know you have the authority to make a decision:* Don't let the other person trick you into admitting that you have authority.
- *Don't fall into the trap of thinking that splitting the difference is the fair thing to do:* Splitting the difference doesn't mean down the middle, because you can do it more than once.
- *Always ask for a trade-off:* Anytime the other side asks you for a concession, ask for something in return.
- *Good guy/bad guy:* It's an effective way of putting more pressure on the other person without creating confrontation.
- *Nibbling:* Using the nibbling gambit, you can get a little bit more even after you have agreed on everything.
- *Taper concessions:* Taper concessions to communicate that the other side is getting the best possible deal.
- *Withdrawing an offer:* You can do it by backing off your last price concession or by withdrawing an offer to include freight, installation, and so on.
- *The decoy:* Use a decoy to take attention away from the real issue in the negotiation.

- *Red herring:* This is a phony demand that can be withdrawn, but only in exchange for a concession.
- *Cherry picking:* Ask for alternatives and then pick the best parts from multiple choices.
- *Escalation:* Raising demands after both sides reach an agreement.
- *Time pressure:* The rule in negotiating is that 80 percent of the concessions occur in the last 20 percent of time available.
- *Being prepared to walk away:* Project to the other side that you will walk away from the negotiations if you can't get what you want.
- *The fait accompli:* This occurs when one negotiator simply assumes the other will accept an assumed settlement rather than go to the trouble of reopening the negotiations.
- *Ultimatums:* Ultimatums are very high-profile statements that tend to strike fear into inexperienced negotiators.

Questions

4. Do any of these tactics seem unethical? Negotiation presents a fertile area for ethical transgressions, with relatively little guidance as to ethical limits. The ethics of negotiation are addressed in Chapter 7.
5. Is there a difference between hard, competitive negotiation and "dirty" bargaining tricks? If so, how would you distinguish them?
6. Are there any gambits or techniques that you could add to Dawson's list?
7. If the tactics listed by Dawson were used against you, what would you do? If any of these behaviors did produce an adverse result for your client, what would be your approach the next time you found yourself matched against this opponent?

Note: Responses to Competitive Hardball and Difficult People

Some of the books and articles cataloging competitive negotiation tactics also prescribe competitive antidotes that could be used in response. Most of these reactive "hardball" tactics are either responses in kind or intended to notch up the positioning in a dance of "one-upmanship." The most effective countermove or response to sharp competitive tactics will depend on the context of the negotiation, your relationship with the other negotiators, your alternatives to continued negotiations, the strength of your own position, your goals in the negotiation, and the information available to you. The key to any effective response is being able to recognize aggressive and deceptive tactics and understanding their potential effect in distorting your perspective and masking the opposition's weaknesses.

There are alternatives to responding in kind to hardball tactics or ending the negotiation. The behavior can be recognized and labeled for what it is and then dismissed by making light of it, or you can just ignore it. You can be direct by making it clear that the tactic is not working and is interfering with either of you getting what you want out of a possible deal or settlement, and that it will not be tolerated. In effect, you can discuss and set ground rules for further negotiations. Hardball tactics are most commonly used in the absence of an ongoing relationship or friendship. Taking time to become friendlier before the bargaining begins or emphasizing the likely continuing contact or repeat plays following this negotiation might discourage hardball tactics — or it might not.

The subject of responding to aggressive moves is related more generally to how we can best negotiate with people we consider difficult. Seminars and training programs are frequently offered to help us deal with "difficult people." The proliferation of these programs, including ones offered for attorneys, reflects the commonly experienced frustration most of us have had in trying to work or negotiate with others whom we perceive as being insensitive, obstinate, selfish, overly competitive, or generally unreasonable. It is an interesting paradox that experience with difficult people should be so common when few, if any, of us view ourselves as being difficult. Do you think the people you consider difficult believe themselves to be so? Studies show that opponents usually see us as more demanding and less reasonable than we view ourselves (Thomas and Pondy, 1977).

William Ury, in his book *Getting Past No: Negotiating with Difficult People* (1991), outlines problem behavior from difficult people in negotiations and offers five easy-to-remember counter-tactics, to which we have added our summary of his advice:

Stage One: Don't React — Go to the Balcony. This means controlling your own behavior and distancing yourself from your natural impulses and emotions. Become an observer to an opponent's bad behavior rather than getting sucked into the game.

Stage Two: Disarm Them — Step to Their Side. Don't fight your opponent, join him. Defuse anger, fear, and suspicion. Feel his pain and empathize, without agreeing to his demands or conceding.

Stage Three: Change the Game — Don't Reject . . . Reframe. Ask questions to figure out what motivates the difficult behavior. Reshape the negotiation to address the issue you want to resolve and in the direction you want it to move.

Stage Four: Make It Easy to Say Yes — Build Them a Golden Bridge. Make your devised outcome the opponent's idea, involve him in the solution, and help him "save face" and look good. Act more like a mediator than an adversary.

Stage Five: Make It Hard to Say No — Bring Them to Their Senses, Not Their Knees. Now that you have made it easy for the opponent to say yes, educate him so it is difficult to say no. Make it clear that his alternatives are worse than what you are offering.

2.   Cooperative Problem-Solving Approach

Cooperative or collaborative negotiation involves parties in an effort to jointly meet each others' needs and satisfy interests. In their best-selling book *Getting to Yes* (1991), which popularized non-adversarial negotiation, Roger Fisher, William Ury, and Bruce Patton suggest that "you can change the game," so that negotiation need not be positional or competitive. They prescribe an interest-based approach with suggested tactics and the use of objective criteria for joint decisions that they refer to as "principled" negotiation or "negotiation on the merits." *Getting to Yes* is recommended reading in many courses and training classes, so you may be familiar with it. The five basic elements of principled negotiation as listed by Fisher, Ury, and Patton are:

1. *Separate the people from the problem.* The negotiators should focus on attacking the problem posed by the negotiations, not each other.
2. *Focus on interests, not positions.* Distinguish positions, which are what you want, from interests, which are why you want them. Look for mutual or complementary interests that will make agreement possible.
3. *Invent options for mutual gain.* Even if the parties' interests differ, there might be bargaining outcomes that will advance the interests of both. The story is told of two sisters who are trying to decide which of them should get the only orange in the house. Once they realize that one sister wants to squeeze the orange for its juice, and the other wants to grate the rind to flavor a cake, a "win-win" agreement that furthers the interests of each becomes apparent.
4. *Insist on objective criteria.* Not all disputes and negotiations lend themselves to a "win-win" outcome. An insurance claim for damage to a car may create such a dispute, as each dollar paid by the insurance company is one dollar less for it. (Bargaining about issues of this nature is generally referred to as "zero-sum" bargaining.) Fisher, Ury, and Patton suggest that the parties first attempt to agree on objective criteria to determine the outcome. Thus, instead of negotiating over the value of a destroyed car, both parties might agree that the standard "blue book" price will determine the settlement amount. "Commit yourself to reaching a solution based on principle, not pressure."
5. *Know your Best Alternative to a Negotiated Agreement (BATNA).* The reason you negotiate with someone is to produce better results than you could obtain without negotiating. If you do not know the best you are likely to

obtain without negotiating, you might accept an offer you should reject or might reject an offer better than you can otherwise get. Your BATNA is the measure to decide if you are better off agreeing to a negotiated outcome or pursuing your alternatives, whether it be a trial or a deal with someone else. Your BATNA is the basis of comparison to protect you from bad negotiating decisions and permits the exploration of imaginative solutions to satisfy your interests.

Note: Positions vs. Interests

   The central theme of cooperative negotiation is that the negotiators focus on the parties' underlying interests rather than on the positions they take. Interest-based bargainers begin with the assumption that a party's position is simply one way (and often not the most efficient or effective one) to satisfy a need or interest. In most disputes parties have multiple interests of varying intensities. In Chapter 2 we looked at the triangle of conflict and presented the three components of satisfactory settlements as the three "Es": economic, emotional, and environmental. These relate to the interests that cooperative negotiators attempt to meet in working toward an integrative resolution. Similarly, *Getting to Yes* explains interests in terms of "basic human needs," including security, economic well-being, a sense of belonging, recognition, and control over one's life (1991, 48). These needs or interests can be further explained as follows:

- *Process interests*. People have a "process" interest in having disagreements resolved in a manner they consider fair. This usually includes the opportunity to tell their story and have the feeling that they have been understood. A cooperative negotiator will sometimes address an opponent's process interest by listening quietly while he vents angry emotions or accusations, then demonstrating, for example, by summarizing what has been said, that while the listener does not agree with what the speaker has said, he has heard and made an effort to understand it — so-called active listening ("So if I understand you correctly, you believe that . . . "). Participants may also have an interest in having a negotiation proceed in an orderly and predictable way.
- *Personal interests*. Most people have a personal interest in feeling respected in their work and as human beings, and in being seen as acting consistently with what they have said in the past and in accordance with their moral standards. Negotiators might address these personal interests by treating everyone courteously and attending to "face saving" needs.

- *Relational interests*. The parties might also have an interest in preserving or creating an ongoing relationship. This is particularly true in contractual disputes, because the very existence of a contract indicates that the parties once saw a benefit in working together, but it can also be true in disputes that arise from less formal connections. Examples of situations with relational interests include divorce and child custody disputes, land use controversies between neighbors, workplace disputes, and disagreements between companies and longtime customers.
- *Economic interests*. Disputants usually have economic or substantive interests. This is where most negotiations begin and where many end unsuccessfully because other interests are not addressed. Economic interests are most easy to state in the form of demands and offers, which are statements of positions. These positions may be misleading when viewed only in terms of dollars. People need money to satisfy other needs, whether material, social, or emotional. Finding out how the money will be used or what needs it will satisfy is essential to fashioning an interest-based agreement or integrative outcome.

Fisher, Ury, and Patton recognize that it is not always easy in negotiations to identify interests, as distinguished from positions. The technique they recommend is to ask "Why?" Why do you want a particular outcome, and why does the other side take the position it does? Do not ask the person with whom you are negotiating "Why?" to seek justification of his position or challenge it, "but for an understanding of the needs, hopes, fears, or desires that it serves" (1991, 44). If you understand why the person wants what he is insisting upon, you can better explore how his interests can be met so you can get from him what you need.

A variation of the cooperative approach, or perhaps another label for it, is *problem solving*. Problem-solving negotiators employ intensely cooperative, interest-based tactics. Problem solvers focus almost exclusively on finding solutions that will maximize the value of the deal for both parties. Problem solvers do not want to obtain a better outcome for their client at the expense of their counterpart and insist on using genuinely neutral principles to accomplish the task of allocating benefits. Negotiation is viewed as a collaboration to solve the challenge of finding opportunities for creating additional value through complementary interests. An early voice for the problem-solving approach to negotiation summarized the process as follows: "The creative problem-solving approach outlined here depends on two structural components: (1) identifying the parties' underlying needs and objectives, and (2) crafting solutions, first by attempting to meet those needs directly, and second, by attempting to meet more of those needs through expanding the resources available. By utilizing such a framework for negotiations, the parties should recognize the synergistic advantage of such an approach over the adversarial and manipulative strategies of zero-sum negotiations" (Menkel-Meadow, 1984).

B. The Tension Between Creating Value and Claiming Value

The negotiation concepts popularized by *Getting to Yes*, whether labeled as cooperative or problem solving, have been widely taught and very influential since the book first appeared in 1981. However, some experienced negotiators believe the underlying theory and tactics espoused by Fisher, Ury, and Patton are naive and could set up adherents to this approach for failure. One frequently cited critic is James White, a well-respected professor and longtime teacher of negotiation. Professor White's review, excerpted next, is followed by comments from Professor Fisher.

❖ **James J. White,** *Pros and Cons of "Getting to Yes"; and Roger Fisher, Comment on White's Review*

34 J. Legal Educ. 115 (1984)

Getting to Yes is a puzzling book. On the one hand it offers a forceful and persuasive criticism of much traditional negotiating behavior. It suggests a variety of negotiating techniques that are both clever and likely to facilitate effective negotiation. On the other hand, the authors seem to deny the existence of a significant part of the negotiation process, and to oversimplify or explain away many of the most troublesome problems inherent in the art and practice of negotiation. The book is frequently naive, occasionally self-righteous, but often helpful. . . .

Unfortunately the book's emphasis upon mutually profitable adjustment, on the "problem solving" aspect of bargaining, is also the book's weakness. It is a weakness because emphasis of this aspect of bargaining is done to almost total exclusion of the other aspect of bargaining, "distributional bargaining," where one for me is minus one for you. . . . [S]ome would describe a typical negotiation as one in which the parties initially begin by cooperative or efficiency bargaining in which each gains something with each new adjustment without the other losing any significant benefit. Eventually, however, one comes to bargaining in which added benefits to one impose corresponding significant costs on the other. . . .

One can concede the authors' thesis (that too many negotiators are incapable of engaging in problem solving or in finding adequate options for mutual gain), yet still maintain that the most demanding aspect of nearly every negotiation is the distributional one in which one seeks more at the expense of the other. My principal criticism of the book is that it seems to overlook the ultimate hard bargaining. Had the authors stated that they were dividing the negotiation process in two and were dealing with only part of it, that omission would be excusable. That is not what they have done. Rather they seem to assume that a clever negotiator can make any negotiation into problem solving. . . . To my mind this is naive. By so distorting reality, they detract from their powerful and central thesis.

Chapter 5, entitled "Insist on Objective Criteria," is a particularly naive misperception or rejection of the guts of distributive negotiation. Here, as elsewhere, the authors draw a stark distinction between a negotiator who simply takes a position without explanation and sticks to it as a matter of "will," and the negotiator who is reasonable and insists upon "objective criteria." Of course the world is hardly as simple as the authors suggest. Every party who takes a position will have some rationale for that position; every able negotiator rationalizes every position that he takes. Rarely will an effective negotiator simply assert "X" as his price and insist that the other party meet it.

The suggestion that one can find objective criteria (as opposed to persuasive rationalizations) seems quite inaccurate. . . . To say that there are objective criteria . . . in the case of a personal injury suit for a million dollars or an $800,000 judgment, is to ignore the true dynamics of the situation and to exaggerate the power of objective criteria. Any lawyer who has been involved in a personal injury suit will marvel at the capacity of an effective plaintiff's lawyer . . . to give the superficial appearance of certainty and objectivity to questions that are inherently imponderable. . . . Their suggestion that the parties look to objective criteria to strengthen their cases is a useful technique used by every able negotiator. Occasionally it may do what they suggest: give an obvious answer on which all can agree. Most of the time it will do no more than give the superficial appearance of reasonableness and honesty to one party's position. . . .

The author's consideration of "dirty tricks" in negotiation suffers from more of the same faults found in their treatment of objective criteria. At a superficial level I find their treatment of dirty tricks to be distasteful because it is so thoroughly self-righteous. The chapter is written as though there were one and only one definition of appropriate negotiating behavior. . . . The authors seem not to perceive that between "full disclosure" and "deliberate deception" lies a continuum, not a yawning chasm. They seem to ignore the fact that in one sense the negotiator's role is at least passively to mislead his opponent about his settling point while at the same time to engage in ethical behavior.

Finally, because the book almost totally disregards distributive bargaining, it necessarily ignores a large number of factors that probably have a significant impact on the outcome of negotiations. . . . There is evidence that the level of the first offer, and the pace and form of concessions all affect the outcome of negotiation, yet there is no consideration of those matters. Doubtless the authors can be forgiven for that. No book of 163 pages can be expected to deal with every aspect of negotiation. Yet this one suffers more than most, for implicitly if not explicitly, it seems to suggest that it is presenting the "true method." . . .

Comment by Roger Fisher

. . . White is more concerned with the way the world is, and I am more concerned with what intelligent people ought to do. One task is to teach the truth, to tell students the unpleasant facts of life, including how people typically negotiate. But I want a student to negotiate better than his or her father. I see my task as to give the best possible prescriptive advice, taking into account the way other human beings are likely to behave as well as one's own emotions and psychological state. . . .

The world is a rough place. It is also a place where, taken collectively, we are incompetent at resolving our differences in ways that efficiently and amicably serve our mutual interest. It is important that students learn about bluffing and hard bargaining, because they will certainly encounter it. It is also important that our students become more skillful and wise than most people in dealing with differences. Thus to some extent, White and I are emphasizing different aspects of what needs to be taught. . . .

The most fundamental difference between White's way of thinking and mine seems to concern the negotiation of distributional issues "where one for me is minus one for you." . . . By focusing on the substantive issues (where the parties' interests may be directly opposed), White overlooks the shared interest that the parties continue to have in the process for resolving that substantive difference. How to resolve the substantive difference is a shared problem. Both parties have an interest in identifying quickly and amicably a result acceptable to each, if one is possible. How to do so is a problem. A good solution to that process-problem requires joint action. . . .

The guts of the negotiation problem, in my view, is not who gets the last dollar, but what is the best process for resolving that issue. It is certainly a mistake to assume that the only process available for resolving distributional questions is hard bargaining over positions. In my judgment it is also a mistake to assume that such hard bargaining is the best process for resolving differences efficiently and in the long-term interest of either side. . . .

White seems to find the concept of "raw power" useful for a negotiator. I do not. For a negotiator, the critical questions of power are (1) how to enhance one's ability to influence favorably a negotiator on the other side, and (2) how to use such ability as one has. My ability to exert influence depends upon the cumulative impact of several factors: skill and knowledge, the state of our relationship, the legitimacy of our respective interests, the elegance of a proposed solution, my willingness and ability to commit myself, and the relative attractiveness to each side of its best alternative. In advance of a negotiation I can work to enhance each of those elements . . .

Without knowing the particular subject matter of a negotiation or the identity of the people on the other side, what is the best advice one can give to a negotiator? People may prefer to ask different questions, but I have not yet heard better answers to the question on which we were and are working. . . .

Questions and Note

8. Are you more persuaded by White or Fisher? Is Professor Fisher naive, or is Professor White too skeptical? Can they both be correct in some ways?

9. Have you experienced situations in which you were open and cooperative initially and then felt that you might have revealed too much or been too accommodating, so that you did not get what you wanted for yourself? If you were in that same situation again, would you behave differently? What are the trade-offs?

10. If a positional negotiator views the person across the table as an opponent, and if an adversarial bargainer views that person as an adversary, then what is the most apt designation for the person at the table with a cooperative or problem-solving negotiator?

11. Does an attorney's reputation for openness and cooperation present a particular attraction to a client willing to pay a premium for that attorney to engage in "hard bargaining" or sharp tactics on his behalf? (For an interesting real-life example, see David McKean and Douglas Frantz's *Friends in High Places: The Rise and Fall of Clark Clifford*, 1995.)

12. Can "problem-solving" negotiation occur if only one side wants to pursue this approach?

The distributional bargaining to which Professors White and Fisher refer occurs when a single, quantitative issue is being negotiated or all apparent possibilities of joint gain have been exhausted. Negotiation by a tourist over the cash price of an item from a transient merchant at a bazaar is a simple example of a zero-sum distributional game, in which a dollar more for the seller is a dollar less for the purchaser and no future relationship is anticipated. Where the possibility exists to go beyond a zero-sum situation and create additional value, such as in the Microsoft–Stac dispute reported earlier, the negotiation becomes more complex and tactical choices must be made.

The next reading, from an influential book by David Lax and James Sebenius, introduces the "negotiator's dilemma," the tension that exists between the behaviors that tend to create value and those that individually claim the value jointly created. They identify some of the sources of creating value in negotiation and suggest open communication and sharing information to avoid leaving joint gains on the table. The critique by Gerald Wetlaufer, which follows our note on differences and joint gains, is more cautionary about buying into "win-win" negotiation and advises against sharing certain information, at least for the pecuniary reasons offered by Lax and Sebenius.

❖ **David A. Lax and James K. Sebenius,** *The Manager as Negotiator: Bargaining for Cooperation and Competitive Gain*

29, The Free Press (1986)

The Negotiator's Dilemma: Creating and Claiming Value

We assume that each negotiator strives to advance his interests, whether they are narrowly conceived or include such concerns as improving the relationship, acting in accord with conceptions of equity, or furthering the welfare of others. Negotiators must learn, in part from each other, what is jointly possible and desirable. To do so requires some degree of cooperation. But, at the same time, they seek to advance their individual interests. This involves some degree of competition.

That negotiation includes cooperation and competition, common and conflicting interests, is nothing new. In fact, it is typically understood that these elements are both present and can be disentangled.

Deep down, however, some people believe that the elements of conflict are illusory, that meaningful communication will erase any such unfortunate misperceptions. Others see mainly competition and take the cooperative pieces to be minimal. Some overtly acknowledge the reality of each aspect but direct all their attention to one of them and wish, pretend, or act as if the other does not exist. Still others hold to a more balanced view that accepts both elements as significant but seeks to treat them separately.... [W]e argue that all these approaches are flawed.

A deeper analysis shows that the competitive and cooperative elements are inextricably entwined. In practice, they cannot be separated. This bonding is fundamentally important to the analysis, structuring, and conduct of negotiation. There is a central, inescapable tension between cooperative moves to create value jointly and competitive moves to gain individual advantage. This tension affects virtually all tactical and strategic choice. Analysts must come to grips with it; negotiators must manage it. Neither denial nor discomfort will make it disappear.

Warring Conceptions of Negotiation

Negotiators and analysts tend to fall into two groups that are guided by warring conceptions of the bargaining process. In the left-hand corner are the "value creators" and in the right-hand corner are the "value claimers."

Value Creators

Value creators tend to believe that, above all, successful negotiators must be inventive and cooperative enough to devise an agreement that yields considerable gain to each party, relative to no-agreement possibilities. Some speak about the need for replacing the "win-lose" image of negotiation with "win-win" negotiation, from which all parties presumably derive great value. . . .

Communication and sharing information can help negotiators to create value jointly. Consider the case of a singer negotiating with the owner of an auditorium over payment for a proposed concert. They reached impasse over the size of the fee with the performer's demands exceeding the owner's highest offer. In fact, when the amount of the fixed payment was the issue, no possibility of agreement may have existed at all. The singer, however, based his demand on the expectation that the house would certainly be filled with fans while the owner projected only a half-capacity crowd. Ironically, this difference in their beliefs about attendance provided a way out. They reached a mutually acceptable arrangement in which the performer received a modest fixed fee plus a set percentage of the ticket receipts. The singer, given his beliefs, thus expected an adequate to fairly large payment; the concert hall owner was happy with the agreement because he only expected to pay a moderate fee. This "contingent" arrangement . . . permitted the concert to occur, leaving both parties feeling better off and fully willing to live with the outcome.

In addition to information sharing and honest communication, the drive to create value by discovering joint gains can require ingenuity and may benefit from a variety of techniques and attitudes. The parties can treat the negotiation as solving a joint problem; they can organize brainstorming sessions to invent creative solutions to their problems. They may succeed by putting familiar pieces of the problem together in ways that people had not previously seen, as well as by wholesale reformulations of the problem.

Roger Fisher and Bill Ury give an example that concerns the difficult Egyptian Israeli negotiations over where to draw a boundary in the Sinai. This appeared to be an absolutely classic example of zero sum bargaining, in which each square mile lost to one party was the other side's gain. For years the negotiations proceeded inconclusively with proposed boundary lines drawn and redrawn on innumerable maps. On probing the real interests of the two sides, however, Egypt was found to care a great deal about sovereignty over the Sinai while Israel was heavily concerned with its security. As such, a creative solution could be devised to "unbundle" these different interests and give to each what it valued most. In the Sinai, this involved creating a demilitarized zone under the Egyptian flag. This had the effect of giving Egypt "sovereignty" and Israel "security." This situation exemplifies extremely common tendencies to assume that negotiators' interests are in direct opposition, a conviction that can sometimes be corrected by communicating, sharing information, and inventing solutions. . . .

We create value by finding joint gains for all negotiating parties. A joint gain represents an improvement from each party's point of view; one's gain need not be another's loss. An extremely simple example makes the point. Say that two young boys each have three pieces of fruit. Willy, who hates bananas and loves pears, has a banana and two oranges. Sam, who hates pears and loves bananas, has a pear and two apples. The first move is easy: they trade banana for pear and are both happier. But after making this deal, they realize that they can do still better. Though each has a taste both for apples and oranges, a second piece of the same fruit is less desirable than the first. So they also swap an apple for an orange. The banana-pear exchange represents an improvement over the no-trade alternative; the apple orange transaction that leaves each with three different kinds of fruit improves the original agreement — is a joint gain — for both boys.

The economist's analogy is simple: Creativity has expanded the size of the pie under negotiation. Value creators see the essence of negotiating as expanding the pie, as pursuing joint gains. This is aided by openness, clear communication, sharing information, creativity, an attitude of joint problem solving, and cultivating common interests.

Value Claimers

Value claimers, on the other hand, tend to see this drive for joint gain as naive and weak minded. For them, negotiation is hard, tough bargaining. The object of negotiation is to convince the other guy that he wants what you have to offer much more than you want what he has; moreover, you have all the time in the world while he is up against pressing deadlines. To "win" at negotiating — and thus make the other fellow "lose" — one must start high, concede slowly, exaggerate the value of concessions, minimize the benefits of the other's concessions, conceal information, argue forcefully on behalf of principles that imply favorable settlements, make commitments to accept only highly favorable agreements, and be willing to outwait the other fellow.

The hardest of bargainers will threaten to walk away or to retaliate harshly if their one-sided demands are not met; they may ridicule, attack, and intimidate their adversaries. . . . At the heart of this adversarial approach is an image of a negotiation with a winner and a loser: "We are dividing a pie of fixed size and every slice I give to you is a slice I do not get; thus, I need to claim as much of the value as possible by giving you as little as possible."

A Fundamental Tension of Negotiation

Both of these images of negotiation are incomplete and inadequate. Value creating and value claiming are linked parts of negotiation. Both processes are present. No matter how much creative problem solving enlarges the pie, it must still be divided; value that has been created must be claimed. And, if the pie is not enlarged, there will be less to divide; there is more value to be claimed if one has helped create it first. An essential tension in negotiation exists between cooperative moves to create value and competitive moves to claim it.

[T]he concert hall owner may offer the singer a percentage of the gate combined with a fixed fee that is just barely high enough to induce the singer to sign the contract. Even when the parties to a potential agreement share strong common interests, one side may claim the lion's share of the value an agreement creates. . . .

The Tension at the Tactical Level

The tension between cooperative moves to create value and competitive moves to claim it is greatly exacerbated by the interaction of the tactics used either to create or claim value.

First, tactics for claiming value (which we will call "claiming tactics") can impede its creation. Exaggerating the value of concessions and minimizing the benefit of others' concessions presents a distorted picture of one's relative preferences; thus, mutually beneficial trades may not be discovered. Making threats or commitments to highly favorable outcomes surely impedes hearing and understanding others' interests. Concealing information may also cause one to leave joint gains on the table. In fact, excessive use of tactics for claiming value may well sour the parties' relationship and reduce the trust between them. Such tactics may also evoke a variety of unhelpful interests. Conflict may escalate and make joint prospects less appealing and settlement less likely.

Second, approaches to creating value are vulnerable to tactics for claiming value. Revealing information about one's relative preferences is risky. . . . The information that a negotiator would accept position A in return for a favorable resolution on a second issue can be exploited: "So, you'll accept A. Good. Now, let's move on to discuss the merits of the second issue." The willingness to make a new, creative offer can often be taken as a sign that its proposer is able and willing to make further concessions. Thus, such offers sometimes remain undisclosed. Even purely shared interests can be held hostage in exchange for concessions on other issues. Though a divorcing husband and wife may both prefer giving the wife custody of the child, the husband may "suddenly" develop strong parental instincts to extract concessions in alimony in return for giving the wife custody.

In tactical choices, each negotiator thus has reasons not to be open and cooperative. Each also has apparent incentives to try to claim value. Moves to claim value thus tend to drive out moves to create it. Yet, if both choose to claim value, by being dishonest or less than forthcoming about preferences, beliefs, or minimum requirements, they may miss mutually beneficial terms for agreement.

Indeed, the structure of many bargaining situations suggests that negotiators will tend to leave joint gains on the table or even reach impasses when mutually acceptable agreements are available.

Note: Differences Can Create Joint Gains

Lax and Sebenius go on to summarize the differences that can lead to joint gains and creation of value. In an article published in 2002, they elaborate on differences that may be the source of unrealized value. These differences can be summarized as follows:

- Differences in relative valuation or priorities can lead to exchanges, directly or by "unbundling" differently valued interests. The apple and orange fruit exchange noted in the reading is an example of differences in relative valuation that create trading value.
- Differences in tolerance for risk and *risk aversion* suggest insurance-like risk-sharing arrangements in negotiated transactions. A risk-averse litigant may be willing to discount what she will receive or pay more as a certain amount rather than bear the risk of losing at trial. If the opposing side is more risk tolerant, they can be rewarded by paying less or receiving more because they are not so averse to the risk of trial.
- Differences in *time preference* can lead to altered patterns of payments or actions over time. If a claimant needs money immediately and a defendant has a reserve set aside for settlement of the claim, a quick payment can create value for both sides and enhance the chance of an agreement.
- Different *capabilities* can be combined. Companies with complementary capabilities can negotiate deals and mergers to create value that neither could achieve alone. For example, a company with strong production capacity can combine forces with a company that has sophisticated marketing and distribution abilities to collectively enhance profitability and create value between them.
- Differences in *cost/revenue structure* can create cost-saving trades. For example, if a butcher, who gets meat wholesale, can trade meat with a shoe merchant, who gets shoes wholesale, they have created value for themselves by each getting what would not otherwise be available to them at wholesale cost.
- Differences in *forecasts* can lead to contingent agreements when the items under negotiation are uncertain and themselves subject to different probability estimates, or when each party feels that it will fare well under, and perhaps can influence, a proposed contingent resolution procedure. In a negotiation over executive compensation where the prospective executive has a more optimistic view of her abilities to produce revenue than does the company, she may agree to a lower salary with a higher bonus contingent on revenue increases. Both negotiating sides might feel better off because they have structured an employment deal based on their own forecasts and have, in effect, created value for themselves.

- Other differences (evaluation criteria, the importance of precedent, the value of personal reputation, constituency attitudes, the organizational situation, conceptions of fairness, and so on) can also be fashioned into joint gains. For example, a law firm being threatened with a suit by a former clerk for sexual harassment might be willing to settle a claim for much more if it is cast as payment for wrongful termination.

These "differences" relate to the role perceptions play in understanding conflict, as explained in Chapter 3, particularly by Rummel in his excerpt on "The Subjectivity Principle." You will note that we have come full circle in connecting the cause of conflict — different perceptions that are all in our heads — to a suggested approach for constructively resolving conflicts, recognizing the different perceptions and trading on them.

❖ **Gerald B. Wetlaufer,** *The Limits of Integrative Bargaining*

85 Geo. L.J. 369 (1996)

It is now conventional wisdom that opportunities for integrative bargaining are widely available, that they are often unrecognized and unexploited, and that as a result both parties to negotiations and society as a whole are worse off than would otherwise have been the case. The failure to recognize and exploit these opportunities may reflect a failure of education, curable either by reading or by attending a course or seminar. It may reflect the "I'm right, you're wrong, and I can prove it" style of discourse associated with law school education and historically male modes of moral reasoning. Or it may be the result of the "negotiator's dilemma" in which the open and cooperative tactics thought appropriate to integrative bargaining are systematically exploited and driven out by the more combative tactics generally associated with distributive bargaining — starting high, conceding slowly, concealing and misrepresenting one's own interests, arguing coercively, threatening, and bluffing.

If the problem at hand is our failure to recognize and exploit opportunities for integrative bargaining, the solution, we are told, is to shift away from the tactics of distributive bargaining and toward the tactics appropriate to integrative bargaining: cooperation, openness, and truthtelling. Individual negotiators should embrace these tactics not because they are good or ethical, or because they will help to build a better society, but instead because they will promote the individual's immediate pecuniary self-interest. . . .

The proponents of integrative bargaining usually assert that opportunities for such bargaining are widely, if not universally, available. Lax and Sebenius, in the most important contribution yet made to our understanding of these matters, catalogue the opportunities for integrative bargaining.

Their list includes differences between the parties in terms of (1) their interests, (2) their projections concerning possible future events (3) their willingness to accept risks, and (4) their time preferences regarding payment or performance. . . . All four of these circumstances will sometimes, but only under certain further conditions and with certain important qualifications, afford opportunities for the parties to expand the pie through integrative bargaining. . . .

[The author next argues and attempts to demonstrate that the listed differences between negotiating parties rarely provide opportunities to lastingly expand the pie and create joint, integrative gains. He discusses negotiating "contingent agreements," which you will read about in the next chapter.]

A final claim that can now be evaluated is that opportunities for integrative bargaining necessarily imply that it is in a negotiator's immediate pecuniary self-interest to engage in the tactics of cooperation, openness, truthtelling, honesty, and trust. First, I have demonstrated that opportunities for integrative bargaining, especially meaningful opportunities for integrative bargaining (e.g., where the pie may be made to expand and to stay expanded), exist within a narrower range of circumstances than sometimes has been claimed. Some of the differences cited by Lax and Sebenius simply do not create opportunities for integrative bargaining. Others, namely those involving different assessments regarding future events, create opportunities to expand the pie only if the parties are willing to bet on their projections. And even when the parties are willing to bet, there will be opportunities for integrative bargaining only some of the time and only in ways that will sometimes prove self-defeating in the sense that the pie may eventually return to its original size. If the pie shrinks back, one or both of the parties will be worse off than they had expected to be and, potentially worse off than they would have been had they not entered the agreement. Other circumstances named by Lax and Sebenius — multiple issues differently valued, differing projections concerning future events, differing time preferences, differing levels of risk aversion — sometimes offer opportunities for integrative bargaining but sometimes do not. Although the general claim is made that opportunities for integrative bargaining provide a reason, based solely on immediate pecuniary self-interest, to engage in openness and truthtelling, those opportunities are considerably less pervasive than has been announced. Thus, this argument for openness and truthtelling is, in that degree, narrower and less persuasive.

Second, even within the range of circumstances in which there are significant opportunities for integrative bargaining, the bargainer must almost always engage in distributive bargaining as well. Therefore, it is in the bargainer's self-interest not just to adopt the tactics of openness and truthtelling that are said to be appropriate to integrative bargaining, but somehow also to adopt the tactics of truth-hiding and dissimulation that are said to be appropriate in distributive bargaining. However we might manage these incompatible tactics, this situation presents at most a weak and highly qualified argument for openness and truthtelling. Moreover, the argument for openness and truthtelling is not an argument for openness and truthtelling with respect to everything, but instead, is limited to information useful in identifying and exploiting opportunities for integrative bargaining. Thus, an opportunity for integrative bargaining will present an occasion for a certain amount of truthtelling with respect to one's relative interest in various issues (or one's projections about the future or aversion to risk) without also presenting even a weak argument for truthtelling with respect to one's reservation price. . . .

If there is a general case for cooperation, openness, and truthtelling in negotiations, that case is multidimensional and parts of it are expressly ethical. Certainly, because there are opportunities for integrative bargaining, a measure of openness and truthtelling is sometimes warranted as a matter of a negotiator's immediate pecuniary self-interest. Similarly, a negotiator's long-term pecuniary self-interest may sometimes be served by openness and truthtelling because of the costs that may be associated with a reputation for sharp dealing. But it is also true that a negotiator's pecuniary self-interest is, at best, only a portion of his true self-interest. Thus, it may be in his true self-interest to accept some pecuniary costs for the sake of living in a community in which cooperation, truthtelling, and ethical behavior are the norm. Moreover, Plato's Socrates may have been right when he argued that a person who has some combination of wealth and virtue may be happier and better off than a person who has more wealth but less virtue. . . .

We have, in certain respects, allowed ourselves to be dazzled and seduced by the possibilities of integrative or "win-win" bargaining. That, in turn, has led to a certain amount of overclaiming. The reason, I think, is that if we hold these possibilities in a certain light and squint our eyes just hard enough, they look for all the world like the Holy Grail of negotiations. They seem to offer that which we have wanted most to find. What they seem to offer — though in the end it is only an illusion — is the long-sought proof that cooperation, honesty, and good behavior will carry the day not because they are virtuous, not because they will benefit society as a whole, but because they are in everyone's individual and pecuniary self-interest. But however much we may want "honesty" to be "the best policy" in this strong sense, the discovery of integrative bargaining has not, at least so far, provided that long-sought proof.

Perhaps the time has finally come to consider the possibility that this proof will always elude us, for the simple reason that the world in which we live does not, in this particular way, conform to our wishes. Even if there is just the chance that this is so, and it looks much more like a certainty than a chance, it would be appropriate to acknowledge the ultimate insufficiency of understanding self-interest in narrowly pecuniary terms. It would be appropriate to attend in a systematic way to the facts that, even when it is contrary to our pecuniary self-interest, relationships matter; that we care about our reputations, not just for effectiveness but also for decency and good behavior: that we care about living in — and helping to create — communities in which pecuniary self-interest is not the only language that is spoken; and that Plato's Socrates may have gotten it right. And it would be appropriate to acknowledge the central importance of the ethical case against certain forms of competitive and self-interested behavior, especially those forms of behavior, central to the process of negotiations, that involve misrepresentations and other conduct that imposes harm upon others.

Questions

13. Are the suggestions made by Lax and Sebenius for creating value by focusing on differences equally applicable to settlement of legal disputes and to deal-making negotiations? What differences on the above list could be utilized in settling a claim for damages by an injured driver against an insurance company?

14. Do Gerald Wetlaufer's comments reflect the same concerns as those of James White? Is there any fundamental difference in their expressed view of "win-win" negotiation or in how negotiators should behave? If so, how do they differ?

15. Professor Wetlaufer concludes that being open and cooperative in negotiations might not benefit immediate pecuniary interests, but that relationships matter and that Plato may have been correct in teaching that virtue is more important than wealth. Even if we believe this is true when we negotiate for ourselves, as lawyers can we trade off a client's potential gain for our personal sense of virtue?

16. Do the immediate pecuniary interests of the client and the longer-term interests of the attorney in maintaining good working relations with other lawyers create a conflict of interest between attorney and client?

C. Choosing an Effective Approach

Problem

Assume that you have established yourself as an effective attorney with a good reputation for your straightforward, cooperative style. You have been a guest lecturer at local law schools about civility in the practice of law and the importance of maintaining a credible professional reputation. Your largest individual client, the president of a regional bank, which your firm also represents, has retained you to represent him in a divorce action initiated by his wife, knowing that you have experience in domestic relations practice. He explains that his highest priority is to retain total control of the bank with no share of the bank stock going to his wife, even though the law might give her a claim to some of it. He wants you to seek for him primary custody of their two middle-school-aged children, for whom he and his wife have both been active parents, so you can use that as a bargaining chip later to assure his retention of the bank stock. What would you tell him? Who should decide negotiation strategies and approaches, you or your client?

1. *Negotiating Within Your Comfort Zone*

Being cooperative, problem solving, competitive, or adversarial is, at least in part, a matter of choice. The choice you make depends on a number of factors: The subject of the negotiation, the expectations of your client, ethics considerations, the customs and conventions where the negotiation occurs, the interrelation between issues, the past or anticipated future relationship between the parties and between the attorneys, your counterpart's negotiation approach, the amount of time available, and the amount at stake can all influence your approach to negotiation. The biggest factor, however, is your own comfort zone, formed by your personality and values. To the extent that how you negotiate is driven by personality and values, it could be better described as a matter of style rather than approach. Behavioral style is in large part a function of who you are. Choosing a style that does not fit your personality and values, if not a recipe for failure, is likely to make your work as a negotiator difficult and dissatisfying. To succeed as a professional and find satisfaction in what you are doing, you must negotiate within your personal comfort zone.

Defining our negotiating comfort zone is not always an easy task. It is a common desire to be liked rather than disliked. We know that we are more likely to be liked when we are cooperative and giving than when we are adversarial and taking. However, we also know that winners are admired, and we want to be respected for vigorously representing our clients' interests and succeeding when we negotiate on their behalf. Law students without legal experience may hold the view of attorneys popularized in movies and television series as hard-charging, aggressive lawyers. The dramatic, adversarial scenes popularly portrayed in dramatized jury trials may be transposed in our minds to all opposing lawyer interactions. As a result, many students have a latent fear that their preference for cooperation and friendliness will not serve them or their clients well in negotiation.

Other students may have thrived on competition and winning in sports and other contests. We know that law students are a self-selected group of achievers who have succeeded, at least academically, and made it into law school through a competitive admissions process. Competition appears to be encouraged by the legal system, where cooperation and generosity may be viewed as a virtuous but less valued quality. So it is understandable that some students are conflicted about whether negotiation should be appro-ached as a professional game in which their competitive qualities are let loose and rewarded with success.

Those of you who have enjoyed competition know from your experience that good competitors can be friendly, gracious, and ethical. Similarly, not all competitive negotiators manifest an adversarial persona. A pleasant and respectful personal style is not necessarily inconsistent with competitive negotiation, any more than being cordial in competitive sports is inconsis-tent with wanting to win. The style you choose in negotiation may depend on how you define the game and the relationship you want with your nego-tiation counterpart.

Your negotiation style might also depend in large measure on your ingrained personality pattern. If personality patterns drive how we and oth-ers approach negotiation, can we discern those patterns in ourselves and others, and how can we benefit from the information?

Because personality does matter in how we interact with others, how we deal with conflict, and how we negotiate, researchers have attempted to test and measure personality traits that influence these functions. The *Thomas-Kilmann Conflict Mode Instrument* (or "Thomas Kilmann test") is one of the best methods available to assess one's tendencies as a negotiator and is administered in some law school negotiation courses. This widely used per-sonality test measures five dimensions of how individuals deal with conflict and negotiation to determine their degree of assertiveness and/or coopera-tion. The Thomas-Kilmann Instrument asks test takers to respond to 30 statements (for example, "I feel that differences are not always worth worry-ing about" or "I make some effort to get my way") and self-score their answers. The results give the taker a profile of how strongly she scores in all five categories: Competitor, Accommodator (sometimes also called Coop-erator), Avoider, Compromiser, and Collaborator (sometimes called Prob-lem Solver).

One of the strengths of the test is that it provides relative scores rather than a simple yes–no or categorical placement: When you take the test, you receive a score along a continuum from very high to very low as a Competi-tor, for instance. Test takers receive scores in all five categories. This gives the taker a nuanced portrait of herself as a composite of several sometimes-conflicting tendencies. Each of the Thomas-Kilmann style categories has advantages and disadvantages in negotiation.

The five categories of conflict management styles are:

- *Competing:* High on assertiveness and low on cooperation;
- *Accommodating:* Low on assertiveness and high on cooperation;
- *Avoiding:* Low on assertiveness and cooperation;
- *Collaborating:* High on assertiveness and cooperation; and
- *Compromising:* Moderate on assertiveness and cooperation.

Another personality test is the *Five-Factor Model* of personality, also known as the Big Five taxonomy. This test is used extensively in experimental psychology to determine the five major categories describing broad personality traits, and has been applied to negotiation outcomes as well (see Barry and Friedman, 1998). The five factors that comprise the test are:

- *Extroversion:* Sociable, assertive, and talkative;
- *Agreeableness:* Flexible, cooperative, and trusting;
- *Conscientiousness:* Responsible, organized, and achievement oriented;
- *Emotional stability:* Secure and confident; and
- *Openness:* Imaginative, broad-minded, and curious.

The best known and most widely referred to personality test is the *Myers-Briggs Type Indicator*. You might have taken this test. It is administered more than 2 million times a year by large companies, the U.S. government, and academic institutions. It is the subject of countless research studies and articles, including ones that analyze the impact of personality variables on negotiation (see Peters, 1993). The Myers-Briggs measures four personality dimensions:

- introverted or extroverted;
- sensing or intuitive;
- thinking or feeling; and
- perceiving or judging.

There is now considerable literature on the role of personality in negotiation styles and outcomes, based on studies of personality test results and experimental research. However, the utility of this literature for instructional purposes is limited because of the lack of consensus among the studies and the limitations of their methodology. The following reading recognizes those limitations, but offers answers to the questions most often asked about personality and negotiation.

❖ **Sheila Heen and John Richardson,** *"I See a Pattern Here and the Pattern Is You": Personality and Dispute Resolution*

in The Handbook of Dispute Resolution 202 (M.L. Moffitt and R.C. Bordone eds., 2005)

Anyone who has more than one child knows that differences in personality are real. The first born may be quiet, eager to please, and shy in new situations. His sister comes along and is an extrovert — smiling early and befriending strangers as a toddler. These traits may remain constant throughout life as the firstborn becomes a writer and his sister makes friends easily and often as a college student, professional, and retiree. . . .

The hard question is this: are there ways to describe the differences in people's personalities that can be useful in conducting and advising negotiations? After all, negotiation is all about dealing with people, getting along with them, and persuading them. Shouldn't knowing how people are different (and what to do about it) be an integral part of negotiation theory and strategy?

One would think so. And yet, the intersection of dispute resolution and personality is a tangle of confusion and contradiction. It is not unexplored territory — scholars have tried to find answers. And it is interesting — there is fascinating work going on and much speculation about what is being learned. Yet there are few clear, satisfying answers to questions that interest dispute resolution professionals most: Are particular personalities better negotiators? Should I negotiate differently with different personalities? And what about when the people and their problematic personalities really are the problem?

[After reviewing the most widely used personality tests, their limitations, and the literature about the reported results, the authors address six questions asked about personality and negotiation.]

1. *Is there really such a thing as personality differences?* It certainly seems so. Whether hard wired by genes or chemical mix, prompted by experience or influenced by the context, two people in a similar situation will often respond differently. This may be particularly so in the pressurized context of a dispute.

Personality researchers attempt to identify and isolate traits that are consistent across situations and different between individuals. This is where things get tricky. Human beings are complex enough, and adaptable enough, that defining and tracking traits, particularly through the dynamic process of negotiation, has proven very difficult.

2. *Or are there particular personality traits that give better outcomes?* With the exception of cognitive ability (more is better), there is no strong answer in the current research. Although you can find small-scale studies suggesting this or that trait is helpful, you can also find studies that say it does not improve outcomes.

3. *Okay, so should I negotiate differently with different personality types?* The biggest obstacle to setting your negotiation strategy based on the other person's personality is figuring out what it is. Because people act differently in different situations, researchers have found that people consistently misperceive the personality traits of those with whom they negotiate or are in dispute.

The best advice is to be aware of your own tendencies, have a broad repertoire of approaches and strategies, and be able to engage difficulties constructively as they come up. Pay attention to particular behavior you see, rather than trying to globalize how the other person "is." And if one approach doesn't seem to be working, try another.

4. Isn't it true that some disputes are hopeless because people's personalities just aren't going to change?

It is certainly true that there are limits to what can change, and that some differences between people are harder to reconcile than others. And there are definitely limits to *your ability to change the other person's personality*.

Yet the impulse to throw up our hands and attribute the problem to the other person's personality flaws is a dangerous one. It blames the other person for the dispute, blinding us to our own contributions to the problem. It may also encourage us to give up on a relationship or dispute too easily or too quickly, when finding a way to work together with less frustration remains possible.

In addition, there are at least three paths forward that personality finger-pointing ignores. Remember that human beings' *behavior* can often change without a grand *personality* change. You might shift the context — offering a private caucus or written channel of communication, for example. You can try to influence the other person's behavior by influencing the story he or she tells about what's going on. Or you might try changing your contribution to the dynamic between you. The other person is reacting both to you and to his or her own experiences, tendencies, and stories, and that's a complex enough set of factors to suggest that progress is possible.

Finally, do not underestimate people's ability to change over time. As a person ages, encounters different life experiences, and makes the transition to new phases in life (where he or she may feel more secure or happier, or have more room for reflection for example), his or her traits and tendencies evolve. You may find that your personality gradually moves into a different era, one you would not have predicted from where you stand now.

5. Why is personality profiling so popular, if it's so inconclusive? People love to talk about themselves. And they especially love to talk about other people. Personality profiling also fits our interest in simplifying the world and the infinitely complex relationships in it. Researchers have long documented the effects of the fundamental attribution error, where we believe we know why people act the way they do, and tend to attribute especially bad behavior to their problematic personality.

People are so complicated that we can't really describe them with few enough variables to meet our needs for parsimony. People can only keep about seven items in their head at one time, before they go into cognitive overload. So they make up something that they can handle in their heads, whether or not it is accurate.

6. So why pay attention to personality at all? The fields of personality and negotiation are both relatively young. Our ability to map interaction in negotiation and dispute resolution, and to recommend paths of influence, is in its infancy. And our ability to isolate traits and trace them through complex interaction is still maturing.

Still, familiarity with common differences between individuals is useful. It reminds us that not every approach to influence works with every person. It can help us generate diagnostic hypotheses about why a negotiation is in trouble ("Ah! We may proceed to closure at different paces"), and come up with prescriptive advice to try out. It may also help us be more forgiving of others' seemingly crazy behavior if we can spot it as a difference in the way the two of us see and respond to the world.

Familiarity with personality differences can also be a self-reflection and coaching tool for yourself. It can help you identify and work on behavior that doesn't come naturally to you. It can also help you explain your behavior to others: "I've learned that I'm not very comfortable making commitments before I have a chance to think things through. Can you give me the weekend and we'll nail this down on Monday?" Becoming familiar with some of the traits that affect your ability to mediate, negotiate, or respond well to disputes can help you become more aware of the situations that bring out these traits, and other choices you might make.

Questions

17. Are the style categories and personality dimensions used by the three test instruments just different ways to label the same personality traits, or do they really measure different aspects of personality?

18. After 18 years or more as a student and as an experienced test taker, if your negotiation course readings and class discussion gave you the impression that your instructor valued collaboration more than avoidance or competition, do you think your responses to the statements on the Thomas-Kilmann test (e.g., "I feel that differences are not always worth worrying about" or "I make some effort to get my way") might be influenced by the instructor's values or not provide a totally accurate measure of your conflict style?

19. Given that all three of the personality tests described above rely on self-assessment answers, do you think the results are likely to match the assessment of your personality by opponents, family, friends, and colleagues? Does your style differ when negotiating with a close friend compared to negotiating professionally?

20. Do you feel that personality testing is helpful as an aid to better understand and improve how you negotiate? Does your answer depend on your view of whether personality traits and behavior can be altered? Do you consciously take stock of the personality type of your counterparts when negotiating? Are there ways you can find out about their personalities before engaging with them?

2. *Effectiveness and Style*

As you know, negotiation is usually done in private and accompanied by confidentiality, so there is little opportunity to compare results. How lawyers behave in negotiation and what they do is not fully known. Lawyers' tales of negotiations, as well as personality tests, are filtered through the lens of the tellers' perceptions. Unless negotiations can be systematically observed on a grand scale, we will never know what really works best to produce desired negotiated outcomes. Few lawyers ever "lose" a negotiation, or tell about it if they believe they did not do well. Spoken and written "war stories" of successful negotiations are not reliable descriptions of what typically occurs, or even of what occurred in the reported negotiation. (There do not appear to be any books on "How I Failed as a Negotiator.") Obstacles to the study and profiling of negotiations leave new lawyers little reliable guidance on what is successful in negotiation and how to weigh the polar tensions they may feel between competition and cooperation to negotiate effectively within their comfort zone.

Two studies help fill the void of information about how lawyers negotiate and which behaviors and styles are effective. Both studies are necessarily limited because they rely on attorneys responding to questionnaires and reporting their perceptions of effective and ineffective negotiation behavior by their opponents in recent negotiations. Nonetheless, both studies provide sources of information about how lawyers negotiate and what is considered effective, as well as ineffective. Because the studies were similar and conducted more than 20 years apart, we can obtain clues about changes over time in how attorneys negotiate (see Schneider, 2000).

The news from the studies, is both good and bad. The good news for students struggling with the tension of deciding on their negotiation comfort zone and not knowing if what they are inclined to do is the right way to negotiate is that there is no one right way.

Both competitive and cooperative styles can be effective approaches to negotiation if done well and with integrity. Being an effective competitive negotiator does not require the use of tricks or deceit. Some competitive techniques can be legitimate ways to pursue negotiation goals, provided they are not carried to extremes. Being a cooperative negotiator need not be based on naiveté or being a pushover. Cooperative attorneys, who appear from the studies to predominate in numbers and perceived effectiveness, are most successful when they are mindful of the interests they are pursuing and set limits on their cooperation.

The studies indicate that although the percentage of attorneys who are adversarial has increased, about two-thirds of lawyer negotiators are classified as cooperative. The rating of cooperative negotiators as more effective than adversarial negotiators has increased. Again, it should be noted that adversarial attorneys are also rated as effective, but in a much lower proportion. Some admirable behaviors of negotiators (like preparation, a focus on the client's interests, and high ethical standards) are shared by effective competitive and effective cooperative attorney negotiators.

The bad news is that the more recent study reported that adversarial negotiators are becoming more extreme and unpleasant. The terms most frequently used to describe them are more negative than 20 years ago. This might not bode well for the legal profession or for clients, if the reports are accurate, because this group as a whole appears less effective as negotiators than previously reported.

3. *Cooperation vs. Competitiveness — Who Decides?*

Generally clients get to choose the objective of negotiation, and lawyers use their professional judgment in selecting the means of obtaining the client's objectives. Of course, it's not quite so simple. In matters of litigation, the lawyer may owe the client an ethical obligation of zealous advocacy in pursuit of a client's interests. Some scholars interpret the ethical norms to mean, "the final authority on important issues of strategy rests with the client; and the client may discharge his lawyer at will, but the lawyer has only limited ability to withdraw from representation" (Gilson and Mnookin, 1995). Mnookin and Gilson believe that a lawyer who wishes to pursue a cooperative approach, with sensitivity for long-term professional relationships with other attorneys, may not be able to do so in the litigation context, or at least that the client calls the negotiation shots. They also point out that the client can fire the lawyer at will if the lawyer seems more cooperative than the client wishes, but that ethical norms do not always allow the lawyer to quit if the client insists on a more aggressive strategy.

Professor Robert Condlin believes that lawyers must be substantively competitive in negotiating for clients but can choose their own personal style. Competitive attorneys can adopt a cordial and respectful persona in their negotiations, although this can be a fine and difficult distinction. Condlin refers to this tug between a client's wishes for the lawyer to defect from a pattern of cooperation and the lawyer's desire for long-term cooperation as the "bargainer's dilemma." Like the prisoners' dilemma, different negotiation tactics may be called for if the situation is viewed as a single- or multiple-round game. Clients tend to view litigation and some deals as one-round events. Lawyers usually view their negotiation with other lawyers as unlimited multiple rounds, where any defect will bring future retaliation and a blemished reputation (Condlin, 1992). We will return to this issue in Chapter 7, where we probe deeper into negotiation ethics.

CHAPTER
5

The Negotiation Dance — Step by Step

A. Negotiation Stages and Approaches

Negotiation, whether competitive, cooperative, or a mixed approach, can be viewed as occurring in stages. Even though lawyer negotiation is often not a tidy process, breaking negotiation into stages is a way to help understand and analyze the process. There is, however, no script — all negotiations do not follow the same lineal staging and each stage will not necessarily be completed in all negotiations.

Listed below are the activities typically occurring in seven stages of competitive or cooperative negotiation. The activities within each stage can be mixed or alternated between competitive and cooperative, bearing in mind the warning that cooperation is commonly driven out by competitiveness. Of course, the labels "competitive" and "cooperative," like all one-word descriptions, are too simple. Adversarial and problem-solving, positional and interest-based, or distributive and integrative may better capture the behavioral contrast. Although each pair of bipolar negotiation labels may signify nuanced differences, we will use them synonymously. Finally, note that although some of the activities and tasks within the two approaches are similar, the sequence of stages may vary between positional and interest-based approaches. For example, making demands and offers comes earlier in positional negotiation and later in interest negotiation, following the exchange of information, if at all.

© 2009 Jay Folberg

Stage	Competitive/adversarial approach	Cooperative/problem-solving approach
1. Preparation and Setting Goals	➤ Planning and research ➤ Counseling client about negotiation ➤ Assessing power of each party ➤ Formulating positions and bottom line ➤ Setting goals	➤ Planning and research ➤ Counseling client about negotiation ➤ Assessing needs of each party ➤ Formulating best alternative to negotiated agreement (BATNA) and reservation point ➤ Setting goals

Stage	Competitive/adversarial approach	Cooperative/problem-solving approach
2. Initial Interactions	➤ Setting tone ➤ Establishing credentials and authority ➤ Making first demand or offer	➤ Setting tone ➤ Establishing rapport and trust ➤ Agreeing on agenda
3. Exchanging and Refining Information	➤ Asking questions ➤ Offering overstated or understated valuations ➤ Informational bargaining ➤ Formal discovery ➤ Stating positions (often exaggerated)	➤ Asking questions ➤ Sharing assessments or appraisals ➤ Information exchange ➤ Informal discovery (I'll show you mine, if you'll show me yours) ➤ Stating needs or interests
4. Bargaining	➤ Argument and persuasion ➤ Making concessions ➤ Forming coalitions and holding out	➤ Proposing principles ➤ Applying principled criteria ➤ Trading off priorities and brainstorming solutions
5. Moving Toward Closure	➤ Using power and threats ➤ Creating time crisis ➤ Evaluating offers	➤ Examining BATNAs ➤ Agreeing on deadlines ➤ Decision analysis
6. Reaching Impasse or Agreement	➤ Possible impasse ➤ Compromising ➤ Adding conditions	➤ Possible, but less likely, impasse ➤ Reaching mutual decisions through joint problem solving ➤ Creating alternative outcomes
7. Finalizing and Writing Agreements	➤ Preparing opposing drafts of agreement ➤ Negotiating over drafts ➤ Approval, ratification, and buy-in (if necessary)	➤ Memorializing terms ➤ Concurring on single text agreement ➤ Approval, ratification, and buy-in (if necessary)

Note and Questions

Professor Williams, in his article "Negotiation as a Healing Process," part of which is excerpted in Chapter 2, refers to negotiation as a ritual. He goes on to say:

In law school we learn that no two cases are alike, and in our culture we assume that no two people are alike. We might surmise from this that no two negotiations are alike. Fortunately, this is only partially true. One of the defining characteristics of a ritual, including the ritual of negotiation, is that it provides an accepted structure for and sequencing of events. As a general proposition, then, we can say *the ritual of negotiation unfolds in predictable stages over time.*

The predictability helps explain why so many lawyers lose patience with the process; it is highly repetitive, and thus not as stimulating as new adventures would be. This aspect of ritual is well captured by W. John Smith when he says, "*ritual* connotes . . . behavior that is formally organized into repeatable patterns. Perhaps the fundamental and pervasive function of these patterns is to facilitate orderly interactions between individuals." The point could not be more clear. Negotiation is a highly repetitive process. Without predictable patterns, the negotiators could not hope to achieve orderly interaction with each other. As Smith explains: "Ritual behavior facilitates interactions because it makes available information about the nature of events, and about the participants in them, that each participating individual must have to interact without generating chaos." The task now is to develop a working knowledge of the predictable stages of the negotiation process. (Williams, 1996, 33)

1. Have you found negotiations in which you were involved to be predictable in process? What types of negotiations are most likely to follow a ritualistic or predictable pattern? Might there be different negotiation rituals depending on what is being negotiated and the setting of the negotiation?
2. How might the stages of negotiation or the activities in each stage differ if the negotiation follows the creating and claiming approach suggested in the excerpt from Lax and Sebenius in Chapter 4?
3. Can you think of how concurring on a single text agreement, listed on the chart as Stage 7 — "Finalization," might be taken up out of order and used in earlier stages to help formulate choices, bargain, and reach decisions? For a fascinating application of the single text procedure in reaching agreement between Israel and Egypt at Camp David, see Jimmy Carter's book *Keeping Faith: Memoirs of a President* (1982).

B.   Getting Ready to Negotiate

Watching a good negotiator or hearing about an effective negotiation can give the impression that it comes easily and that success is the result of intuitive ability, cleverness, and quick thinking. However, similar to trial practice, appellate advocacy, or any other disciplined endeavor, success in negotiation is in large part the result of planning, research, and preparation. The famous quote by Antoine de Saint-Exupery that "a goal without a plan is just a wish" is applicable to negotiation.

The following excerpt provides a helpful blueprint for effective negotiation preparation that is likely to maximize results in most bargaining situations by refining your BATNA and reservation point, as well as by anticipating your opponent's bargaining zone.

1.   *Preparation*

❖ **Russell Korobkin,** *A Positive Theory of Legal Negotiation*

88 Georgetown L.J. 1789 (2000)

[The author posits two negotiation situations, one a potential transaction for the purchase by Esau of Jacob's catering business and the other a potential settlement of a suit by Goliath against David for battery.]

All observers of the negotiation process agree that painstaking preparation is critical to success at the bargaining table . . . "Internal" preparation refers to research that the negotiator does to set and adjust his own RP [reservation point or price]. "External" preparation refers to research that the negotiator does to estimate and manipulate the other party's RP.

1.   Internal Preparation: Alternatives and BATNAs

A negotiator cannot determine his RP without first understanding his substitutes for and the opportunity costs of reaching a negotiated agreement. This, of course, requires research. Esau cannot determine how much he is willing to pay for Jacob's business without investigating his other options. Most obviously, Esau will want to investigate what other catering companies are for sale in his area, their asking prices, and how they compare in quality and earning potential to Jacob's. He also might consider other types of businesses that are for sale. And he will likely consider the possibility of investing his money passively and working for someone else, rather than investing in a business.

Alternatives to reaching an agreement can be nearly limitless in transactional negotiations, and creativity in generating the list of alternatives is a critical skill to the negotiator. The panoply of alternatives is generally more circumscribed in dispute resolution negotiations. If Goliath fails to reach a settlement of some sort with David, he has the alternative of seeking an adjudicated outcome of the dispute and the alternative of dropping the suit. Most likely, he does not have the choice of suing someone else instead of David, in the same way that Esau has the choice of buying a business other than Jacob's.

After identifying the various alternatives to reaching a negotiated agreement, the negotiator needs to determine which alternative is most desirable. Fisher and his coauthors coined the appropriate term "BATNA" — "best alternative to a negotiated agreement" — to identify this choice. The identity and quality of a negotiator's BATNA is the primary input into his RP.

If the negotiator's BATNA and the subject of the negotiation are perfectly interchangeable, determining the reservation price is quite simple: The reservation price is merely the value of the BATNA. For example, if Esau's BATNA is buying another catering business for $190,000 that is identical to Jacob's in terms of quality, earnings potential, and all other factors that are important to Esau, then his RP is $190,000. If Jacob will sell for some amount less than that, Esau will be better off buying Jacob's company than he would be pursuing his best alternative. If Jacob demands more than $190,000, Esau is better off buying the alternative company and not reaching an agreement with Jacob.

In most circumstances, however, the subject of a negotiation and the negotiator's BATNA are not perfect substitutes. If Jacob's business is of higher quality, has a higher earnings potential, or is located closer to Esau's home, he would probably be willing to pay a premium for it over what he would pay for the alternative choice. For example, if the alternative business is selling for $190,000, Esau might determine he would be willing to pay up to a $10,000 premium over the alternative for Jacob's business and thus set his RP at $200,000. On the other hand, if Esau's BATNA is more desirable to him than Jacob's business, Esau will discount the value of his BATNA by the amount necessary to make the two alternatives equally desirable values for the money; perhaps he will set his RP at $180,000 in recognition that his BATNA is $10,000 more desirable than Jacob's business, and Jacob's business would be equally desirable only at a $10,000 discount.

Assume Goliath determines that his BATNA is proceeding to trial. He will attempt to place a value on his BATNA by researching the facts of the case, the relevant legal precedent, and jury awards in similar cases, all as a means of estimating the expected value of litigating to a jury verdict. If Goliath's research leads to an estimate that he has a 75% chance of winning a jury verdict, and the likely verdict if he does prevail is $100,000, then using a simple expected value calculation ($100,000 × .75) would lead him to value his BATNA at $75,000.

For most plaintiffs, however, a settlement of a specified amount is preferable to a jury verdict with the same expected value, both because litigation entails additional costs and because most individuals are risk averse and therefore prefer a certain payment to a risky probability of payment with the same expected value. Goliath might determine, for example, that a $50,000 settlement would have the equivalent value to him of a jury verdict with an expected value of $75,000, because pursuing a jury verdict would entail greater tangible and intangible costs such as attorneys' fees, emotional strain, inconvenience, and the risk of losing the case altogether. If so, Goliath would set his RP at $50,000. On the other hand, it is possible that Goliath would find a $75,000 verdict more desirable than a $75,000 pretrial settlement. For example, perhaps Goliath would find additional value in having a jury of his peers publicly recognize the validity of his grievance against David. If Goliath believes that such psychic benefits of a jury verdict would make a verdict worth $10,000 more to him than a settlement of the same amount (after taking into account the added risks and costs of litigation), he would set his RP at $85,000. . . .

Internal preparation serves two related purposes. By considering the value of obvious alternatives to reaching a negotiated agreement, the negotiator can accurately estimate his RP. This is of critical importance because without a precise and accurate estimation of his RP the negotiator cannot be sure to avoid the most basic negotiating mistake — agreeing to a deal when he would have been better off walking away from the table with no agreement.

By investigating an even wider range of alternatives to reaching agreement and by more thoroughly investigating the value of obvious alternatives, the negotiator can alter his RP in a way that will shift the bargaining zone to his advantage. Rather than just considering the asking price of other catering companies listed for sale in his town, Esau might contact catering companies that are not for sale to find out if their owners might consider selling under the right conditions. This could lead to the identification of a company similar to Jacob's that could be purchased for $175,000, which would have the effect of reducing Esau's RP to $175,000 and therefore shifting the bargaining zone lower. Goliath's attorney might conduct additional legal research, perhaps exploring other, more novel, theories of liability. If he determines that one or more alternative legal theories has a reasonable chance of success in court, Goliath might adjust upward his estimate of prevailing at trial — and therefore the value of his BATNA of trial — allowing him to adjust upward his RP.

2.   External Preparation: The Opponent's Alternatives and BATNA

Internal preparation enables the negotiator to estimate his RP accurately and favorably. Of course, the bargaining zone is fixed by *both* parties' RPs. External preparation allows the negotiator to estimate his opponent's RP. If Esau is savvy, he will attempt to research Jacob's alternatives to a negotiated agreement as well as his own alternatives. For example, other caterers might know whether Jacob has had other offers for his business, how much the business might bring on the open market, or how anxious Jacob is to sell — all factors that will help Esau to accurately predict Jacob's RP and therefore pinpoint the low end of the bargaining zone. This information will also prepare Esau to attempt to persuade Jacob during the course of negotiations to lower his RP. . . .

It is worth noting that in the litigation context both parties often have the same alternatives and the same BATNA. If plaintiff Goliath determines that his BATNA is going to trial, then defendant David's only alternative — and therefore his BATNA by default — is going to trial as well. In this circumstance, internal preparation and external preparation merge. For example, when Goliath's lawyer conducts legal research, he is attempting to simultaneously estimate the value of both parties' BATNAs. Of course, just because the parties have the same BATNA, they will not necessarily estimate the market value of it identically, much less arrive at identical RPs. Research suggests that an "egocentric bias" is likely to cause litigants to interpret material facts in a light favorable to their legal position, thus causing them to overestimate the expected value of an adjudicated outcome. Consequently, it is likely that, examining the same operative facts and legal precedent, plaintiff Goliath will place a higher value on the BATNA of trial than defendant

David. This difference in perception often will be offset, however, by the fact that plaintiff Goliath is likely to set his RP, or the minimum settlement he will accept, below his perceived expected value of trial to account for the higher costs and higher risk associated with trial, while defendant David is likely to set his RP, or the maximum settlement he will agree to pay, above the expected value of trial for the same reasons. As long as the parties' preference for settlement rather than trial outweighs their egocentric biases, a bargaining zone will still exist, although it will be smaller than it would be if the parties agreed on the expected value of trial. Research also suggests that both parties are likely to be more risk averse when they are less confident in their prediction of the expected value of trial. In other words, the less confident the parties are in the value that they place on the BATNA of trial, the larger the bargaining zone between the RPs is likely to be.

---

2.   Setting Goals

In addition to thinking through the least you can accept, or your reservation point, it is also helpful to formulate goals and set high expectations. High expectations lead to better outcomes, as discussed in this excerpt by Richard Shell.

❖ **G. Richard Shell,** *Bargaining for Advantage: Negotiation Strategies for Reasonable People*

28, Penguin (2006)

Goals: You'll Never Hit the Target if You Don't Aim

In Lewis Carroll's *Alice's Adventures in Wonderland,* Alice finds herself at a crossroads where a Cheshire Cat materializes. Alice asks the Cat, "Would you tell me please, which way I ought to go from here?" The Cat replies, "That depends a good deal on where you want to get to." "I don't much care where —" says Alice. "Then it doesn't matter which way you go," the Cat replies, cutting her off.

To become an effective negotiator, you must find out where you want to go — and why. That means committing yourself to specific, justifiable goals. It also means taking the time to transform your goals from simple targets into genuine — and appropriately high — *expectations.* . . .

Our goals give us direction, but our expectations are what give weight and conviction to our statements at the bargaining table. We are most animated when we are striving to achieve what we feel we justly deserve.

So it is with negotiation. Our goals give us direction, but our expectations are what give weight and conviction to our statements at the bargaining table. We are most animated when we are striving to achieve what we feel we justly deserve. The more time we spend preparing for a particular negotiation and the more information we gather that reinforces our belief that our goal is legitimate and achievable, the firmer the expectations grow . . .

What you aim for often determines what you get. Why? The first reason is obvious: Your goals set the upper limit of what you will ask for. You mentally concede everything beyond your goal, so you seldom do better than that benchmark.

Second, research on goals reveals that they trigger powerful psychological "striving" mechanisms. Sports psychologists and educators alike confirm that setting specific goals motivates people, focusing and concentrating their attention and psychological powers.

Third, we are more persuasive when we are committed to achieving some specific purpose, in contrast to the occasions when we ask for things halfheartedly or merely react to initiatives proposed by others. Our commitment is infectious. People around us feel drawn toward our goals. . . .

Goals Versus "Bottom Lines"

Most negotiating books and experts emphasize the importance of having a "bottom line," "walkaway," or "reservation price" for negotiation. Indeed, the bottom line is a fundamental bargaining concept on which much of modern negotiation theory is built. It is the *minimum acceptable level* you require to say "yes" in a negotiation. By definition, if you cannot achieve your bottom line, you would rather seek another solution to your problem or wait until another opportunity comes your way. When two parties have bottom lines that permit an agreement at some point between them, theorists speak of there being a "positive bargaining zone." When the two bottom lines do not overlap, they speak of a "negative bargaining zone" . . .

A well-framed goal is quite different from a bottom line. As I use the word, "goal" is your *highest legitimate expectation* of what you should achieve. . . .

Researchers have discovered that humans have a limited capacity for maintaining focus in complex, stressful situations such as negotiations. Consequently, once a negotiation is under way, we gravitate toward the single focal point that has the psychological significance for us. Once most people set a firm bottom line in a negotiation, that becomes their dominant reference point as discussions proceed. They measure success or failure with reference to their bottom line. Having a goal as your reference point, by contrast, prompts you to think you are facing a potential "loss" for any offer you receive below your goal. And we know that avoiding losses is a powerful motivating force. This power is not working as strongly for you when you focus solely on your bottom line.

What is the practical effect of having your bottom line become your dominant reference point in a negotiation? Over a lifetime of negotiating, your results will tend to hover at a point just above this minimum acceptable level. For most reasonable people, the bottom line is the most natural focal point. Disappointment arises if we cannot get the other side to agree to meet our minimum requirements (usually established by our available alternatives or our needs away from the table), and satisfaction arises just above that level. Meanwhile, someone else who is more skilled at orienting himself toward ambitious goals will do much better. Not surprising, research shows that parties with higher (but still realistic) goals outperform those with more modest ones, all else being equal.

To avoid falling into the trap of letting our bottom line become our reference point, be aware of your absolute limits, but do not dwell on them. Instead, work energetically on formulating your goals, ... [T]est the other side's reaction to your goal. Then, if you must, gradually re-orient toward a bottom line as that becomes necessary to close the deal. With experience, you should be able to keep both your goal and your bottom line in view at the same time without losing your goal focus. Research suggests that the best negotiators have this ability. ...

If setting goals is so vital to effective preparation, how should you do it? Use the following simple steps:

1. Think carefully about what you really want — and remember that money is often a means, not an end.
2. Set an optimistic — but justifiable — target.
3. Be specific. ...
4. Get committed. Write down your goal and, if possible, discuss the goal with someone else.
5. Carry your goal with you into the negotiation.

Set an Optimistic, Justifiable Target

When you set goals, think boldly and optimistically about what you would like to see happen. Research has repeatedly shown that people who have higher expectations in negotiations perform better and get more than people who have modest or "I'll do my best" goals, provided they really believe in their targets. ...

Once you have thought about what an optimistic, challenging goal would look like, spend a few minutes permitting realism to dampen your expectations. *Optimistic goals are effective only if they are feasible; that is, only if you believe in them and they can be justified according to some standard or norm.* ... [N]egotiation positions must usually be supported by some standard, benchmark, or precedent, or they lose their credibility. ...

Commit to Your Goal: Write It Down and Talk About It

Your goal is only as effective as your commitment to it. There are several simple things you can do that will increase your level of psychological attachment to your goal. First, as I suggested above, you should make sure it is justified and supported by solid arguments. You must believe in your goal to be committed to it.

Second, it helps if you spend just a few moments vividly imagining the way it would look or feel to achieve your goal. Visualization helps engage our mind more fully in the achievement process and also raises our level of self-confidence and commitment . . .

Third, psychologists and marketing professionals report that the act of *writing a goal down* engages our sense of commitment much more effectively than does the mere act of thinking about it. The act of writing makes a thought more "real" and objective, obligating us to follow up on it — at least in our own eyes.

Questions

4. Can you explain the difference between BATNA and RP?
5. Can you explain the difference between goals and expectations?
6. Does the advice to set high expectations work only if the other side does not follow the same advice? Will setting high expectations, particularly if done by both sides to a negotiation, likely lead to larger "negative bargaining zones," as explained by Shell, and thus more frequent impasse? Is there a way for two optimistic negotiators to deal with this and reach agreement?
7. If expectations in negotiation are, in part, a function of previous success and failure, as Shell suggests, how does a new lawyer set expectations? Would a client be well advised to seek out a lawyer who has had well-known recent success in trials and negotiations on the theory that "success breeds success?" How might you leverage someone else's success with a similar case to your advantage in a negotiation?

For an in-depth scholarly discussion of the role of aspirations in settlement negotiations, see Korobkin (2002). Korobkin concludes that high aspirations may help negotiators reach better results, but at the cost of a greater risk of impasse and personal dissatisfaction in not fully achieving the expectations created by high aspirations.

---

3. *Negotiation Preparation Checklists*

There are many negotiation preparation checklists available to guide you prior to communicating with opposing counsel. A comprehensive, multi-page negotiation checklist, providing an inventory of helpful questions from which you can choose, is available on the companion Web site for this book. You will want to create a personal checklist to use in preparing for negotiations in both litigation and transactional settings. Using a checklist will help to discipline your thinking, so you may eventually not need the list.

Note: Computer-Assisted Preparation

The questions to ask yourself in preparation will, in part, depend on your negotiation style and the subject of the negotiation. The purposes of your negotiation preparation are to determine your strategy, BATNA, reservation point, first offer, and management of concession. Similarly, you will use the information generated from your preparation to anticipate what your opponent perceives, values, and will do during the negotiations.

Today's technology makes it possible to obtain and capture on a computer program the information necessary to prepare, generate options, value trade-offs, and anticipate the moves of a negotiation opponent. If computers can be used to research law, play chess (calculating the probable moves of an opponent and choosing the best move from all available options), engage in sophisticated market research, anticipate terrorist attacks, and plot wars, they should be of help in preparing for negotiations.

Googling or Binging your negotiation counterparts and checking them out on social and professional networking sites is an easy way to learn about their background and experience. You can use the Web to obtain clues about how they might negotiate, the value they might place on items of potential trade, and their interests. Knowing more about an opponent can also aid in establishing trust and rapport. Please don't forget that the people with whom you negotiate will likely use their computers to learn all they can about you.

Another value of the Web is to help you calculate your BATNAs. What both sides to a negotiation previously had to guess at, and as a result probably perceived differently, can now be determined by a computer search. For example, the cost of replacing equipment or an object of art can quickly be found by a search in a truly worldwide marketplace. Thus, the creation of objective criteria to propose for resolution of an anticipated issue can be easily researched and prepared in advance. You can better research jury awards for similar injuries and court decisions on questions that might have to be decided if your negotiation fails. Diligent computer research may also reveal the outcome of similar negotiations.

Commercially available software programs can help you analyze the negotiation style that is most comfortable for you and determine the approach likely to be used by your negotiating counterpart, provided some questions can be answered about them. The programs can also assist you in designing concessions and assigning relative values to them. They collect input that is used to suggest the best opening offer and counteroffers. These programs can also formulate questions for you to ask during a negotiation and predict the actions of an opposing negotiator, along with recommended strategies for you to use. Finally, they can help you value and decide on outcomes once proposals emerge.

Although these programs are sophisticated with a type of built-in negotiation intelligence, like with any productivity software, the quality of the result ultimately depends on the input you provide. If nothing else, a good negotiation software program can provide a guide for what you should do to be well prepared to negotiate and what the alternative approaches may be. They can also catalog tactics you might not have considered and organize ideas and data helpful to you before commencing a negotiation. At the time of this writing the most comprehensive and user-friendly negotiation preparation software is Negotiator Pro, available at *www.negotiatorpro.com.* This program assesses negotiator styles based on responses to questions about each negotiator and then offers strategies of how to negotiate with the profiled personality type. A unique feature includes an international negotiation analysis where parties can learn about cultural differences.

C.   Initial Interaction

1.   *Trust and Rapport*

How we feel about those with whom we negotiate is a critical element to whether an agreement will be reached. Just as you may feel you can quickly "read" the character and trustworthiness of those you face, so others are forming a quick impression of you. The maxims that "you never get a second chance to make a first impression" and "first impressions matter" need to be considered as you prepare for and commence a negotiation.

The impression you make on an opponent will probably be formed, in part, before you meet. If the negotiation is of significance you and your opponent will find out what you can about one another. Your reputation will precede you into the negotiation. In addition to informal inquiries among those with whom you have previously negotiated or had other professional contact, the Internet opens your public history, both accomplishments and mistakes, for all to see. So your preparation for a negotiation, in terms of the impression you make and whether you can be trusted, involves your entire professional life. Although a misimpression can be corrected, it is an uphill struggle because of what we know about self-fulfilling prophecies and the selective way we view evidence to support earlier impressions. Trust is more likely to develop between negotiators if they see one another as similar. Similarity of backgrounds, experience, values, tastes, or group identity helps develop rapport and smoothes the way to trust. There is a delicate balance when opening a negotiation session between engaging in "small talk" that might establish a shared interest, affiliation, or acquaintance for the purpose of creating rapport, and getting to the point regarding the issues in dispute. However, taking time to learn enough about your counterpart to find commonalities and the opportunity to establish a personal connection as the basis for trust is usually time well spent.

The flip side of trust, distrust, inhibits negotiation. Distrust tends to be reciprocated and becomes a self-fulfilling prophecy engendering negative behavior and selective perceptions that confirm the reasons for not trusting one another. Distrust is an obstacle to the exchange of information and collaboration or joint problem solving.

Unless negotiators know one another socially or have had positive professional experiences together, mistrust is more the norm at the beginning of a negotiation because you know the other side can prevent you from getting something you want. So, setting a positive tone and early moves to build trust are important. If you can start on a positive note, you can build a momentum of trust that can carry the negotiations through difficult times. Trust initiated through good listening, sincere compliments, or small opening concessions builds upon itself through reciprocity. Consider the following dramatic example of creating trust by paying attention to local custom and the offering of a small gift.

❖ **Robert Benjamin,** *Terry Waite: A Study in Authenticity*
Adapted from *http://www.mediate.com,* **Summer 2002**

Terry Waite has been both hostage negotiator and hostage. He was instrumental in gaining the release of two Anglican [p]riests held captive by the Libyan leader Omar Khadafy, and subsequently was himself taken hostage for five years by a militant group associated with the Ayatollah Khomeini in Iran. As a negotiator, Waite had to deal face to face with a man who fit the mold of most negotiators' "worst-fear scenario" when his and other people's lives were on the line.

In 1983, in the course of ongoing hostilities between the United States and the United Kingdom and Libya, Colonel Omar Khadafy lashed out at the West by taking hostages. The conventional wisdom about the Colonel was that he was quite simply a "madman" — the principal "evildoer" of his time. If trust, as it is often stated, is a pre-requisite for negotiation, then Khadafy was a poor prospect. Many cautioned against trying to negotiate with someone so erratic, unpredictable and downright evil. Given the situation, Waite, of course, saw little alternative except to negotiate; Khadafy was the only one who had the authority to order the hostages' release.

After making contact through circuitous sources, Waite's introductory meeting with Khadafy could not have inspired less confidence. Just getting to the meeting was daunting. Without benefit of car, body guard, or protection of any kind, he was required to walk across a sports stadium playing field, where the bodies of those executed or tortured the night before by Khadafy security forces were laid out from one side to the other.

Waite abided by cultural tradition and presented Khadafy with a gift — a book on Islam. Given the circumstances and gravity of the situation, that act seems absurdly silly and out of place, but was not. It served to alter the atmosphere of the discussions and set the stage. Waite knew he could not just "cut to the chase" and any chance he might have of success required awareness and attention to ritual. A delighted Khadafy was thus offered the opportunity to talk about Middle East history and reciprocate Waite's initial gesture. The Westerner Waite had to stifle his urge to talk directly about the situation at hand. They bided time, talking only indirectly around the present circumstance. This was, however, a necessary dance paying homage to Koranic traditions and building a measure of trust.

Question and Note

8.   What are some of the ways that a negotiator in the United States can create trust with a counterpart that he knows only by reputation or by Googling? Might your answer be different if the context is the negotiation of a transaction, rather than the settlement of a lawsuit?

Considerable research has been done on ways to build rapport and influence attitudes for purposes of marketing and sales. Much of this research has applicability to negotiation and can be put to good use, provided it is implemented subtly enough that you appear sincere and don't come across as a salesman. One core finding of the research is that people tend to reciprocate small favors and concessions by giving more than they receive (see Cialdini, 2001).

In our chart of negotiation stages at the beginning of this chapter, we listed first demands and offers as part of initial interactions under the competitive/adversarial approach, but omitted them in the interest-based approach. Interest-based negotiators seek to establish a positive relationship and exchange information before discussing proposals. We will return to demands and offers after the following discussion about gathering and managing information.

D.   Exchanging and Refining Information

The task of finding out all that you can about the other side, their needs, their case, their BATNA, and other factors affecting their reservation point

is a significant part of the preparation stage and pervades the entire negotiation process. Similarly, disclosing and managing information in your control that may shape the other side's perceptions or that they want to know is
also a continual part of the process. Exchanging and refining information
are listed as a separate step only to emphasize their importance in the process and to recognize that there are points in the negotiation where information is expected to be exchanged formally or informally. This "stage" could
just as well have been listed before initial interactions and offers. Exchanging and refining information is a dynamic that continually shapes expectations and effects negotiation and decision making. Information may be
bargained before negotiating over outcomes.

A hallmark of effective negotiators, whether competitive or cooperative,
is their ability to listen, their propensity to ask questions, and their desire to
continually gather information. (As will be presented later, information is
power in negotiations.)

1.   *Listening and Questioning*

Lawyers are often characterized as good talkers, who love to argue. In court,
being a "silver-tongued" attorney may be valued. In negotiations, as in conversations, being a good listener and knowing how to obtain information
through the use of questions is more important than talking. This is true in
interacting with clients when preparing to negotiate for them, as well as in
negotiating. The old wisdom that "we were born with one tongue and two
ears so that we can hear from others twice as much as we speak," is good
advice for negotiators.

If you can learn what is in the brain and heart of an opponent, you can
make a personal connection, satisfy their needs, and get what you want at the
lowest possible cost. If you actively allow others to openly express themselves, they usually will tell you what you want to know. The more you talk,
the less they can say, and the less you can listen and learn. We seldom learn
anything new by speaking. The key lesson here is easy: Talk less and listen
more. When you do speak in a negotiation, do so in a way that elicits more
information, directly or indirectly, or that helps shape the negotiation.
Sometimes giving information is a way to get information, but know when
and how to listen.

Research results confirm that effective negotiators are better at eliciting
information and do more of it than less effective negotiators. Disclosing
information, whether by arguing the merits of your case or asserting your
position early on, generally results in worse outcomes than first asking questions and listening. Neil Rackham and John Carlisle studied the behavior of
English labor and contract negotiators. The more successful negotiators
asked twice the number of questions asked by less successful negotiators and
spent twice as much time acquiring information. Effective negotiators tested

their understanding of what was said and summarized what they heard (Rackman and Carlisle, 1978).

Their research supports what psychologists and interviewers have known: The most effective listening is active listening. Active listening is the opposite of deadpan, silent, passive listening. During active listening you focus your energy on what the speaker is communicating and provide responses that encourage the speaker to open up and say more. In active listening you hear not only the content, but also identify the emotion or sentiment expressed. You then briefly restate in your own words the feeling and some of the content you heard communicated so the speaker can confirm, clarify, or amplify. Most important, your response lets speakers know you heard what they said and that you care about how they feel.

The following selection provides a guide for active listening and purposeful questioning when you are negotiating.

❖ **Lee E. Miller and Jessica Miller,** *A WOMAN'S GUIDE TO SUCCESSFUL NEGOTIATING*
66, McGraw-Hill (2002)

Active Listening

There are numerous ways to encourage others to talk so you can find out what their real concerns are. These techniques are referred to as active listening and include the following:

Reflect Back
Restate what the other person has said in your own words. This ensures that you correctly understand what has been said, and it also shows the other person that you are trying to see things from their perspective. For example, if someone says, "I can't understand how you could come up with such an unworkable solution to our problem," you might paraphrase that by stating, "I guess we don't understand what your real needs are here."

Clarify
When something is not clear or you want a better understanding of what has been said, you can ask for clarification. For example, in response to the previous statement, you might say, "I don't understand. What do you mean by unworkable?" Or you could ask them to explain: "Why do you think it's unworkable?" In addition to giving you additional information, clarifying signals that you care about their concerns.

Encourage
Nod and smile, lean forward when others are talking, look them in the eye, and occasionally interject phrases such as "I see," "Go on," or "Really." This will encourage those who are speaking to expand upon what they are saying. The more they speak, the more information you will get. Again, by

engaging in this behavior, you signal your willingness to listen and your interest in what is being said.

Acknowledge Effort

Provide positive reinforcement when the speaker tries to work with you or says something you agree with. For example, you might respond by saying "I appreciate your efforts," or "That's a good point." This will encourage further efforts to find common ground with you.

Recognize Feelings

It often helps to address the feelings that people may be experiencing but not openly sharing. In response to the statement that "The proposal is unworkable," you could reply, "I see that you're frustrated with how the discussions are proceeding." Recognizing others' feelings often defuses anger and allows them to open up. This is frequently necessary before you can move on to problem solving.

Summarize

When you believe that you understand the other person's point of view, summarize your understanding of what has been said and ask whether your understanding is correct. Do the same when you reach an agreement on a particular issue. Summarizing helps to prevent misunderstandings, and you should use it continually throughout the course of negotiations. When done on an ongoing basis, it reinforces that the parties are making progress and encourages continued efforts toward reaching an agreement.

It doesn't do much good to listen, however, if you don't act on what you hear. Don't be afraid to stray from what you had planned to say if you get signals the other side is not receptive to the approach you are taking. Moreover, nothing works better than using what the other side says. You can achieve many of your objectives just by listening carefully to what is being said and agreeing to those points that are helpful. That is why it is always best to listen first.

Purposeful Questioning

Good negotiators ask different types of questions for different reasons, from open-ended, information-gathering questions to focused questions intended to lead someone to a specific conclusion. The two primary reasons for asking questions during negotiations are to get information or to support your argument. How you ask a question will depend on what you are trying to achieve.

Ask Open-Ended Questions

You should ask open-ended questions if your goal is to obtain information or to find out what the other person is thinking. Open-ended questions can't be answered with a yes or a no. They usually begin with "who," "what," "where," "when," "why," or "how," which allow for wide latitude as to responses. Their unstructured nature often enables you to find out what the real issues are and how you might satisfactorily resolve them. Open-ended questions such as "Tell me how you reached that conclusion" can also give you an insight into how someone else thinks.

Often, asking the right question at the right time can give you the information you need to completely turn around a negotiation. I recall one such situation. . . . I was practicing law, representing an executive who was taking a job with a new company and being asked to relocate from California to Connecticut. We had worked out the major issues — salary, bonus, stock options — to his satisfaction. The new company had a generous relocation policy, but it provided for only a 30-day temporary living allowance. My client's daughter was a senior in high school and he was not going to move his family until after she graduated. So he asked the company to pay his temporary living expenses for one year. The company representative insisted that they could not deviate from their relocation policy. My client was equally adamant and felt that if the company was taking such a bureaucratic approach to his request, it was probably not a place where he would want to work. Just when I thought the deal was about to fall through, I asked a question that allowed us to successfully conclude the negotiation. What was this brilliantly insightful question? It was simply "Why?" More specifically, I told the vice president of human resources that I couldn't understand why we were arguing about this issue. He explained that the relocation policy was written that way because the company had been burned by a senior executive who, after being paid temporary living expenses for well over a year, could not get his wife to move and rejoined his previous company. Having been embarrassed once, the vice president was not about to ask for another exception to the policy. Understanding his reasons for refusing our seemingly reasonable request enabled us to readily resolve the problem. We agreed that if my client did not move his family to Connecticut, he would repay the company for his temporary living expenses. This allowed the vice president to ask for and receive a modification to the relocation policy without the fear of looking foolish if things didn't work out. . . .

One purpose of asking open-ended questions is to keep the other side talking. The more someone talks, the more likely they are to provide valuable information. An added benefit is that it helps you develop a relationship with that person, which, in and of itself, is helpful. When you ask questions of others, people feel that you are working with them to find solutions, not negotiating against them.

Ask "Why?"

As mentioned above, often the most useful question you can ask is "Why?" Asking why works particularly well as a response to statements such as, "We can't agree to that" or "That would be contrary to policy." When you ask, "Why can't you agree to that?" or "Why do you have that policy?," you are calling for a reasoned response. After you are given a reason, you can make a case that the reason is not applicable in this instance. Alternatively, you have an opportunity to satisfy the other side's objections.

Repeat Back in Question Form

Another way to ask why is to use a variation on the reflecting back technique described above. Simply repeat what has just been said, but in question form . . . reflecting back the other side's own words when a proposal is not reasonable can be very effective. Similarly, when people make unqualified statements such as, "We never do that," a simple "Never?" will force them to either confirm that this is really the case, or, more likely, cause them to retreat to something like, "Except in very unusual circumstances." Once you get that kind of admission, you are well on your way to making your case because now you know what argument to make: that yours are unusual circumstances and require an exception to the normal practice. Once someone concedes that exceptions have been made in the past, it becomes much harder to claim that you don't deserve the same treatment.

Answer Questions with Questions

Sometimes you can answer a question with a question. If you don't want to respond to a particular question or you want to understand why someone is asking a particular question, you can respond by asking, "Well, what do you think?" If you do this too often you may appear evasive and argumentative, but using this approach sparingly can be effective.

Ask What They Would Do

Finally, if you find yourself at an impasse, you can always ask what they would do if they were in your position. This can sometimes completely change the dynamics of the negotiations by forcing the other side to come up with a solution to the problem, rather than trying to convince you that there is no problem. In doing so, a solution may emerge that would be acceptable to you or could be made so with slight modification.

Questions

9. The selection above on active listening and questioning is excerpted from a book written as a guide for women. Do you consider the advice given to be gender specific? Do you think men or women are generally better listeners? Why?

10. Are there times when active listening or responding to a question with a question should not be used? When would you find these techniques annoying or counterproductive?

11. The use of silence to elicit additional information after someone stops speaking can also be effective in situations other than negotiation. The silence should be accompanied by continued eye contact to convey an expectation or invitation for more information.

> Have you used this method with friends, a spouse, or children? Do you think you are susceptible to this technique when used by others?

2. *Managing Information*

Effective negotiators also know how to manage information and thoughtfully determine when and what information to provide. Generally, it is better to receive more information than you provide, but this is not an absolute. The distinction between managing information and purposely deceiving is a thin line and will be examined in the section on negotiation ethics.

The following selection provides advice and discusses issues regarding obtaining and providing information. Professor Nelken first focuses on managing and bargaining for information in distributive situations and then on the benefits and concerns of sharing information in more integrative negotiations. The separation between distributive and integrative negotiation is not always clear, so her comments may apply to both.

❖ Melissa L. Nelken, *Negotiation: Theory and Practice*
41, Anderson Publishing (2007)

In the course of the negotiation, you will try to learn things about the other party's case, and about his perception of your case, that you don't know when the negotiation starts. He, of course, will do the same with you. Another important aspect of preparation, then, is deciding what you need to find out before you actually make a deal. Without considering what information you need to gather in the early stages of the negotiation, you will not be able to gauge how well the actual situation fits the assumptions you have made in preparing to negotiate. You may have overestimated how much the other party needs a deal with you, or underestimated the value he places on what you are selling. Only careful attention to gathering information will enable you to adjust your goals appropriately. In addition to what you want to learn, you also have to decide what information you are willing, or even eager, to divulge to the other party — for example, the large number of offers you have already received for the subject property — and what information you want to conceal — for example, the fact that none of those offers exceeds the price you paid for the property originally. Managing information is a central feature of distributive bargaining, and you have to plan to do it well.

A beginning negotiator often feels that she has to conceal as much as possible, that virtually anything she reveals will hurt her or be used against her. . . . [Y]ou are more likely to feel this way if you have not thought through your case and prepared how to present it in the best light that you realistically can. If you choose when and how you will reveal information, rather than anxiously concealing as much as possible, you gain a degree of control over the negotiation that you lack when you merely react to what your counterpart says or does. Increasing the amount of information you are prepared to reveal, and reducing the amount you feel you absolutely must conceal, will help you make a stronger case for your client. In addition, the more willing you are to share information that the other party considers useful, the more likely you are to learn what you need to know from your counterpart before you make a deal.

Using Outside Sources

As part of your preparation, you need to consult outside sources of information to help you understand the context of a given negotiation. You will need data about the subject of the negotiation — market prices, alternate sources of supply, industry standards, market factors affecting the company you are dealing with, and so on. In addition, information about the parties and their representatives from others who have negotiated with them in the past will be helpful in planning your strategy. You will also want to learn about any relevant negotiation conventions, for example, the convention in personal injury litigation that the plaintiff makes the first demand. . . .

Bargaining for Information

A central aspect of distributive bargaining is bargaining for information. In the course of planning, you have to make certain working assumptions about the motives and wishes of the other side, as well as about the factual context of the negotiation. In addition, we all have a tendency to "fill in" missing information in order to create a coherent picture of a situation. For a negotiator, it is imperative to separate out what you know to be true from what you merely believe to be true by testing your assumptions during the early stages of the negotiation. Otherwise, you risk making decisions based on inaccurate information and misunderstanding what the other side actually tells you. . . .

Many negotiators forget that they start with only a partial picture of the situation, and they push to "get down to numbers" before learning anything about the other side's point of view. Yet the relevant facts of a situation are not immutable; they are often dependent on your perspective. Knowing the other side's perspective is a valuable source of information about possibilities for settlement. The most obvious way to gather that information is by asking questions, especially about the reasons behind positions taken by the other party. Why does a deal have to be made today? How good are her alternatives to settlement with you? What is the basis for a particular offer? Asking questions allows you to test the assumptions that you bring to the negotiation about both parties' situations. Questions also permit you to gauge the firmness of stated positions by learning how well supported they are by facts. In addition, the information you gather can alert you to issues that are important (or unimportant) to your counterpart, opening up possibilities for an advantageous settlement if you value those issues differently.

In addition to asking questions, you have to learn to listen carefully to what the other party says, to look for verbal and nonverbal cues that either reinforce or contradict the surface message conveyed. If someone tells you that he wants $40,000-50,000 to settle, you can be sure that he will settle for $40,000, or less. If he starts a sentence by saying, "I'll be perfectly frank with you . . . ," take whatever follows with a large grain of salt and test it against other things you have heard. Asking questions is only one way to gather information, and not always the most informative one. You also have to listen for what someone omits from an answer, for answers that are not answers or that deflect the question, for hesitations and vagueness in the responses that you get. There is no simple formula for what such things mean, but the more alert you are for ways in which you are not getting information in a straightforward way, the better able you will be to sort through the information that you get. . . .

One of the most effective and underutilized methods of bargaining for information is silence. Many inexperienced negotiators, especially lawyer-negotiators, think that they are paid to talk and are not comfortable sitting quietly. If you can teach yourself to do so, you will find that you often learn things that would never be revealed in response to a direct question. When silences occur, people tend to fill them in; and because the silence is unstructured, what they say is often more spontaneous than any answer to a question would be. Since you are interested in gathering new information in the course of the negotiation, it is useful to keep in mind that if you are talking, you probably aren't hearing anything you do not already know. Therefore, silence is truly golden. . . .

Sharing Information

All that has been said so far about integrative bargaining suggests that lawyers will only be able to do a good job if they share substantive information about their clients' needs and preferences and look for ways to make their differences work for them in the negotiation. According to Follett (1942, p. 36), "the first rule . . . for obtaining integration is to put your cards on the table, face the real issue, uncover the conflict, bring the whole thing into the open." This is a far cry from the bargaining for information that characterizes distributive negotiations, where each side seeks to learn as much as possible about the other while revealing as little as it can. The more straightforward and clear the negotiators' communications are, the fewer obstacles there will be to recognizing and capitalizing on opportunities for mutual gain. This means, first, that they must be clear about their clients' goals, even if they are open as to the means of reaching those goals. In addition, there must be sufficient trust between them so that both are willing to reveal their clients' true motivations. Such trust may be based on past experience, but it may also be developed in the course of a negotiation, as the negotiators exchange information and evaluate the information they have received. It does not have to be based on an assumption that the other side has your best interest at heart, but only that he is as interested as you are in uncovering ways that you can both do better through negotiation. Self-interest can keep both sides honest in the process, even where there might be a short-term gain from misrepresentation. Of course, the need to share information in order to optimize results creates risks for the negotiators as well. . . .

Flexibility, rather than rigid positions, is key to integrative bargaining, since the outcome will depend on fitting together the parties' needs as much as possible. When the negotiators share adequate information, they may end up redefining the conflict they are trying to resolve. For example, what seemed a specific problem about failure to fulfill the terms of a contract may turn out to be a more fundamental difficulty with the structure of the contract itself. A better outcome for both sides may result if the contract is renegotiated. . . .

Strategic Use of Information

There is also anxiety because the amount of shared information needed for integrative bargaining to succeed may be more than a distributive bargainer wants to reveal. For example, a distributively-inclined buyer may prefer that his counterpart think that time of delivery, which he does not care much about, is very important to him, so that he can exact concessions on other aspects of the deal by "giving in" to a later delivery to accommodate the seller. Since it is hard to know in advance what issues will be most significant to the other side, it can be difficult to decide how much information to share and how to evaluate the quality of the information you receive about your counterpart's priorities. The fear of being taken advantage of often results in both sides' taking preemptive action focused on "winning" rather than on collaborating. Sometimes such strategies are effective; but they are also likely to impede or prevent what could be a fruitful search for joint gains.

E.   The Timing of Demands and Offers

As we noted earlier, the timing of offers and demands may vary between positional and interest-based approaches. Positional bargainers tend to make demands and offers early. Their initial interaction may commence with the presentation of a demand. The filing of a lawsuit without prior negotiation of the claim is one way to assert a demand and start negotiations. In contrast, interest-based negotiators seek information from their counterpart and prefer to establish a positive relationship before discussing proposals. One purpose of the information sought and perhaps exchanged is to discover interests that might lead to an acceptable solution that creates value, even if there might later be more competitive bargaining to allocate the added value.

Whether you prefer a competitive or cooperative approach, there will be negotiations in which you must decide if it is better to make the first offer or invite an offer from the other side. (Offers and demands are used here synonymously.) If choosing to make the first offer, should it be extreme, modestly favorable, exactly what you expect, or equitably calculated to be fair to all and maximize collective value? If the first offer is made by the other side, should you flinch, as recommended by Dawson, counteroffer immediately, or process the offer and come back with an exaggerated counteroffer or one closer to your reservation point? How does formulating the initial offer relate to what we have learned about perceptions, ripeness, anchoring, preparation, the role of expectations, and trust?

The negotiation guidebooks are full of advice on making offers, much of it contradictory. There appears to be consensus that in distributive negotiations, more extreme or aggressive offers result in more favorable outcomes. (However, an exaggerated offer can come before or after learning the other side's opening position.) This consensus, focused on distributive negotiation, doesn't help you on how to start an integrative negotiation. The first selection below, which is based on Professor Williams's extensive empirical research of lawyer negotiators, weighs the advantages and disadvantages of three different opening strategies. Each strategy assumes that both sides seek to establish the illusion that they are inalterably committed to their opening positions. The second excerpt explores when to make the first offer and how to respond to an initial offer. It reviews the power of the first offer as an anchor, which you learned about in Chapter 3.

❖ **Gerald R. Williams and Charles Craver,** LEGAL NEGOTIATION
79, West Publishing (2007)

. . . The lawyers articulate their opening positions. At this early stage in the dispute, that exchange is not as simple as it appears. The facts are not all in, the legal questions are not fully researched, and unforeseen developments loom on the horizon. In the face of these uncertainties, the negotiators must leave themselves a certain amount of latitude, yet they must develop credible opening demands and offers . . .

[T]here are essentially three strategies that can be used in framing an opening position. . . . Negotiators may adopt the *maximalist strategy* of asking for more than they expect to obtain, they may adopt the *equitable strategy* of taking positions that is fair to both sides, or they may adopt the *integrative strategy* of searching for alternative solutions that would generate the most attractive combination for all concerned. Each strategy has its own strengths and weaknesses.

Maximalist Positioning

Arguments for maximalist positioning begin with the assumption that the opening position is a bargaining position, and that no matter how long bargainers may deny it, they expect to come down from them to find agreements. Maximalist positioning has several advantages. These position statements effectively hide the bargainer's real or minimum expectations, they eliminate the danger of committing to an overly modest case evaluation, they provide covers for them while they seek to learn real opponent positions, and will very likely induce opponents to reduce their expectations. They also provide negotiators with something to give up, with concessions they can make, to come to terms with opponents. This last factor may be especially important when opponents also open high, and negotiators are required to trade concessions as they move toward mutually agreeable terms. These advantages may lead many to believe that negotiators who make high opening demands, have high expectations, make relatively small and infrequent concessions, and are perceptive and unyielding fare better in the long run than their opponents.

The potential benefits of the maximalist position need to be weighed against its potential demerits, which are those associated with competitive/adversarial strategies. . . . The most important weakness is the increased risk of bargaining stalemates. Competent opponents will prefer their non-settlement alternatives to the unreasonable demands and supporting tactics of the maximalist negotiators, unless the opponents themselves can devise effective strategies to counter such maximalist behaviors. We observe in the data that competitive attorneys at all levels of effectiveness are rated as making high opening demands. Yet, by definition, effective competitive/adversarials use the strategy proficiently, while ineffective competitive adversarials do not. We are forced to conclude that in the legal context the maximalist strategy does not consistently bring high returns for those who use it — only for those who employ it effectively. How high demands can be without losing their effectiveness depends on several considerations. One is the nature of the remedy being sought. By their nature, contract damages are less inflatable than personal injury damages, for example, and negotiators who multiply their contract damages as they do their personal injury claims will undermine their own credibility. Another consideration is local custom. Specialized groups within the bar develop norms and customs that provide measures against which the reasonableness or extremism of demands can be evaluated. Not all high demands are the same. Some demands lack credibility on their face by their inappropriateness and lack of congruity in the context in which they are made. But the level of demands is not the sole factor. The data suggest that effective competitive/adversarial negotiators are able to establish the credibility and plausibility of high demands by relying on convincing legal argumentation. Ineffective competitive/adversarials lack the skills to do this, and, in the absence of convincing support, their high demands lack credibility.

Finally, it should be noted that the effectiveness of high demands will depend upon the opponents against whom the high demands are made. In cases where opponents are unsure of the actual case values, high opening demands by maximizing negotiators have the desired effect. The opponents, unsure of case values, use the maximizer's high opening demands as standards against which to set their own goals. However, when the opponents have evaluated their cases and arrived at appropriate value judgments, the opponents interpreted maximizer high opening demands as evidence of unreasonableness. This causes maximizer credibility to be diminished, and the likelihood of bargaining breakdowns increases.

Equitable Positioning

Equitable positions are calculated to be fair to both sides. Their most notable proponent, O. Bartos, challenged the assumption of maximalist theorists that both sides to negotiations are trying to maximize their own payoffs or benefits. He argued that a competing value is also operative — that negotiators feel a cooperative desire to arrive at solutions fair to both sides. In support of this argument, he cited not only humanistic literature defending equality as an essential ingredient of justice, but also anthropological and sociological studies confirming the widespread existence and operation in society of an egalitarian norm of reciprocity. Bartos conducted numerous theoretical and experimental negotiation studies which lead him to believe that the human desire to deal fairly with others is preferable to a more competitive strategy.

This equitable approach is considered as the most economical and efficient method of conflict resolution. It minimizes the risk of deadlock and avoids the costs of delay occasioned by extreme bargaining positions. Bartos recommended that negotiators be scrupulously fair and that they avoid the temptation to take advantage of naive opponents. He cautioned that the equitable approach requires trust, which allows both sides to believe they are being treated fairly. Nonetheless, trust must be tempered with realism. It is out of trust that negotiators make concessions, but if their trust is not rewarded or returned in fair fashion, further concessions should be withheld until their opponents reciprocate. Equitable negotiators do not always open negotiations with statements specifying their desires to achieve mutually beneficial solutions. Rather, they open with positions that show they are serious about finding fair agreement, and they trustingly work toward midpoints between their reasonable opening position and the reasonable opening positions of their opponents. Unless both sides come forward with reasonable opening positions, it will be difficult for one side to compel the other to move toward an equitable resolution. Referring back to the data on cooperative/problem-solving and competitive/adversarial negotiators, we intuitively suspect that Bartos' equitable negotiators are cooperative/problem-solvers. This observation is borne out by the extremely high ratings received by cooperative/problem-solving attorneys on characteristics such as trustworthy, ethical, honest, and fair. Just as with our analysis of maximalist positioning by competitive/adversarial attorneys, it must be pointed out that the use of equitable positioning by cooperative/problem-solving attorneys does not always generate satisfactory results. It is obviously satisfactory as used by effective cooperative/problem-solvers, but it is likely to be deficient when used by ineffective cooperative/problem-solvers. We must conclude that the positioning strategy, whether maximalist or equitable, does not guarantee success. Whichever approach is used, it must be employed with care and acumen or it will not be effective.

Integrative Positioning

Integrative Positioning involves more than opening demands and offers. It describes an attitude or approach that carries through the other stages of the negotiation, and is an alternative to pure positional bargaining. The most effective advocates of this method have been Roger Fisher and William Ury who advise negotiators to avoid positioning completely. Among business people, the method is seen as the art of problem solving. Integrative negotiators view cases as presenting alternative solutions, and they believe that chances for reaching agreements are enhanced by discovering innovative alternatives reflecting the underlying interests of the parties, and seeking to arrange the alternatives in packages that yield maximum benefit to both parties. This strategy is often identified with exchange transactions involving many variables, and is generally seen as having limited utility in personal injury actions, for example, where the fundamental issue is how much money defendants are going to pay plaintiffs — a classic distributive problem. . . .

❖ **Deepax Malhotra and Max H. Bazerman,** *Negotiation Genius*
27, Bantam Books (2007)

Should You Make the First Offer?

The primary benefit of making a first offer in negotiation is that it establishes an *anchor*. An anchor is a number that focuses the other negotiator's attention and expectations. Especially when the other party is uncertain about the correct, fair, or appropriate outcome, they are likely to gravitate toward any number that helps them focus and resolve their uncertainty. As it turns out, first offers tend to serve this purpose well: they anchor the negotiation and strongly influence the final outcome. . . .

The power of anchors is substantial. Research has shown that anchors affect even those with negotiation experience and expertise. In one remarkable demonstration of the power of anchors, professors Greg Northcraft and Margaret Neale invited real estate agents to evaluate a house that was for sale. The agents were allowed to walk through the house and neighborhood, and were given the Multiple Listing Service (MLS) information sheet that provided details about the house, including its size and dimensions, the year it was built, the amenities included, etcetera. They were also given detailed information about other properties located in the same neighborhood. The information provided to each agent was identical with one exception: the "list price" on the MLS sheet that was given to the agent was randomly picked from one of the following: (a) $119,000, (b) $129,000, (c) $139,000, or (d) $149,000. In real estate, the list price is the "first offer" made by the seller. Thus, this study manipulated the first offer to see whether it would affect the perceptions of experienced real estate agents. After seeing the house and reading all of the information, agents were asked to evaluate the house on four dimensions:

1.   What is an appropriate list price for this house? *(Appropriate List Price)*
2.   What do you estimate is the appraisal value of this house? *(Appraisal Value)*
3.   As a buyer, what is a reasonable amount to pay for the house? *(Willingness to Pay)*
4.   What is the lowest offer you would accept as the seller? *(Lowest Acceptable Offer)*

[The chart] graphs the responses to these questions by agents who were provided each of the list prices. As you can see, agents were strongly influenced by whichever list price they were arbitrarily assigned! On every measure, those given a higher list price thought the house was worth more than did those given a lower list price. Furthermore, when the agents were asked whether their answers had been influenced *at all* by the list price given to them on the information sheet, more than 80 percent of them said no.

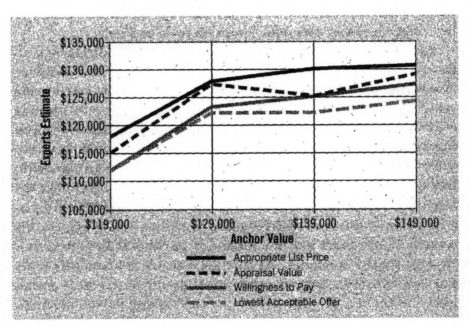

. . . [W]hether you should make the first offer or not depends upon how much information you have. If you believe you have sufficient information about the other side's reservation value, it pays to make a reasonable (i.e., *sufficiently* aggressive) opening offer that anchors the discussion in your favor. If you suspect that you may not have enough information about the ZOPA [zone of possible agreement], you'd be wise to defer an opening offer until you have collected more information. In this case, it may even be a good idea to let the other party make the first offer. You might forgo the opportunity to anchor the negotiation, but you also avoid the downside of not anchoring aggressively enough. Notice that a lack of information can also lead you to anchor *too* aggressively, demanding an amount that might offend the other side and drive them away. In other words, asking for too little diminishes the amount of value you can capture; asking for too much diminishes your chances of consummating the deal. . . .

How Should You Respond to Their Initial Offer?

When the other party makes the first move, you become vulnerable to the effects of anchoring. Because anchoring effects can be very subtle, this is likely to be true even if you are aware of these effects. However, there are a number of ways you can protect yourself from being overly influenced by the other side's anchor:

Strategy 1: Ignore the Anchor

The best thing to do in the event that the other party makes an aggressive first offer — whether high or low — is to ignore it. This doesn't mean you should pretend you didn't hear it. Rather, respond to this effect: "Judging by your offer, I think we might be looking at this deal in very different ways. Let's try to bridge that gap by discussing . . . ." In this manner, you can shift the conversation to an entirely different topic, one that allows you to reassert control of the discussion.

Strategy 2: Separate Information from Influence

Every offer is a combination of *information* and *influence*. The other party's offer tells you something about what she believes and what she wants (information), but it also has the power to derail your strategy (influence). Your task is to separate the information contained in the particulars of the offer (and the way in which it was made) from the other side's attempt to influence your perceptions. The best way to stave off influence is to stick to your original game plan. If you walked in with a prepared first offer, don't allow the other side's anchor to soften it. This does not mean that you should ignore substantial information that changes your beliefs about the actual ZOPA. For example, if the other side has just provided credible evidence that she has an attractive offer from a competitor of yours, this might be reason to adjust your counteroffer. However, it is important to realize that anchors will affect perceptions and counteroffers even in the absence of any real information provided to you. For example, the negotiator's mind can sometimes fail to distinguish between these two statements:

- *Information and Influence:* "We have received a better offer from Company X. As a result, we think your initial offer is low. We would like you to increase it to $7 million."

- *Influence Only:* "As you know, there are other companies with whom we do business. We have spoken with them. As a result, we think your initial offer is low. We would like you to increase it to $7 million."

The first statement provides some (but not much) substantive information that should prompt you to think about whether to accept, challenge, or question the statement being made. The second statement simply reiterates what you already knew, but uses phraseology that helps the other side emphasize its anchor. Thus, you have every reason to ignore this statement.

Strategy 3: Avoid Dwelling on Their Anchor

Many negotiators believe that if someone anchors aggressively, you should push them to justify the anchor, thereby exposing the frivolous nature of their extreme demands. This is a dangerous strategy. Why? Because the more an anchor is discussed in a negotiation, the more powerful it becomes. If you ask the other party to justify their offer or discuss it further (e.g., "How did you come up with that number?"), you increase the power of that anchor to define the negotiation parameters. Almost always, your counterpart will find a way to frame the negotiation such that their offer makes at least a modicum of sense.

On the other hand, you do not want to miss out on the opportunity to learn something new about the deal or about your counterpart's perspective. To resolve this dilemma, try the following: if you are surprised by their offer, probe a little to find out if there is in fact any substantive new information that you can obtain. If no such information is forthcoming, quickly shift attention away from the anchor by sharing your own perspective and defining the negotiation in your terms.

Strategy 4: Make an Anchored Counteroffer, then Propose Moderation

Finally, if it is not possible to ignore or dismiss the other party's anchor, you should offset its influence by making an aggressive counteroffer. In doing so, you retain the ability to capture as much of the ZOPA as possible. However, countering aggression with aggression comes at a risk: the possibility that both parties will become entrenched and reach an impasse. To mitigate this risk, you should offset their anchor with an aggressive counteroffer, and then suggest that you need to work together to bridge the gap. In addition, you should offer to make the first move toward moderation by discussing your own perspective (i.e., by justifying your aggressive counteroffer). This allows you to deflate their anchor while shifting from an aggressive exchange to a quest for common ground. For example, in response to an aggressive anchor, you might say:

> Well, based on your offer, which was unexpected, it looks like we have a *lot* of work ahead of *us*. From our perspective, a fair price would be closer to $X [your counter-anchor]. I will explain to you how *we* are valuing this deal, but it appears to me that

if we are to reach any agreement, we will both have to work together to make it happen.

Strategy 5: Give Them Time to Moderate Their Offer Without Losing Face

If the other party's initial offer is *very* extreme — far outside the ZOPA — you may need to inform them that their offer is not even a basis for starting the discussion. This assertion should be followed by information regarding your own perspective and a candid invitation to reopen negotiation — from a very different starting point. . . .

To illustrate the point that your first offer or demand should not be so extreme that your opponent walks out of the room, consider the following scene from a popular book and movie. The non-fiction story chronicles the negotiation and trial of the claims of eight families in Woburn, Massachusetts, who sued the corporate owners of a tannery and chemical plants for cancer-related illnesses and deaths of their children. Even food and gifts could not prevent an impasse.

❖ **Jonathan Harr,** *A CIVIL ACTION*
277, Vintage Books (1996)

After a few minutes, the lawyers took their assigned seats at the table. Schlichtmann began talking about how he and his partners took only a few select cases and worked to the exclusion of all else on those. (This was Schlichtmann's way of saying there was no stopping them.) He said he wanted a settlement that would provide for the economic security of the families, and for their medical bills in the future. The families, he continued, weren't in this case just for money. They wanted an acknowledgment of the companies' wrongdoing, Schlichtmann said, a full disclosure of all the dumping activities.

"Are you suggesting there hasn't been a full disclosure?" Facher asked. "No," said Schlichtmann, who was suggesting exactly that, but now made an effort to avoid confrontation. "But as part of a settlement, we want a disclosure that the judge will bless." Another condition of settlement, he added, was an agreement that the companies clean their land of the toxic wastes, and pay the costs for cleaning the aquifer.

None of the defense lawyers had touched any of the food or drink. As Schlichtmann spoke, he saw Facher reach for a bowl of mints on the table and slowly unwrap the foil from one. Facher popped the mint into his mouth and sucked on it, watching Schlichtmann watch him.

Schlichtmann talked for fifteen minutes. Then Gordon laid out the financial terms of the settlement: an annual payment of $1.5 million to each of the eight families for the next thirty years; $25 million to establish a research foundation that would investigate the links between hazardous wastes and illness; and another $25 million in cash.

Cheeseman and his partners took notes on legal pads as Gordon spoke. Facher examined the pen provided courtesy of the Four Seasons, but he did not write anything on his pad. Facher studied the gilt inscription on the pen. It looked like a good-quality pen. These figures, he thought, were preposterous. They meant that Schlichtmann did not want to settle the case, or else he was crazy. Maybe Schlichtmann simply wanted to go to trial. This opulent setting, and Schlichtmann sitting at the table flanked by his disciples like a Last Supper scene, annoyed Facher. Where was Schlichtmann getting the money for all this?

When Gordon finished, silence descended.

Finally Facher stopped studying the pen. He looked up, and said, "If I wasn't being polite, I'd tell you what you could do with this demand."

Cheeseman had added up Gordon's figures. By Cheeseman's calculations, Schlichtmann was asking a total of four hundred ten million over thirty years. "How much is that at present value?" Cheeseman asked Gordon.

Gordon replied that he would rather not say. "Your own structured-settlement people can tell you that."

Facher took a croissant from the plate in front of him, wrapped it in a napkin, and put it into his pocket. That and the mint he had consumed were the only items the defense lawyers had taken from the sumptuous banquet that Gordon had ordered.

Cheeseman and his partners asked a few more perfunctory questions about the terms of disclosure, which Schlichtmann answered. Facher had gone back to studying the pen. "Can I have this?" he said abruptly, looking at Schlichtmann.

Schlichtmann, appearing surprised, nodded. Facher put the pen into his breast pocket. "Nice pen," he said. "Thank you."

Then Facher got up, put on his coat, and walked out the door. Frederico, who had not uttered a word, followed him.

Cheeseman and his partners stood, too, and in a moment, they followed Facher.

Schlichtmann and his colleagues sat alone on their side of the table. Gordon looked at his watch. The meeting had lasted exactly thirty-seven minutes, he announced. "I guess we're going to trial," Gordon added.

Schlichtmann was surprised, but only for a moment. He looked at his colleagues and shrugged. "We're going to get a jury in two weeks," he said. "The pressure's on them."

Conway got up and paced the room and smoked a cigarette. He didn't feel like talking. There was nothing to discuss. They'd gotten nothing out of this so-called settlement conference, not even information from the other side. He put on his coat and, along with Crowley, walked up Tremont Street back to the office.

Questions and Note

12.   How did Schlichtmann go wrong? What advice offered by Shell and by Williams and Craver might have been helpful for Schlichtmann in making his demand?

13.   Might local custom and the experience of opposing counsel, as well as the evaluation done by the other side, have been contributing factors to the defense walkout in the above scene? What would you have done differently than Schlichtmann in this situation?

In formulating your first proposal, whether it be a demand or offer, it is advised that you determine the most aggressive proposal for which you can state a credible justification. Never demand so much or offer so little that you can't explain the reason for it. Be able to phrase your first offer as "I propose this because . . ." This will minimize the "Schlichtmann effect."

F.   Bargaining

Bargaining takes many forms and is not confined to a specific stage in the negotiation process. The term "bargaining" is more associated with the competitive/distributive approach. Phrases like "searching for solutions" and "problem solving" are frequently used to describe a more cooperative/integrative approach. However, at some point in any negotiation there must be movement from the differences that brought the parties to the table toward the agreement that will resolve the dispute or create a deal. Whether the movement results from arguments and persuasion or from proposed principles and criteria may be more a matter of semantics and tone than of real difference. For example, lawyers in negotiating a settlement of a lawsuit may agree, expressly or implicitly, that legal principles and precedent will be the criteria for settlement. Does this reduce the role of argument and attempts at persuasion regarding what case precedent is most analogous and applicable to the matter in dispute? A hallmark of integrative negotiation is trading off a lower priority to satisfy one more personally important. Is this not a form of bargaining concession?

1.   Managing Concessions

Concessions are the compromises you make after your opening offer to move the negotiation forward, particularly in competitive bargaining. Usually the concessions you make are offered in return for those your negotiation opponent offers. Making concessions can be done strategically in recognition that the timing, amount, and nature of concessions are a form of communication by which each side sends signals about priorities and reservation points. The pattern of concessions forms a message. By carefully considering what you want to communicate you can manage concessions to shape the message, particularly about how close you are to your reservation point. (Diminishing concessions signal you are close.)

The timing of offering concessions can be telling and must also be considered carefully. Concessions given in rapid succession early on may signal risk aversion or desperation. Giving away too much in the initial stages of negotiation depletes the reserve of concessions that can be offered later, when they may be more appreciated.

By planning and using concessions strategically, you can influence the outcome of the negotiation. The flip side of anything that can be used strategically is that a similar or counterstrategy might be used to manipulate you. So be aware that the concession signals from a competitive bargainer can be deceptive and may mislead an adversary about how far the bargainer will go. The following reading is an exploration of concessions and their use, as explained by a leading negotiation trainer.

❖ **Theron O'Connor,** PLANNING AND EXECUTING AN EFFECTIVE CONCESSION STRATEGY

Bay Group International (2003)

Concessions and the Negotiating Process

It is the concession piece of the negotiation process — the bargaining, the give-and-take, the "horse-trading," what the parties are willing to give up in order to reach an agreement — that will be discussed here. There are two principal sets of tasks to consider. The first is how to create the most advantageous negotiation context within which a concession strategy can be implemented. The techniques to establish a favorable negotiation context are discussed elsewhere in this volume. The second critical consideration is how to effectively handle the *execution* of the concession strategy or plan once the context has been established. This piece will focus upon the execution phase.

It should be noted that the many parts of the negotiation process are not strictly sequential. Rather, they occur and reoccur throughout the negotiation and must be attended to iteratively. That is particularly true of concession patterns. Often attention to concessions is mistakenly deferred until late in the game and concessions are used tactically, rather than strategically, as a closing tool.

Planning and Executing an Effective Concession Strategy

Once a desirable negotiating context has been established, the concession strategy can be executed. Whether to concede, when to concede, what to concede, how to concede are among a number of important considerations to keep in mind in dealing with concessions. Skilled negotiators develop plans for managing the process of making concessions, and thereby exert more control over the negotiation process. Conceding without a plan can doom you to failure in negotiation.

Concessions Should Be Made Only as Required

Notwithstanding that a sophisticated concession strategy has been developed — replete with creative and cost effective negotiables — no concessions should be made unless they are demanded by the other side. If the other side is willing to accept the initial proposal, then there has probably been a failure to accurately gauge the unexpectedly high value perception of the other side and a failure to take a sufficiently ambitious opening position. That error ought not to be compounded by then freely granting concessions from the largesse that has been built into the plan. While this should go without saying, there is often the temptation to "throw something in" simply because it is unexpectedly still there.

Concessions Should Be Made Slowly and Reluctantly

At the early stages of the negotiation, the focus should be on continuing to shape and influence the value perception of the other side and continuing to uncover and evaluate their wants and needs. With the range of reason advantageously set, it is imperative to hold the line and show resolve with respect to the value proposition and opening position. Reluctance to make concessions early on tends to increase their value in the mind of the other negotiator when they are in fact granted. Care should be taken, however, not to communicate too aggressive and inflexible a stance.

Try Not to Be the First to Make a Concession

If possible, get the other party to move first. Take the time to test the resolve of the other side by asking for concessions and suggesting ways that interests might be satisfied by them. First concessions can carry strong signals as to the flexibility of the other negotiator and can help calibrate the distance between the party's positions. Do not hesitate to make a concession, however, if it seems necessary to keep the negotiation going.

Get Something in Return for Any Concession

Concessions should be made in the context of trades or exchanges rather than given simply to see if the other side's point of satisfaction might be found. Demanding a concession in return both reinforces the value of what is being conceded and signals the resolve of the negotiator making the concession. It also helps to build the process of give and take and stimulate movement toward agreement.

First Concede Low Cost Negotiables That Represent High Value to the Other Side and Vice Versa

Having prioritized and ranked those things which might be offered to satisfy the wants and needs of the parties, it is important to evaluate each opportunity in terms of what might be offered that would be perceived to provide the highest possible value to the other side at the lowest cost. Likewise, in seeking concessions from the other side, it is important to seek concessions of high perceived value at comparatively low cost to them.

Use a Concession Pattern Designed to Leverage Fundamental Interests

Concession patterns communicate predictable messages to the other side. Holding firm and making one big concession at the end sends one message; making one large early concession and then holding firm sends another message. Making incremental but growing concessions sends one message; making incremental but diminishing concessions sends another message. Driving value early on and then executing a concession pattern of a large concession first and then progressively smaller ones often can be the most powerful pattern of all. It communicates resolve, then flexibility, and then diminishing returns moving toward closure.

Conclusion

It is critical to the ultimate success of the negotiation to deal with the concession process early on — even prior to initial contact — both to build the most advantageous context and to develop a strategy for execution of the concession plan. The context-building activities, anchoring, framing, positioning, setting high opening targets, discovering interests and negotiables, and managing emotions and behaviors, help to develop a robust value proposition and to stretch the range-of-reason within which an optimal outcome can be achieved.

Concession execution guidelines help to ensure that the negotiator will not give up too much too soon and that an appropriate balance will be maintained between self-interested competitiveness on the one hand and relational collaboration on the other. The concession execution guidelines are:

> *No Concession Unless Needed*
> *Get the Other Party to Make First Concession*
> *Concede Slowly and Reluctantly*
> *Get Something in Return*
> *Concede to High Value from Low Cost/Vice-Versa*
> *Use Advantageous Pattern*

Rigorous integration of both phases, building context and concession execution — from beginning to end — create the highest likelihood of successful negotiation.

Problem 1

Assume you are negotiating a personal injury claim on behalf of an injured pedestrian, and liability is not clear. You have spoken with the insurance claims adjuster five times. Each time you have conceded an additional $1,000 off your initial written demand of $80,000, while offering new information or arguments in support of your claim. What do you think the adjuster might be communicating to you with each of the following concession patterns (he would use only one of these four patterns), and how would each pattern influence your recommendation to your risk-averse client about accepting a $47,000 settlement after your fifth round of negotiation?

	A	B	C	D
1.	$ 0	$ 3,000	$40,000	$47,000
2.	$ 0	$ 6,000	$45,000	$47,000
3.	$ 0	$12,500	$46,500	$47,000
4.	$ 0	$25,000	$47,000	$47,000
5.	$47,000	$47,000	$47,000	$47,000

2.   Value-Creating Trades and Brainstorming

A type of bargaining also occurs in cooperative, problem-solving negotiation. The focus is more on finding the best fit of interests rather than on gaining a one-sided advantage. The following reading proposes a way to generate value-creating options and trade-offs. The technique of brainstorming to generate more creative options based on different interests and values is described.

❖ **Robert H. Mnookin, Scott R. Peppet, and Andrew S. Tulumello,**
Beyond Winning: Negotiating to Create Value in Deals and Disputes

37, Harvard University Press (2000)

Generate Value-Creating Options

Now . . . look for value-creating trades. But this is not as easy as it might appear. Many negotiators jump into a negotiation process that inhibits value creation. One side suggests a solution and the other negotiator shoots it down. The second negotiator proposes an option, only to be told by the first why it can't work. After a few minutes of this, neither side is willing to propose anything but the most conventional solutions. This method mistakenly conflates two processes that should be engaged in separately: generating options and evaluating them.

It often helps to engage in some sort of brainstorming. The most effective brainstorming requires real freedom — however momentary — from practical constraints. . . . [There are two ground rules for brainstorming.]

* No evaluation
* No ownership

Premature evaluation inhibits creativity. We are all self-critical enough, and adding to our natural inhibitions only makes matters worse. When brainstorming, avoid the temptation to critique ideas as they are being generated. This includes avoiding even congratulatory comments about how great someone else's idea is, murmurs of approval, and backslapping. When you signal such approval, you send the implicit message that you're still judging each idea as it is generated — you're just keeping the *negative* comments to yourself. That does not encourage inventiveness. The goal is to liberate those at the table to suggest ideas. One person's idea may seem crazy, but it may prompt another person to suggest a solution that might otherwise have been overlooked. There will be time enough for evaluation. The idea behind brainstorming is that evaluation should be a separate activity, not mixed with the process of generating ideas.

The second ground rule of brainstorming is: *no ownership of ideas*. Those at the table should feel free to suggest anything they can think of, without fear that their ideas will be attributed to them or used against them. Avoid comments such as: "John, I'm surprised to hear you suggest that; I didn't think you believed that idea made much sense." John should be able to suggest an idea *without believing it*. Indeed, those at the table should feel free to suggest ideas that are not in their best interests, purely to stimulate discussion, without fear that others at the table will later take those ideas as offers.

In preparing for negotiations, brainstorming is often employed behind the table with colleagues in order to generate ideas. For many negotiators, however, it may feel very dangerous to engage in this activity with someone on the other side. Our own experience suggests, nevertheless, that by negotiating process clearly, brainstorming can also be productive across the table.

How do you convey these ground rules to the other side? You can get the point across without sounding dictatorial or rule-obsessed. Just explain what you're trying to achieve and then lead by example. . . . Generating these possible options may broaden the parties' thinking about the terms of their negotiated agreement.

Many of these options demonstrate that a negotiator's interests can often be met in a variety of ways. And often the simplest solution is to compensate one side by adjusting the price term . . . to accommodate the parties' needs and concerns. . . . In many deal-making situations, such "side-payments" can be an effective way to adjust the distributive consequences of value-creating moves. . . .

What happens to interest-based, collaborative problem-solving when you turn to distributive issues? Some negotiators act as if problem-solving has to be tossed overboard when the going gets tough. We could not disagree more. In our experience, it's when distributive issues are at the forefront that problem-solving skills are most desperately needed . . .

Sometimes, of course, you won't be able to find a solution that satisfies both sides. No matter how hard you try, you will continue to disagree about salary, the amount to be paid in a bonus, or some aspect of a dispute settlement. Norms may have helped move you closer together, but there's still a big gap between the two sides. What should you do?

Think about process. How can you design a process that would fairly resolve this impasse? In a dispute settlement, you might be able to hire a mediator to address the distributive issues that are still open. Is there anyone both sides trust enough to decide the issue? Could you put five possible agreements into a hat and pick one at random?

Procedural solutions can often rescue a distributive negotiation that has reached an impasse. They need not involve complicated alternative dispute resolution procedures that cost money and time. Instead, you can often come up with simple process solutions that will resolve a distributive deadlock and allow you to move forward.

Changing the Game

Not everyone approaches negotiation from a problem-solving perspective. The basic approach described in this chapter — with its emphasis on the sources of value creation and the importance of a problem-solving process — obviously departs from the norm of adversarial haggling. To be a problem-solver, a negotiator must often lead the way and change the game. . . .

Conclusion

The tension between value creation and value distribution exists in almost all negotiations. But as our teaching and consulting have shown us, many people tend to see a negotiation as purely one or the other. Some people see the world in zero-sum terms — as solely distributive. We work hard to demonstrate to people that there are nearly always opportunities to create value. Others believe that, with cooperation, the pie can be made so large that distributive questions will disappear. For these negotiators, we emphasize that there are always distributive issues to address. . . .

The problem-solving approach we have suggested here will not make distributive issues go away or this first tension of negotiation disappear. But it does outline an approach that will help you find value-creating opportunities when they exist and resolve distributive issues efficiently and as a shared problem. . . .

Question

14. Assume you represent the plaintiff family suing for wrongful death of a husband/father killed by a drunk driver. Bargaining has reached an impasse, with your last demand at $1 million and the defendant's last offer at $800,000 (combining a $500,000 insurance limit and defendant's personal funds). Would you consider brainstorming? If you knew that the affluent defendant was facing sentencing for vehicular manslaughter and a letter from your client could be beneficial to her, would this open the door to value creation? The following letter was written to the sentencing judge following brainstorming, which resulted in settlement of the case. (All names have been changed.) Is an ethical problem raised by the use of this letter to settle a wrongful death claim against a drunk driver?

> To whom it may concern:
> We are the mother and surviving widow of the deceased, David Baron, whose death has left us and his three young sons behind. We write this letter to request leniency for Ms. Dorian.
>
> Mistakes were made by both Ms. Dorian and David, and we have all paid an enormous price. At this point, we do not believe that these consequences should be further multiplied by sending Ms. Dorian to jail.
>
> We understand that this was an isolated incident of drinking and driving for Ms. Dorian and she seems truly sorry for what happened. She has taken steps to deal with the drinking problem and she has done her best to compensate us and the three boys for our loss. We believe it is time for everyone to put this tragedy behind them and to begin building new lives in its aftermath.
>
> We want to ask that Ms. Dorian be placed on probation for a period of time. We would like to see her participate in programs and organizations for victims and substance abusers in the criminal justice system. We think David would agree.
>
> Thank you for your time and consideration.
>
> Sincerely,
> Judith Baron and Martha Baron

3. Multiparty Bargaining — Coalitions and Holdouts

Legal disputes and transactions often involve multiple parties. The negotiation dynamic and trades then become more complex and there may be sub-bargaining within the more comprehensive negotiation. In a multiparty lawsuit, a plaintiff must negotiate with the defendants and the defendants are likely to negotiate with each other. If there is also more than one plaintiff, negotiations occur on both sides of the table and across it. In multiparty transactions, there is a mix of complementary and competing interests that may require many negotiations within the larger negotiation context.

A key difference between two-party and multiparty bargaining is the formation of coalitions. A coalition forms when two or more parties discover that they have complementary interests or that they can form side deals. They can then leverage their combined bargaining strength against the others or reach a deal that leaves out another bargainer. It is the possibility of freezing someone out of participating in the deal or blocking a deal that gives a coalition leverage. The more parties, the more possible alliances or coalitions there are. The bargaining gets both more extracted and complex as each party weighs their bargaining options with each of the other parties and the possible combinations. Bargaining can become very strategic. Because there are different payoffs possible with each combination and these are not immediately known, coalitions may dissolve and change before a final agreement is reached.

An example of a classic coalition arises when an injured driver sues another driver, the dealer who sold the defendant her car, the automobile manufacturer, and the auto repair shop that last serviced the defendant's car. Although naturally allied in their defense against the injured plaintiff, because of joint and several liability each defendant has individual interests that may motivate him or her to bargain separately with the plaintiff and form a coalition against the remaining defendants. So if the auto dealership bargains with the plaintiff to pay a limited amount that caps the dealer's liability and reduces its actual payout if the plaintiff recovers full damages from the other defendants, then a coalition of interests is formed against the remaining defendants. The settling defendant may agree to stay in the case to testify favorably and also avoid creating the "empty chair" defense. (This is known as a "Mary Carter" agreement and is discussed in Chapter 8. See *Abbot Ford, Inc. v. The Superior Court of Los Angeles County; Ford Motor Co.*, 43 Cal. 3d 858 (1987).) A similar coalition situation can occur in a breach of contract case or any other type of case involving multiple defendants or plaintiffs.

Another aspect of multiparty cases and transactions that can change the bargaining process is the prospect of one or more parties holding out from a settlement or deal knowing that the others want to close the deal and will pay proportionately more to bring in the holdout. A settlement requirement of unanimity among multiple parties in a negotiation increases the strategic motivation for one party to hold out for more and also increases the chance of a negotiation impasse. For example, one of four partners may hold out in negotiations to sell their business to a suitor unless the holdout is paid more than the other partners. One of several property owners may hold out until all other property owners have sold to a developer so he may demand more in order for the complete transaction to close. (For an analysis of the added complexities and obstacles to settlement created in multiparty situations, see Mnookin, 2003.)

Multiparty disputes and transactions, which create the prospect of coalitions and holdouts, complicate the bargaining phase and require more detailed analysis of the potential payoffs and negotiation leverage. Correctly anticipating the behaviors and moves of others in multiparty bargaining situations can be particularly valuable. Game theory combines mathematical and economic concepts to calculate and quantify what others are likely to do in response to what you do. Game theory principles can be useful to systematically assess the probable actions of opponents in multiparty negotiations. (See Baird, Gertner, and Picker, 1994; Kaplow and Shavell, 2004.)

Just as there may be a payoff for one seller in a multiple-seller situation or one plaintiff in a multiparty claim who holds out to be the last to agree, there are situations in which being the first defendant to settle is advantageous. Plaintiffs may, in effect, offer an attractive discount to the first to settle to obtain one defendant's cooperation and then leverage that agreement as pressure against the remaining defendants. The following excerpt illustrates such a situation in a class action negotiation.

❖ John M. Poswall, *The Lawyers: Class of '69*
248, Jullundur Press (2003)

On Monday morning, Leon and Bishop did what appeared to be poor strategy in negotiations. They went to the turf of their opponent to talk settlement — into the luxurious 28th floor conference room of the largest defense law firm in Northern California. There, overlooking the San Francisco Bay, they met with the firm's senior litigation partner, Martin Crosby, Jr., flanked by his committee of defense attorneys representing the various levels of defendants. A number of corporate senior vice presidents were also in evidence, each being given careful deference by his representative attorney. Jack Merchant was absent. . . .

"We're all realists here," Crosby went on. "All professionals. Litigation is costly, even when we win. I'll be candid with you. I think class actions are legal blackmail and should be resisted forcefully. But my clients, our clients," he corrected himself, gesturing with his hands to the assembled group, "are willing to resolve the matter now to save the costs of litigation. Of course, if the matter proceeds, this offer will be withdrawn, and I can give you my personal assurance, Mr. Goldman, that we are prepared to spend whatever it takes to win." . . .

"We're prepared to pay your class of clients $1 million" — Crosby said $1 million very slowly to let it sink in — "for any real or imagined slight they have endured and," he looked at Leon closely, "$1 million in fees and costs to your firm for its efforts in this matter." . . .

"Marty" — he knew no one called Martin Crosby, Jr., anything but Mr. Crosby — "you invite me over here, threaten me, and then insult me and my clients, and conclude with offering me what amounts to a bribe to sell out my clients. I think I should report you to the State Bar." . . .

Leon smiled. . . . He stood up, leaned on the table with both hands, and spent a few seconds on each corporate vice president, after passing his eyes over their attorneys.

"Here's how it's going to be, gentlemen. We will settle with each group separately. The first group will pay the least; the next a bit more; and so on. The last to settle will pay the most." . . .

"You should know that I met with Jack Merchant [a defense attorney not in the room] on Saturday and Sunday, and we have arrived at a settlement, signed last night, that includes all of the provisions I just outlined. The lenders group of defendants have agreed to pay $40 million in settlement with our guarantee that each remaining group will pay more."

He shifted his eyes around the room again. He sensed the shock bordering on panic.

"So gentlemen, I suggest each of you call me when you are ready."

He turned and walked to the door. . . .

G.   Moving Toward Closure

1.   *The Role of Power and Commitment*

Negotiation is often discussed in terms of power and how each side to a negotiation can use its power to move the negotiation in the direction it desires and get what it wants from the other side. Power comes from the mind of your negotiating opponents. If they believe that you can provide them what they want or deny it to them, then relative to them, you have power. Again, perception becomes reality for purposes of negotiation. What someone wants may be material or emotional. It may be a desire to gain something new or not to lose what they have. So, you have power if you control what your opponent wants, including peace of mind, looking good, or not being harmed — provided they think you will exercise your control.

Power is linked to commitment. If it is perceived that you are committed to do what another wants, or not do it, only if they give you what you want, then you have power to obtain what you want. For example, a hostage taker may have added power if one of several hostages is shot.

Power may be a factor from the beginning to the end of negotiation. However, the perception of power often changes as the process goes forward. Because power is in the mind of the perceiver, what is communicated verbally and nonverbally during the course of a negotiation determines how power is perceived at the time decisions must be made. Both parties will attempt to display or exercise the power they have over the other to move the negotiation to a successful closure. Each may communicate their power, or attempt to create a perception of power, by threats, displays of absolute commitment, or disclosure of better alternatives for themselves and worse alternatives for the opponent.

Getting to Yes did not place emphasis on negotiation power and was criticized for not addressing the topic more. In the article that follows, Roger Fisher, the lead author of *Getting to Yes*, takes up the subject of negotiating power and ties it to commitment. He defines power and expands the traditional concepts of power in a way that makes using power consistent with being a principled negotiator.

❖ **Roger Fisher,** Negotiating Power: Getting and Using Influence
_____
**in Negotiation Theory and Practice 127, Program on Negotiation Books
(J. Z. Rubin and W. Breslin eds., 1991)**

Getting to YES (Fisher and Ury, 1981) has been justly criticized as devoting insufficient attention to the issue of power. It is all very well, it is said, to tell people how they might jointly produce wise outcomes efficiently and amicably, but in the real world people don't behave that way; results are determined by power — by who is holding the cards, by who has more clout.

At the international level, negotiating power is typically equated with military power. The United States is urged to develop and deploy more nuclear missiles so that it can negotiate from a position of strength. Threats and warnings also play an important role in the popular concept of power, as do resolve and commitment. In the game of chicken, victory goes to the side that more successfully demonstrates that it will not yield.

There is obviously some merit in the notion that physical force, and an apparent willingness to use it, can affect the outcome of a negotiation. How does that square with the suggestion that negotiators ought to focus on the interests of the parties, on the generating of alternatives, and on objective standards to which both sides might defer? . . .

How Should We Define Negotiating Power?

If I have negotiating power, I have the ability to affect favorably someone else's decision. This being so, one can argue that my power depends upon someone else's perception of my strength, so it is what they *think* that matters, not what I actually have. The other side may be as much influenced by a row of cardboard tanks as by a battalion of real tanks. One can then say that negotiating power is all a matter of perception.

A general who commands a real tank battalion, however, is in a far stronger position than one in charge of a row of cardboard tanks. A false impression of power is extremely vulnerable, capable of being destroyed by a word. In order to avoid focusing our attention on how to deceive other people, it seems best at the outset to identify what constitutes "real" negotiating power — an ability to influence the decisions of others assuming they know the truth. We can then go on to recognize that, in addition, it will be possible at times to influence others through deception, through creating an illusion of power. Even for that purpose, we will need to know what illusion we wish to create. If we are bluffing, what are we bluffing about? . . .

Categories of Power

My ability to exert influence depends upon the combined total of a number of different factors. As a first approximation, the following six kinds of power appear to provide useful categories for generating prescriptive advice:

1. The power of skill and knowledge
2. The power of a good relationship
3. The power of a good alternative to negotiating
4. The power of an elegant solution
5. The power of legitimacy
6. The power of commitment. . . .

1. The Power of Skill and Knowledge

All things being equal, a skilled negotiator is better able to influence the decision of others than is an unskilled negotiator. Strong evidence suggests that negotiating skills can be both learned and taught. One way to become a more powerful negotiator is to become a more skillful one. Some of these skills are those of dealing with people: the ability to listen, to become aware of the emotions and psychological concerns of others, to empathize, to be sensitive to their feelings and one's own, to speak different languages, to communicate clearly and effectively, to become integrated so that one's words and nonverbal behavior are congruent and reinforce each other, and so forth. . . .

The more skill one acquires, the more power one will have as a negotiator. These skills can be acquired at any time, often far in advance of any particular negotiation.

Knowledge also is power. Some knowledge is general and of use in many negotiations, such as familiarity with a wide range of procedural options and awareness of national or negotiating styles and cultural differences. A repertoire of examples, precedents, and illustrations can also add to one's persuasive abilities.

Knowledge relevant to a particular negotiation in which one is about to engage is even more powerful. The more information one can gather about the parties and issues in an upcoming negotiation, the stronger one's entering posture. . . .

2. The Power of a Good Relationship

The better a working relationship I establish in advance with those with whom I will be negotiating, the more powerful I am. A good working relationship does not necessarily imply approval of each other's conduct, though mutual respect and even mutual affection — when it exists — may help, the two most critical elements of a working relationship are, first, trust, and second, the ability to communicate easily and effectively.

Trust.   Although I am likely to focus my attention in a given negotiation on the question of whether or not I can trust those on the other side, my power depends upon whether they can trust me. If over time I have been able to establish a well-deserved reputation for candor, honesty, integrity, and commitment to any promise I make, my capacity to exert influence is significantly enhanced.

Communication.   The negotiation process is one of communication. If I am trying to persuade some people to change their minds, I want to know where their minds are; otherwise, I am shooting in the dark. If my messages are going to have their intended impact, they need to be understood as I would have them understood. . . .

3.   The Power of a Good Alternative to Negotiation

To a significant extent, my power in a negotiation depends upon how well I can do for myself if I walk away. In *Getting to YES*, we urge a negotiator to develop and improve his "BATNA" — his Best Alternative To a Negotiated Agreement. One kind of preparation for negotiation that enhances one's negotiating power is to consider the alternatives to reaching agreement with this particular negotiating partner, to select the most promising, and to improve it to the extent possible. This alternative sets a floor. If I follow this practice, every negotiation will lead to a successful outcome in the sense that any result I accept is bound to be better than anything else I could do. . . . The better an alternative one can develop outside the negotiation, the greater one's power to affect favorably a negotiated outcome.

4.   The Power of an Elegant Solution

In any negotiation, there is a mélange of shared and conflicting interests. The parties face a problem. One way to influence the other side in a negotiation is to invent a good solution to that problem. The more complex the problem, the more influential an elegant answer. Too often, negotiators battle like litigators in court. Each side advances arguments for a result that would take care of its interests but would do nothing for the other side. The power of a mediator often comes from working out an ingenious solution that reconciles reasonably well the legitimate interests of both sides. Either negotiator has similar power to effect an agreement that takes care of some or most of the interests on the other side.

5.   The Power of Legitimacy

Each of us is subject to being persuaded by becoming convinced that a particular result ought to be accepted because it is fair; because the law requires it; because it is consistent with precedent, industry practice, or sound policy considerations; or because it is legitimate as measured by some other objective standard. I can substantially enhance my negotiating power by searching for and developing various objective criteria and potential standards of legitimacy, and by shaping proposed solutions so that they are legitimate in the eyes of the other side. . . .

To retain his power, a wise negotiator avoids advancing a proposition that is so extreme that it damages his credibility. He also avoids locking himself into the first principle he advances that he will lose face in disentangling himself from that principle and moving on to one that has a greater chance of persuading the other side. In advance of this process, a negotiator will want to have researched precedents, expert opinion, and other objective criteria, and to have worked on various theories of what ought to be done, so as to harness the power of legitimacy — a power to which each of us is vulnerable.

6. The Power of Commitment

There are two quite different kinds of commitments — affirmative and negative:

(a) Affirmative commitments
    (1) An offer of what I am willing to agree to.
    (2) An offer of what, failing agreement, I am willing to do under certain conditions.
(b) Negative commitments
    (1) A commitment that I am unwilling to make certain agreements (even though they would be better for me than no agreement).
    (2) A commitment or threat that, failing agreement, I will engage in certain negative conduct (even though to do so would be worse for me than a simple absence of agreement).

Every commitment involves a decision. Let's first look at affirmative commitments. An affirmative commitment is a decision about what one is willing to do. It is an offer. Every offer ties the negotiator's hands to some extent. It says, "This, I am willing to do." The offer may expire or later be withdrawn, but while open it carries some persuasive power. It is no longer just an idea or a possibility that the parties are discussing. Like a proposal of marriage or a job offer, it is operational. It says, "I am willing to do this. If you agree, we have a deal." . . .

A negative commitment is the most controversial and troublesome element of negotiating power. No doubt, by tying my own hands I may be able to influence you to accept something more favorable to me than you otherwise would. The theory is simple. For almost every potential agreement there is a range within which each of us is better off having an agreement than walking away. Suppose that you would be willing to pay $75,000 for my house if you had to; but for a price above that figure you would rather buy a different house. The best offer I have received from someone else is $62,000, and I will accept that offer unless you give me a better one. At any price between $62,000 and $75,000 we are both better off than if no agreement is reached. If you offer me $62,100, and so tie your hands by a negative commitment that you cannot raise your offer, presumably, I will accept it since it is better than $62,000. On the other hand, if I can commit myself not to drop the price below $75,000, you presumably will buy the house at that price. This logic may lead us to engage in a battle of negative commitments. Logic suggests that "victory" goes to the one who first and most convincingly ties his own hands at an appropriate figure. Other things being equal, an early and rigid negative commitment at the right point should prove persuasive.

Other things, however, are not likely to be equal.

The earlier I make a negative commitment — the earlier I announce a take-it-or-leave-it position — the less likely I am to have maximized the cumulative total of the various elements of my negotiating power.

The Power of Knowledge

I probably acted before knowing as much as I could have learned. The longer I postpone making a negative commitment, the more likely I am to know the best proposition to which to commit myself.

The Power of a Good Relationship

Being quick to advance a take-it-or-leave-it position is likely to prejudice a good working relationship and to damage the trust you might otherwise place in what I say. The more quickly I confront you with a rigid position on my part, the more likely I am to make you so angry that you will refuse an agreement you might otherwise accept.

The Power of a Good Alternative

There is a subtle but significant difference between communicating a warn-ing of the course of action that I believe it will be in my interest to take should we fail to reach agreement (my BATNA), and locking myself in to precise terms that you must accept in order to avoid my taking that course of action. Extending a warning is not the same as making a negative commitment. . . .

The Power of an Elegant Solution

The early use of a negative commitment reduces the likelihood that the choice being considered by the other side is one that best meets its interests consistent with any given degree of meeting our interests. If we announce early in the negotiation process that we will accept no agreement other than Plan X, Plan X probably takes care of most of our interests. But it is quite likely that Plan X could be improved. With further study and time, it may be possible to modify Plan X so that it serves our interests even better at little or no cost to the interests of the other side.

Second, it may be possible to modify Plan X in ways that make it more attractive to the other side without in any way making it less attractive to us. To do so would not serve merely the other side but would serve us also by making it more likely that the other side will accept a plan that so well serves our interests.

The Power of Legitimacy

The most serious damage to negotiating power that results from an early negative commitment is likely to result from its damage to the influence that comes from legitimacy. Legitimacy depends upon both process and substance. As with an arbitrator, the legitimacy of a negotiator's decision depends upon having accorded the other side "due process." The persuasive power of my decision depends in part on my having fully heard your views, your suggestions, and your notions of what is fair before committing myself. And my decision will have increased persuasiveness for you to the extent that I am able to justify it by reference to objective standards of fairness that you have indicated you consider appropriate. That factor, again, urges me to withhold making any negative commitment until I fully understand your views on fairness. . . .

The Power of an Affirmative Commitment

Negative commitments are often made when no affirmative commitment is on the table. . . . To make a negative commitment either as to what we will not do or to impose harsh consequences unless the other side reaches agreement with us, without having previously made a firm and clear offer, substantially lessens our ability to exert influence. An offer may not be enough, but a threat is almost certainly not enough unless there is a "yesable" proposition on the table — a clear statement of the action desired and a commitment as to the favorable consequences which would follow.

Conclusion

This analysis of negotiating power suggests that in most cases it is a mistake to attempt to influence the other side by making a negative commitment of any kind . . . at the outset of the negotiations, and that it is a mistake to do so until one has first made the most of every other element of negotiating power.

This analysis also suggests that when as a last resort threats of other negative commitments are used, they should be so formulated as to complement and reinforce other elements of negotiating power, not undercut them. In particular, any statement to the effect that we have finally reached a take-it-or-leave-it position should be made in a way that is consistent with maintaining a good working relationship, and consistent with the concepts of legitimacy with which we are trying to persuade the other side. . . .

Note and Questions

Getting to Yes is one of the world's best-selling books and has been translated into every major language. Since its first publication in 1981, it has become the reference point for writing on negotiation. Other writers either agree and expand on its concepts or take issue with Fisher and Ury, as we have read in excerpts by James White and Roger Dawson. Roger Fisher has responded to some of the criticisms of cooperative/ principled negotiation by either conceding that *Getting to Yes* presents abbreviated concepts that need to be further expanded and specifically applied, or by elaborating on their principled theories and countering the criticisms.

15.   Does the above essay by Professor Fisher on negotiating power depart from the principles of *Getting to Yes*? How is it consistent or inconsistent?
16.   Does an affirmative commitment always create more power than a negative commitment or threat? Are threats ever appropriate in negotiation? If so, when and under what circumstances?
17.   Have you experienced or heard reports of threats that seemed irrational, but succeeded in getting the threatening party what it wanted?

Note: Irrational Threats, Absolute Commitments, and Perception of Power

The selections you have read are all premised on rational behavior to get what your client wants through negotiation. Expressed and implied threats can also be conveyed very powerfully when viewed as irrational. Nikita Khrushchev gained immense power when, as premier of Russia, one of only two countries with a nuclear arsenal in the 1950s, he pounded his shoe on the table at the United Nations in an apparent fit of anger. An irrational, impulsive leader with his finger on the nuclear button had more power to get his way than a rational, restrained person, at least in the short run.

A threat does not become powerful unless the recipient believes the person making the threat has the capacity to carry it out. Khrushchev's behavior at the United Nations was powerful because it was known that the Soviet Union had nuclear capacity. Power can also come from creating the illusion that you have capacity to harm others. Iraq's Saddam Hussein was attributed with more power than he actually had because of our impression that he had weapons of mass destruction. This illustrates the statement that your power comes from the mind of your negotiating opponents.

A commercial negotiator can exert persuasive power by threatening to end a negotiation so that both sides will lose what they want, even if the result is irrational. The threat of going to trial over a small monetary dispute, for example, may seem irrational. However, if the commitment appears real and the means exist for the threat to proceed, the power of irrationality may prevail. The apparent irrationality may be explained by an absolute commitment to prevail, but it is no less effective. If in a game of "chicken" an opposing driver, headed toward you on a narrow road, removed her steering wheel and threw it out the window, would you get off the road? Would you be more persuaded to concede if you thought the oncoming driver was carrying a load of dynamite and you were on a road wide enough for only one vehicle?

The road-chicken example of the power of commitment and many others are discussed in an essay by Thomas Schelling, who shared the 2005 Nobel Prize in Economics for his writing on noncooperative bargaining and game theory. Schelling also provides this example of the power of irrational threats: "[I]f a man knocks at your door and says that he will stab himself on the porch unless given $10, he is more likely to get the $10 if his eyes are bloodshot." Schelling equates bargaining power with the firmness of one's commitment as communicated to an opponent. A sophisticated, rational negotiator has difficulty appearing obstinate and may have trouble bluffing. Threats and commitment to an outcome may be more believable from a madman or from someone irrevocably locked into a position by outside influences. Schelling cites examples of leverage derived from being locked into a position, including the added international bargaining power of a U.S. President negotiating under a congressional mandate on tariffs and a labor leader's leverage in negotiating with management following a union vote to strike if a set wage limit is not met.

Schelling notes that his examples have instructive characteristics in common:

> First, they clearly depend not only on incurring a commitment but on communicating it persuasively to the other party. Second, it is by no means easy to establish the commitment, nor is it entirely clear to either of the parties concerned just how strong the commitment is. Third, similar activity may be available to the parties on both sides. Fourth, the possibility of commitment, though perhaps available to both sides, is by no means equally available; the ability of a democratic government to get itself tied by public opinion may be different from the ability of a totalitarian government to incur such a commitment. Fifth, they all run the risk of establishing an immovable position that goes beyond the ability of the other to concede, and thereby provoke the likelihood of stalemate or breakdown. (1960, 22-28)

Power need not be based on the capacity to harm others. It can come from the positive ability to help others meet their needs. If they believe that you can provide them with what they want or deny it to them, then relative to them, you have power.

We know that perceptions can be manipulated to project power that otherwise would not exist. Perception becomes reality for purposes of negotiation. A classic example of perceived power resulting from illusion is portrayed in L. Frank Baum's popular tale the *Wizard of Oz*, which was made into the classic 1939 film featuring Judy Garland as Dorothy. The Wizard was created by the special effects of a meek, old man to be an image of power. The Wizard was able to create power and meet the needs of Dorothy and her rag-tag friends by manipulating their perceptions, and thus he also fulfilled his interest in banishing the Wicked Witch of the West. If only success in life and negotiation could be as easy as following the yellow brick road.

2. *Deadlines and Final Offers*

The well-known maxim that work expands to fill the time available applies to negotiation. Negotiations often continue until time runs out. As available time to conclude an agreement decreases, slow-moving or stalled negotiations seem to move toward closure. Concessions are offered and compromises are sometimes reached near the forced end of negotiations even though they would not be considered at the earlier stages. As Dawson noted in *Secrets of Power Negotiating*, quoted in Chapter 4, "the rule in negotiating is that 80 percent of the concessions occur in the last 20 percent of time available." More competitive negotiators will attempt to take advantage of any perceived need of the other side to conclude a deal, while hiding their own need for quick closure. However, creative solutions also materialize for more cooperative negotiators as available time comes to an end. Experienced cooperative negotiators will discuss their time constraints and agree on a time frame for the negotiation.

The passage of time may be associated with costs or lost opportunities. Time is money in many situations. More often than not, both sides want to conclude an agreement as soon as practical. However, time and delay may be more costly for one side in a negotiation. An injured plaintiff may not have the financial resources to hold out during a protracted negotiation for payment of a claim, whereas the insurance company on the other side may benefit from delay if its claim reserves are earning interest. It is this type of asymmetrical time pressure that gives an advantage to one side and is subject to manipulation.

When it is to one party's favor to move to closure, particularly if it believes that it is advantageous to prevent the other side from exploring other alternatives or opportunities, that party will impose an accelerated deadline. The deadline may be linked to a concession or a desired sweetener in exchange for accelerating closure. ("Order now and receive a free set of 'Ginza' knives.") The deadline may be imposed to accept the entire last offer or end the negotiation. ("Accept this settlement amount by 5 p.m. or we go to trial.") A take-it-or-leave-it deadline proposal is referred to as an "exploding offer."

Deadlines can also be used to test if the other side is serious about settlement. Of course, any test can fail and the side imposing the deadline must be willing to live with the consequences. Consider the use of the bold and strategic deadline imposed by the plaintiff's attorney in a class-action civil rights lawsuit brought by African-American customers against the Denny's restaurant chain.

❖ **Guy T. Saperstein,** *Civil Warrior: Memoirs of a Civil Rights Attorney*
384, Berkeley Hills Books (2003)

Tom Pfister showed up with the President of Denny's and began to present Denny's offer, as we sat and listened in our conference room. He explained what corrective action Denny's was willing to undertake, and, in some cases, had already undertaken. Much of that already was required under the agreement with the United States Department of Justice and we had no quarrel with the requirements of that agreement, except that it didn't go far enough. Then Tom addressed the damage issues, explaining that Denny's would donate $3 million to various civil rights groups. . . . I interrupted Tom before he finished, demanding, "Is that it? Is that all the money you're offering?" Tom said it was. So I said, "OK, I've heard enough" . . .

"You indicated Denny's is willing to donate $3 million to various civil rights groups. That is fine, but as far as I'm concerned, that is your client's charity. It has nothing to do with our lawsuit. We are not seeking charity, we are seeking damages for Denny's reprehensible behavior. You can give $3 million away to any group or groups you want, but you will get no credit from us for that. Frankly, I was astonished and angered at your money offer, as it bore no relation to the seriousness of our lawsuit. Your offer left me with the feeling that time spent in settlement negotiations with Denny's is time wasted. Therefore, I am going to tell you what Denny's has to do to maintain credibility with me. By 10 a.m. tomorrow morning, Denny's has to offer a *minimum* of $20 million to settle damage claims of the class. That $20 million offer which Denny's is going to make tomorrow morning will NOT settle this case. It is only Denny's down payment — a tangible expression of good faith that will allow Denny's to continue these discussions. In the end, Denny's will have to pay far more than $20 million to settle this case."

Tom and his cohort left the room. We went back to my office. The mood was heavy with gloom. No one said a word in support of what I had done; several attorneys quietly voiced negative opinions: "We overplayed our hand"; "They won't be back"; "It'll be a long time before we have settlement discussions again in this case." I responded, "We broke them today. Just watch."

I walked into the office the next morning around 9 a.m. Tom Pfister was sitting in our reception area, waiting for me. Tom, a former USC basketball player, and still trim and athletic, rose to his full height of about 6' 3", shook my hand, and said, "You've got your $20 million."

Negotiations in the above case continued until a settlement was reached that included the payment by Denny's of $54.4 million, then the largest settlement in a public accommodations case in American history. This example also illustrates the power of commitment, the power of legitimacy, and the power of a good alternative, all explained by Roger Fisher in the previous selection. Guy Saperstein's power to successfully make this bold demand was enhanced by Denny's lawyers' awareness that Saperstein had tried and won a total of $250 million in a class action gender discrimination case against State Farm Insurance companies.

Note: The Effect of Scarcity and Deadlines

Moving to closure by imposing deadlines or making an "exploding offer," which becomes unavailable if not accepted by a deadline imposed by the offerer, is a tactic in negotiation to take advantage of what is known as the "scarcity effect." The scarcity effect enhances the value of a desired item by making it appear less available or fleeting. We tend to pay more for something now if we believe it will not be available later. If something we want seems readily available, we tend to value it less and are less motivated to act decisively to obtain it. As examples, a New Yorker might never visit the Statue of Liberty until she discovers she must move to the Midwest, or the price of existing Volkswagen convertibles was bid up when it was announced that no more would be made.

Scarcity is enhanced if we discover that others want what we want, particularly if the item is limited in quantity or unique. A common ploy to close a negotiation is to suggest, directly or indirectly, that there is someone else interested in the deal if you do not accept it or that another offer is pending. (Lying about the existence of a competing offer is an ethical issue, as we will see in Chapter 7.)

Introducing deadlines into a negotiation is a way to create a vanishing opportunity or scarcity. Deadlines may be imposed by one side in the form of a threat, or created by external factors, like the end of a tax year. Time limits or deadlines can also be agreed to between the negotiating parties. Mutually imposed deadlines help structure negotiations and ensure a finite conclusion. So deadlines can be used cooperatively in negotiations, as well as in a unilateral, threatening way. Of course, agreed-upon deadlines can be extended by agreement and unilateral deadlines may also be subject to negotiation.

3.   Decision Tree Analysis

Moving toward closure by evaluating offers in light of probable BATNAs and making decisions about what is on the negotiation table may be aided by the use of decision tree analysis. Decision tree analysis provides a tool for making decisions in a rational, methodical, quantitative way, particularly in the face of uncertainty. Regularly taught in business schools to quantify strategic business choices, decision tree analysis has more recently been adopted within the legal community as an aid to decision making in complex litigation and in negotiations.

Decision tree analysis is a graphic version of the decision process we often engage in intuitively when we make common life decisions. Suppose, for example, that you are planning to go out, but it is threatening to rain. You listen to the weather report to learn the probability of rain to make a decision about taking an umbrella. After learning the percentage chance of rain, you then determine how far you have to walk to calculate the probable risk and degree of getting wet. Next you calculate the discomfort and damage depending on how you are dressed. Each decision is discounted or multiplied by the next to make a rational final choice. The higher the likelihood of rain, the less far the walk need be before deciding to carry an umbrella. The more casually you are dressed, the lower the need to take an umbrella.

Making decisions in litigation and business settings can become more complicated because of the number of choices, the number of possible consequences and their probability, and the impact of decisions at each stage on later choices. More than intuition may be needed to make a rational series of decisions and keep track of the probabilities along the way. Decision tree analysis can help with this task.

The first step in decision tree analysis is to convert a set of possible decisions into a graphic format — a decision tree graph. The decision tree displays possible decision choices and the probable consequences of each choice. The decision tree graph then leads to the next set of decision choices on a new limb of the tree and all of those probable outcomes. The decision maker works through the tree graph in sequence, one limb at a time, and makes decisions based on the most favorable probable outcomes expressed in quantitative sums. The process is both logical and intuitive.

Decision tree analysis is also helpful because it requires that we and our clients write down all the explicit factors to be considered. This methodical process discourages us from taking mental shortcuts that leave out important points and considerations that should be factored into our clients' decisions. Going through a decision tree analysis with a client, in addition to promoting rationality, prevents misunderstandings and second guessing about strategic choices.

The following explanation will help you understand how to create and read decision trees as an aid to making decisions about settlement of pending litigation, even if you went to law school — because math is not on the LSAT.

❖ **Richard Birke,** *Decision Trees — Made Easy*
(2004)

Evaluating what a lawsuit is worth is difficult. The use of decision trees can make this difficult task somewhat easier. However, much of the literature on decision trees is too complicated for the average practitioner to use. This very short piece is an attempt to make this important tool more accessible.

Every negotiation or mediation of a legal dispute involves a comparison between the last offer made by the other side and the expected value of continuing on with litigation (or arbitration). On the one hand, there is a sure thing (the offer), and on the other is a risky alternative (litigation/adjudication).

In some cases, the client is unsure of how to compare the value of an offer to settle to the value of continuing litigation. In these cases, the client would do well to understand how to use a simple decision tree. The tree would help them determine the ballpark for an appropriate settlement.

There are seven simple steps that any person can take that will enable them to set up and use a decision tree to help them evaluate their claim. These are:

1. Use numbers when speaking about probability.
2. Pare the case down to no more than four major areas of uncertainty (fewer is better).
3. Learn to set up a simple tree in a logical order.
4. Assign probabilities based on the strengths and weaknesses in the case, working from left to right.
5. Add in the financial awards associated with the various ways the case might end.
6. Do the math to solve the tree.
7. Add in costs as appropriate.

Using Numbers

When lawyers talk about the value of trial with their clients, they tend to shy away from using numbers to express probabilities. This reluctance is understandable — law is not an exact science, and lawyers fear overpromising. So instead of saying "we have a 90% chance of winning," lawyers use phrases like "we have a good shot at winning" or "our case is strong." In workshops I have run in which I ask lawyers to assign a number to these phrases, they exhibit spreads of more than 50% between the intended probability and the understood probability. That is, the lawyer could say "we have a good shot," intending to express that the case is a winner 40% of the time, and the client could understand that the lawyer expressed an 80% likelihood. Words simply do not adequately express probabilistic estimates. Lawyers have to buckle under and start using numbers.

Determining the Significant Uncertainties

Lawsuits may be complicated, but disputes about the value of these lawsuits typically boil down to a small handful of disagreements between the parties. Ask what are the areas about which the parties are really far apart, and the answers are often differences like one side believes that a motion in limine will be granted and the other believes it will be denied. One side believes that their client will be believed by the jury and the other side believes that the client will be easily impeached. Each side is optimistic that the judge will use their jury instruction. The potential number of such disagreements is vast, but in any particular lawsuit, the number of really significant areas of disagreement is small. These disagreements represent the significant uncertainties in the case.

Setting up Trees

I like to think of decision trees as roadmaps with a few intersections, and each intersection has some discrete number of forks in the road. The intersections represent the areas of uncertainty and the number of forks represents the number of ways the issue could come out. For example, in a simple tort case in which the uncertainties are "will plaintiff prove duty," "will plaintiff prove breach," and "will plaintiff prove causation," there are three intersections, each with two forks — one for yes and one for no. Some intersections in some cases could have more than two forks. In a case in which one of the major areas of uncertainty is the credibility of a witness, there could be a fork representing "jury believes every bit of testimony," another for "jury believes nothing," and a third for "jury believes some but not all." Similarly, an intersection representing the various monetary awards that a jury might assign could have many forks.

An easy way to make sure that the tree is set up in a logical manner is to start at the left and move chronologically through the dispute. Our tort case might have duty as the first intersection, breach as the second, and causation as the third. A tree might be set up in a different manner (perhaps in order of most contested issue to least), but a chronological effort usually yields a competent result.

Each fork in the tree will end at a terminal point, and the package of terminal points represents all the different ways that a case could come out. In our tort liability case, there are four terminal points. One is where plaintiff fails to prove duty, in which case the lawsuit is over. The second is where plaintiff proves duty, but fails to prove breach, in which case the lawsuit is over. The third is where plaintiff proves duty and breach but not causation, and the fourth is where plaintiff proves all three elements.

Probabilities

First, look at each intersection and write down all the reasons why a case may travel each fork. In the tort case, the fork labeled "plaintiff proves duty" will have a yes fork and a no fork. The reasons why the case might go to the yes fork may be that plaintiff has good witnesses, a friendly judge, a good legal ruling or case, etc. The reasons why the case might go to the no fork might be related to uncertainty about witnesses, opposing legal case law, etc.

Analyze the factors that surround each intersection and then fill in the probabilities from left to right, and be careful not to double-count factors in your analysis. For example, imagine a case in which plaintiff was very concerned that a witness who would testify about duty and about breach might not show up for the trial. This might result in plaintiff assigning a lower probability to "prove duty," and it may appear again in the "prove breach" intersection. However, it would be incorrect to discount the case two times because of this witness. If the witness doesn't show up, plaintiff will not prove duty, and the case will not ever get to the "prove breach" intersection. Put another way, if plaintiff is at the "prove breach" intersection and is assigning a probability to that intersection, plaintiff has to take into account the fact that the witness has shown up. If you fill in from left to right and you take into account what has already happened in the intersections to the left, you will not run into dependent variable problems because you will have only counted each factor one time.

Add in the Awards

The awards attached to winning a lawsuit are sometimes clear — imagine our tort case involves an insurance policy with limits far below the value of the injuries, and that there is no possibility of an award in excess of the limits. So everyone in this case would know that if plaintiff prevailed, the award would be $1,000,000. In other cases, the awards might be highly variable, and that uncertainty would be another intersection in the tree with an appropriate number of forks.

Solving the Tree

Now comes simple math. Each terminal point consists of a probability and a value. Assume for the moment that each element of our tort case has a 50/50 probability. That means that 50% of all cases result in a terminal point we can call "P didn't prove duty." The award is 0. The second terminal point "proved duty but not breach" will have a 25 percent probability (50% of 50%) and a value of 0. The third, "proved duty and breach but not causation" will have a 12.5% chance and a value of 0. The final terminal point shows a 12.5% chance of obtaining a $1,000,000 award value. A 50% chance of 0 is

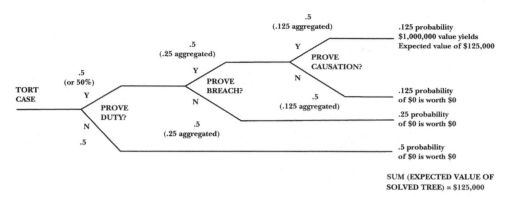

Figure-3 — The Tree solved

worth 0, a 25% chance of 0 is worth 0, a 12.5% chance of 0 is worth 0, and a 12.5% chance of a million dollars is worth $125,000. The sum is $125,000, and that is the solution of the tree.

Deduct Costs

If the trial would cost plaintiff $100,000 — win or lose — we can deduct $100,000 from the solution of the tree, so that the net value of this lawsuit would be $25,000.

However, sometimes the costs vary depending on the nature of the uncertainties. For example, if the case has been tried already and is pending appeal, the uncertainties may be "will appellant win at the court of appeal" and "if they do, will they win at a new trial?" In this instance, if appellant loses at the court of appeal, they bear the costs of pursuing the appeal win or lose. If they win at the court of appeal and go to a new trial, they bear the cost of pursuing the appeal and the cost of the new trial. Thus the deductions of costs come not from the total expected value of the case, but at the end of each terminal point.

Still Not Simple Enough?

Here's a simple analogy that I like to use that helps me think of how these trees work. Imagine that there are 100 runners at the start of a race. The race course has a number of unmarked intersections. At each intersection, some number of runners will run in a way that brings them closer to the finish line, and some will turn in ways that will run them into a ditch, out of the race. Only runners who run the whole race will get a financial prize, and the rest will get nothing, and they may pay a fee for running.

Our 100 runners start, and 50 of them turn one way at the intersection of "prove duty" street and "don't prove duty" street. The 50 who run one way are still in the race with many intersections ahead, and the other 50 have run into a ditch and are out of the race. The remaining 50 split equally at the intersection of "prove breach" street and "don't prove breach" street, send 25 more into a ditch and 25 still in the race. At our third intersection, half run into a ditch and half run to the finish line where they each get a $1,000 prize. The average prize for each runner entering the race is $125, and if it cost each runner $100 to enter the race, the average take home reward is $25. If someone were to offer an individual runner $50 to buy her spot in the race, the runner would be well advised to take the money.

Of course, this assumes that the runner was in the race just for the money, and not to prove something to the defendant, or to herself, or to create a precedent. If the motivation for litigating has little to do with money, the decision tree is not a useful tool.

This is a very boiled-down discussion of a very well-studied topic. There are many wonderful, complex works on risk analysis, and the purpose of this short section is to whet your appetite. If this teaser was too much for you, then simply be aware that you can hire a consultant to help you in the appropriate case. If, on the other hand, this piece was not enough, then go to a search engine and find works by Marc Victor, Howard Raiffa, Bruce Beron, David Hofer, Marjorie Aaron, and others. They will help you get your fill.

Note: The Problem with Risk Analysis and Decision Trees

Decision trees create a mathematical model for risk analysis of the trial alternative to settlement. Although decision trees can be very helpful tools, they are based on what we know and, as Professor Birke points out, depend on "guesstimates." Even experienced trial attorneys and judges can only guess at a party's percentage chance of prevailing on a given set of facts, which are seldom clear. Some risk factors (uncertainty) come from factors that we may fail to build into our risk model or decision tree. For example, the decision tree might not factor in the possible bankruptcy of the defendant or his insurance carrier, or the death of a key witness. Nassim Taleb in his book, *The Black Swan* (2007), argues that in real-world situations there is always more that we don't know than we do, and that we tend to overvalue the known and undervalue the unknown and thereby expose ourselves to the most consequential risks when we least expect the outcome. Taleb reminds us that the "black swan" (his metaphor for highly consequential, improbable events) is produced in messy real-world circumstances where the gap between what we know and what we think we know can become dangerously wide. He postulates that our modern taste for data and "objective" decision-making models have increasingly undermined this part of the risk inquiry.

More questions about lawyer risk analysis are raised by a recent study of 4,532 civil litigation cases over a 44-year period. This study found that decisions to reject settlement offers and proceed to trial very often resulted in court outcomes no better than had the offer been accepted. Comparing the actual trial results with the rejected pretrial settlement offers, the study finds that 61 percent of plaintiffs and 24 percent of defendants obtained an award at trial that was the same as or worse than the result that could have been achieved by accepting the opponent's pretrial settlement proposal. Although plaintiffs experienced adverse trial outcomes more frequently than defendants, the financial costs incurred by defendants when they lost their litigation wagers were significantly higher than plaintiffs' error costs. The decision errors were worse in the most recent three years studied than in the previous 40 years, even with modern attention to jury verdict information and decision tree analysis. The average cost of "decision error," as the co-authors term these adverse trial outcomes, was $43,100 for plaintiffs and $1,140,000 for defendants during the 2002-2005 period (Kiser et al., 2008).

Questions

18. Is there any reason to think that the use of decision trees for case settlement would be favored more by plaintiffs or more by defendants? Why?

19. If you created a decision tree to assist you and your client in evaluating a case for settlement purposes, would you share it with the opposing side? Under what circumstances might you reveal it?

20. Are opposing sides likely to agree about the determinant events or decision points for constructing a decision tree? Are they likely to agree on the probability percentages assigned at each decision node, or the chance of the other side winning?

21. Would a decision tree be helpful in evaluating and settling a case on appeal? What would an appellate case decision tree look like, and how many branches would there be?

H. Impasse or Agreement

Although a negotiation may appear to be moving toward closure, some gaps or differences can still exist. Both sides must assess if what is on the table is or is not better than no agreement. Adversarial negotiators may see this as the time to add new demands or conditions, and competitive bargainers may test an opponent's resolve by threatening to end the negotiation. More cooperative negotiators will see the need for joint problem solving and explore the possibility of improving the outcome for both sides. Several endgame moves or collaborative strategies are available to bring closure. Some of these focus on closing remaining economic gaps in the settlement or transaction, and some look for agreement by attending to matters beyond money. We now look at some approaches to breaking impasse.

1.   Apologies

Some negotiations reach an impasse even though economic considerations do not seem to present an obstacle. Progress on substantive matters may stall because something gets in the way of a final agreement, but it is not always clear what that "something" is. As you now know, negotiated settlements depend on satisfaction of three sets of needs — economic, emotional, and environmental — that form the three sides of the settlement triangle, presented in Chapter 2. It may be difficult to quantify the emotional and environmental factors, but there are ways to satisfy emotional and social needs in a manner that creates value. Offering something other than money that fills a felt need can be worth more to the recipient than is given up by the offering party. An apology and its acceptance illustrate this point.

The most readily identified words indicating an apology are "I'm sorry." This usually marks the beginning of an apology, but the most effective apologies contain several elements:

1.   Expressing regret for the wrong suffered (I'm sorry)
2.   Manifesting sympathy for the injury or hurt
3.   Admitting responsibility or blame
4.   Promising forbearance — not to do it again
5.   Offering repair or compensation

Saying you are sorry and showing sympathy without admitting fault is a partial apology that might help, but it can also make matters worse if perceived as insincere or a brush-off. A "full apology" would include at least the first three elements on the list. The third element, admitting fault, in many situations is the key component of an apology. However, admitting fault can be legally dangerous because the admission may be admissible evidence at trial to establish liability. The two elements of providing assurances that the wrong will not happen again and offering compensation create the perfect apology package.

The hoped-for counterpart or trade-off for an apology is forgiveness. Forgiveness may create value by filling needs for both the recipient and the forgiving party. An apology, even if not full or perfect, and expressions of forgiveness can unlock a stalled negotiation and facilitate closure. Although we have placed this material on apology at a late stage of the "negotiation dance" when impasse occurs, an apology that precedes negotiation or is offered in the earliest stages may be most effective. In resolving some disputes, the amount of compensation or other substantive considerations may be secondary to an apology and resulting forgiveness. In other cases, an apology might not matter or could be seen as manipulative.

The role of apologies in settling cases has become a subject of increased interest as states consider legislation providing evidentiary protection or "safe harbor" for apologies made by people who have done harm to those on the receiving end of a tort or wrong. We will revisit the role of apologies in the next section on mediation. Several significant law review articles have examined the appropriateness and effect of apologies on settlement, most drawing on psychological literature and anecdotal experience (see, e.g., O'Hara and Yarn, 2002; Taft, 2000; Cohen, 1999; Robbennolt, 2003).

Notes and Questions

22. In what type of cases would an apology be most effective to bring closure? What needs might an apology fill? Are there types of cases in which an apology would be counterproductive or inappropriate?

23. A highly publicized apology from basketball star Kobe Bryant in 2004 played a role in the dropping of criminal rape charges by the recipient of the apology and the settlement of a related civil suit. Do you think the following apology by Mr. Bryant was a spontaneous, benevolent gesture, or the result of careful drafting and negotiation by attorneys? What policy issues are raised by this apology, the subsequent dropping of criminal charges, and the negotiated settlement in 2005 that resolved the civil suit? What considerations and motivations, from both sides, prompted the inclusion of the specific wording that was used? What purpose did this apology serve?

> First, I want to apologize directly to the young woman involved in this incident. I want to apologize to her for my behavior that night and for the consequences she has suffered in the past year. Although this year has been incredibly difficult for me personally, I can only imagine the pain she has had to endure. I also want to apologize to her parents and family members, and to my family and friends and supporters, and to the citizens of Eagle, Colorado.
>
> I also want to make it clear that I do not question the motives of this young woman. No money has been paid to this woman. She has agreed that this statement will not be used against me in the civil case. Although I truly believe this encounter between us was consensual, I recognize now that she did not and does not view this incident the same way I did. After months of reviewing discovery, listening to her attorney, and even her testimony in person, I now understand how she feels that she did not consent to this encounter.
>
> I issue this statement today fully aware that while one part of this case ends today, another remains. I understand that the civil case against me will go forward. That part of this case will be decided by and between the parties directly involved in the incident and will no longer be a financial or emotional drain on the citizens of the state of Colorado.

2.   *Splitting the Difference and Dealing with Impasse*

A deceptively simple concluding technique often used in both competitive and cooperative negotiations is "splitting the difference." The rationale for splitting the difference and a couple of caveats about agreeing to it are discussed in a popular book by Richard Shell. Professor Shell also offers advice on what to do when the remaining gap causes the negotiation to reach impasse.

❖ **G. Richard Shell,** *Bargaining for Advantage: Negotiation Strategies for Reasonable People*

185, Penguin (2006)

Perhaps the most frequently used closing technique is splitting the difference. Bargaining research tells us that the most likely settlement point in any given transaction is the midpoint between the two opening offers. People who instinctively prefer a compromise style like to cut through the whole bargaining process by getting the two opening numbers on the table and then splitting them right down the middle.

Even in cases in which the parties have gone through several rounds of bargaining, there often comes a time when one side or the other suggests that the parties meet halfway between their last position. In situations in which the relationship between the parties is important, this is a perfectly appropriate, smooth way to close.

Why is splitting the difference so popular? First, it appeals to our sense of fairness and reciprocity, thus, setting a good precedent for future dealings between the parties.... Each side makes an equal concession simultaneously. What could be fairer than that?

Second, it is simple and easy to understand. It requires no elaborate justification or explanation. The other side sees exactly what you are doing.

Third, it is quick. For people who do not like to negotiate or are in a hurry, splitting the difference offers a way out of the potentially messy interpersonal conflict that looms whenever a negotiation occurs.

Splitting the difference is such a common closing tactic that it often seems rude and unreasonable to refuse, regardless of the situation. This is taking a good thing too far, however. There are at least two important situations in which I would hesitate to split the difference.

First, you should be careful that the midpoint being suggested is genuinely fair to your side. If you have opened at a reasonable price and the other party opened at an aggressive one, the midpoint is likely to favor the other party by a big margin. So don't split the difference at the end if there was a lack of balance at the beginning. Second, when a lot of money or an important principle is on the line and relationships matter, quickly resorting to a splitting may leave opportunities for additional, creative options on the table....

When the gap between offers is too wide to split, another friendly way to close is to obtain a neutral valuation or appraisal. If the parties cannot agree on a single appraiser, they can each pick one and agree to split the difference between the two numbers given by the experts.

What Happens if Negotiations Break Down?

The concession-making stage of bargaining sometimes ends with no deal rather than an agreement. The parties reach an impasse. In fact, a no deal result is sometimes the right answer. No deal is better than a bad deal. . . .

In addition to escalation problems, the parties may start too far apart to close the gap. Many times there are miscommunications, misunderstanding, and simple bad chemistry that the parties fail to overcome. Now what?

Jump-Starting the Negotiation Process

Perhaps the easiest way to overcome impasse is to leave yourself a back door through which to return to the table when you get up to leave it. "In light of the position you have taken," you might say as you pack your bags, "we are unable to continue negotiations at this time." An attentive opponent will pick up on your use of the words "at this time" and tactfully ask you later if the time has come to reinitiate talks. This back door also allows you to contact the other side at a later date without losing face.

If the other negotiator leaves in a genuine fit of anger, he may not be very careful about leaving a back door open. If so, you should consider how you can let him back in without unnecessary loss of face. You must, in one expert's phrase, build him a "golden bridge" across which to return to the table. Such bridges include "forgetting" that he made his ultimatum in the first place or recalling his last statement in a way that gives him an excuse for returning.

When miscommunication is the problem, a simple apology may be enough to get the parties back on track. If the relationship has deteriorated beyond apologies, changing negotiators or getting rid of intermediaries altogether may be necessary.

In America, the sport of professional baseball lost nearly two full seasons in the 1990s because of an impasse in negotiations between the players' union and the club owners. The team owners from the big cities wanted to limit the size of team payrolls. The team owners from smaller cities wanted the team owners from big cities to subsidize their franchises. The players wanted more money. It was a three-ring circus. The breakthrough came when the owners hired a new negotiator — a lawyer named Randy Levine — to represent them at the table. Levine acted in the role of mediator as much as advocate and brought a high degree of both credibility and creativity to the process that, according to one participant, "broke the dam of mistrust" that had built up between the parties. Another move that helped move the talks beyond impasse was getting all parties to agree to stop talking to the press and taking public positions that made it hard for them to compromise at the table.... [P]ublic commitments can help you stick to your goals, but there comes a time when it is in everyone's interest to get unstuck from their positions. In a high stakes negotiation such as a labor strike, this often means getting the parties out of the spotlight so they can work in private.

The worst impasses are the products of emotional escalation that builds on itself: My anger makes you angry, and your response makes me even angrier.... The solution to this sort of collision, in business deals as well as wars, is what I call the "one small step" procedure. One side needs to make a very small, visible move in the other side's direction, then wait for reciprocation. If the other party responds, the two can repeat the cycle again, and so on. Commentator Charles Osgood, writing about the Cold War in the early 1960s, created an acronym for this process: GRIT (Graduated and Reciprocated Initiatives in Tension Reduction).

Egypt's late prime minister, Anwar Sadat, used the "one small step" technique to deescalate the Arab-Israeli conflict when he flew to Jerusalem on November 19, 1977 and later met with Prime Minister Menachem Begin. By simply getting off a plane in Israel — a very small step indeed — Sadat demonstrated his willingness to recognize Israel's existence. This move eventually led to the Camp David peace accords and Israel's return of the Sinai Peninsula to Egypt.

An executive once told me a bargaining story that nicely sums up how the "one small step" process can work in everyday life. Two parties were in a complex business negotiation. Both were convinced that they had leverage, and both thought that the best arguments favored their own view of the deal. After a few rounds, neither side would make a move.

Finally one of the women at the table reached in her purse and pulled out a bag of M&M's. She opened the bag and poured the M&M's into a pile in the middle of the table.

"What are those for?" asked her counterparts.

"They are to keep score," she said.

Then she announced a small concession on the deal — and pulled an M&M out of the pile and put it on her side of the table.

"Now it's your turn," she said to the men sitting opposite.

Not to be outdone, her opponents put their heads together, came up with a concession of their own — and pulled out two M&M's. "Our concession was bigger than yours," they said.

The instigator of the process wisely let the other side win this little argument and then made another concession of her own, taking another M&M for herself.

It wasn't long before the parties were working closely together to close the final terms of the deal. Call this the M&M version of the GRIT process. Any similar mechanism that restarts the norm of reciprocity within the bargaining relationship will have a similar, helpful effect.

Overall, when parties reach an impasse, it is usually because each sees the other's demands as leaving it below its legitimate expectations. Eventually, if the parties are to make any progress, they must change their frame of reference and begin seeing that they will be worse off with no deal than they would be accepting a deal that falls below their original expectations.

Sometimes this transition takes time. The impasse must be allowed to last long enough that one or both parties actually alter their expectations. A final agreement must be seen as a gain compared with available alternatives.

Questions

24.   Have you ever "split the difference" to conclude a negotiation or sale? Looking back, was that the best way to close the deal? Are you now sure you were not manipulated into an outcome or price that was more favorable to the other side? Have you used this closing tactic to your advantage?

25.   Do you agree with Shell that impasse can often be helpful? If so, when? Why would anyone plan an impasse as part of their negotiating strategy?

3.   Logrolling and Packaging

You should now be familiar with the concept that value is created through negotiation when what is received in trade is worth more to the recipient than to the provider. Logrolling involves conceding on low-priority interests to satisfy high-priority interests. Legislators logroll when they trade their vote on a matter of little concern in their district for another legislator's vote on an important issue in their own district. For example, a congressman from Montana might agree to vote for a federal rapid transit subsidy bill in return for a New York City congressman's vote for federal animal grazing subsidies. Logrolling creates value, because both legislators are better off if both bills pass than if neither passes. The New York congressman strongly favors the rapid transit bill, while only moderately opposing the grazing bill, and the Montana legislator strongly favors the animal grazing bill and only moderately opposes the rapid transit bill.

You should also understand that the difference between overlapping reservation points, or "bottom lines," of negotiators creates a bargaining zone within which agreement is likely. Differences in the value that negotiators place on multiple items or promises allow for integrated solutions that expand the bargaining zone. Packaging multiple items, adding items to the mix, and taking advantage of an expanded zone of possible agreement can help close a deal. Packaging requires flexibility and creativity because the negotiators may have initially perceived the negotiation to be fixed on a single item or a more limited set of trade-offs. Selling a car by including a longer warranty or a reduced-price luxury package is a sales example of packaging. When negotiating for office space, the landlord may not budge on the rent but will include in the package the use of his building crew to make office improvements or the use of free conference rooms.

Packaging is also used in negotiating the settlement of lawsuits. An agreement may not be possible based on the claim in litigation, but a universal settlement that resolves other pending or potential claims between the same parties or those aligned in interest may expand the bargaining range, and allow more high-priority/low-priority trade-offs that allow an agreement to be reached. It was this type of packaging that led to the "universal" settlement of the Microsoft v. Stac litigation described in Chapter 4. Each side agreed to drop its claims in the lawsuit in exchange for cross-licensing all of their existing patents as well as future ones over five years and Microsoft agreed to pay Stac license royalties totaling $43 million over 43 months, while also investing $39.9 million for a 15 percent equity stake in Stac. Although most often associated with problem-solving negotiation, packaging and logrolling are frequently utilized by competitive negotiators at the end of the day. Effective negotiators, regardless of their general approach, will do what it takes to reach a settlement or complete a deal if they end up getting more than they have to give up.

4.   Agree to Disagree: Contingent Agreements

If impasse is reached because of different predictions of future events or disagreement over risks, an agreement might be structured based on these differences. In short, you can agree to disagree and write contingent outcomes into the deal.

Recognition of different views and probability assessments of uncertain events can help conclude a negotiation and result in an agreement that builds on differences by rewarding the side that most accurately predicts an unknown future event or outcome. An impasse over the amount of rent for a new restaurant can be resolved by the landlord agreeing to a lower base rent for the skeptical or risk-averse renter, with an additional amount to be determined by the restaurant's revenue. A personal injury settlement negotiation that is stalled because of different predictions about the ongoing need for medical treatment can be resolved by a lump sum amount, with a contingent amount based on the speed of recovery.

Agreeing to disagree and leaving economic questions open to uncertain results through the use of contingent agreements has a down side. The uncertainty and the temptation to manipulate the contingencies on which future rewards are based can create moral dilemmas and future disputes. The nature, potential, and dilemmas of contingent agreements are discussed in the next reading.

❖ **Michael Moffitt,** CONTINGENT AGREEMENTS: AGREEING TO DISAGREE
ABOUT THE FUTURE

87 Marquette L. Rev. 691 (2004)

"That won't happen." "Yes, it will." "No, it won't." "Will too." "Will not."

Negotiators generally find no shortage of things about which to disagree. For example, negotiators seeking to resolve a dispute often have sharply differing perceptions of the past. What happened? Whose decisions and actions caused the effects in question? How does their conduct compare with expectations or duties? In some circumstances, settlement is impossible without resolution of these backward-looking questions. A significant component of classical dispute resolution theory suggests that one might overcome impasse by shifting the focus of conversations toward the future. Sometimes, however, the shift to a forward-looking exploration merely provides fertile, new grounds for disagreement. Rather than arguing about what happened, the negotiators argue about what will happen. A wholesaler asserts that demand for the product will skyrocket in the future, and the retailer suspects otherwise. A defendant points to the relatively minor and temporary injuries caused in a car crash, but the victim fears that currently undetected injuries may manifest themselves down the road. Instinct may suggest that one negotiator will need to persuade the other about the likelihood of future uncertain events. Instead, genuinely held disagreements about the future present an important opportunity for negotiators to discover an attractive trade. The vehicle for capturing this potential is the contingent agreement.

Structurally, a contingent agreement is one in which the parties identify the universe of possible future conditions and agree to take on different obligations in each of those conditions. The simplest contingent deals are those in which the future has only two possible relevant conditions. X will happen, or it will not. If X happens, the terms of our deal are ABC; otherwise, we will do DEF. If I think X is unlikely to happen, I will be happy to give you terms you prefer for ABC, in exchange for terms I favor for DEF. Believing that she will get the work finished on time, an author signs a lucrative book contract with a very harsh penalty for late completion. Buyer loves Seller's house, but really wants a property with off-street parking. Seller firmly expects that the city council will approve a variance required for construction of a new garage, but Buyer is less confident about the likelihood of getting approval. Buyer agrees to purchase the property from Seller at a reduced price, with a substantial additional payment to Seller if the City Council grants a variance within the next twelve months. Negotiators can craft attractive trades by establishing obligations that are contingent on a future uncertain event that affects each side's valuation of the agreement.

Contingent agreements can also include variable terms, pegged to some benchmark to be measured in the future. I think interest rates will increase over the next few months, and you think they will go down. If I am loaning you money today, we will each be happy to agree to a deal with a floating interest rate. A school board is nervous about the future level of state funding to the districts, while the teachers' union is optimistic. The teachers' union agrees to a wage and benefit increase tied to a particular line in next year's state budget. The plaintiff believes that he may suffer long-term health effects of exposure to the defendant's product, while the defendant believes no significant health risks exist. The defendant agrees to pay specified medical monitoring expenses for the plaintiff and to assume any future medical costs associated with exposure. Parties to a joint venture agree to final, binding resolution of their intellectual property dispute by an appointed arbitrator. Without the possibility of contingent agreements, uncertainty regarding future conditions can make distributive decisions (for example, who gets how much money) difficult. By linking the allocation of resources to an externally measurable variable, negotiators can sometimes overcome otherwise paralyzing disagreements about the future.

Contingent agreements also present an opportunity to create favorable incentives. Some negotiated deals involve no future relationship between the negotiators and are self-executing. Buying a trinket in a marketplace involves a simple exchange of money for goods. In more complex circumstances, however, ongoing relationships exist and implementation of the agreement takes place over time. When the negotiated deal involves more than a simple, one-time exchange, parties' behavior after the agreement is relevant. Contingent agreements can help to create incentives for parties to behave well after the terms of the deal are fixed. A company may agree to tie a sales executive's compensation to sales performance, thus promoting sales-maximizing behavior out of the executive after the deal is signed. The health ministry of a developing country approaches a prospective donor, seeking support for particular health sector programs. Both the prospective donor and the developing country want to see multiple sources of funding. They agree to a matching program under which the donor will contribute an amount equal to the funds the ministry secures from other sources, giving the ministry officials added incentive to garner resources. In some contingent deals, one party can affect the likelihood of the contingent trigger — the salesman can make more sales calls, the ministry officials can approach more donors. Contingent agreements can affect parties' behavior after the agreement.

Precisely because contingent agreements can affect parties' behaviors, some contingent agreements risk creating conditions of moral hazard. Moral hazard is a condition in which one party, under the terms of an agreement, may undetectably or uncontrollably behave in a way that is adverse to the other party. How quickly do you take the speed bumps when you are driving a rental car? Moral hazard suggests that many drivers will drive more cautiously over the bumps if they are driving their own cars because they consider the long-term effects of their driving behavior. Athletes' contracts often contain contingent incentive clauses. If the athlete scores a certain number of points, for example, he or she receives additional money. Moral hazard arises when, toward the end of the season, a team notices that the athlete is only a few points away from the triggering contingent event. Will the team structure its play to enable the athlete to achieve the statistical goal? If an agent's contract provides for a thirty percent commission on sales this year, but only a ten percent commission in future years, the agent will have an incentive to push deals into the current year — even if the deal he or she could have struck next year would have been on terms more favorable to the company. Negotiators crafting a contingent agreement should foresee the possibility of moral hazard and, where appropriate, structure incentives and disclosures to minimize the incentive for subsequent adverse behavior. . . .

Contingent agreements may affect negotiators' perceptions of "winning" and "losing." Classical negotiation advice counsels negotiators to conceive of negotiations in terms other than win-lose, pointing to the risk that competitive behavior may cloud opportunities for joint gains. In one respect, contingent agreements may present an opportunity for negotiators to avoid the necessity of identifying a winner. Rather than forcing one side to concede on its forecast, contingent agreements permit (in fact, require) both sides to maintain their conflicting predictions about the future. At the time of the agreement, therefore, each side can declare "victory," to the extent such a declaration is important. On the other hand, contingent agreements have the nature of a wager or a bet. Unless one counts the sheer joy of gambling as a victory, both sides cannot win a wager. The contingent event either happens or it does not. Either way, one side may be disappointed. In some organizational cultures, failure is punished more harshly than success is rewarded. A negotiator fearful of identifiable failure (for example, a wager that visibly did not pay off) may forgo an elegant contingent agreement in favor of a less efficient non-contingent deal. Elegantly structured contingent deals may help to reduce the risk of visibly "losing." For example, if the plaintiff fears that a jury may award him nothing, and a defendant fears a runaway jury award of millions, the two could agree to a small guaranteed recovery in exchange for a cap on the maximum recovery. The losing party at trial will then be grateful to have made the contingent agreement, and the winner's regret will be dampened by having won a favorable verdict. . . .

A final, often overlooked, factor dissuading parties from crafting contingent deals is that parties place some value on certainty and finality. Particularly for negotiators embroiled in a dispute, achieving resolution may have an inherent value independent of the terms of the deal. Many disputants find it emotionally costly to carry around uncertainty. A contingent agreement does not represent complete finality, as at least some of the terms are yet to be determined. Uncertainty also can be costly for economic reasons. A company with an uncertain liability or benefit on its books faces considerable challenges in planning appropriate reserves of money, for example. If a company has a large collection of similar contingent agreements, it may be able to spread the risks and allocate money accurately in the aggregate. Similarly, some circumstances may permit parties to manage risks through the use of hedging instruments such as futures or options. Such allocations are not generally available to all individual negotiators, potentially making contingent agreements less attractive. For a contingent agreement to be appropriate in a given context, therefore, the perceived benefit it captures for each negotiator must exceed the transaction costs of discovering and implementing the agreement.

Negotiators arguing about the past sometimes "agree to disagree," preferring instead to focus on what they will do moving forward. Negotiators with differing perceptions of the future should similarly agree to disagree — using contingent agreements to capture the potential benefits of their differences.

Problem 2

Assume you are negotiating with a small law firm interested in hiring you as an associate. The firm is offering you a lower salary than other firms are paying new associates. You do not want to accept a lower salary, but your employment options are limited and you believe the firm has up-side potential. What terms of agreement might you suggest that could benefit you and be attractive to the firm?

I. Finalizing and Writing the Agreement

After you reach decisions about how a case will be settled or a deal will be structured, your work as a lawyer is not complete. The relief you feel in reaching an agreement can induce you to neglect the important task of how the agreement will be worded and how the remaining details will be determined. Issues of implementation and execution may remain to be determined. The old maxim that "the devil is in the details" is an apt warning. Often a negotiated settlement about the amount to be paid or an agreement "in principle" triggers another set of negotiations, this time over the formal terms of the settlement agreement itself. Lack of clarity about the terms of the agreement can result in perceptual differences about what was decided and the unraveling of the agreement. Inattention to how the agreement is written can also put your client's interests at risk of intentional overreaching by the other side or unintentional differences of interpretation that do not favor your client. Not memorializing the agreement in writing as quickly as possible can lead to unnecessary expenses if more time is required to reconstruct exactly what was agreed or if uncertainty develops about the outcome. If you did well negotiating, the favorable result for your client can lead to buyer's remorse, causing the other side to look for ways to change the non-finalized terms or reject the not yet enforceable agreement.

A negotiated business transaction is usually memorialized in the form of a written contract that incorporates the terms of the deal and follows general contract principles. An agreement to settle a legal claim may have different characteristics and requirements. A release of claims, a dismissal or other disposition of the underlying lawsuit, enforceability by entry of judgment or liquidated damages, how and when money will be paid or performance of obligations will occur, costs, expenses, and tax aspects — all of these issues must be considered when writing an agreement to settle a lawsuit. Ambiguities must be avoided; a settlement document is written to resolve an existing dispute, not foster a future one.

It is also important to attend to the psychological and relationship aspects of closing the deal. Never celebrate a victory in the presence of an opponent. If you can leave the other side feeling they did well, there will be fewer questions regarding implementation of the agreement. The relationship is also strengthened if no one feels they were bested and if clients on both sides have reason to think they were well represented. (It is for this reason that a good negotiator on the other side will not give you an honest critique or tell you that you could have done better.) Even if the parties will not have an ongoing relationship, the attorneys may have future professional contact. There is value in the rapport that carries forward to future negotiations when each side is satisfied with the outcome and great cost if an opponent feels compelled to "get even" at the next opportunity because of regret over an outcome.

Both relationship and legal practicality issues involved in finalizing negotiated agreements, whether transactional or settlement based, are addressed in the next reading.

❖ **Charles B. Craver,** *Effective Legal Negotiation and Settlement*

212, Lexis (4th ed., 2001)

Leave Opponent with Sense They Got Good Deal

As the overall terms are being finalized, negotiators should remember how important it is to leave their opponents with the feeling they got a good deal. If their adversaries are left with a good impression, they will be more likely to honor the accord and more likely to behave cooperatively when the parties interact in the future. Some advocates attempt to accomplish this objectively by making the final concession on a matter they do not highly value. Even a minimal position change at this point is likely to be appreciated by the other side. Others try to do it by congratulating their opponents on the mutually beneficial agreement achieved. Individuals must be careful, however, not to be too effusive. When negotiators lavish praise on their opponents at the conclusion of bargaining interactions, those individuals tend to become suspicious and think they got a poor deal.

Take Time to Review Agreement

When bargaining interactions are successfully concluded, many participants are anxious to terminate their sessions and return to other client matters. As a result, they fail to ensure a clear meeting of the minds. If both sides
are not in complete agreement, subsequent misunderstandings may negate
their bargaining efforts. To avoid later disagreements, the participants
should take the time to review the specific terms agreed upon before they
adjourn their discussions. In most instances they will encounter no difficulties and will merely reaffirm the provisions they have achieved.

Endeavor to Draft Final Agreement

Once the Competitive/Distributive, Closing, and Cooperative/Integrative
Stages have been completed and a final accord has been achieved, many
negotiators are readily willing to permit opposing counsel to prepare the
settlement agreement. While this may save them time and effort, it is a risky
practice. It is unlikely that they and the opponent would employ identical
language to memorialize the specific terms agreed upon. Each would probably use slightly different terminology to represent his or her own perception of the matter. To ensure that their client's particular interests are
optimally protected, bargainers should always try to be the one to draft the
operative document.

No competent attorney would ever contemplate the omission of terms
actually agreed upon or the inclusion of items not covered by the parties'
oral understanding. Either practice would be wholly unethical and would
constitute fraud. Such disreputable behavior could subject the responsible
practitioner and his or her client to substantial liability and untoward legal
problems. Why then should lawyers insist upon the right to prepare the final
accord? It is to allow them to draft a document that unambiguously reflects
their perception of the overall agreement achieved by the parties.

Each provision should be carefully prepared to state precisely what the
drafting party thinks was mutually agreed upon. When the resulting contract is then presented to the other party for execution, it is quite likely that
it would be reluctant to propose alternative language, unless serious questions regarding the content of particular clauses were raised. Doubts tend to
be resolved in favor of the proffered document. This approach best ensures
that the final contract will most effectively protect the interests of the party
who drafted it.

Review Opponent's Draft Carefully

If negotiators are unable to prepare the ultimate agreement, they should
be certain to review the terms of the document drafted by the other side
before they permit their client to execute it. They should compare each provision with their notes and recollections of the interaction, to be positive that
their understanding of the bargaining results is accurately represented.
They should be certain that nothing agreed upon has been omitted and that

nothing not agreed upon has been included. If drafters suggest that certain new terms are mere "boilerplate," reviewers should make sure those terms do not alter the fundamental substantive or procedural aspects of their agreement.

Unabashed Questioning of Drafts

Agreement reviewers should not hesitate to question seemingly equivocal language that may cause future interpretive difficulties or challenge phrases that do not appear to describe precisely what they think was intended by the contracting parties. Since practitioners now use word processors to draft contractual documents, it is easy to accommodate additions, deletions, or modification. Bargainers should never permit opponents to make them feel guilty about changes they think should be made in finally prepared agreements. It is always appropriate for non-drafting parties to be certain that the final language truly reflects what has been achieved through the negotiation process. If the other side repeatedly objects to proposed modifications because of the additional work involved, the participant suggesting the necessary alterations can quickly and effectively silence those protestations by offering to accept responsibility for the final stages of the drafting process. It is amazing how expeditiously these remonstrations cease when such an easy solution to the problem is suggested!

Tact in Questioning

When negotiators reviewing draft agreements discover apparent discrepancies, they should contact their opponents and politely question the pertinent language. They should not assume deliberate opponent deception. It is always possible that the persons challenging the prepared terminology are mistaken and that the proposed terms actually reflect what was agreed upon. The reviewers may have forgotten modifications quickly accepted near the conclusion of the negotiation process. It is also possible that the drafting parties made honest mistakes that they would be happy to correct once they have examined their notes of the bargaining interaction. Even when document reviewers suspect intentional deception by drafting parties, they should still provide their opponents with a face-saving way out of the predicament. The best way to accomplish the desired result is to assume honest mistakes and give the drafters the opportunity to "correct" the erroneous provisions. If reviewers directly challenged opponent integrity, the dispute would probably escalate and endanger the entire accord.

Vigilance Against Underhanded Tactics

In recent years, a few unscrupulous practitioners in the corporate area have decided to take advantage of the drafting stage of large documents to obtain benefits not attained during the negotiation process. They include provisions that were never agreed upon, or modify or omit terms that were jointly accepted. They attempt to accomplish their deceptive objective by providing their opponents with copies of the agreement at the eleventh hour, hoping that time pressure will induce their unsuspecting adversaries to review the final draft in a cursory manner. Lawyers who encounter this tactic should examine each clause of the draft agreement with care to be certain it represents the actual accord achieved. If necessary, they should completely redraft the improper provisions. If their proposed terms are rejected by opposing counsel, they should insist upon a session with the clients present to determine which draft represents the true intentions of the parties. When this type of meeting is proposed, deceitful drafters are likely to "correct" the "inadvertent misunderstandings" before the clients ever get together. If a client session were to occur and the other side enthusiastically supported the deceptive drafting practices of their attorneys, it would be appropriate for the deceived lawyers to recommend that their client do business with another party.

Addressing Unforeseen Ambiguities and Problems

On some occasions, ambiguities or actual disagreements may be discerned during this stage. Negotiators should not allow these difficulties to destroy their previous progress. When good faith misunderstandings are found, the advocates should strive to resolve them before they terminate their current interaction. At the conclusion of the Closing or the Cooperative/Integrative Stage, the parties tend to be in a particularly accommodating frame of mind. They feel good about their bargaining achievements and are psychologically committed to a final accord. It is thus a propitious time to address newly discovered problems. If they do not deal with these issues now, they are likely to encounter greater difficulties when these questions arise at a later date.

Writing and Signing Items as Safeguard

A few unscrupulous negotiators attempt to obtain a tactical advantage by deliberately creating "misunderstandings" as final agreements are being drafted. They hope to extract additional concessions from unsuspecting opponents as these seeming ambiguities are being resolved. Individuals who suspect that their adversaries may employ this tactic should insist on a careful review of the basic terms at the conclusion of the bargaining process. They should write out these items and have their opponents sign the draft to indicate their concurrence. This practice makes it difficult for adversaries to later create disingenuous "misunderstandings" that can be used to obtain unreciprocated benefits for their own side.

Note: Structured Settlements, Ratification, and Single Text
Agreements

Structured settlements are commonly used where damages are substantial or otherwise difficult to meet in one lump-sum payment and in
cases of catastrophic injury or in significant settlements where the plaintiff is a minor. In a structured settlement, the amount recovered by the
plaintiff is paid over time in installments. The defendant funds the payments by purchasing an annuity or bond, or by establishing a trust from
which the plaintiff receives periodic payments. The structure can be tailored to meet a variety of circumstances. For example, an injured child
whose future earning capacity is impaired by an accident may receive a
sum now for medical expenses and escalating monthly payments beginning at age 18 for supplemental income. Experts are readily available to
help structure the future payments and offer annuities for a time-
discounted payment.

There are many situations where final authority to sign an agreement
rests with someone not directly part of the negotiation. This can result
in another opportunity to reopen negotiations to obtain approval of an
absent authority and, in the process, for one side to "nibble" at what was
thought to be an agreed deal. They might take advantage of asymmetrical timing needs or an opponent's investment in the anticipated outcome. Clarification of who has ultimate authority and whose signature
is necessary to create an enforceable agreement should occur before the
negotiation begins. (Issues of enforcement and defenses are covered in
Chapter 8.)

The settlement of some disputes or transactions requires ratification
by a constituent group. The resolution of labor-management controversies may require ratification of union members. Some corporate issues
may require a vote of stockholders. Disputes involving municipalities
and other public bodies may rest upon final approval of elected councils
or boards. Again, it is helpful to agree at the outset of negotiations on
the approval/ratification process and on mechanisms to help ensure
that those engaged in the negotiation have the confidence of the final
decision makers. Good faith deposits or penalty provisions if approval
is not forthcoming may help guard against last minute manipulations
and disappointments.

The most effective way to ensure approval and ratification of "stakeholders" or interested parties not at the table is to involve those who
hold final authority in the negotiation or to structure steps that require
interim approval or endorsement along the way. If the stakeholder
group becomes invested in the process and aware of the value being created, as well as the BATNAs involved and the concessions leading to the
proposed agreement, its members are more inclined to concur with

what they feel part of than if presented with an up-or-down vote on what appears to be a fait accompli. A gradual "buy-in" is more likely to result in endorsement than an after-the-fact request, even if a group process complicates the negotiation.

One method used by mediators can also be of help in direct negotiation, particularly when ratification may be required. The single-text approach of building an agreement by writing the provisions or sections together at the table and then circulating that section for approval before the next section is written was made famous by President Jimmy Carter during the Camp David negotiations between Egypt and Israel (see Carter, 1982). The resulting document grows section by section with the buy-in of all approving parties along the way. The completed agreement then reflects a joint effort that was grown to maturity by those who feel an ownership of what was built together. Of course, the pieces of an agreement are interrelated and final approval must await the completed document, so there is no guarantee that the end terms of a single text agreement will be accepted. However, using a single text approach and getting buy-in along the way makes it more likely that there will be concurrence on the cumulative final document that represents the resulting agreement.

Questions

26. What other situations may require approval, formal or informal, of a negotiated settlement or deal?
27. What are the potential advantages and disadvantages of a structured settlement?

CHAPTER
6

Gender, Culture, and Race

A. Moving Beyond Gender Stereotypes

A generation ago, the issue of gender in negotiation was addressed as a question of how women should approach bargaining in a male-dominated profession. Although this issue has not totally disappeared, it is no longer the central question. More than half of law students are women, and quantitative gender balance among attorneys will soon approach equanimity. If there is a "male" model of practice, it is no longer necessary that women conform to it. Nor is it any longer necessary to ask whether women can succeed as negotiators. Experience and research have clearly shown that women can excel in all lawyering roles including negotiation. We have seen that negotiation is increasingly approached as a process of problem solving and that effective negotiation draws upon a different set of qualities and skills than those associated with stereotyped male competitiveness. The game, as well as the players, has changed and the old stereotypes of gender-based behavior are also changing, if not forgotten.

The fact that women have taken their place at the negotiation table does not necessarily mean that gender is irrelevant in negotiation. Questions remain about whether men tend to negotiate differently than women, whether negotiating with someone of the other gender is different than when a negotiating opponent is of the same gender, and whether any differences can be used to advantage or disadvantage. There is also a question of whether men and women tend to communicate differently — whether we speak the same language. In considering matters of gender, as well as culture and race, it is important to note that there are no generic beings, no common man or woman. Every individual is unique, defined by genetic makeup, environment, and personal experience. Emphasizing gender differences detracts from considering women and men across culture, class, race, ethnicity, age, and gender orientation. However, culture and perhaps chromosomes foster some male- and female-associated behaviors that identify us with our gender and set us apart. The phenomenon of selective perceptions, and its children, stereotyping and self-fulfilling prophecies, along with attribution errors, magnify these differences and create cognitive traps that may shape and limit how we interact with those of the opposite gender when negotiating. The way to open these traps is to understand our individual uniqueness, as well as our gender differences, and work with them. Even if there are no actual differences, the belief by some that differences exist between male and female approaches to bargaining can be as important as reality in driving their behavior. Gender stereotyping may not be important to a new generation of enlightened lawyers who experience and assume more equality than previous generations, but gender may influence older lawyers and clients.

Carol Gilligan has written about a theory of moral development, which has been much cited and discussed in negotiation literature. Her theme is that men and women think and speak differently when confronted with ethical dilemmas. Gilligan distinguishes a feminine "ethic of care" with a masculine "ethic of justice" and believes that these gender differences in moral perspective are due to contrasting images of self:

> My research suggests that men and women may speak different languages that they assume are the same, using similar words to encode disparate experiences of self and social relationships. Because these languages share an overlapping moral vocabulary, they contain a propensity for systematic mistranslation, creating misunderstandings which impede communication and limit the potential for cooperation and care in relationships. (1982, 173)

Several more recent books provide guides for women on how to succeed at negotiating in what is assumed to be a male-dominated environment. Some, in effect, educate women to negotiate more like men. Some advise women on how to take advantage of what are described as feminine differences and qualities. Others rewrap traditional negotiation lessons in a package designed for the female market. The next reading describes the shadow negotiation — the often determinative negotiation within a negotiation — and provides a helpful guide for both men and women. The book from which this passage is taken draws on some of the principles previously developed, including hidden agendas, the role of trust and rapport, and reciprocity of listening to demands and making concessions. However, the authors caution that a seemingly even playing field may slope against women.

❖ **Deborah M. Kolb and Judith Williams,** *The Shadow Negotiation: How Women Can Master the Hidden Agendas That Determine Bargaining Success*

20, Simon & Schuster (2000)

The Shadow Negotiation

As we talked to women about what happens when they negotiate, we learned that a good idea alone rarely carries the day. Negotiations are not purely rational exercises in problem solving. They are more akin to conversations that are carried out simultaneously on two levels. First there is the discussion of substance — what the bargainers have to say about the problem itself. But then there is the interpersonal communication that takes place — what the talk encodes about their relationship. Yes, people bargain over issues, but they also negotiate how they are going to negotiate. All the time they are bargaining over issues, they are conducting a parallel negotiation in which they work out the terms of their relationship and their expectations. Even though they seldom address the subject directly, they decide between them whose interests and needs command attention, whose opinions matter, and how cooperative they are going to be in reaching an agreement. This interchange, often nonverbal and masked in the positions taken on issues, has a momentum all its own, quite apart from the substance of what is being discussed.

We call this parallel negotiation the *shadow negotiation*. This shadow negotiation takes place below the surface of any debate over problems. As bargainers try to turn the discussion of the problem to their advantage or persuade the other side to cooperate in resolving it, they make assumptions about each other, what the other person wants, his or her weaknesses, how he or she is likely to behave. They size each other up, poking here and there to find out where the give is. They test for flexibility, trying to gauge how strongly an individual feels about a certain point.

How you resolve the issues hinges on the actions you take in the shadow negotiation. If you don't move to direct the shadow negotiation, you can find the agreement tipping against you. The shadow negotiation is no place to be a passive observer. You can maneuver to put yourself in a good position or let others create a position for you. Your action — or inaction — here determines what takes place in the negotiation over problems.

Impressions count. Slight changes in positioning can cause a major shift in the dynamics within the shadow negotiation. You want to move into a position from which you can claim your place at the table. At the same time, you need to encourage your counterpart to collaborate with you in fashioning an agreement that works for both of you.

The Twin Demands of the Shadow Negotiation: Advocacy and Connection

To hold your own in the shadow negotiation, you don't have to be brash or aggressive. You do need to be an advocate for your interests. Through strategic moves you position yourself in the shadow negotiation so that the other party takes your demands seriously. You also turn any attempts to put you on the defensive. In effect, your advocacy defines your claim to a place at the table. It tells the other side not only that you are going to be an active player, but that you will not and do not need to settle for less than you deserve.

Active positioning is critical to how you negotiate the issues. The impressions you create in the shadow negotiation determine how much give and take there will be over the issues. If you are unsure of yourself or doubt whether your demands are justified or legitimate, you will have a tough time convincing others to give them much weight. Bargainers are quick to ferret out points of weaknesses, where you are tentative or vulnerable. You must be ready to move in the shadow negotiation not just to promote your interests but to block any attempt to undermine your credibility.

The messages you send in the shadow negotiation establish your advocacy. But you cannot pay attention only to gaining an advantage for your demands and to how you are positioned in the negotiation conversation. Any good solution requires compromise, concessions, and creativity on both sides. Concentrate only on your agenda, promote it at the other party's expense, and she has little incentive to cooperate. Regard her as an enemy and pretty soon she starts acting like one — blind to the interests you share.

To find common ground, you have to work together, not against each other. This is where the *skills of connection* come into play. It takes sensitivity and responsive action to draw out what other people have on their minds in a negotiation. Often these hidden agendas are their real agendas. Unless bargainers are explicitly encouraged to talk about them, they will hesitate, fearing that any candor will be used against them. They don't want to tip their hand.

There is a pragmatic reason behind this attentiveness to relationship building in the shadow negotiation. Show the others involved that you value them and their ideas, and there is a good chance they will reciprocate. You'd be surprised how quickly they become more open in voicing the reasons for their demands *and* more receptive to listening to yours. But establishing a connection with the other party does a good deal more than facilitate equal airtime. When you each feel free to engage in an open exchange that flows both ways, you can confront the real issues rather than their proxies. Different perspectives surface and point to other, more creative ways of resolving the issues than either of you can contemplate on your own.

Advocacy and connection go hand in hand in successful negotiation, and you establish the terms of both in the shadow negotiation. Using strategic moves and turns, you create your own space in the conversation. You cannot let a need for responsive and open exchange hold your own interests hostage. You must lay the groundwork for dialogue with a forceful advocacy. The other person has to have something and someone to connect with for the skills of connection to work. But those skills hold a larger promise. They enable you to build a relationship across differences so that you are both committed to working collaboratively on a mutual solution.

What Does Gender Have to Do with Negotiation?

Almost without exception, the women we interviewed could analyze a problem or a situation with great skill. Yet they stumbled in the shadow negotiation. The reason became clear the more we talked with them. Problems can be and often are gender neutral. But surprising things happen in negotiation. Unrecognized expectations and unwarranted assumptions come into play. And gender often sets them off.

Because we experience negotiation in such a personal way, we look for personal reasons why being a woman matters more at some times than at others. Something in the chemistry of this party negotiation, we figure, makes gender an issue. But even when we don't have a strong visceral reaction, gender colors our experience. Any negotiation is caught in a web of influence, social values, and informal codes of conduct. Social norms or standards that seem at first blush to have nothing to do with gender might generate troubling expectations about what we should and can do as women. Resources are often unevenly divided along gender lines. As a result, what appears to be a benign or even playing field might, in fact, slope against us.

Gender Frameworks

To a great extent, how we see gender determines how we deal with its effects in the shadow negotiation. We can consider being a woman a hindrance in negotiation and take seriously Professor Higgins's exhortation in *My Fair Lady*: "Why can't a woman be more like a man?" Alternatively, we can celebrate our differences and adopt the approach of Sally Field and Dolly Parton in the movie *Steel Magnolias*. When Steel Magnolias negotiate, they tap feminine strengths to temper confrontational impulses and encourage collaborative exchange. Or we can focus on the social dynamic set in motion when common yardsticks used to measure performance don't fit a woman's experience.

Professor Higgins' Advice

For the Professor Higginses of this world, the gender glass is half empty for women. They are not, by nature, bad negotiators. Socialized to be mothers and caretakers, they have never been schooled in the art of hard-nosed bargaining. They can, however, learn the "rules of the game." A woman need not fare badly in a salary negotiation or put in a double shift at home and at work. If she has not been able to argue her case for equal pay for equal work or prevent her colleagues from taking over her, she can study how to be more assertive, more strategic in her thinking, and less emotional.

The Professor Higgins approach is a remedial one. It assumes that individual deficiencies can be patched up with sufficient study and rigorous discipline: Passivity, for example, is a personal liability that can be corrected by training. The fault rests squarely on the particular woman's shoulders. She needs a "cure." Conveniently overlooked is the extent to which that cure will always be incomplete. No matter how hard a woman tries to learn the rules of the game, she will always play the game as a woman. Adopting aggressive behavior or a more "masculine" way of speaking in a negotiation can backfire. Instead of gaining her a voice and acceptance, it can provoke censure or backlash.

Remedial programs like these hold out a dubious promise: If you patch yourself up — fill in your obvious deficiencies and acquire the necessary skills — you can play the game as well as, or better than, many men. By recommending the wholesale assimilation of "good" masculine qualities, however foreign, advice like this encourages a woman to blame only herself when she is underpaid, overworked, or simply overlooked, invisible. The fault lies with her — in some inadequacy, in something she did or failed to do — not in the imbalances in the system itself.

The Steel Magnolias' Answer

Wait a minute, some critics say. Femininity is *not* an encumbrance. It gives a woman an edge, assets she can use to her advantage. Rather than lament the lack of assertive independence or competitive drive in women, why not celebrate an expressive, emotional, caring femininity? Women, through their capacity to mother and from their subordinate status at work, have developed not just coping mechanisms but real strengths. Empathy, an intuitive aptitude for collaboration, the ability to connect with others rather than to remain distanced as an independent actor, an instinctive feeling for "relationship" — these skills and inclinations carry an unrealized advantage in the new interconnected world of business. Women, it is suggested, build rapport and reach joint solutions more easily than men do precisely because they cooperate and empathize more naturally.

This thinking successfully challenges the notion that women are in some way deficient or inadequate. It runs into difficulty, however, when it assumes that a constellation of certain traits and qualities makes up the "female essence." This premise washes out differences among women. The problem is not that women do not have these special qualities. Many do. But others enjoy the challenge of competition; they are not by nature *only* concerned with others.

There is also some wishful thinking involved in declaring feminine attributes unqualified assets uniformly useful in negotiation. These "feminine" skills, far from being an advantage, can undermine a woman when she negotiates. If she is not careful, her attachment to relationship can be exploited and used against her. Of course, the helpful female colleague does not mind shouldering the lion's share of the work and ending up with none of the credit. Of course, a woman negotiating a severance package will sacrifice her financial interests to maintain cordial relations with her former employers. Taken to extremes, the feminine advantage does not gain a woman much credit when she negotiates.

While her empathetic male counterpart earns praise for his "people" skills, she is just acting like a woman. And if she is really successful, she is accused of being manipulative, of using feminine wiles to get her way. That is the flint behind the honey in Steel Magnolia's voice, the reason for the hint of the pejorative in the term's common usage.

There is a more damaging objection. Praise of the "feminine," when unqualified, makes it easy to discount or ignore the extent to which influence follows gender lines. As one commentator put it, an emphasis on women's special qualities of caring and nurturing amounts to a "setup to be shafted." In an unequal world, such critics argue, difference will always mean less and women will generally get less when they negotiate. In other words, the doubts women experience about their ability to do well often tell more about status, about bumping up against seemingly immovable walls and ceilings, about having less clout, than they reveal about underappreciated skills and abilities.

We are using the exaggerations of Professor Higgins and the Steel Magnolia for effect. They point to the extremes in the advice directed at women, but they also illustrate the extent to which we personalize the challenges gender creates in negotiation. On the one hand, it is our weakness and so we need to remedy it. On the other, it is *our* strength, but we must be wary in how we use it. But not all the challenges gender poses in negotiation are rooted in personal causes. However inclined we as individuals might be to view supposed differences as a handicap or a strength, a woman quite simply has to work harder than a man to get what she wants in a negotiation. . . .

The Yardstick Explanation

Gender is not a "woman's" problem — a question of whether women have deficiencies or special qualities. Although gender figures in most human relations, we deny its pervasiveness, preferring instead to see egalitarian gender neutrality in our relationships and in our organizations. Yet to a large extent, we still maintain implicit standards for behavior that can have a different impact on women than men. Standards generally reflect the experience of the people setting them. And, by and large, men do the setting in our society. As a result, their experience becomes the yardstick for measuring what is normal. And, in a masked exercise of power, that standard is then rather cavalierly assumed to be gender neutral. . . .

The authors of *The Shadow Negotiation* are esteemed and experienced in negotiation research and education. Their book has generally been well received and popular. However, some critics have questioned categorizing negotiators by gender and juxtaposing behaviors of women on a binary scale of male-female distinctions. The following reading raises some of these issues.

❖ **Amy Cohen**, *Gender: An (Un)Useful Category of Prescriptive Negotiation Analysis*

13 Tex. J. Women & L. 169 (2003)

. . . [R]epresentations of gender as either male-female difference or male-female similarity, as the basis for describing interpersonal skills and theoretical analysis, draw artificial parameters around the range of behavioral

and communicative capabilities available to us each to imagine and perform. Naming negotiating skills and analysis as "masculine" versus "feminine" in the first instance is of little, if any, pedagogical advantage and
potentially considerable pedagogical harm insofar as such binary coding
works to narrow and normalize the emancipatory possibilities inherent in
the process of learning and achieving. In arguing for a pedagogy of negotiation that decodes behaviors and skills as masculine and feminine, I begin
with a detailed look at Deborah Kolb and Judith Williams' construction of
gender and women bargainers in *The Shadow Negotiation: How Women Can
Master the Hidden Agendas that Determine Bargaining Success*. I focus on *The
Shadow Negotiation* because it presents a recent, widely acclaimed, and perhaps the most extensive attempt to link feminist theory and empirical
research with prescriptive negotiation advice.... Much of their advice is
written in second person — the "you" is presumably female throughout.
Kolb and Williams begin by critiquing conventional "rational" (read: masculine) negotiation advice to "take the people out of the problem" and suggest
that as individuals bargain over issues, they are simultaneously negotiating
the terms of their relationships, albeit in the "shadow." Thus, Kolb and Williams propose we learn to focus on active interpersonal positioning — both
assertive and collaborative — within the "shadow negotiation" in order to
best resolve the issues that form the substance of the "real" negotiation.

Unsurprisingly, if not ironically, the "shadow" is also the location of gendered expectations and frustrations. In aiming to allow women a nonessen-
tialized space to overcome stereotypical gender barriers, Kolb and Williams
reject paradigmatic, if purposefully oversimplified, liberal feminist (Professor Higgins's advice) and cultural feminist (Steel Magnolias' answer)
attempts to resolve the tension they assume exists between women and
negotiation. Namely, they discount conventional wisdom suggesting that
with equal access to personal and institutional resources, individual women
will negotiate just like individual men. Instead, they remind us "she will
always play the game as a woman." Alternatively, they admit there is a risk of
unqualified praise of women as empathic and relational that may cloud differences among women. Nonetheless, they conclude that even though
"many" women do have "these special qualities," such feminine skills
become structural liabilities in real world negotiations where yardsticks of
success are typically correlated with "masculine" experience and standards.

Ultimately, "the effective negotiator," they tell us, "turns out to look
remarkably like a man": independent, self-confident, active, objective, and
unruffled by pressure. Kolb and Williams are correct in their observation
that this reified model hurts men and women alike — men when they show
their "feminine" side and women when they fall short of the "masculine"
ideal, for "no woman, however competent, can pull off what is essentially a
male performance." Thus, their prescription is not a matter of choosing
between masculine and feminine styles, but rather encouraging women to
draw on "all our skills" as we learn to recognize and manage gendered
behavioral patterns and expectations in the shadow negotiation.

However, in maintaining a binary distinction between what is feminine and what is masculine as the basis for prescriptive negotiating advice, as well as in creating a "shadow" as the locus of the interpersonal that can be analyzed separately from the substance of the problem, Kolb and Williams solidify the categories of analysis they in fact attempt to discredit. Perhaps even more importantly, by encouraging women to place "ourselves" in negotiations based on descriptive assumptions about the way we as women are, they draw unnecessary parameters around their own useful and seasoned interpersonal negotiating advice that limit our range of imagining the ways in which individuals and groups might communicate with each other. . . .

The challenge for women, then, is to "learn how to use their strengths and manage the dual impressions of femininity and strategic resolve." Thus, for women learning the art and science of negotiation, gender is the point of entry; it is the preexisting condition we bring to the table and then use to position ourselves as we interact with other parties. However, the conclusion that women do not fare as well as men, Kolb argues, follows not from our skills or abilities, but rather from the technical and rational prescriptions underlying conventional negotiation advice that excludes a "subjective and embedded feminine approach." . . .

Thus, "as women," Kolb and Williams tell us in *The Shadow Negotiation*, "we take our differences and our competence into every negotiation. These can be turned to our advantage, but they have to be recognized as valuable. . . . We need, in effect, to revise the standard." Using gender both as a descriptive indicator of women bargainers and as a method of feminist critique, Kolb, together with Williams, provides a series of behavioral and analytical skills to help women negotiate effectively in a feminine voice. . . .

Questions

1. Is the legal negotiation table still slanted against women? Are there situations in which it might be slanted against men? Can you give examples?

2. Are female law students a self-selected group that does not reflect the characteristics described by Kolb and Williams? For a general report on gender differences in negotiation, see Babcock and Laschever (2003).

3. If relationships matter and effective negotiation results from making connections and problem-solving skills, could men benefit by signing up for seminars on how to negotiate like a woman?

4. The above selection and the literature on gender and negotiation focuses on male perceptions of females and, to a lesser extent, on female perceptions of males. Isn't the perception that women have of women, and that men have of men, just as important in explaining our negotiation approaches and behaviors? Do you believe from

what you have read and experienced that patterns between women negotiating with one another would be significantly different than negotiations between men? If so, how?

5. Might gender orientation be a factor in negotiation style? What effect might it have, and why?

6. Do you agree with the statement by Kolb and Williams that "a woman quite simply has to work harder than a man to get what she wants at a negotiation"?

B.   Cultural Differences, or Why the World Is Not Boring

We tend to be most comfortable and trusting among people like ourselves and most fascinated with those who are different. Negotiating with people from other cultures can be challenging because trust and rapport affect negotiations, as do cultural values and traditions, which color what we perceive.

Cultural differences are difficult to discuss and apply to negotiation because the meaning of culture is elusive. Like gender, focusing on culture lends itself to stereotypes and creates a risk of substituting categorical norms for the uniqueness of individuals. Cultural considerations are so complex and ever-changing in our globalized world that defining a person by identity to a single culture and using that identity to predict values or behavior is prone to error.

However, because it is helpful to have clues about how our negotiating counterparts perceive the world and perhaps value things differently than us, cultural variations should be considered. Sensitivity to cultural differences can assist in preparing for negotiations, interpreting behavior, and providing ideas for how impasse can be avoided and value might be created in a negotiation. Cultural awareness can also help us avoid unintended consequences of what we say and do, as well as alert us to what others may anticipate from us because of our own cultural identity.

Cultural classifications are similar to many conveniences in life that we use but wish we did not need. Like automatic home appliances, disposable products, computers, and other of life's shortcuts, we may wish we did not need them, but we cannot seem to live without them. We use culture as a label or shortcut about categories of people with whom we do not confidently identify. We know that there are shortcomings to this convenience, but we use it anyway. We know that no culture or grouping of people is monolithic or truly homogenous. Although a group of people may have some common characteristics, those characteristics are not distributed or shared uniformly. Even if we could be sure of the nature of a group, few people are part of only one cultural identity. So we can never be sure of which of several cultural influences will be most applicable. Will the culture of a person's national origin, ethnicity, religion, schooling, professional identity, or economic class predominate in a particular contextual situation? Finally, can we ever know if the culture of the last generation, when cultural norms for that group may have been identified or popularized, is the behavioral or value norms of that group today? We know that cultural generalizations, although convenient, are inherently unreliable. In constitutional parlance, they are necessarily underinclusive and overinclusive.

With all of these caveats, cultural considerations are of great interest because we feel we need all the help we can get in better understanding others. Travel guides feature a section on the culture you will encounter in another country. One book claims to provide clear and concise information on how to negotiate in 50 different countries that account for 90 percent of the world economy (Llamazares, 2009). Sociologists and political scientists, among others, study the impact of culture. People regularly talk about cultural behavior and analogize that culture is the software of the mind. Most books on negotiation include advice on how to utilize cultural awareness and knowledge to improve negotiation results. The next article explains both the value and shortcomings of using cultural categories. The perception errors referred to by Professor Sebenius, by now, should be familiar to you.

❖ **James K. Sebenius,** *Caveats for Cross-Border Negotiations*

18 Negot. J. 122 (2002)

While some of the work on culture and negotiation is at best superficial, much of the relevant academic literature is well grounded and accompanied by careful statements as to its limits and the conditions under which it should apply. While holding on to the truth that some characteristics do systematically vary across national borders, however, there is often a general uneasiness about unwarranted use of purported cross-cultural insight.... My objective is to make analysts and negotiators more sophisticated consumers of this advice by suggesting four classes of caveat, each with a slightly tongue-in-check name that will, I hope, be usefully evocative.

1. The John Wayne v. Charlie Chan Fallacy: Stereotyping National Cultures

Start with the obvious: All American negotiators are not like John Wayne and all Chinese negotiators are not like Charlie Chan. . . . In the face of such internal variation, we wisely caution ourselves against mindless stereotyping by nationality (as well as by gender, religion, race, profession, or age). Even so, in many situations it remains all-too-common to hear offhand remarks such as "all Chinese negotiators..." (as well as generalizations about "women" . . . or "engineers"). To combat this, a strong version of the anti-stereotyping prescription calls for ignoring nationality altogether in preparing for negotiation.

That advice is too strong. Nationality often does have a great deal to do with cultural characteristics, particularly in relatively homogeneous countries like Japan. The careful work of many researchers confirms significant associations between nationality and a range of traits and outcomes. . . . It would be foolish to throw away potentially valuable information. But what does information on a particular group's behavioral expectations or deeper cultural characteristics really convey? Typically, cultural descriptions are about central *tendencies* of populations that also exhibit considerable "within-group" variation. . . .

Inferences about individuals from central tendencies are often misleading or wrong. *You negotiate with individuals, not averages.*

But viewing the world without the aid of stereotypes is difficult. Forming stereotypes is a natural reflex that helps order the overflow of information that barrages people. Social psychologist Ellen Langer argues that a solution to the negative effects of stereotyping is "mindfulness," which she defines as a willingness to create new categories, an openness to new information, and an awareness that more than one perspective exists. Rather than straining against forming stereotypes, a more realistic strategy is to allow stereotypes room to change, multiply, and adapt to new information.

In sum, remember that "national traits" — as well as traits supposedly associated with gender, ethnicity, etc. — are *distributions* of characteristics across populations, not blanket descriptions applicable to each individual. Be very cautious about making inferences about characteristics of specific individuals from different groups — even where the groups are, on average, sharply different. Avoid stereotyping and the "prototypicality" error of assuming an individual will exhibit the most likely group characteristic. Even if U.S. negotiators are on average more impatient, deal-focused, and individually oriented than their Chinese counterparts, be careful not to help amplify that stereotype in the mind of the other side. . . .

2.   The Rosetta Stone Fallacy: Overattribution to National Culture

National culture clearly matters. But there is a tendency to see it as the Rosetta Stone, the indispensable key to describe, explain, and predict the behavior of the other side. Of course there are many possible "cultures" operating within a given individual. . . . National culture can be highly visible but, obviously, it is only one of many possible influences. For example, Jeswald Salacuse surveyed executives from a dozen countries to determine national tendencies on ten important bargaining characteristics, such as negotiating goal (contract v. relationship), orientation (win-win v. win-lose), formality level, communication style, risk-taking, etc. While his results showed significant national differences, he also analyzed the data according to profession and occupations of the respondents such as law, engineering, marketing, the military, diplomacy, accounting, etc. These categories, too, showed systematic association with different bargaining styles. Finally, Salacuse could also differentiate many of these characteristics by gender. Other extensive studies extend and elaborate analogous findings. Nationality often matters when considering someone's bargaining characteristics but so too does gender, ethnicity, functional specialty, etc. . . . [N]ational culture is but one of many "cultures" that can influence bargaining behavior. . . .

Attribution Bias

Cultural differences, often evident in surface behavior, are easy to see; richer contextual factors frequently are not. In unfamiliar cross-border settings, factors like strategic incompatibility, politics, or even individual personality are less likely to be "blamed" for undesirable outcomes. The powerful but unconscious tendency to overattribute behavior to culture, all too often clouds negotiators' vision of the full range of factors that can affect a negotiation. Psychologists have extensively documented this dynamic, a systematic tendency to focus on supposed characteristics of the person on the other side of the table, rather than on the economic or other powerful contextual factors. . . . The antidotes? First, remember that "culture" doesn't just mean nationality; instead there are many potentially influential "cultures" at work. Second, beyond "culture" are many other factors that have potential to affect negotiation behavior. Nationality can carry important information, but with many other cultures and many other factors at work, you should be careful not to treat your counterpart's passport as the Rosetta Stone.

3.   The "Visual Flying Rules" at Night Fallacy: Falling Prey to Potent Psychological Biases

Self-Serving Perceptions of Our Own Side

There is a powerful tendency, formally studied as "biased assimilation," for people to interpret information in negotiation self-servingly. For example, experiments give a number of people identical information about a pending court case but randomly assign them to the role of plaintiff or defendant. When each person is asked for his or her private assessment of the probability that the plaintiff will win, those assigned the role of plaintiff on average give much higher odds than those (randomly) assigned to the role of defendant (but, again, on the basis of identical information). People tend to "believe their own lines" or self-servingly interpret information. . . . And this tendency runs deep: Back in the 1950s, researchers conducted an experiment at a boy's camp, sponsoring a jelly bean hunt among the campers. After the hunt, the boys were shown an identical picture of a jar of jelly beans. Each boy evaluated the total number of beans in the jar according to whether he was told the jar belonged to his own team or to the other side. The same photograph was estimated to contain many more beans when it was presented as "your team's" and far fewer when it was alleged to be the "other side's."

Partisan Perceptions of the Other Side

If our capacity to process information critical of our own side is flawed, it is even more the case for our assessments of the other side in a conflict or negotiation. In part, this stems from the in-group/out-group phenomenon. Persons from different cultures, especially on the opposite side of the bargaining table, are more readily identified as belonging to an out-group, or the Other. Once that labeling is in place, powerful perceptual dynamics kick in (beyond the tendencies toward stereotyping and overattribution). Robert Robinson describes extensive research over the last 40 years, documenting an unconscious mechanism that enhances "one's own side, portraying it as more talented, honest, and morally upright" while simultaneously vilifying the Other. This leads to a systematic exaggeration of the other side's position and the overestimation of the extent of the actual conflict. As a result, negotiators are often unduly pessimistic about their ability to find common ground, and can be unwilling to pursue it.

Self-Fulfilling Prophesies

Such partisan perceptions hold the power to change reality by becoming self-fulfilling prophesies. The effects of labeling and stereotyping have been documented thoroughly to show that perceptions have the power to shape reality. . . . At the negotiating table, the same principle holds true: Clinging firmly to the idea that one's counterpart is stubborn, for example, is likely to yield intransigence on both sides, precluding the possibility of a compromise that might have occurred had the label of "obstinacy" not been so rigorously affixed.

In short, just as a pilot trying to navigate by visual flight rules at night or in a storm is prone to dangerous misjudgments, the psychology of perception in cross-cultural situations is rife with biases. Not only do we stereotype and overattribute to nationality, we are also poor at interpreting information on our own situation, vulnerable to partisan perceptions of the other side, and likely to act in ways that become dangerously self-fulfilling.

4.   St. Augustine's Fallacy: "When in Rome . . ."

Assume that you have undertaken a full analysis of the culture of the person you will meet on the other side of the bargaining table. St. Augustine gave the classic cross-cultural advice: When in Rome, do as the Romans do. While this admonition certainly has merit, it is not always good advice- . . . much better options may be available. For example, learning that the Chinese, on average, are more hesitant than North Americans to take risks is only a first step. Clearly, a responsive strategy would not mimic this hesitancy, but effectively anticipate it.

Rather than learning to behave as the Romans do (while in Rome or elsewhere), strategies should accommodate the degree of cross-table understanding each side has of the other. For example, consider the best approach for a U.S. manager on his first visit to Japan dealing with a Yale-educated Japanese executive who has worked extensively in Europe and North

America. Here it would be sensible to let the Japanese take the lead. If a negotiator is far more familiar with a counterpart's culture than vice versa, the best strategy might be to embrace the counterpart's negotiating "script." If both sides are equally "literate," an improvisational and mutually-accommodating approach might be most appropriate. A lower degree of familiarity dictates bringing in locally familiar expertise, perhaps on your side and perhaps even as a mediator.

A great deal depends on how familiar you are with "Roman" culture and how familiar your "Roman" counterpart is with your culture. And of course you want to avoid the previous fallacies as well. The nationalities across the table from each other may be Chinese and U.S., but both players may be regulars on the international business circuit, which has its own, increasingly global negotiating culture. Again, assess — etiquette, deeper traits, negotiation-specific expectations, and caveats; do not assume and project your assumption onto your counterpart.

In Conclusion

Cross-cultural negotiation analyses offer insight as to systematic differences in gestures and body language, etiquette and deportment, deeper behavioral traits, as well as organizational decision-making processes and forms of corporate and public governance. Accurately applying the very real insights from such studies can be challenging, but the difficulties perhaps lessened by thinking of four unlikely categories that themselves derive from cultures most dissimilar: John Wayne and Charlie Chan, the Rosetta Stone, VFR at night, and St. Augustine.

Note: Research on Culture and Negotiation

Professor Sebenius provides important caveats about the limits of cultural references. He also concludes that cultural analysis offers insight into systematic differences about how people from different cultures negotiate. With his caveats in mind, we now turn to some of the salient features that research indicates do distinguish the way people from different cultures negotiate.

The negotiation approaches and behaviors common within a culture are related to other aspects of that culture and are based on societal values, social structure, and modes of communication. The three distinguishing features most often mentioned in relation to negotiation norms within a culture are the value of individualism versus collectivism, egalitarianism versus hierarchy, and direct versus indirect modes of communication. Understanding these norms is helpful in forming working assumptions about different cultures and also in understanding our own values. The sharpest differences between societal values are often framed as differences between Eastern and Western cultures; however, this is too simple and can be misleading. The counter-posed sets of values can be summarized as follows:

- *Individualism versus collectivism:* Some societies appear to value individual needs over the collective needs of the group. Economic rewards, as well as social standing, are based on individual accomplishments. Individual autonomy is more important than societal interests. Individual rights tend to be most highly valued. In contrast, other societies place a higher priority on the interdependence of individuals and their social obligations to one another. Collective interests are valued more highly than individual rights.
- *Hierarchy versus egalitarianism:* This cultural juxtaposition distinguishes societies in which power and status are seen as vertical rather than horizontal. In hierarchical societies, social superiority is based on others being socially inferior, and deference is given to those who are higher on the social and economic ladder. In egalitarian societies there are no social castes, and social status is undifferentiated.
- *Direct versus indirect communication:* In more direct communicating societies information is explicit, with minimum nuance, and can be readily understood regardless of the context. Meaning is on the surface rather than embedded in other layers of pretext or context. People in societies with more indirect communication embed the meaning of their words in the context of the situation. Meaning must be inferred to be fully understood.

Interdisciplinary research is increasingly focusing on cultural variations in negotiation. Although very interesting, much of the research is highly theoretical and is written in research parlance. Practical application of the research findings is just starting to emerge and should be of considerable value to negotiators, subject to the caveats explained by Professor Sebenius.

Much of the research and writing on culture as a factor in negotiation focuses on cultural norms as traits we should be aware of in those with whom we negotiate, particularly across borders. If the research on cultural norms is reliable, our own cultural identity can offer clues to others about our negotiating tendencies and can provide us personal insight into our negotiating behaviors and responses. Even though our own cultural or group identity may influence how we perceive ourselves and how others view us, these categorical attributes are subject to error and oversimplification to the point of being misleading and insulting. This limitation will not stop others with whom we negotiate from generalizing about us in a way that might affect their behavior toward us. Just as important, our self-identity helps shape our beliefs, emotions, and behaviors. This can have an impact on how we negotiate.

If you would like to test your own cultural, gender, or racial sensitivities and biases online, go to *https://implicit.harvard.edu/implicit/demo/selectatest.html*, where you will have the opportunity to participate in a Web-based research study. The results can be revealing and might be discussed in class.

Questions

7. What is the dominant culture with which you identify? Is this the same culture that those who do not know you well would assume you belong to? Are there other cultural subgroups that help define who you are? Are there stereotypes that opposing negotiators might have about you? Is there any way you can use those likely stereotypes to your advantage?

8. Does the downside of thinking about people as part of a cultural group outweigh the possible benefit of grouping people to help understand their values and anticipate their behavior?

9. Do you agree that "culture is the lens through which we make sense of the world"? If so, is there any doubt that people of different cultures will see the world so differently that world conflict is inevitable? Is conflict and how to deal with it culturally defined? For a comprehensive and instructive collection of provocative readings on both culture and gender as they relate to conflict, see Chew (2001).

10. Based on selection, training, and shared values, do lawyers constitute a cultural subgroup that helps others understand them and predict their behavior? Is your answer the same for doctors, accountants, or clergy?

C.   Is Race a Factor in Negotiations?

Earlier studies on race as a factor in negotiation outcomes found significant differences based on race (Ayers, 1991, 1995). These studies compared prices arrived at for new cars in the Chicago area between white and black testers posing as otherwise similar buyers. Although cited in the negotiation literature as disturbing evidence that African-Americans "often get worse outcomes in negotiations," this evidence cannot be extrapolated to indicate that race is a predictor of negotiation skill. These studies documented discrimination in the offers that sales personnel made to African-American versus Caucasian testers, rather than differences in negotiating ability among the testers. Indeed, the studies were later introduced as evidence of discrimination in a class-action law suit against General Motors Acceptance Corporation (see Hawkins, 2004).

We live in an age in which an African-American U.S. President has been elected, an increasing number of professionals are people of color, and many more people identify themselves as interracial or blended. Even though discrimination still exists and race may matter in important social justice issues, does it make a difference in negotiation among lawyers, who are a self-selected group of achievers with similar training?

We are not aware of empirical data about race as a factor in negotiation among attorneys, but Professor Charles Craver, who has taught negotiation for more than 25 years, has tracked simulated negotiation outcomes by gender and race among law students. In the next reading, Professor Craver presents the results and notes how race can influence negotiation encounters. He introduces his article by discussing one specialized practice of negotiation where client statistics can be accessed — sports agents, many of whom are lawyers. The disproportionately small percentage of African-American sports agents sets the stage for his report on negotiation outcomes between law students.

❖ **Charles B. Craver,** *Race and Negotiation Performance: Does Race Predict Success as a Negotiator?*

8 ABA Disp. Resol. Mag. 22 (Fall 2001)

In major league baseball, nineteen percent of the players are black. As of 1992, 150 of the 200 agents registered with Major League Baseball Players Association had active clientele; black agents accounted for a mere three percent of this 150. In professional football, sixty-nine percent of the players are black, but black agents comprise only fourteen percent of the registered agents with active files. Worse yet, more than eighty percent of the NBA's players are black, but less than ten percent of them have black agents.

Why are many prominent black athletes reluctant to retain black agents to represent them? One factor undoubtedly concerns the high profile success of white agents such as David Falk in basketball and Leigh Steinberg in football, and the ability of these super-agents to attract draft-eligible black athletes. Another may involve the fact that "many black players have internalized racial stereotypes about blacks and thus, discriminate against their own people." These athletes may privately believe that white agents can negotiate better contracts than black agents....

Real, Perceived Racial Differences

Negotiations involving participants from diverse ethnic backgrounds frequently develop differently than bargaining interactions involving persons from similar backgrounds. People tend to negotiate more cooperatively with opponents of the same race and culture than with adversaries of different races and cultures. Apparently, similarity induces trust and reduces the need for each interactor to maintain a particular "face" in the other's eyes. . . .

Students I have taught at various law schools over the past 25 years have often allowed their stereotypical beliefs to influence their bargaining encounters. Many of my students — regardless of their ethnicity — think that Caucasian males are the most Machiavellian and competitive negotiators. They expect these men to employ adversarial and manipulative tactics to obtain optimal results for themselves. On the other hand, numerous students expect African-American, Asian-American, and Latino-American negotiators to be more accommodating and less competitive. Even members of one race often stereotype other members of the same race. When opponents fail to behave in the anticipated manner, the bargaining process may be adversely affected.

Despite the unreliability of many stereotypical beliefs and the absence of more recent surveys, several empirical studies have found a few relevant differences between black and white interactants. Blacks tend to be high in terms of Interpersonal Orientation (IO). High IO individuals are more sensitive and responsive to the interpersonal aspects of their relationships with others. This tendency should make blacks more effective negotiators. Because bargaining outcomes are directly affected by the interpersonal skills of the participants, high IO individuals should be able to achieve better results than their low IO cohorts.

During verbal encounters, blacks tend to speak more forcefully and with greater verbal aggressiveness than whites. In competitive settings, this trait might enhance the bargaining effectiveness of individuals with these traits, while in cooperative situations it might undermine their ability to achieve mutual accords. When they interact with others, blacks tend to make less eye contact while listening to others than do whites, which may be perceived by speakers as an indication of indifference to what is being said or of disrespect toward the speaker. Such behavior might undermine the ability of the persons with minimal eye contact to establish the kind of rapport that can advance bargaining discussions.

Most negotiators tend to employ a cooperative/problem-solving or a competitive/adversarial style when they bargain with others. Cooperative/problem-solvers tend to be open with their information, prefer to use objective criteria to guide their discussions, and endeavor to maximize the joint return achieved by interactants, while competitive/adversarials tend to be less open with information, focus more on stated positions than objective factors, are manipulative, and attempt to maximize their own side's return. White negotiators usually employ relatively consistent bargaining styles, while black negotiators tend to adopt styles that are reflective of the race of their opponents. Blacks tend to perform more effectively when they compete with whites and when they cooperate with other blacks.

Statistical Findings

... This study evaluates the possible relationship between race and performance on negotiation exercises. The Null Hypothesis is that there is no correlation between race and the results students achieve on Legal Negotiation course exercises. The Alternative Hypothesis is that there is a relationship between race and the results students achieve on Legal Negotiation course exercises.

Although I have 16 years of Legal Negotiation course data at George Washington University, I decided to focus on the data covering the past nine years because the classes I taught from 1986 through the spring of 1992 contained insufficient numbers of black students to permit meaningful statistical comparisons....

The statistical data ... provide strong support for the Null Hypothesis ... for three of the nine years, the mean negotiation scores for white students were slightly above the mean scores for black students, while for the other six years, the mean negotiation scores for black students were slightly above the mean scores for white students.

Implications

Individuals who commence negotiations with people of different races should appreciate the need to establish trusting and cooperative relationships before the serious substantive discussions begin. This approach should significantly enhance the likelihood of mutually beneficial transactions. The preliminary stage of their interaction may be used to generate a modicum of rapport. Negotiators should try to minimize the counterproductive stereotypes they may consciously or subconsciously harbor toward persons of their opponent's ethnicity. If negotiators anticipate difficult interactions as a result of such usually irrational preconceptions, they are likely to generate self-fulfilling prophecies. If negotiators conversely expect their opponents to behave more cooperatively and less manipulatively because of their ethnicity, they may carelessly lower their guard and give their opponents an inherent bargaining advantage. Negotiators must also try to understand any seemingly illogical reactions their opponents may initially exhibit toward them as a result of those individuals' stereotyping of them.

If the first contact negotiators have with opponents indicates that those persons are expecting highly competitive transactions, they should not hesitate to employ "attitudinal bargaining" to disabuse their opponents of this preconception. They should create cooperative physical and psychological environments. Warm handshakes and open postures can initially diminish combative atmospheres. Cooperative negotiators can sit adjacent to, instead of directly across from, opponents. In a few instances, it may be necessary to directly broach the subject of negative stereotyping, since this may be the most efficacious way to negate the influence of these feelings.

People who participate in bargaining transactions should recognize that the specific circumstances and unique personal traits of the individual negotiators — rather than generalized beliefs regarding ethnic characteristics — determine the way in which each interaction evolves. Each opponent has to be evaluated and dealt with differently. Is that individual a cooperative or a competitive bargainer? Does the other side possess greater, equal, or less bargaining power concerning the issues to be addressed? What bargaining techniques are likely to influence that person? What negotiating techniques has that individual decided to employ, and what are the most effective ways to counter those tactics? As the instant transaction unfolds, each negotiator will have to make strategic changes to respond to unanticipated disclosures or to changed circumstances.

When negotiators find themselves attributing certain characteristics to opponents, they must carefully determine whether those attributes are based on specific information pertaining to those particular opponents or to vague generalizations regarding people of their race. If people bargained only with individuals of the same race, they would quickly realize how different we all are. Some opponents would behave cooperatively, while others would act in a competitive manner. Some would exhibit win-lose tendencies, while others would evidence win-win attitudes. Techniques that would be effective against some opponents would be ineffective against others.

The nine years of Legal Negotiation course data evaluated by me indicates the absence of any statistically significant correlation between student race and the results achieved on negotiation exercises. These findings would suggest that even if cultural and behavioral differences between black and white students exist, those differences have no impact on students' ability to achieve beneficial negotiation exercise results.

Questions

11. Is race distinguishable from culture for purposes of negotiation? If so, what is the difference?

12. Are the "differences between black and white interactants," as cited by Professor Craver, valid? Are any generalizations about the speaking patterns, eye contact, or bargaining style of black people in comparison to white people reliable or of any value? In a multicultural, increasingly blended society, is race relevant?

13. Are there any possible factors or explanations for the disproportionate number of African-American sports agents other than the high profile of white agents and "internalized racial stereotypes," as noted by Professor Craver?

14. Is there any different explanation for the relatively few female sports agents?

15. If other bargainers assume that male Caucasian negotiators are "Machiavellian and competitive," how might this affect the bargaining process? Could a white male minimize such assumptions? How?

CHAPTER
7

The Ethical Negotiator

A. Deception vs. Disclosure

As a lawyer, you will find yourself governed by rules that may seem both contradictory and personally uncomfortable. Ethics codes forbid you from lying in court but permit you to lie in negotiation, at least as most non-lawyers would define lying. Even if you would not deceive or lie on your own behalf, the obligation to be a zealous advocate for clients will confront you, as a lawyer, with the dilemma of deciding how far to go in gaining a negotiation advantage for your client by misstating or not revealing information.

This dilemma has contributed to an image problem for our profession. "Lawyer" is considered by many to be synonymous with "liar." The 1997 movie *Liar, Liar,* featuring actor Jim Carrey, was advertised by displaying the words "Lawyer, Lawyer," crossed out, with "Liar, Liar" written over them in red. This theme was repeated in the first scene of the film, where the lawyer's son is asked in his kindergarten class what his father does for a living. He innocently tells the class that his father is a "liar." The public image of lawyers is also reflected in unflattering and prolific jokes ("How do you know when a lawyer is lying? When his lips are moving.").

Because negotiation occurs in private, usually without clients present, there is little check on what is said or not said in negotiation between lawyers. The ethics rules for negotiation are not precise and are sometimes contradictory, especially regarding what must be revealed to an opposing party. These elements result in constant and challenging choices facing attorneys in terms of ethics, morality, and negotiation effectiveness.

Ethics rules attempt to provide a guide for lawyers on how to balance our obligation to a client's interests and the integrity of the profession in a negotiation, but the specifics of applying the rules are elusive. Ethical limits can be found in each state's Rules of Professional Conduct or Code of Professional Responsibility and in its case and statutory law. The American Bar Association's (ABA's) Model Rules of Professional Conduct are the basis for most state ethics rules. The beginning point is Rule 4.1, which states that a lawyer shall not "knowingly (a) make a false statement of material fact or law to a third person; or (b) fail to disclose a material fact to a third person when disclosure is necessary to avoid assisting a criminal or fraudulent act by a client, unless disclosure is prohibited by Rule 1.6."

A serious limitation of knowing what should or should not be revealed is the qualification that only "material" facts must be revealed. The official comment to Rule 4.1 states that "under generally accepted conventions in negotiation, . . . estimates of price or value placed on the subject of the transaction" are not considered material, nor are "a party's intentions as to an acceptable settlement of a claim" covered by Rule 4.1's prohibitions against making false statements. (See Comment 2.)

Also, as you may recall, Rule 1.6 protects client confidences. So an attorney whose client reveals a bottom line, or any other information that the client regards as confidential, cannot disclose that information, unless the client authorizes the disclosure. In effect, the requirement that a lawyer may not reveal client confidences swallows the rule requiring disclosure, even of most criminal conduct.

The net result of the ethical rules is that lawyers in negotiation can lie about some things, but not others. You can puff and bluff because that's the expected convention. So, as a lawyer you can tell the other side that "this is a seven-figure case if it gets to a jury," even though you believe a verdict would not exceed $500,000, or that your client's bottom line is $100,000 when it is really $80,000. However, you cannot say your client sustained a broken neck, knowing that she did not. In other words, deception is still considered an acceptable aspect of negotiation, but only to a point. (See the next chapter for the limits imposed by contract law.) This creates a dilemma for the ethical negotiator and lends itself to a lot of debate and literature on the subject.

Richard Zitrin and Carol Langford in their book, *The Moral Compass of the American Lawyer* (1999), refer to lawyers engaging in "strategic speaking" when they shade the truth while negotiating. According to them, negotiation necessarily "involves some measure of misleading the opponent [and] concealing one's true position. . . . Negotiation is not, and never will be, a matter of 'putting all our cards on the table'" (165). Zitrin and Langford summarize lawyers' excuses for lying in negotiation:

- "I didn't lie," which includes "My statement was literally true" (although misleading), "I was speaking on a subject about which there is no absolute truth," and "I was merely putting matters in the best light."
- "I lied, if you insist on calling it that, but it was . . . ": "ethically permissible" (and thus okay); "legal" (and thus okay); "just an omission"; or "ineffectual," because it was just a white lie or because it was simply not believed.
- "I lied, but it was justified by the very nature of things." This includes situations where lying is considered part of the rules of the game, such as negotiations, where most lawyers feel that candor defeats the very purpose of the exercise.
- "I lied, but it was justified by the special ethics of lawyering," especially the duties owed clients: loyalty, confidentiality, and, of course, zealous representation.

- "The lie belongs to someone else," usually the client, so that the lawyer is "just the messenger."
- "I lied because my opponent acted badly." This includes "self-defense," or "having to lie" before the opponent does, and lying to teach the opponent a lesson, or because bad behavior means the opponent has forfeited any right to candor.
- "I lied, but it was justified by good consequences," that is, justice triumphed. . . .

Professor Longan, in the next reading, provides hypotheticals that highlight some of the ethical issues in negotiation. In considering these hypotheticals, he analyzes the ABA Model Rules and opinions on point, but goes beyond these in urging consideration of both what is wise and most effective in the long run.

❖ **Patrick E. Longan,** *Ethics in Settlement Negotiations: Foreword*

52 Mercer L. Rev. 810 (2001)

A. The Limits of Representations

. . . You represent the plaintiff in a breach of contract action. You are seeking lost profits. What can you say in negotiations about the lost profits if:

1. Your expert has come to no conclusion about their cause.
2. Your expert has told you the breach did not cause the lost profits.
3. Your expert has given you a range between $2,000,000 and $5,000,000 for the lost profits.
4. Your expert says the maximum lost profit is $2,000,000.
5. You do not have an expert; your client says the loss was $5,000,000.

It is common in negotiation for each side to emphasize the strength and persuasiveness of its evidence. On the other hand, each side in discovery has the opportunity to explore the other side's evidence. In this scenario, each side would be entitled to a report and a deposition of the other's testifying expert. Any statement about the expert would be a statement of fact. Because of the importance of expert testimony to this case, any statement of this sort would be material. The lawyer must be careful to tell only the truth to avoid violating Rule 4.1. Good lawyers, however, will test the assertions in discovery, consistent with the now-famous Russian proverb, "Trust, but verify."

Beyond the rules of ethics, however, it is proper to ask what the best strategy is for a lawyer in this negotiation. Here, any statement about the expert's conclusions probably will be the subject of discovery. If the statement is found to be false, the lawyer who made it will lose some credibility. That loss, which will likely survive the conclusion of this particular case and affect negotiations with the other lawyer in future cases, will cause these future negotiations to be more strained, more lengthy, and probably less fruitful. To the extent that the lawyer gains a reputation for untruthfulness as a result of statements about the expert, the lawyer may be impeding all his or her future negotiations. In other words, this hypothetical involves a happy situation in which it is both the right strategy and the smart strategy to tell the truth. . . .

In this breach of contract action, can you:

1. tell opposing counsel that you will not settle for less than $3.5 million when you have authority to settle for $2 million?
2. tell opposing counsel that five major buyers stopped buying from your client after the breach, knowing that they stopped buying for other reasons?

As discussed, comment 2 to Model Rule [4.1] defines statements about settlement authority not to be material. Technically, therefore, the lawyer should feel free to lie about his or her authority. Another strategy, however, and one that may be more effective in the long run, is simply to deflect any questions of authority with statements such as, "You know neither one of us can discuss our authority — let's talk about a fair settlement of this case." The reason a deflection may be more effective in the long run is the same reason exaggerations about the expert's conclusions may cause long term harm. You may be ethically permitted to lie about your authority, but if you do it, and the other lawyer catches you at it, he or she will not trust you again.

The misleading statement about the lost customers raises a persistent and subtle issue for lawyers about the use of language. The statement is literally true. These customers have left, and they did so at a time after the defendant's breach. The only reason the statement is made, however, is in the hope that the defendant will make the leap and conclude that the customers left because of the breach or, at least, that the plaintiff will attempt to prove that they did. The statement is, therefore, an intentionally misleading, sly use of language. It is reminiscent of former President Clinton's response to a question before the grand jury about his deposition testimony: "It depends on what the meaning of is is." The lawyer who engages in this type of deception is more clever, perhaps, than a straightforward liar, but the lawyer is no less worthy of condemnation. Once again, however, we can rely on the power of reputation to deter lawyers (at least those who care about their reputations) from engaging in these tactics. Word gets around.

B. Disclosure of Factual Errors

The second hypothetical concerned a duty to disclose facts when the other lawyer has made a settlement offer containing obvious mistakes:

You represent the husband in a divorce action. You receive from opposing counsel a proposed property settlement with the following errors: (1) a transcription error that undervalues an asset; (2) an arithmetical error that undervalues an asset; (3) a valuation by purchase price of an asset when market value is much higher. All the errors work to your client's advantage. What, if anything, should you do about them?

To the extent that the first two errors are "scrivener's errors" (the other lawyer missed a typographical error or failed to add the numbers correctly), the lawyer has the duty to correct the mistakes. The third problem may raise more difficult issues because the error may come from opposing counsel's conscious but erroneous judgment about what valuation is best for his or her client. Can the lawyer in the hypothetical take advantage of his or her adversary's error in judgment?

The question is a species of a fundamental, recurring question in an adversarial system. The lawyer owes a primary duty of loyalty to the client. In most respects, the lawyer is not expected to be his or her brother's keeper. One answer to the particular ethical question presented is to say that it is not the interesting or important question. The client is not perpetrating a fraud or a crime by taking advantage of a bad lawyer on the other side. There is no duty to disclose under Rule 4.1.

Abiding by the rules of ethics, however, is necessary but not always sufficient for good lawyering. Ethically, the lawyer need not correct every misstep of opposing counsel. But sometimes correcting the mistake would be the wise thing to do. For example, if the mistakes involved in the proposal were fundamental mistakes, ones that under the law of contract the opposing party would provide grounds later to void the transaction, then the lawyer may best serve his or her client by alerting opposing counsel to the mistakes now. If the parties to the transaction will have a continuing relationship, such as shared responsibility for minor children, the best strategy might be to correct the mistakes and buy some trust, which may be sorely needed later. Here, as in many situations, ethics tells you the options available, but the lawyer must still exercise good judgment among the options.

C. Disclosure of Legal Errors

The final hypothetical . . . highlighted the fact that Model Rule 4.1 forbids a lawyer from making a material misrepresentation about the law. The hypothetical does so in the context of an interaction with a young lawyer who is operating under a mistake about the state of the law:

> You represent the defendant in a personal injury case. In negotiation with plaintiff's counsel (a young, relatively inexperienced lawyer), it becomes clear to you that this lawyer believes his or her client's potential recovery is limited by a tort reform statute. You know that this statute has been found unconstitutional by the state supreme court. May you, and should you, correct opposing counsel's mistake about the law?

Most practicing lawyers would not think twice about taking advantage of this younger lawyer. Again, the client is not perpetrating a fraud or a crime, and the client might be very happy to save some money because his or her adversary's lawyer is clueless. No rule of legal ethics requires the lawyer to be the opposing party's lawyer also. No rule requires that lawyers settle cases only on "fair" terms.

Again, however, the strictly ethical inquiry cannot end the discussion. For example, lawyers might find that taking advantage of the mistake in particular circumstances, such as a horrific injury to a young child, would be morally wrong although ethically permissible. The lawyer is free to counsel the client about nonlegal matters, such as the morality of leaving the injured child unable to obtain the life-long care the child needs. The lawyer is even free to seek to withdraw if assisting in a settlement under these circumstances would be repugnant to the lawyer. Here, as in the prior examples, the best lawyers consider all the circumstances and determine first whether the rules of ethics require a particular course of action and, if they do not, what under all the circumstances is the wisest choice. . . .

Questions

1. Assuming that a lawyer can lie about a client's bottom line and matters of value in negotiation without violating ethical rules, when might doing so be a good tactic, and when not? What is the tactical advantage of candor? If there is reason to be candid when not ethically required, should it be selective candor depending on the situation or is a uniform policy of candor more advantageous? Why?

2. Should the client have a say in what is revealed in the above hypotheticals? If you disagree with your client, must the client's wishes govern? (See the next section, Client Control v. Lawyer Integrity, for discussion of these issues.)

3. Zitrin and Langford suggest that "instead of putting lawyers in the position of having to lie, as the rule does now, it could simply forbid lawyers from asking their opponents their ultimate positions on value" (168). Would this be an effective, or at least preferable, solution to the dilemma between zealous representation and candor? Why or why not?

4. Is there any reason to behave differently toward people in negotiation than you would in other interactions? In other words, what distinguishes negotiation from interpersonal interactions generally? (For an interesting analysis of this question, see Cohen, 2001.)

5. There is much debate and also some case law on what is "a material fact" that must be revealed in a negotiation pursuant to Model Rule 4.1(a). For example, if you are representing a client injured in an automobile accident, need you reveal the client's death prior to finalizing settlement of a claim for his injuries? Why or why not? (See *Kentucky Bar Assn. v. Geisler*, 938 S.W. 2d 578 (1997).)

6. Assuming that your client in the above question was alive at the

> initiation of the claim and the beginning of negotiation, the question
> raises an issue of what must be revealed when facts change or when
> what was revealed earlier is no longer true. This occurs frequently
> in the context of formal discovery. If a response to a question asked in
> formal discovery is no longer true, rules of civil procedure generally
> require an attorney to inform the opposing side of the change. (See
> FRCP Section 26(e).) If a fact material to a negotiation changes, is
> silence on the part of the knowing attorney a violation of Model
> Rule 4.1? Should the ethics rules governing attorneys permit silence
> when rules of procedure would require correction? Can you arti-
> culate a meaningful distinction? (See White, 1980.)
> 7. How does what Rule 4.1 requires of lawyers compare with your per-
>   sonal moral values? If your personal ethics are more restrictive than
>   the rules, is there a risk that your interests might conflict with those
>   of your client? This topic is covered in the following section.

B. Client Control vs. Lawyer Integrity (Conflicts of Interest)

Ethical issues in negotiation are often compounded for lawyers because
their interests are seldom in complete congruity with those of their client's.
As we saw in Chapter 4 (Cooperation vs. Competiveness — Who Decides?),
when lawyers are employed to negotiate for principals, the interests in the
timing, costs, trade-offs, goals, and relationships involved in a settlement
may be different for the lawyer than for the client. However, lawyers work for
clients and, at least to some extent, clients get to call the shots. ABA Model
Rule 1.2(a) states that "A lawyer shall abide by a client's decisions concerning the objectives of representation . . .and shall consult with the client as to
the means by which they are to be pursued. A lawyer shall abide by a client's
decision whether to accept an offer of settlement of a matter." This rule distinguishes the end goal, decided by the client, from the means of achieving
it, decided by the lawyer in consultation with the client. The rule is clear that
the decision whether to settle and under what terms is the client's choice.
The application of the rule to how lawyers should negotiate is less clear.

We suggested earlier, in discussing cultural identities, that being a lawyer
identifies you with what may be considered a cultural subgroup. Another way
to view the relationship between lawyers is to analogize the relationship
among lawyers to a "community." Whether viewed as a community or sub-
culture, lawyers have long-term relationships with one another and repeatedly interact in ways that have their own norms of behavior and shared
expectations. This may be in contrast to the relationship of clients to the
legal/judicial system, which is likely to be a one-time occasion. A potential

conflict exists between the client's interest in maximizing gain from a one-time transaction or settlement and a lawyer's longer term interest in maintaining credible and amicable relations with other lawyers. The gain from deceit and lying may benefit a client at the expense of the lawyer's reputation and relationships within the community.

Both economic and ethical considerations may conflict with your ideals and commitment to self-defined professional integrity and honesty. Preserving your client's confidences may prevent you from candidly discussing with an opposing lawyer how your client has asked you to negotiate or giving your counterpart warning that she should be cautious.

Questions

8. If a client you represent in the sale of a business instructs you to make a first offer of $1,000,000 to eventually sell for his target of $500,000, can you refuse because you feel the bloated offer compromises your integrity? If you do refuse, over the client's objection, is the representation necessarily ended? Can you make the first offer to opposing counsel with a wink and not be breaching a client confidence?

9. Does Model Rule 1.2(a), which divides bargaining decision responsibilities along an end-means line (client decides the end goal, lawyer decides the means of obtaining client's goal), provide a helpful distinction for you?

10. Is there a cleaner end-means line when representing an injured tort claimant than when representing a businessperson in a commercial transaction? Is an insurance company that retains a lawyer to defend a personal injury claim more likely to control the means of lawyer negotiating than is an injured plaintiff? Do different ethics rules apply to lawyers depending on who employs them?

A conflict may also exist between a client's personal economic needs, which drives her to value an attractive settlement offer more than societal interests, and a lawyer's ideals, which may focus more on broader policy concerns. This conflict can cut the other way if an idealistic client wants to reject a settlement on principle when the lawyer is coveting the immediate fee payoff.

Consider the settlement situation described in the following example and the conflicts it raises.

❖ **Richard Zitrin and Carol M. Langford,** THE MORAL COMPASS OF THE
AMERICAN LAWYER

183, Ballantine Books (1999)

E.J. Boyette was a forty-eight-year-old computer programmer when he died, leaving a wife and five kids. Always active, Boyette had worked out three times a week, and on the weekends he rowed with a group of guys he knew from college. Shortly after his forty-seventh birthday he noticed that he was getting tired easily and was often short of breath. He made an appointment with his doctor, who referred him to a cardiologist. After extensive tests, the cardiologist recommended surgical placement of a new kind of heart valve from the Jones/Henning/Wharton Company that had been highly praised in all the medical journals.

At first everything seemed fine. Boyette was released from the hospital, started mild workouts, and had even begun dreaming of joining his rowing mates on the water again. But after three months Boyette's physical condition began deteriorating quickly. In another month he was dead. His widow consulted attorney Andrea Hardy, partner in a small firm that represents plaintiffs in injury cases. . . .

Now eighteen months later, after extensive discovery and a review of thousands of documents, Andrea and her paralegal have just found a memo that seems to show that the company knew its first-generation heart valves had design flaws that could cause some patients to get worse and even die. She and her paralegal can barely contain their excitement. They quickly draft a new and very specific demand for the other side to produce more documents, which Andrea believes will include the smoking gun she can use to prove that the manufacturer knew the heart valves were defective. . . .

On the appointed day for delivery, Andrea is surprised to find Burger himself [chief defense counsel] at her office. He asks if they can talk.

"Look," he says, "I'll hand over these documents in a minute. I think you know what's in them. But there's something I'd like you to consider. We'll offer you five million dollars right now to settle the case. There are just two conditions: the amount we pay must be secret, and the documents you've gotten from us must be returned. All of them, including copies." Andrea is dumb-struck. Until this moment Burger had maintained his client's innocence and never breathed a word about settlement. She knows $5 million is a lot more than she's likely to get for a case at trial, even with punishment damages. And the fee would easily be the largest her firm has ever received. She's sure the documents in George Burger's briefcase include the smoking gun she'd been looking for.

Andrea tells Burger that she'll have to review the documents and discuss things with her client before making a decision. "Fine," says Burger, "I'll give you a week." Later that day, with her paralegal and her law partners gathered around her, Andrea reads three memos from senior Jones/Henning/Wharton officials that conclusively prove that the manufacturer knew that the heart valve's design was defective before Mr. Boyette's valve was implanted. One memo summarizes 107 incidents in which the valve was considered a contributing cause in a patient's death. The other two discuss how the company should deal with the design flaw, eventually concluding that nothing should be done to take it off the market until a new product could be developed to replace it.

Andrea knows she must talk to Mr. Boyette's widow. But she ponders what to advise her about accepting Burger's offer. She loves her practice because she gets to expose dangerous products, not conceal them. She knows that if she agrees to keep the documents secret, other people with heart valves like Mr. Boyette's could be in danger, even die. But she also knows the guiding principle that her first duty is to her client, not the public at large. And the amount her client has been offered is enormous. . . .

She was not surprised when John Boyette called the next day to say that the family had met, discussed the offer, and decided to accept it.

Questions

11. After describing the $5 million Boyette secret settlement, Zitrin and Langford discuss some state laws that ban secret settlements to prevent protection of public health and safety. What are the arguments for and against statutory restrictions on secret settlements involving claims of defective products, fraud, and malpractice? Should lawyers be required to report such settlements? Why or why not? (See Doré, 1999; Zitrin, 1999.)

12. How can you as a lawyer deal with this type of conflict or the more common one of the client's desire to have her lawyer shade the truth or conceal adverse bargaining information?

Problem 1

Assume that you are a third-year law student who has landed a plum job as an associate with a boutique intellectual property law firm to commence after graduation. You were to be paid $160,000 a year. Although a very good law firm, the written offer, which it prepared and you accepted, was an absolute commitment on the part of the firm with no conditions. Since your acceptance, economic conditions have worsened and the type of litigation in which the firm primarily engages has declined. A couple of weeks ago you met with the managing partner, Jerome Higgins, who cordially explained the circumstances and indicated that the firm needed to cancel the employment arrangement but wanted to be fair with you. You indicated that you relied on the early offer and turned down other employment offers during the law school interview season, which is now concluded. You also truthfully revealed that you had rented a new apartment and purchased a car in reliance on the employment agreement. You acknowledged that economic conditions have tightened since you accepted the offer, but pointed out that the offer was unconditional and that the bad economic times would make it difficult for you to find a comparable position.

You agreed that you would meet again with Mr. Higgins in a few weeks to discuss severance terms. While discussing your situation with your IP law professor, he told you of an alum who recently was appointed General Counsel for a tech startup and had asked him for a recommendation of a graduating student who might be interested in working with him. He passed on your name and you have been offered the position at a starting salary of $120,000 to commence immediately following the Bar exam. Although the position pays less than the law firm job, you are thrilled because of the excitement of the startup and the unique opportunity it presents, as well as the fact that he other job offer was withdrawn. You plan to accept the Associate General Counsel position. However, you first want to talk with Mr. Higgins to see what you can work out with him regarding the breach of your employment contract by his law firm. You are truly concerned about your immediate economic needs and your heavy student loan debt. Although Higgins's law firm may not be expanding, you are aware of its high per-partner income and the firm's solid economic base. You would like to get as much from them as you can. You know that if you personally negotiate with Mr. Higgins, you will feel compelled to tell him about your new job offer, even if he doesn't ask. If you do that, your severance package won't be worth much.

Can you hire a lawyer to negotiate for you and not tell the lawyer about your pending job offer? If you do tell the lawyer about the other job offer, would she be acting unethically not to disclose it if Higgins does not ask if you have other offers? If Higgins does ask about what you have done to mitigate damages, then must your attorney reveal the other offer? Can your lawyer insist on revealing the terms of the other job offer even if you instruct her not to do so? If you were to switch roles, would you agree to negotiate on behalf of someone in these circumstances? What would you advise your client to do and why?

Mnookin, Peppet, and Tulumello, after posing a similar situation to that above, offer advice on how to grapple with the ethical dilemma when your client wants you to mislead the other side, as well as how lawyers may in fact signal a warning to other lawyers without directly communicating confidential client information.

❖ **Robert H. Mnookin, Scott R. Peppet, and Andrew S. Tulumello,**
Beyond Winning: Negotiating to Create Value in Deals and Disputes

282, Harvard University Press (2000)

What If My Client Wants Me to Mislead the Other Side?

Seek to Understand the Client's Choice

If a client is asking you to mislead the other side, the first step, as always, is to try to understand why. In what ways does this request make sense for the client? Put yourself in her shoes. If you were the client, would you propose the same thing that she's proposing?

By identifying the incentives that motivate your client to ask you to mislead the other side, you may be able to relate better to the client as you talk about his request. The key is to learn why the client thinks you should manipulate the truth. What does he see as the advantages? What does he see as the risks? What are the client's concerns? By listening and demonstrating understanding, you can often draw out the client to talk about the underlying choice of strategy.

Raise Your Concerns Explicitly

Lawyers also must learn to discuss ethical dilemmas explicitly. You can find yourself in a very uncomfortable situation if neither you nor your client is willing to discuss ethical conflicts. Learning to have such conversations productively is a critical skill.

If your client asks you to mislead the other side, you should negotiate with her and try to help her understand your views. You must explain that you don't want to violate established rules of professional responsibility, and that you don't want to do something that isn't in your client's best interests. You don't want to go against your personal beliefs, and you don't want to do something that hurts your reputation. By explaining your interests and perspective — while continuing to demonstrate understanding for the client's views — you can begin a conversation about the dilemma you face.

Ed's lawyer, for example, would want to explain that in the face of questioning by Mr. Jenks he would either have to tell the truth about a competing offer or refuse to answer a direct question. "That would probably give away the issue right there," Ed might say. "Couldn't you just say 'No, he has no other offers'?" "No," his lawyer might explain. "I can't lie about a material piece of information like that. And I've got to tell you, it would probably amount to fraud. Given that sooner or later he's going to find out whether you're working again, lying about it could cause serious problems later."

Remember That Your Reputation Is a Valuable Asset

Clients sometimes want to use a lawyer's reputation for honesty as a cover for their own unethical behavior. If a lawyer is known for telling the truth, this reputation can be a perfect smokescreen for throwing the other side off track. If your client persuades you to lie, however he may take advantage of your reputation for his own short-term gain, disregarding the long-term effect on your career and well-being.

We learned of a recent example in a divorce case. After discovering that his wife had hired an attorney, the husband hired an outstanding family lawyer — known in his community as an honorable problem-solver. The two lawyers had done many divorce cases together in the past and had built up a great deal of trust. Ordinarily they did not rely on formal discovery procedures, choosing instead to exchange information informally. This saved their clients a great deal of time and money.

The husband in this case insisted that his lawyer not disclose certain financial information to the other side unless forced to do so through formal discovery. The husband's lawyer faced a real ethical dilemma. When his colleague proposed that they informally exchange information as they had in the past, what was he to do? He knew that if he disclosed partially but withheld the information in question, it would go against his counterpart's clear expectation and would ultimately hurt his own reputation as an honest negotiator. At the same time, he was obligated to obey his client's wishes not to disclose the financial information.

Ultimately, he chose to refuse to engage in the informal information exchange process with the other attorney. This implicitly signaled, of course, that this divorce was unlike the others they had negotiated together before. Many lawyers had told us that in such situations they are likely to signal to the other side that the normal rules of play are suspended and that the baseline professional ethics rules are all that should be expected. One lawyer told of a case in which he entered the room where the negotiation was to occur, sat down across the table from a long-time colleague, and simply said "On guard." Both knew immediately that their normal collaborative rules of engagement were temporarily suspended.

Such signaling raises difficult ethical issues, of course. On the one hand, why should a client be able to gain distributive advantage by hiding behind his lawyer's reputation? Doesn't that disserve the attorney's other clients who rely on his problem-solving abilities? By refusing to engage in the informal discovery process that was based on trust, doesn't the lawyer merely give his client what the client would get from any other attorney that *didn't* have a reputation for honesty? On the other hand, is it ever legitimate for an attorney *not* to do something that would maximize the distributive benefit for a given client? If a lawyer's approach conflicts with his client's, would the best approach be simply to withdraw?

In our view, withdrawal is one possible solution. In practice, as we've discussed, however, lawyers *and clients* face real financial and logistical constraints that may make withdrawal unattractive. Once an attorney has worked with a client over time, the lawyer has built up a store of knowledge and experience relevant only to that client, and the client has invested time and money in educating his lawyer about the particulars of the case. Under such circumstances, rather than withdraw, it seems reasonable for an attorney to signal to the other side that for this negotiation they should not expect anything beyond what the formal discovery rules require.

The lesson we draw, however, is that lawyer-client preparation is essential. As a lawyer-client relationship begins, an attorney must be clear with his client about his problem-solving orientation and what that requires. If a lawyer is unambiguous about what he will and won't do, the client can make an informed choice about which lawyer to retain. Such ethical conflicts are thus much less likely to arise.

Lawyers' fees and how they are determined may influence how lawyers negotiate on behalf of both plaintiffs and defendants. Herbert Kritzer discusses this factor and particularly how a contingent fee arrangement may influence negotiation decisions.

❖ Herbert M. Kritzer, *Fee Arrangements and Negotiation*
21 L. & Socy. Rev. 341 (1987)

My central argument is that discussions of the settlement process, and particularly of manipulations of that process, must consider the interests of *all* involved in litigation. Regular participants in litigation are well aware of this point. In my series of interviews with corporate lawyers and their clients in Toronto regarding the impact of fees and fee shifting a number of respondents mentioned the importance of taking into account the interest of the opposing lawyer. For example, a litigation partner in a firm with one hundred lawyers said, "If you can satisfy the lawyer [with regard to his fee], you'll be a lot closer to settlement." A lawyer for a large retailer similarly stated that to achieve settlement, "you need to provide an incentive for the [opposing] lawyer." Yet despite the evidence that litigation lawyers do not selflessly ignore their own interests, little attention has been paid to how these interests affect settlement and negotiation.

I am not suggesting that lawyers engage in questionable actions for financial gain. The argument is more subtle: Lawyers, like all of us, when forced to make a choice for which there is no definitive answer, will tend to select the option that is in their own interest. In other words, the financial incentives of their work will often influence the decisions, and it is not coincidental that they will personally benefit from these choices. Thus, although the plaintiffs' bar may truly believe that the contingent fee is the poor man's key to the courthouse door, this belief is shaped by the fact that the key to the courthouse also brings clients — and therefore a livelihood — to the plaintiffs' lawyers. Elsewhere I have pointed out that the relationship between lawyers and clients is shaped by professional, personal, and business considerations, the last, at their most basic, meaning income (and income streams.) But what is the significance of this type of analysis for settlement and negotiation? . . .

Contingent fee lawyers in cases with modest amounts at stake have an incentive to arrive quickly at a settlement, even if that settlement is not the best for the client. Whether this means that the fee arrangement directly affects the amount of time the lawyer spends on settlement negotiations (although I could in fact find no systematic difference in time spent on such activities between hourly and contingent fee lawyers), the same theoretical considerations apply to the content of the actual negotiation. Specifically, since the contingent fee lawyer is to receive a share of the ultimate recovery, she has an incentive to see to it that the recovery can in fact be shared.

A contingent fee lawyer who sought nonmonetary resolutions of her clients' cases, even if those resolutions were better from the clients' perspectives, would soon go out of business unless some alternate payment method were available for such settlements (e.g., fee shifting, whereby the defendant pays the plaintiff's attorney for his time, or a central fund, created by taxing contingent fees, from which the lawyer could receive compensation).

. . . Although lawyers are professionals who are concerned with the needs and interests of their clients, their behavior is nonetheless influenced (note the use of *influenced* rather than *determined*) by the forces of economic rationality or necessity or both, and this influence is felt as well in the lawyers' means of negotiating. If we want lawyers to consider actively what Menkel-Meadow calls the problem-solving approaches to negotiation, we must insure that their livelihood is not dependent upon adversary approaches to negotiation.

Questions

13.   Might there be some settlements that are better from the client's perspective, but not necessarily in the economic interests of the plaintiff's lawyer? What is the meaning of the saying that "all contingent fee settlements need to be divisible by 3"?

14.   Do contingent fee arrangements create an attorney-client conflict of interest? Should they be considered unethical? Why or why not?

15.   Would Kritzer's suggestion, that contingent fees be replaced by a fee shifting method where the defendant pays the plaintiff's attorney for time spent or a tax on contingent fees to create a central lawyers' fee fund, eliminate attorney-client conflicts of interest in settlement or create new ones? Would you support these "reforms"?

C. Good Faith vs. Threats, Exposure, and Coercion

Although it can be hoped that lawyers will be retained to negotiate only when the client desires to reach an agreement and bargain in good faith, there may be occasions when settlement is not the goal or when compromise for purposes of agreement is not an option. On occasion a client may pursue negotiation for purposes of delay or distraction, to obtain information from a competitor, or to harass. As previously discussed, clients have the right to decide the purpose and objectives of negotiation, but lawyers can usually decline to represent a party or withdraw. Indeed, ethical rules may require the lawyer to withdraw if continued representation will result in violation of ethical rules. (See ABA Model Rule 1.16(a)(1).)

There is no general ethical duty to bargain in good faith, but if the parties have agreed by contract to negotiate in good faith, for example, before ending a business relationship or going to court, they may be held to their bargain. In some labor management disputes under the National Labor Relations Act, 29 U.S.C.A. 158(d), there may be a good faith negotiation requirement. Rules of court and court orders may also require "good faith" negotiation or mediation before a dispute will be heard.

Even if good faith in negotiation is not required, ethical rules and contract law limit certain types of "bad faith" bargaining. A prohibition against bad faith negotiation is indicated by ABA Model Rule 4.4, which states:

> "*Respect for Rights of Third Persons*: In representing a client, a lawyer shall not use means that have no substantial purpose other than to embarrass, delay, or burden a third person, or use methods of obtaining evidence that violate the legal rights of such a person."

Tort law, contract law, and criminal law may also restrict the use of threats, extortion, and some forms of coercion. However, threatening to file a civil lawsuit to resolve the matter in dispute when the lawyer has a good faith basis for the claim is not prohibited. (See Restatement, Second of Contracts, Sec. 175, Comment (b) (1981).) Indeed, every legal negotiation carries, at least, an implicit threat that if agreement is not reached, further action will be taken or alternatives will be pursued. Adversarial negotiations and pressure from clients may tempt lawyers to go further and use threats of unrelated legal action or exposure of wrongdoing if negotiation demands are not met. The law, rather than ethical rules, may be used to decide when threatening exposure of wrongdoing or a ruinous lawsuit becomes criminal extortion, and also when lying becomes fraud.

A threat by a lawyer to punch an opponent in the nose if a demand is not met is clearly unethical and criminal. A threat to do something adverse to your opponent, even if not unlawful, only for the purpose of gaining an advantage in a negotiation, presents more challenging issues. For example, deciding to expose or not expose an opposing lawyer's unethical behavior in conjunction with a negotiation may place you between the proverbial "rock and a hard place." Power imbalances may also create questions of intimidation in the negotiation process, as might the otherwise legitimate threat of filing a class action against a modest-sized company if monetary demands are not met. In addition to being ethically risky, threats may jeopardize the enforceability of a settlement because of duress or other contract grounds for voiding or rescinding agreements.

The article that follows addresses some of these issues and is included to help you understand that even though the limits of what lawyers can do in negotiations are murky, tort, contract, and criminal law do impose outer limits on negotiation conduct and communications. It explains negotiation constraints, particularly where there is unequal power.

❖ **Robert S. Adler and Elliot M. Silverstein,** *When David Meets Goliath: Dealing with Power Differentials in Negotiations*

5 Harv. Negot. L. Rev. 1 (2000)

. . . Although the superior bargaining power of one party, standing alone, does not generally provide the basis for invalidating an agreement, the law does set limits within which bargainers must operate. These limits apply both with respect to the terms that can be negotiated and to the methods one can use to influence an opponent to agree to the terms. They are premised on the assumption that at some point in the bargaining process, power advantages can produce inequities so pronounced that the law must step in to protect the weak. In negotiations involving power imbalances, most abuses arise when the stronger party, either through threats or other overt displays of power, intimidates the other into entering an agreement so one-sided that it offends reasonable sensibilities. Of course, not all bargaining abuses result from overt power displays. Some arise from shifting the balance of power by exploiting trust or employing deceit.

Depending on the nature of the abuse, the law may take different approaches — regulating modestly where "arm's length" conditions exist or expansively where a "special relationship" requires protection for particularly vulnerable individuals. Where special relationships exist, special protections apply.

A. Undue Influence

When a relationship of trust and dependency between two or more parties exists, the law typically polices the relationship closely and imposes especially stringent duties on the dominant parties. For example, although tort law generally imposes no obligations on citizens to assist those in danger, the courts take the opposite position when they determine that a special relationship exists. In those cases, the courts unhesitatingly find an affirmative duty to rescue.

Contract law imposes similar duties in the case of agreements involving undue influence in special relationships. Where one party — because of family position, business connection, legal authority or other circumstances — gains extraordinary trust from another party the courts will scrutinize any agreements between them with great care to ensure fairness. Common examples of special relationships include guardian-ward, trustee-beneficiary, agent-principal, spouses, parent-child, attorney-client, physician-patient, and clergy-parishioner. To treat negotiations in these settings as arm's length interactions would invite "unfair persuasion" by the dominant parties either through threats, deception, or misplaced trust. Accordingly, the law imposes special obligations on those who play the dominant role in such relationships, requiring them to exercise good faith and to make full disclosure of all critical facts when negotiating agreements with dependent parties. In determining whether a dominant party in a special relationship exerted undue influence, the courts generally look to the fairness of the contract, the availability of independent advice, and the vulnerability of the dependent party. An agreement entered into as a result of undue influence is voidable by the victim.

B. Protections in Arm's Length Transactions

Under the "bargain theory" of contracts, parties negotiate at arm's length to exchange consideration. An arm's length transaction is one in which the parties stand in no special relationship with each other, owe each other no special duties, and each acts in his or her own interest. The vast majority of contracts fall within the arm's length category, which means that no special obligations of disclosure, fair dealing or good faith are generally required. This is not to suggest that parties are free to operate without rules, but it does mean that they are accorded substantial leeway in negotiating contracts. They certainly maintain the freedom to assume even foolish and shortsighted contractual obligations, so long as they do so knowingly and voluntarily. Once one of the parties acts in a patently abusive manner, however, the law does provide protection, as, for example, with fraud, duress, and unconscionability.

1. Fraud

Negotiated agreements, to be binding, must be entered into by the parties in a knowing and voluntary manner. Lies undermine agreements by removing the "knowing" element from the bargain. That is, one induced by misrepresentations to purchase a relatively worthless item of personal property typically buys the product "voluntarily" — in fact, eagerly — with enthusiasm generated by the false promise of the product's value. The catch is that because of the defrauder's lies, the victim has unfairly lost the opportunity to "know" the precise nature of what he or she has bought. Lies of this nature clearly alter the normal contractual dynamic, unfairly shifting power from the victim to the defrauder. Because of the dramatic impact that fraud has on the power balance in negotiations, we necessarily review this doctrine.

In its classic formulation, common law fraud requires five elements: (1) a false representation of a material fact made by the defendant, (2) with knowledge or belief as to its falsity, (3) with an intent to induce the plaintiff to rely on the representations, (4) justifiable reliance on the misrepresentation by the plaintiff, and (5) damage or injury to the plaintiff by the reliance. Fraud entitles the victim to void the transaction and permits him or her to pursue restitution or tort damages. A false representation may be made in several ways — through a positive statement, through misleading conduct, or by concealing a fact that the defrauder has a duty to disclose....

2.   Duress

Coercion, whether express or implied, takes many forms. One party, for example, might threaten to take its business elsewhere if its terms are not met. Another might threaten to file suit if its financial claims are not resolved. Still another might insist that it will no longer provide a discount or expedited delivery if a deal cannot be struck. These threats, designed to exert pressure on an opponent to secure his or her cooperation, generally fall into a category that the law would consider to be hard bargaining, but not illegal. At some point, however, coercion becomes objectionable. How does one distinguish between proper and improper behavior? Unfortunately, there is no clear dividing line. As various commentators and courts have stated, threats per se are acceptable; only wrongful threats are forbidden. What makes one threat "wrongful" and another not depends on the circumstances of each case. To constitute duress, threats must be of a particularly virulent nature....

Threatened action need not be illegal — even acts otherwise legal may constitute duress if directed towards an improper goal. For example, a threat to bring a lawsuit — normally a legitimate form of coercion — becomes abusive if "made with the corrupt intent to coerce a transaction grossly unfair to the victim and not related to the subject of such proceedings." Similarly, a threat to release embarrassing, but true, information about another person, although abhorrent, would not constitute duress (in the form of blackmail) unless accompanied by an improper demand for financial or other favors.

Should negotiators with a decided power advantage feel inhibited from pushing for as hard a bargain as they can in light of the law of duress? Generally, no. Judging from the language in the courts' opinions, hard bargainers should have little to fear from the doctrine of duress. Nothing in the law of duress prevents negotiators from pushing to the limits of their bargaining power or from taking advantage of the economic vulnerabilities or bad luck of their opponents. Trouble arises only when a party makes threats that lapse into the illegal, immoral and unconscionable. Of greater impact on negotiators concerned about legal protections is the law of unconscionability, to which we now turn.

3. Unconscionability

The doctrine of unconscionability functions to protect bargainers of lesser power from overreaching by dominant parties. Invoked in a variety of cases under the Uniform Commercial Code and elsewhere, the term has never been precisely defined, no doubt to provide greater flexibility in its use. . . .

What is an unconscionable contract? Given that the UCC drafters deliberately avoided an explicit definition, one cannot simply and easily capture the concept. At a minimum, an unconscionable contract is one "such as no man in his senses and not under delusion would make on the one hand and no honest and fair man would accept on the other." Unconscionability seeks to prevent two evils: (1) oppression and (2) unfair surprise. In a seminal analysis, Professor Arthur Allen Leff labeled these two concepts "substantive" and "procedural" unconscionability, respectively. Substantive unconscionability includes the actual terms of the agreement; procedural unconscionability refers to the bargaining process between the parties. . . .

Virtually all cases in which unconscionability arises as an issue involve significant disparities in bargaining power, but that, standing alone, rarely justifies a finding of unconscionability according to most courts and commentators. What draws judicial fire is when the party endowed with superior bargaining power imposes an extremely unfair and one-sided agreement on the weaker. In effect, the stronger party oppresses the weaker party through the application of brute power, thereby removing any real "choice" from the victim. Accordingly, inequality of bargaining power seems a generally necessary, but not sufficient, condition of unconscionability. . . .

How concerned should a negotiator be — especially one with superior bargaining power — that pursuing an advantage in a contract will result in a court ruling that the agreement is unconscionable? Our best answer: some, but not much. For the most part, the courts have taken a cautious approach to finding unconscionability in negotiated agreements. The vast majority of successful unconscionability claims involve poor, often unsophisticated, consumers challenging oppressive adhesion contracts foisted on them by retail merchants or credit sellers. . . . No doubt this reflects the general view that persons of greater sophistication suffer less contractual abuse and need less protection. . . .

Questions

16. If you become aware that an opposing lawyer is lying about a material fact, like the amount of medical damages incurred by a client, what should you do? Must you report the lie to the Bar? Should you first confront the lawyer or state your intent to report? Might this be considered a threat? Must you wait until after the negotiation is completed to report the ethical breach?

17. Suppose during a lawsuit you receive a copy of a letter from your

opponent instructing one of their witnesses to lie under oath. May you use this letter in settlement negotiations? May you use the threat of a bar disciplinary proceeding or a criminal prosecution for obstruction of justice? In exchange for a favorable settlement, may you agree not to report the opponent's instructions? (See ABA Comm. on Ethics and Professional Responsibility, 1992.)

18.   There is a generally recognized privilege for statements made in the course of judicial proceedings. (See *Silberg v. Anderson*, 50 Cal. 3d 205 (1990), holding that a letter with threats of criminal prosecution sent in the course of judicial proceedings is privileged.) Should a threat of physical violence be covered by this privilege?

19.   Assume a client asks you to represent her against a prominent, wealthy man she claims had forced sex with her. She wants you to inform him that if he reasonably compensates her, she will not "go public." Would you accept this assignment, and, if so, how might you proceed? Do you risk criminal prosecution or a civil action against you for extortion? (See *Flatley v. Mauro*, 18 Cal.Rptr.3d 472 (2004).)

20.   The greatest power differentials in negotiation are associated with consumer cases and bargaining where one side is not represented by an attorney. Can undue influence and unconscionability in negotiations occur when all parties are represented by competent lawyers? By definition, if undue influence or unconscionability is found to void a settlement or transaction negotiated by lawyers, do incompetence and malpractice exist?

Problem 2

Your client is a small business tenant who is involved in a civil dispute with his landlord regarding whether the lease entitles him to use certain space in the basement of the building for the storage of inventory items. You have requested that the landlord give your client access to the space, but the landlord will not agree unless your client pays significantly more rent. During the course of negotiations you discover that the landlord has failed to maintain the property in accordance with local building codes, and this may subject him to criminal prosecution. Can you inform the landlord that you intend to report him to the appropriate authorities if he fails to agree to your settlement terms? (See Peter H. Geraghty, Making Threats, ABA 2008, *www.abanet.org/media/youraba/200810/article11*.)

D.   Ethics Reform and New Forms of Practice

1.   *Reform Proposals and Guidelines*

The absence of a rule explicitly prohibiting deception by lawyers during negotiation has disturbed many who feel that a change in lawyer ethics is necessary to promote honesty and correct the lawyer-liar image. For decades there has been a debate within the Bar about prohibiting false statements of fact in negotiation, whether material or not. The ABA, when drafting the Model Rules in the early 1980s, considered requiring that lawyers be "fair" in negotiations and not permit "unconscionable" agreements, but these requirements, following much debate, were rejected as untenable. Some believe the ethics requirements should be enhanced to promote honesty and professional integrity. For others, requiring truthfulness in all matters relating to negotiation would be naive and undermine the enforceability of negotiated agreements, particularly when truthfulness regarding nonmaterial facts is not required of those who are not lawyers. An array of proposals has been urged to formally change Model Rule of Professional Conduct 4.1, which prohibits only lying about material facts, and Comment 2, which acknowledges and does not disapprove the use of deception about bottom lines and puffery about value. The rule would be easy to rewrite, but the revisions could be difficult to sell and enforce. (For a specific proposal, see Alfini, 1999.)

The Litigation Section of the ABA in 2002 approved Ethical Guidelines for Settlement Negotiations. Although the Guidelines do not change the ABA Model Rules, they do suggest best practices and aspirational goals that go beyond the rules regarding honesty in negotiation. (See *www.abanet.org/ litigation/ethics/settlementnegotiations.*)

The ABA's Commission on Evaluation of the Rules of Professional Conduct, known as the "Ethics 2000 Commission," resulted in a slight change to Comment 2 of Rule 4.1. The official comment now states that "a party's intentions as to an acceptable settlement of a claim are *ordinarily* not in the category of facts" where candor can be expected (see Mahoney, 2002).

The prevailing view is opposed to requiring fairness as a matter of lawyer ethics and against prohibiting lawyers from making false statements regarding "nonmaterial" facts. This practical, minimalist view of regulating lawyer negotiation is rooted in our adversary legal system and a lawyer's duty to his client of loyalty and confidentiality.

2.   *Collaborative Law, Cooperative Practice, and Mindfulness*

A movement by some lawyers to commit to a nonadversarial, interest-based approach and more openness in how they represent clients may have a more profound impact on lawyering ethics and the negotiation of disputes than changes in ethics rules alone. The discontent with the practice of adversarial law, fueled in part by the tension created between the expectation of zealous representation and the desire for personal integrity, has caused some lawyers to explore other models of practice. These efforts have been thoughtful and courageous, as well as controversial. Individual lawyers have reshaped their practices by emphasizing aspects of representation that they find more comfortable and rewarding. We have previously covered the problem-solving approach in contrast to adversarial negotiations. This approach changes the practice paradigm and has implications for personal standards of professional integrity.

Some lawyers have gone further, forming regional groups of practitioners who pledge between them to abstain from litigation and adhere to enhanced standards in their interactions. The most notable example is the collaborative law (CL) movement in domestic relations, where subscribing lawyers contract with clients about standards and limits of representation. A collaborative lawyer will not represent the client if the case goes to court and will not mislead another lawyer during negotiations. (For an explanation of the collaborative practice model, see Lawrence, 2003; Tesler, 2001.)

The basic elements of CL, as explained by Pauline Tesler, one of its founders, are:

- Each party is represented by separate counsel specially trained to provide effective collaborative representation.
- All parties and attorneys sign a binding participation agreement providing that the attorneys are retained solely to facilitate reasonable, efficient settlement of all issues (a "limited purpose" retention).
- The agreement commits all participants to good-faith negotiations, without the threat of or resort to litigation during the pendency of the collaborative process. All parties agree to provide early, voluntary, continuing disclosure of all information that a reasonable decision maker would need to make an informed decision about each issue in the dispute. If a party refuses to disclose information that counsel considers relevant and material to the dispute, collaborative counsel commit to withdraw and/or terminate the process. In other words, although collaborative lawyers remain bound by attorney-client privilege, they will not assist a client to participate in bad faith in the collaborative process or to misuse the process for undue advantage.
- Clients are free to terminate the process at any time and seek third-party dispute resolution, including litigation, but if any party does so, all attorneys are disqualified from participating in any way in nonconsensual third-party proceedings brought by any party to the dispute against any other party or parties.
- If the process is terminated and litigation follows, the collaborative agreement may give the court jurisdiction to make awards of attorneys'

fees and costs against any party who has misused the collaborative process for delay, deception, or other bad-faith purposes. The collaborative lawyers, however, could not be witnesses in such proceedings.

(See Tessler, 2003.)

CL practice is designed to encourage parties to stay in the negotiation process, but this may cause some clients to feel stuck, having invested time and money and then being at risk of losing their lawyer if the collaborative process terminates and the conflict continues. Ethical issues have been raised about attorneys limiting their practice to provide clients with representation only if the other side collaborates. Several states, including Kentucky, Pennsylvania, and New Jersey, have examined CL practice in light of Model Rule of Professional Conduct 1.2(c), which requires informed client consent before lawyers can limit the scope of their practice, and Rule 1.7, which prohibits representation if there is a conflict of interest with the lawyer's responsibilities to others. The CL lawyer's commitment to other CL attorneys, as well as her own interest in a limited practice, raises conflict of interest questions. Several ethics opinions have found that these two provisions create a duty for a CL lawyer to assess whether the limitation and commitment are in the client's best interest and screen cases for CL appropriateness. Clients must be clearly informed about the risks of the process. Although considerable effort has been made by proponents of CL to expand the practice to non-family civil matters, the effort has not met with much success (see Lande and Mosten, 2010; Peppet, 2008). The Colorado Bar Association's Ethics Committee ruled in 2004 that the disqualification provision, a hallmark of CL, violates the lawyer's duty of client loyalty and creates a non-waivable conflict of interest:

> It is the opinion of this Committee that the practice of Collaborative Law violates Rule 1.7(b) of Colorado Rules of Professional Conduct insofar as a lawyer participating in the process enters into a contractual agreement with the opposing party requiring the lawyer to withdraw in the event that the process is unsuccessful. The Committee further concludes that pursuant to Colo.RPC 1.7(c) the client's consent to waive this conflict cannot be validly obtained.

The comment to Rule 1.7 explains:

> Loyalty to a client is also impaired when a lawyer cannot consider, recommend or carry out an appropriate course of action for the client because of the lawyer's other responsibilities or interests. The conflict in effect forecloses alternatives that would otherwise be available to the client.

Despite the controversy over the withdrawal aspect, or perhaps because of it, the Uniform Law Commission in 2009 voted to adopt the Uniform Collaborative Law Act. The Act recognizes CL as an ADR process. It also articulates requirements for informed client consent to participate and a duty upon lawyers to protect the safety of clients from domestic violence during the collaborative process. The Act was sent to the ABA House of Delegates in 2010 for its consideration and, if approved, was to be sent to states for adoption (see Schepard, 2009, *http://lawprofessors.typepad.com/family_law/2009/week30/index.html*).

A variant on CL is known as "cooperative law." Interestingly, the Colorado ethics opinion distinguished cooperative law from CL. It found that cooperative law is not per se unethical because it "lacks the disqualification agreement found in Collaborative Law." As explained by Professor John Lande, its principal advocate, cooperative practice, also involves a "participation agreement" between lawyers and parties setting out a negotiation process with a goal of reaching a resolution that is fair for all parties. These agreements vary and may include terms committing to negotiate in good faith, act respectfully toward each other, disclose all relevant information, use jointly retained experts, protect confidentiality of communications, and refrain from formal discovery and contested litigation during negotiation. The participation agreement may provide for use of a mediator or a "cooling off" period before engaging in contested litigation. It may also state that if the parties do litigate, the lawyers would focus solely on the merits of the issues. The process generally begins before the parties file a lawsuit or soon afterward. The process typically involves "four-way meetings" with the parties and lawyers, although some negotiation may be directly between the lawyers or parties when appropriate.

The main difference between cooperative practice and CL, as noted in the Colorado ethics opinion, is that the participation agreement in cooperative practice does not include a "disqualification agreement" or "withdrawal agreement," so that if any party chooses to litigate (or threatens litigation), the lawyers are not disqualified from representing the parties, and there is no need to hire new lawyers. In addition to this distinction, there may be other differences in tailoring the procedure to the particular circumstances. For example, cooperative practitioners may not use four-way meetings as much or involve as many other professionals in the meetings as in collaborative practice. (See Lande, 2009.)

Another developing concept and practice that may influence how some lawyers negotiate is "mindfulness" in lawyering. Although difficult to simply describe and pigeonhole, mindfulness derives from meditative qualities that put immediate demands in a larger perspective. Mindfulness builds individual capacity for non-judgmental awareness of ourselves and all around us. It amounts to paying attention, being present, and developing insight through concentration. It is a way of being that focuses the practitioner on the big picture and not only on the discrete transaction of the moment. Mindfulness redirects the context of practice to the integrity of the person and the system, rather than the immediate needs of the situation. Mindfulness focused on ethical decision making and compassion is not necessarily the opposite of adversarialness, but they may be difficult to reconcile. (See generally Riskin, 2006.)

Mindfulness is finding its way into law school curricula, law firm programs, and legal publications. An issue of the Harvard Negotiation Law

Review was dedicated to meditation and mindfulness in the practice of ADR. One commentator in that Review, Professor Scott Peppet, takes on the logical extension of mindfulness, perhaps tongue-in-cheek, to reach an analogy between the mindful lawyer and a saint or holy man and then questions whether two saints could negotiate. His article helps put our earlier consideration of Model Rule 4.1 in perspective and recasts the question of whether a lawyer can reconcile personal integrity with the conduct allowed, if not required, by Model Rule 4.1.

❖ **Scott R. Peppet,** Mindfulness in the Law and ADR: Can Saints Negotiate?

---

7 Harv. Negot. L. Rev. 83 (2002)

. . . [I]magine that, at the extreme, a diligent mindfulness practitioner might eventually reach a state of complete dedication to an ethical life. I will call this person a "saint" because she adopts a more conscientious stance toward her relations with the world and others than most of us will ever achieve. Our saint would also have to be sufficiently strong-willed to live up to her moral commitments. She must have developed herself to the point that the contingencies of her life — her history, attachments, psychology, and emotions — no longer lead her to act against these deeply-held beliefs. She is so mindful as to be somewhat frightening.

What sort of ethical commitments would our saint adopt? For the sake of argument, I will assert that at the very least such a person would commit to both honesty and fairness, resolving neither to deceive nor to take advantage of other human beings for her own ends and to respect and take others' interests into account. There is good reason to believe that a very mindful person would adopt such a saintly view of life. Even without turning extensively to religious doctrine, one can imagine that our saint would be consistently non-partisan when it came to her own and others' interests. . . .

Consider the negotiating standards of two holy men, one a willing buyer and the other a willing seller. If their personal commitments to holiness prevented them from making the slightest misrepresentation or from engaging in any abuse of their bargaining positions, how would the ultimate outcome of their negotiations differ from the outcome achieved by two lawyer negotiators? If deceit truly is inherent to negotiation, the outcome achieved by the holy men could not be defined as the product of a negotiation. . . .

Not everyone agrees with this characterization, but it is certainly common. Perhaps the best example of this sort of thinking is, again, Model Rule 4.1's permission of misrepresentations about reservation price. According to the Rule's Comments, misleading statements of this sort are permitted because "under generally accepted conventions in negotiation, certain types of statements ordinarily are not taken as statements of material fact." Although the Rules do not say so explicitly, this Comment seems to imply that barring all types of misrepresentation would demand too much — it would make negotiation as we normally understand it impossible.

I disagree with this view . . . . Although many negotiators may deceive and manipulate, I see nothing that requires one to do so, nor do I think that one can be effective only by doing so. Negotiation requires parties to manage different and sometimes conflicting interests to determine whether a jointly-created outcome can be found that is more satisfying than any self-help alternative. Two saints could honestly disclose their alternatives and reservation values, their interests and priorities, and still face a variety of challenging decisions regarding how best to maximize achievable joint gain and divide the pie. Even for the enlightened there would likely be no easy answer as to whether to give more of the economic surplus in a transaction to the person who needed it more, wanted it more, or deserved it more. Two saints might disagree about how to classify a used car in the "blue book" scheme, or about when an employment agreement should vest an executive's stock options. I see no reason to redescribe their interaction over these matters as something other than negotiation merely because they chose to avoid dishonesty or manipulation.

I must make one caveat, however. One can imagine a person who becomes so universal in her views — so detached from the particulars of her individual position — that she no longer values her own interests at all. Her only interest becomes to serve others' interests. Although it is difficult to imagine how two such people could interact (wouldn't they merely circle each other endlessly, each trying to help the other?), I think the introduction of even one such person into what would otherwise be a negotiation does require redescription of the interaction as something other than bargaining. In this extreme circumstance there would not be two people with differing or conflicting interests; only one with interests and another with a desire to serve. There would be nothing to negotiate about — person A would express needs and person B would satisfy them to the best of B's ability.

Finally, one might object that lawyers have a duty to compete. If a lawyer refuses to do so because of ethical commitments that include consideration of an opponent's interests, then even if we cannot redescribe that lawyer's interactions as something other than negotiation, perhaps we should simply decide that the person can no longer be a lawyer. Robert Condlin, for example, has written that lawyers "must use any legally available move or procedure helpful to a client's bargaining position. Among other things, this means that all forms of leverage must be exploited, inflated demands made, and private information obtained and used whenever any of these actions would advance the client's stated objectives. . . ." If negotiating lawyers will not play the game, they should be disqualified as players.

Although it opens yet another difficult line of argument, I think it unlikely that a saint, or even just a very reflective person, would decide, like Condlin, to prioritize client loyalty over the saint's already-discussed ethical commitments. As Riskin explains, mindfulness loosens one's attachments — one's loyalties. This is, again, what suggests that these practices might aid in adopting a more universal perspective on moral questions. It also suggests, however, that a loyalty-driven ethic, peculiar to one's particular duties to a particular client, will be relatively unpersuasive to our saint as compared to the basic obligations to honesty and fairness. . . .

Questions

21. How might a "disqualification agreement," as used in collaborative practice, benefit a client?

22. What might be the barriers to the acceptance of collaborative law in general civil cases?

23. If cooperative practice does not involve a disqualification agreement, how does it differ from more traditional practice by competent attorneys, who attempt to negotiate settlements before initiating litigation?

24. Would a "saint," as described by Professor Peppet, who negotiates on behalf of a client, be subject to discipline by the Bar for failing to make the client's interests a priority and for not being a zealous advocate? Would you retain such a saint as your lawyer for purposes of negotiation?

25. Would you change Rule 4.1 and the comments to it? If so, what would you change and why?

26. A corporate defendant may desire to restrict a plaintiff's lawyer from representing other plaintiffs with similar claims or may feel vulnerable to future lawsuits based on information the plaintiff's lawyer obtained through discovery. As part of a negotiated settlement, the defendant in this situation may request that the plaintiff's attorney agree not to represent other plaintiffs with similar claims. Such a provision would contravene Model Rule 5.6, which provides, "A lawyer shall not participate in offering or making . . . an agreement in which a restriction on the lawyer's right to practice is part of the settlement. . . . " What do you think is the rationale and justification for this prohibition?

27. Is the "mirror test" the ultimate guide for negotiation ethics? That test takes into account your own values following a completed negotiation by asking, "Can you look at yourself in the mirror and feel okay?"

CHAPTER

8

The Law of Negotiation

A. How Law Impacts Negotiation

The purpose of most negotiation by lawyers is to reach an agreement to settle a claim or transact a business deal. The resulting agreement is a contract intended to be enforceable. Contract law is in play during negotiations and becomes the focus when enforcing or challenging a negotiated agreement. The basic contract principles of offer, acceptance, and consideration are the foundation of understanding the law of negotiated agreements. When a negotiated agreement is challenged, it is most often on contract-based grounds, such as failure of consideration, fraud, misrepresentation, or duress.

A related legal issue in negotiations conducted by lawyers is what authority the lawyer, as agent, has to commit the client, as principal, to an agreement. Questions about a lawyer's authority to represent a party's interests in settlement negotiations and bind the client can surface when a settlement or transaction is challenged. Case law and statutory limits on remedies and lawyer's fees can also result in collateral litigation, particularly in class actions where negotiations may create a conflict between the interests of the plaintiff class and its attorneys. (See, e.g., *Evans v. Jeff D.*, 475 U.S. 717, 106 S. Ct. 1531 (1986).) The imprecise drafting of settlement agreements may create subsequent litigation about what was covered and what was mutually intended as a settlement. The law relating to releases, confidentiality provisions, and promises to do or not do something in the future can be critical in fashioning a lasting negotiated settlement.

Most settlement negotiation occurs in the "shadow of the law," in the sense that the prospect of the law of the case and what would happen in court if the claim is litigated influence bargaining (see Mnookin and Kornhauser, 1979). The substantive law of the matter being negotiated affects lawyer negotiations and forms the backdrop for bargained outcomes. So the entire law school curriculum bears in some way on the process, substance, and outcomes of negotiations by lawyers.

We will focus on four areas in which the law may shape negotiation conduct. First, negotiated settlements can be encouraged by allocating attorneys' fees and litigation costs based on the reasonableness of rejected settlement offers. We examine both statutory and case law regarding offers of settlement and fee shifting. Second, strategic moves by lawyers to settle with only some of several defendants have spawned appellate decisions about the consequences when some defendants settle and others do not. We look at "Mary Carter" agreements, as these secret, selective settlements have become known. Third, because a settlement agreement is a contract, this chapter reviews how the law may limit the extent to which the settlement can be enforced if it is the result of fraud, misrepresentation, or duress. Finally, lawyers must be aware that what they do or fail to do as negotiators for clients can lead to charges of professional malpractice. We include material on potential claims by disappointed clients against their lawyers after the negotiation is concluded.

Other areas of law that can significantly impact negotiations are not covered here, but should be noted. Insurance coverage issues and the role of insurance in paying settlement agreements loom in the background of tort and other settlement negotiations, but this topic cannot be adequately presented in a general ADR course. Similarly, the tax aspects of settlements, which can influence negotiation tactics and outcomes, must be saved for a more specialized course. There are also distinct legal issues and possible reporting requirements regarding settlements when bankruptcy lurks in the shadows or when the negotiation may impact publicly traded securities. Specific factors of which negotiators must be aware may also exist in domestic relations, environmental, and civil rights cases, particularly when courts must approve the settlement. Class actions create unique issues about the fairness of settlements and the need for court approval. Settlement discussions may postpone filing an action and a question may arise about whether negotiation can stop a statute of limits from running and barring the claim. Finally, because the law generally encourages negotiation and settlement, evidentiary rules preclude the use at trial of some statements and conduct resulting from efforts to compromise and resolve disputes (see Federal Rule of Evidence 408). What follows is intended to help familiarize you with a few critical areas in which the law does matter in lawyer negotiations and to help you spot potential red flags.

B.   Offers of Settlement and Fee Shifting

1.   *The American Approach*

Attorney's fees and costs of bringing or defending a lawsuit are a major factor in negotiating the settlement of a dispute. Whether legal action is threatened or pending, each side must consider in its risk analysis the potential costs of court proceedings. Favorable verdicts must be discounted by the amount required to obtain them. Modest victories in court can be dwarfed by the costs expended, particularly for attorney's fees. Anticipation of litigation costs affect reservation price calculations and can have a profound influence on negotiations.

In the United States the general rule is that each party pays its own legal expenses. This rule is modified by statute for some causes of action, like civil rights cases, or by pre-dispute contractual agreements. In contrast to the "American rule," England and most of Europe impose expenses on the losing party by awarding costs to the prevailing party. The "English rule," as this approach is known, tends to discourage litigation and increase the incentive to settle, particularly for those of limited means, by increasing the costs of losing. "Loser pays" legislative proposals in the United States have been favored by business defendants as part of "tort reform" to discourage frivolous lawsuits.

One problem with "loser pays" is defining who is the "loser." For example. is the person who obtains a verdict of $10,000, after bringing a lawsuit claiming damages of $1 million and rejecting an offer of $100,000, a winner or loser? A modified loser-pays approach is to allow a defendant to offer a judgment against itself for a designated amount. This offer, if not accepted, then becomes the benchmark to decide who the winner is at trial. This approach, known as an "offer of judgment," is embodied in Federal Rule of Civil Procedure (FRCP) 68, which has many state counterparts and variants. Pursuant to this rule, a plaintiff who rejects the defendant's formal, unconditional settlement offer, made within a specified time prior to trial, and is awarded less than the offered amount, is responsible for the defendant's court cost and fees incurred after the date of the offer. It is important to note that court costs and fees, as used in the rule, do not include actual attorney's fees, but may include certain discovery expenses from the time the offer is made, as well as statutory costs. Although the cost-shifting mechanism of FRCP 68 is available only for defendants, it is thought to provide an incentive for more reasonable offers of settlement.

Offers of judgment under Rule 68 can also be used strategically in negotiations and can be used to signal information in both directions. Consider the use of a cost-shifting offer and counteroffer, as well as attorney-client decision making, in the following story of a medical malpractice case against Dr. Wallace Bondurant, described as "rich, influential and above the law — a selfish crusader determined to save his career from the courts, regardless of the consequences" (from the back cover of *Harmful Intent*).

❖ **Baine Kerr,** *HARMFUL INTENT*

73, Jove Books (2000)

He was stunned by the statutory offer of settlement. . . .

Not its amount, $60,000, insult-level, or the accompanying disparagement of Moss's case, or the tactic. Basteen presented the offer under the costs statute that provided that if not accepted within ten days all defense costs from that point forward would be assessed against the plaintiff and her attorney if she fared more poorly at trial. It was a standard Basteen ploy that forced plaintiff's lawyers to explain to clients the statute's mighty downsides, driving a wedge in their relationship and intimidating fainter hearts, colder feet, or weaker knees than Terry Winter's.

What blew Moss away was Bondurant's having authorized any settlement at all. . . .

To Bondurant, settlement implied an admission of professional unworthiness. Never would he authorize a dime.

But Basteen could not have faxed the offer without Bondurant's consent. Moss thought again of the look in his eyes at his office. The timing was also telling, eleven days before his deposition. What did he not want to talk about?

Moss was ethically required to run through with his client the offer and the risks of the statutory costs award if they did worse than sixty grand with a jury. . . .

"Terry. Bondurant wants to settle."

"Settle what?"

"Your case. He will pay you money if you dismiss your lawsuit against him."

It was a formulation that apparently had not occurred to her. "Is that good news?"

Moss explained the offer, the sixty thousand, the requirement of confidentiality, that the ball was in their court, he needed to respond, and quickly. He gave her the rap about the statute and potential defense costs award. "What do I tell him?"

"You're the lawyer."

"I can't make this call. Ethical rule. I make recommendation only. You have to decide. It needs to be an informed decision, so I explain the facts and the tactics, give you my opinion, and you tell me what to do."

"*I* tell *you* what to do?"

"I advise. You decide."

"You are s___ me." There was a period of contemplation that made Moss a little nervous. "You do all this work for which I'm paying nothing and I still call the shots?"

"Some shots. The big ones. I s___ you not."

"Wow."

"But I'm not working for free, Terry. Payday comes at settlement time. One third plus costs are reimbursed, which would leave you barely half of this, maybe thirty-five thousand. So you need to reject it. It's an opener. There's much more money there."

"O.K. Tell him to stick it."

"How about a counter?"

"I don't know. What do you think?"

"Something big, round, and fat."

"Tell him I'll walk away for a cool million. Hear that, girls?"

"My recommendation exactly."

Question

1. What message was the defendant, Dr. Bondurant, sending with this offer "under the rule?" Is this an effective way to initiate settlement negotiations?

---

2. *Rule 68 and Its Expansion*

There are explicit and implicit requirements for making an FRCP 68 offer of judgment. Failure to follow the requirements can defeat the recovery of costs and have adverse consequences. The principal requirements to invoke FRCP 68 and most of its state counterparts include

- The offer must be in writing.
- The offer must be served more than ten days before the trial begins (when the actual hearing commences), although the time requirement can vary state by state.
- The terms and amount of the offer must be clear.
- The acceptance must be in writing and unconditional.

Once an offer of judgment is made, it is irrevocable until the trial begins and it is then considered withdrawn and inadmissible as evidence. Because the offer is treated as unconditional, there is no relief to a defendant for a unilateral mistake or misstated offer. On occasion this can result in a windfall for an accepting plaintiff. In *BMW of North America, Inc. v. Krathen*, 471 So. 2d 585 (1985), BMW offered a written settlement in the amount a purchaser paid for a new car claimed to be a "lemon." The plaintiff accepted the offer, which was silent about returning the car. The Florida Court of Appeals affirmed the trial court's ruling that the offer could not be clarified or withdrawn. The purchaser was entitled to keep the full amount offered for settlement and the car.

The important question of how an FRCP 68 settlement offer affects a statutory right to attorney's fees was answered by the Supreme Court in *Marek v. Chesny*, 473 U.S. 1, 105 S. Ct. 3012 (1985). The plaintiff brought a civil rights cause of action pursuant to a federal statute that provides attorney fees if the plaintiff "prevails." The rejected FRCP 68 offer of a lump sum judgment was more than plaintiff's eventual recovery of damages, but less than the total of damages added to recoverable fees, including attorney's fees, at the end of trial. The Court was asked to decide if the right to statutory attorney fees was lost when the judgment obtained for damages was less than the rejected FRCP 68 offer. The majority held that post-offer costs and fees recovered were not part of the amount to be compared with the FRCP 68 settlement offer and, therefore, plaintiff's attorney's fees were not recoverable.

Justice Brennan in his dissent in *Marek* noted that the Judicial Conference, which proposes the wording of the Federal Rules, and Congress have on multiple occasions considered amending FRCP 68 to include attorney's fees, as well as other costs, and to make the same mechanism available to plaintiffs as well as defendants. Congressional bills continue to propose expansion of FRCP 68 to increase its impact on promoting settlement. This ongoing interest in amending FRCP 68 is prompted, in part, by a sense that in its current form FRCP 68 is not enough of an incentive in the negotiating process to make a meaningful difference in settlement rates and fails to shift enough expense risk to plaintiffs if they reject an offer. Although the frequency with which FRCP 68 is invoked in negotiating lawsuit settlements is not regularly tracked, its incidence of use is thought to be relatively light.

On the other hand, increasing the economic incentive or coercion for plaintiffs to settle may diminish access to courts by less wealthy plaintiffs attempting to right wrongs or pursue public interest causes. This concern, along with the complexities of expanding FRCP 68, has defeated attempts to broaden the Federal Rule. However, the beat goes on to promote more negotiated settlements by increasing settlement incentives and litigation disincentives. The issue is sometimes framed in terms of putting more "teeth" in FRCP 68.

Experimentation at the state level provides experience that may pave the way for change to FRCP 68. Alaska has adopted an offer of judgment rule that allows an award of attorney's fees in most cases. A declining percentage of the offerer's attorney's fees are awarded according to how long after discovery is completed the offer is made. Arizona and Nevada allow attorney fees on a more restrictive basis in their variations on FRCP 68. California, in section 998 of its Civil Procedure Code, allows plaintiffs as well as defendants to make cost-shifting offers of judgment that also apply to arbitration proceedings. California has experimented with adding attorney's fees to costs as part of its offer of judgment rule, but on a pilot project basis in only two counties (see Summer, 2003).

Questions

2. Does the Court's holding in *Marek* defeat the incentive to bring civil
    rights cases as intended by Congress when it provided for recovery
    of plaintiffs' attorneys' fees?

3. Could some of the problems of determining if an FRCP 68 offer was
    better than the outcome at trial be avoided by requiring that the
    offer must be at least 25 percent greater than the final judgment?
    Would this approach be fairer to the plaintiff when confronted with
    deciding to accept or reject an offer of settlement? How might
    such a requirement affect the negotiation dynamic? (A similar
    25-percent margin of error proposal was part of a 1995 ABA task
    force package of suggested changes to FRCP 68. Some state statutes
    and court rules provide for a 10-percent differential.)

4. Earlier in Chapter 3, you read about loss aversion and the role it can
    play in influencing negotiators. Professor Ed Sherman suggests
    "that a well heeled defendant is less likely to be deterred from
    defending a weak suit by the threat of having to pay its opponent's
    attorneys' fees than a plaintiff from prosecuting a possibly merito-
    rious suit. Since plaintiffs are generally more risk averse than defen-
    dants, a 'loser pays' rule impacts disproportionately on plaintiffs'
    access to the courts" (Sherman, 1998, p. 1863). Is it convincing to
    you that well-heeled defendants are less risk averse than less finan-
    cially well-off plaintiffs?

5. You also read earlier about the tendency of parties and lawyers to be
    overly optimistic about the strength of their case and their chance
    of winning. If both sides in a case are confident about their chance
    of prevailing, does a "loser pays" rule promote or impede settle-
    ment? Are both sides likely to insist on more in their negotiations
    because each believes the other will have to pay all costs and fees fol-
    lowing trial?

6. Do the statutes allowing attorney's fees to prevailing plaintiffs in
    civil rights, private attorney general, and environmental suits create
    ethical dilemmas for attorneys negotiating settlement of these
    cases? Often, attorneys negotiate the amount of statutorily allowed
    fees at the same time they seek substantive payments for their cli-
    ents. The defendant may seek trade-offs of lower attorney's fees, or
    waiver of fees, in exchange for a higher payment to the client. This
    principal-agent conflict can pit client interests against those of the
    lawyer. The Supreme Court addressed this issue in *Evans v. Jeff D.*,
    475 U.S. 717, and held that the plaintiff's waiver of statutory attor-
    ney fees to obtain a better settlement for his client would not be set

aside and that the trial court could consider the propriety of such a trade-off on a case-by-case basis. Is the ethical dilemma greater for the plaintiff's attorney confronted with a coercive offer to waive or reduce fees to obtain a better settlement for her client or for the defendant's attorney whose client insists that the trade-off be proposed? Do you feel that such proposals for a fee waiver or reduction should be ethically prohibited?

3.   Does FRCP 68 Create More Risk Taking Rather Than Less?

The study referred to in Chapter 5 of 4,532 civil litigation cases over a 44-year period was based on California Code of Civil Procedure Section 998, the California equivalent of FRCP 68, intended to encourage settlement by financially penalizing parties whose trial result is worse than the settlement offer made by an adversary. That study shows that Section 998 inspired offers could be counterproductive. Parties who received settlement offers under Section 998 were more likely to take aggressive settlement positions, resulting in financially adverse outcomes, than were those in the study who didn't receive such offers. The decision error rate (defined as getting less at trial than the pretrial offer) for plaintiffs who risked the imposition of statutory financial penalties for not accepting written settlement offers was 83 percent, compared with 61 percent for plaintiffs who did not receive such offers. Similarly, defendants faced with statutory penalties for unreasonable settlement positions exhibited a decision error rate of 46 percent, compared to an error rate of 22 percent for defendants who did not negotiate under the threat of statutory penalties. These findings complement other empirical and experimental studies indicating that legislation intended to increase settlement rates or curb risk-taking settlement negotiation behavior may be ineffective. Whether this particular California statutory procedure provokes risk-taking behavior, the co-authors caution, is unclear, as other factors may cause the high decision error rates associated with the procedure (see Kiser et al., 2008).

Problem 1

You are serving as a representative of the Law Student Section on an ABA task force to suggest revisions to FRCP 68, which has not been substantively changed since 1946. The task force is composed of attorneys representing plaintiffs and defendants, as well as several judges. The judges report that the use of FRCP 68 appears to be declining. Several amendments to the Rule have been proposed, including adding attorney's fees to costs when the Rule is invoked, creating mutuality by allowing plaintiffs to propose an FRCP 68–triggering settlement, and requiring a 10 percent differential between the judgment and the settlement offer. What, if any, changes would you support and why? What additional information would you find helpful? Are there any other amendments to FRCP 68 that you might suggest?

C. Mary Carter Agreements

Negotiation between a plaintiff and multiple defendants can get legally and ethically complex. When one or more of multiple defendants with joint and several liability settles with a plaintiff and the others do not, it is commonly referred to as a "Mary Carter" or sliding-scale agreement. The settling defendant typically makes a deal with the plaintiff on the maximum amount that defendant will pay, regardless of the trial outcome or later settlement by plaintiffs with other defendants. The agreement also allows a decrease in the settling defendant's payment if the plaintiff obtains more from all defendants combined than the total amount of damages (sliding scale). In other words, the settling defendant caps his liability while potentially benefiting from plaintiff's success against the remaining defendants. It is possible that the settling defendant will pay nothing if plaintiff collects from the other defendants the full amount of damages (a "zero bottom" settlement.)

Mary Carter agreements are named after the Florida case of *Booth v. Mary Carter Paint Company,* 202 So. 2d 8 (Fla. App. 1967) in which the plaintiff, Booth, brought a negligence action against multiple defendants for the motor vehicle death of his wife. During settlement negotiations, the defense counsel for two of the defendants made a deal with the plaintiff, separately from Mary Carter Paint Company, also a defendant in the case, as to the maximum amount that they would pay. The signing defendants were not released from liability and remained in the case, which was tried to a jury, unaware of the settlement agreement. Mary Carter Paint Company lost its post-trial objections to the secret settlement deal, which could have resulted in it paying the entire settlement (but did not). The Florida Court of Appeal upheld the partial settlement agreement.

Mary Carter agreements typically involve four major features:

1. The plaintiff is guaranteed a certain amount of recovery from the settling defendant[s].

2. The dollar liability of the settling defendant[s] is limited to the guaranteed amount and may be reduced by plaintiff's recovery from other defendants.
3. The agreement between the settling defendant and the plaintiff is kept secret from the jury and often from the nonsettling defendants.
4. The settling defendant remains in the lawsuit.

Although a few states have banned Mary Carter agreements, most allow some form of this negotiated partial settlement, even if on a case-by-case basis or referred to by another name. In Arizona, for example, this type of selective settlement is known as a "Gallagher covenant," from the case of *City of Tucson v. Gallagher*, 14 Ariz. App. 385, 483 P.2d 798 (1971). California relies on the wording of a state statute (CCP 877 and 877.6) to allow "sliding scale recovery agreements," provided the value of the settlement indicates it was entered in "good faith." As the California Supreme Court explained in *Abbot Ford, Inc. v. The Superior Court of Los Angeles County; Ford Motor Co.*, 43 Cal. 3d 858 (1987), the negotiated cap amount and other financial obligations must be within a reasonable range of the settling defendant's proportional share of liability.

One reason for the California requirement of "good faith" or proportionality is that a Mary Carter agreement between a plaintiff and one of multiple defendants stops a codefendant/tortfeasor with joint and several liability from cross-complaining or suing the settling defendant for contribution. The plaintiff may want to keep secret from the jury that one of multiple defendants has settled or capped their payment to the defendant. This desire for secrecy is to avoid the "empty chair" defense, where the missing defendant will be blamed by the other defendants as the cause of plaintiff's loss. The plaintiff will prefer to keep the secretly settling defendant in the case and obtain favorable testimony from the settling defendant, who still appears to be adverse to the plaintiff even though their interests are now aligned. This presents a policy question of whether the jury should know about the new complementary interests between the plaintiff and the settling defendant, who may pay less if the nonsettling defendants are required to pay more. (See *Alcala Co., Inc. v. S. Ct.*, 49 Cal. 4th 1308, 1317, 57 Cal. 2d 349, 354 (1996).)

D.   Common Law Limits — Fraud, Misrepresentation, Duress, and Mistake

A settlement agreement is usually drafted to bind the parties to each do something, like paying money, or refraining from actions, most often from pursuing a lawsuit. If there is not compliance with the settlement terms, the agreement can be enforced as a contract. Courts are called upon to enforce settlement agreements and, on occasion, to rescind them or declare their meaning. Defenses of fraud, misrepresentation, or duress may be invoked. Courts, in applying the common law when enforcing, or declining to enforce settlement agreements, in effect set limits on bargaining behavior. Those limits are discussed in the following article.

❖ **Russell Korobkin, Michael Moffett, and Nancy Welsh,**
The Law of Bargaining

87 Marq. L. Rev. 839 (2004)

When a negotiated agreement results from false statements made during the bargaining process, the common law of tort and contract sometimes holds negotiators liable for damages or makes their resulting agreements subject to rescission. The common law does not, however, amount to a blanket prohibition of all lying. Instead, the common law principles are subject to the caveats that false statements must be material, the opposing negotiator must rely on the false statements, and such reliance must be justified. Whether reliance is justified depends on the type of statement at issue and the statement's specificity. A seller's specific false claim ("this car gets 80 miles per gallon gas mileage") is actionable, but his more general claim ("this car gets good gas mileage") is probably not, because the latter statement is acknowledged as the type of "puffing" or "sales talk" on which no reasonable buyer would rely.

While it is often said that misrepresentations of fact are actionable but misrepresentations of opinion are not, this statement is not strictly accurate. Statements of opinions can be false, either because the speaker does not actually have the claimed opinion ("I think this Hyundai is the best car built in the world today") or because the statement implies facts that are untrue ("I think this Hyundai gets the best gas mileage of any car"). But statements of opinion are less likely to induce justified reliance than are statements of specific facts, especially when they are very general, such as a claim that an item is one of "good quality."

Whether reliance on a statement of fact or opinion is justified depends significantly on the context of the negotiation and whether the speaker has access to information that the recipient does not. A seller "aggressively" promoting his product whose stated opinions imply facts that are not true is less likely to find himself in legal difficulty if the veracity of his claims are easily investigated by an equally-knowledgeable buyer than if his customer is a consumer unable to evaluate the factual basis of the claims. The case for liability is stronger still when the negotiator holds himself out as being particularly knowledgeable about the subject matter that the expressed opinion concerns. Whether a false statement can be insulated from liability by a subsequent disclaimer depends on the strength and clarity of the disclaimer, as well as on the nature of the false statement. Again, the standard is whether the reasonable recipient of the information in total would rely on the statement at issue when deciding whether to enter into an agreement.

It is universally recognized that a negotiator's false statements concerning how valuable an agreement is to her or the maximum she is willing to give up or exchange in order to seal an agreement (the negotiator's "reservation point," or "bottom line") are not actionable, again on the ground that such false statements are common and no reasonable negotiator would rely upon them. So an insurance adjuster who claimed that $900 was "all he could pay" to settle a claim is not liable for fraud, even if the statement was false. The law is less settled regarding the status of false statements concerning the existence of outside alternatives for a negotiator. A false claim of an offer from a third-party is relevant because it implies a strong reservation point, so a negotiator might logically argue that such a claim is no more actionable than a claim as to the reservation point itself. But courts have occasionally ruled that false claims of a specific outside offer are actionable, on the ground that they are material to the negotiation and that the speaker has access to information that cannot be easily verified by the listener's independent investigation.

The most inscrutable area of the law of deception concerns when a negotiator may be held legally liable for failing to disclose information that might weaken his bargaining position (rather than affirmatively asserting a false claim). The traditional laissez-faire rule of caveat emptor eroded in the twentieth century, with courts placing greater disclosure responsibility on negotiators. It is clear that any affirmative action taken to conceal a fact, including the statement of a "half-truth" that implies a false fact, will be treated as if it were an affirmative false statement. Beyond this point, however, the law becomes murky. Although the general rule is probably still that negotiators have no general disclosure obligation, some courts require bargainers (especially sellers) to disclose known material facts not easily discovered by the other party.

Just as the law places some limits on the use of deceptive behavior to seal a bargain, so too does it place some limits upon negotiators' ability to use superior bargaining power to coerce acquiescence with their demands. In general, negotiators may threaten to withhold their goods and services from those who will not agree to their terms. Courts can invoke the doctrine of duress, however, to protect parties who are the victims of a threat that is "improper" and have "no reasonable alternative" but to acquiesce to the other party's demand, such as when one party procures an agreement through the threat of violence, or through the threat to breach a prior agreement after using the relationship created by that agreement to place the victim in a position in which breach would cause non-compensable damage. Judicial intervention is most likely when the bargaining parties' relationship was not arms-length. For example, the common law provides the defense of undue influence to negotiators who can show that they were dependent upon and thus vulnerable to the other, dominant negotiator. . . .

Problem 2

Your client successfully sued Goodyear for damages resulting from a defective hose and valve that they manufactured. The verdict was for $1.3 million, but you appealed because the award did not grant pre-judgment interest. The Court of Appeals remanded to the trial court for determination of interest. The parties agreed as to the dates from which interest should be calculated, but their calculations about the amount of interest owed were apart by several hundred thousand dollars. Goodyear sent an e-mail offering to negotiate a settlement, in which it accidentally overstated the damages it owed by $550,000. You accepted immediately. While Goodyear was drafting the satisfaction of judgment, it noticed its mistake and sent a revised document, with $550,000 deducted. You refused to sign and instead moved the district court to enforce the "settlement agreement." The district court did so, and Goodyear appealed.

What argument might Goodyear make to overturn the district court decision? What would you argue in support of the favorable ruling? Are some things too good to be true? (See *Sumerel v Goodyear Tire & Rubber Co*, Colorado Court of Appeals, May 27, 2009.)

E.   Negotiation Malpractice

Client dissatisfaction, after the fact, with a settlement or transactional agreement negotiated by their attorneys is not uncommon. An agreement that seemed appealing at the time it was obtained, when uncertainty, fear of the worse alternatives, and time pressure drove acceptance, may, with hindsight, be unsatisfactory. A good negotiated result is attributed to a strong case and a resolute client; a marginal result, after the dynamics and trade-offs of the negotiation are forgotten, is attributed to poor representation.

The frequency of complaints filed against attorneys for malpractice in negotiations is not precisely known, but Professor Epstein, in her article that follows, thinks the number is high. Even though there is a general requirement that clients must agree to a negotiated settlement or transaction before it becomes final, consent to the result is not a total barrier to a claim of malpractice. Clients have reason to rely on the professional expertise, skill, and integrity of the attorney negotiating in their behalf and may sue when that reliance is misplaced.

Malpractice is grounded in tort and requires proof of the classic tort elements:

- Duty to the plaintiff
- Breach of that duty
- Causation
- Damages

Proving causation and damages is difficult in claims of negotiation malpractice because, as we have suggested throughout this text, there is no one right or sure way to negotiate. Damages cannot be easily established by comparing a negotiated outcome to a trial result that did not occur or to another negotiation with all the same variables. Richard Posner, Chief Judge of the Seventh Circuit, stated the issue and the challenge succinctly:

> Proof of causation is often difficult in legal malpractice cases involving representation in litigation — the vast majority of such cases — because it is so difficult, yet vital, to estimate what difference a lawyer's negligence made in the actual outcome of a trial or other adversary proceeding. How many criminal defendants, required as they are to prove that their lawyer's ineffective assistance prejudiced them, succeed in overturning their convictions on this ground? Proof of causation is even more difficult in a negotiating situation, because while there is (at least we judges like to think there is) a correct outcome to most lawsuits, there is no "correct" outcome to a negotiation. Not only does much depend on the relative bargaining skills of the negotiators, on the likely consequences to each party if the negotiations fall through, and on luck, so that the element of the intangible and the unpredictable looms large; but there is no single "right" outcome in a bargaining situation even in principle. Every point within the range bounded by the lowest offer that one party will accept and the highest offer that the other party will make is a possible transaction or settlement point, and none of these points is "correct" or "incorrect." (*Nicolet Instrument Corp. v. Lindquest & Vennum*, 34 F.3d 453 (7th Cir. 1994))

Lawyers have both procedural and substantive duties when advising and representing clients in negotiations. The procedural duties reflect ethical responsibilities that lawyers have toward clients. Breach of procedural duties, as well as the substantive ones, results in malpractice. Procedural requirements that are often the gravamen of malpractice claims against attorney negotiators include the following:

- Duty to communicate settlement offers to client (see ABA Model Rule 1.4(a))
- Duty to not exceed authority given by client in making or accepting offers (see ABA Model Rule 1.2(a))
- Duty to be diligent (see ABA Model Rule 1.3)
- Duty to reveal conflicts of interest (see ABA Model Rule 1.7) and not trade off clients' interests to cover up attorney error (see ABA Model Rule 1.7(2))

Substantively, lawyers owe their clients the duty to know the law and properly advise clients on how law and practice impact their situation. Accurate information is necessary for clients to make informed decisions about settlement. The test for purposes of malpractice is commonly stated as whether the attorney exercised that degree of skill, prudence, and diligence in investigating facts, legal research, and giving legal advice that lawyers of ordinary skill and capacity would in similar situations.

Only disappointed clients sue their lawyers. Domestic relations is an area of legal practice in which client expectations are often unrealistically high, as are emotions. It is not unusual for clients to have second thoughts and be disappointed with a negotiated settlement. "Buyer's remorse" can lead to claims against lawyers following an accepted settlement, particularly in divorce. Consider the following malpractice case and the lessons you can learn from it.

❖ Ziegelheim v. Apollo

128 N.J. 250, 607 A.2d 1298 (1992)

HANDLER, J.

. . . In September 1979, Mrs. Ziegelheim retained defendant, attorney Stephen Apollo, to represent her in her anticipated divorce action. Because this appeal relates to the trial court's granting of summary judgment against plaintiff, we assume for the purposes of our decision that all of the facts she alleges relating to Apollo's handling of her divorce are true. According to Mrs. Ziegelheim, she and Apollo met on several occasions to plan various aspects of her case. She told him about all of the marital and separate assets of which she was aware, and they discussed her suspicion that Mr. Ziegelheim was either concealing or dissipating certain other assets as well. In particular, Mrs. Ziegelheim told Apollo that she thought her husband had $500,000 hidden in the form of cash savings and bonds. Accordingly, she asked Apollo to make a thorough inquiry into her husband's assets, including cash, bonds, patents, stocks, pensions, life insurance, profit-sharing plans, and real estate. . . .

According to Mrs. Ziegelheim, Apollo failed to discover important information about her husband's assets before entering into settlement negotiations with Mr. Ziegelheim's attorney, Sheldon Liebowitz. Apollo hired an accountant who valued the marital estate at approximately $2,413,000. Mrs. Ziegelheim claims that the accountant substantially underestimated the estate because of several oversights by Apollo, including his failure to locate a bank vault owned by Mr. Ziegelheim; to locate or determine the value of his tax-free municipal bonds; to verify the value of his profit-sharing plan at Pilot Woodworking, a company in which he was the primary shareholder; to search for an estimated $500,000 in savings; to contact the United States Patent Office to verify the existence of certain patents he held; to inquire into a $1,000,000 life insurance policy naming an associate of his as the beneficiary; to verify the value of certain lakefront property; and to verify the value of his stock holdings. She alleges that had Apollo made a proper inquiry, it would have been apparent that the marital estate was worth approximately $2,562,000, or about $149,000 more than the accountant found....

In sum, Mrs. Ziegelheim was to receive approximately $333,000 in alimony, $6,000 in contributions to insurance costs, and $324,000 in property, the last figure representing approximately fourteen percent of the value of the estate (as appraised by Apollo and the accountant). Mr. Ziegelheim was to receive approximately $2,088,000 in property, approximately eighty-six percent of the value of the estate.

When testifying before the court immediately after the settlement was read into the record, both Mrs. Ziegelheim and Mr. Ziegelheim stated that they understood the agreement, that they thought it was fair, and that they entered into it voluntarily. Mrs. Ziegelheim now asserts, however, that she accepted the agreement only after Apollo advised her that wives could expect to receive no more than ten to twenty percent of the marital estate if they went to trial. She claims that Apollo's estimate was unduly pessimistic and did not comport with the advice that a reasonably competent attorney would have given under the circumstances. Had she been advised competently, she says, she would not have accepted the settlement....

The trial court ruled in favor of defendant on all counts. It noted that Mrs. Ziegelheim had stated on the record that she understood the settlement and its terms, that she thought the terms were fair, and that she had not been coerced into settling....

In accepting a case, the lawyer agrees to pursue the goals of the client to the extent the law permits, even when the lawyer believes that the client's desires are unwise or ill-considered. At the same time, because the client's desires may be influenced in large measure by the advice the lawyer provides, the lawyer is obligated to give the client reasonable advice. As a legal matter progresses and circumstances change, the wishes of the client may change as well. Accordingly, the lawyer is obligated to keep the client informed of the status of the matter for which the lawyer has been retained, and is required to advise the client on the various legal and strategic issues that arise.

In this case, Mrs. Ziegelheim made several claims impugning Apollo's handling of her divorce, and the trial court dismissed all of them on Apollo's motion for summary judgment. As we explain, we believe that the trial court's rulings on several of her claims were erroneous....

On Mrs. Ziegelheim's claim that Apollo negligently advised her with respect to her chances of winning a greater proportion of the marital estate if she proceeded to trial, we conclude, as did the Appellate Division, that there was a genuine dispute regarding the appropriate advice that an attorney should give in cases like hers. According to the expert retained by Mrs. Ziegelheim, women in her position — who are in relatively poor health, have little earning capacity, and have been wholly dependent on their husbands — often receive upwards of fifty percent of the marital estate. The expert said that Mrs. Ziegelheim's chances of winning such a large fraction of the estate had she gone to trial would have been especially good because the couple had enjoyed a high standard of living while they were together and because her husband's earning capacity was "tremendous" and would remain so for some time. Her expert's opinion was brought to the trial court's attention, as was the expert report of Mr. Ziegelheim. If plaintiff's expert's opinion were credited, as it should have been for purposes of summary judgment, then Apollo very well could have been found negligent in advising her that she could expect to win only ten to twenty percent of the marital estate.

Apollo urges us to adopt the rule enunciated by the Pennsylvania Supreme Court in *Muhammad v. Strassburger, McKenna, Messer, Shilobod and Gutnick*, 526 Pa. 541, 587 A.2d 1346 (1991), that a dissatisfied litigant may not recover from his or her attorney for malpractice in negotiating a settlement that the litigant has accepted unless the litigant can prove actual fraud on the part of the attorney. Under that rule, no cause of action can be made based on negligence or contract principles against an attorney for malpractice in negotiating a settlement. The Pennsylvania Supreme Court rationalized its severe rule by explaining that it had a "longstanding public policy which encourages settlements."

New Jersey, too, has a longstanding policy that encourages settlements, but we reject the rule espoused by the Pennsylvania Supreme Court. Although we encourage settlements, we recognize that litigants rely heavily on the professional advice of counsel when they decide whether to accept or reject offers of settlement, and we insist that the lawyers of our state advise clients with respect to settlements with the same skill, knowledge, and diligence with which they pursue all other legal tasks. Attorneys are supposed to know the likelihood of success for the types of cases they handle and they are supposed to know the range of possible awards in those cases.

As we noted in *Levine v. Wiss & Co*, 97 N.J. 242, 246, 478 A.2d 397 (1984), "One who undertakes to render services in the practice of a profession or trade is required to exercise the skill and knowledge normally possessed by members of that profession in good standing in similar communities." We have found in cases involving a great variety of professionals that deviation from accepted standards of professional care will result in liability for negligence. . . . Like most courts, we see no reason to apply a more lenient rule to lawyers who negotiate settlements. *After all, the negotiation of settlements is one of the most basic and most frequently undertaken tasks that lawyers perform* [emphasis is court's]. . . .

The fact that a party received a settlement that was "fair and equitable" does not mean necessarily that the party's attorney was competent or that the party would not have received a more favorable settlement had the party's incompetent attorney been competent. Thus, in this case, notwithstanding the family court's decision, Mrs. Ziegelheim still may proceed against Apollo in her negligence action.

Moreover, another aspect of the alleged professional incompetence that led to the improvident acceptance of the settlement was the attorney's own failure to discover hidden marital assets. When Mrs. Ziegelheim sought to reopen her divorce settlement, the family court denied her motion with the observation that "[a]mple opportunity existed for full discovery," and that "the parties had their own accountants as well as counsel." The court did not determine definitively that Mr. Ziegelheim had hidden no assets, but stated instead that it "suspected that everything to be known was known to the parties." The earlier ruling did not implicate the competence of counsel and, indeed, was premised on the presumptive competence of counsel. Hence, defendant cannot invoke that ruling now to bar a challenge to his competence. Mrs. Ziegelheim should have been allowed to prove that Apollo negligently failed to discover certain assets concealed by her former husband. . . .

In holding as we do today, we do not open the door to malpractice suits by any and every dissatisfied party to a settlement. Many such claims could be averted if settlements were explained as a matter of record in open court in proceedings reflecting the understanding and assent of the parties. Further, plaintiffs must allege particular facts in support of their claims of attorney incompetence and may not litigate complaints containing mere generalized assertions of malpractice. We are mindful that attorneys cannot be held liable simply because they are not successful in persuading an opposing party to accept certain terms. Similarly, we acknowledge that attorneys who pursue reasonable strategies in handling their cases and who render reasonable advice to their clients cannot be held liable for the failure of their strategies or for any unprofitable outcomes that result because their clients took their advice. The law demands that attorneys handle their cases with knowledge, skill, and diligence, but it does not demand that they be perfect or infallible, and it does not demand that they always secure optimum outcomes for their clients. . . .

Questions

7. The Supreme Court of New Jersey opinion in *Ziegelheim v. Apollo* states that "In holding as we do today we do not open the door to malpractice suits by any and every dissatisfied party to a settlement." Does the New Jersey court, in allowing the negligence action against the attorney to proceed, shut the door or, indeed, leave it wide open?

8. The court advises that "Many such claims could be averted if settlements were explained as a matter of record in open court in proceedings reflecting the understanding and assent of the parties." This advice may be practical in divorce cases, where the court is asked to approve and incorporate the marital settlement agreement into a court judgment, but is this cautionary step practical at

> the conclusion to most lawsuit settlements? Does this help explain why settlement agreements often do recite the facts, premises, and underlying reasons for the settlement?
>
> 9. Is the *Ziegelheim v. Apollo* case likely to be tried following this remand? If you represented defendant Apollo, how would you negotiate a final settlement of the Ziegelheim claim, and what amount would you anticipate it would take to conclude this matter?

The New Jersey Supreme Court in the Apollo case expressly rejects the reasoning of the Pennsylvania Supreme Court in *Muhammad v. Strassburger et al.*, which barred a client who accepted a negotiated settlement from suing his attorney in the absence of fraud. The *Muhammad* decision has been rejected by other courts, as illustrated by *Apollo*. In the following article, Professor Epstein explains why courts have rejected the *Muhammad* opinion reasoning and then contrasts malpractice actions arising from the negotiation process from other types of malpractice cases. She also offers advice on how to defend and avoid malpractice claims when clients initially accept a negotiated settlement.

❖ **Lynn A. Epstein,** *Post-Settlement Malpractice: Undoing the Done Deal*

46 Cath. U. L. Rev. 453 (1997)

Clients voice their approval to mediators and judges as a settlement agreement is reached. A release is signed, the file is closed, and from the lawyer's perspective, another case ends. The settled case joins an overwhelming majority of civil cases that are resolved in pretrial settlement. Buried within this figure, however, is a more troubling statistic: Over twenty percent of civil cases will be resurrected in the form of malpractice actions initiated by dissatisfied clients. In those instances, and for various reasons substantiated by expert opinions, the client will charge that they could have received a better result in the settlement even though the client knowingly and willingly agreed to end the case.

In every state except Pennsylvania, a client is permitted to proceed with the theory that his attorney negligently negotiated an agreement despite the fact that the client consented to settlement. In *Muhammad v. Strassburger, McKenna, Messer, Shilobod & Gutnick*, the Pennsylvania Supreme Court determined that an attorney is immune from malpractice based on negligence where the client consented to settle. Court decisions after *Muhammad*, however, have uniformly rejected immunity for the attorney, permitting post-settlement malpractice actions to proceed in the same manner as the prototypical malpractice case.

This Article analyzes the Pennsylvania Supreme Court's decision to bar malpractice lawsuits based on settled cases. This Article then contrasts the opinion with the contradictory majority rule in other states. Next, this Article addresses the difference between mainstream malpractice actions and those malpractice actions arising from the negotiation of settled cases....

Muhammad and Its Successors

Conventional wisdom dictates that attorneys settle cases effectively, as an estimated ninety-five percent of civil cases are resolved by settlement. Yet, an emerging trend of post-settlement malpractice claims threatens the integrity of the settlement negotiation process. While malpractice actions are on the rise, most attorneys reasonably believed they were insulated from liability because the client had consented to settlement, and because there was no affirmative wrongdoing by the attorney. Because so many factors influence a client's decision to settle, and because so many individuals, such as judges and mediators, are a part of the process, it would appear fundamentally unfair to hold the attorneys solely responsible for such malpractice claims. This is buttressed by a majority viewpoint which looks unfavorably upon malpractice claims that require the judiciary to infiltrate the negotiation process, a process traditionally viewed as immune from judicial scrutiny.

Balancing these competing interests, the Pennsylvania Supreme Court barred such malpractice actions to foster the negotiation and settlement process. In *Muhammad*, the Pennsylvania Supreme Court held that, absent fraud, an attorney is immune from suit by a former client dissatisfied with a settlement that the former client agreed to enter....

The court emphasized that this immunity extends to specific cases where a plaintiff agreed to settlement in the absence of fraud by the attorney. This is distinguished from the instance when a lawyer knowingly commits malpractice, conceals the wrongdoing, and convinces the client to settle in order to cover up the malpractice. According to the court, in this instance, the attorney's conduct is fraudulent and actionable....

Muhammad has suffered widespread criticism and is uniformly rejected in every reported opinion reviewing post-settlement legal malpractice litigation.... While most courts are expeditious in determining that an attorney is not absolutely immune from legal malpractice actions when the client consents to settlement, they are also uniform in expressing a desire to foster protection over the negotiation process.

Courses of Action for Attorneys Confronting Post-Settlement Malpractice Claims

A.   The Contributory/Comparative Negligence Defense

In a post-settlement malpractice action, an attorney should defend the action by claiming client contributory/comparative negligence. The defense should be presented by introducing evidence of the client's subjective reasons for settling the case.

The client contributory/comparative negligence defense is generally recognized in legal malpractice actions; however, some courts do not permit the issue to reach a jury. This reluctance is supported by the Restatement (Third) of Law Governing Lawyers, which asserts that the client contributory negligence defense is available in jurisdictions that recognize the same defense to general negligence actions. The Restatement cautions, however, that the lawyer/client relationship imposes fiduciary duties by which "clients are entitled to rely on their lawyers to act with competence, diligence, honesty, and loyalty." The lawyer/client relationship imposes numerous duties on the lawyer, while imposing few on the client. Yet, this cannot relieve clients from accepting responsibility for their own acts or omissions which result in unfavorable settlements.

Courts that permit the client comparative negligence defense, however, proceed with caution, premised on the view that attorneys should not be permitted to circumvent responsibility to former clients under the guise that the client should have known how to respond or act. Thus, even when a legal document contains simple English that needs no interpretation by a lawyer, the defense of client contributory negligence has been barred in certain jurisdictions....

Courts should, however, permit the comparative negligence defense to proceed to the fact finder where the client settled a claim and now seeks to hold an attorney liable for malpractice committed in the negotiation of that settlement. In a majority of post-settlement malpractice claims, the former clients do not claim they did not understand the settlement agreement. Instead, this majority group freely admits they voluntarily entered into settlement, conceding they understood the agreement and abandoned their right to a trial. Only after settlement did these former clients contend there was "something else" their former lawyer should have done to secure a better result.

Although there will be cases where the client is genuinely aggrieved by a negligent attorney, the majority of post-settlement malpractice litigation arises from the client's own conduct. In those cases, the comparative fault defense should be considered by the fact finder.

While the comparative fault defense is available in the typical legal malpractice action, its use has been limited in post-settlement malpractice litigation.... [Courts] provide minimum guidelines to which an attorney should adhere in advising a client regarding settlement.... [T]he lawyer should hold an appreciation of (1) the relevant facts; (2) the present and future potential strengths and weaknesses of his case; (3) the likely costs, both objectively (monetarily) and subjectively (psychological disruption of business and family life) associated with proceeding further in the litigation; and (4) the likely outcome if the case were to proceed further.

Many cases of legal malpractice occur from "perceived" negligence by attorneys who fail to adhere to the [above] criteria. Common practice dictates that attorneys review the four factors in detail with their client prior to settlement. In post-settlement malpractice litigation analysis, courts tend to focus only on the result obtained (the settlement sum) to gauge the lawyer's liability exposure, ignoring the traditional factors preceding settlement. Hence, an attorney wishing to marshal an effective defense must take pre-settlement steps aimed to protect his client's interest. This will safeguard against subsequent malpractice claims within the framework developed by the courts.

B. The "Release and Settlement Agreement": Solidifying the Deal

The "release and settlement agreement" is the final written document ending the litigation and, in many instances, the lawyer-client relationship. An historical review of related lawyer-client concern over apparent complications arising from contingency fee arrangements creates an additional post-settlement malpractice defense. To assure a client's comprehension of contingency fee contracts, many state bar associations require clients and attorneys to review and execute a "statement of client rights" which thoroughly explains the contingency fee agreement. This statement obligates the attorney to adhere to specific reporting and accounting requirements concerning fees throughout the client's case. It also provides the client with a remedy against unscrupulous attorneys.

Similar to the "statement of client rights," an attorney should be required to provide a client with a statement of the case before settlement. This statement would precisely articulate the ramifications of settlement and act as written confirmation of the attorney's work on the case. . . .

CONCLUSION

Post-settlement malpractice actions are quite unique. While the Pennsylvania Supreme Court effectively banned these lawsuits, providing former counsel immunity rather than engaging in the arduous analysis inherent to malpractice litigation, the better course of action is to permit attorneys to present the client comparative fault defense. This will allow an attorney to present evidence of the client's subjective reasons for settling the litigation. Additionally, through the use of a pre-settlement statement of the case form, attorneys will provide their clients sufficient information to adequately prepare for a successful negotiation and settlement process.

Concluding Note

In the *Muhammad* case, Justice Larsen wrote a stinging dissent accusing the majority of creating a "LAWYER'S HOLIDAY" by barring malpractice against lawyers for negligence committed in the negotiation of civil settlements. He reasoned by comparison, "If a doctor is negligent in saving a human life, the doctor pays. If a priest is negligent in saving the spirit of a human, the priest pays. But if a lawyer is negligent in advising his client as to settlement, the client pays." Justice Larsen's dissent reflects the general view that most courts have taken in rejecting the Pennsylvania Supreme Court's protection of the negotiation process from claims of malpractice.

When negotiation malpractice cases do proceed to a jury trial, the jury is required to assess the negotiated outcome. The dilemma of evaluation confronted in these cases is "compared to what?" Most often the comparison is to the likely result if the negotiated claim proceeded to trial. This requires, in effect, a "trial within a trial." Although this approach is thought to apply an objective standard, it does not take into account the give and take of the negotiation process and the subjective, or nonmonetary interests, that may in reality have driven the negotiation. The "trial within a trial" approach reverts to a distributive negotiation model that launders out integrative aspects that favorably distinguished negotiation from trial.

Judging a negotiated outcome by an objective, monetary gauge fails to factor in the interest-based approach to which most of the new negotiation literature is directed. It raises the same concerns as does grading law students at the end of a negotiation course only on the quantitative, money results of a final negotiation role-play. As expressed by Epstein, "every aspect of a negotiated settlement, particularly its conclusion, is a subjective evaluation premised on the client's needs and desires, coupled with the various influences that affect that client's ultimate desire to settle" (Epstein, *infra*, 463). Gauging a lawyer's liability exposure only on the monetary result obtained can have a chilling effect on good integrative bargaining by attorneys.

Professor Epstein proposes that attorneys protect themselves from malpractice claims by regularly using a form entitled, "Pre-Settlement Statement of Client's Case," which the client is to sign before settlement. This form memorializes all the facts, assessments, and advice that were considered to decide upon settlement. The concluding sentence of the form states ". . . your attorney may use this document as a defense in a malpractice action if permitted by law." Although not a release per se, it is clearly intended to relieve the attorney of malpractice liability.

This "CYA" approach might or might not be effective protection, but is it the way you want to practice law? Each of us must ask how a precautionary approach with an eye ahead to defending malpractice claims will influence our relations with clients and impact our interaction with other attorneys. Will fear of malpractice hinder our nimbleness and creativity as negotiators? Was the *Muhammad* decision correct in its premise that opening up negotiation to after-the-fact legal scrutiny may impede negotiation and discourage settlement? If so, will judicial resources and client interests be adversely impacted?

As you consider these questions, please be aware that malpractice verdicts against lawyers for their good faith efforts in negotiating on behalf of clients appear to be rare. Doing your best and keeping clients informed is the most effective prevention. Satisfied clients whose needs are met, including the need to know you have faithfully attended to their interests, do not sue their lawyers.

PART II

Mediation

CHAPTER
9

Mediation—The Big Picture

A. Introduction

1. *The Process of Mediation*

a. What Is Mediation?

Mediation is a process of assisted negotiation in which a neutral person helps people to reach agreement. The process varies depending on the style of the mediator, the nature of the dispute, and the wishes of the participants. Mediation differs from direct negotiation in that it involves the participation of an impartial third party. The process also differs from adjudication in that it is consensual, informal, and usually private. The participants need not reach agreement, and the mediator, who is usually selected by the participants, has no power to impose an outcome.

In some contexts you may find that this definition does not fully apply. The process is sometimes not voluntary, as when a judge requires litigants to participate in mediation as a precondition to trial. In addition, mediators are not always entirely neutral; a corporate lawyer, for instance, can apply mediative techniques to help colleagues resolve an internal dispute, despite the fact that he is in favor of a particular outcome. Occasionally mediation is required to be open to the public, as when a controversy involves governmental entities subject to "open meeting" laws. Finally, a mediator's goal is not always to settle a specific legal dispute; the neutral may focus instead on helping disputants improve their relationship or complete a transaction.

There is an ongoing debate within the field about what mediation should be. To some degree this results from the different goals that participants have for the process: Some focus only on settlement of a claim and seek to obtain the best possible monetary terms, whereas others seek to solve a problem and still other participants enter mediation to improve a difficult relationship. The increasing application of mediation to areas such as family and criminal law also raises serious questions of policy. This text focuses on "civil" mediation, involving legal disputes outside the area of collective bargaining, because this is what you are most likely to encounter in lawpractice. However, to give you a sense of the flexibility of mediation, we also present other perspectives on the process.

b.   What Do Mediators Do?

Mediators apply a wide variety of techniques. Depending on the situation, a settlement-oriented mediator may use one or more of the following approaches, among others:

- Help litigants design a process that ensures the presence of key participants and focuses their attention on finding a constructive solution to a dispute.
- Allow the principals and their attorneys to present legal arguments, raise underlying concerns, and express their feelings directly to their opponents, as well as hear the other side's perspective firsthand.
- Help the participants focus on their interests and identify imaginative settlement options.
- Moderate negotiations, coaching bargainers in effective techniques, translating communications, and reframing the disputants' positions and perceptions.
- Assist each side to assess the likely outcome if the case is litigated, and to consider the full costs of continuing the conflict.
- Work with the disputants to draft a durable agreement and, if necessary, to implement it.

c.   What Is the Structure of Mediation?

Because mediation is informal, lawyers and clients have a great deal of freedom to modify the process to meet their needs. In practice, good neutrals and advocates vary their approach significantly to respond to the circumstances of particular cases. That said, a typical mediation of a legal dispute is likely to proceed through a series of stages.

Premediation

Before the disputants meet to mediate, the neutral often has conversations with the lawyers, and sometimes also with the parties, to deal with issues such as who will attend the mediation and to address emotional and other issues. Lawyers can use these contacts to start to build a working relationship with the mediator and educate him about their client's perspective on the dispute and obstacles that have made direct negotiations difficult.

The Opening Session

Many mediations begin with a session in which the parties, counsel, and mediator meet together. The content and structure of such a session varies considerably, depending on the participants' wishes and the goals of the process. When mediation is focused on reaching a monetary settlement, the joint session is likely to be dominated by arguments of lawyers, perhaps followed by questions from the neutral. If the goal of the process is to find an interest-based solution or to repair a ruptured relationship, then a mediator is much more likely to encourage the parties themselves to speak and to attempt to draw out underlying issues and emotions.

Private Caucusing

After disputants have exchanged perspectives, arguments, and questions and obtained a "read" on one another, most commercial mediators adjourn the joint session to meet with each side individually in private "caucuses." The purpose of caucusing is to permit disputants, counsel, and the mediator to talk candidly together. Keeping the parties separated, with communications channeled through the mediator, also allows the neutral to shape the disputants' dialogue in productive ways.

When the mediation process is focused on monetary bargaining, the participants usually spend most of their time separated, with the mediator shuttling back and forth between them. If, however, parties are interested in exploring an interest-based resolution or repairing a broken relationship, then the mediator is more likely to encourage disputants to meet together extensively so that they can work through emotions and learn to relate productively with each other.

Joint Discussions

Even when a mediation is conducted primarily through private caucusing, neutrals sometimes ask disputants to meet with each other for a specific purpose. This might be to examine tax issues in a business breakup, explore a licensing agreement to resolve a patent claim, or deal with a difficult emotional issue in a tort case. In most mediations, whether or not conducted through caucusing, the lawyers and perhaps also the parties meet at the end of the process to sign a memorandum of agreement or decide on future steps.

Follow-Up Contacts

Increasingly the mediation process is not limited to the occasions on which the mediator and disputants meet together. If a dispute is not resolved at a mediation session, then the neutral is likely to follow up with the lawyers or parties, and may facilitate telephone or e-mail negotiations or convene additional face-to-face sessions if the parties wish.

Variations in Format

The model we have just discussed represents a "default" model for legal mediation, but you will encounter significant variations in the field. Mediators who handle family disputes, for example, often remain in joint session during the entire process, and some mediators are experimenting with no-caucus formats in other kinds of civil cases.

At the same time, in several states the practice of holding an opening session in legal mediations is declining. Some legal mediators, acting at the request of litigators, often begin the process with only a cursory opening session or none at all, and spend virtually all their time in private caucusing. Others meet with each side before the opening session. The advantages and disadvantages of these and other formats are discussed later.

2.   The Value of Mediation

The growing popularity of mediation reflects an important change in the legal culture. What, in the eyes of parties and their lawyers, are the potential benefits of going to mediation? Consider the comments and data that follow.

a.   Viewpoints of Lawyers

Diane Gentile, Dayton

My practice is focused on employment law. These claims deal with one of the most important aspects of peoples' identity — their work. In addition, they often involve serious allegations of wrongdoing. Both sides in these disputes often have good reason to want a confidential solution. One example [is] a case I handled involving a worker and supervisor. Several years before the two had had a consensual intimate relationship, but the worker later accused her supervisor of sexual harassment. For the employer, the claim was a potential nightmare. The fact that the supervisor had at first denied the existence of the earlier relationship made it even more difficult. Moreover, because the employer was a nonprofit organization that depended in part on public funds, the potential for negative publicity could have crippled the organization. As soon as we received notice of the plaintiff's suit we suggested mediation. After nine hours of difficult discussions we had a resolution, and the organization's relief was limitless.

Mediation is effective in part because it allows the parties to talk about many things that will never be considered relevant by a court. When they are allowed to speak freely, often in private to a mediator offering a sympathetic ear, material just spills out, and afterward people are often much more willing to compromise. Mediation also allows for nonlegal relief, which is particularly important in employment cases: changes to a file to reflect a voluntary quit rather than termination, for example, or agreement on what the company will say to a future employer asking for a reference.

Stephen Oleskey, Boston

I use mediation extensively in commercial cases to deal with a wide variety of obstacles. My goals depend on the nature of the situation. In one recent case, for example, the problem was anger: The parties had been talking off and on for two years, but both were so upset that they could not focus productively on settlement. At the same time, with several hundred million dollars at stake, neither side could bear the risk of a winner-take-all trial. Mediation created the context for a rational discussion of the merits and risks. In another case, we used mediation to get a group of corporate and political stakeholders to come to the same place and focus intensively on a case that some of them had not previously thought through.

Occasionally, I've used a mediator to give a message to a client — or the other side's client — that was hard for a lawyer to deliver. In a few cases, it's been the way that the mediator has framed the discussions: her choice of what issues to focus on, or the statement that, "We'll stay here until midnight if we have to, to get this done," that tells the parties that this is the time to make the difficult choices, put all their money on the table, and work out a deal if possible.

Mary Alexander, San Francisco

My practice focuses on personal injury cases, including auto accident, product liability, and defective design claims. Years ago we settled cases only on the courthouse steps, but courts in California now push parties to mediate long before trial. Often a case will not settle at court-ordered mediation, but the process gets lawyers talking and often leads to an agreement.

The single most useful service provided by mediators in my practice is to provide a reality check for clients. People often come into a lawyer's office with very real injuries, but unrealistic expectations about what they can obtain from the court system. They have heard somewhere about a large award and assume that it is typical, when in fact it is not. Clients are often in dire financial straits and physical pain, making it hard for them to listen to a lawyer's warnings about trial risk. When a mediator, especially a former judge, explains the realities of present-day juries — often in language that turns out to be very similar to what I had said earlier — it makes a real impression. Clients are able to become more realistic, and to accept a good offer when it appears. Even if the courts did not order it, I would elect to mediate almost every significant case.

Katherine Gurun, Former General Counsel, Bechtel Corporation

Our business involved complex construction and engineering projects. It was built around long-term relationships with suppliers and partners. Things inevitably went wrong — equipment failed, customers encountered financial problems, and so on. We had to resolve these issues, but in a way that kept our relationships healthy. Mediation became our most powerful and successful process for accomplishing this.

The flexibility of mediation is its most useful quality. In the disputes we encountered at Bechtel, the complex nature of the issues almost always required several sessions, often spread over a period of months. During adjournments, people could confer with their organizations and the mediator could work on one or both sides. Overall, ADR reduced Bechtel's litigation costs phenomenally; just as important, it avoided the management distraction caused by formal litigation.

We also used mediation in international disputes. Here cultural differences were an important consideration. Many of our foreign partners were in mediation for the first time, and it was particularly important to find a neutral who "knew both sides of the fence." Asian executives seemed especially comfortable with the mixture of joint and private meetings, because the structure accommodated their preference for conferring and reaching a consensus within the team at each point in the process. Europeans sometimes seemed troubled by mediation's lack of formality, but I found that its adaptability was what made the process so effective.

Paul Bland, Public Justice, Washington, D.C.

There are two major situations in which I find mediation helpful as a litigator for a public interest organization. The first is when we challenge widespread practices; for example, a group of HMOs flagrantly violating a statute. Inside counsel sometimes cannot believe that their organization has violated any law, simply because all of their peers are doing the same thing. In such cases I ask for mediation with a former judge or well-regarded private lawyer — someone who can convincingly tell the other lawyer that her client has a genuine problem.

Another indicator for mediation is when I suspect that defense counsel is not being candid with his own client. Many firms I encounter are completely ethical — they fight hard but fair. Some lawyers, however, seem to "milk" clients, playing on defendants' instinctive belief that they've done nothing wrong and billing them unnecessarily for a year or two. Mediation can be the best way to get the truth to an unrealistic client. I often have to work to get such cases into mediation. I have resorted to coming up to a defense counsel, in the presence of his client, and saying, "This looks like a perfect case for mediation." Or I might write to defense counsel and make an explicit request that he transmit the letter to his client. The hardest part of mediation is sometimes to get the other side into the process.

Patricia Lee Refo, Phoenix

My caseload consists primarily of large commercial disputes. We use mediation in most of our cases — I sometimes joke that we lawyers have worked ourselves into a place where we can't settle cases by ourselves anymore! I don't believe that a bad settlement is better than a good trial. I am convinced, though, that in the right situation, a mediator can add a great deal of value. Sometimes the problem is that both sides have the same facts, but they view them very differently. A mediator may not be able to convince a client to change his viewpoint, but she can make the client understand what the other side can do with the facts at trial. It's often the first time the client has heard the reaction of someone who comes to the case completely fresh.

There are also issues in business cases over which people become quite invested and emotional — for example, did someone violate an agreement in bad faith. Mediation allows clients to vent their feelings in private, making it easier for them to compromise later in the process. I recently encountered a mediator who said that he didn't "do venting." I find that aspect of the process often to be crucial, and I won't use neutrals who can't handle it. Mediators can also be helpful by "cutting to the chase," focusing on the few issues that will really matter at trial. This frees parties from arguing over every point, and moves them toward making settlement decisions.

Harry Mazadoorian, Former Assistant General Counsel and ADR Coordinator, CIGNA Corporation

I've used mediative methods often in working out business relationships. Insurers, for example, often make investments in joint venture and partnership deals. It's impossible to predict the future, and as the project goes on and circumstances change, issues often arise about how the parties should share unexpected benefits and responsibilities. I remember one alternative energy venture that nearly broke down when money ran short and additional contributions were required from the participants. At first the lawyers focused on parsing the language of the contract, but as we talked I was able to persuade them to explore options that redistributed costs so that each partner could bear them most easily, and potential benefits in ways that they would be felt most strongly. Once the partners dropped their focus on legalese and looked instead at their specific needs, the conflict was quickly resolved. The greatest music to my ears in these situations was always to hear an executive say, "I just don't know how to get this done." I knew that if I could get the attention of high-level decision makers — ideally, get top people from both sides to sit down at lunch and commit to trying to work it out — success was nearly assured.

b.   Business Perspectives

In recent years researchers have questioned companies about their use of ADR. A 2004 survey of corporate general counsel, for example, found that the respondents had mixed attitudes toward binding arbitration, but supported the use of mediation. Asked "What is your company's attitude toward nonbinding mediation clauses in its [domestic business] agreements?" the respondents gave these answers:

Strongly Favor	31%
Slightly Favor	29%
Neutral	25%
Slightly Disfavor	8%
Strongly Disfavor	7%

General counsel at large companies were more likely than others to support mediation clauses, with 35 percent strongly favoring and only 1 percent strongly disfavoring their use (*www.fulbright.com*). We discuss the issues raised by contractual mediation clauses in Chapter 14.

One of the first companies to make aggressive use of mediation was the Toro Corporation, which produces a wide variety of consumer goods including lawn mowers, snow blowers, and other power tools, and as a result is subject to personal injury claims, some of them serious and complex. Here is a description of Toro's ADR program.

❖ **Ashby Jones,** *House Calls*

Corporate Counsel 4 (October 2004)

Resolving cases before legal expenses pile up certainly isn't a novel corporate strategy. But over the past decade, few companies have pushed settlements for product liability claims as aggressively and systematically as Toro. . . . The program has been in place since 1991, and Toro says it will [have saved more than] $100 million in litigation costs. . . .

Toro has cut the cost of handling each claim it receives by some $80,000, from $115,000 to only $35,000 — a figure that includes lawyers' fees, verdicts, and payouts — according to "product integrity manager" Andrew Byers. The head of Toro's settlement program, Byers boasts that his company hasn't "set foot in a courtroom" on a product liability claim since 1994.

. . . Within days of receiving word from a dealer or customer that someone was injured while using Toro equipment, [one of Toro's paralegals] sets up a visit to the victim's home to talk about what happened and ultimately discuss a settlement, regardless of whether a victim has made a demand for money. "I make it clear that they really have nothing to lose [by meeting with us]," says Kelly. "The [injured parties] aren't obligating themselves to anything." . . . Inside, usually over coffee, the paralegal asks the victim to recount the accident. She listens attentively, nods sympathetically, and expresses regret "that such an unfortunate incident had to happen."

If Kelly and Gotzian are unable to resolve a case, they suggest a mediation between the plaintiff's lawyer and [Toro settlement counsel] — typically with a mediator Toro has used before. Plaintiffs' lawyers who have negotiated with Toro say they are happy to get a satisfied client and a chunk of cash for just a couple of hours' worth of work. "There was really little downside to trying mediation," says Joseph Baggett, a solo practitioner in Oroville, California. Baggett mediated — and settled — a case against Toro on behalf of a man who cut off his toe while using a Toro mower. "We knew we could just walk away from the table [and sue] if we felt we weren't being treated fairly."

. . . Toro admits that it routinely pays claims that probably would collapse in court. For instance, the company settled with Joseph Baggett's client for $25,000 even though, as Baggett concedes, some protective guards were removed from the mower after it left the store.

It's clear that Toro hasn't started a revolution throughout corporate America with its mass settlement approach. But a few big companies have adopted Toro-like programs. Neither Johnson & Johnson nor DuPont, for example, settle as aggressively as Toro. But [work by] settlement counsel has cut the "cycle time" of DuPont's average lawsuit from around 24 months to between six and eight months. "When you're saving 18 months' worth of outside counsel fees, that adds up in a hurry," counsel says. Mazza adds that DuPont's willingness to settle cases earlier hasn't increased its average settlement fee.

After Toro, General Electric might well have the most aggressive settlement approach in the country. According to P. D. Villarreal, [GE's] approach has worked. "We've always settled more cases than we've taken to trial," he says. "But now we're getting them settled much earlier." And that has helped the company keep its outside counsel costs flat despite the fact that since 1998 GE has grown its gross revenues by 25 percent. "There are very few categories of cases that this approach doesn't work with," adds Villarreal. . . .

Other chief legal officers simply don't want to be seen as an easy mark for plaintiffs and their lawyers — and insist on backing up their products, whatever the cost. "If you make products that you feel are well made and safe, your instinct is to stand behind them when others attack them," says James Buda, the general counsel at Peoria, Illinois–based Caterpillar, Inc.

Toro's Byers scoffs at the idea that an aggressive settlement policy creates a "soft target" for enterprising plaintiffs lawyers. He says that from 1986 to 1991, the five years prior to the start of its settlement approach, Toro received 640 injury-related claims. From 1991 to 1996 and from 1996 to 2001, that number actually declined, to 536 and 404, respectively. "Look, you can stand on principle all you want, but we've saved millions handling claims this way," says Byers.

Questions and Notes

1. Why do you think the concern that Toro's willingness to mediate all claims would spur more lawsuits did not materialize?
2. If you were the lawyer for a person injured by a Toro product, would you advise her to participate in its settlement process? What factors would be important in your decision?
3. One issue that Toro faced was persuading plaintiff counsel that the invitation to mediate was not merely a pretext for "free discovery" or "below-market" settlements. To overcome such suspicions, Toro developed a list of references — plaintiff lawyers who had worked with Toro and could vouch for its sincerity.

---

c. Is It Right for Every Dispute? Is It Fair?

Few would argue that mediation is appropriate for every controversy. Even those who generally favor its use agree that the process might not be effective in the following situations, among others:

*   A disputant is not capable of negotiating effectively. This may occur, for example, because the person lacks legal counsel or is suffering from a personal impairment.
*   One side in the controversy wants a judicial decision to use as a benchmark to settle or discourage similar cases.
*   A party fears a settlement that may stimulate "copycat" claims.
*   A litigant requires a court order to control an adversary's conduct.
*   One of the disputants is benefiting from the existence of the controversy, for example, to inflict pain or delay making a payment.
*   A party needs formal discovery to evaluate the strength of its legal case.
*   A crucial stakeholder refuses to join the process.

Some commentators also see mediation as inherently unjust, arguing that the very informality of the process allows the intrusion of prejudice that is suppressed by more formal procedures. Mediation, it is argued, also facilitates case-by-case resolutions that siphon off pressure for law reform (although nothing prevents parties from mediating the content of a consent decree).

Other critics concede that ADR may be useful generally, but object to its application to specific areas such as spousal abuse cases. By suggesting that legal standards are only one point of reference, they say, ADR opens the way for the exploitation of unsophisticated parties. Such criticism is particularly strong in situations in which participation in mediation is mandatory, as when parents litigating over child custody are required to go through ADR as a precondition to obtaining a court hearing. Other writers have suggested that minorities tend to do less well in certain forms of mediation. Still another issue is whether ADR gives an advantage to "repeat players" such as corporations and insurers. Some studies have also called into question a basic premise of court-related mediation programs — that they reduce the duration of cases. All of these critiques raise significant policy issues that are discussed in more depth in Chapter 14.

Questions

The article regarding Toro Corporation's use of mediation describes the company's initial approach to injured persons as follows:

> From the moment the victims answer [the paralegal's] knock on the door, they're assaulted by nice. Kelly and Gotzian avoid business garb; instead they don Toro polo shirts and khaki pants. They explain that they're not lawyers, a point the company takes very seriously. "Bring a sharply dressed lawyer to one of these meetings, and immediately you'll see the walls go up," says Byers. "If Carol and Helen were attorneys, this program simply wouldn't work."

Two leading professors had these comments about Toro's approach to settlement:

> "I can't imagine that the plaintiffs are truly getting what they deserve," says Laura Nader, a professor of law and anthropology at the University of California, Berkeley . . . "The [Toro] plaintiffs are giving up one of their most fundamental rights — the right to our court system." But Stephen Gillers, a legal ethics expert at New York University School of Law, retorts, "These plaintiffs are free to walk away at any time: They're not getting [coerced] into anything."

4. Do you agree more with Professor Nader or Professor Gillers? Why?
5. Should potential defendants be prohibited as a general rule from approaching injured parties who do not have a lawyer? What rule would you suggest?

3. *Examples of Mediation in Action*

a. **Death of a student**

Note: Confidentiality is one of the most important attributes of mediation. The facts in the following account that have not previously been published have been approved by attorneys for both parties.

In August 1997 Scott Krueger arrived for his freshman year at the Massachusetts Institute of Technology. Five weeks later, he was dead. In an incident that made national headlines, Krueger died of alcohol poisoning following an initiation event at a fraternity. Nearly two years later Krueger's parents sent MIT a demand letter stating their intent to sue. The letter alleged that MIT had caused their son's death by failing to address what they claimed were two long-standing campus problems: a housing arrangement that they said steered new students to seek rooms in fraternities, and what their lawyer called a culture of alcohol abuse at fraternities.

MIT's lawyers saw the case as one that could be won. An appellate court, they believed, would rule that a college is not legally responsible for an adult student's voluntary drinking. Moreover, under state law the university could not be required to pay more than $20,000 to the Kruegers (although that limit did not apply to claims against individual university administrators). MIT officials felt, however, that a narrowly drawn legal response would not be in keeping with its values. They also recognized that there were aspects of the institution's policies and practices — including those covering student use of alcohol — that could have been better. MIT's president, Charles M. Vest, was prepared to accept responsibility for these shortcomings on behalf of the university, and felt a deep personal desire for his institution to reach a resolution with the Krueger family. MIT also recognized that defending the case in court would exact a tremendous emotional toll on all concerned. The Kruegers would be subjected to a hard-hitting assessment of their son's behavior leading up to his death, whereas MIT would be exposed to equally severe scrutiny of the Institute's culture and the actions of individual administrators. Full-blown litigation in a case of this magnitude was also sure to be expensive, with estimated defense costs well in excess of $1 million.

The question, as MIT saw it, was not whether to seek to engage the Kruegers in settlement discussions, but how. The university decided to forego a traditional legal response and reply instead with a personal letter from President Vest to the Kruegers, which noted the university's belief that it had strong legal defenses to their claims, but offered to mediate.

The Kruegers responded with intense distrust. Tortuous negotiations ensued. The parents eventually agreed to mediate, but only subject to certain conditions: At least one session would have to occur in Buffalo, where the Kruegers lived. MIT would have to offer a sincere apology for its conduct; without that, no sum of money would settle the case. There would be no confidentiality agreement to prevent the parents from talking publicly about the matter, while at the same time any settlement could not be exploited by MIT for public relations purposes. The Kruegers would have the right to select the mediator. And, President Vest would have to appear personally at all the mediation sessions. The university agreed to most of the conditions and the mediation went forward.

MIT's lawyers believed that it was important that the Kruegers' lawyers and the mediator understand the strength of the university's defenses, but plaintiff counsel knew that subjecting the Kruegers to such a presentation would make settlement impossible. To resolve the dilemma, the lawyers bifurcated the process. The first day of the mediation, which the Kruegers would not attend, would focus on presentations by lawyers and would be held in Boston. One week later the mediation would resume at a conference center located a 40-minute drive outside Buffalo, this time with the Kruegers present. Their counsel selected that location so that "no one could leave easily." On the second day the Kruegers would personally meet President Vest, and the parties would begin to exchange settlement proposals.

Counsel had agreed that the mediator, Jeffrey Stern, should begin the day by having a private breakfast with Mr. and Mrs. Krueger and their lawyers. The Kruegers vented their anger, first to Stern and later to President Vest. "How could you do this?" they shouted at Vest, "You people killed our son!" They also challenged Vest on a point that bothered them terribly: Why, they asked him, had he come to their son's funeral but not sought them out personally to extend his condolences? Vest responded that he had consulted with people about whether or not to approach the Kruegers and was advised that, in light of their anger at the institution, it would be better not to do so. That advice was wrong, he said, and he regretted following it.

Vest went on to apologize for the university's role in what he described as a "terrible, terrible tragedy." "We failed you," he said, and then asked, "What can we do to make it right?" Mrs. Krueger cried out again at Vest, but at that point her husband turned to her and said, "The man apologized. What more is there to say?" Their counsel, Leo Boyle, later said that he felt that, "There's a moment . . . where the back of the case is broken. You can feel it. . . . And that was the moment this day." The mediator gradually channeled the discussion toward what the Kruegers wanted and what the university could do.

Hard bargaining followed, much of it conducted though shuttle diplomacy by the mediator. In the end the parties reached agreement: MIT paid the Kruegers $4.75 million to settle their claims and contributed an additional $1.25 million to a scholarship fund that the family would administer. Perhaps equally important, President Vest offered the Kruegers a personal, unconditional apology on behalf of MIT that no court could have compelled and that would not have been believed if it were. At the conclusion of the process Vest and Mrs. Krueger hugged each other. For MIT the settlement, although expensive, made sense: It minimized the harm that contested litigation would have caused to the institution. And, most important, the university felt that it was the right thing to do.

What did the mediator contribute to the process? During the first day, Stern questioned both lawyers closely about the legal and factual issues, creating a foundation for realistic assessments of case value later in the process. The initial money offers put forth by each party were far apart, but the mediator put them into context so that neither side gave up in frustration. According to plaintiff counsel Brad Henry, Stern's greatest contribution was probably the way he responded to the Kruegers' feelings: "What he did most masterfully was to allow a lot of the emotion to be directed at him. He allowed it almost to boil over when it was just him with the Kruegers, but later he very deftly let it be redirected at President Vest and the university. . . . He also prepared Charles Vest for the onslaught. . . . Mediation can be like a funeral — especially with the death of a child. He mediated the emotional part of the case, and then let the rest unfold on its own."

Questions

6.   What barriers made it difficult for the parties in the Krueger case to negotiate with each other directly? In what ways was mediation likely to be more effective than direct negotiation at overcoming them?
7.   What goals did the university have in proposing mediation? What did the student's family appear to be seeking from the process?
8.   What did the Kruegers obtain in mediation that they could not have won at trial?

---

b.   United States et al. v. Microsoft Corporation

In one of the highest profile antitrust cases in U.S. history, the Justice Department, later joined by several states, sued the Microsoft Corporation, arguing that it had monopolized certain markets in computer software. While the case was pending, judges twice ordered the parties into mediation processes, which are described in the following readings.

❖ **James Laflin and Robert Werth,** UNFINISHED BUSINESS:
ANOTHER LOOK AT THE MICROSOFT
MEDIATION: LESSONS FOR THE CIVIL LITIGATOR

12 Cal. Tort Rep. 88 (April 2001)

On November 18, 1999, twelve months into a case that was eventually to last eighteen, U.S. District Judge Thomas Penfield Jackson announced the appointment of Richard A. Posner, the Chief Judge of the Seventh Circuit Court of Appeals in Chicago, to serve as mediator in the Microsoft antitrust case. . . . Posner was neither a practiced diplomat nor experienced mediator. However, he brought other credentials to the table. He had gained recognition as one of the most capable, influential members of the federal bench, and a recognized authority in the field of antitrust law. . . .

Posner's mission as a mediator was to induce Microsoft and the government to shed what he referred to as "emotionality" and come to a rational compromise. At the outset, the parties met for lunch at a private club, in what would turn out to be the only face-to-face meeting of the entire mediation process. In attendance were lawyers representing Microsoft, the Justice Department and three attorneys general representing the nineteen states who joined as plaintiffs in the suit. In describing the protocol, Posner indicated he would refrain from evaluating the strength of either side's case, "try to deflate unrealistic expectations" and keep all talks in confidence. Each side was asked "to make a detailed presentation of the facts and remedies it would consider." Posner promised to devote himself almost full time to the process.

To mitigate "emotionality" Judge Posner ordered separate meetings for at least the first month, the government each Monday, Microsoft each Tuesday. Two months later the process had evolved into a form of shuttle diplomacy interspersed with the judge's email inquiries seeking additional information. He began, in the words of one Microsoft negotiator, "growling at the other side, growling at us." After two months of work Posner outlined the first draft of a settlement proposal. Over the next several months, some nineteen draft proposals were exchanged via Posner, who edited them into his own language and emailed them either to Microsoft's General Counsel, or the chief of the Justice Department's Antitrust Division. Copies went to the chair of the association of the nineteen state attorneys general.

By mid-February, negotiations had stalled. Neither side believed that the other was open to a compromise, and both sides were often confused. At Microsoft, this was reflected by [General Counsel] Bill Neukum[,] who said of Posner, "You keep asking yourself, 'Is he wearing his hat as a mediator, trying to motivate people to narrow their differences and come together, or is he speaking as the Chief Judge of the Seventh Circuit, who's an expert on antitrust law?'" Compounding this confusion, neither side could be sure whether, or which, terms contained in the successive draft proposals originated with Judge Posner or came directly from their adversary.

From late February 2000 through the end of March, Posner had extensive telephone conversions with Microsoft, sometimes with [Chairman William] Gates directly, and with Justice Department attorneys, in which successive draft agreements were negotiated and refined. In early March Gates seemed close to accepting the deal reflected in draft fourteen, which Posner forwarded to the Justice Department and the states. The states were given ten days to accept, or Posner would terminate the process. The state attorneys general made it clear that Joel Klein [chief of the Justice Department team] was not their spokesperson and responded separately to the proposal. The states were angry with both Posner and Klein. As one state official said, "Posner was more interested in dealing with Gates and Klein and didn't perceive that he had nineteen other parties to the lawsuit. . . . He got enamored of talking to Gates. And he's not a mediator by training, and lacked basic mediation skills."

Posner was prepared to summon the parties to Chicago for direct face-to-face negotiations starting on March 24th. Their options would be to accept the basic terms contained in the most recent draft, or face termination of the mediation. More emails and telephone conversations between Posner and the two sides ensued. Meanwhile, the states had communicated their disapproval of parts of draft eighteen and added further conditions. Posner now realized he would have to negotiate with the nineteen state attorneys general to develop a single government proposal. Then, even if that could be accomplished, he would still have to negotiate the divide between the government stakeholders and Microsoft. That night he telephoned Microsoft and Klein and announced that his mediation effort was over.

The Microsoft case went to trial and the court found that Microsoft had violated antitrust laws. Judge Jackson ordered a breakup of the company, and Microsoft appealed. Several months later the court of appeals upheld some of the trial court's findings of antitrust violations, rejected others, and disapproved the court's breakup remedy. Criticizing the conduct of the trial judge, particularly his decision to talk privately with a reporter, the appeals court appointed a new judge to preside over the case. Other changes had occurred: While the appeal was pending, a new president had taken office and the Justice Department had announced that it would no longer seek a breakup of the company. Before resuming hearings, the second trial judge again referred the Microsoft case to mediation. The following reading summarizes its results.

❖ **Eric Green and Jonathan Marks,** *How*
We Mediated the Microsoft Case

The Boston Globe, A23 (November 15, 2001)

Mediators never kiss and tell. But within the bounds of appropriate confidentiality, lessons can be learned from the three-week mediation marathon that led to Microsoft's settlements with the Department of Justice and at least nine states. Federal District Judge Colleen Kollar-Kotelly took over the case after the Court of Appeals partially affirmed the prior judge's findings that Microsoft had violated antitrust laws. . . . Neither the mediation nor the settlements would have happened if Kollar-Kotelly had not acted to suspend litigation and order settlement negotiations. The judge's Sept. 28 mandate was blunt: "The Court expects that the parties will . . . engage in an all-out effort to settle these cases, meeting seven days a week and around the clock, acting reasonably to reach a fair resolution." The court gave the parties two weeks to negotiate on their own, ordering them to mediation if they couldn't reach agreement by then. The court bounded its "24/7" timetable by ordering the parties to complete mediation by Nov. 2. . . . Tight timetables command attention. In mediation, just as in negotiation, time used tends to expand to fit time available. A firm deadline gets the parties to focus. . . .

We are both mediators, with 40 years of combined experience. . . . But we are not experts in the applicable law or the disputed technology. . . . Even had we had such expertise, our objective would not have been to try to craft our own settlement solution and sell its merits to the parties. We believed that the only chance of getting all or most parties to a settlement was for us to work intensively to help them create their own agreement. Our "job one" was to facilitate and assist in the gestation, birth, and maturing of such an agreement. We had to be advocates for settlement — optimistic and persistent — but not advocates for any particular settlement. . . .

Reaching a settlement required working with adversarial parties with very different views about a large number of technologically and legally complicated issues. When we arrived on the scene, the parties had begun exchanging drafts of possible settlement terms. . . . After initial separate briefings, we moved the process into an extended series of joint meetings, involving representatives of the Antitrust Division, the state attorneys general and their staffs, and Microsoft. No party was left out of the negotiations. The bargaining table had three sides. . . .

Throughout most of the mediation the 19 states and the federal government worked as a combined "plaintiffs" team. We worked to ensure the right mix of people, at the table and in the background. The critical path primarily ran through managing and focusing across-the-table discussions and drafting by subject matter experts — lawyers and computer mavens — with knowledge of the technological and business complexities gained through working on the case since its inception. The critical path also required working with senior party-representatives who could make principled decisions about priorities and deal breakers.

[As a result of the mediation, Microsoft, the Justice Department, and ten state attorneys general reached agreement.] Even as settlement advocates we have no quarrel with the partial settlement that was achieved. . . . Successful mediations are ones in which mediators and parties work to identify and overcome barriers to reaching agreement. . . . Successful mediations are ones in which, settle or not, senior representatives of each party have made informed and intelligent decisions. The Microsoft mediation was successful.

Note: The remaining nine attorneys general filed objections to the settlement with the trial judge, but both the trial and appeals courts upheld its terms.

Questions

9. Neutrals reveal their own definition of mediation by the manner in which they practice it. Looking at the techniques that Judge Posner applied, what appeared to be his concept of how mediation should work?

10. In what ways did mediators Green and Marks view the process differently?

11. Green and Marks emphasize the importance of deadlines. Do you think the judge could have achieved the same settlement result by setting a firm trial date and ordering the parties to negotiate with each other directly?

c. **Mediating as an Interested Party**

❖ **Stephen B. Goldberg,** MEDIATING THE DEAL: HOW TO MAXIMIZE
VALUE BY ENLISTING A NEUTRAL'S HELP AT AND AROUND
THE BARGAINING TABLE

24 Alternatives 147 (2006)

If you've ever been part of an organizational team preparing to negotiate an agreement with another organization, you probably have faced this frustrating task: aligning your individual interests, other team members' interests, and those of your company as a whole.

For instance, imagine that you're the sales vice president for an automobile manufacturer, and that you're in charge of the corporate team responsible for negotiating a contract for the sale of next year's models to a large car-rental firm. As sales VP, you want to boost sales by offering as many models as possible. The production representative wants to offer as few models as possible, to streamline the production process. The finance VP doesn't care how many models are offered, but wants an accelerated payment schedule to maximize this year's cash flow. Meanwhile, the legal representative wants contract terms that will maximize your company's protection in the event the buyer declares bankruptcy.

How can you coordinate these different interests while ensuring that the team meets its overall corporate goal of achieving a good deal? An obvious, though infrequently used, source of expertise can help: a professional mediator. . . .

A few years ago, I was asked to serve as a facilitator for and adviser to a corporate team from a telecommunications firm that was preparing to negotiate with five other telecom companies on the division of radio spectrum for cellular telephone relay satellites. . . . All team members were knowledgeable about the cell phone industry, and some were experts on satellite transmission. I knew little of the former and nothing of the latter. I was concerned about how much I could contribute to the team's success. As the internal negotiations progressed, however, I discovered that I could perform a valuable function. . . .

Using my mediation skills, I assisted the team in developing a common position that each department regarded as sufficiently protective of its interests. . . . The bulk of my work took place prior to external negotiations. I first met separately with each team member and key personnel in that member's department to get a sense of the interests underlying each department's position and the relative importance of each interest. For example, I learned that certain aspects of the new technology were less dear to the engineers than others and could be dropped from their demands if more important aspects were protected. . . .

Once I knew the core interests of each department, I engaged in "shuttle diplomacy," trying out proposed tradeoffs with each department. I then assembled the entire team to see if the team members could agree on an overall position. With my knowledge of key interests and possible tradeoffs, [r]eaching overall agreement was not difficult. Next, the operations VP assessed whether the common position fully represented overall corporate interests. His alterations led to a further round of mediated internal negotiations that formed a corporate position acceptable to all. . . .

Mediator's Role: External Negotiations

What happened next was perhaps the most surprising aspect of the experience. During the inter-corporate negotiations among the various telecom firms, I sat silently in the back of the room. Only during recesses did I talk, advising "my" team. . . .

The other negotiating teams became curious about the silent "outsider" and began questioning me about my role. On learning that I was a professional mediator with no direct stake in the amount of spectrum gained by my team, other teams began presenting proposals to me. They asked whether I thought the proposals would appeal to my team, and made some of my suggested changes to improve their acceptability. Thus, I ended up mediating not only among different members of my team but also between my team and some of the other teams. The result was a successful negotiation leading to an agreement on most issues. . . .

There is an alternative to using an outside mediator to assist the firm, organization, or corporation in preparing for negotiation. If there exists someone in the company, perhaps in the legal department, who has no personal or departmental stake in the negotiation's outcome, is trusted by all participants, and has mediation skills and experience, that person could serve as negotiation adviser. So, too, could someone from the company's outside law firm, subject to the same qualifications — and subject to the fact that this person, too, would be a sort of outsider. . . .

Questions

12. Have you seen an example of a person who acted as a "quasi-mediator," in the sense that he or she brought people together to make agreements without any formal title or role as a mediator? What was his or her formal role?
13. Have you ever seen someone take on a quasi-mediative role in a family or community setting?

---

4. The Evolution of Legal Mediation

The public thinks of dispute resolution primarily in terms of court trials. Court access to remedy wrongs and enforce legal rights is central to American democracy and we have fashioned a system of rules to ensure fair trials and provide a finely tuned system of public justice. However, litigation, with all of its procedural protections, is slow, costly, and relatively inflexible. The process is also centered on lawyers, restricting the roles and options for the disputing parties. Finally, the remedies available through adjudication are limited to what can be enforced through courts; most commonly, judicial resolutions consist of money judgments.

In part because of these limitations, alternatives to adjudication have long existed. Mediation has probably existed for nearly as long as humans have lived together — think, for example, of a village elder assisting members of a tribe or village to settle a quarrel. History offers many examples of the use of mediative processes. Thousands of years ago, Chinese villagers were accustomed to resolving disputes through the assistance of respected leaders, and commercial disputes were mediated in England before the Norman invasion.

Modern American mediation began in response to the rise of organized labor. Following initiatives in several states, Congress in 1898 authorized railroads and their unions to invoke mediation and in 1913 created a Board of Mediation and Conciliation to deal with such cases. Labor mediation expanded greatly in the first half of the twentieth century, and the process began to be applied to other legal disputes. By the early 1920s, for example, mediation programs for civil cases existed in courts in New York, Minneapolis, Cleveland, and other cities. Following World War II legal reformers began to promote the use of mediation in other subject areas, with special emphasis on using mediation to lower the frequency of divorce.

Civil mediation received a powerful boost during the late 1970s from prominent jurists who believed that the justice system was in crisis. Although some have argued that this concern was overstated (Galanter, 1983), it led judges, academics, and bar leaders to advocate increased use of ADR. During the same period, leaders at the local level argued for using mediation to deal with neighborhood disputes, and support continued to grow for applying mediation in family cases (Folberg and Taylor, 1984).

During the 1980s courts and litigators experimented with the use of mediation to resolve civil disputes outside the divorce arena. At first lawyers approached the process cautiously, concerned that their willingness to mediate would be interpreted by opponents as weakness. Bar leaders and judges, however, continued to voice support for the process and, equally important, corporations began to throw their weight behind the use of ADR to reduce the cost of litigation and the risk of uncertain verdicts. Some 4,000 companies, for example, have signed a formal pledge undertaking to consider ADR before resorting to traditional litigation, and more than 1,500 law firms have signed a similar pledge; the corporate version of the pledge appears in Chapter 20.

In 1990 Congress mandated that every federal district court create a plan that incorporated ADR to control litigation delay, and in 1998 it reaffirmed that requirement. By the mid-1990s most state and federal courts had established court-connected ADR programs for a wide variety of civil disputes, and mediation quickly became by far the most popular process used in such programs (Stienstra et al., 1996). The 1990s also saw federal and state government agencies using mediation more frequently to resolve public disputes. As one measure of the growth of the process, by the end of the decade states had enacted more than 2,000 statutes that mentioned mediation (Cole et al., 2008).

As the use of mediation became more widespread, some commentators questioned whether the process, particularly as applied in court-connected programs, might stifle law reform, condemn low-income groups to a second-class form of justice, prejudice abused women and children, or disadvantage the powerless. At the same time new data called into question some of the premises of the mediation movement, for example that court ADR programs sped the processing of cases (Kakalik et al., 1996), although other studies found that mediation did generate significant savings of time and money (Stienstra et al., 1997; Stipanowich, 2003). We explore these policy issues more deeply in Chapter 14. Although the recognition of these complex issues has shaped mediation debate and practice, none has prevented mediation from growing rapidly in popularity.

B. Goals and Mediator Styles

1. Goals for the Process

When you participate in mediation as an advocate, what will be your goal for the process? The answer may seem simple: to settle a legal dispute as favorably as possible. But the question is often more complex. Parties' goals in the process vary widely. For example, an organization that advocates ADR in business disputes stresses that "Mediation provides a framework for parties to . . . achieve remedies that may be outside the scope of the judicial process- . . . maintain privacy . . . preserve or minimize damage to relationships and reduce the costs and delay of dispute resolution" (CPR Institute, 1999). By contrast, a prominent personal injury lawyer has described the process as

> an opportunity — a time for you, as the legal representative of your client, to avoid putting your client through the litigation "mill" . . . and get results. . . . It is a means of essentially "selling" your client's lawsuit to a buyer, who buys off the expense and exposure of an ongoing lawsuit. The client has the money to begin the life restructuring process and has avoided the pressures and uncertainties of litigation. . . . (Kornblum, 2004)

The goals you pursue in mediation may change greatly from one situation to another, and should influence your choices about structuring the process. As a lawyer representing clients you might have one or more of the following purposes for electing to mediate.

a.   Resolve a Legal Claim on the Best Possible Monetary Terms

When litigators enter mediation, their goal is usually to settle a legal dispute. Most trial lawyers take a narrow approach to the process, discussing only legally relevant facts and issues and setting a goal of obtaining the best possible monetary payment in return for ending the case. When litigators talk about mediation they often reflect this perspective. One lawyer, for example, has said, "The effective advocate approaches mediation as if it were a trial . . . the overwhelming benefit of mediation is that it can reduce the cost of litigation" (Weinstein, 1996).

Perhaps in response, commercial mediators often see their primary role as facilitating distributive bargaining over money. One neutral, for example, wrote that, "In the typical civil mediation, money is the primary (if not the only) issue" (Contuzzi, 2000), and another has said, "The goal of resolution is always the same: allowing the parties to negotiate to a 'reasonable ballpark,' in which they, with the help of the mediator, identify 'home plate' based on what a jury will consider 'a reasonable verdict range'" (Max, 1999).

In the typical commercial dispute, then, litigants and counsel are likely to enter the process assuming that it will focus primarily on legal arguments and positional bargaining over money. Although this kind of negotiation often produces less-than-optimal results, a mediator can do a great deal to assist parties even when money is the only issue over which the disputants are willing to bargain.

> *Example:* An inexperienced plaintiff's lawyer was representing an automobile accident victim in negotiations with the defendant's insurer. The victim had suffered broken bones and had out-of-pocket damages totaling $6,000. Requested by the defendant's adjuster to make a settlement demand, the plaintiff counsel asked for $1.2 million. The adjuster was incredulous: In her experience, plaintiff lawyers rarely demanded more than ten times the "out-of-pockets." She refused to "dignify" the plaintiff's "wild number" with a response, and the result was a complete breakdown of talks.
>
> The case went to mediation. In a private meeting with the plaintiff and his counsel, the mediator asked about their goals in the negotiation. The lawyer said that he was willing to be flexible and the client indicated that he was seeking a much more modest amount than the $1.2 million demand might suggest. The neutral asked the plaintiff lawyer to make a new offer at a much lower level. She offered to tell the adjuster that the plaintiff had done this only to accommodate the mediator's request that both sides "cut to the chase," and that the plaintiff expected the defendant to respond in a similar vein. Three hours later the case settled at $27,500.

b.   Develop a Broad, Interest-Based Resolution

As we have seen, parties to legal disputes often have interests that go far beyond money, and settlements that respond to these concerns can provide greater value to disputants than a purely monetary outcome. Some lawyers employ mediation to facilitate interest-based bargaining and obtain creative resolutions. One text for corporate attorneys, for example, emphasizes that "The process creates an opportunity to explore underlying business interests [and] offers the potential for a 'win-win' solution . . .' (Picker, 2003), while another describes the process as providing "a framework for parties to . . . privately reveal to the mediator in caucus sensitive interests that may assist the mediator to facilitate broad solutions" (CPR Institute, 1999).

Example: A company that processed hazardous chemical waste and one of its residential abutters had been embroiled for years in a series of disputes over the company's applications for licenses to expand its operations. They eventually agreed to mediate. Although the parties at first focused exclusively on the meaning of certain state hazardous waste regulations, the mediator noted that the abutter became most angry when he mentioned the company's practice of parking large trucks filled with waste on the street across from his house. The company insisted that such situations resulted from unpredictable traffic jams at the plant, but the abutter maintained that the problem showed the company's basic callousness about its neighbors' safety.

As he spoke with the parties, the mediator found that the company also wanted to end the practice and could do so if it could widen its driveway to accommodate two trucks at a time. This was impossible because the driveway was wedged against the abutter's land. That land was not, however, being used. As part of a settlement, the mediator convinced the abutter to convey a narrow strip of his unused land to the company. The company in turn agreed to widen its driveway, thus solving the truck parking problem for everyone and increasing the value of the abutter's remaining land.

c. Repair the Parties' Relationship

Parties sometimes enter mediation not so much to obtain specific terms of settlement as to repair their relationship. The act of filing suit is usually understood as a decision to sever any connection between the parties (Galanter, 1983), but many believe that "mediation has as its primary goal the repair of the troubled relationship" (Fuller, 1971).

Example: An Austrian company that marketed a process to stop soil erosion along river banks and a principal officer of its U.S. affiliate were in a dispute. The plaintiff was the founder of the company, who had trained the other protagonist, a young American woman, to create a subsidiary to sell his process in the United States. The woman modified the process in the belief that the original version would not fit the American market. This triggered a violent disagreement with the founder. Faced with the prospect of resolving the dispute or declaring bankruptcy, the shareholders and executives agreed to meet.

The founder arrived at the mediation and sat rigid and silent as others talked. When the mediator asked him to give his perspective on the situation he refused: His position was stated in a letter that everyone had received. What else needed to be said? Still, the mediator asked if he would read the letter aloud to ensure that everyone heard him clearly. As the founder began to read, feelings began to show under his stolid exterior. The woman responded angrily and they began to argue. It seemed to be a classic daughter/mentee-grows-up-and-challenges-father/mentor situation. Eventually the two went to a corner and talked animatedly for more than an hour.

Afterward, in a calmer atmosphere, the mediator led the principals through a discussion of the challenges facing the firm and how they might solve them. Under the leadership of a new CEO not linked to either protagonist, painful changes were agreed to and the company survived.

d. Change the Parties' Perspectives

In a still broader view, the purpose of the mediation process is not to obtain a specific outcome but rather to assist parties in transforming their perspectives on the dispute and each other, a change that might or might not lead to an improvement in their relationship. Advocates of this approach, known as "transformative" mediation, believe that the disputants should be allowed to take charge of the mediation process with the mediator serving simply as a resource to facilitate conversations. The transformative approach is described in more detail later.

e. Choices Among Goals

Although a particular mediation can have more than a single purpose, the process can be viewed as falling along a continuum (see Figure 1).

Figure 1.

Potential Goals in Mediation

| Monetary result | Interest-based solution | Repair of the relationship | Transformation of perspectives |

How likely is it in practice that if an attorney seeks a goal, he will be able to achieve it — how often, in other words, can parties in civil or "commercial" mediation expect to leave the process with a purely monetary settlement, an interest-based solution, or a relationship repair?

The answer will be heavily influenced by the nature of the case, the attitudes of clients and counsel, and the skills and goals of the mediator. Relationship repair in mediation is often not feasible; in most automobile tort cases, for example, there is no prior relationship to revive. Even when a dispute does arise in a relationship, the parties often litigate bitterly before mediating, and in such situations repairing the relationship is very difficult. Sometimes, however, both sides recognize that it is in their interest to heal their rupture. This is most common in settings in which the parties' past connection has been strong and their alternatives to relating are not attractive.

One example is a quarrel between a divorcing couple over parenting their children. Relationships can be important in commercial settings as well; partners in small businesses, like the Austrian-American venture described above, may have a strong interest in seeking a repair of a troubled relationship because neither is able to buy out the other and continued conflict will destroy the enterprise. A study of mediations of civil disputes arising from relationships (excluding unionized labor and divorce cases, and large enough to justify the retention of lawyers) found a pattern of outcomes shown in Figure 2.

Figure 2.
Outcomes of Legal Mediation in "Relationship" Cases

Repair of relationship	*Integrative term and money, but no repair*	*Money terms only*	*Impasse*
17%	30%	27%	27%

Figure 2 shows that when parties mediate a legal dispute arising from a significant prior relationship using a professional mediator, about 15 to 20 percent of the time they are able to repair their relationship, roughly 30 percent of the time they achieve a settlement with at least one significant integrative term in addition to money,[1] there is a 25 to 30 percent probability of a simple money settlement, and there is a 25 to 30 percent likelihood of impasse. Interestingly, focusing only on cases that settled, agreements that contained a relationship repair or one integrative term totaled 47 percent, a much higher percentage than pure money settlements, which totaled 27 percent (Golann, 2002). Another study found that nonmonetary terms were included in most settlements of contract disputes, but seldom in personal injury (mainly auto accident) cases (Wissler, 2006).

As a lawyer you are likely to encounter many situations in which a client's only goal is to end a relationship with an adversary on the best possible terms. The data suggest, however, that in cases that arise from a prior relationship, it is feasible more often than not to obtain agreements that include at least one term of significant value to the parties apart from money, and that in a small but appreciable percentage of cases, the parties repair their relationship.

---

1. Examples of integrative terms in business disputes included an agreement among parties breaking up a partnership that one partner would have the exclusive use of certain billing software, or that the ex-partners would continue to share office space. In employment cases, companies agreed to terms such as temporarily maintaining the health coverage of a departing employee or changing records to reflect a voluntary resignation rather than a termination, and employees sometimes agreed never to apply for employment with the company again. Releases of liability and confidentiality agreements were not counted as integrative terms in the survey because they were typically assented to as a matter of course.

Question

14. In what types of disputes are the parties likely to find it difficult or costly to sever their connection? In what kinds of cases should it be relatively easy to do so?

2. Mediator Styles

One key issue that you will confront when representing clients in mediation is selecting a neutral. Most communities now have a large number of mediators, and different neutrals have widely varying styles. Depending on the dispute and the personalities and goals of the participants, you may select different types of mediators. Indeed, experienced lawyers sometimes look for a mediator who can best influence the *other* party to the dispute.

a. Classifying Styles

It is possible to classify mediators according to the goals they pursue and the methods they use to achieve them, and to show the results graphically, as in the following reading.

❖ **Leonard L. Riskin,** *Retiring and Replacing the Grid of Mediator Orientations*

21 Alternatives 69 (April 2003) and 12 Alternatives 111 (Summer 1994)

[A decade ago, there was] a vast and diverse array of processes . . . called mediation. Yet there was no accepted system for distinguishing among the various approaches. As a result, there was great confusion in the field about what mediation is and what it should be. . . . Looking back, I like to think about this confusion in terms of three gaps between mediation theory — that is, what the well-known writings and training programs, mainly those focusing on civil, non-labor mediation, said mediators did or should do — and mediation practice — that is, what mediators actually did.

First, mediation theory held that mediators don't evaluate, make predictions about what would happen in court, or tell parties what to do. In practice, however, many mediators evaluated and told people what to do. Second, mediation theory said that mediation was intended to address the parties' underlying interests or real needs, rather than, or in addition to, their legal claims. Quite commonly, however, mediations in civil disputes — especially those that were in the litigation process, or might be — were narrow and adversarial. The third disparity between theory and practice concerned self-determination. The "experts" touted mediation's potential for enhancing self-determination. Yet in practice, many mediation processes did not fulfill that promise.

These gaps between theory and practice produced a number of problems. The most salient problem concerned evaluation [a mediator's willingness to give an opinion as to the likely outcome of a case in adjudication, or to propose terms of settlement]: Sometimes parties went into a mediation thinking they were not going to get an evaluation, but got one nevertheless — without consenting to it or preparing for it. And sometimes the reverse happened: Parties who thought they would get an evaluation, because they were analogizing mediation to some judicial settlement conferences, didn't get one. Similarly, parties who entered a mediation thinking it would focus either broadly or narrowly often were surprised to find the opposite focus. And some mediators gave short shrift to party self-determination by exercising extensive control of the focus and even the outcome.

For all these reasons, great ambiguity suffused most conversations about mediation. In addition, many parties, potential parties, lawyers, and mediators did not recognize the existence of numerous choices about what would happen in a mediation and that someone would make those choices, either explicitly or implicitly. [To address these problems, I proposed a system for classifying mediator orientations.] It focused primarily on two of the gaps: evaluation by the mediator and problem-definition (which was my vehicle for addressing the tendency of many commercial mediators to focus on positions, in the form of claims of legal entitlements, rather than underlying interests). . . .

. . . The classification system [starts] with two principal questions: 1. Does the mediator tend to define problems narrowly or broadly? 2. Does the mediator think she should evaluate — make assessments or predictions or proposals for agreements — or facilitate the parties' negotiation without evaluating? The answers reflect the mediator's beliefs about the nature and scope of mediation and her assumptions about the parties' expectations.

Problem Definition

Mediators with a narrow focus assume that the parties have come to them for help in solving a technical problem. The parties have defined this problem in advance through the positions they have asserted in negotiations or pleadings. Often it involves a question such as, "Who pays how much to whom?" or "Who can use such-and-such property?" As framed, these questions rest on "win-lose" (or "distributive") assumptions. In other words, the participants must divide a limited resource; whatever one gains, the other must lose. The likely court outcome — along with uncertainty, delay and expense — drives much of the mediation process. Parties, seeking a compromise, will bargain adversarially, emphasizing positions over interests.

A mediator who starts with a broad orientation, on the other hand, assumes that the parties can benefit if the mediation goes beyond the narrow issues that normally define legal disputes. Important interests often lie beneath the positions that the participants assert. Accordingly, the mediator should help the participants understand and fulfill those interests — at least if they wish to do so.

The Mediator's Role

The evaluative mediator assumes that the participants want and need the mediator to provide some directions as to the approximate grounds for settlement — based on law, industry practice, or technology. She also assumes that the mediator is qualified to give such direction by virtue of her experience, training, and objectivity.

The facilitative mediator assumes the parties are intelligent, able to work with their counterparts, and capable of understanding their situation better then either their lawyers or the mediator. So the parties may develop better solutions than any that the mediator might create. For these reasons, the facilitative mediator assumes that his principal mission is to enhance and clarify communications between the parties in order to help them decide what to do. The facilitative mediator believes it is inappropriate for the mediator to give his opinion, for at least two reasons. First, such opinions might impair the appearance of impartiality and thereby interfere with the mediator's ability to function. Second, the mediator might not know enough — about the details of the case or the relevant law, practices, or technology — to give an informed opinion.

Mediators usually have a predominant orientation, whether they know it or not, based on a combination of their personalities, experiences, education, and training. Thus, many retired judges, when they mediate, tend toward an evaluative-narrow orientation.

Yet mediators do not always behave consistently with the predominant orientations they express. . . . In addition, many mediators will depart from their orientations to respond to the dynamics of the situation. . . . [As an] example: an evaluative-narrow mediator may explore underlying interests (a technique normally associated with the broad orientation) after her accustomed narrow focus results in a deadlock. And a facilitative-broad mediator might use a mildly evaluative tactic as a last resort. For instance, he might toss out a figure that he thinks the parties might be willing to agree upon, while stating that the figure does not represent his prediction of what would happen in court. . . . Many effective mediators are versatile and can move from quadrant to quadrant (and within a quadrant), as the dynamics of the situation dictate, to help parties settle disputes. . . .

I appreciate the insight of Professor George Box: "All models are wrong. Some are useful." No graphic can capture the rich complexity of real life. Nevertheless, I hope that this grid will be useful.

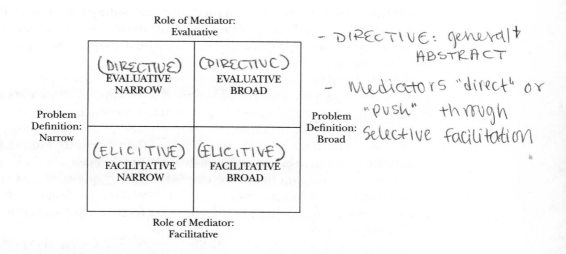

Role of Mediator: Elicitive and Directive

Professor Riskin has refined his grid by replacing the word "evaluative" with "directive" and "facilitative" with "elicitive" (the "broad" versus "narrow" continuum remains the same) for the following reasons.

> First, the terms "directive" and "elicitive" more closely approximate my goals for this continuum, which [are] to focus on the impact of the mediator's behavior on party self-determination. Second, the term "directive" is more general and abstract than "evaluative" and therefore may cover a wider range of mediator behaviors. . . . Using the terms "directive" and "elicitive" also can help us recognize that mediators can direct (or push) the parties toward particular outcomes through "selective facilitation" — directing discussion of outcomes the mediator favors, while not promoting discussions of outcomes the mediator does not favor — without explicitly evaluating a particular outcome. (Riskin, 2003d)

Most writing on mediator styles continues to use evaluative-facilitative terminology, and we will use those terms in this book. Students interested in exploring the issue of mediator style more deeply should read Professor Riskin's articles referenced in the bibliography.

Question

15. Have you seen a demonstration or video of the mediation process? Using the Riskin grid, how would you classify the mediators whom you observed?

b. Do Mediators Have a Single Style?

Do legal mediators use a single goal orientation and style throughout their practice, or at least during a single mediation? To investigate this issue, one of the authors filmed several mediators mediating the same civil case in role-play format. He found, as Professor Riskin suggests, that good neutrals do not maintain a single orientation, but instead adapt their approach to fit the circumstances of a dispute.

Indeed, the filmed mediators often changed their style repeatedly during a single meeting with a party. All began in a broadly facilitative mode, asking about the parties' business and personal interests, but were usually met with narrowly evaluative comments from the lawyers, who focused on arguing the strength of their legal cases. The mediators adjusted to the lawyers, remaining facilitative but focusing on legal issues and facts. Periodically during the process, most mediators returned to "broad" questions, asking about clients' interests and suggesting nonmonetary solutions. Some of the disputants responded by moving toward a broader focus, and others continued to remain narrowly evaluative.

The experiment confirmed Riskin's observation that successful legal mediators are not consistently either facilitative or evaluative. The neutrals in the study did become increasingly evaluative over the course of each mediation, but their advice usually focused on the bargaining situation — how the other side was probably seeing the situation and what negotiating approach was likely to be effective ("If you make that offer, I'm concerned that they will react by . . . ") rather than the legal merits.

As the process continued, mediators became more willing to ask questions and make comments that suggested a view, or at least skepticism, about the disputants' legal arguments. However, when neutrals did make an evaluative comment they almost always framed it in general terms ("The evidence on causation seems thin . . . I'm concerned that a court might. . . . ").

Although commentators tend to speak in terms of a mediator's "preferred style," the stylistic changes of the mediators in the experiment seemed to be driven much more by who they were dealing with — the personalities and attitudes of the parties and lawyers — than by the tendencies of the mediators. The advocacy of the lawyers and decisions by the clients (for example, was a party representative willing to consider resuming a broken relationship?), in other words, counted for more than a mediator's orientation in happened during the process.

Questions

16. What type of mediator would you select if you were a lawyer representing the following clients?
     a. The family of the deceased MIT student.
     b. The chemical company in the abutter-chemical company case.
     c. The plaintiff in the "$1.2 million demand" personal injury mediation.

3. *Mediative Approaches and Techniques*

This section examines forms of mediation that you are likely to encounter in practice. As ADR has evolved, a wide variety of approaches have gained acceptance. Most lawyer-mediators focus on civil cases — that is, disputes involving the kinds of tort, contract, property, employment, and statutory claims that you have studied in law school, compared to marital or collective bargaining disputes. These are commonly referred to as "commercial" cases and the neutrals who handle them as commercial mediators. Commercial mediators almost all use a caucus-based format, and discussions in such cases tend to focus on what courts would consider legally relevant and on exchanges of money offers.

Mediators who specialize in divorce and other disputes between family members, by contrast, usually avoid caucusing and place more emphasis on the parties' nonmonetary interests. The setting in which mediation occurs — for example, whether it is an all-day affair or a two-hour process — also affects how the process develops. The following readings give a flavor of several models.

a. **Commercial Mediation**

Mediators who focus their practice on commercial disputes tend to use similar methods to conduct the process. A legal mediator's overall goal is to stimulate constructive negotiations. If mediation is invoked it is usually because parties are unable to negotiate effectively on their own because they are frustrated by barriers. A commercial mediator might therefore begin by seeking answers to two questions:

- What obstacles are preventing the parties from settling this dispute themselves?
- What strategy is most likely to overcome these barriers?

A mediator's understanding of what is keeping the parties apart will deepen over the course of a mediation, and the obstacles themselves may change as the process goes forward. Ideally a mediator's strategy would be attuned to each case. In practice, however, this might not be possible. Many commercial mediators use a similar sequence of techniques to deal with the barriers most likely to be present, customizing their approach as they go along. This section, written in the form of advice to a novice mediator, describes a six-step strategy.

A Basic Commercial Strategy

1. Build a Foundation for Success

The Challenge: Missing Elements — People, Data, Interactions.   Negotiations often fail because some essential element is missing. One side may have the wrong people — a key decision maker may be missing, or one of the bargainers may be so emotional he cannot make good decisions. At other times, parties do not have the data they need to settle: Defense counsel may not, for instance, know how the claimed damages were computed and without this information cannot get authority to settle. Such problems are difficult to fix once mediation begins and the clock begins to run.

The Response: Identify Issues and Address Them in Advance.   To identify and resolve such problems, it is best to start before the parties meet to mediate. The first step is to ask the lawyers for mediation statements and set up telephone conversations with each of them. Ask each attorney who he plans to bring and who needs to attend from the other party. If a decision maker is absent, work to bring her to the table. If key information is missing, suggest that a party provide it. Mediators can elicit information and persuade people to attend in circumstances in which the same request would be rejected if made by a party.

> *Example:* A company bought a shipping line, and later sued an accounting firm for allegedly overstating the enterprise's profitability and misleading it into overpaying. The buyer's lawyer called the mediator ahead of time to warn that it was crucial for his client, the buyer's CEO, to attend the mediation. However, he said, the CEO would not come unless the managing partner of the defendant did as well, and the plaintiff would not commit to attend first. The mediator called the defense attorney, who agreed that the principals should attend but said that his client also did not want to be the first to agree to come.
>
> The neutral decided to ask each side to tell her privately whether its principal would come if the other did so. When they both answered positively, she announced that both decision makers had agreed to attend.

Alternatively, you might learn that one of the participants needs more time to talk, for instance, because he is in the grip of strong emotions. With the opponent's assent you can meet privately with a disputant ahead of time, allowing people to begin to work through difficult emotions and arrive at mediation more ready to make decisions. Or a lawyer might ask that you use an unusual format for the process itself.

2. Allow Participants to Argue and Express Feelings

Challenge: Unresolved Process and Emotional Needs.   If parties don't settle, it's often because someone wants something more than particular settlement terms. A litigant might be looking instead for a process: the opportunity to appear before a neutral person, state his grievances, and know he has been heard. Or a party may have a need to express strong feelings directly to an adversary.

People may enter litigation expecting to have this opportunity, only to learn that emotions are relevant only if they serve a strategic purpose, such as supporting a claim for damages. As a result, disputants can remain trapped in feelings of anger and grief for years, never having a chance to speak freely. Until they feel heard out, however, parties are often not ready to settle.

Response: An Opportunity to Speak and Feel Heard. Mediation is not a court session and mediators are not judges, but the process can give parties the experience of receiving a hearing. They can see their lawyer argue their case, or present it themselves, and listen to an opponent's arguments. The mediator will not decide the dispute and might never even express an opinion about the merits, but she can demonstrate she has heard the disputants. The experience of telling one's story and feeling heard out by a neutral person can have a surprising impact on a person's willingness to settle. Arguing the merits also focuses participants on the facts and legal principles relevant to the controversy, and knowing that a neutral person will be listening encourages them to think through their arguments and avoid extremes.

This aspect of the process often has an emotional component as well. The need to express strong feelings to one's adversary is a very human one, felt by executives and mailroom clerks alike. At various points parties can express some of their feelings about the dispute and each other.

Example: A state trooper began a high-speed chase of a drunk driver in a small New England town. The driver ran a stop sign; straining to keep up, the policeman hit a third car that was crossing the intersection. The trooper was unhurt, but the driver of the third vehicle died instantly. He was a 17-year-old boy, only weeks away from his high school graduation.

The driver's family sued the state, arguing the trooper had been negligent in ignoring the stop sign. It was a typical tort case in which a jury would have to decide whether the officer had acted carelessly. Defense counsel investigated, looking for facts to show the victim had been drinking or careless. It seemed, however, that the boy was a model student, in fact the valedictorian of his class, and had left behind a loving family. On the other hand, the trooper was showing initiative in giving chase to a dangerous driver. It was a difficult case, but one the defense thought could be won, and counsel began the usual process of discovery.

Two years later, as trial approached, the defense decided to make a settlement offer. It was rejected. Defense counsel waited a few weeks and then made a more substantial offer. The word came back from the plaintiffs' lawyer that his clients would not settle. Why, the defense counsel asked: Didn't the family understand that juries in the area had been very hard on claimants lately, and the trooper had a reasonable defense? The plaintiffs' lawyer was apologetic, but said the family was adamant and refused even to make a counteroffer. Instead, he suggested they mediate, and emphasized that the family wanted to begin with a meeting with the trooper.

> Defense counsel agreed to mediate but resisted the idea of a joint meeting:
> What was the point of having angry people rehash the facts, given that the evi-
> dence was largely undisputed and the state, not the trooper, would pay for any
> settlement? Eventually, however, they agreed to the process.
>
> The opening session was an extraordinary event. The victim's mother,
> father, and sisters came; they talked not about the case, but about their lost
> son and brother. The mother read a poem to the trooper describing the hopes
> she had had for her dead son, and the life she knew they would never be able
> to share.
>
> The officer surprised everyone as well. Although he maintained he had not
> been negligent, he said he felt awful about what had happened. He had three
> sons, and had thought over and over about how he would feel if one of them
> were killed. He had asked to be assigned to desk work, he told the family,
> because he could no longer do high-speed chases.
>
> The parties did not reach an agreement that day, but as the family walked
> out one of the children turned to the trooper. "It's been three years since my
> brother died," she said, "and now I feel he's finally had a funeral." Two weeks
> later the defense settlement offer was accepted.

Emotional discussions are often uncomfortable for people and temporarily make them angrier, but over the course of a process difficult conversations can help disputants let go of feelings and consider settlement. You
can achieve a great deal simply by allowing the parties to talk about feelings
and disagreements in a controlled setting; Chapter 10 describes techniques
for managing this successfully.

3. Moderate the Bargaining

Challenge: Positional Tactics Leading to Impasse.   Negotiators often have
trouble reaching settlement because they use a positional approach to bargaining, trading monetary concessions until they reach agreement. We have
seen that positional bargaining can be successful but that it often makes
negotiators frustrated and angry, for example when one side makes an offer
that the other perceives as "insulting."

Response: Become the Moderator of the Process.   Ideally a mediator could
avoid adversarial bargaining over money entirely by convincing parties to
focus on principles and interests. In commercial mediation, however, parties
usually arrive suspicious of each other, focused on legal issues, and determined to engage in money bargaining. A mediator's only practical option
in such cases is often to facilitate the process the parties want while looking
for an opportunity to move them toward a more effective approach.

One way to facilitate money negotiations is to act as a coach. You can, for
example, ask a bargainer to support its number with an explanation ("I'll
communicate it, but if they ask how you got there what should I tell them?"),
or help a disputant assess how a planned tactic will work ("What do you think
their response will be if you start at $10,000?").

If coaching is not enough, a mediator can become a moderator, giving bargainers advice about how to keep the process moving ("If you want them to get to $100,000 with the next round, I think your offer to them needs to be in the range of 700 to 800K. . . . "). By using these steps in combination with a continuing discussion of the case, a mediator can often orchestrate a "dance" of concessions to move the parties toward settlement.

4.   Seek Out and Address Hidden Issues

Challenge: Disregard of Hidden Issues and Missed Opportunities.   Negotiations in legal cases are often blocked by hidden psychological obstacles, which could include the following:

Strong feelings. We have talked about the usefulness of drawing out feelings in premediation discussions or the opening session, but this is often not possible. Participants in commercial mediation typically arrive with "game faces on," presenting a businesslike demeanor even as feelings boil beneath the surface. When this occurs, simply giving a disputant the chance to express emotions is often not enough.

Unexploited opportunities for gain. We know that negotiators can often create more valuable outcomes by including nonmoney terms in settlement agreements, but that parties typically enter commercial mediation focused on legal arguments and expecting to bargain solely over money.

Response: Probe for and Deal with Hidden Issues.   Even as you are carrying out other tasks, look for clues to hidden emotions and overly narrow approaches to settlement. Chapter 10 describes ways to promote more valuable settlements and deal with emotional issues.

5.   Test the Parties' Alternatives; If Necessary, Evaluate the Adjudication Option

Challenge: Lack of Realism About the Outcome in Adjudication.   Participants in legal disputes often justify hard bargaining positions in terms of the merits of the dispute. They are asking for a great deal or offering little, they say, because they have a strong legal case. The problem, however, is that that both parties usually claim that they will win in court.

To some degree parties bluff about litigation options to justify their bargaining positions and do not expect to taken literally. To a surprising degree, however, disputants actually believe their clashing predictions. Even when a mediator points out to parties that their predictions of success are inherently impossible (one believes that it has a 70 percent chance of winning, for instance, and the other thinks it has a 60 percent chance of prevailing), their confidence remains unshaken: It is the other side, they say, that is being unrealistic. There are two basic causes for disputants' distorted thinking about legal alternatives. One is lack of information; the other, an inability to interpret the data disputants do have accurately.

Response: Foster an Information Exchange.   A first response to a disagreement over the legal merits is to help parties exchange information. Modern discovery rules are meant to require each side to disclose key evidence, but it is often surprising how little one party knows about the other's case even after years of litigation.

As a mediator, you can be an effective facilitator of information exchange. If, for example, a plaintiff has explained its theory of liability in detail but has given no explanation for its damage claim, you can suggest it flesh out damages to help the defendant get authority to settle. Parties will often respond cooperatively to a mediator's request, although they would have refused the same inquiry coming from their opponent.

> *Example:* A sales manager who had been fired by a computer software company sued his former employer for violating his contract. The company maintained that the termination was lawful. The case remained in discovery for years and then went to mediation. As the neutral caucused with the parties, it quickly became apparent that a major component of the manager's claims was equity options in the company. The plaintiff, however, had never been able to obtain the internal financial reports needed to value the options. He assumed that the company was concealing its wealth and intended to go public in the near future, an event that would make his options very valuable.
>
> Questioned about this in caucus, the company CEO said that he had ordered the data withheld from the plaintiff because "It's none of his business!" In fact, the company was only marginally profitable and everyone's options were "under water" — essentially worthless.
>
> The mediator suggested to the CEO that if there really was no pot of gold in the case, he could help settle it by letting the plaintiff know this. The CEO agreed, and the parties reviewed the financial data together. Within an hour the plaintiff was persuaded that his potential damages were much lower than he had thought, and a settlement was worked out that included verification of the company's financial representations and termination of the options.

Response: Reality Test.   Even when parties have the relevant information, we have seen that they often do not interpret it accurately. Another way to help to solve merits-based problems is therefore to help disputants analyze their legal case. The least intrusive way is through questions that help parties focus on evidence and issues they have missed. It is important both to ask questions pointed enough to prompt someone to confront a problem and to avoid comments so tough the disputant concludes the mediator as taken sides against her.

Questions and analysis.   Begin with open-ended questions asked in a spirit of curiosity; in this mode, you are simply trying to understand the dispute and the parties' arguments. ("Tell me what you think are the key facts here," or "Can you give me your take on the defendant's contract argument?")

Your questions can progress gradually from open-ended queries ("Have you thought about . . . ?") to more pointed requests ("They are resisting making a higher offer because they believe you won't be able to prove causation . . . What should I tell them?"). You might also want to take a party through an analysis of each element in the case, using systematic questions to prevent disputants from skipping over weaknesses.

Discussing the merits can help to narrow litigants' disagreement about the likely outcome in adjudication for several reasons. For one thing it helps counteract disputants' tendency to be overoptimistic. It also assists lawyers who are dealing with an unrealistic client, and can give a disputant a face-saving excuse for a compromise it secretly knows is necessary.

Evaluative feedback.   In some cases questions and analysis are not enough; a disputant might be wedded to an unrealistic viewpoint or require support to justify a settlement to a supervisor. In such situations a commercial mediator may go further, and offer an opinion about how a court is likely to decide a key issue or even the entire case. Evaluations can be structured in a wide variety of ways; for example, "My experience with state court judges is that they usually deny summary judgment in this kind of situation," or "If the plaintiff prevails on liability, what I know of Houston juries suggests they would value damages at somewhere between $125,000 and $150,000."

> *Example:* A lawyer was pursuing a tort claim on behalf of a baseball coach at a private school who had recently died from unclear causes. The lawyer's theory was that the coach's death was due to "multiple chemical sensitivity" triggered by turf treatments. The school's position was that this theory was unfounded, but even if it was true, such a claim was barred by the state worker's compensation law, which prevented employees from suing employers in tort. The school's representatives said, however, they were willing to offer special benefits to the coach's family as a purely voluntary gesture.
>
> During the joint session the plaintiff's lawyer played heavily on the "sympathy" card and at the same time threatened that the coach's widow was ready to rally alumni to attack the school for its stinginess. In response to the mediator's questions in caucus, the lawyer admitted privately to problems with his legal case. He asked the mediator not to opine about legal issues, however, because he thought as a tactical matter he would do better relying on a mix of threats and sympathy than his legal claim. The school, on the other hand, asked the mediator to point out to the plaintiff how weak the claim really was.
>
> The mediator carried both sides' messages to the other, but did not give either one an explicit opinion about case value. The result was an agreement.

One key point to note is that you should never say how you *personally* would decide the case, but rather should frame your opinion as a *prediction* of the attitude of an *outside decision maker*. Expressing one's personal opinion about what is "right" or "fair" in a dispute is almost always a bad idea, because it is likely to leave a listener feeling that the mediator has taken sides against him. Properly performed, a neutral evaluation can be helpful in producing an agreement, but a poorly done or badly timed opinion can be quite harmful. This is a controversial issue that is discussed in more depth in Chapter 10.

6.   Break Bargaining Impasses

Challenge: Closing the Final Gap.   Often barriers to agreement are too high, causing bargaining to stall and provoking an impasse.

Response. A mediator has several options for dealing with a stalled bargaining process.

Persevere and project optimism.   The first bit of advice might seem simple but embodies a basic truth: When in doubt, persevere. Parties get stuck at some point during a mediation, often during the late afternoon or early evening, when energy levels decline and each side has made all the compromises it feels it ought to and more. The key thing to remember at this point is that the mediation probably *will* succeed; if you can keep the parties talking, they will find a solution. The disputants will be looking for signals about whether it is worth continuing and it is important to send positive ones if possible within the bounds of reality.

> *Example:* The dispute involved a Silicon Valley executive who sued his company after being fired. The mediator continued to work, even after each attorney told him privately the case could not settle. Finally, at 9 p.m., the parties reached agreement. As the mediator went over the settlement terms the defendant's lawyer exclaimed, "They kept beating you up and you just kept going. You were like . . . like . . . the *Energizer Bunny!*"
>
> At first the mediator found the idea of being compared to a drum-beating pink toy a bit demeaning. But as he thought more about it, the comparison was apt. A commercial mediator's job, he thought, is to advocate settlement until the parties tell him unequivocally to stop, and he sees no plausible way to change their minds.

Return to a prior tactic.   Another option is to return to an earlier stage or tactic. You might wonder why, if an approach has not worked once, it would be successful the second time around. Surprisingly often, however, something that was rejected earlier will evoke a positive response later in the process. Peoples' emotional states shift over the course of a mediation as they learn new facts and realize their original strategy is not working. As a result, they often become more open to compromise.

Invite the disputants to take the initiative.   Another simple tactic is to ask the disputants to take the initiative. You could say, "What do you think we should do?" and then wait quietly. If disputants realize they cannot simply "hang tough" and demand that the mediator produce results, they sometimes offer surprising ideas.

Test flexibility privately.   Another option is to test the disputants' flexibility in private. Parties may refuse to offer anything more to an opponent, but be willing to give private hints to you. You could, for example, ask "What if?" questions ("What if I could get them down to $150,000; would that be acceptable?") or propose bracketed bargaining ("Could we agree that the parties will negotiate between $100,000 and $150,000?").

Adjourn and follow up.   If the disputants are psychologically spent or have run out of authority, the best response may be to adjourn temporarily. You can follow up with shuttle diplomacy by telephone, propose a second, shorter mediation session, or set a deadline to prompt parties to make difficult decisions.

A Basic Commercial Strategy

Challenges	*Responses*
1. Missing elements: people, data, emotions	• Contact counsel beforehand to initiate a relationship and learn about the dispute. • Arrange for information to be exchanged and decision makers to attend. • If necessary, meet with participants ahead of time to begin working on difficult issues.
2. Lack of opportunity to present arguments and express feelings	• Provide disputants with a "day in court" to argue their case. • Create a setting in which they can express their feelings. • Encourage participants to listen to each other.
3. Positional tactics leading to impasse	• Encourage principled and interest-based approaches, but support money bargaining if parties want to use it. • Advise bargainers about the likely impact of tactics. • If necessary, coach or moderate the bargaining.
4. Hidden issues	• Probe for emotional obstacles. • Identify personal and business interests. • Treat emotional and cognitive problems. • Encourage the parties to consider imaginative terms.
5. Lack of realism about the outcome in adjudication	• Encourage exchanges of information. • Ask about legal and factual issues. • Point out neglected issues; lead an analysis of the merits. • If necessary, predict the likely court outcome on one or more issues.

6. Inability to reach agreement   • Persevere, remaining optimistic.
                                         • Invite the disputants to take the
                                           initiative.
                                         • Repeat earlier tactics.
                                         • Adjourn and follow up.

This six-step strategy will produce success in many situations, particularly
when a case is relatively straightforward and the parties have a strong incentive to settle, and provides a solid foundation on which to premise a mediative effort. No single set of strategies, however, can overcome all obstacles.
Experienced mediators use this basic strategy as a foundation, modifying
their approach to deal with the specific obstacles they encounter in each dispute. We discuss other options in Chapter 10.

Questions

17. What goals is a mediator using the "Basic Strategy" seeking?
18. Using Professor Riskin's grid, how would you classify the style of a
     mediator applying the preceding advice: Broad or narrow? Facili-
     tative or evaluative?

b.   No-Caucus Approaches

Although commercial mediators typically employ a joint-session-follo-
wed-by-caucusing format, some neutrals conduct all, or almost all, of the
process in joint session. Many mediators of marital disputes, for example, do
most or all of their work with both parties present, in part to build a better
working relationship between the spouses around issues such as parenting
and in part out of concern that caucusing would exacerbate the air of suspicion that often hangs over such cases. Disputes arising from close business
relationships have many of the characteristics of a family quarrel and also
might lend themselves to the use of a no-caucus format. Some believe that
no-caucus techniques should be used not whenever parties are seeking a better understanding of their situation and creative agreements. The following
reading describes one such approach.

❖ **Gary Friedman and Jack Himmelstein,** CHALLENGING
  CONFLICT: MEDIATION THROUGH UNDERSTANDING

xxv **(2008)**

Introduction to the Understanding-Based Model

One of the keys to the power of the Understanding-based model of mediation is that it is a real alternative . . .

[W]e work from a base of four interrelated core principles.

- First, we rely heavily on the power of *understanding* rather than the power of coercion or persuasion to drive the process.
- Second, the primary *responsibility* for whether and how the dispute is resolved needs to be with the parties.
- Third, the parties are best served by *working together* and making decisions together.
- Fourth, conflicts are best resolved by *uncovering what lies under* the level at which the parties experience the problem. . . .

The Power of Understanding

In the traditional approach to resolving conflict, the coin of the realm is the power of coercion. When parties disagree, the exertion of control through the use of threat, persuasion, manipulation, or the imposition of an external authority is considered inevitable, necessary, and proper. That is true not only in the traditional adversarial model of resolving disputes but also in many of the seemingly differing models of alternative dispute resolution that have evolved. While we do not pretend to be able to totally eliminate coercion in our approach, we try to bring the power of understanding to bear wherever possible as the gateway to resolution.

Understanding proves central along several dimensions of helping parties to deal with their conflict. One, of course, is the substance of the conflict. We support each party in gaining as full an understanding as possible of what is important to him or her in the dispute, as well as what is important to the other party. Understanding is also critical in creating a working relationship between the parties and the mediator that makes sense to all. And understanding can prove crucial in helping the parties to recognize the nature of the conflict in which they are enmeshed and how they might free themselves from its grasp.

We want *everything* to be understood that may be important to the parties in resolving their differences . . .

Party Responsibility — Let the Parties Own Their Conflict

"Let the parties own their conflict" means it is important to remember and honor that it is the parties' conflict. *They* hold the key to reaching a resolution that best serves them both. And *they* have the power and responsibility, if they are willing, to work together toward that resolution. For us, that does not mean simply that the parties must ultimately agree to any final settlement of their dispute. *Party responsibility* means the parties understand what is substantively at stake for both and craft a resolution best for all. It also means the parties actively participate in shaping the mediation process by making ongoing choices, along with the mediator, as to the course it will take.

Thus, the *parties exercise responsibility* not only in determining the substantive result — the *what* of the problem, but they also participate actively in deciding the *how* — the way the mediation proceeds. For us, the *what* and the *how* are inextricably related; and the parties' active involvement in shaping the *how* is more likely to lead to their creating a better result on the *what*.

This does not mean that the mediator plays a passive role, yielding to the parties in determining the course of the mediation. Rather . . . we view the mediator's role as both active and interactive with the parties. This stands in contrast to the assumption within the traditional approach to conflict that it is the professional who needs to assume active responsibility for the resolution of the controversy.

The mediator, too, is responsible. The mediator's responsibility is directed to supporting the parties in *their ability to make choices together based on their growing understanding*. *Understanding* ensures that those choices will be informed.

Working Together

We believe that the best way for mediators to support parties in resolving their dispute is for the parties to work together and make decisions together. We appreciate that for many professionals, this is one of the most striking and questionable aspects of our approach. Most mediators regularly meet separately with the different parties ("caucusing"). Our goal is to work together with the parties directly and simultaneously. We will address at length in this book why we work in this way and how we do so. Here we highlight a few of the bases on which this core principle rests.

We work in this way because it creates better solutions for the parties. We do it also because we believe it best honors the parties while also contributing to what we view as a critical need in society for developing better ways for people to go through conflict.

We do not believe that our approach to mediation with its emphasis on the parties working together, or any particular approach to mediation, is the answer to all conflicts. We do think that for those people who are motivated and capable of working together, there are many benefits. We have seen that succeed for thousands of individuals and organizations. . . .

Going Under the Conflict

Einstein is credited with saying that "you cannot resolve a conflict at its own level." The point for us in Einstein's words is that when it comes to dealing with conflict, we need not only breadth of understanding but depth as well. That means recognizing that conflict has an inner life and being open to that dimension. Repeatedly, we find that the basis for resolving conflict comes from examining with the parties, as best as we are all willing and able what *underlies* their dispute.

. . . This deeper level of understanding can make all the difference and therefore merits a special place in our core principles. The inquiry into what lies beneath takes place in each aspect of the conflict.

First, we work with the parties to understand what *underlies the substance of the conflict*. As we noted earlier, we help both sides identify what is truly important to each in the dispute — not only *what* they want but *why* they want it . . . [T]he goal is for the parties to ultimately be able to take each other's views into account along with their own as the foundation for a solution that is individually suited to all parties. . . .

Second, we work with the parties to understand *what underlies their conflict* in terms of how it may have them trapped in their dynamic. . . . Conflict is rarely just about money, or who did what to whom. It also has a subjective dimension — the emotions, beliefs, and assumptions of the individuals caught within the conflict. This subjective dimension includes feelings, such as anger and fear, the need to assign blame, and the desire for self-justification . . .

We are not suggesting that the answer to every conflict is that a little understanding magically changes the dynamics between the parties and resolves the problem. What we are suggesting is that understanding can begin to help the parties appreciate how they have become caught in this ricocheting trap and lead to a way out . . .

The Non-caucus Approach

Many other approaches to mediation recommend that the mediator shuttle back and forth between the parties (caucusing), gaining information that he or she holds confidential. Our central problem with caucusing is that the mediator ends up with the fullest picture of the problem and is therefore in the best position to solve it. The mediator, armed with that fuller view, can readily urge or manipulate the parties to the end he or she shapes.

The emphasis in our approach, in contrast, is on *understanding* and *voluntariness* as the basis for resolving the conflict rather than persuasion or coercion. We stress that it is the parties, not the professionals, who have the best *understanding of what underlies* the dispute and thus are in the best position to find the solution . . .

The parties' motivation and willingness to *work together* is critical to the success of this approach. Mediators often assume that the parties (and their counsel) simply do not want to work together, and therefore keep the parties apart. In our experience, many parties (and counsel) simply accept that they will not work together and that the mediator will be responsible for crafting the solution. But once educated about how staying in the same room might be valuable, many are motivated to try it. If the parties (and the mediator) are willing, *working together* throughout can be as rewarding as it is demanding, as the mediations recounted in this book illustrate.

Role of Law and Lawyers

Mediators tend to be divided in how they approach the role of law in mediation. [W]e welcome lawyers' participation *and* we view it important to include the law. We do not, however, assume that the parties will or should rely solely or primarily on the law. Rather, the importance the parties give to the law is up to them. Our goals are (1) to educate the parties about the law and possible legal outcomes and (2) to support their freedom to fashion their own creative solutions that may differ from what a court might decide. In this way, the parties learn that they can together reach agreements that respond to both their individual interests and their common goals while also being well informed about their legal rights and the judicial alternatives to a mediated settlement.

We also want to respond to a common perception and challenge that working in this way is simply not realistic for most conflicts and most people. When we hear that critique, we are reminded of similar statements three decades ago when it was the legal profession directing the challenge at the very idea of mediation where parties would decide for themselves. Now, too, the challenge is from many lawyers (not all), and they are joined, ironically, by a good number of mediators. Our response now — as it was then — is that many parties in conflict, if given the opportunity, can and want to do it. . . .

Example: A caucus-oriented mediator took on a case involving the dissolution of a design firm. One of the partners, whose specialty was marketing, had taken an inside position with a large client of the firm, while her partner, who focused on supervising the execution of projects, had decided to continue the business on her own. The two women remained friendly, but the situation had created tension around setting the terms of the remaining partner's buyout of her colleague's interest in the firm. The partner who handled production was anxious at the prospect of becoming solely responsible for the business and plainly felt somewhat abandoned. Her marketing colleague, by contrast, tended to take an everything-will-work-out approach to life, and found it hard to credit her partner's concerns.

The partnership's corporate lawyer recommended that they mediate the issues between them. In light of their long history of working together cooperatively, he suggested that they do so without lawyers present, but with each having a personal attorney available for consultations between sessions. The mediator ordinarily used a caucus-based format, but he decided in this case to keep the two women together throughout their discussions. He felt that with some assistance they could negotiate directly, and was concerned that if he held separate meetings it would be taken as a signal that their disagreements were more serious than they were. Most important, the partners themselves expressed a preference for face-to-face discussions. The mediation went forward in a joint-meeting format, although each woman occasionally talked with the mediator privately by telephone. The memo of agreement was written out and initialed in an ice cream shop located under the partnership's offices.

Questions

19.   What potential advantages would a no-caucus model provide, as compared to a caucus-based approach, in a typical commercial contract dispute? What drawbacks?

20.   Can a no-caucus model be effective when the disputants believe that the only issue in the case is money? If they insist on limiting bargaining to money?

21.   In the case example, the mediator had occasional private conversations with each party over the telephone. Although neither party appeared to feel excluded as a result, what concerns might a no-caucus mediator have about this technique?

22.   In terms of the Riskin Grid, how would you chart the style of a mediator who uses an "understanding-based" process?

c.   All-Caucus Mediation

While some mediators advocate spending the entire process in joint session, an increasing number of disputants in commercial mediation — civil litigators and, it appears, the parties who hire them — do not want to meet together at all. More and more mediators report that at the request of lawyers they do not hold a substantive opening session in commercial cases.

Instead, the mediator is likely to bring the parties together for a short meeting to introduce themselves to each other and permit her to explain ground rules such as confidentiality. Disputants do not make substantive statements in each other's presence, however, and after introductory comments adjourn into private caucuses, where they spend the rest of the process. Some mediators do not hold even an introductory meeting — disputants go into separate rooms on arrival and the mediator conducts the entire process in caucus format.

❖ **Pam Smith,** SEPARATING OPPONENTS KEY TO
JAMS NEUTRAL'S SUCCESS

The Recorder 4 (June 20, 2006)

The lawyers who bring their cases before William Cahill . . . can't predict if they'll lay eyes on their opponents.

The retired San Francisco Superior Court judge dispenses with the initial joint session practiced by many mediators. "Sometimes it takes two hours to undo the bad feelings that that creates," he said.

Instead, he meets separately with each party at the beginning of the day to assess whether to bring the attorneys, their clients or both into the same room. On rare occasions, opponents don't see much more of each other than the signatures that dress a settlement at the end of the day, Cahill said.

Litigator Michael Early first picked up on that technique in a case before Cahill, though he says he's since noticed more mediators doing away with those initial group presentations.

"Except in exceptional [cases], it tends to get more sides entrenched in their positions and starts the mediation off with the confrontation that mediation is supposed to avoid."

Questions

23. Why might counsel in a civil case prefer a pure-caucus model? Why might the parties?
24. What are potential advantages and disadvantages of this model? In what kinds of cases might it work well or poorly?
25. Would Gary Friedman and Jack Himmelstein agree that mediation is "supposed to avoid . . . a confrontation"? Why do you think litigators might favor this approach?
26. Is it significant that the mediator described in the article is a former judge? What might be the pluses and minuses of selecting a former judicial officer as a mediator?

Problem 1

Assume you are a mediator who uses the "Basic Strategy" described above. Two lawyers ask you to mediate a contract dispute between an IT firm and a manufacturer. The dispute involves a $1.4 million contract the parties signed 18 months ago to create software for workstations that control the manufacturing of sensors used in cars' automatic braking systems.

The manufacturer says that the software was delivered late and is unreliable, stopping production and costing the company lost profits on the contract of more than $3.5 million. The developer agrees that there have been delays and problems, but attributes them to "scope creep," saying that the original project was to create software to manage no more than 50 workstations performing no more than 15 operations, but over the contract life this number expanded to 175 stations and 25 operations, greatly increasing the complexity of the required software. It says it is entitled to $400,000 in unpaid fees for work it has done to date, and that the entire contract, with its larger scope, will cost nearly $2 million.

- Would you suggest a caucus or no-caucus process for this dispute? Why?
- Would you agree to use the opposite format if the lawyers in the case strongly wanted to do so? What would you tell them if you did?

4.   Is There More to Mediation Than Technique?

The discussion so far might give the impression that while mediators' styles vary widely, the key differences involve choices of format and tactics. The mediation process, however, involves subtle personal influences that are more important than any particular format or technique.

❖ **Daniel Bowling and David Hoffman,** Bringing Peace into
the Room: The Personal Qualities of the Mediator and
Their Impact on the Mediation

16 Negotiation J. 5 (January 2000)

Empirical studies of the mediation process consistently show high rates of settlement, as well as high levels of participant satisfaction. These favorable results seem to occur regardless of mediation styles or the philosophical orientation of the individual mediator (e.g., evaluative vs. facilitative; transformative vs. problem-solving). Indeed, the history of mediation, as well as our own experience, shows that mediation sometimes works even when the mediator is untrained. Is there some aspect of the mediation process — wholly apart from technique or theory — that explains these results?

Some might say that mediation works because it provides a safe forum for airing grievances and venting emotion (that is, it gives people their "day in court"), and this can be done even with an unskilled mediator. Others might point to the use of active listening and reframing — skills that many people have, whether or not they have had any formal mediation training. Still others may focus on the use of caucusing and shuttle diplomacy — again, techniques that do not necessarily require specialized training.

We believe all of these techniques are important. We also believe that mediation training is vitally important. However, there is a dimension to the practice of mediation that has received insufficient attention: the combination of psychological, intellectual, and spiritual qualities that make a person who he or she is. We believe that those personal qualities have a direct impact on the mediation process and the outcome of the mediation. Indeed, this impact may be one of the most potent sources of the effectiveness of mediation. . . . As mediators, we have noticed that, when we are feeling at peace with ourselves and the world around us, we are better able to bring peace into the room. Moreover, doing so, in our experience, has a significant impact on the mediation process. . . .

Our starting point is to reflect on how we ourselves developed as mediators. For us, and for many of our fellow mediators, the process seems to involve three major "stages." Although we describe these aspects of our development sequentially, for some mediators they may occur in a different order, overlap, or occur to some degree simultaneously.

First, as beginning mediators, we studied techniques [and] looked for opportunities to practice these skills. A period of apprenticeship ensued. . . .

The second stage of our development involved working toward a deeper understanding of how and why mediation works. In seeking an intellectual grasp of the mediation process, we hoped to find the tools with which to assess the effectiveness of various techniques . . . and better understand what we were doing, why we were doing it, and the meaning of the process for our clients. . . .

The third stage of our growth as mediators is the focus of this article, and we consider it to be the most challenging frontier of development. For us, the third aspect begins with the mediator's growing awareness of how his or her personal qualities — for better or worse — influence the mediation process. . . . It is about being a mediator, rather than simply doing certain prescribed steps dictated by a particular mediation school or theory. . . . More specifically, it is the mediator's being, as experienced by the parties, that sends the message. . . .

The Mediator's "Presence"

This brings us to the heart of our thesis — namely, that there are certain qualities that the mediator's presence brings to the mediation process that exert a powerful influence, and enhance the impact of the interventions employed by the mediator. . . . Central to this way of looking at mediation is the recognition that the mediator is not extrinsic to the conflict (any more than the therapist is wholly separate from the issues addressed in therapy). . . .

Subtle Influences

If we accept the view that, notwithstanding impartiality, mediators are inevitably engaged in creating a relationship with the parties, a relationship in which their personal qualities will influence the parties' ability to negotiate successfully — we are led inevitably to the next question: What are the qualities in the mediator that will contribute to a successful relationship with the parties, one that will support reorganization of this conflict "system"? . . .

In our work as mediators, integration comes in part from developing a strong identification with our role: the transition from feeling that "I am someone who mediates" to realizing that "I am a mediator" — from seeing mediation as work that we do to seeing it as an integral part of our identity. . . . [T]hese theories suggest that we as mediators "create" the conflict resolution process through our perception of the participants, the conflict, and our role in it as conflict resolvers. . . . Accordingly, who we are — i.e., the personal qualities we bring into the mediation room — begins to take on larger significance. . . . The effectiveness of our interventions often arises not from their forcefulness but instead from their authenticity. . . .

Implications for Mediation Practice

. . . Integration is a quality that we may never fully achieve but are continually developing. It is a quality which, we believe, mediators should foster because (1) it provides a model for the parties — bringing peace, if you will, into the room; and (2) by subtle means which are more easily described than understood, the "integrated" mediator's presence aligns the parties and mediation process in a more positive direction.

Questions

27.   Are the qualities described in this reading more compatible with some models of mediation or negotiation you have read about than with others? Which ones?

28.   In the mediations in the *Microsoft* case, what quality did Judge Posner appear to "bring into the room"? What did Green and Marks try to project?

29.   Does it appear to matter that Posner conducted the process primarily by telephone and e-mail, whereas Green and Marks met with the parties in face-to-face sessions? Do you think a mediator can communicate "presence" to the parties without being physically present?

CHAPTER
10

A Deeper Look into the Process

This section delves more deeply into the mediation process, examining the techniques mediators use to assist persons in conflict. We organize the discussion around three topics: process skills, psychological and emotional forces, and barriers arising from disagreement over the legal merits.

Before focusing on mediation technique, we should ask: How much do specific skills, whether good listening, analytic ability, or creativeness, matter to a mediator's success? The following article describes how the lawyers who hire commercial mediators answered this question.

❖ **Stephen B. Goldberg and Margaret L. Shaw,** *Further Investigation into the Secrets of Successful and Unsuccessful Mediators*

26 Alternatives 149 (2008)

This article reports the results of . . . a continuing research project. . . . [W]e surveyed people who had participated in mediation as representatives of disputing parties — typically attorneys — to determine their responses to the question of what led to mediation success.

The most frequently cited behavior correlated to mediator success involved the mediator's ability to gain the parties' confidence. . . . Tops on the list — referred to by an average of 60% of the mediation advocates . . . — was that the mediator was friendly, empathic, likable, etc. Examples of the respondents' comments include:

- "He is a genuinely nice guy. People like to be around other people whom they like — especially someone you have to spend hours with in a high-stakes situation."
- "She demonstrates compassion for the client, which makes the client feel that she is working hard on her behalf and tends to make the client trust her."

The next most frequently cited reason for mediator success — referred to by an average of 53% of the mediation advocates — was that the mediator had high integrity, as demonstrated by his or her honesty, neutrality, trustworthiness, protection of confidences, etc. Examples of these comments include:

- "He has honesty and integrity. We had absolute confidence that he would not reveal information we did not want revealed to the other side."
- "Another essential quality is her personal integrity — as it is essential to any mediator. Both sides trust that the information she relays is accurate, and that she's not putting a spin on things to help her get where she needs to go."

Rounding out the top three most frequently cited reasons for mediator success, and referred to by an average of 47% of the mediation advocates, was that the mediator was smart, well-prepared, or knew the relevant contract or law. Examples . . . include:

- "She's extremely smart. That plays out in several ways, such as creativity in finding solutions."
- "He was an extraordinarily quick study who was able to master the underlying facts and issues of a complex case well enough to be credible in his discussion of the strengths and weaknesses of each party's position."

The confidence-building attributes referred to above were cited by respondents as key elements of mediator success more frequently than were the various skills used by mediators to bring about agreement. The most frequently mentioned mediator skills were patience and persistence (referred to by an average of 35% of the mediation advocates); providing useful evaluations or reality-testing regarding the likely outcome of the dispute in court or arbitration (33%); and asking good questions and listening carefully to responses (28%).

Some comments relating to the mediator's patience and persistence include: "Her patience was outstanding. The parties were very far apart: We didn't give this case a chance for success. . . . However, her patience resulted in a settlement."

Comments involving the mediators' provision of useful evaluations or reality-testing . . . include: "She readily identifies — and expresses in a non-confrontational fashion — the most significant weakness or downside in each party's position."

Comments involving the importance of asking good questions and listening carefully to responses include: "I think primarily he's a good listener, which is key for a mediator to be successful . . . ."

The central conclusion . . . is that a — if not *the* — core element in mediator success is the mediator's ability to establish a relationship of trust and confidence with the disputing parties.

A.   Process Skills

Among the most important ways in which mediators can help parties deal with conflict are to:

*   Listen, and show that they understand
*   Reframe communications
*   Identify interests and develop options for settlement
*   Manage positional bargaining successfully

If you are in the role of a neutral, think about how you can use these skills in your cases — and why applying them may be difficult in practice. As a lawyer selecting mediators, ask yourself whether process issues appear to be obstacles to settlement in your case and, if so, whether candidates have the skills needed to overcome them.

1.   Listening

Most mediators would agree that of all the skills needed to be an effective neutral, the most important is to be a good listener. This is harder than it may seem, especially for those of us who are inclined by temperament and training to identify issues, discard irrelevancies, and make decisions quickly. It is often difficult, as we listen to clashing viewpoints, to restrain our instinctive wish to pass judgment. Doing so requires us to put aside, if only temporarily, some important skills we have learned in law school in favor of a different approach to listening. To understand the importance of listening, consider the following account of one of America's most famous expeditions.

   In 1804, acting on orders of President Thomas Jefferson, Meriwether Lewis and William Clark set out on a journey across the unexplored American continent. After wintering on the Pacific coast, they began the long trip home. The party reached the Bitterroot Mountains of Idaho, where they expected to recover horses they had left behind with a local tribe. The horses were essential; without them, the party could not survive their passage through the arid mountains. This reading describes what happened next, with quotations from Meriwether Lewis's journal.

❖ **Stephen E. Ambrose,** *Undaunted Courage*
Touchstone Books, 361 (1996)

That day, the Americans chanced on Chief Cut Nose with a party of six. Cut Nose had been off on a raid the previous fall, but Lewis had heard of him and knew he was regarded as a greater chief than Twisted Hair. The Indians and white men rode on together, and soon encountered Twisted Hair with a half-dozen warriors. It was Twisted Hair who had agreed to keep the Americans' horses through the winter — he had been promised two guns and ammunition as his reward. The captains were naturally delighted to see him. But he greeted the white men very coolly. Lewis found this "as unexpected as it was unaccountable."

Twisted Hair turned to Cut Nose and began shouting and making angry gestures. Cut Nose answered in kind. This continued for some twenty minutes. The captains had no idea what was going on, but clearly they had to break it up. They needed the friendship of both chiefs if they were to get through the next three weeks, and they needed their horses if they were to have any chance of getting over the mountains.

The chiefs departed for their respective camps, still angry with each other. An hour later, [the expedition's interpreter] returned from hunting. The captains invited Twisted Hair for a smoke. He accepted, and through [the interpreter] explained that the previous fall he had collected the expedition's horses and taken charge of them. Cut Nose then returned from his war party and, according to Twisted Hair, asserted his primacy among the Nez Perce. He said Twisted Hair shouldn't have accepted the responsibility, that it was he, Cut Nose, who should be in charge. Twisted Hair said he got so sick of hearing this stuff that he paid no further attention to the horses, who consequently scattered. But most of them were around, many of them with Chief Broken Arm.

The captains invited Cut Nose to join the campfire. He came and "told us in the presents (*sic*) of the Twisted Hair that he the Twisted Hair was a bad old man that he woar two faces." Cut Nose charged that Twisted Hair had never taken care of the horses but had allowed his young men to ride them and misuse them, and that was the reason Cut Nose and Broken Arm had forbidden him to retain responsibility for the animals. The captains said they would proceed to Broken Arm's camp in the morning, and see how many horses and saddles they could collect. This was satisfactory to Twisted Hair and Cut Nose, who had calmed down considerably after being allowed to tell their sides of the story. The next day, everyone moved to Broken Arm's lodge. There the expedition recovered twenty-one horses, about half the saddles, and some ammunition.

Questions

1. What was the dispute here?
2. Did either chief change his mind? If not, why was the meeting helpful?
3. If this encounter had been a mediation, what would one call the meeting hosted by Lewis and Clark?
4. What might have happened if Lewis and Clark had responded by giving an opinion as to who was at fault, rather than simply listening?

❖ **Richard Salem,** *The Benefits of Empathic Listening*

Conflict Research Consortium, University of Colorado (2003)

Empathic listening (also called *active* listening or *reflective* listening) is a way of listening. Though useful for everyone involved in a conflict, the ability and willingness to listen with empathy is often what sets the mediator apart from others involved in the conflict.

How to Listen with Empathy

Empathy is the ability to project oneself into the personality of another person in order to better understand that person's emotions or feelings. Through empathic listening the listener lets the speaker know, "I understand your problem and how you feel about it, I am interested in what you are saying and I am not judging you." The listener unmistakably conveys this message through words and non-verbal behaviors, including body language. In so doing, the listener encourages the speaker to fully express herself or himself free of interruption, criticism, or being told what to do. It is neither advisable nor necessary for a mediator to agree with the speaker, even when asked to do so. It is usually sufficient to let the speaker know, "I understand you and I am interested in being a resource to help you resolve this problem." [In the words of Madelyn Burley-Allen], a skilled listener:

- takes information from others while remaining non-judgmental and empathic,
- acknowledges the speaker in a way that invites the communication to continue, and
- provides a limited but encouraging response, carrying the speaker's idea one step forward.

Empathic Listening in Mediation

Parties to volatile conflicts often feel that nobody on the other side is interested in what they have to say. The parties often have been talking at each other and past each other, but not with each other. Neither believes that their message has been listened to or understood. Nor do they feel respected. Locked into positions that they know the other will not accept, the parties tend to be close-minded, distrustful of each other, and often angry, frustrated, discouraged, or hurt.

When the mediator comes onto the scene, she continuously models good conflict-management behaviors, trying to create an environment where the parties in conflict will begin to listen to each other with clear heads. For many disputants, this may be the first time they have had an opportunity to fully present their story. During this process, the parties may hear things that they have not heard before, things that broaden their understanding of how the other party perceives the problem. This can open minds and create

receptivity to new ideas that might lead to a settlement. In creating a trusting environment, it is the mediator's hope that some strands of trust will
begin to connect the parties and replace the negative emotions that they
brought to the table.

Mediator Nancy Ferrell questions whether mediation can work if some
measure of empathy is not developed between the parties. She describes a
multi-issue case involving black students and members of a white fraternity
that held an annual "black-face" party at a university in Oklahoma. At the
outset, the student president of the fraternity was convinced that the annual
tradition was harmless and inoffensive. It wasn't until the mediator created
an opportunity for him to listen to the aggrieved parties at the table that he
realized the extraordinary impact his fraternity's antics had on black students. Once he recognized the problem, a solution to that part of the conflict was only a step away. . . .

Guidelines for Empathic Listening

Madelyn Burley-Allen offers these guidelines for empathic listening [the
guidelines have been edited]:

1. *Be attentive*. Be interested. Be alert and not distracted.
2. *Be noncritical*. Allow the speaker to bounce ideas and feelings off you.
   Don't indicate your judgment.
3. *Indicate you are listening by:*
   • Making brief, noncommittal responses ("I see . . .").
   • Giving nonverbal acknowledgment, for example by nodding your
     head.
   • Inviting the speaker to say more: for example, "Tell me about it" or
     "I'd like to hear about that."
4. *Follow good listening ground rules:*
   • Don't interrupt.
   • Don't change the subject, or move in a new direction.
   • Don't rehearse a response in your own head.
   • Don't interrogate with continual questions.
   • Don't give advice.
   • Do reflect back to the speaker:
     — What you understand.
     — How you think the speaker feels.
5. *Don't let the speaker "hook" you emotionally*. Don't get angry or upset or
   allow yourself to get involved in an argument.

The ability to listen with empathy may be the most important attribute of
interveners who succeed in gaining the trust and cooperation of parties to
intractable conflicts and other disputes with high emotional content. . . .

Do executives appreciate empathy? William Webster, a former federal appeals judge who also served as Director of the CIA and FBI, later became a mediator. He was once asked to name the book that he had found most useful in his work as a neutral in complex corporate disputes. Webster's response: "When my wife and I had teenagers, I found Dr. Haim Ginnott's book, *Between Parent and Child*, very helpful . . . and I find it equally useful now." Dr. Ginnott emphasizes how important it is for parents to listen to children empathically, without expressing judgment on what they say. This, Judge Webster was suggesting, is one of the most important skills that a mediator can bring to a dispute — apparently as useful with executives as with upset children.

Problem 1

Your client is going through a difficult divorce and has engaged you to negotiate the terms of dissolution of the marriage. Your client and her husband have been separated for two months. They have two children — a boy, seven, and a girl, ten. He is a partner in a local law firm, and she is a teacher who has been a homemaker since the birth of their second child.

Your client is extremely angry at her spouse. Her feelings are crystallized around an affair he had with a co-worker a year ago. She complains, however, that the husband was never really committed to the marriage. He enjoyed weekend golf more than spending time with their young children; neglected her emotionally; did not attend many of the children's after-school activities, pleading the press of work; and failed to give her any support during the illness and death of her father two years ago. Your client has demanded that you get the maximum possible recovery from him and "not pull punches." She calls you about every second day to describe her most recent run-in with the husband about payments for household expenses and visitation with the children, and regularly sends you documents that she thinks may be helpful in proving his neglect and ability to pay high alimony.

a. Do you think that you would have any difficulty listening empathically to this client? Why? What might you do to deal with such a problem?
b. Would you have any concern about sending your client into mediation? What qualities would you look for in selecting a mediator for this case?
c. What, if anything, would you want to tell the mediator in advance?

2. *Reframing*

The root of many disagreements is that people see the same dispute in quite different ways. As you read in Chapter 3, the "frame" that a person puts on a situation will influence, in particular, whether he will see a proposal for settlement as a net loss or gain, and this in turn will strongly affect his decision about whether to settle. Helping disputants to reach agreement often requires finding a way to modify their perspectives, or frames, on a controversy, or at least to allow them to appreciate that an opponent honestly sees the same situation differently. One powerful technique for doing so is known as "reframing."

❖ Ken Bryant and Dana L. Curtis, REFRAMING
(2004)

To "reframe" a statement (in mediation lingo) is to recast the statement in more neutral terms, giving the speaker, as well as his mediation partner(s), the chance to look at the problem differently, in a more positive way. The new statement offered by the mediator to accomplish this goal is the "reframe."

How It Works

Let's assume for the moment that a mediation participant has made a statement using value-laden (negative) language. The statement is guaranteed to make the other party angry or defensive if simply left floating in air. The task and challenge for the attentive mediator is to quickly find a positive, constructive interpretation of the assertion. (It helps if you simply assume that every behavior, including a rude comment, is appropriate, given some context, or frame.)

Before you can restate or paraphrase, of course, you must be certain you have heard the original statement correctly, which involves a heavy dose of active listening. Your goal is to accurately reflect the message sent by the speaker, while simultaneously molding the statement into an aid for easier communication. In other words, the speaker must be comfortable that you heard what was said, the other party must not be offended by your restatement, *and* the new version (yours) should point the conversation in a constructive direction.

Restating the Message

You might try restating the message by:

- Redirecting the thrust of the negative assertion, i.e., away from persons verbally attacked to problems inherent in the complaint.
- Narrowing or broadening the gist of the allegation by pinpointing a single problem, or generalizing the issues to include basic policy decisions.
- Forming a question: e.g., "Is there a specific issue you would like to work on? Is there another possible explanation for what happened?"
- Shifting the focus from problems to opportunities: "Recognizing that you feel the status quo is intolerable, do you have some ideas about what changes are needed?"

- Simplifying a complex statement of a dispute, by choosing a single issue which can be addressed immediately.
- Categorizing the speaker's concerns to be dealt with either on a "most important," "easiest to deal with first," or some other useful basis.
- Neutralizing the original statement by excising ad hominem attacks and generalizing the issues, while retaining the essential elements of the message.

It bears repeating: *Confirm the accuracy of your reframe.* You can confirm your reframe by simply asking, "Is that what you meant?" Or, "Have I expressed your concerns accurately?" Additional, and even more effective, confirmation can be obtained by using your powers of observation of the speaker's non-verbal communication. Check the body language: posture, facial expression, muscle tension, skin coloring, and breathing pattern. Remember, studies indicate that more than ninety-three per cent of human communication is non-verbal.

Why Reframe?

Your purpose is not only to change the harsh effect of the words used by the speaker, but also to create a new dynamic in the mediation. Reframes can change the focus of the speaker's statement, and the mediation, from

- Blame and guilt, to problem-solving
- Past to future
- Judgmental to non-judgmental
- Position to interest
- Ultimatum to aspiration

It probably goes without saying that reframing can, by lowering emotional temperature, increase the efficiency of the mediation process.

Reframing as a Joke

Consider that reframing is the essence of a good joke: What seems to be one thing suddenly shifts and becomes something else. Example: "What do Alexander the Great and Smokey the Bear have in common?" (Answer: their middle names). When you reframe a statement, you shift the speaker's perception, even if just a little. The shift can get creative juices flowing and enhance discussions of options for resolution.

"Meaning" Reframe and "Context" Reframe

Meaning

There was a man who was compulsive about cleaning his house. He even dusted light bulbs. He made his family take their shoes off in their living room. His view of fulfillment as a father and husband was reflected in his home's cleanliness. The problem: He was driving his family crazy. The man was asked to visualize his living room rug, white and fluffy, not a spot anywhere. He was in seventh heaven. Then he was asked to realize that his vision meant he was totally alone, and that the people he cared for and loved were nowhere around. He ceased smiling, and felt terrible, until he was asked to visualize "a few footprints" on the carpet. Then, of course, he felt good again. This is a "meaning" reframe, where the stimulus in the world doesn't actually change, but the meaning does.

Context

A father complained that he and his wife hadn't done a very good job in raising their daughter, because the daughter was so stubborn. The father, a successful banker, acknowledged that he had acquired traits involving tenacity and a stubborn quality needed to protect himself. The father was asked to look at his daughter and to realize that he had taught her how to be stubborn and to stand up for herself, and that this gift might someday save her life. Imagine, he was asked, how valuable that quality will be when *his* daughter goes out on a date with a man who has bad intentions. This is a "context" reframe, demonstrating that every behavior in the world is appropriate in some context. Being stubborn may be judged bad in the context of a family, and becomes good in the context of banking and in the context of a man trying to take advantage of a young girl. When faced with an assertion about the meaning of an event or a person's conduct, the mediator might ask, "What *else* might that conduct mean?" A context reframe can be handled by asking, "Where would this behavior be *useful*?"

Finding the appropriate reframe for negative or non-useful assertions during mediation is hard work and takes practice. No two circumstances will be the same. More often than not, you will not be quite sure if your reframe was useful. Sometimes you will know it was not. There is, however, no such thing as failure, only feedback. You will learn as you try different approaches, and your mediation partners will benefit from your dedication to improving your skills.

Perjury, or just hardball? During mediation of a case arising from a failed partnership, the defendant's attorney argued vehemently that the plaintiff's lawyer had committed malpractice in drafting the partnership contract. This accusation inflamed the plaintiff side, requiring the mediation to be temporarily adjourned. A few days later the plaintiff lawyer produced a recently-signed affidavit in which a key witness not only rebutted the defendant's version of events, but went on to say that the defense lawyer had told him that he would be given free legal counsel if he changed his story, arguably an incentive to perjure himself.

Defense counsel, told by the mediator about this in caucus, stood up and said angrily that he would not stand for being accused that way. The mediator replied that he thought the abetting-perjury innuendo was simply a "high inside fastball," thrown by the other side in response to the defense attorney's own "hardball" charge of malpractice. The defense lawyer, who did not really want to walk out and did not mind being characterized as a tough player in front of his client, accepted the reframing of his adversary's accusation as a professional sports tactic and sat down. Both the perjury and malpractice issues tacitly dropped out of the case.

3. *Identifying Interests*

One of the themes of this book is that bargainers can create value and smooth the path to settlement by using interest-based techniques. It is also true, however, that competitive approaches tend to dominate settlement negotiations in legal disputes.

Why is it so difficult to use interest-based approaches in the context of a lawsuit? It is not that disputants don't know the value of such techniques. Most commercial disputes arise from contracts, and mediators report that most of the contracts they deal with contain significant interest-based terms. Litigants, in other words, arrive at mediation with a record of having created interest-based bargains in the very document over which they are now quarrelling. Once in litigation, however, they usually stop looking for creative options and focus solely on money. Why might this occur? Among the reasons for this are:

- Mutual mistrust
- Role limitations
- Lack of knowledge/limitations of the commercial format

Mutual Mistrust

The first obstacle is the air of suspicion that permeates most commercial cases. To implement interest-based solutions, litigants usually will be required to work together in the future. It is possible to reach interest-based settlements that do not involve future performance, of course: A divorcing couple, for instance, might decide to take turns in dividing their furniture, allowing each to choose the pieces he or she wants most. But the strongest interest-based settlements usually involve parties working together, or one side providing a service or product for the other, after the settlement takes effect.

The problem is that by the time two parties have become involved in a lawsuit, they are usually deeply suspicious of each other. They may distrust the other side's *competence*: An owner, for example, might mistrust a contractor's ability to complete a construction project. An even more serious problem exists when a party suspects an opponent's *intentions*. A buyer, for example, might believe that a supplier intentionally underbid a project, intending to make a profit through shoddy work.

A mediator who proposes a relationship repair to litigating parties risks being met with a response such as: "You've known these people for only a few hours. When we first met them they seemed competent, too, so we're not surprised they look that way to you. It took a lot of bad experience for us to learn what they're really like. No way are we going back into a deal with them!"

This illustrates a pervasive phenomenon, one psychologists call *attribution bias*. Litigants tend to assume the worst about their opponent's motives, viewing every ambiguous step with suspicion.

In legal conflicts parties' suspicions are magnified by the litigation process itself. Filing suit requires a plaintiff to accuse a defendant of errors or wrongdoing, and parties often exaggerate their claims for tactical purposes. Disputants arrive at mediation, in other words, having accused an opponent or having been accused themselves of behavior unworthy of any good professional. Even if parties know that accusations against them were exaggerated for tactical purposes, they are likely to be embarrassed to admit it. The following responses can help alleviate this distrust.

Confront the Issue Directly.   There is little point in pretending that feelings of anger or mistrust do not exist, or in asking bitter parties to let bygones be bygones. It is better to acknowledge that each side does have serious concerns about whether they can work together in the future.

Promote Confidence-Building Measures.   Having admitted a problem exists, a mediator can begin to work on it. Most important is to change people's doubts about their adversary's intent. If parties trust an opponent, they may excuse a failure of performance, but as long as they doubt the other side's good faith, repairing a relationship is extremely difficult. Sometimes explaining how the problem arose is enough to restore trust.

> *Example:* A franchisor and franchisee were in a dispute over the franchisor's alleged inability to deliver services and the franchisee's failure to pay a $60,000 quarterly fee. It became clear any settlement would require continuing the franchise relationship. The franchisor, however, would not consider this, arguing that the franchisee was a deadbeat who had made up his allegations simply to avoid paying the fee. Asked about this, the lawyer for the franchisee explained that his client had been planning to make the payment and had only withheld it because the attorney told him to do so.
>
> The mediator knew the opposing lawyers in the case respected each other, and asked the franchisee and his attorney if the lawyer would be willing to go into the franchisor's caucus room to explain why the payment had not been made. He suggested the lawyer go in alone, so there would be less suspicion he was simply protecting his client.
>
> The lawyer went into the other caucus, explained that the franchisee had acted on his instructions, and answered questions. After talking privately the franchisor team told the mediator that the franchisee had gotten bad legal advice, but they were now less concerned about his good faith and willing to consider restructuring the franchise.

Provide Certainty. People strongly prefer certain outcomes over ones that involve even a small amount of risk — what psychologists call the "attraction to certainty." As a result parties attach much less value to an offer if they see a chance the other side will not carry it out. Interest-based settlements suffer from this, because it is usually easier to determine whether an opponent has paid a sum of money than whether it has adequately carried out a cooperative activity.

It is usually not possible to eliminate the risk of implementation entirely, but it may be possible to convince a party a risk is manageable. To do this a mediator can analyze less-than-certain proposals carefully so that parties understand that a risk is minor in objective terms. ("What you're asked to assume here is that the defendant will make payments under the new schedule. But the proposal gives you a judgment in escrow and a guarantee of attorneys' fees if you have to collect. Do they really have any incentive not to make a payment — and if they do miss one, can't you bring them into line pretty quickly?")

Role Limitations

The next barrier is the people who attend legal mediations. Mediation representatives can be "wrong" in two different respects: their roles and their lack of knowledge. Consider first the problem of role.

Once parties define a dispute as a matter that requires the threat or filing of a lawsuit, they usually hire lawyer-litigators as their representatives, both to conduct the litigation and to discuss settlement. As a result, when parties enter mediation, litigators usually act as spokespersons. Litigators have special skills but a narrow method of approaching problems, tending to assume that they have been hired as gladiators and focusing only on the legal aspects of a dispute and money remedies. Litigators are also in a bind because they have been hired as legal gladiators. Unless a litigator has strong credibility with her client, she will be reluctant to mention "soft" options for fear of seeming weak or disloyal to the cause.

The most likely way to deal with this as the mediator is to talk privately with the litigators, asking how to raise interest-based issues and offering to take responsibility for promoting alternatives. Another avenue is to talk directly with the principals, relying on the lawyers not to squelch the conversation.

Lack of Information/Limitations of the Commercial Format

Even when mediation representatives are willing to consider nontraditional remedies, they often lack the necessary information to do so. Bargainers usually are either litigators or persons with checkbook authority. Interest-based solutions, however, require people who can think "outside the box" of court remedies. The more imaginative an option is, the more likely it is that new people and information will have to be brought into the mediation to develop it.

This is especially difficult in commercial mediations, however, because they are usually scheduled for only a single day. A one-day format confronts mediators interested in exploring interests with a difficult choice: Encourage parties to devote time and energy to gathering data, contacting experts, and exploring an imaginative option, or seek a simple deal based only on money.

One option is to hold premediation conversations to begin to identify interests and assemble the information and expertise needed to explore them during the mediation. Another is to adjourn to permit a creative idea to be considered. There are drawbacks to stopping, but the following is a case in which it proved effective.

> *Example:* A computer manufacturer brought a warranty claim against a chip maker who had inadvertently supplied it with defective chips. The parties agreed that the chip maker was competent and the problem was caused by an adhesive compound supplied by an outside company. The manufacturer argued, however, that the chip maker was legally responsible for the problem.
>
> The chip maker said it did not have enough cash on hand to pay the tens of millions of dollars the manufacturer was demanding, and eventually proposed making a low-seven-figure payment and providing additional compensation in the form of discounts on future orders. The manufacturer agreed to the concept, conceding privately to the mediator that it expected to need the chip maker's products. However none of the people at the mediation knew what kinds of products the manufacturer would need from the defendant over the next few years.
>
> The parties agreed to adjourn for a month so their product teams could confer about a new chip the defendant had under development. Two months later, a deal was worked out that included cash and a discount on future orders.

4.　*Managing Positional Bargaining*

Competitive or positional tactics are a common source of bargaining impasse. We have seen that the problem of "dividing the pie," however large it can be made, exists in almost every situation. Competitive approaches and positional bargaining are common in mediation, and a primary challenge for commercial mediators is to manage it effectively. When the process gets into difficulty, a mediator's best options are to offer information, advice, and coaching. One can, for example:

- Ask about their thinking
- Ask about the underlying message
- Ask about the likely response
- Ask for private information about goals
- Offer advice

Ask About Their Thinking

Often a party who uses positional tactics has not thought through its strategy, or has adopted a poor one. If a party gives a mediator an extreme offer, the neutral can ask how it was formulated ("Can tell me how you got to that?"). The tone should be one of curiosity, not disagreement — assume that the bargainer has a reason and try to understand it. Once you know what a bargainer intends by making a tough positional offer it is possible to discuss whether there are other ways to achieve the purpose.

Ask About the Underlying Message

Numbers, like words, have meanings and every money offer carries an implied message. Positional bargainers may, for example, make an extreme offer to express anger ("There — *that's* what I think of your case!") or frustration ("If the court system were fair, this is what we'd be paid!"), or to suggest that the other side has not been reasonable ("Until they are realistic we're not going above $15,000.").

When a money offer arrives without an explanation, the recipient must decide what it means, and disputants' tendency is to interpret an adversary's signals in the worst light. You can ask a bargainer to say explicitly what he intends to communicate by an offer and suggest less disruptive ways to send it. ("If you want me to tell them how angry you are with their behavior, I can do that. In terms of an offer that will tempt them to make serious concessions, though, I wonder. . . .")

Ask About the Likely Response

The next step can be to ask a party to think about, or predict, the other side's response. ("Let's try to game this out . . . If you drop to 1.675 million from 1.7 as a first move, what do you think they'll do?") Thinking about an adversary's response can give a party some of the satisfaction of taking an extreme position without actually doing so. If you think the disputant is not predicting the likely reaction realistically, you can offer your own assessment ("If you start at $5 million, I think they'll assume you need a settlement well into seven figures, and you may get a response in the $20,000 range.").

Ask for Private Information About Goals

If a party insists on making a tough proposal, you can at least ask for private information about its ultimate goal ("I understand you don't want to put any money on the table now. But just for my information, where would you be willing to go if, for example, I could get them down to actual damages?").

Offer Advice

Positional bargainers are tempted to act as if they do not want an agreement at all, provoking impasse, and it can be tempting to offer advice to head off the problem. Be careful about doing so early in the process, and bear in mind that tone of voice and phrasing are as important as what is said. That said, in a caucus format a mediator may be able to give each side valuable suggestions about what is needed to provoke movement from the other.

B.   Emotional Issues and Cognitive Forces

Disputes often fail to settle because the people involved are emotionally at odds with each other. Strong feelings may be provoked by the incident that gave rise to the dispute or by something that happened afterward. Recall, for example, how the parents of the deceased MIT student became even angrier because the university president did not greet them at their son's funeral. Strong emotions can disrupt communication and produce irrational decision making. And, as we saw in the context of negotiation, cognitive forces can provoke disputes and prevent bargainers from making good decisions even when they are calm. We explore in this section how mediation can deal with emotional and cognitive forces.

1.   Strong Feelings

Both mediators and lawyers can contribute greatly to the process of settlement by dealing with emotional forces. To do so, you do not have to become a pseudo-therapist or take on other inappropriate roles. You must, however, be willing and able to listen to strong expressions of feelings without becoming flustered or squelching them. The following responses can be effective in dealing with emotional issues:

- Identify the issue
- Allow venting: listen, acknowledge, empathize
- If necessary, trace the issue back to its source
- Provide, or arrange for, a response
- Treat continuing problems
- Extend the process or adjourn for a time

Identify the Issue

Legal disputes almost always stimulate strong feelings, but the parties usually arrive at mediation with "game faces" on, not showing emotions unless they are part of the legal case. A person whose legal claim involves emotional distress, for example, may be willing to describe her feelings, but executives and lawyers typically present "businesslike" faces even when they are boiling inside. A mediator or advocate's first task, therefore, is often to discover what emotions are affecting the participants.

A person's feelings may be apparent from facial expressions, body language, tone of voice, or the way he relates to people on the other side of the table. Often, however, a neutral or lawyer has to ask questions to dig out emotional issues. Attorneys or parties can probe for emotions in a joint session, but it is often easier for a mediator to do so in the private setting of a caucus.

The mediator must be willing to accept brush-offs at the outset, remembering that a question that is turned aside at first may be answered later as the participant comes to trust the mediator. The right approach, therefore, is to be both diplomatic and persistent.

> *Example:* A mediator was attempting to settle a claim by an auto dealer that a banker had unfairly foreclosed on his loan and driven him into bankruptcy, then sold his property at a bargain price to a business associate. During the first caucus, when the mediator remarked to the plaintiff how crushing the experience must have been, his lawyer interrupted, saying, "Never mind that — I want to know what they'll offer to settle this thing." The discussion returned to the bargaining situation.
>
> The mediator raised the emotional issue again during a second meeting a week later. This time, the auto dealer hesitated and looked at his attorney. Gesturing expansively, the attorney said, "Joe, tell him how you felt when the bank foreclosed on you. . . ." A torrent of feelings about scheming lenders, the unfair way the public views car dealers, and other angry emotions poured out.

Allow Venting: Listen, Acknowledge, Empathize

Once an emotional issue has been identified, you must decide how to deal with it. In some situations, simply allowing the disputants to vent their feelings directly to each other or privately to the mediator is enough to clear the air. An attorney might, for example, warn a mediator that his client has something to get off her chest, asking the neutral to make clear in opening comments that frank expressions of feelings are welcome and to be prepared to draw them out.

If a party does express a strong emotion, someone should respond. The first-level response is simply to acknowledge that the feeling exists. The appropriate reaction will vary depending on the nature of the issue; a lawyer's anger over an opponent's litigation tactics, for example, is very different from the feelings of a victim of sexual abuse. Whether you are in the role of lawyer or neutral, you can often accomplish a good deal by listening to the aggrieved party and simply showing that you have heard and understood her feelings ("I understand that the deposition was a very frustrating experience for you"). In some cases, you can go further to sympathize with the person's situation.

A listener does not need to agree with a party's view of the facts to sympathize with the party's emotional reaction to them. Indeed, mediators in particular need to be careful to keep the issue of what happened separate from how a disputant feels about it. By characterizing a situation in terms of "if," one can imply gently that there might be other ways of interpreting the underlying facts. You might say, for instance, "If I felt that I'd been cheated by a business partner, I'd probably feel the same way you do," or "I can understand your frustration, given your belief that the company never tried to respond to your complaints."

Finally, you do not have to *fix* the problem. This is a lawyer's (and beginning mediator's) instinctive reaction to many emotional situations; solutions, after all, are what we are inclined by temperament and training to look for. But many situations are not "fixable" in any conventional sense. It might help instead to think of the role as similar to that of a mourner at a funeral: You cannot change what has happened, but the very fact that you are present and showing concern provides solace to the bereaved.

Retrace the Issue to Its Source

Often acknowledging or empathizing with the emotion is not enough: The person remains "stuck" in the feeling. When this occurs, it can help to trace the emotion back to the events that stimulated it. A lawyer can sometimes do this through tactful questions, delivered in a tone that suggests that she is genuinely curious to know the answers. Again, it is easier for a mediator to do this because he is not viewed as an adversary. The listener might, for instance, encourage a disputant to describe how the situation developed.

By asking a disputant to trace the history of a dispute from her perspective, you can often discover the reasons for her feelings and begin to identify areas in which emotion is affecting her settlement decisions. When a mediator asks about the past, he also allows the party the opportunity to reexamine her underlying assumptions.

Arrange a Response

Even more can be accomplished with emotional issues if a mediator brings an adversary into the process in a constructive way. A neutral may, for example, be able to persuade one party to listen to the other express feelings and then acknowledge having heard what was said. Disputants are sometimes able to go even further to express empathy. In fact, within the confidential setting of mediation, with the parties communicating directly with each other and with less concern about admitting liability, one disputant might even express regret or apologize to another.

Treat Continuing Problems

Sometimes people are upset not by a past event, but by an opponent's current conduct. If, for example, one side is angry over what it sees as an opponent's improper tactics, the issue should be handled as a process problem. If, by contrast, the irritation is caused by a condition outside the negotiation process, a mediator can approach it as a hidden substantive issue.

Example: A mediator was moderating discussions between a man and a woman who were breaking up their partnership. The mediator pushed to wrap up the case because he knew that the man was anxious to start a new job, and the woman was pregnant. The woman partner, however, canceled a session at the last minute. The mediator learned from a friend that she had been diagnosed with a serious genetic problem that would affect her unborn child, and she was agonizing over it.

Exploring the issue of scheduling gingerly with both partners, the mediator decided that it would make sense to delay the process. An adjournment would create additional issues, however, because the woman was upset that her partner was making efforts to collect the partnership's outstanding bills. The man had meant this as a gesture of assistance, but the woman interpreted it as a maneuver to change the value of the receivables and thus the sale price of the business. The mediator worked out an agreement by which the male partner would handle day-to-day finances under agreed criteria, and there would be a two-week adjournment of the mediation.

Extend the Process or Adjourn for a Limited Time

Highly emotional disputants, especially at the outset of a case, might need time to work through their feelings. Few mediators would suggest waiting for months for feelings to cool, but it is sometimes sensible to adjourn a settlement process for a day or a week to give a participant more time to adjust psychologically to the need to compromise.

Questions

5. Why might a mediator find it easier to identify an emotional obstacle than a lawyer in direct bargaining?
6. Which of the techniques described above could a lawyer apply with an angry opponent?
7. Which might an attorney apply with her own emotional client?

Note: Apology in Mediation

One of the potentials of mediation is that it provides a setting in which disputants can apologize more easily than in direct negotiation. In part this is because the process is confidential, making it possible for a party to express regret without concern that the gesture will be thrown back at him if the case does not settle. In part also it is because of the atmosphere created by the process itself — the mediator's "presence in the room." Mediators in commercial cases report that it is very unusual for litigants to apologize to each other, but when it does occur it can have a major impact.

As you know from your earlier reading, how an apology is made is crucial to its effectiveness. Professor Jennifer Robbenolt (2003) found that whereas full apologies lessened the likelihood that plaintiffs in a tort case would reject offers and go to court, a partial apology — one viewed by the listener as insincere — was usually worse than nothing, lowering the chances of settlement. For more on the impact and legal issues involved in apologies see the articles by Professor Jonathan Cohen and Deborah Levi in the bibliography.

Questions

8. In April 2001, a U.S. spy plane made an unauthorized emergency landing on China's Hainan Island after colliding with a Chinese fighter jet and causing the loss of the Chinese pilot. The Chinese refused to release the 24 American crew members until the United States issued an apology. The U.S. apology read:

> Both President Bush and Secretary of State Powell have expressed their sincere regret over your missing pilot and aircraft. Please convey to the Chinese people and to the family of pilot Wang Wei that we are very sorry for their loss. Although the full picture of what transpired is still unclear, according to our information, our severely crippled aircraft made an emergency landing after following international emergency procedures. We are very sorry the entering of China's airspace and the landing did not have verbal clearance, but very pleased that the crew landed safely. We appreciate China's efforts to see to the well being of our crew.

What elements of an apology does this statement contain? How might it have contributed to the release of the U.S. crew?

9. In the mediation of the student death claim described in Chapter 9, what do you think made the apology by the president of MIT effective?

2. *Personal Issues in Dealing with Emotion*

Many attorneys and mediators find dealing with intense emotion one of the most difficult aspects of their work. As you read the following dialogue, ask yourself if the lawyer's comments describe your own reaction to emotional situations.

A Dialogue Between a Lawyer and a Psychologist

Lawyer: The fact is, I sometimes don't feel that I'm being professional when I work with emotions. It's not what lawyers do.

Psychologist: That's interesting — What *does* make you feel as if you're acting like a professional?

L: Dealing with facts and arguments, analyzing issues, generating strategies and, most important, solving problems . . .

P: Well, those are clearly professional activities, and they are often invaluable to clients. My only concern would be not to rush into them too soon. In an emotional situation — and people who feel that they've been hurt or treated unfairly are often quite emotional — people *can't really listen until they feel they've been heard.* You might think that you can predict their story because you have heard so many similar ones, but even if you are right, they won't feel heard until they've told it. In fact, they may need to review the story with you in order to hear it themselves and become open to different ways of resolving the problem. Rushing to analyze can get in the way of disputants figuring out what is important to them . . .

I sometimes think of people in this situation as being like a tightly closed fist: One option is to help them strike with that fist. Another is to counsel them about their chances of winning the fight. But it could be even more useful to help them uncurl their fist, so that they can grasp other possibilities. Strategizing with "closed fist" clients who don't know what they feel or why they feel it is often unproductive. The issues they present are often only a smokescreen for other, more important concerns. Lawyers or mediators who charge ahead to focus on legal or bargaining issues may find themselves going off in a direction that the client may later resist or even sabotage . . . .

L: I think it's sitting without doing anything that often strikes us lawyers as meaningless.

P: OK, I'm hearing how important it is to feel that you are *doing something specific* to feel like a responsible professional. It's true that usually more is needed than silence; we need to find a way for lawyers to experience listening, and even encouraging the expression of emotions, as an active, professional activity in and of itself . . . .

L: Another problem is that lawyers often feel lost in long discussions about emotions — they seem directionless.

P: It's true that exploring emotional territory makes it difficult to have a clear agenda. Your questions and interventions need to be guided by what emerges as important to the client as she tells her story . . . .

L: Actually, many of us became lawyers to avoid dealing with these messy emotional issues. I've sometimes said that hearing people out is like "draining pus from an infected wound."

P: Ugh — I can understand why you wouldn't be enthusiastic about doing it. That metaphor also helps me understand why I've rarely heard "venting" described by lawyers as anything more than a necessary evil, to be gotten out of the way as quickly as possible. But allowing people to vent emotions doesn't have to be distasteful, and it does have a purpose and goal — it's just that *you* are not the one setting the goal. It might help to imagine a litigant's experience as a dark room filled with noxious fumes; "venting" is an opportunity to open the windows, release the blinding smoke and let in fresh air so your client can think more clearly.

L: Are you saying that venting moves inevitably toward clarity?

P: Not necessarily — people can just spin their wheels and go even deeper into the same old rut. We all know couples who've been having the same argument for years. That's where the active aspect of listening comes in. If it's not clear to you how a disputant got from point A to point B, you can ask for an explanation (e.g., "I hear that A happened and then B, but I'd like to understand better how you are connecting them"). The answer may be even more clarifying for the client than it is for you. If there's a lot of fuzziness about how A led to B, that may be where unarticulated feelings are hiding.

Active listening stays focused on encouraging the client to tell her story fully, but it also offers opportunities for lawyers to use their organizational skills to bring clarity . . . .

L: Many of us worry that if we start to let parties express emotions, the situation will blow up. It'll be like uncapping a volcano — lava everywhere! And people will get burned.

P: In fact, no one can cap an emotional "volcano," and even if you could it might not be a wise course. The pressure is there and denying it may fuel it further. If you don't drain emotional pressures off, they will find their own escape routes — often to fuel more arguments and hardened positions.

If you want to think of emotional release as a volcano erupting, think of your job as allowing the lava to escape, while at the same time channeling it away from the "village" and into a safe area. There are ways to channel discussion so that it does not disrupt the process of settlement or your relationship with the parties. Just by modeling respectful listening yourself and establishing ground rules for how people express themselves, you can channel emotional "lava." Perhaps the most important rule I enforce in working with families is to ask each participant to focus on his own experiences, feelings, and wishes, without accusing or analyzing the motives of the other side . . . .

L: Again, as I think about it, the more usual problem is that most parties come to mediation with "game faces on." They act as if there is no emotional issue, when I suspect they are simmering inside.

P: Yes, in therapy, too, clamming up is by far the more common and challenging response to emotional turbulence. The listening techniques we've been discussing are the most effective ways I've found to get at buried emotions.

L: The final obstacle is litigators — the people who usually hire legal mediators. One might fairly ask: If the lawyers don't want to get into an emotional issue, how can we do it without offending them?

P: I wonder if you're reading them right? A major problem may be that a litigator's role as an advocate armored for battle often makes it hard for her to explore a client's mixed feelings. I think a mediator could make himself quite valuable as someone prepared to handle the messy emotions that some attorneys don't feel in a position to confront, yet know are preventing a resolution of the dispute.

Question

10.   Could any of these factors lead you to avoid dealing with intense emotions in a legal dispute? Which seem most significant?

3.   *Cognitive Forces*

We saw in Chapter 3 that the effect of psychology on decision making is not limited to emotions; cognitive forces often prevent persons from making good decisions even when they are calm. Of the numerous cognitive forces that affect disputing we will focus on two — selective perception and optimistic overconfidence — that impair disputants' ability to assess the merits of a case, and two others — reactive devaluation and loss aversion — that distort parties' judgment about bargaining decisions.

a.   Selective Perception

Example: Students at Harvard Law School are preparing to negotiate the settlement of a personal injury case. Before they begin, they are asked to make a private prediction of their chances of winning based on their confidential instructions. What the students don't know is there is nothing confidential about the instructions: Both sides have received exactly the same data, with different labels. Because both sides have the same information, they should come out with the same answers, but this is not what occurs.

In fact, hundreds of law and business students told to negotiate for the plaintiff assess her chances of winning as being nearly 20 percent higher than students who are assigned to the defense. The two sides' predictions total nearly 120 percent. Asked to estimate what damages a jury will award if the plaintiff does win, there is a similar disparity: Plaintiff law students estimate her damages at an average of $264,000, whereas defense negotiators looking at the same data estimate a verdict of only $188,000.

What caused these distortions? It was not due to disparities in information, because both sides had the same facts. Nor was it due to lack of experience: When experienced litigators training to be mediators were assigned roles in the same problem, their predictions were similarly distorted. Disagreements like these are a serious barrier to settlement, because parties understandably resist accepting an outcome worse than their honest (but inflated) estimate of the value of their case.

Humans instinctively form a viewpoint or image of any new situation — in mediation terms they create a "frame" in which they view a dispute. People then process any new information they receive about the situation through their existing frame. When a person receives data that conflicts with his frame it creates clashing images in his mind — *cognitive dissonance.* The human brain tries to eliminate this dissonance by unconsciously filtering out data that conflict with its existing frame.

This tendency to disregard data is known as selective perception. Selective perception most likely explains, for example, the results of the Harvard experiment, and it can pose a serious problem in mediation. A typical litigant will quickly form an opinion about who is right in a controversy, and most people instinctively assign that role to themselves. Once a disputant adopts a viewpoint, however, he unconsciously filters out data that conflict with his "take" on the case. At the same time he gives full weight to information that reaffirms it, becoming even more convinced that his initial view was correct. Mediators often encounter cases in which the facts are largely undisputed but parties disagree vehemently about who will win in court. Each litigant's perspective seems plausible to itself, because selective perception has caused it to disregard the evidence that contradicts it.

To deal with the problem of selective perception, consider these options:

- Encourage the parties to speak
- Use charts and other visual aids
- Explicitly question gaps
- Ask disputants to summarize the other side's key points

Encourage the Parties to Speak

One excellent option is to encourage parties to speak for themselves, either during an opening session or in ad hoc tête-à-têtes with a counterpart on the other side. The reason is that a party is much more likely to listen to the opposing party than to a lawyer. Fairly or not, disputants tend to view the attorney on the other side as a hired gun and to disregard what she says. Listeners are usually also suspicious of what opponents say, but are likely to listen more carefully to them, if only to see whether the speaker makes an admission or misrepresentation about what happened. As a result, both lawyers and parties pay better attention to statements made by an opposing party.

Use Charts and Other Visual Aids

Lawyers are accustomed to dealing with printed documents, especially the proverbial "fine print." Nonlawyers, by contrast, may absorb information more effectively when it is presented in other formats. A disputant who misses information in a memo, for example, might be able to understand it if it is presented or reinforced with a chart or graph. Similarly, data that are skipped over in black and white may be remembered if highlighted in color, and information that fades out on a printed page can become clearer if written on a whiteboard.

Explicitly Question Gaps

The most straightforward way to deal with a gap in a disputant's assessment of data is to ask about it, in effect shining a spotlight on the omitted item. We give suggestions for how to ask questions in the next section.

Ask for Help in Understanding the Other Side's Points

Asking disputants to summarize an opponent's argument may push them to confront its strength or focus attention on an issue. However, disputants are usually reluctant to do this in an opponent's presence. Instead, in the privacy of a caucus you can:

* Express doubt about what the other side is saying and ask for help ("I'm not sure which is their main argument on the contract issue . . . what do you understand them to be saying?").
* Note that the disputant has been living with the case much longer and so probably better appreciates the opponent's position.
* If a summary seems erroneous or incomplete, point this out diplomatically ("Hmm . . . what I thought I heard was more that . . .").

b.   Optimistic Overconfidence

Assessing the value of a legal case requires predicting events that are uncertain, for example, how an unknown jury will react to evidence that may or may not be admitted. These assessments are often unreliable. For one thing, people are consistently overconfident about their ability to assess uncertain data. Why is this? The problem is that when we don't know something — even a fact that we aren't expected to have at our fingertips — we are either embarrassed to admit our ignorance or simply feel a competitive urge to be right. So we give a more precise answer than our knowledge can support.

The tendency to be overconfident becomes even stronger when a person acquires a personal stake in the outcome. In psychological experiments, for example, subjects who placed a small bet that a horse would win a race were consistently more confident about their ability to predict the outcome than people who had not placed a bet.

There is a related problem. When people in an uncertain situation are asked to estimate the likelihood of a good or bad outcome, they consistently underestimate the chances of an unfavorable result. The reason, it appears, is that we like to believe that we are in control of events and thus able to bring about good results, even when we cannot. In addition to being overconfident of our ability to predict the future, we are overoptimistic that future outcomes will be favorable to us.

How do these forces affect negotiations over lawsuits? Lawyers are often asked to estimate the outcome of court proceedings when they have little basis for offering an accurate assessment. Under pressure to appear expert, they are particularly likely to be overconfident about the accuracy of their estimates. To make matters worse, both lawyers and clients "bet" on cases by investing time and money in them, which accentuates their tendency to be overconfident in the face of uncertainty.

To counteract the tendency to be overoptimistically overconfident:

- Discuss best and worst-case scenarios
- Focus on the most likely outcome, a mediocre result
- Distance "bettors" from their "horses"

Discuss Best- and Worst-Case Scenarios

If a disputant has misevaluated a case because she is using a false point of comparison, it is helpful to present other examples, making the risk of loss more concrete in the litigant's mind. Parties are more likely to listen to warnings about bad outcomes if you first acknowledge the possibility of a good one. You might begin, therefore, by admitting that a big win is possible for the party and discussing it. Having covered the best possibility, one can move on to other, less attractive outcomes, for example, by asking a lawyer if he has seen bad results in this kind of case. Discussing adverse outcomes also harnesses the power of loss aversion, discussed later.

Focus on the Most Likely Outcome, a Mediocre Result

Another option is to draw a litigant's attention to the most likely outcome in the case, which is often a mediocre result rather than a clear victory for either side. Parties who see only win-or-lose possibilities, and focus only on the better one, need to be reminded that many judgments fall in the middle. A tort case, for instance, might result in a ruling that the defendant is liable but that the plaintiff is contributorily negligent, resulting in a modest award. To the extent that a mediocre result replaces an outright win as the benchmark for evaluating a settlement, compromise will appear more attractive.

Distance the "Bettor" from His "Horse"

A mediator can reduce the "bettor" effect by making a party feel less invested in his prediction. You might, for instance, suggest that money a litigant has already spent on a case — its bet — is a "sunk" cost that cannot be recovered regardless of the outcome and is therefore irrelevant to decisions about the future. The real issue is whether to spend new money — to place an additional "bet" — on a case that has not been a winner so far.

c. Reactive Devaluation

Imagine that you are defense counsel in a lawsuit. Your opponent is demanding that you pay $100,000 to settle, but appears sure that you will never agree. Now you decide to offer that sum. Is your adversary pleased? To the contrary, her first reaction is likely to be that she has undervalued the case: It must be worth more than $100,000, because you are the enemy and would never offer her a fair deal. The tendency people have to reject offers made by anyone they see as an adversary is what was described in Chapter 3 as "reactive devaluation." A bargainer's instinctive response to an opponent's offer is reminiscent of the comedian Groucho Marx, who vowed never to join any club that would have him as a member.

Probably a mediator's single greatest advantage is that he is not subject to reactive devaluation. Potential ways to deal with this barrier include:

- Offer a proposal as your own
- Discuss the merits of an idea in the abstract
- Offer a disputant a choice
- Accredit an adversary's proposal

Offer a Proposal as Your Own

If as a mediator you float a proposal, for instance, that a contractual relationship be restructured or parties agree to an expert appraisal of a disputed piece of property, the disputants are likely to listen politely. They will not devalue your proposal automatically, as they would if it came from the other side.

There are two dangers in doing so, however. First, if the listener thinks you are simply communicating an idea generated by an adversary, devaluation will apply with full force. Second, if the listener thinks you have endorsed a skewed proposal, he may decide you have taken sides against him. It is therefore important to think through not just whether an idea makes sense in the abstract, but also how a partisan listener will interpret it. Citing objective criteria or principles to support your ideas is also useful; even if the listener is not convinced by them, it will help reassure him that even if you are mistaken, you are acting in good faith.

Discuss the Merits of an Idea in the Abstract

The flip side of disputants' tendency to devalue ideas because opponents favor them is that if an opponent has not yet agreed to an option, devaluation is less likely to occur. Put another way, a hypothetical offer is not yet cursed by the fact the other side is actually willing to make it. If the party agrees that an offer not yet on the table might be acceptable, it is at least partially "inoculated" against being devalued if the other side later signs on.

Presenting an offer as out of reach also takes advantage of the so-called scarcity principle — the fact that people instinctively want things that are not available. To take advantage of this effect, test out proposals as uncertain possibilities even if you are fairly sure you can persuade the other side to agree to them ("You know, I think if we could ever get them up to $100,000, it would be worth serious consideration. What do you think?").

Offer a Disputant a Choice

If you present two or three settlement options and indicate the opponent has not decided in favor of any of them, it is less likely they will be devalued ("I think I may be able to convince the defendant either to pay the money within 60 days or over a year at a reasonable rate of interest. Which would you prefer?"). People usually like the feeling of having a choice, even if none of the proposals is very attractive. (Think of a child who is inveigled into going to bed by being asked whether he would prefer red or blue pajamas.)

Accredit an Adversary's Proposal

If you genuinely believe an adversary's proposal is constructive, you can say so, using your credibility to persuade the listener it is worth considering. In doing so you might want to note that the proposal has flaws from the perspective of the listener — it almost certainly will — but may be worth considering. Be careful, however, not to sacrifice your relationship with a party by advocating a solution it sees as seriously biased.

d.   Loss Aversion

We have seen that disputants often develop an opinion about the "right" outcome in a case early in the process, based on statements by friends, comments by attorneys, stories they see in the media about superficially similar cases, and other sources. In addition to stimulating selective perception, such opinions then become a mental benchmark for settlement decisions. For example, a tort plaintiff might hear on television about a $500,000 verdict in a case that seems similar to his. The plaintiff then begins to think of $500,000 as the right amount at which to settle his claim. Two years later a mediator may suggest that information produced in discovery has lowered the chance of winning and that verdicts in this kind of case rarely exceed $100,000. The plaintiff, however, feels a strong sense of loss at being asked to settle for less than his $500,000 benchmark.

Loss aversion is both a cognitive effect and a source of emotion that distorts judgment, because feelings of loss are quite painful.

> *Example:* Students at Stanford University who had expected to attend a seminar without charge are told after they arrive they will each have to pay $20 when they leave the room to cover unexpected expenses. They can, however, spin a roulette wheel with three chances in four of paying nothing and one chance of having to pay $100. The odds thus discourage gambling — because the average cost of spinning the wheel is ¼ of $100, or $25, the smart choice is to pay $20. However, 70 percent of the students tested chose to spin the wheel. Having expected to pay nothing, they apparently experienced the demand for $20 as an unwelcome loss and were willing to take an unreasonable risk to avoid it.

People involved in legal disputes behave much like the Stanford students, often taking unreasonable risks to avoid what they see as a "loss." To deal with feelings of loss, consider the following:

- Identify loss benchmarks
- Recharacterize the situation
- Suggest new terms

Identify Loss Benchmarks

The first task is to identify the benchmarks by which disputants are measuring losses or gains. You can do so, for example, by asking parties what they think would be a fair outcome and how they arrived at their opinion. Remember not to argue with a party — your goal at this point is to identify the issue, not to resolve it.

Recharacterize the Situation

Because loss calculations are inherently subjective, you can reduce feelings of loss by persuading a disputant to use a more realistic benchmark.

> *Example:* A discharged employee brought an age discrimination claim against his employer and became convinced his claim would bring $200,000 or more. Over two years of litigation, however, he got no settlement offers at all and became increasingly frustrated with his ex-employer's bad faith.
>
> The case eventually went to court-ordered mediation. After five hours of discussion, the employer put $40,000 on the table. From the perspective of the employee's initial goal this was extremely disappointing, and he complained about this to the mediator. In response, the mediator said, "For two years now, you've seen nothing at all. The defendant has ignored you! But now we've got his attention and there's forty thousand dollars on the table. The challenge at this point is to find out just how far you can push him, *then* decide if you want to take it."
>
> The employee listened, seeming to take satisfaction at having finally forced the employer to pay attention to his grievances. His focus shifted to how to "push" the employer to its limit, measuring progress from the employer's offer rather than his prior benchmark.

Suggest New Terms

Feelings of loss are more painful when there is only a single issue in play, making each party's loss easily measurable. Thus, for instance, loss aversion is such a problem when parties engage in positional bargaining over money. By contrast, when there are multiple issues under consideration, losses are harder to measure. If a new issue is introduced into the mix, disputants often have no benchmark for measuring what they ought to get or seeing the outcome as a loss.

> *Example:* Former Secretary of State Henry Kissinger is said to have ascribed his success in mediating agreements between Arabs and Israelis to the tactic of "making the deal so complicated no one could tell who was winning." In essence, he used complex proposals attuned to the parties' sensitivities to distract the parties from measuring agreements against their prior benchmarks.

C.   Merits-Based Barriers

Lawyers who negotiate over legal disputes instinctively apply one of the key lessons of good bargaining practice — not to settle for less than the value of one's best alternative to a negotiated agreement. In legal disputes each side's clearest alternative is usually the same: to submit the case to adjudication. But the fact that disputants have the same alternative does not mean that they agree about its value; in practice parties' disagreement over likely outcomes is a major obstacle to settlement.

Litigators tend to assume that if they cannot settle it is because the other side has misevaluated its case. But as we saw from the discussion of optimistic overconfidence, *both* sides in a dispute, as well as their lawyers, commonly make overoptimistic judgments. In such situations part of the challenge for lawyers and mediators is to bring the parties' assessments closer together so that a settlement will seem less unfair. How can this be done?

1.   *Responses to Lack of Information*

One obstacle to settlement is often a simple lack of information: People sometimes assess their alternatives incorrectly because they do not have enough data, or the data they have are not accurate. Lawyers often say, for example, "It's too early to settle; I don't know the case well enough." Sometimes, however, negotiators claim to have all relevant data, but a neutral observer can see that their arguments are laced with gaps and assumptions. It is also possible that each side has information but that their versions of key events conflict.

It is often surprising to an outsider how little litigants know about each other's claims and defenses even after years of discovery. Court rules are designed to stimulate full disclosure of relevant information, but in practice discovery often fails because litigants "hide the ball," concealing evidence from each other for as long as possible. Even when parties do learn legally relevant facts, they often lack information about other important issues. As a result, a mediator can often make significant progress simply by arranging for an informal exchange of information among disputants. As one example, remember the case described in Chapter 9 between a discharged executive and his employer, in which the parties litigated for years before the plaintiff learned in mediation that a major component of this claim had no value, opening the way to settlement.

Among the steps a mediator can take to solve disagreements that stem from information problems are the following:

* Arrange an exchange of information
* Moderate a joint discussion
* Direct attention to nonmerits information

Arrange an Information Exchange

A mediator can often arrange for a more effective exchange of relevant information than occurs in most discovery proceedings. Litigants are usually more forthcoming because they hope to settle the case, wish to cooperate with the neutral, and trust the mediator to shield them from a one-sided process. Mediation's special confidentiality rules, discussed in Chapter 15, allow disputants to share data with less fear of being harmed if the case does not settle.

Moderate a Joint Discussion

Disputants often have never looked at information together to clear up misunderstandings and understand its significance to the other side. If parties can talk civilly with each other, it often makes sense to ask participants, or a subset of them, to meet to discuss an issue. Such discussions can expose misunderstandings, as well as giving people the experience of working cooperatively.

Direct Attention to Nonmerits Information

All this assumes, of course, that the parties are focusing on the right information. We have seen that new, nonlegal data can help parties construct more valuable settlement packages.

2. *Intermediate Techniques*

Even when litigants have complete information, cognitive forces often influence them to disagree about the value of their litigation alternative. Mediators and bargainers can use the following approaches to help disputants who have information but seem to be evaluating it poorly:

*   Ask questions
*   Lead disputants through an analysis of possible outcomes
*   Point out worst-case scenarios
*   Stress transactional costs

Ask Questions

The safest approach is to ask questions about the parties' factual and legal assumptions. This is the essence of the tactic known as "reality testing." Questions are particularly useful at the outset because one does not need to have developed an analysis to ask them. It is worth stressing that reality testing does not require a mediator to give her own opinion about an issue. For example, a mediator might:

*   Ask a plaintiff, "Can you help me understand how you calculated the figure of $5 million in lost profits? Are there any documents I could look at to flesh that out?"
*   Ask a defendant, "Is there a precedent for your argument that a judge will have to throw out the punitive damages claim? The plaintiff says that the circuit court ruled the other way; is there anything to the contrary I can show him?"
*   Draw attention to a problem that a party has ignored: "You're looking for $2 million in damages, but I see insurance coverage of only $250,000. How do you think you can collect a judgment that favorable?"

One useful tactic is to ask each party to suggest questions to present to the other. This allows you to raise an argument as coming from the other side and put yourself in the stance of being willing to present a reply on the party's behalf ("The defense is arguing that there is no proof of emotional distress — can you give me something I can take to them on this?").

Lead Disputants Through an Analysis of Possible Outcomes

Another option is to take a disputant through a point-by-point analysis of the case, covering each aspect of liability, damages, and enforcement of a judgment. This can pinpoint problems glossed over or forgotten during informal discussion, and counteract litigants' persistent tendency to filter out unfavorable information.

Point Out Worst-Case Scenarios

Although the concept of the "best alternative to a negotiated agreement," or BATNA, is useful, parties often take it too literally. They focus only on their *best* alternative to a settlement and ignore the most likely result or worst possible outcome.

You should make an effort to ensure that each side considers less-favorable-but-possible scenarios. You might play on risk aversion, for instance, by probing the impact of a total loss in the case and requesting each lawyer to estimate for her client the risk that it will occur. Focusing on worst-case scenarios also lets a mediator harness the psychological power of loss aversion; if disputants begin to measure an unattractive but certain settlement against the possibility of a total loss, compromise might seem more attractive.

You can also focus attention on the most likely outcome, a mediocre one. In a tort case, for instance, this might be a finding that the defendant is liable but that the plaintiff is contributorily negligent and receives reduced damages. Doing this helps counterbalance the human tendency to focus on dramatic events such as a huge victory, rather than the more common mediocre result.

Stress Transactional Costs

Parties will often accept a settlement that is worse than they expect to do in court, because by doing so they avoid additional costs of litigation. People almost always understand this problem in general terms, but often have not realistically considered how much it will cost to pursue their case through trial. To address this you can ask disputants what it will cost to continue the case. If a party's estimate seems unrealistic, ask questions or go through an analysis of what is likely to happen if there is no settlement.

3.   Evaluation of the Likely Outcome in Adjudication

When bargaining reaches an impasse and the reason is disagreement over who will win in court, many lawyers expect mediators to give an opinion on the issue. Evaluation is a controversial topic, and this section explores the issue.

Keep in mind as you read that legal issues are not the only topics on which a mediator can express a viewpoint. He might, for instance, suggest what offer a party should make, how a proposal is likely to be received by an adversary, the likely meaning of an opponent's move, or whether a particular offer satisfies a person's personal interests. Doing any of these things requires that a mediator "evaluate" something. The classic form of mediator evaluation, however, is to offer an opinion about how a court will decide a legal issue or about the monetary value of a claim.

a.   Should Mediators Evaluate?

No one argues that mediators should use evaluation as a first resort, and court-related ADR programs that focus on evaluating cases have declined greatly in popularity. Still, commercial mediators may think that offering advice about legal issues is part of what they have been hired to do, and there is often no clear dividing line between facilitative and evaluative interventions.

Other mediators, however, believe that evaluation should not be part of mediation at all. For a mediator to offer advice, they say, interferes with core values of the process such as the right of parties to make their own decisions. Consider the following perspectives on this issue.

❖ **Lela P. Love,** *The Top Ten Reasons Why Mediators Should Not Evaluate*

24 Fla. St. U. L. Rev. 937 (1997)

... The debate over whether mediators should "evaluate" revolves around the confusion over what constitutes evaluation and an "evaluative" mediator. ... An "evaluative" mediator gives advice, makes assessments, states opinions — including opinions on the likely court outcome — proposes a fair or workable resolution to an issue or the dispute, or presses the parties to accept a particular resolution. The ten reasons that follow demonstrate that those activities are inconsistent with the role of a mediator.

I.   *The Roles and Related Tasks of Evaluators and Facilitators Are at Odds*

Evaluating, assessing, and deciding for others is radically different than helping others evaluate, assess, and decide for themselves. Judges, arbitrators, neutral experts, and advisors are evaluators. Their role is to make decisions and give opinions. To do so, they use predetermined criteria to evaluate evidence and arguments presented by adverse parties. The tasks of evaluators include: finding "the facts" by properly weighing evidence; judging credibility and allocating the burden of proof; determining and applying the relevant law, rule, or custom to the particular situation; and making an award or rendering an opinion. The adverse parties have expressly asked the evaluator — judge, arbitrator, or expert — to decide the issue or resolve the conflict.

In contrast, the role of mediators is to assist disputing parties in making their own decisions and evaluating their own situations. A mediator facilitates communications, promotes understanding, focuses the parties on their interests, and seeks creative problem-solving to enable the parties to reach their own agreement. Mediators push disputing parties to question their assumptions, reconsider their positions, and listen to each other's perspectives, stories, and arguments. They urge the parties to consider relevant law, weigh their own values, principles, and priorities, and develop an optimal outcome. In so doing, mediators facilitate evaluation by the parties.

These differences between evaluators and facilitators mean that each uses different skills and techniques, and each requires different competencies, training norms, and ethical guidelines to perform their respective functions. Further, the evaluative tasks of determining facts, applying law or custom, and delivering an opinion not only divert the mediator away from facilitation, but also can compromise the mediator's neutrality — both in actuality and in the eyes of the parties — because the mediator will be favoring one side in his judgment.

Endeavors are more likely to succeed when the goal is clear and simple and not at war with other objectives. Any task, whether it is the performance of an Olympic athlete, the advocacy of an attorney, or the negotiation assistance provided by a mediator, requires a clear and bright focus and the development of appropriate strategies, skills, and power. In most cases, should the athlete or the attorney or the mediator divert their focus to another task, it will diminish their capacity to achieve their primary goal. "No one can serve two masters." Mediators cannot effectively facilitate when they are evaluating.

   I. *Evaluation Promotes Positioning and Polarization, Which Are Antithetical to the Goals of Mediation . . .*

   II. *Ethical Codes Caution Mediators — and Other Neutrals — Against Assuming Additional Roles . . .*

  III. *If Mediators Evaluate Legal Claims and Defenses, They Must Be Lawyers; Eliminating Non-Lawyers Will Weaken the Field . . .*

  IV. *There Are Insufficient Protections Against Incorrect Mediator Evaluations . . .*

   V. *Evaluation Abounds: The Disputing World Needs Alternative Paradigms . . .*

  VI. *Mediator Evaluation Detracts from the Focus on Party Responsibility for Critical Evaluation, Re-Evaluation and Creative Problem Solving . . .*

 VII. *Evaluation Can Stop Negotiation . . .*

VIII. *A Uniform Understanding of Mediation is Critical to the Development of the Field . . .*

  IX. *Mixed Processes Can Be Useful, But Call Them What They Are! . . .*

❖ **Marjorie Corman Aaron**, *Merits Barriers: Evaluation and Decision Analysis*

in D. Golann, Mediating Legal Disputes 145 (2009)

A mediator's ultimate weapon for influencing divergent case assessments is to offer an evaluation. Evaluation is an important, risky, and controversial tactic that should be carefully considered, structured, and delivered.

To understand the difference between evaluation and other mediator interventions, consider this metaphor. If mediators were doctors, fostering an information exchange might be the equivalent of recommending exercise and diet. Helping lawyers and parties to rigorously analyze their own views on disputed issues would be like administering medicine with potentially uncomfortable side effects.

Mediator evaluation would be akin to surgery. Just as surgery can range from an arthroscopic procedure to a major operation, evaluation can vary from small and low-risk to comprehensive and potentially threatening. Most people would not choose a doctor whose first response to every illness was to bring out a scalpel. At the same time, few would feel comfortable with a physician who refused to perform surgery regardless of need. The challenge for a mediator is to know when and how to perform evaluative "surgery" in the safest possible way.

What do we mean by "evaluation"? In this context it means forming and expressing one's views regarding the likely outcome in adjudication. Evaluation can focus on single issue ("It seems doubtful the statute of limitations defense will be successful.") or the overall outcome ("The plaintiff is likely to win."). It can be expressed as a range ("I think damages could run between $125,000 and $175,000."), a numeric probability ("I would estimate a 40 percent chance of success."), or a precise number ("I predict a $500,000 award in this case in Randolph County."). An evaluation can be expressed with certainty ("I am fairly sure the plaintiff will win . . . ") or left vague ("I have some doubts about how a jury might react to . . . ").

The idea that parties and lawyers evaluate their own cases is not controversial. However we have seen that a party's numbers may be seriously distorted. . . .

Lawyers and parties who enter mediation often expect the neutral to evaluate the issues. Having educated a mediator about their case, disputants anticipate that she will think about what she has heard. Professional mediators are not "potted plants" and do in fact form judgments much of the time. Lawyers and parties are thus reasonable to ask a mediator "What do you think?," "How do you see this argument?" or "Where do you predict the damages will fall out?," and if a mediator refuses to answer they may feel frustrated.

On the other hand, many mediators can recount a time they provided an evaluation, were rebuffed, and soon thereafter the process ground to a halt. Experienced lawyers talk of frustration with mediators who announce a "reasonable settlement number" and then alienate or entrench clients by trying to push the outcome toward their opinion. Because evaluation can be powerful both negatively and positively, it is critical for mediators to evaluate appropriately, skillfully and with minimum collateral damage, just as a surgeon must choose the optimal technique to achieve a goal with minimum post-operative harm.

Benefits

Evaluation can cause litigants to question and reevaluate their own judgments and "bottom lines." When a neutral who has listened thoughtfully to a presentation of facts and arguments disagrees with a litigant's prediction of victory, the party may be motivated to rethink its position. Evaluation can, for example, help to overcome the impact of selective perception and other cognitive forces discussed earlier.

...A mediator evaluation can also satisfy a litigant's emotional desire for "my day in court." An evaluation approximates the civil justice paradigm — both sides present their stories and arguments and a neutral renders a judgment — but within the safer, non-binding confines of mediation. Having presented their cases to a neutral, even one without a black robe, parties may feel less need to do it again before a judge.

A mediator's evaluation can also provide psychological or professional cover to litigants who realize negotiation concessions are necessary, but do not want to move from an entrenched position without a rationale. Business representatives, insurance adjusters, government officials, and even individuals who feel obligated to family members, often use evaluations to protect them from after-the-fact criticism.

Disputants can use evaluation as a convenient scapegoat for a difficult decision, even when the disputant privately agrees with the assessment. ("Once the mediator said the case was worth $100,000, there was no way I was going to be able to settle it for any less. . . .")

Dangers

Mediator evaluation can also create a serious risk of harm to the process, making settlement more difficult. First and foremost, mediators who evaluate risk damaging their credibility as neutrals. As long as litigants trust a mediator is impartial, they are willing to consider options, listen to questions, and make painful compromises. When a mediator evaluates, however, a participant may conclude the mediator has "gone over to the other side," assuming that because the mediator thinks the other side will win, the mediator must want settlement to be skewed in the other side's favor. When the mediator next asks for compromise in such circumstances, the disputant is likely to resist.

If these risks are not enough, consider the following additional concerns. A "global" opinion of case value may freeze the bargaining process, because neither side wants to accept a settlement worse than the neutral's number even when it would be wise to do so. In these circumstances a mediator's evaluation becomes a take-it-or-leave-it offer to both sides.

The expectation of a mediator evaluation can also discourage bargaining. After all, why confront painful decisions about concessions when the neutral may soon vindicate one's position? Disputants may also assume the mediator will place her evaluation between their last offers, and thus be concerned that offering additional concessions will simply shrink the zone in which they can "win" in the evaluation.

The expectation of an evaluation also changes the focus of the dialogue. Participants emphasize their legal arguments, seeking to persuade the mediator as judge and jury. This, in turn, can cause parties to become even more convinced of the strength of their arguments and angry at the other side's advocacy. Evaluations also tend to distract the parties' (and perhaps also the mediator's) attention away from non-legal barriers to settlement and creative solutions. And if the real barrier to agreement is a party's unresolved feelings or a similar non-legal issue, evaluation will be irrelevant.

Given its inherent dangers, our fundamental advice regarding mediator evaluation is: "Only when necessary, and with humility." To us "necessary" means evaluation should be undertaken as a strategy of last resort, when it appears to be the only way to break a negotiation deadlock. At that point even if all the risks of evaluation come to pass they are of no ultimate consequence, because the case probably would not settle in any event.

Questions

11.   Do Professor Aaron's arguments answer any of Professor Love's concerns? Which are not addressed?

12.   a.   The Federal Court for the Northern District of California has adopted the following rules for its court-connected mediation program:

> . . . As promptly as possible during the mediation the mediator should identify the issues and discuss them with the parties. . . .

Is a mediator who does this engaging in evaluation under Professor Love's definition? Professor Aaron's?

b.   The rules go on to say:

> In some cases the mediator may consider suggesting specific settlement terms. Such action is not required, or even appropriate, in every case, and should generally be employed only if the parties request it and the mediator concludes it will aid the parties and counsel in reaching a settlement. Any such settlement recommendation should be based on the mediator's experience or other knowledge concerning jury verdicts and settlement value.

If the parties request a mediator to make a suggestion, is it still "evaluation"? Would Professor Love object to this if a mediator, responding to the parties' request, based a settlement recommendation on an assessment of their underlying interests rather than the litigation value of the case?

13.   The Supreme Court of Virginia has adopted the following rule for court mediators:

> The mediator may offer legal information if all parties are present, or separately if they consent, and shall inform unrepresented parties or those parties who are not accompanied by legal counsel about the importance of reviewing the mediator's legal information with legal counsel. Also, the mediator may offer evaluation of strengths and weaknesses of positions only if such evaluation is incidental to the facilitative role and does not interfere with the mediator's impartiality or the self-determination of the parties.

Does this rule respond to Professor Love's concerns about evaluation? Which ones?

14.   To what degree are the problems of mediator evaluation eliminated if all parties in the process are represented by counsel?

b.   If a Mediator Does Evaluate, How Should It Be Done?

Assuming that a mediator does evaluate the merits, a key issue is what substantive standard he should apply. There are several possible criteria:

- A mediator can offer a *prediction of what will happen* if a particular issue or the entire matter is adjudicated. Here the mediator is not saying how he personally would decide the issue, but rather is assessing how a judge, jury, or arbitrator in that jurisdiction, with all *their* quirks and foibles, is likely to respond. To put it another way, in this model the mediator is offering a "weather forecast" about the atmosphere in some future courtroom, but not advocating rain. This is the classic form of mediator evaluation.

- Alternatively, a mediator can give an *expert judgment about what happened or a personal view of what is fair*. Here the neutral is assuming the role of advisory arbitrator in the case. This is the most dangerous form of evaluation, because the loser is likely to feel, with justification, that the neutral has taken sides against him. And the mediator's personal view of a case is irrelevant, because he is almost always disqualified from sitting in judgment on it.

- Finally, a mediator may not evaluate the legal merits at all, but instead *assess the bargaining situation*. Here the neutral is giving an estimate of what each side needs to do to get an agreement, given the current state of mind of the other party. A neutral might say, for instance, "Given how they are feeling in the other room, my sense is that you'll need to go to six figures if you want a deal today." This is probably the least dangerous form of evaluation, because the mediator is simply assessing the opponent's attitude, without indicating that he thinks that it is fair or agrees with it.

❖ **American Bar Association Task Force on Improving Mediation Quality,**
                               FINAL REPORT

                                    (2008)

"Analytical" Techniques Used by the Mediator

Information from Focus Groups, Surveys, and Party Interviews

The Task Force collected substantial amounts of data about user perceptions of mediators utilizing analytical techniques in mediation. We observed
in our focus groups that many reasonably sophisticated mediation users in
civil cases want mediators to provide certain services, including analytical
techniques. A substantial majority of survey participants (80%) believe some
analytical input by a mediator to be appropriate.

Other survey questions focused more specifically on user attitudes about
specific kinds of input by the mediator. The following percentages of our
users surveyed rated the following characteristics important, very important
or essential:

- 95% — making suggestions;
- about 70% — giving opinions;

In addition, we asked survey participants to indicate the proportion of cases
in which a particular activity would be helpful. The following percentages of
users thought the listed activities would be helpful in about *half or more* of
their cases (emphasis added):

- 95% — ask pointed questions that raise issues;
- 95% — give analysis of case, including strengths and weaknesses;
- 60% — make prediction about likely court results;
- 100% — suggest possible ways to resolve issues;
- 84% — recommend a specific settlement; and
- 74% — apply some pressure to accept a specific solution.

On the other hand, nearly half of the users surveyed indicated that there
are times when it is not appropriate for a mediator to give an assessment of
strengths and weaknesses, and nearly half also indicated that it is sometimes
not appropriate to recommend a specific settlement. User reservations on
these issues should give pause to mediators who routinely offer such analysis and opinions . . . .

There is an interesting contrast between user and mediator survey
responses when asked about recommending a specific settlement.

- Eighty-four percent (84%) of users . . . but only 38% of mediators
  . . . thought it would be helpful in half or more cases.
- 75% [of users but only 18% of mediators] thought it would be helpful in
  most [to] all . . . cases.

Similarly, when asked about applying some pressure to accept a specific solution,

- 64% of the users responded favorably for most or all or almost all cases and 75% for half or more cases.
- Among mediators, however, only 24% responded favorably for most or all or almost all cases, while only 30% responded favorably for half or more of their cases.

The opinions of parties who were interviewed differed from . . . lawyers on the issue of whether mediators should state their opinions about settlement terms. While only a minority of lawyers objected to this, six parties out of twelve stated that mediator comments such as "I think this is the best offer you're going to get," are inappropriate. An even higher percentage, eight out of eleven parties, objected to mediators telling them what to do, as in "You should accept this offer," or "If I were you, I'd offer $70,000 and be done with it."

Questions

15. Why do you think a much higher proportion of attorneys than neutrals in the ABA survey favor mediators giving opinions and applying "pressure" to settle?
16. What accounts, do you think, for the differences of opinion between attorneys and clients?

Does a disputant's reaction to evaluation differ depending on what issue the mediator evaluates, or the reasons the neutral gives? Consider the following survey of parties' reactions to evaluation in court-connected mediation programs.

❖ **Roselle P. Wissler,** *To Evaluate or Facilitate? Parties' Perceptions of Mediation Affected by Mediator Style*

7 Disp. Resol. Mag. 35 (Winter 2001)

Some commentators have argued that if a mediator evaluates the merits of a case instead of using a more purely facilitative approach, the parties will feel that the mediator is less neutral. The parties will also have less opportunity to participate in the mediation process and to determine its outcome, will not gain a better understanding of the other side's position and their own interests, and will be less satisfied with mediation. Four recent studies of mediation in civil and domestic relations cases provide the opportunity to empirically test the effect of mediator style on parties' perceptions. . . . No consistent differences were observed in the pattern of findings between the studies of civil cases and the studies of domestic relations cases.

When the mediator evaluated the merits of the case, no negative effects on parties' perceptions of mediation or the mediator were observed in any of the studies. Instead . . . parties were more likely to say that the mediation process was fair and the mediator understood their views. They were also more likely to say that they had enough opportunity to express their views, had input in determining the outcome, were satisfied with the outcome and gained a better understanding of their own interests. Importantly, parties who reported that the mediator evaluated the case did not feel more pressure to settle.

In contrast, when the mediator recommended a particular settlement, parties were *less* likely to say that the mediation process was fair and the mediator was neutral [and] parties were more likely to feel pressured to settle. When the mediator suggested possible options for settlement, parties were more likely to say that the mediation process was fair and that the mediator was neutral and understood their view. By far the strongest and most consistently positive effects on parties' perceptions were observed when the mediator encouraged the parties to express their feelings and summarized what they said. (These actions were examined only in the domestic relations studies.)

In summary, if the mediators evaluated the merits of the case and even made some suggestions about possible settlements, the parties had more favorable perceptions of mediation with virtually no negative repercussions, as long as the mediators did not recommend a specific settlement.

Questions

17. According to the ABA and Professor Wissler, which evaluative interventions are more dangerous and which less so? Assuming that parties do not object to certain forms of evaluation, does this answer Professor Love's concerns?

18. Imagine that you are counsel for MIT in the student death case described in Chapter 9. Can you imagine circumstances in which you would want the mediator to give an evaluation? If so, what would you want evaluated?

19. Now assume that you are counsel for the plaintiffs in the same case. How, if at all, might an evaluation be useful to your side?

20. If you agree with Professor Love, how would you want a mediator to respond to a situation in which you and your opposing counsel disagreed vehemently about the likely outcome at trial and you thought the other lawyer was being unrealistic? What if your own client appeared to be overly optimistic?

> ### Problem 2
>
> Read the following exchanges, taken from the mediation of a commercial breach of warranty case. The plaintiff entered the mediation with a demand of $1.5 million, based on out-of-pocket damages of about $250,000, an additional $200,000 in intangible damages, and a demand for treble damages under a state unfair business practices statute. The defense had made no offer of settlement prior to the litigation. The mediator formed an initial impression that the plaintiff would face significant obstacles in proving liability and find it difficult to establish damages beyond the out-of-pocket sum. As to each exchange, ask yourself:
>
> - Is the mediator here "evaluating" or only "reality testing"?
> - If so, what issues are being evaluated?
> - Is the mediator acting in a manner likely to incur resentment?

i. A Caucus Meeting with the Defense

Mediator: Well, all right, you heard the frustration from the plaintiff side, and you said you were surprised by it. What I'm hearing from [the vice president of the plaintiff company] is that he feels that there has never been a dialogue, acknowledgment of their difficulties and, most importantly to them, I guess, an offer of cash to settle this dispute. I'm hearing from you that you are not willing to make a specific settlement offer at this point. If you can't authorize me to bring back a specific number to the plaintiff . . . what I'd like to have is a feel for the range that you are in that I could communicate to them, so that they would have a sense of where things are going.

Defense counsel: We will respond if they come down to a range of reasonableness, but their demand of $1.5 million is just in the stratosphere. I know that you're experienced, and I'm going to rely on you to digest what our view of the damages are and speak to them and maybe tell them what the real world is like: A million five is just not the real world.

Mediator: Well, what if the plaintiff were willing at this point to accept an amount that would allow them to recoup their out-of-pocket costs, and were perhaps looking for a little bit extra to put away in case their soft damages become a reality: Would you think that was a more reasonable place for them to be?

Defense counsel: Well, that would be a more reasonable place for them to *start*, and then we have to discount that number for the risk that they won't be able to prove liability at all.

ii. Meeting with the Plaintiff

Plaintiff counsel: The bottom line is — what is their bottom line? What's their offer? That's what we have been trying to get at for two years.

Mediator: I think there is a number that they would pay, which maybe will turn out to be a number that you would accept. But they haven't told me what it is yet. I don't think you're going to find out what they'll pay unless you get past this impasse. I see you as being at an impasse so far because they see you as "up in the clouds," and because you see them as completely recalcitrant "stones" who won't offer a thing. In fact, I don't see them as stones refusing to deal — I think they *will* deal. But they want to have some confidence that they are in the right universe with you, and if I can give them that confidence, then we'll get a number out of them. A better indication of what you're really looking for is what I need.

iii.   Second Meeting with the Defense

Mediator: What is it going to cost to try this case?
Defense counsel: Oh, about $25,000.
Mediator: Wow, that's a bargain . . . You really think you can do it for that?
Counsel: Most of the discovery is done, and my rates are reasonable.
Mediator: Well, you're going to need an expert . . . They'll get an expert . . . It'll get expensive.

iv.   Meeting with the Defense Late in the Process

Inside counsel: You don't have to do this now, but if at some point if you could explain to me if you think we are being too optimistic about our chances at trial. I just don't see very much risk here.
Mediator: Well, I think the following . . . So far, the court has been willing to accept the plaintiff's case on their "res ipsa" theory that incidents of this type just don't occur without somebody being negligent. It looks as if the judge will let the case go to the jury on that theory. As a result, I think you run the risk that the jury will seize the appealing simplicity of the plaintiff's argument, and if it does it will find against you.

You have a credible, viable defense, and I think that this significantly reduces the likelihood that the plaintiff will prevail. But the likelihood that the other side will win on liability, given their *res ipsa* argument, is probably at least 50-50, and maybe better than that.

Note: Issues for Advocates

The use of evaluation also presents practical issues for lawyers. As counsel to a disputant you should think about the following questions:

- Do you want your mediator to give an evaluation at all?
- If the mediator does evaluate, at what point in the process and on what issues should she do so? Would you prefer to have the evaluation done in joint session or in caucus?
- Is the other side likely to ask for evaluative feedback? If so, how should you respond?

- Is the mediator likely to offer evaluative comments on her own initiative? What can you do to influence this?
- What do you want the mediator to see before making an evaluation?

We discuss how a lawyer can use evaluation to best advantage in Chapter 12.

CHAPTER
11

Representing Clients: Preparation

The next two chapters focus on the lawyer's role in mediation. We have described how the mediation process can facilitate disputants' ability to communicate and bargain with each other. We now explore how advocates can use the process to best advantage.

Lawyers' expectations upon entering mediation, and the tactics they use when working with mediators, are changing in significant ways. A decade ago lawyers approached mediation like processes with which they were familiar — direct bargaining and settlement conferences conducted by a judge.

In this traditional model, assent to mediation is a signal: By committing to engage in an intensive and expensive process, parties confirm to each other that they are serious about settling. Lawyers who embrace this model often see mediation as a way to bargain competitively with less risk of impasse than direct negotiation. The process tends to be dominated by legal arguments and exchanges of money offers in a caucus format. If, as often occurs, positional tactics lead to impasse, the mediator takes over and evaluates the case and/or suggests a settlement, which often amounts to a take-it-or-leave-it offer to the litigants.

This concept of mediation is still prevalent, but lawyers increasingly approach the process in other ways. They are more likely to use mediators in a variety of roles, supporting both competitive and creative strategies. Good advocates see themselves as bargaining not only with the other side but also with the mediator in what becomes a three-sided process. Attorneys may negotiate with a mediator, for example, over what he will say to their opponent ("I'd prefer if you stressed that . . ."), ask for information ("Has he calmed down yet?"), and bargain over tactics ("We'd like you to hold off on giving an evaluation for now"). Indeed, mediated negotiations sometimes have more than three sides; a lawyer might, for example, enlist a mediator to help persuade her client to compromise. We explore the practical questions raised by attorney tactics in Chapter 12 and ethical issues in Chapter 15.

A. An Overview

1. Identify Your Goals

The first issue when planning for mediation is your client's goal in the process. Are you seeking the best possible money outcome? An imaginative solution? Repair of a relationship? Your objective should influence the approach you take to the process and how you relate to the mediator.

If your goal is to solve a problem or repair a relationship, you can treat the mediator almost as a member of your team, revealing interests and soliciting the neutral's advice about how to achieve them, and if the focus is on relationship repair both lawyer and mediator may gradually withdraw to give the parties an opportunity to reconnect.

If, however, your goal is to get the best possible money outcome, your relationship with a mediator will be more complex. You can continue to take advantage of the neutral's knowledge, for example by asking about hidden obstacles, and as long as you employ principled bargaining techniques you and the neutral can work together cooperatively. At the point, however, that you begin to compete with the other side for the best possible terms, your goals and those of the neutral are no longer the same, because the mediator cannot take sides.

Legal mediators have significant power, whether or not they decide to use it. Although mediators cannot compel parties to settle, they can greatly influence the *process* of bargaining, opening opportunities for advocates to mold the process to meet their clients' needs. Whatever your goals, you can use the mediation process to advantage by approaching it actively and exploiting its special characteristics.

Questions

1. What would you have said before taking this course was the typical goal of a lawyer settling a lawsuit? Has your perspective changed?
2. What do you think the typical client in civil litigation wants to achieve through mediation?

Problem 1

Your client is a business in a dispute with a supplier of software services over the quality of the supplier's performance under a contract. Given the expected costs of litigating the issue, you have recommended that the client consider mediating before a complaint is filed, and the client has reluctantly agreed.

The client sees the goal as simply to collect as much as possible for the interruptions and lost profits caused by the supplier's bad work, and has estimated damages at $1.5 million. The client would also like to recoup as much as possible of the roughly $500,000 it has paid the supplier so far, and secure cancellation of its obligation to pay $200,000 more due under the contract terms.

You see the merits of the case as doubtful. The rupture seems to have been caused more by ambiguities in the scope of work in the contract and the rather rigid approach taken by your client's IT director than by lack of competence in the supplier — although the supplier's performance can certainly be faulted. You also doubt that, as a practical matter, you could collect most of the past payments even if you won. You see ways in which the supplier could continue to provide services to your client, and think that this might be more effective as compensation than a legal judgment.

1. What problems might you encounter in raising your concerns with the client?
2. What could you say to the client about goals in this mediation and how to accomplish them?

2. An Overview of Strategy

We believe that over time more lawyers and parties will come to view mediation as a method to solve problems. At present, however, most attorneys in mediation are litigators who tend to see the process as a way to facilitate competitive bargaining over money. To prepare for what you are likely to encounter in practice, we examine how counsel can approach a legal mediation process that includes a large element of competitive bargaining. To provide you with tools to adapt to the future, we also discuss how to represent a client in a problem-solving process.

a. Commercial Mediation Processes

We begin with a reading that focuses on some errors an adversarial mind-set can produce. Inherent in listing errors are messages about what lawyers can do to be effective. As you read, think about these questions.

Questions

3. Have you made any of the mistakes Arnold describes in an exercise in this course?

4.   Which errors do you think you are most likely to make in an actual
     case?

❖ Tom Arnold, TWENTY COMMON ERRORS IN MEDIATION ADVOCACY

13 Alternatives 69 (1995)

Trial lawyers who are unaccustomed to being mediation advocates often
miss important opportunities. Here are twenty common errors, and ways to
correct them.

Problem: Wrong Client in the Room

CEOs settle more cases than vice presidents, house counsel, or other
agents. Why? For one thing, they don't need to worry about criticism back at
the office. Any lesser agent, even with explicit "authority," typically must
please a constituency which was not a participant in the give and take of the
mediation. That makes it hard to settle cases.

A client's personality also can be a factor. A "Rambo" who is highly self-
confident, aggressive, critical, unforgiving, or self-righteous doesn't tend to
be conciliatory. The best peace-makers show patience, creativity and sometimes tolerance for the mistakes of others. Of course, it also helps to know
the subject.

Problem: Wrong Lawyer in the Room

Many capable trial lawyers are so confident that they can persuade a jury
of anything (after all, they've done it before) that they discount the importance of preserving relationships, as well as the common exorbitant costs
and emotional drain of litigation. They can smell a "win" in the court room,
and so approach mediation with a measure of ambivalence.

Transactional lawyers, in contrast, having less confidence in their trial
outcome, sometimes are better mediation counsel. At a minimum, parties
should look for sensitive, flexible, understanding people who will do their
homework, no matter what their job experience. Good preparation makes
for more and better settlements. A lawyer who won't prepare is the wrong
lawyer. Good mediation lawyers also should be good risk evaluators and not
averse to making reasonable risk assumptions.

Problem: Wrong Mediator in the Room

Some mediators are generous about lending their conference rooms, but
bring nothing to the table. Some of them determine their view of the case
and like an arbitrator urge the parties to accept that view without exploring
likely win-win alternatives. The best mediators can work within a range of
styles. . . . Ideally, mediators should fit the mediation style to the case and the
parties before them, often moving from style to style as a mediation

progresses, relatively more facilitative at the beginning and more instructive or directive as the end comes into view. Masters of the questioning process can render valuable services whether or not they have relevant substantive expertise.

When do the parties need an expert? When do they want an evaluative mediator, or someone of relevant technical experience who can cast meaningful lights and shadows on the merits of the case and alternative settlements? It may not always be possible to know and...fit the choice of mediator to your case. But the wrong mediator may fail to get a settlement another mediator might have finessed.

Problem: Wrong Case

Almost every type of case, from antitrust or patent infringement to unfair competition and employment disputes, is a likely candidate for mediation. Occasionally, cases don't fit the mold, not because of the substance of the dispute, but because one or both parties want to set a precedent. For example, a franchisor that needs a legal precedent construing a key clause that is found in 3,000 franchise agreements might not want to submit the case to mediation. Likewise, an infringement suit early in the life of an uncertain patent might be better resolved in court; getting the Federal Circuit stamp of validity could generate industry respect not obtainable from ADR.

Problem: Omitting Client Preparation

Lawyers should educate their clients about the process and the likely questions the mediator will ask. At the same time, they need to understand that the other party (rather than the mediator) should be the focus of each side's presentation.

Problem: Not Letting a Client Open for Herself

At least as often as not, letting the properly coached client do most or even all of the opening, and tell the story in her own words, works much better than lengthy openings by the lawyer.

Problem: Addressing the Mediator Instead of the Other Side

Most lawyers open the mediation with a statement directed at the mediator, comparable to opening statements to a judge or jury. Highly adversarial in tone, it overlooks the interests of the other side that gave rise to the dispute. Why is this strategy a mistake? The "judge" or "jury" you should be trying to persuade in mediation is not so much the mediator as the adversary. If you want to make the other party sympathetic to your cause, most often at least it is best not to hurt him. For the same reason, plenary sessions should demonstrate your client's humanity, respect, warmth, apologies, and sympathy. Stay away from inflammatory issues, which are better addressed by the mediator in private caucuses with the other side.

Problem: Making the Lawyer the Center of the Process

Unless the client is highly unappealing or inarticulate, the client should be the center of the process. The company representative for the other side may not have attended depositions, so is unaware of the impact your client could have on a judge or jury if the mediation fails. People pay more attention to appealing plaintiffs, so show them off.

Prepare the client to speak and be spoken to by the mediator and the adversary. He should be able to explain why he feels the way he does, why he is or is not responsible, and why any damages he *caused* are great or only peanuts. But he should also consider extending empathy to the other party.

Problem: Failure to Use Advocacy Tools Effectively

You'll want to prepare your materials for maximum persuasive impact. Exhibits, charts, and copies of relevant cases or contracts with key phrases highlighted can be valuable visual aids. A ninety-second video showing one or more key witnesses in depositions making important admissions, followed by a readable-sized copy of an important document with some relevant language underlined, can pack a punch.

Problem: Timing Mistakes

Get and give critical discovery, but don't spend exorbitant time or sums in discovery and trial prep before seeking mediation. Mediation can identify what's truly necessary discovery and avoid unnecessary discovery.

One of my own war stories: With a mediation under way and both parties relying on their perception of the views of a certain neutral vice president who had no interest in the case, I leaned over, picked up the phone, called the vice president, introduced myself as the mediator, and asked whether he could give us a deposition the following morning. "No," said he, "I've got a board meeting at 10:00." "How about 7:30 a.m., with a one-hour limit?" I asked. "It really is pretty important that this decision not be delayed." The parties took the deposition and settled the case before the 10:00 board meeting.

Problem: Failure to Listen to the Other Side

Many lawyers and clients seem incapable of giving open-minded attention to what the other side is saying. That could cost a settlement.

Problem: Failure to Identify Perceptions and Motivations

Seek first to understand, only then to be understood. [B]rainstorm to determine the other party's motivations and perceptions. Prepare a chart summarizing how your adversary sees the issues: Part of preparing for mediation is to understand your adversary's perceptions and motivations, perhaps even listing them in chart form. Here is an example, taken from a recent technology dispute:

Plaintiff's Perceptions:

Defendant entered the business because of my sound analysis of the market, my good judgment and convictions about the technology.

Defendant used me by pretending to be interested in doing business with me.

Defendant made a low-ball offer for my valuable technology. Another company paid me my asking price.

Defendant's Perceptions:

I entered the business based on my own independent analysis of the market and the appropriate technology that was different from plaintiff's. . . .

Plaintiff misled me with exaggerated claims that turned out to be false.

I made plaintiff a fair offer; I later paid less for alternative technology that was better.

Problem: Hurting, Humiliating, Threatening, or Commanding

Don't poison the well from which you must drink to get a settlement. That means you don't hurt, humiliate, or ridicule the other folks. Avoid pejoratives like "malingerer," "fraud," "cheat," "crook," or "liar." You can be strong on what your evidence will be and still be a decent human being. All settlements are based upon trust to some degree. If you anger the other side, they won't trust you. This inhibits settlement.

The same can be said for threats, like a threat to get the other lawyer's license revoked for pursuing such a frivolous cause, or for his grossly inaccurate pleadings. Ultimatums destroy the process and destroy credibility. Yes, there is a time in mediation to walk out — whether or not you plan to return. But a series of ultimatums, or even one ultimatum, most often is counterproductive.

Problem: The Backwards Step

A party who offered to pay $300,000 before the mediation, but comes to the mediation table willing to offer only $200,000, injures its own credibility and engenders bad feelings from the other side. Without some clear and dramatic reasons for the reduction in the offer, it can be hard to overcome the damage done.

The backwards step is a powerful card to play at the right time — a walk away without yet walking out. But powerful devices are also dangerous. There are few productive occasions to use this one, and they tend to come late in a mediation. A rule of thumb: Unless you're an expert negotiator, don't do it.

Problem: Too Many People

Advisors — people to whom the decision-maker must display respect and courtesy, people who feel that since they are there they must put in their two bits worth — all delay mediation immeasurably. A caucus that with only one lawyer and vice president would take twenty minutes, with five people could take an hour and twenty minutes. What could have been a one-day mediation stretches to two or three.

This is one context in which I use the "one martini lunch." Once I think that everyone present understands all the issues, I will send principals who have been respectful out to negotiate alone. Most come back within three hours with an oral expression of settlement. Of course, the next step is to brush up on details they overlooked, draw up a written agreement and get it signed. But usually those finishing touches don't ruin the deal.

Problem: Closing Too Fast

A party who opens at $1 million and moves immediately to $500,000 gives the impression of having more to give. Rightly or wrongly, the other side probably will not accept the $500,000 offer because they expect more give. By contrast, moving from $1 million to $750,000, $600,000, $575,000, $560,000, $550,000, sends no message of yield below $500,000, and may induce a $500,000 proposal that can be accepted. The "dance" is part of communication. Skip the dance, lose the communication, and risk losing settlement at your own figure.

Problem: Failure to Truly Close

Unless parties have strong reasons to "sleep on" their agreement, to further evaluate the deal, or to check on possibly forgotten details, it is better to get some sort of enforceable contract written and signed before the parties separate. Too often, when left to think overnight and draft tomorrow, the parties think of new ideas that delay or prevent closing.

Problem: Breaching Confidentiality

Sometimes parties to mediation unthinkingly, or irresponsibly, disclose in open court information revealed confidentially in a mediation. When information is highly sensitive, consider keeping it confidential with the mediator. Or if revealed to the adversary in a mediation where the case did not settle, consider moving before the trial begins for an order in limine to bind both sides to the confidentiality agreement.

Problem: Lack of Patience and Perseverance

The mediation "dance" takes time. Good mediation advocates have patience and perseverance.

Problem: Misunderstanding Conflict

A dispute is a problem to be solved together, not a combat to be won.

b.   Problem-Solving Approaches

❖ **Harold Abramson,** *MEDIATION REPRESENTATION: ADVOCATING IN A
PROBLEM-SOLVING PROCESS*

1 NITA (2004)

The mediation process is indisputably different from other dispute resolution processes. Therefore, the strategies and techniques that have proven so effective in settlement conferences, arbitrations, and judicial trials do not work optimally in mediation. You need a different representation approach. . . . Instead of advocating as a zealous adversary, you should advocate as a zealous problem-solver. . . .

. . . Many sophisticated and experienced litigators realize that mediation calls for a different approach, but they still muddle through mediation sessions. They are learning on the job. . . .

As a problem-solver . . . you do more than just try to settle the dispute. You creatively search for solutions that go beyond the traditional ones based on rights, obligations, and precedent. . . . To [do this], you develop a collaborative relationship with the other side and the mediator, and participate throughout the mediation process in a way that is likely to result in solutions that are enduring as well as inventive. . . .

You should be a constant problem-solver. It is relatively easy to engage in simple problem-solving moves such as responding to a demand with the question "why?" in order to bring to the surface the other party's interests. But it is much more difficult to stick to this approach throughout the mediation process, especially when faced with an adversarial, positional opponent. Trust the problem-solving approach. And, when the other side engages in adversarial tactics — a frequent occurrence in practice — you should react with problem-solving responses, responses that might even convert the other side into a problem-solver.

Also strive to create a problem-solving process when your mediator does not. Your mediator may fail to follow this approach (even though he professes to foster one) because he lacks the depth of experience or training to tenaciously maintain a consistent approach throughout the mediation process. Or, your mediator may candidly disclose his practice of deliberately switching tactics based on the needs of the parties — a philosophy that . . . undermines the problem-solving approach.

Finally, for the skeptics who think that problem-solving does not work for most legal cases because they are primarily about money, I offer three responses. First, the endless debate about whether or not legal disputes are primarily about money is distracting. Whether a dispute is largely about money varies from case to case. You have little chance of discovering whether your client's dispute is about more than money if you approach the dispute as if it is only about money . . . .

Second, if the dispute or any remaining issues at the end of the day turn out to be predominately about money, then at least you will have followed a representation approach that may have created a hospitable environment for dealing with the money issues. A hospitable environment can even be beneficial when there is no expectation of a continuing relationship between the disputing parties. Third, the problem-solving approach provides a framework for resolving money issues. . . .

In short, the problem-solving approach provides a comprehensive and coherent approach to representation that can guide you throughout the mediation process. By sticking to this approach, you will be prepared to deal with the myriad of unanticipated challenges that inevitably arise as mediation unfolds.

B.   Entering the Process

1.   *Should You Mediate?*

The first issue is whether to mediate at all. In general, you should recommend mediation if two conditions are met:

- There appear to be potential settlement terms more favorable for each side than it could achieve by other means — a precondition for almost any negotiation. In the context of a legal dispute this usually means a settlement better than the likely outcome in adjudication, taking into account all the risks and costs of continuing the conflict.
- Obstacles make it difficult or impossible for the parties to negotiate a settlement directly, but those barriers might be overcome with the help of a mediator.

It is worth remembering that people can elect to mediate for reasons other than settlement, for instance to set up an efficient discovery plan or improve a relationship. The fact that complete agreement does not appear realistic, in other words, is not always a reason to reject mediation.

There are also reasons why you might validly recommend that a client not enter mediation, at least at the present time. These factors — for example, the need to establish a benchmark or precedent — are described in Chapter 9.

2.   *If So, When?*

Assuming that mediation is appropriate, when is the right time to undertake it? Sometimes there is no choice: You may be required to mediate by a contract clause or court order. If you can choose, however, the question is an important one, and to answer it you and your client must again consider goals.

If your primary objective is to solve a problem or restore a relationship, it is usually best to mediate quickly. If not, the parties' positions are likely to harden and one of them may replace the relationship with a new one, making a repair much more difficult.

If relationships are not a priority, then the issue of timing is more complex. By delaying mediation, lawyers might be able to improve a client's bargaining position, for instance by winning a round in court. In attempting to do so, however, the client will incur costs and its opponent may react in kind. The American legal system does not ordinarily allow litigants to recover their legal expenses and almost never reimburses the nonlegal costs of conflict. As a result parties must bear the expenses they incur by attempting to improve their bargaining position, and as each side's investment in the conflict increases, loss aversion becomes a larger obstacle to agreement.

Disputants tend to enter legal mediation at particular points along the litigation continuum, most often when they face either a sharp increase in cost or the risk of a significant loss. Natural points to discuss settlement are before a formal legal action is filed, after preliminary discovery, in the shadow of a significant court ruling, and shortly before trial.

Before a Formal Legal Action Is Filed

Parties in a relationship, such as a supplier and customer, may opt to mediate as soon as possible. Likewise, a discharged employee may decide to mediate before filing a formal claim to avoid inflaming feelings on both sides. Whenever disputants decide to enter mediation before suing, they accept a trade-off: Each side has less information, but also avoids the cost of litigating to obtain it. In an effort to control expenses, disputants appear to be entering pre-suit mediation more often.

After Preliminary Discovery

Parties may file suit and undertake limited discovery, for instance document requests, but mediate before undertaking costly, adversarial processes such as depositions. One commentator has noted that:

> One approach . . . is to follow the 80-20 rule: 80 percent of the relevant information that parties learn from discovery often comes from the first 20 percent of the money they spend. Tracking down the last, difficult-to-obtain data is the most expensive part. . . . If parties conduct initial core discovery, they may find all they need to know in order to resolve the case appropriately. Following this approach, parties can agree to take abbreviated depositions of the key witnesses and then proceed to ADR. . . . Often this will give them everything they need to determine their negotiation position with reasonable accuracy. (Senger, 2004)

In the Shadow of a Significant Ruling

Parties sometimes elect to mediate when they are at or near a significant point in the litigation process such as a motion for summary judgment. One might think that if one side were willing to mediate because it feared a loss, its opponent would refuse to do so in hope of a win. As we have seen, however, humans are much more sensitive to losing than to winning, and as a result both parties in a case may agree to mediate at the point at which they risk sustaining a serious loss in adjudication.

Shortly Before Trial

This has been the traditional point at which to pursue settlement for several reasons. First, as trial approaches, attorneys must prepare intensively, imposing costs on them and/or their clients. Second, trial represents the ultimate win–lose event, triggering strong feelings of loss aversion. Finally, there are cultural assumptions about the "right" time to broach settlement: In the legal community this used to mean that mentioning mediation early in a case was considered a sign of weakness, whereas raising the issue on the eve of trial was acceptable, an assumption that no longer appears true.

3. Initiating the Process

In the past lawyers were often reluctant to propose mediation out of concern that an adversary would see it as a sign of weakness. That attitude has largely disappeared — as one litigator remarked in Chapter 9, many lawyers now seem to find it easier to propose mediation than direct negotiation. Lawyers have several options for initiating mediation.

Point Out That Settlement Discussions Are Inevitable

Given the increasing rarity of trials, it is nearly inevitable that parties will settle at some point. You like to litigate — it's what you do for a living. But given that few cases are tried, the parties will be talking settlement sooner or later; why not do it now and save everyone the cost of litigation?

Cite a Rule

Some court systems require counsel to participate in ADR or make a good-faith effort at settlement in every case. Counsel can cite such rules, suggesting the parties design their own process rather than be pushed into a court "one-size-fits-all" program. Even if no judicial mandate exists, it may be possible to approach an ADR administrator or clerk and ask the court to suggest mediation.

Rely on a Policy

If you represent an organization with a uniform policy of exploring ADR early in every dispute, cite it as the reason for suggesting mediation. The most prominent example of such a policy is the "CPR Pledge" discussed in Chapters 9 and 21.

Invite a Third Party to Take the Initiative

Another option is to ask a private neutral or a provider organization to approach an adversary to advocate that the parties mediate. Although the opponent will probably know that you initiated the contact, this lets you avoid having to "sell" the process personally.

So far we have assumed that the challenge is to persuade one's opponent to mediate. In some situations, however, the obstacle is one's own client. In the words of a litigator:

> There are no hard and fast rules as to when that perfect moment has arrived to mediate, [but] one point is clear. Before you begin, recognize that the first obstacle to starting the dialogue early may well be your own client, particularly if you have not represented him in the past. He may wonder if you lack confidence in yourself or the case if you push for settlement too early. On the other hand, if you don't mention settlement to the more sophisticated client, he may well wonder whether you are looking to "milk" a case that will likely never be tried. As such, begin with the adversary only after you have reached a consensus with your own client. (Stern, 1998)

C. Structuring the Mediation

1. *Select the Right Mediator*

The most important issue in arranging for mediation, apart from agreeing on who will attend, is to choose the right neutral. In most areas, mediation is very much a buyers' market, with many qualified mediators seeking assignments. This poses a problem for neutrals, but an opportunity for advocates looking for the right mediator.

What should you look for? One guide is the survey quoted at the start of Chapter 10 of what experienced lawyers value in commercial mediators. Another approach is to think about what specific obstacles are making it difficult to negotiate in your case and look for a mediator with the qualities needed to overcome them. If, for example, the key problem is that your opponent (or your client) has an abrasive manner, a mediator with strong process skills may be the best choice. If a party needs "cover" to justify a difficult compromise, a neutral with strong evaluative credentials may be helpful. If the problem is anger, a neutral who can handle emotion may be what is called for. In many situations more than one barrier exists, calling for someone with a blend of abilities.

Mediators vary greatly in characteristics. You will usually be able to choose among candidates with experience as litigators, judges, and transactional lawyers, as well as professionals in fields ranging from psychotherapy to engineering. The goal is to find a person with qualities that match the needs of the case.

You can obtain information about neutrals from:

- Biographical material and writings by the mediator.
- Recommendations and comments from colleagues.
- A conversation with the prospective neutral. Counsel, for example, sometimes talk with prospective mediators, either jointly or individually.

Example: In the student death case described in Chapter 9, the defense attorney decided to allow the Kruegers' lawyer to select the mediator. In part this was because they insisted on the right to do so and in part because the defense respected plaintiff counsel's ability to choose wisely.

The Kruegers selected a mediator who regularly handled personal injury claims for plaintiffs, but they had other concerns as well. It was important that the mediator be willing to work to customize the process, and that he or she be respected by defense counsel so the University would listen to his or her recommendations. Plaintiff counsel also knew that the discussions would be extremely emotional, and it was therefore crucial that the mediator have the ability to absorb and manage intense anger and grief.

The mediator's final qualification was unique: In a conversation with the mediator, the plaintiff lawyer discovered that he had once lost a college-age son himself.

Questions

5. Texas mediator Eric Galton has suggested that transactional lawyers are better advocates in mediation because "they negotiate better, more creatively and are more acutely aware of business solutions which may be advantageous to their clients."
    a. Assuming this is true, in what types of legal disputes would a transactional lawyer be best suited to represent clients in mediation or serve as a mediator?
    b. What might you sacrifice by selecting a transactional lawyer rather than a litigator as your representative in mediation?
6. Assume that the other side proposes a mediator and you learn that the opponent has mediated with this neutral more than a dozen times. What should you do in response? Should it matter if it is the opposing party or lawyer who has had experience with the neutral?
7. If you wish to propose a mediator with whom you have worked repeatedly, how might be a good way to do so?
8. Assume you represent a party in a role-play assigned by your teacher. You are in the process of selecting a neutral. What qualities would you look for in a mediator for the case? Obtain biographies of actual mediators in your community, decide whom you would prefer or object to, and prioritize the candidates in terms of attractiveness.

9. Can you think of a case in which the gender or race of the mediator might make a difference? If so, how would you handle neutral selection in such cases? If not, how would you respond if the other lawyer seemed to be taking race or gender into account?

2. *Ensure the Presence of Necessary Participants*

We know that mediation is an intensely personal process, and as a result the presence of the right people is perhaps the single most important factor in its success. Consider the following example from San Francisco mediator Jerry Spolter:

> This may come as a surprise, but there is nothing wrong with communicating ex parte with a mediator or prospective mediator. In fact, it's usually the smart and right thing to do to secure the best result for your client. So don't be bashful. Talk to your mediator.
>
> A recent mediation session I conducted highlights what can happen when you leave your mediator in the dark. Everything went great for about five hours. . . . The joint session was textbook material, with lots of helpful information exchanged; the private caucuses peeled away postured "positions" to reveal the parties' real interests. And then it happened: Although the physician accused of malpractice was in the room, the doc wouldn't make a move until his personal attorney gave the OK.
>
> Unfortunately, the personal attorney was on a chairlift in the Sierra with a dead battery in her cell phone. And since this was a malpractice case requiring the doc's consent, "my" mediation was suddenly in trouble. To make matters worse, the doc's insurance representative had to consult two "invisible-hierarchy" decision-makers to discuss increasing authority.
>
> If only I had received a heads-up beforehand, we could have resolved the authority problems in advance and taken advantage of the momentum we had generated that day to settle the case. (Instead, the parties are now scurrying around trying to acquire the necessary authority to put Humpty-Dumpty back together again.)

Parties

There is a good deal that lawyers can do beforehand to ensure that the right people are at a mediation. Who these people are in each case depends again on your objectives.

- If the primary goal is to repair a personal relationship, then the presence of the principals themselves, to talk out problems and regain the ability to relate with each other, is usually essential.
- If parties have little or no relationship, as, for example, in a dispute between a corporate landlord and a former commercial tenant, the presence of principals may be less important, provided those at the table have full authority to settle.

- If the objective is to work out an imaginative solution, then you need participants able to think outside the box and with enough information to identify and flesh out useful options. Working out a novel solution to a business dispute, for instance, often requires executives rather than lawyers.
- If the only goal is to settle a legal claim on the best possible money terms, as is true of many routine negligence cases, the priority may be to get bargainers with the authority to do so.

If the parties are individuals, they should be personally present. Corporations and other organizations, however, must act through agents. Some representatives, such as an executive with a personal stake in defending the decision at issue, are positively harmful to the process. Others might lack the right kind of expertise; an outside litigator, for instance, might be a good representative in bargaining over the trial value of a claim, but wrong for a process focused on resolving an emotional employee grievance.

Negotiators routinely claim to have "full authority," but in practice their ability to agree is usually limited. Disputants also routinely conceal their authority even from mediators, for fear that admitting to authority will be interpreted as a willingness to make concessions. To deal with this, ask opposing counsel who will attend for the other side, and check with your own client about their authority; a person's title and role may offer an indication of his ability to make a hard decision. But as the following story illustrates, it is sometimes difficult even to determine who can make a decision for your own client.

❖ **Bennett G. Picker,** *Navigating Relationships: The Invisible Barriers to Resolution*

2 Amer. J. of Mediation 41 (2008)

Most mediation advocates and party representatives, when preparing for mediation, primarily focus on one relationship that significantly impacts resolution — the relationship between plaintiff and defendant.

A trial lawyer will often pause in the middle of a negotiation or mediation and wonder, "Why hasn't the other side made a realistic offer? Don't they understand their risk?" The question ignores the fact that "they" — those on the other side — frequently do not function as a cohesive unit with the capacity to either make a collective decision or speak with one voice.

For example in a recent mediation involving an alleged breach of a long-term supply agreement, the corporate plaintiff's representatives each entered the process with considerably different perspectives on the "ideal outcome" for the company. As the mediator, I spent well over an hour in a private caucus session with the company's CEO, CFO, general counsel and general manager. After exploring the positions and interests of the parties, we began discussing the plaintiff's response to a proposal by the defendant.

Initially, the plaintiff's several representatives stood in total disagreement with each other.

The CEO argued that the defendant should pay a large sum of money, readily admitting that the result would directly affect the size of the bonus he would receive at the end of the year. The CFO expressed concern about the timing of any payment, conscious of maximizing reported earnings in the current year. The general counsel of the company warned that everyone in the room represented the "client" — the company — and had a duty as fiduciaries to maximize shareholder value [and] Wall Street values long-term streams of revenue more highly than a one-time payment of cash. . . . The general manager who originally determined that the defendant breached the contract simply wanted a court to affirm the breach had occurred and that she had made the correct decision.

During the caucus I conducted what was, in essence, an internal mediation with the plaintiff's representatives to get all of them on the same page. . . . Even though the CEO had the ultimate decision-making power in this dispute, internal differences of opinion presented a serious potential barrier to resolution — a barrier invisible to the defendant. . . .

To maximize the opportunity for success, advocates . . . should pay extra attention to the relationships among and between the representatives of the client. [C]ounsel to the parties [should] ask who in [their] company really "owns" the dispute. They can then assemble a team to define goals, discuss "authority," and try to align the varying interests and perspectives of the key players. . . .

Sometimes the key decision makers are not parties at all. A husband, for instance, might look to his wife for advice, or a company may be unable to make a deal without permission from its insurer. There is no easy way to resolve this issue. Wise lawyers know, however, that a mediator can help them obtain the participation of key persons.

In asking a neutral for assistance, lawyers benefit from several forces. First, having agreed to mediate, disputants usually feel an interest in establishing a good relationship with the mediator. Mediators, too, acquire a stake in the process and have a bias toward inclusion. Better, a mediator will think, to ask for the presence of a person who later proves unnecessary than to lack a key decision maker at crunch time. You can take advantage of an opponent's wish to humor a mediator and the neutral's own investment in the process by enlisting the neutral's help to bring in key participants.

Example: A high-tech company was suing a former employee who had left and then recruited her software team to join her at a competitor. For technical reasons the new employer was not a party to the litigation, although it had agreed to indemnify the defendant for any liability arising from her activities.

The plaintiff company and the defendant employee agreed to mediate, but the general counsel of the competitor refused to attend, arguing that her company was not a party in the case and she could not justify traveling across the country simply to watch.

In response the plaintiff lawyer first agreed to mediate, and then lobbied the mediator to secure the presence of the missing lawyer. He began by stressing to the mediator how important the general counsel would be to the success of "our" process. After several conversations the mediator persuaded the general counsel to join all sessions of the mediation by conference call, and her presence proved crucial to reaching agreement.

Questions

10.   Neutrals come to mediation from very different careers. What background might make a mediator more or less willing to take active steps to bring the right people into the process?
11.   How could you test for this quality when selecting a neutral?

3.   Draft an Agreement to Mediate

Attorneys can use a mediation agreement to deal with the following issues:

- What rules of confidentiality will apply, and who will be bound by them?
- Who will pay the cost of the process, and in what proportions?
- Under what conditions can the mediator evaluate legal issues?
- How can a party terminate its participation in the mediation?
- Can the mediator be called to testify in subsequent litigation?
- Will ongoing litigation be stayed or claims tolled while mediation occurs?

However, a lawyer's ability to mold an agreement is often limited, because most ADR provider organizations use standard mediation engagement forms. Examples of mediation agreements appear in the Appendix.

4.   Influence the Format

We have seen that mediation can occur in a wide variety of formats. If you see a reason to change the "default" process, alert the mediator to this in advance. Again, the choice depends on objectives.

- If the goal is to repair a relationship, you will probably want the clients to have as much opportunity to talk directly as possible. This suggests a longer opening session, private meetings between the principals, or both.

- In a highly emotional case it might be useful for a party to meet with the mediator ahead of time and for the neutral to carefully structure the party's interactions with the other side.
- In factually complex cases it may be necessary to arrange advance meetings and lengthy opening statements, perhaps supported by experts.
- Where the condition of property is at issue, as in construction and environmental disputes, it might make sense to take a site view.

> *Example:* In the MIT–Krueger mediation the lawyers modified the format in several ways:
>
> - They divided the process into two days, the first day involving only lawyers and focused on legal arguments, and the second bringing together all the stakeholders and issues.
> - To satisfy the Kruegers' need to feel the University was coming to them, the second meeting was held near the parents' home.
> - To discourage a walkout and set an informal tone, the second session was held at a rural conference center.
> - To create an opportunity for the parents to express their anger and grief, the mediator began the second day by having breakfast with the Kruegers and their lawyer.
> - The "formal" mediation began with a joint session in which the parties could speak directly to each other and express emotions. The process then evolved into caucusing.
> - At the end, the Kruegers and President Vest came together and hugged.
>
> Very few cases are as emotional as the Krueger case, but the modifications give a sense of how much freedom imaginative lawyers have to vary the format of mediation to achieve their objectives.

5. *Deal with the Special Issues of Court-Mandated Mediation*

The discussion to this point has assumed that you have freedom to design the mediation process in cooperation with the other side. Sometimes, however, your client may be required to engage in mediation by a contract clause or a court. In states such as Florida, Texas, and California, for example, most civil cases must go through mediation as a precondition to trial.

Courts may order parties to mediate but leave process choices to them, with court rules available only as a default. Many jurisdictions, however, impose significant restrictions on the process. Litigants might be able to opt out of such restrictions by agreement, but in the context of litigation this can be difficult to do.

If you have a case that is subject to mandatory mediation, whether by contract or court rule, ask yourself whether the mandated process is adequate and, if not, how to respond. In assessing adequacy, think about these issues:

- Will you have a role in choosing the neutral? Some programs require parties to select a mediator from panels. Others assign a mediator to each case, or give parties the option to select a private mediator themselves.
- Who will be required to be present? Many courts require parties to send representatives with "full settlement authority," creating serious problems for organizations with cases pending in several different jurisdictions.
- Will you be able to brief the mediator in advance?
- Will you be required to pay for the process? Some programs are free, whereas others use private neutrals.
- Will you be required to mediate within a limited time frame? Court-related mediation can range from an hour or less to a full day, with the option to extend by agreement. If the process is time-limited, even good mediators will feel pressure to "cut to the chase" to produce progress quickly, limiting consideration of broad issues.
- What confidentiality guarantees does the program offer?
- Can you modify the process by agreement? If so, will the other side agree to the changes you want?

If you do not want to mediate at all, or decide that the mandated process is inadequate, you should consider these questions:

- Is it possible to opt out or apply for an exemption?
- If not, what is the minimum you have to do to comply? (See the discussion of "good faith participation" requirements in Chapter 14.)
- Are there penalties for nonparticipation or noncompliance? Can the mediator report to the court concerning the parties' cooperation? Can the court ask the mediator to recommend how it should rule on unresolved issues, as occurs in some California family courts?

To gather information, talk with a local lawyer or program administrator and review the program rules.

We discuss the legal and policy issues presented by court-related mediation in Chapters 14 and 15.

D.   Preparing to Mediate

To plan for mediation, think not only about what you will do as an advocate, but also about the roles you want your client and other team members to take. This includes at least three issues: developing a negotiation plan, considering whether to exchange information, and coaching your client.

1. Develop a Negotiating Plan

Texts often speak of the art of "mediation advocacy" but you now know that while lawyers may make semiformal opening statements, most of the process consists of a mixture of discussion and bargaining. You should plan for mediation in much the same way as for direct negotiation, and points made in the context of negotiation about preparation apply here as well. You will want, for example, to consider the parties' alternatives to agreement, principles that each side can cite, underlying interests, and potential options for settlement.

You should also, however, plan to take advantage of the special aspects of mediation — the presence of the neutral and the format of the process. The next chapter describes several ways in which lawyers can "borrow a mediator's powers." Here is advice from competitive and cooperative perspectives.

a. A Competitive Viewpoint

❖ **Robert M. Smith,** *Advocacy in Mediation: A Dozen Suggestions*

26 San Francisco Att'y 14 (June/July 2000)

Your strongest ally, if you can make him or her an ally, is the mediator. It is the mediator's neutral voice that is most powerful in carrying your argument to the other side. This is true even if the mediator asks a lawyer to put on the chalkboard the strongest points of the case, then unveils the board to the other side.

The mediator knows you — indeed, everyone — is trying to manipulate, or con, him or her. Manipulation is as much a given as the coffee machine. But often — perhaps usually — the mediator is aware of the con. Good advocates know when to stop the con, show some trust, and make a straighter, and more reasonable, argument. Honesty can buy an advantage.

Play the Odds

When you go to a commercial mediation, there is, statistically, close to an eighty-five percent chance of settling the case. This means you should probably prepare as if the mediation session will be the last step in the case, and prepare your client accordingly. To tell the client, for example, that we are all just going through the motions and then find yourself in serious end-game bargaining is not prudent.

Black-Tie Affair

Often — we all know this — lawsuits bobble along like a play in search of a theater; they need a defining event before both parties and lawyers get serious.

Mediation is an event — probably the event. If the mediator is effective, everyone will focus on the matter in a way that they haven't before.

The Art of Scribbling

This is the time to do your best brief. Mediators read them — they get paid to. And this may be all they know about the case before you troop in. The mediator is likely to ensure that the parties, as well as the lawyers, see the brief and consider your most forceful arguments, or what a neutral sees as your most forceful arguments. It may be worth considering their impact on the plaintiff or the defendant when sections are pointed out to them.

Sharing Can Be Beautiful

You might consider whether you want to give a copy of the brief to the other side, as well as to the mediator. But you can give only a portion of the brief to the other side — or the whole brief, with only a secret annex going to the mediator (for instance, "I think the claims rep was himself a party to a similar squabble two years ago"). The process is what you make of it. Flexible, it bends to your imaginative sculpting.

We Don't Accept Cash Here

Some have pointed out the power of an apology, appropriately timed and tendered. But advocacy may also involve asking for a non-economic concession — even one you know you likely won't get; it may put other demands in a new, or reframed, perspective.

About Reframing

Once discussions have foundered, the mediator knows that the parties are not likely to move on their own. It is up to the mediator to step back and find a new perspective or approach. You should anticipate the possible reframing, or you may not like the suddenly unfamiliar perspective. Be reframed, not hung.

A las Cinco de la Tarde

"At five in the afternoon" is a repetitive line in a poem by Federica Garcia Lorca. It has to do with a death, not mediation. But I sometimes think of it when discussions bog down after hours of negotiation because it is about five in the afternoon that the role of poetic imagination is sometimes called into play in mediations. You hope the mediator did not lose his or her imagination in the second year of law school; part of what you are paying for is creativity. But when the clock strikes — or beeps — in a soundless room, your own imaginative suggestion may prove sublime advocacy.

b.   A Problem-Solving Approach

The following reading is addressed to problem-solving advocates, but applies to other styles as well.

❖ **Harold Abramson,** *Mediation Representation:*
Advocating in a Problem-Solving Process

NITA 221 (2004)

[*Note:* Professor Abramson recommends that advocates begin their preparation by analyzing the overall nature of the dispute, doing necessary research, and resolving issues of structure such as who will attend. Having done this, lawyers should consider the following issues.]

   . . . Identify three components of the mediation representation formula: interests, impediments, and ways the mediator might contribute to resolving the dispute.

1. Goal:
    * Identify Interests to Meet: Your Client's
    * Identify Interests to Accommodate: The Other Side's
2. Goal: Identify Impediments to Overcome . . .
3. Identify Mediator's Possible Contributions to Resolving the Dispute.

Approaches to Dispute

You want the mediator to use the following approaches [select among the options for each item]:

* Manage the process by primarily facilitating, primarily evaluating, or following a transformative approach.
* View the problem broadly or narrowly.
* Involve the clients actively or restrictively.
* Use caucuses extensively, selectively, or not at all.

Useful Techniques

You want the mediator to use his or her techniques to [select one or more]:

* Facilitate the negotiation of a problem-solving process.
* Promote communication through questioning and listening techniques.
* Deal with the emotional dimensions of the dispute.
* Clarify statements and issues through framing and reframing.
* Generate options for settlement (e.g., brainstorming).
* Separate process of inventing settlement options from selecting them.
* Deal with power inequalities.

- Overcome the impediments to settlement.
- Overcome the chronic impediment of clashing views of the court outcome.
- Close any final gaps (consider your preferred methods for closing gaps).
- Deal with _____.

Questions

12. Assume that you are a competitive advocate in an exercise assigned by your teacher. Your goal is to get the best possible money outcome for your client. How would you answer the questions on Professor Abramson's checklist?
13. Now assume that you have a problem-solving orientation in the same case. How would your answers change?

2. Exchange Information

One of the key aspects of any negotiation is exchanging information, and part of mediation's value is its ability to enhance the flow of data between the parties. What information will be relevant depends again on your goals. If the process turns on money then legal evidence and arguments are likely to be key. If your purpose is to repair a relationship, knowing the "why" behind a disputed action will be important. If the objective is to create a new business arrangement, then financial data might be more useful. As a rule, negotiations that focus on imaginative options require a much broader base of information than discussions that revolve solely around money. You should think about two types of data:

- What information will your client need to make a good settlement decision?
- What information will help persuade your adversary to agree to the terms you are seeking?

We saw in Chapter 10 that advocates can enlist a mediator's help with an adversary; the neutral might also be able to help you explain to your client why it makes sense to give an opponent "free discovery."

a. Exchanging Data with the Other Party

Disputants usually need less data to mediate effectively than to try the same case. Still, especially if parties mediate early in a dispute, one side may lack the information necessary to assess the value of its litigation alternative or determine whether an imaginative option is viable. An insurance adjuster, for example, might not be able to obtain the authority needed to settle a claim without documents verifying the plaintiff's medical expenses, and a plaintiff lawyer might be unable to accept a reasonable settlement offer until he is satisfied there is no "smoking gun" lurking in the defendant's files.

Consider what data you and your opponent need to negotiate successfully, and whether you can arrange this through direct discussions or would benefit from the assistance of a mediator.

Example: A town sued a company for negligently designing a solid-waste treatment plant. It complained that the sludge produced by the plant, which it had expected to be able to market as fertilizer, was not solid enough; not only did farmers refuse the sludge, but it could not be stored effectively. Before going forward with expensive litigation, the parties agreed to mediate.

When the outside counsel for the defendant received the parties' pre-mediation statements, she realized that the town had described here client's alleged design errors in great detail, but had given no explanation of how it calculated its $3 million damages demand. Without an explanation, the lawyer could not get authority from her client's insurer to offer a significant settlement.

The lawyer contacted the mediator, who explained the problem to the town's lawyer and recommended that he provide a damage calculation to the defense. A day later it arrived, totaling slightly more than $1.7 million. Counsel reviewed the document and passed it along to the insurer, who arrived at mediation with the authority to close a deal.

Questions

14. What types of data gathered before mediation might help an advocate avoid some of the "twenty errors" described by Tom Arnold?
15. Assume that you are the lawyer in an exercise assigned by your teacher. What additional information would help you mediate? What data might the other attorney ask you for?

b. Educating the Mediator

In smaller cases and court-connected programs, neutrals sometimes are told almost nothing about the dispute in advance. In privately conducted mediations, however, lawyers typically make an effort to orient, and begin to persuade, the neutral before they meet to bargain. Pre-mediation communications can take at least three forms: written statements, organizing discussions, and private conversations.

Written Statements

Parties commonly send a mediator written statements, sometimes called "briefs" or "submissions," in advance.

- Is it better to prepare a customized brief, or use an existing pleading? A customized document has obvious advantages, but particularly in smaller cases it might make sense to use an existing pleading such as a summary judgment brief or pretrial memorandum. Most mediators are also willing to receive information in letter format.
- Is it preferable to submit the statement on an ex parte basis, or exchange it with opposing counsel? Mediators usually prefer that lawyers exchange statements so they are free to discuss one side's points with the other. Even if you exchange statements, however, you are ordinarily free to provide the mediator with a confidential statement in a letter or email for her eyes only.
- What should be in the statement? Most mediation briefs describe the facts of the dispute, the litigation history, legal arguments, and perhaps the prior bargaining. Of more interest to a mediator, but rarely covered even in private statements, are:
  — What nonlegal concerns are present in the case?
  — What barriers have made direct bargaining difficult? Are there, for example, personal or emotional issues affecting a party?
  — Who are the key decision makers?
  — Are there creative ideas that might help resolve the dispute?

Organizing Discussions

In complex legal cases, mediators often schedule joint meetings with counsel to discuss organizational questions such as who will be present at the mediation. These discussions usually occur through conference calls and are typically limited to lawyers, but clients and experts participate occasionally.

Private Conversations

Often lawyers do not seek to talk with mediators ahead of time, or limit any conversation to legal issues. Both are mistakes. Pre-mediation conversations offer exceptional opportunities to shape a neutral's initial "take" on a dispute. As you talk with the mediator, think about covering nonlegal obstacles, the personal dynamics of the participants, and potential settlement options, not merely legal points. Mediators have trouble assimilating long oral presentations about unfamiliar disputes, and will in any case get a more complete summary of the case from the written briefs.

In addition to attorney–mediator conversations, lawyers and clients may benefit from meeting, or at least talking by telephone with, the neutral before the process begins. You might seek out a meeting:

- To permit a client to work through emotions or get to know the mediator.
- To present sensitive or complex data or proposals.
- To allow the mediator to meet with a key witness or decision maker who will not be present at the mediation session.

Questions

16. You are representing a party in an exercise assigned by your teacher. What might be helpful for you or your client to tell the mediator in a private conversation before the process begins?
17. You have sent your mediation statement to your adversary and the mediator. The other side now sends its confidential statement to the mediator alone. What can you do in response? How might you have avoided this problem?

3. Preparing the Client

As we have noted, mediation is primarily a process of negotiation, but one that varies in significant ways from direct bargaining. Attorneys usually conduct direct negotiations outside their clients' presence, but in mediation the clients are ordinarily present and the mediator has conversations with them. At the same time, in the typical commercial mediation disputants spend much of their time isolated from each other and interact mainly through the neutral. Because of these structural differences, lawyers need to cover the following topics, in addition to the usual issues in preparing a client for any negotiation.

- How the format of mediation differs from negotiations to which the client is accustomed, including:
  - The expected procedure (for example, will the process be held in joint session, caucuses, or a mixed format?).
  - The client's role in each setting.
- The background, personality, and likely approach of the mediator. Is she likely to change style, for example, from an empathic to evaluative approach?
- What confidentiality rules will apply to the process, and what gaps and exceptions exist.
- What role the client will play in the process. In particular,
  - What kinds of questions should the client expect?

— What should the client volunteer or not reveal? Explain that it is appropriate to decline to answer questions from opponents and even the mediator.

— May the client be invited to meet privately with the other principal?

- What the other side might say and do.
- How you and the client will coordinate. For instance, will one of you talk and the other listen? One play "good cop" and the other "bad cop"? The client should know that it is appropriate to ask the mediator to leave the room so you can talk privately.
- What role you as lawyer will play. Be sure the client understands that although your overall goal — getting the best possible result — remains the same, your tactics will need to be adapted to the nature of the process. In particular you might take a more conciliatory tone than you would in a courtroom, so as not to antagonize the other side as you explore a deal. You might also not mention some favorable evidence, holding it for later use.

❖ **Thomas Arnold,** *Client Preparation for Mediation*
----
15 Corp. Couns. Q. 52 (April 1999)

In adjudicative processes (both arbitration and court trials), it is common for the advocacy to be an attack upon the good faith, integrity, and alleged wrongs of the other. . . . Necessarily that attack angers the other party, stirs up animosity, and interferes with any settlement effort.

In mediation the intent is to move the parties together, to treat the dispute as a problem to be solved together by respectful partners rather than a combat to be won. It is not the neutral but the other *party* and counsel that are the critical persons to be persuaded. So you don't hurt or disparage them: You seek out, you court, their good will and understanding. From this and other differences between mediation and adjudicative processes, you will see that advocacy and exhibit preparation. . . are poles apart as between mediation and adjudication. In this paper I list key client and some lawyer preparation pointers for mediation.

Who Represents the Client?

Who is the choice client representative for this mediation? A bellicose, unforgiving, inflexible, arrogant, and/or big-risk-taking personality? A wet rag personality who might give away the store? A person whose concessions at the mediation inherently imply criticism of his own prior actions, or his boss's prior actions? A temperate-mannered somebody who knows the subject matter, knows the values of the likely trade-offs? An open-minded person with quiet courage but no arrogance? Merely discussing these considerations and what available person is the best client representative with the client contact . . . becomes importantly educational . . . as to how he should undertake to conduct himself. . . .

First Impression

Upon arrival at the mediation, [the client should be cautioned to] be friendly and respectful, and attempt to build trust with the adversaries. Most settlements involve some degree of trust between client to client, client to counsel, counsel to counsel . . . so it is important to start developing trust at the first opportunity. . . .

Confidentiality

Acquaint the client with the rules and realities of confidentiality. Emphasize what not to say in plenary session, and that it's okay simply to decline to answer some questions. Only some, not all, disclosures in mediation are confidential. . . . Once learned in a mediation, . . . information can still be discovered by regular discovery processes and used, even though it may not be attributed to the . . . mediation.

Consider Strengths and Weaknesses

Counsel in a preparation session should have the client write down all of the weaknesses and strengths in his/her case, and discuss and evaluate each with counsel. It is important that counsel strain hard to be objective. . . .

Don't Argue

The client should be cautioned not to argue with the other party or try hard to "win" the . . . case. The stock in trade in most legal negotiation is the other party's (and your own) risk of a substantial loss at important expense. But arguing hard and aggressively to get an admission . . . is usually counterproductive. Just be sure the other party truly knows their risks. . . .

Know Which Questions to Answer

The client should be advised to answer questions from the other lawyer without exaggeration, honestly, carefully, and correctly. And he or she should also know which questions to quietly, simply decline to answer. Some lawyers try to use mediation as if it were primarily a discovery tool. You must make material disclosures for the process to work, but you don't have to tell the other side everything (for example, information subject to the attorney-client privilege). . . .

Become Familiar with "The Dance"

Plan with the client how you might handle the first . . . rounds of offers and counter-offers to convey subliminal messages. Plan not to be disturbed by an outlandish initial offer by the other party, but to turn it to . . . advantage by showing how ridiculous it is. . . .

Consider Speaking Out

When the parties can understand the issues, as is usual in commercial and many other disputes, encourage them to speak up during the mediation and participate in the negotiation.

End the Battle Within the Camp

Within a "party" there often are many constituencies . . . with different interests or viewpoints, for example, a partner, the vice-president . . . , the union, the board, the marketing manager. They may be represented at the mediation by one, two, or three persons, or some of them by no one. . . . Not infrequently, the most important and destructive disputes are between constituencies on the same side. In multi-faction situations, counsel and the client business representatives at the mediation must each be sure to address all internal disputes before they face the other side.

Don't Look Like a Klutz

This goes for you and the client, but the client is more likely to need the reminder. It is important to show the client off in the mediation as someone who would be an appealing witness in any court process, should mediation fail. People pay more to, and accept less from, a party with jury appeal.

Be Prepared for Down Time

There is often some idle time during mediation, while the other party meets with the mediator in private caucus, so the client should bring work or reading material. . . .

Plan for a Long Session

Let the client know that it will be necessary to make sure work and children are taken care of all day — until 7:30 in the evening or later, if need be. It is a good idea to talk to the mediator in advance about termination times. Some mediators like the pressure of late hours and work on past midnight if there is even a little movement in parties' positions; some quit at 6:00 p.m. no matter what is going on.

Bow Out Gracefully

Advise your client that when the process ends, you should each shake hands with your opposite number and say "Thank you," even if there's no settlement. Many settlements follow shortly after a mediation, when the right flavor is left in the mouth of an adversary . . . .

Questions

18. What aspects of the mediation process do you think a typical plaintiff in a personal injury case is unlikely to understand? What might a business executive find surprising in mediation of a contract dispute?

19. Tom Arnold's underlying theme is that a lawyer needs to prepare a client differently for mediation than for litigation. Which of his suggestions would you *not* follow if you were preparing a client for a hearing in court?

20. Any advice must be adapted to the needs of specific situations. As one example, Arnold advises that clients be told to assume an "empathetic" role. In what kinds of disputes would empathy be likely to be productive? Are there situations in which it might be the wrong emotion to show?

CHAPTER
12

Representing Clients: During the Process

We now focus on the stage in the mediation process at which the parties and mediator convene together to talk and bargain. This is what many lawyers think of as the "actual" mediation, but you now know that effective advocacy begins well before the parties meet in person.

There is relatively little written about advocacy outside commercial mediation. This could be due to the fact that in the traditional family-mediation format and in "transformative" mediation attorneys do not appear at mediation sessions. The most common noncommercial formats do not offer attorneys very much opportunity for advocacy. We therefore discuss advocacy in the context of commercial mediation, the form of the process in which lawyers do play significant roles.

A.   Joint Meetings

1.   *The Opening Session*

a.   Should You Have an Opening Session?

Most mediators prefer to begin the process with an opening session attended by all the disputants. Lawyers, however, regularly suggest that the parties dispense with the opening stage and go directly into caucusing. Each side already knows the other's arguments, they say: What benefit could there be to repeating them? Or, they warn, the session will simply inflame their clients. Moreover, time is limited: Why not get right to the bargaining? There is often some truth to each of these concerns, and as noted, the practice of holding opening sessions seems to be dying out in some locales. Still, however repetitive or uncomfortable an opening session may appear, you should be reluctant to ask that it be omitted entirely.

The key point is that this is probably the only time in the entire litigation process that you will have the opportunity to talk directly to the principal on the other side and inform her of the facts and considerations you think she should bear in mind when deciding whether to settle the case. In ordinary litigation you will rarely encounter the opposing principal, other than in formal, adversarial settings such as depositions and court hearings. The opening session in mediation is a unique opportunity to avoid the obstructions imposed by court rules and opposing counsel and communicate directly with the person who has the authority to grant the concessions you seek.

You could, of course, send opposing counsel a letter and request that he forward it to his client, but writing has a very narrow "bandwidth" by comparison with direct, informal conversation. Don't let the opportunity pass to present your message directly to the decision maker on the other side.

> *Example:* A retired executive bought an antiques company, only to conclude a few months later that the seller had deceived him about its condition. He filed suit, then agreed to mediate. The mediator called each lawyer before the mediation to ask about process issues. The purchaser's lawyer said he thought his client would welcome the chance to talk and asked the mediator to encourage the principals to participate. The attorney for the seller, asked about this, agreed to an opening session, but warned that her client was an "engineer-type" who would not want to say much.
>
> The purchaser showed up with a four-page single-spaced text. He described how he'd entered the deal in good faith, only to find himself betrayed by deceptions ranging from inflated inventory to a clientele outraged at the prior owner's failure to meet shipping dates. After 30 minutes the purchaser finished and the seller began to talk. Belying his counsel's prediction, he spoke articulately and at length.
>
> There ensued a back-and-forth discussion between the principals in which the attorneys participated. When the discussion became heated and repetitive, the mediator deferred to the lawyers' request they move into caucusing. Still, the opening session went on for 2½ hours, and later that day the case settled.

If you do have a reason for avoiding a joint meeting, raise this with the mediator in advance and work out an agreement about how to proceed. Remember, though, that you have options between complete cancellation of the opening session and the "usual format." You could, for example, ask that the session be limited to comments by parties, not attorneys, or that the mediator conduct the session entirely in "Q and A" format.

> Question
>
> 1.   Can you think of any type of dispute in which an early joint meeting is likely to be counterproductive? What format would you use instead?

You will want to use an opening session to best advantage. To do so, consider these questions:

- What is special about opening sessions in mediation?
- What is my goal for this stage of the process?
- How can I structure the session for maximum impact?
- What can the mediator do to help me do so?

b. What Is Special About the Opening Session?

An opening session in commercial mediation resembles a court hearing in that attorneys and parties engage in advocacy in the presence of a neutral moderator. Unlike a judicial hearing, however, mediation is a "cool" medium, and sessions usually take place in rooms much smaller and less imposing than a courtroom. Parties are seated only a few feet away from each other, and the mediator sets an informal tone. As a result, a subdued style of advocacy is usually more effective than courtroom rhetoric.

A calmer, less formal presentation also makes sense because of the nature of the audience. Unlike a court hearing, in mediation you have two quite different audiences: the opposing party and the mediator. The mediator is willing to listen but has no power to make a decision, whereas the opponent has the ability to decide but will resist agreeing with what you say. Decision makers from both sides will also be personally present at an opening session, something usually not true in direct negotiations.

c. What Is Your Goal?

Advocates' overall purpose for the opening session is usually to create the conditions for successful communication and bargaining later in the process, but beyond that their approach will depend on their ultimate objective.

Foster a Working Relationship

A lawyer can use an opening session, and perhaps also the casual interactions that often occur as people assemble, to foster a better working relationship with an opponent. This does not necessarily mean repairing a past connection, although that might be desirable. Instead the goal at this stage is typically more modest — to create a good framework for the parties to bargain later. You can do this, for example, by demonstrating that you are serious about settlement and are willing to make principled compromises to reach one. Or you can use the opening session to help emotional or angry participants work through feelings preventing them from bargaining well.

Gather Information

You can also use the opening session to gather information. In a joint meeting, unlike discovery or court proceedings, disputants can talk informally. Attorneys and clients also have the opportunity to observe the people on the other side and perhaps also the chance to speak directly with the opposing principal. (The other side, of course, has the same opportunity to "size up" you and your client.)

Focus the Discussion on Key Issues

Another option is to use the opening session to focus discussion on issues helpful to your case or that create a platform for effective bargaining. If, for example, you want to emphasize the evidence (or lack of it) supporting the plaintiff's damage claims, you can alert the mediator beforehand that this issue is significant and focus attention on it through your comments. If your primary goal is to explore an interest-based solution, you can use the opening session to send signals about this as well, either directly or through the mediator. Neither side can control the agenda of an opening session, but attorneys who take the initiative can significantly influence it.

Persuade an Opponent

You can also use the opening session to begin the task of persuading an opponent to compromise. If this is the objective, you should usually focus your advocacy on the opposing decision maker. You will have other chances to talk with the mediator, but this could well be your only opportunity to speak directly to the other party. The goal is usually to convince the other side that it is in its own best interest to compromise. Opponents are more likely to do so if they believe that:

- You are serious about seeking a settlement; they can therefore probably gain something tangible by compromising, and it will not be a one-sided process.
- You are open to options that will advance their interests.
- If discussions fail, however, you believe that you have a good alternative to settlement and they do not.
- You are willing to compromise, but will accept impasse sooner than an unfair result.

d.   How to Present the Opening for Maximum Effect

How Should You Frame Your Presentation?

What Format Should You Use?   The fluid nature of mediation gives you great freedom to customize a presentation. For example, you can:

- Speak yourself, or involve your client or other team members.
- Restrict the presentation to legal issues, focus on personal or business interests, or discuss other topics.
- Rely solely on a verbal presentation, or incorporate media such as PowerPoint slides and video. Within fairly broad limits you can take as much time as you need.

If, however, you plan to say nothing or take an unusual length of time, need special equipment, or have unusual elements in your presentation, alert the mediator to this so she can facilitate your approach and alert you to any problems it might create.

Remember that exhibits and videos are likely to have a greater impact in mediation than in a courtroom, because the room is smaller and documents can stay "on the table" for hours. Evidence also cannot be excluded: If an item is inadmissible your opponent will probably point that out, but evidence that would never get before a jury can still have an effect, especially on lay parties.

> *Example:* A plaintiff lawyer found an embarrassing email sent by the defendant's CEO. She had it blown up on a 2-by-3-foot board, which she set up as she talked. The words seemed to fill the conference room, to the evident discomfort of the defendant team.
>
> When the lawyer turned the floor over to the other side, the defense attorney took the board down and set it facing the wall. But as the plaintiff counsel began her rebuttal she put the board back up, underlying the fact that the words would return to bedevil the defense.

Although a mediator has no power of decision, his views about a case may affect the bargaining. Bear in mind that a mediator's views will usually flow from the briefs and documents he reads, augmented by observations of the people present at the mediation. This means that like trial, mediation has:

- A *primacy effect*: The evidence and people a mediator actually observes are more vivid, and thus usually have more impact on decisions, than data the neutral only hears about.
- A *melding effect*: When a mediator cannot personally observe a witness she is likely to place the person in a category ("nurse," "retired accountant," etc.), and then make an assumption about how a fact-finder would react to a typical member of that group.

These effects apply in the opening session — it is at this point that the mediator gets his first view of people whose persuasiveness as witnesses he may have to evaluate. The opposing party and lawyer may have seen the witness before, but the mediator will not and will have to imagine whatever he cannot see.

Conversely, whereas the mediator may have reviewed key documents, the opposing decision maker might not have seen them or understood their significance. If you have a person or document that strongly supports your case, consider bringing the witness or item into the mediation room and making it part of your presentation.

Remember also that once the mediation session begins the mediator will not have much leisure time to read though new documents or court opinions. If you must present a document for the first time at the mediation, highlight or make a copy of the key passages.

Who Should Speak?   Unlike statements at trial, openings in mediation can include several people: lawyers, parties, experts, and witnesses. Most lawyers are inclined to take the lead in the opening session and treat it like an informal pretrial hearing or business negotiation. A better approach is to take advantage of this freedom in the format to use as a spokesperson whoever is likely to have the most impact on the other side and the neutral.

Look for ways to involve your client in opening meetings. Opponents tend to "tune out" the opposing attorney, but they are usually interested in hearing from principals: They represent the "horse's mouth," and might make a mistake or offer hints about concessions. Mediators also seek out contact with parties for some of the same reasons, paying close attention to what they say. Statements by your client will therefore usually have a greater impact than the same words from you. Parties who participate effectively in an opening session can significantly affect how an opponent views them as witnesses, future partners, or negotiators.

- In a personal injury or employment case, in which pain and suffering or emotional distress is often an important element of a claim, a plaintiff who can persuasively describe how he has suffered increases the settlement value of his case. Whenever a person is likely to be a significant witness in adjudication, his participation at mediation can affect the other side's estimate of the value of the case.
- When parties wish to repair a relationship or the principals cannot avoid relating with each other, for instance if they have children together, one party's participation in mediation can affect the other side's willingness to revive a working relationship. Again, statements made by one principal to another almost always have greater impact than comments made by a lawyer or through a mediator.
- If interests are the focus, parties can often articulate their concerns more persuasively if they speak themselves.
- If one side doubts an opponent's commitment to settling, the principal may be able to dispel those concerns by participating in the opening session.

You could, for example, summarize the legal arguments in the case and then ask the client to describe key factual events, or cover liability and let the client describe the effect of the case on her family or business. If you do want your client or the other party to speak, prompt the mediator in advance to encourage principals to comment.

All this assumes, of course, that a client presents himself positively. If a client is obnoxious, inarticulate, or unappealing, then her participation will lower an opponent's opinion and make it harder to achieve her objectives. In such situations it is better for the person to remain silent if possible.

If you don't want your client put on the spot, warn the mediator about this. If a client is inarticulate or an unattractive witness, you have no obligation to put him on display. If you do want your client to participate, go over with him in advance what he will say and how to present it, as you would with a witness at a trial or deposition. In particular:

- Remind your client that the setting is informal and that he can take a break to consult with you at any time. Discuss how you and the client will communicate, for example, how to signal a need for a break.
- Alert him that he may be asked questions or given the chance to speak in joint sessions in mediation, but that unlike in a courtroom, he has no obligation to do so even if the mediator asks.
- If you don't want your client to answer a question, intervene and respond yourself. If you don't wish to seem rude, say that you would prefer to discuss the issue in caucus.

What Tone to Take?   Mediation is an informal process that combines discussion with bargaining. Speakers should therefore use a conversational tone, usually focused on the key opposing decision maker.

If the speaker is discussing background facts that are familiar to the other side, he should address the neutral. If the issue involves past incidents between principals, or a party is attempting to explain a misunderstanding, apologize, or empathize with an adversary, he should speak directly to the concerned person. If the purpose is to show the client's effectiveness as a witness, then it is usually best to address the other side and the mediator at once, like a judge and jury.

If it is necessary to make an accusation, for example, that the other side has committed fraud, it is usually better to address comments to the neutral, to make listeners feel less "assaulted" and more willing to listen. Mediators with backgrounds as judges also sometimes prefer that participants speak directly to them.

Question

2. You represent a company that vacated commercial space because of dissatisfaction with the condition of the building. Your client is being sued by a corporate landlord for rent due under the lease. Both sides have agreed to mediate. Apart from the basic issue of liability, which you see as a 50–50 proposition, you believe that the landlord ignored its responsibility to maintain the building and as a result would not be awarded much even if it did establish a technical violation of the lease. How can you use the opening session to make the landlord aware of its risk at trial?

e.   How to Take Advantage of the Mediator's Presence

Shaping the Agenda

Chapter 11 described how a mediator can influence the negotiation agenda. If you would like to have an issue discussed in the opening session, ask the mediator to encourage this. If you don't want to raise the topic yourself, ask the mediator to do so. You might also want to avoid issues; it is difficult to avoid a topic entirely, but if your client will be upset by discussion of a certain issue, you can alert the mediator to discourage or contain it. Mediators can also help with issues of timing and structure; if, for example, you want a recess between an opponent's presentation and your own, ask the mediator ahead of time to suggest a break.

Muting Adversarial Reactions

If you need to make adversarial statements, for example, accusing the other side of intentional misconduct, a mediator can at least partially "defang" your role and make it easier to present the issue.

> *Example:* An American pharmaceutical company terminated its Brazilian distributor, alleging that its sales were disappointing and that it had the right to cancel the contract on 90 days' notice. The distributor filed suit in Texas state court, alleging that the American company had hired away the distributor's chief salesman, persuading him to break his noncompetition agreement, and had encouraged him to begin soliciting the same clients he had developed while on the Brazilian company's payroll.
>
> The distributor's lawyer told the mediator before the opening session that his client had emails showing that the American company's executives had begun talking with the disloyal salesman a full three months before he left. The lawyer planned to argue that the U.S. company had intentionally stolen the employee away, in knowing violation of his contract with the Brazilian distributor. Recognizing that the American company's executives might take umbrage at these charges, the distributor's lawyers asked the mediator to prepare them for what would happen.
>
> In his opening comments the mediator said, "I've asked each lawyer to state their case unvarnished and with the gloves off. The parties may find what they say upsetting, but I've asked them to do this because we have to be aware of what will happen in court if this case does not settle."

Gathering Information

If you want to gather information during the opening session, ask the mediator to:

*   Raise certain issues himself, or
*   Suggest that the parties ask each other questions or discuss the case.

> *Example:* A contractor was sued by an owner for allegedly mispouring the concrete slab on which a building had been erected. Before the mediation the attorney warned the mediator, "We cannot figure out how the plaintiff got its number of $750,000 to fix the foundation. Even assuming it's our problem, our contractors are coming in with figures in the $300,000 range. This is the major element of their damages and the difference is driving our assessment of what we'd pay to settle. Can you ask them to flesh out their estimate, or suggest it would be useful to have a discussion in the joint session about the calculation of repair costs?"

2. *Other Joint Formats*

We have seen that commercial mediation typically relies on private caucusing, but that does not mean that parties must spend all their time after the opening session separated from each other. Caucusing can be useful but it also imposes significant limitations. Don't let yourself fall into a caucus format as a matter of routine without thinking first about whether other approaches might be more effective in a particular case.

Caucusing is most useful when disputants want to focus primarily on legal issues and monetary offers, or when they are too emotional or unskilled in bargaining to interact effectively. If, however, parties wish to repair a relationship or work out inventive or complex solutions, direct discussions are often effective because they allow the people most concerned or knowledgeable about a situation to talk with each other. Even when a case is "only about money," it may be useful for opponents to talk directly to deal with emotions, address complex factual issues, or clarify misunderstandings. The flexible nature of mediation allows participants to change the structure on an ad hoc basis. This creates another opportunity for sophisticated counsel to use the process to their advantage.

Here is another example:

> *Example:* A manufacturer and a trucking company had a productive relationship for more than a decade, with the trucker distributing the manufacturer's products throughout the southern United States. Then their relationship went sour. The manufacturer sued the trucking company, claiming it had fraudulently inflated its costs by overstating mileage and padding other charges. After two years of intense litigation, the parties agreed to mediate.
>
> The mediation process began with an unusual twist: The plaintiff's lawyer called ahead of time to suggest that the mediator ask the defense whether they could dispense with the usual opening statements by lawyers and instead have the two CEOs meet privately. The mediator raised the issue with defense counsel who agreed, subject to the neutral being present during the conversation.
>
> The three retired to a room, leaving the lawyers behind. The plaintiff executive opened the discussion by retracing the companies' earlier good relationship and their later problems. He suggested the breakdown had been provoked in part by a wayward manager he had hired away from the trucking company but had recently let go. The executive then made a settlement offer. The defendant CEO said he needed to run it by his lawyers.
>
> The parties went into caucuses and bargained intensely for hours, reducing an initial $900,000 gap to $30,000 — a demand of $300,000 against an

offer of $270,000. At that point, however, the defense refused to make another offer, expressing frustration at the plaintiff's unreasonableness.

As the mediator searched for ways to break the impasse, the defendant CEO suddenly pulled a quarter out of his pocket. "See this?" he asked. "You check — It's an honest quarter. I'll flip him for it!" "For what?" "The 30," he replied. "Let's see if he's got the ****s to flip for it!" The mediator looked at the trucker's lawyer: Was this serious? The attorney shrugged his shoulders; "It's OK with me. Why don't you take Jim down and present it to them. But you should do the talking; Jim's feeling really frustrated by all this." Why not? the mediator thought; it was better than anything he had to suggest.

The neutral led the defendant CEO into the plaintiff's conference room and, with a smile, said, "Jim has an idea to break the deadlock. It's kind of . . . unusual, but you might want to listen to it." In a calm voice and without anatomical references, the CEO repeated his coin-toss offer.

The plaintiff executive grinned. "OK," he said, "But you didn't answer my last move, so the real spread is 50, between my 320 (his last offer before dropping to $300,000) and your 270." They argued over what should be the outcomes for the flip, showing some exasperation but also bits of humor. When the discussion stalled the mediator suggested options to keep it going ("Why not give the 20 to charity?"), but they could not agree and the defendant CEO walked out.

As he left, the mediator walked with him down the hall. "Suppose I could get him to drop to a flat 290," he asked. "Would that do it?" As it turned out, it did.

In this mediation both attorneys' initiatives proved important to settlement. The plaintiff lawyer's proposal that the process begin with a parties-only meeting created an informal connection between the executives that smoothed their later bargaining. And the CEO's idea of a coin toss, which the mediator learned later had been concocted with his lawyer, was key to shaking the parties out of their stalemate.

As this example demonstrates, even in a process in which the parties are separated in caucuses, lawyers can advance their clients' interests by arranging meetings of subgroups of disputants. The mediator will usually be present during such sessions, but this is not always true: In a case described later, the plaintiff's inside counsel asked to meet privately with the defendant's CEO outside the presence of both the outside lawyers and the neutral. Good mediators will usually agree to ask whether people can talk directly with each other, and smart lawyers are not afraid to ask a mediator to vary the usual format. Both understand that mediation is inherently a fluid process.

B.   Caucusing

Because caucusing is dominant in civil mediation outside the family law area, attorneys and mediators you encounter in practice are likely to expect to spend most of the time in caucus format. You will need either to take the initiative to change this assumption or work to reap an advantage from it.

To make the best use of caucuses, you need to prepare in two ways. First, you must adapt bargaining tactics to a situation in which you are communicating with the other side indirectly, through a third person. Second, you need to think about how to deal with the mediator.

> *Example:* During the opening session opposing counsel asks in a challenging tone whether your client, a discharged employee claiming discrimination, ever sought medical care for the emotional distress she is claiming. You immediately step in and order her not to respond, noting that this is a settlement process, not a deposition.
>
> During a later caucus discussion the mediator, in a sympathetic tone, asks your client essentially the same question, and your client begins to explain that she never obtained treatment. You might be more willing to have your client answer in this context, knowing that you could tell the mediator not to reveal what she says, but even if you were reluctant you would not wish to appear uncooperative. You might also be concerned that a failure to answer in the "nonadversarial" setting of a caucus would be interpreted by the mediator as an admission that there was no evidence to support the claim.

The nature of caucusing typically changes over the course of mediation, and we therefore focus on early and later caucuses separately.

1. Early Caucuses

Goals

During the early caucuses you are likely to have some or all of the following goals:

- Relationships:
  - Develop a good working relationship with the mediator.
  - Not harm, and perhaps improve, your relationship with the other side, unless you have decided to adopt a hard-bargainer role.
- Legal issues:
  - Focus attention on favored issues and avoid or minimize unhelpful ones.
  - Gather the data you need to bargain, and provide the other side with information that will induce it to move in your direction.
  - Persuade the other party and the neutral that you have a good alternative to settling or that its alternative is not attractive.
- Interests:
  - Identify nonlegal barriers that have made settlement difficult.
  - Focus the mediator on your interests and identify the key concerns of the other side.
- Bargaining:
  - Start the process of exchanging offers.
  - Encourage or assist the mediator to pursue interest-based options.

Content

You can expect the following to occur in a first caucus meeting. The mediator will emphasize listening and gathering information, while building a working relationship with the attorney and client. He will seek to gather information to help the parties understand each other's perspectives and perhaps also to lower their confidence about prevailing in court. Attorneys pursuing a competitive strategy will want to offer data that support their legal position and perhaps some "ammunition" that the mediator can use with an opponent. Lawyers taking a cooperative, interest-based approach will want to give the mediator information about their underlying needs and those of the other side; cooperative bargainers might also ask for help identifying what is important to an opponent.

Many neutrals in early caucuses will use a principled bargaining style, trying to avoid or minimize positional tactics such as "insulting" first offers meant to jolt the other side. The mediator will invite disputants to offer ideas or concessions to help the process gain momentum, and will be looking for possible openings or at least a private indication of flexibility. Be prepared to offer the mediator something to assist the bargaining process, or to explain you do not believe that is yet appropriate.

Of the potential goals listed above, we focus on two: facilitating exchanges of information and initiating bargaining.

a. Exchange Information and Arguments

In direct negotiation good lawyers often spend considerable time exchanging information and feeling each other out before making explicit offers; it is not surprising that advocates and mediators do so in mediation as well. At this stage a lawyer might pose questions to a mediator that she wants answered by an opponent, or pass on to the neutral points to emphasize in the other room.

Neutrals, for their part, understand that disputants often arrive at mediation without the data they need to make good settlement decisions, and that smart lawyers will seek to use the mediator to convey arguments more effectively to an adversary. Indeed, to the extent that a party's questions, like queries on cross-examination, amount to disguised arguments, mediators are often happy to transmit them as part of their effort to encourage both sides to reassess the value of their case. To understand how lawyers can use mediation to assist the exchange of information, consider the following.

Example: Professional mediators and litigators were put in a role-play situation as part of an experiment to film how advocates use the mediation process. The dispute involved a manufacturer's claim against a supplier for selling a defective product. The manufacturer also sued the supplier's insurer, alleging that the insurer had acted in bad faith by refusing to settle the claim and asking for treble damages. The bad-faith claim hung over the case, inflating the plaintiff's monetary demands and discouraging the defense from making a serious offer.

In defense of the bad-faith allegation, the defendant's counsel pointed out to the mediator in their first caucus meeting that the insurer had a solid basis for denying the claim — the results of tests conducted by an independent expert. At the end of the first caucus meeting she elected to highlight the issue:

Defendant's inside counsel: We hope you'll raise with them that we see the crux of settlement as hinging on the fact that we don't see any evidence to support their case on treble damages. . . .

Mediator: But if they do have evidence, that might influence your bargaining position?

Counsel (smiling): Yes, and if they don't, we hope it influences theirs. . . .

In response, the mediator raised the issue during his meeting with the plaintiff side:

Mediator: Suppose an outside expert reports that he found nothing in the insured's product that could have caused the damage and the insurer then denies the claim on that basis. If all that is true and the expert is credible, how would you then get the insurer into the case?

Plaintiff counsel: Well, it's a problem, no question about it.

Mediator: What percentage chance would you place on the bad-faith claim?

Counsel: Twenty-five percent.

At the conclusion of this caucus meeting the plaintiff agreed to heavily discount the bad-faith claim. What the defense counsel obtained by making her request through the mediator was to focus his discussion with the plaintiff on her issue. She also benefited from the plaintiff lawyer's natural inclination to be candid with the neutral.

Potential Questions

The following are some specific questions a lawyer may have in planning for an early caucus.

- If I have confidential information that supports my analysis of the merits, should I disclose it early in the process or wait?

It is usually better to offer evidence early, while the mediator is focused on gathering information. If you wait until late in the process, the new data will be mixed with bargaining discussions. Recall a case, mentioned earlier, in which a Brazilian company sued an American distributor for allegedly inducing the plaintiff's chief salesman to violate his noncompete contract. To bolster his claim, the Brazilian company's lawyer might say in caucus, "We've located another salesman they tried to solicit in violation of his contract with us. They don't know about this, but it will really make them look bad at trial."

If a party waits to disclose "silver bullet" information until late in the process, when the mediator is pressing each side to make difficult concessions, it risks being heard by the neutral not as genuine data, but as an excuse for avoiding compromise. Late in the mediation a mediator is also likely to give new evidence less weight because he has shifted focus from understanding the case to finding settlement terms.

One reason not to disclose evidence early in the process might be that counsel is not yet convinced that the other side is ready to settle, and if not, wishes to preserve "good ammunition" for another day. If that is the concern, a lawyer can make her reasoning clear to the mediator, or even make settlement a quasi-condition of disclosure: "You can tell them _____, but only if you're confident that it will seal a deal. . . ."

- Should I direct the mediator to take a tough line with the other side, but tell him privately that we are willing to compromise?

Your strategy should flow from your goals. That said, it is usually a good idea to let the mediator know your strategy in general terms so he can warn you of problems and present it most effectively to the other side. Telling the neutral that you are delaying in offering a compromise rather than refusing to ever to do so makes you appear more cooperative.

- Who should make the first offer in mediation?

As a rule, plaintiffs come into mediation having made a demand and will not make another offer until the defense puts an offer on the table ("We won't bid against ourselves."). If a defendant has responded, however, the plaintiff is usually asked to make a concession.

- Should I make an offer during the first caucus meeting?

Assuming it is your "turn" to bid, making an offer in the first meeting might or might not be the best strategy. It depends primarily on whether you think that by simply exchanging information in the first round of caucusing you can learn something valuable or persuade the other side to be more conciliatory. If you decide to wait, don't let yourself be pushed into acting prematurely. Instead of making an offer, you could say that you prefer to wait because you want to talk more about the substantive issues or each side's larger interests before making decisions about settlement.

- Will the mediator be offended if I ask her to leave the room temporarily or don't explain my bargaining goal or strategy?

Don't be bashful about asking a mediator to leave so you can confer with your client, especially when concessions are under consideration. Mediators expect parties to talk confidentially with their lawyers. Indeed the fact that you want to do so could be taken as evidence that you have listened to what the mediator has said. You might say, "This has given us some things to think about. Can we have a few minutes to talk?"

Mediators also understand that lawyers usually do not disclose their entire strategy, because advocates and neutrals do not have the same goal. Neutrals expect that if an attorney makes a factual representation it will be accurate, but not that lawyers will confide in them completely.

Problem 1

You represent the defense in the mediation of an employment discrimination case. A typical plaintiff's claim for damages in such a case consists of lost wages, out-of-pocket expenses, and emotional distress. Of these, the item that is often the largest, and the most subject to dispute, is emotional distress.

Here the plaintiff is demanding $200,000 in emotional distress damages, but you think it is highly unlikely that he will recover more than a modest amount, because he never sought medical care for his alleged condition. Also there are no egregious facts, such as being ordered out of the building summarily in front of other employees, that a fact-finder would think likely to trigger serious distress.

You are in the first round of caucusing. The mediator is coming to meet with you and your client and will then meet with the plaintiff. Outline how you would raise this issue.

---

b. Initiate Bargaining

Advocates in settlement discussions may focus either on monetary goals or creative solutions. The format of mediation allows lawyers to advance either of these goals, or both of them, more effectively.

Interest-Based Bargaining

Although interest-based bargaining is desirable, a basic problem, especially for plaintiffs, is that if they show a willingness to explore nonmonetary terms, their opponent could interpret this as a signal that the party is not committed to its monetary position. (Defense lawyers, by contrast, tend to be receptive to imaginative terms, because they see them as a substitute for paying money.)

Mediation can allow a lawyer to have it both ways to some extent. The advocate can press "publicly," in communications sent through the mediator or in joint session, for the best possible money outcome, and at the same time ask the neutral "privately," in a caucus discussion, to explore nonmonetary options.

Example: A large manufacturer sued a supplier of sensors, alleging that the defendant's product was defective, causing an unacceptable rate of failure in automobiles in which they were installed. The defendant supplier was interested in restoring its business relationship with the manufacturer. Not only had the contract been a source of profit, but the supplier knew that if the manufacturer resumed using its products it was much less likely to make negative comments about the defendant to other customers.

Because the plaintiff knew that the quality failure had been a one-time event caused by a third party that provided defective wiring to the supplier, it was not necessarily opposed to this. Still, it was concerned that the defense would seize on talk of a "win–win" solution to avoid its cash demands, and it badly needed the cash it could gain from a settlement. To deal with this problem the manufacturer's lawyer continued to press for a large money settlement, while indicating to the mediator privately that the plaintiff would not object to renewing the contract if it was additional to, and not a substitute for, a cash payment.

By exploiting the structure of mediation, the plaintiff lawyer in this example was able to pursue distributive and integrative bargaining strategies simultaneously.

A "Hard" Bargaining Strategy

One aspect of mediation not often mentioned is that it offers protection to parties who opt for a competitive approach as well as creative ones. Indeed the structure of mediation often allows attorneys to take tougher stands than they could in direct negotiations. Because the process is seen as a one-time effort, participants in mediation are more reluctant to walk out in response to "insulting" proposals. Bargainers also know that the mediator will work to "scrape the other side off the ceiling" when it erupts at their stubbornness. Lawyers sometimes take advantage of this dynamic to play "tough cop," knowing that good mediators will instinctively take on a good-cop role to keep the process alive.

Example: A manufacturer was in a dispute with its insurer over the insurer's refusal to pay nearly $1 billion in claims against the manufacturer arising from a mass-tort class action. The parties agreed to go to mediation. The insurer's CEO prepared intensively for the process, planning to have a point-by-point discussion of the merits with the manufacturer's representatives.

When the parties convened, however, the plaintiff's inside counsel said that he wasn't interested in discussing legal issues with the CEO; he had listened carefully to his litigation team's analysis, and saw no point in having a debate. He went on to say that he would not make any concessions at all until the insurer first agreed to pay the full amount the manufacturer claimed was due under an "incontestable" section of the policy. That amount, counsel said, was just under $130 million.

The mediation was held in a conference room at a large airport, and in a direct negotiation the insurer's team would very likely have been on the next flight out. The manufacturer's lawyer knew, however, that the mediator would respond to his tactic by cajoling, even begging, the CEO to ignore his opponent's obnoxiousness, look at the big picture, examine the legal risks — and put up a very large amount of money. And that is exactly what happened.

> After hours of talking, the CEO strode into the manufacturer's conference room, wrote "100" on the board, and walked out. Now it was the neutral's job to convince the plaintiff team that although $100 million might seem paltry in light of its claim, from the insurer's perspective it was a large step forward. To counter feelings of reactive devaluation, he argued that the right way to assess the offer was to count up from zero, rather than down from the plaintiff's original demand. In fact, by relying on the protection afforded by the mediation process, the manufacturer's lawyer had been able to take a hard positional stance and obtain a huge first offer from the other side.
>
> Months later the case settled. The turning point came when the manufacturer's counsel — the same lawyer who had refused to discuss the case with the CEO — intervened to change the mediation format. He asked the mediator to invite the CEO to meet him in the lobby of the hotel where the mediation was being held. As the neutral and the lawyers sat in conference rooms, reading newspapers and speculating about what was going on, the two key players sat down over coffee and cut a deal.

As this example illustrates, good lawyers can use mediation to enhance a competitive strategy as well as a cooperative one, in the knowledge that the mediator will work to keep the process from falling apart.

2.   Later Caucuses

As caucusing progresses the tactics of the disputants and the mediator are likely to evolve. Advocates will continue to probe for information, argue the merits, and explore interests, but as the process continues these aspects usually become less dominant. Parties find themselves returning to the same facts and legal arguments, making continued discussion seem repetitive. If the process has followed a creative path, parties in later caucuses often shift their attention from identifying and communicating interests to devising options that satisfy them.

As a result, during the later stages of a process that focuses on monetary demands, caucuses are likely to become progressively shorter, as both sides focus on exchanging and interpreting offers. In one focused on interests, caucuses might actually become longer, as participants focus on finding terms that produce the best possible fit of concerns, and opposing parties or subgroups are likely to meet directly with each other to clarify issues and discuss options.

In later stages of the process mediators also become more active in expressing viewpoints and press parties harder about the cost and risk of litigation and the resulting advantage of compromising. In part this happens because the mediator becomes increasingly confident about her assessment of the participants, the legal issues, and the obstacles blocking agreement. Parties often also become more receptive to the mediator's advice, because they realize that the neutral has listened carefully to their concerns and communicated them to the other side, and perhaps because they realize that their preferred tactics are likely to lead to an impasse. As mediators become more active in the process, lawyers should:

* Be prepared for harder reality testing. Warn clients that the mediator may ask tough questions and disagree explicitly with their arguments; assure them that this is a normal part of the process, and that the neutral is being equally frank with their opponent.
* Be ready to suggest changes in the format, for example, a joint meeting or conversations between subsets of disputants. Ask the mediator to advise you whether the other side would be receptive to such an approach.
* If your client is becoming discouraged, consider asking the mediator for an assessment of how the process is going. If your client is becoming tired or irritable or is pushed too hard, ask the mediator to arrange a break or adjournment.
* As the process nears an end, be ready to bargain with the mediator about whether and how the mediator will use evaluation and other impasse-breaking tactics (discussed below).

a.   Bargaining

As the parties move into what is often difficult and competitive bargaining, lawyers can take advantage of a mediator's presence in several ways.

Use the Mediator to Obtain or Convey Information

One of the paradoxes of mediation is how mediators are expected to treat information that they gather during private caucuses. On the one hand, caucus discussions are to be kept confidential. At the same time, one of mediation's key purposes is to foster better communication, and as long as the parties are separated in caucuses this can happen only if the mediator conveys information between them. How can an advocate take advantage of this tension?

In practice most lawyers in mediation designate very few facts to be held confidential from the other side, and appear to expect a mediator to reveal at least some of what they say in private caucus. A plaintiff lawyer might tell a mediator, for example, "$500,000 is as low as we'll go at this point. You can tell them 500." The attorney knows that the neutral will interpret this to mean that he can tell the other side that the plaintiff is reducing his demand to $500,000. The mediator can also, however, offer a personal opinion — not attributed to the plaintiff — that she thinks the plaintiff will be willing to go further ("at this point") if the defendant makes an appropriate concession.

Experienced lawyers know, in other words, that although mediators will not report sensitive data to the other camp they will usually feel a license to go beyond simply repeating what a party says, to interpret its underlying message and intentions. Unless instructed otherwise, a mediator should convey such information as his own impression and not attribute it to the speaker. The result resembles the way government officials sometimes float trial balloons on a "background" basis. In mediation this tactic has two advantages. First, the listener might be left a bit unsure of whether the other side is sending a signal, giving the sender leeway either to reinforce or back away from its message later. Second, the fact that the mediator is the one making the interpretation makes it appear less manipulative, and therefore less subject to reactive devaluation, than if the signal were attributed to the opposing side.

More generally, advocates should realize that the mediator may well interpret their attitude or intentions in the other room. Lawyers should think about what they wish a mediator to say about them, and state their desires to the neutral. Mediators are not bound to follow such instructions, but the chances that a neutral will do what you want are much greater if you make your wishes known.

Advocates should also consider whether to ask the mediator about the other side's state of mind. If, for instance, a plaintiff seems agitated during an opening session, defense counsel might later ask the mediator, "Has Smith calmed down?" or "If his lawyer recommends a deal, do you think he'll listen?" Alternatively, a lawyer might ask a mediator to collect specific information, such as whether the other side has retained an expert. Lawyers can also ask mediators to explore an adversary's reaction to a potential deal without disclosing their own interest in it.

Questions about what the other side is thinking pose tricky ethical and practical issues for mediators because of the paradox mentioned previously, but that does not mean that counsel should not ask them. Lawyers should be aware, however, that if they ask a neutral for information about their opponent, the neutral may interpret this as permission to provide the other side with the same kind of data about the questioner. As in direct bargaining, in other words, information exchange is a two-way street. That does not mean, however, that asking questions is not helpful, and mediation can amplify the effectiveness of doing so.

To take advantage of the mediator's ability to gather and convey information during the caucusing process:

- Ask the mediator about the other side's attitude and intentions.
- Discuss with the mediator what he will say to your opponent about you.
- Use the mediator as a sounding board for how a potential offer might be received.

Problem 2

You are in the late afternoon of a mediation of a dispute over a large software contract; your client, the buyer of the software, experienced serious business problems because it was defective, and sued for nearly $10 million in out-of-pocket damages and lost profits. You and your client have become frustrated with the slow pace of the bargaining and the defendant's lack of realism. You began with an offer of $5 million, to which the defendant offered $200,000. Your most recent proposal was $2.75 million, with a final "bottom-line" target of $1.9 million. The defense has been inching up, their last move being only from $650,000 to $700,000.

In a private conversation while the mediator is out of the room, your client tells you that he is willing to drop to $2.5 million, but that unless the defendant's next offer "hits seven figures" (i.e., $1 million), he's inclined to pack up and leave. How might the mediator help you? What should you and/or your client say to the neutral?

Assume that the mediator comes back 30 minutes later with a defense offer of $900,000. What should you do now?

Take Advantage of a Mediator's Neutrality

As we have seen, mediators have a key advantage not available to even the best advocate: the simple fact that they are seen as neutral. The phenomenon of reactive devaluation makes humans instinctively suspect anything proposed by an opponent, but mediators can deliver bargainers from at least some of its impact. Take, for example, a situation in which a defendant is stubbornly clinging to an offer of $75,000. The mediator could say to the plaintiff, "You know, I think that if we could ever get them up to $100,000, it would be worth serious consideration. What do you think?" By phrasing the issue in this way, the neutral has done two things. First, she has presented the offer as hypothetical — it is not yet "cursed" by the fact that the defendant is actually willing to make it.

Second, she has tentatively endorsed its reasonableness. If the plaintiff buys into the potential offer, the mediator will have partially "inoculated" it against being devalued if it materializes. Good lawyers instinctively work to take advantage of the advantages conferred by the mediator's neutral status.

Example: In the filmed experiment described earlier, defense counsel's initial response to a high cash demand was to propose that his client provide the plaintiff with future products at a discounted price, but no actual cash. As he made this offer the lawyer was being imaginative, but he also was offering no money so as to deflate the plaintiff's expectations.

Mediator: I've told you that the plaintiff is willing to move significantly from their opening demand. This isn't just the mediator reading tea leaves — they gave me explicit permission to tell you that. . . . But if I go back now and say, "They're willing to give you a discount but . . . *that's it*," we will have a big problem and a short afternoon, I think. . . . But I could be wrong.

Outside counsel: David, we need you to be more . . . *creative* than that. I'm confident that you would say to them that you decided after talking to us that it wasn't fruitful to talk in terms of how many dollars we would give them to settle — that *you* came up with the suggestion for a discount program. . . .

In this instance defense counsel was not able to persuade the mediator to assume authorship of the proposal; the neutral was appropriately concerned that he would seriously damage his credibility if he endorsed an offer that the plaintiff saw as unfair. But the lawyer was not bashful about asking, and in the end he got an excellent result for his client.

Take advantage of a mediator's perceived neutrality by:

- Asking a mediator to deliver unwelcome information to the other side.
- Suggesting that a mediator offer your proposal or argument as his own.
- Requesting the mediator to certify the fairness of a proposal.

Use a Mediator to Carry Out Uncomfortable Tasks

Mediators are freer to use unorthodox tactics to solve bargaining impasses because they needn't worry about maintaining a judge's reserve or showing a litigator's resolve. Attorneys can take advantage of this by asking mediators to take on unconventional tasks.

Example: Two brothers were fighting over the business empire of their deceased uncle. Following years of inconclusive court proceedings, the two agreed to mediate. The parties went through a difficult first day, in part because the mediator encountered ambivalence from the plaintiff. He would make a decision, but then backpedal after the neutral left the room. The defendant's lawyer became angry over this, and the mediator hinted at what was happening.

Defense counsel told the mediator that the plaintiff couldn't decide anything without talking to his wife, and was calling her while the mediator was out of the room. The wife was not at mediation; to alleviate the family's dire financial situation she had taken a job as a bookkeeper at a local store. "Why don't you go talk to her before we meet tomorrow?" the lawyer suggested. With the assent of the plaintiff's attorney, the mediator agreed.

Early the next morning the neutral drove out to the store, walked down to the basement, and amid boxes of auto parts sat down to talk with the plaintiff's wife. After listening to a tearful story of betrayal and sacrifice, he suggested that she accompany him to the mediation — it was her family's future that was being discussed, after all. She agreed, and rode with the mediator to the mediation site. In the ensuing hours the wife proved to be more decisive than her husband, and also better with numbers. The case settled, but absent an outside-the-box suggestion from counsel and a mediator's freedom to respond to it, the process would almost certainly have foundered.

Mediators can take on a wide variety of roles to support a settlement process. They might counsel a distraught litigant, deliver a "hard sell" to a stubborn executive, or act as scapegoat for a difficult compromise. If a mediator does not see the need or seems reluctant to take on an unusual role to promote settlement, counsel should take the initiative to ask the neutral to do so.

Questions

3. Is there any reason that you as an advocate would feel reluctant to ask a mediator to take the kinds of initiatives described previously?
4. What kind of background would make a neutral more likely to agree to take such initiatives? Less open to doing so?

b.   Impasse-Breaking Techniques

Each of the techniques described so far can help an advocate achieve more than is possible in direct negotiation. Suppose, however, that despite your best efforts the bargaining process hits an impasse because of a process issue such as lack of authority, psychological factors such as loss aversion, merits-based problems like misevaluation of the likelihood of winning in court, or some other barrier. How can you use mediation to overcome the problem?

Impasses occur most frequently when negotiators focus narrowly on monetary solutions, but they are possible even during interest-based bargaining. Two parties might agree, for example, that it would be desirable to restore their business relationship, but reach a stalemate in allocating the costs and rewards of the new arrangement. When an impasse does occur, advocates can often take advantage of a mediator's assistance to resolve it. In some instances, however, a lawyer may have to bargain with a mediator over what the neutral will do and how.

Ask the Mediator for Advice

The first suggestion is simple: Ask the mediator for a suggestion about what to do. Mediators have seen many settlement processes. More important, they have had a unique opportunity to observe and talk with both sides. As the process goes on they often acquire a great deal of information about each party's state of mind, approach to bargaining, and priorities for settlement. A mediator will not help one side obtain an advantage over another, and commercial mediators do have an interest in seeing each side compromise as much as possible. But they do share some goals with you and your client. If the negotiation process bogs down, consider asking the mediator for advice about how to restart it.

You can also use a mediator to educate an unsophisticated or emotional client, or to present difficult truths to either or both sides about what is achievable. Possible questions include the following:

- What seems to be the obstacle here? What can we do to resolve it?
- Would a gesture toward the other side help? What would be most effective?
- Is a new combination of terms likely to get a positive response?
- Are other process options available?

Retry an Earlier Step

Many of the interventions discussed in Chapter 10 — reframing, drawing out difficult emotions, assessing the merits, and so on — can be useful at the end of the process as well as at earlier stages. The concept of returning to a tactic may seem strange — after all, if a particular approach wasn't successful when the participants were fresh, why should it be productive when everyone is tired and frustrated?

Necessity, however, can be the mother of invention, in mediation as elsewhere. For example, would a renewed focus on interests produce movement? Does a review of disputed facts appear capable of helping? A party who rejected an option early in the process might become more open to advice as time goes on. The fact that a particular step has been taken earlier in the process, either with or without success, does not mean that it cannot be used again.

Arrange a Discussion Among a Subset of Participants

A variant of retrying a prior technique is to go to a different format. You will recall, for example, that in the "hundred-million-dollar offer" case, the same lawyer who, during the opening session, had flatly refused to discuss issues with the defendant's CEO later asked to talk with him privately, and by doing so resolved the case. In the "$30,000 coin-toss" mediation, defense counsel asked the mediator to arrange for his client to meet the plaintiff's executive, leading to a solution.

Most common is for a person on one team to talk with his counterpart on the other side: lawyers with lawyers, VPs with VPs, experts with experts, and so on. Such discussions can produce genuine insights. Even when this does not occur, however, a new exchange could provide a party with an excuse — a "fig leaf" one might say — to take a step it knows is necessary to revive the process. If nothing else, by demanding even an inconclusive meeting, a bargainer sends the signal that further concessions will not be obtained easily.

Make a Hypothetical Offer

Counsel who will not make a unilateral concession will sometimes authorize a mediator to make an offer in a hypothetical, "if . . . then," format. The goal can be to test the waters, probe the other side's flexibility, or ensure that a potential move will be reciprocated. For instance, a lawyer might say to a mediator, "Given the other side's refusal to go below 250, I cannot see us getting above 100. However, you can tell them that you personally think you could get us to 125 if they would respond by breaking 200."

The hypothetical formula gains added impact if it is presented as a final resolution of the case rather than simply as a new move. By proposing an actual settlement, bargainers take advantage of the fact that disputants will often make a special effort if they can achieve complete peace — the "certainty effect" described in Chapter 10. You might say, "You can tell them that if they could get to 750, you have some optimism that you could convince my client to go there — but only if it would settle the case, once and for all." Hypothetical offers can sometimes short-circuit impasses caused by positional bargaining.

Ask the Mediator to Intervene

If these steps are not effective, another option is to ask a mediator to intervene directly, as described below. Good mediators will delay doing so for as long as possible, knowing that disputants could be alienated by a perception that the neutral is "taking over," or perhaps because the mediator sees intervening as inconsistent with his role. Still, many commercial mediators are prepared to intervene actively in a case if the bargaining process appears to be seriously stalled. If you prefer that a mediator maintain a restrained role in the face of impasse, make that preference known to the neutral. Alternatively, if you want the neutral to become more active, say that.

Next we discuss three interventions used by mediators to resolve impasses — confidential listener, evaluation of the merits, and the mediator's proposal. We also suggest ways in which lawyers can use each tactic to advantage.

Ask for "Confidential Listener"

Sometimes each side in mediation refuses to move to a reasonable position until its adversary has done so. The result is an "After you . . . No, after you" situation in which both sides remain stuck, but each would be willing to compromise if the other did so. In response a mediator may offer to play "confidential listener." This involves asking each side to disclose to the neutral privately how far it would go to settle the case. The mediator can then make a judgment about the real gap between the parties.

Often mediators will then give the lawyers a verbal statement of how far apart they are ("You are quite close — it's really worth making another effort," or "You are far apart, but the difference is less than it would cost to try this case.") The mediator's characterization is intentionally ambiguous and verbal, to preserve the confidentiality of what each side has said. However, each lawyer, knowing what he or she has told the mediator, is able to process the words and make a rough estimate of how apart the parties really are.

The first question about the confidential listener technique is whether you wish the mediator to use it. If so, suggest it; if not, ask the neutral to hold off. Sophisticated lawyers sometimes ask, for example, that a mediator delay doing so and that the parties continue to exchange offers. The next question is how to use the technique to best effect. Lawyers should realize that at this point they are in a three-sided negotiation with their opponent and the mediator. The neutral is not on anyone's side: His goal is simply to obtain a settlement.

What should an advocate tell a mediator who is playing confidential listener? Unless you are in a situation in which a mediator states explicitly that he wants each side's true bottom-line number *and* you believe that he really means it — that unless the parties' positions either touch or come very close, the mediator will terminate the mediation — it is not wise to give your client's actual bottom line. Doing so will place you at a disadvantage in the next stage of the process in which the parties continue to bargain, and might lead your client to dig prematurely into an unrealistic position. For these reasons, experienced mediators often avoid asking litigants for bottom-line numbers at all.

For a competitive bargainer, the challenge in the confidential listener process is to make an offer extreme enough to set up a favorable compromise, but realistic enough to motivate the other participants to continue. A principled bargainer, by contrast, will gravitate toward a proposal that is solidly based on neutral criteria, but also leaves them room to move. A cooperative bargainer will be inclined to answer the mediator honestly and consult about steps to keep the process alive. Parties can couple a response with an indication of intention for the mediator's private information ("Our number is $100,000. That's as far as we're willing to go at this point. Let's see what they come back with.").

One final point: If a neutral does ask for your "bottom line," how should you respond? If you are cooperative and fully trust the neutral, you can answer with complete candor. In other situations, you might want to adopt this response, suggested by a litigator:

> Based on what we currently know about the case and taking into account the arguments, we believe that the offer we have made is the best we could make. Obviously,

we would like to pay less and [they] would like to receive more, but what we might like is not the issue. If you can give me a principled reason why my client should consider paying more, we will consider it; otherwise, we don't believe that any further adjustments are warranted.

[By this response,] you are conveying at least two messages. First, you are flexible. Second, your flexibility is based on principle — meaning the value of the case — not demands, extortion or other extraneous factors. With this response, you have left the door open for dialogue and you have moved the dialogue to the plane of principle rather than petulance. (Stern, 1998)

Ask for an Evaluation

If shuttle diplomacy fails, litigators often ask mediators to evaluate the legal merits of the case. As we have indicated, evaluation is a somewhat controversial technique but one that most lawyers surveyed think can be useful in commercial mediation. The value of an evaluation is not simply in changing opponents' minds, but also those of clients. Whenever, for example, an advocate stops a mediator in the hall and suggests that she give the client her "thoughts" about a case, the neutral knows that she is being enlisted in the difficult task of client education.

Evaluations usually focus on the legal issues in the case — who is likely to prevail in court, what the damages are likely to be, and similar issues. It is possible, however, to have a mediator evaluate broader issues as well. If, for example, a disputant is suspicious that its adversary will not carry out a proposed settlement, the mediator could offer an assessment of that risk, based on what he has observed about the opponent and his experience with other settlements.

Before requesting a mediator's evaluation on a legal issue ask yourself two basic questions. First, is the primary obstacle to settling this case really a disagreement about the outcome in court, or another issue evaluation can address? If the real barrier is something else, evaluation will not be effective. Second, if the mediator does evaluate the merits, are you confident that the result will be helpful — that you will get the opinion you want?

Once you decide to seek an evaluation, the next issue is how to structure it. The first question is what data the mediator will consider. Bear in mind that a mediator's views about a case are usually based on the briefs and documents she sees, augmented by personal observations of people at the mediation. As was mentioned earlier, this means that information presented directly to the neutral has a "primacy" effect and witnesses or evidence that the neutral only hears about tend to be "melded," that is, treated as if they were a typical member of a category of people — an electrician, for example, or police officer.

As a result, if you want a mediator to give full weight to a witness or a piece of evidence, you should show it directly to the neutral. In a construction case, for example, you might ask the mediator to visit the site, or in a commercial case have the mediator meet a key witness. Again, bear in mind that in mediation, unlike a court proceeding, you can arrange for the neutral to see evidence without having to make it available to your opponent.

Take care to ensure that the mediator takes time to give your evidence adequate consideration. Don't assume, for example, that he will read every document you give him. Mediators often receive thick piles of paper in advance, and must review them without knowing what may turn out to be relevant. A neutral who is busy or concerned about keeping costs down is likely to skim through voluminous materials and wait for the parties to tell him what is important. Once the process begins, however, mediators are often reluctant to take long breaks for fear of losing momentum.

If you have documents that are important to a mediator's evaluation, tell him what, specifically, you want him to focus on, provide highlighted copies of key passages, and ask him to examine the evidence before opining. A mediator assisted in this way is less likely to jump to an erroneous conclusion with which you will then be stuck.

A second crucial question is what, exactly, you want evaluated. Don't simply say "the case." Ten years ago mediators routinely provided global opinions about the likely outcome if a dispute were adjudicated. Increasingly, however, mediators think of evaluation as a means to jump-start a stalled negotiation — more like filling a "pothole" in which the "settlement bus" has gotten stuck, than building a road to a predetermined destination. Often a prediction limited to a single issue is enough to put the parties back on the path to settlement. The question, then, is this: What aspect of the case do you want evaluated?

As discussed in Chapter 10, you should not expect every evaluation to take the form of an explicit opinion. Good mediators see evaluation as a spectrum of interventions rather than a single event. They rely on pointed questions, raised eyebrows, and other "shadow" techniques much more than explicit statements to nudge negotiations back on track. When an advocate hears a mediator make such comments, he should realize that the evaluation process is under way, but in a form less likely to provoke resentment than an explicit conclusion. Again, your chances of getting the level of specificity you want are much higher if you ask for it.

If There Is No Agreement, Ask the Mediator to Continue

If a case does not settle at the mediation session, what should an advocate do? One option is to keep trying. If your mediator loses heart, you might have to prompt him to continue. Consider this anecdote related by mediator Benjamin Picker:

Example: An inventor sued a company for patent infringement. The company hired a large law firm to represent it. It was aware, however, that litigation costs in such a case could easily exceed $1 million, and in the meantime its business strategy would be in limbo. The company therefore decided to explore settlement, and it designated a separate lawyer in the firm as "settlement counsel," responsible for seeking an agreement while his colleagues focused on litigating. The lawyer suggested early mediation. The plaintiff agreed, and the parties selected a retired judge as mediator.

At the end of the first day of mediation, notwithstanding a defense offer of several million dollars, the mediator indicated that the parties were far apart and recommended that the process end. The settlement counsel suggested, however, that the mediator instead ask the plaintiff to think about how he would spend the millions of dollars that were on the table, and adjourn the process for a week. The hope was that loss aversion would set in, making the plaintiff reluctant to risk money that was already "his." At the second session, the defense sweetened its offer slightly and the parties reached agreement.

Questions

5. Parties are mediating a dispute concerning the amount due from a commercial real estate developer to a building contractor under a "cost-plus" contract. You represent the developer. The contract provides that the contractor will be reimbursed for its reasonable costs plus a 10 percent profit. The project is complete and all issues have been resolved except one: The contractor has demanded that the developer pay for the cost of benefits in a tax-sheltered retirement plan accrued by the contractor's employees while they were working on the project. Your client believes that the contract, which is silent on the issue, does not call for reimbursement of employee expenses other than wages and usual fringe benefits such as medical care.

The mediation proceeds through an opening session and a lengthy series of caucuses. The law and facts relevant to the issue are exhaustively discussed, but the parties continue to disagree about the merits. You privately evaluate the likely outcome in court at a $650,000 verdict for the contractor, with a potential high of $1 million and a low of zero. You expect the future defense costs in the case to be roughly $75,000. Your client is reluctantly prepared to offer up to $600,000, and if absolutely necessary would go to $700,000. He has no interest in working with this contractor again.

During the afternoon the process gradually focuses on exchanges of money offers. The offers are as follows:

Contractor's demand:	Developer's offer:
$1.5 million	$100,000
$1.3 million	$100,000
$1.25 million	$250,000
$1.2 million (with difficulty)	$275,000
Remains at $1.2 million	Defendant refuses to "bid against myself."

     a.   Assuming that the only term at issue is money, what should you do next on behalf of the developer?

     b.   Suppose that your client sees a possibility of using the contractor to do approximately $200,000 worth of work on another property. What process would you recommend?

6.   You represent the plaintiff in an employment dispute. It is 5 p.m. and you have been mediating for nearly eight hours. You began with a demand of $1.5 million, and in response the defendant offered $25,000. After laborious bargaining, you have dropped to $400,000. You need at least $350,000 in a cash settlement, but could conceivably go to $200,000 if your client were offered a good job back at the company. Unfortunately, the defendant is at only $100,000, having moved there from a prior offer of $85,000. Your client is feeling very frustrated and has told the mediator this. The mediator has gone back to the defense and returned.

     a.   Assume that the defendant suggests that the mediator play "confidential listener" and you agree. What should you tell the mediator?

     b.   Assume instead that the defense suggests a "mediator's proposal." Should you agree?

If Negotiations Fail

Sometimes settlement is genuinely unachievable. Even in such situations a mediator can be of use by helping disputants to design an efficient process of adjudication, for example, by facilitating negotiations over a discovery plan or brokering an agreement on an expedited form of arbitration. To take advantage of mediation even when settlement is not possible:

- Ask the mediator to contact the parties periodically to urge further negotiations.
- Ask the mediator to facilitate agreement on an efficient process of adjudication.

How should an advocate leave an unsuccessful mediation process? A litigator offers the following advice:

> At some point, hours or days after you have started, the mediation process will end. If it ends with an agreement, that is fine. But if you can't reach agreement, accept that as well. Parties and lawyers often get desperate as the mediation nears conclusion, but the dispute remains unsettled. It is possible, but exceedingly unlikely, that the mediation is the last chance to settle the case. More likely, there

will be multiple opportunities — at deposition, at court-ordered settlement conferences, before trial, during trial, even after trial and appeal — to settle. As such, do not despair or let your client despair if you walk away without a deal. Not all cases should be settled, and almost none should be settled on any available terms. Most will eventually settle one way or another, so if you can't settle at the mediation, ask yourself what benefits you can achieve before you part ways.

Occasionally, you can agree to keep talking. Sometimes that dialogue will depend on one side or the other developing more information. Or it might depend on how well a witness does at a deposition or whether a particular motion is granted or denied. Search for partial agreements if feasible or part company respectfully so that the possibility of future negotiation remains open. In all likelihood, settlement will eventually occur and both you and your client will benefit if you keep that probability in mind.

Attorneys too often treat the mediation process simply as a safe place in which to conduct positional bargaining and mediators as mere messengers, trading arguments and offers until they reach impasse. At that point the mediator often takes over the process by making a settlement recommendation or offering an evaluation.

We hope you appreciate that whatever approach you take to bargaining, the mediation process has a great deal to offer. Lawyers who approach mediation actively, looking at a mediator as a consultant, resource, and potential ally, use the process to best effect and obtain optimal outcomes for their clients.

CHAPTER
13

Specific Applications

Mediation is used in a wide variety of subject areas. From its traditional roots in family, union, and construction disputes, it has expanded to employment, environmental, high-tech, and even criminal cases. The application of mediation to specialized fields raises issues of process design, and also poses the question of whether the process is appropriate for every kind of dispute. We explore these issues here. There is a rich literature on the use of mediation in each subject area, and we invite you to read more on applications of particular interest to you.

A. Family Disputes

1. What Is Unique About Family Mediation?

Family disputes involve several factors that make them different from other civil cases. Among them are the following.

Intense Emotions

Marriage is perhaps the most intimate relationship that human beings can enter. People often define themselves around being a husband or wife, and divorce thus strikes at the very heart of their sense of identity and self-worth. This is likely to provoke feelings more intense than those found in almost any other kind of conflict. Marital discord can also trigger deep and sometimes irrational emotions that stem from each spouse's own childhood.

Continuing Relationships

Ordinarily when people fall into disagreement, they have the option to separate. If a couple has children, they usually cannot completely dissociate even when they divorce, however. Instead ex-spouses remain connected in their roles as parents, often for many years. Divorced parents must find ways to share their children's physical presence, financial responsibility, teaching, socializing, and a variety of other tasks. People often find it difficult to cooperate on these issues even when they are happily married. If both parties seek custody, or if a spouse decides to use the children as a weapon in marital conflict, difficulties will multiply.

Impact on, and Participation by, Children

While children are young they are completely dependent on parental decisions about their upbringing. This raises a concern that a spouse who is desperate to escape a marriage or simply not thinking clearly may sacrifice a child's best interests to his or her own wishes. For teenagers, a different problem arises. Older children often have strong wishes about where they want to live and how to lead their lives, and can become third-party actors in disputes over custody and visitation, rejecting agreements worked out by parents and complicating the process of settlement.

Potential for Physical or Emotional Abuse

In domestic conflicts, unlike most civil disputes, there is a real possibility that criminal acts will occur, in the form of physical or emotional abuse. Even when victims do not complain, society has a strong interest in preventing such acts or an abused spouse from giving away rights. This issue is especially acute in states that require couples to engage in mediation as a precondition to gaining access to a court, an issue discussed in Chapters 14 and 15.

Lack of Legal Counsel

Despite the fact that family disputes involve some of people's most basic rights, divorcing spouses are less likely than most litigants to obtain legal advice. Businesses typically have resources to obtain counsel, and in personal injury cases contingent fees or insurance can provide parties with access to lawyers. Family disputes, however, involve disagreements between individuals who often have no means to pay legal costs. This creates a serious risk that participants in family mediation will not get good advice, making it difficult for them to negotiate effectively and putting mediators in an awkward position.

Although there can be problems with the use of mediation in family cases, the consequences of litigating such disputes can be worse. Legal proceedings are often deeply destructive, creating rather than healing emotional scars and exhausting a family's financial resources at the very time its expenses are increasing. Legal battles over custody and visitation, in particular, often have a severe impact on children.

For these reasons, family disputes were among the first cases to be mediated. Most states now mandate that disputes over child custody or visitation go through mediation before entering a courtroom.

We have seen that the process of family mediation differs from traditional civil or commercial mediation in several respects. First, the parties generally remain together throughout rather than separating into caucuses, and mediation occurs in multiple sessions spread over weeks or months. Attorneys are ordinarily not present, although the parties may consult a lawyer between sessions. Because many couples have issues regarding children, there is more need for the process to be interest based and future oriented. Finally, perhaps due to the strong emotional issues present in such cases, most family mediators have in the past been mental health professionals.

2. *Policy Issues*

The very elements that make divorce mediation so appealing compared to the adversarial model also create dangers and raise serious policy issues. Because mediation distinguishes itself as an approach that recognizes divorce and family disputes as both matters of the heart and of the law, there exist issues of how emotional feelings are to be weighed against and blended with legal rights and obligations and what are appropriate subjects for mediation. Because mediation is conducted in private and is less hemmed in by rules of procedure, substantive law, and precedent, questions arise of whether the process is fair and the terms of a mediated agreement are just. This concern for a fair and just result has particular applicability to custody and child support provisions because mediated bargaining occurs between parents, and children are rarely present or independently represented during mediation.

Because mediation represents an "alternative" to the adversarial system, it lacks the precise and perfected checks and balances that are the principal benefit of the adversary process. The purposeful "a-legal" character of mediation creates a constant risk of overreaching and dominance by the more knowledgeable, powerful, or less emotional party. Some argue that the a-legal character of divorce mediation requires all the more careful court scrutiny before mediated agreements are approved and incorporated into a judicial decree. Others argue against court review of mediated agreements. They reason that if the parties have utilized mediation to reach agreement, there is no need for the expense, delay, and imposition of a judge's values — all features of the judicial review process. Questions about the enforceability of agreements to mediate as well as the enforceability of mediated agreements have not been fully answered.

Fairness

In considering whether mediated settlements will be fair and just, we must ask "compared to what"? We know that the great majority of divorce cases currently go by default. The default may be a result of ignorance, guilt, or a total sense of powerlessness. The default could also be a result of an agreement between the parties on distributional questions, eliminating the need for an appearance. The question persists in our present dispute resolution system of whether such agreements are the result of unequal bargaining power due to different levels of experience, patterns of dominance, the greater emotional need of one divorcing party to get out of the marriage, or a greater desire on the part of one of the parties to avoid the expense and uncertainty of litigation.

The current adversarial approach does not require the adverse parties to be represented, nor does it impose a mediator or "audience" to point out imbalances and assure that they are recognized by the parties, as mediation should attempt to do. Pro se divorce, in which there need be no professional intervention prior to court review, is increasingly popular and sanctioned by our existing system. Mediation, at least, provides a knowledgeable third party to help the couple evaluate their relative positions so that they can make reasoned decisions.

The most common pattern of legal representation in divorce is for one party to retain an attorney for advice and preparation of the documents. The other party will often negotiate directly with the moving party's attorney or retain an attorney to do so without filing an appearance. If a second attorney has not been retained, the unrepresented party will often consult with an attorney to determine whether the proposed settlement is "fair enough" not to contest and if all necessary items have been covered or discussed. The reviewing attorney serves as a check, informing the client of any other options to the suggested terms and whether the points of agreement fall within an acceptable range of legal norms. The likelihood of a different court outcome than the proposed agreement is weighed against the financial, time, and emotional expenses of further negotiation or litigation.

A similar pattern of independent legal consultation could, and should, be utilized for review of mediated agreements. Current mediation practice, influenced by ethical restraints, is to urge or require that each divorcing party seek independent legal counsel to review the proposed agreement before it is signed. Although the criteria for independent attorney review of a proposed mediated agreement are not clear, the purpose of the review is no less clear than it is under present "fair enough" practice. The initial mediated agreement is formed in a cooperative environment with the assistance of a neutral person who serves as a check against intimidation and overreaching. Independent legal review by an attorney for one spouse pursuant to a "fair enough" standard would assure at least as great a fairness safeguard as the common reality of our present adversary system. When both parties to the mediation obtain independent legal review, as they should be encouraged to do, there is a double-check of what is fair enough. In some complex cases, other professional review, such as that of a certified public accountant, may be necessary.

Protection of Children

When divorce involves minor children, some argue that the state has a responsibility beyond encouraging the speedy, private settlement of disputes between parents. The state, however, under the well-developed doctrine of parens patriae, has a responsibility for the welfare of children only when parents cannot agree or cannot adequately provide for them. Divorce mediation begins with the premise that parents love their children and are best able to decide how, within their resources, they will care for them.

A mediated agreement is much more likely than a judicial decision to match the parents' capacity and desires with the child's needs. Whether the parents' decision is the result of reasoned analysis or is influenced by depression, guilt, spite, or selfishness, it is usually preferable to an imposed decision that may impede cooperation and stability for the child. In any event, a resolution negotiated by attorneys or reviewed by or litigated before a court is no more likely than a mediated settlement to disclose which outcomes are the result of depression, spite, guilt, or selfishness.

The principal protection that a mediator can offer a child in the context of divorce is to ensure that the parents consider all factors that can be developed between them relative to the child's needs and their abilities to meet those needs. The mediator should be prepared to ask probing and difficult questions and to help inform the parents of available alternatives. The mediator's ethical commitment, however, is to the process of parental self-determination, not to any given outcome.

The Continuing Role of Courts and Attorneys

Increased use of divorce mediation does not remove the courts from the divorce process and would not entirely eliminate adversarial proceedings. We know that some cases cannot be settled or mediated. There must be a fair and credible forum with procedural safeguards and rules to assure the peaceful resolution of disputes for parties who are unable to recognize the benefits that may come from a less coercive process. The threat of court litigation, with all of the human and material expense that it requires, might be the very element that will help some parties cut through their egocentric near-sightedness to see that their self-interests, as well as the interest of the family, may be promoted through mediation rather than a court fight.

To conclude, divorce mediation has been touted as a replacement for the adversary system and a way of making divorce less painful. Although it should be available as an alternative for those who choose to use it, it is not a panacea that will create love where there is hate, or totally eliminate the role of the adversary system in divorce. It may, however, reduce acrimony and postdivorce litigation by promoting cooperation. It might also lessen the burden of the courts in deciding many cases that can be diverted to less hostile and less costly procedures (see Folberg et al., 2004).

3.   An Alternative Process: Transformative Mediation

Chapter 9 described a different kind of mediative process, known as "transformative" mediation, which does not seek to settle disputes but is focused instead on creating a setting in which participants can, if they wish, change the way in which they view themselves and others in the dispute. The following reading describes how transformative techniques are used in divorce and family disputes.

❖ **Robert A. Baruch Bush and Sally Ganong Pope,** TRANSFORMATIVE
     MEDIATION PRINCIPLES AND PRACTICES IN DIVORCE MEDIATION

Divorce and Family Mediation 53 (Folberg et al. eds., 2004)

Why do parties come to divorce mediators, and what is it that mediators can do to best serve them? The parties themselves, as they enter mediation, give varied reasons for their choice, but most fall into the following categories. Saving money and time and avoiding the legal system are at the top of most lists. Reducing hostility and conflict for their own sake and the sake of their children, and developing effective parenting plans, are also important. One party may be more interested in the time-savings and the other in protection of the children. Most all, however, agree that staying out of the legal system is essential. Certainly, with few exceptions, all hope to achieve a fair divorce settlement. . . .

How then are we to understand the "why" of divorce mediation? In our view, all of the above descriptions of clients' goals express their desire to experience a different form of conflict interaction than they have experienced in their private negotiations and than they believe they would find in the legal system. . . . Rather, they want to come out of the process feeling better about themselves and each other. . . .

This conclusion is the result of insights from the fields of communication, developmental psychology and social psychology, among others. According to that view — what we call "transformative" theory — conflict is about peoples' interaction with one another as human beings. It is not primarily about problem-solving, about satisfaction of needs and interests. Certainly there are problems to be solved at the end of a marriage — the assets to be divided, the parenting plan to be created — and certainly parties want to solve those problems. The reality is, however, that they want to do so in a way that enhances their sense of their own competence and autonomy without taking advantage of the other. They want to feel proud of themselves for how they handled this life crisis, and this means making changes in the difficult conflict interaction that is going on between them, rather than simply coming up with the "right" answers to the specific problems.

. . . When we study perceptions of and attitudes towards conflict, we find that what most people find hardest about conflict is not that it frustrates their satisfaction of some interest or project, no matter how important, but rather that it leads and even forces them to behave toward themselves and others in ways that they find uncomfortable and even repellent.... Before the conflict, there is some decent human interaction going on, whatever the context — between people in a family, a workplace, a community. Even divorcing couples were once engaged in some form of decent, even loving, human interaction. Then the conflict arises and, propelled by the vicious circle of disempowerment and demonization, what started as a decent inter-action spirals down into one which is negative, destructive, alienating, and demonizing, on all sides....

Given this view of what conflict entails and "means" to parties, where does conflict intervention come into the picture? In particular, what are divorcing couples looking for when they seek the services of a mediator? One funda-mental premise of the transformative model is that what bothers parties most about conflict is the interactional degeneration itself, and therefore what they most want from an intervene — even more than help in resolving specific issue — is help in reversing the downward spiral and restoring a more humane quality to their interaction....

But how do parties in conflict reverse the destructive conflict spi-ral?... The first part of an answer to this question is that the critical resource is the parties' own basic humanity: their essential strength, and their essen-tial decency and compassion, as human beings.... They move from weak-ness to strength, becoming (in more specific terms) calmer, clearer, more confident, more articulate and more decisive. They shift from self-absorption to responsiveness, becoming more attentive, open, trusting, and more responsive toward the other party.... [T]hese dynamic shifts are called "Empowerment" and "Recognition." Moreover, there is also a reinforcing feedback effect... The stronger I become the more open I am to you. The more open I am to you, the stronger you feel, the more open you become to me, and the stronger I feel.... Why "conflict transformation"? Because as the parties make empowerment and recognition shifts, and as those shifts gradually reinforce in a virtuous circle, the interaction as a whole begins to turn the corner and regenerate....

What divorcing parties want from mediators, and what mediators can in fact provide — with proper focus and skills — is help and support for these small but critical shifts by each party.... The mediator's primary goals are: (1) to foster Empowerment shifts, by supporting but never supplanting each party's deliberation and decision-making, at every point in the session where choices arise (regarding process or outcome); and (2) to foster Recognition shifts, by encouraging and supporting but never forcing each party's freely chosen efforts to achieve new understandings of the other's perspective.

The transformative model does not ignore the significance of resolving specific issues; but it assumes that if mediators do the job just described, the parties themselves will very likely make positive changes in their interaction and, as a result, find acceptable terms of resolution for themselves where such terms genuinely exist.... The transformative model posits that this is the greatest value mediation offers to families in conflict: it can help people conduct conflict itself in a different way. . . .

This is what we have learned from the parties that we have worked with and studied over all these years. . . . The promise mediation offers is real . . . because wise mediators can support the parties' own work, create a space for that work to go on, and — most important — stay out of the parties' way. . . .

Translating Theory into Practice: How Does the Transformative Mediator Work?

. . . *Essential Skills: Avoiding Directive Responses.* The mediator "follows" or accompanies the parties. . . . The transformative mediator is not the director of the discussion. . . . He trusts the parties. He has confidence in them — that they know best — that they know what is right for themselves and their children. He will not attempt to substitute his judgment for theirs. He will not try to steer them in the direction of what he thinks is the best arrangement for them and their children. He will not decide what is fair for them. He respects and trusts the parties to make those decisions. The mediator is not trying "to get the parties to do anything." He is not trying to "get them" to talk to each other, to stop arguments for the sake of the children, or to stay out of court. . . . Probing for the "real, underlying issues" is leading, directive, and disrespectful of the party choice about what to talk about. Following the parties in their discussion will highlight all of the issues the parties choose to put out on the table. . . .

The skills employed by the transformative divorce mediator are simple to describe: listening, reflection, summarizing, questions used to open doors, to invite further discussion on a subject raised by the parties, and to "check in" on what the parties want to do at a choice point in the discussion. . . . They are difficult to employ. It is much easier to allow our directive impulses and positive goals for the parties to steer us into leading and guiding the discussion and, therefore, the outcomes. It is much more difficult to stay with the parties through their cycles of conversation as they develop strength and understanding and become clear about what they want to do. . . .

Questions

1. What do you think are the primary risks to parties in mediating family disputes? Are risks larger in disputes in certain subject areas or involving particular types of litigants?
2. Would you impose any special conditions on mediation of family disputes?
3. In answering the preceding questions, would you distinguish between private mediation, in which parties or lawyers opt for mediation, and court-connected mediation, in which parties may be compelled to engage in mediation by a judge or court rule?

B. Employment Cases

One of the fastest growing areas of mediation practice is employment disputes. These range from contract claims by terminated executives to discrimination charges lodged by hourly employees. In the reading that
follows, practicing mediators analyze the special issues likely to arise in such
cases.

❖ **Carol A. Wittenberg, Susan T. Mackenzie, and
Margaret L. Shaw, EMPLOYMENT DISPUTES**

in D. Golann, Mediating Legal Disputes 279 (2009)

The use of mediation to resolve employment disputes is on the rise. Increasingly, federal district courts are referring discrimination cases to mediation,
and similarly administrative agencies charged with enforcing anti-
discrimination laws are experimenting with mediation programs. Mediation is well-suited to resolving employment disputes for a number of
reasons.

Special Issues

Emotionality

Employment disputes usually involve highly emotional issues. It is said
that loss of one's job is the third most stressful life event, next only to death
and divorce. Whether one's livelihood is at stake, as in a wrongful termination case, or the issue involves a professional relationship that has gone awry,
as in a sexual harassment claim, the dispute occurs in a charged atmosphere.
A mediator can help parties vent their anger and frustrations in a nonjudgmental setting that allows them to feel that their positions have been heard
and to move on to a more productive, problem-solving viewpoint.

One of us, for example, had the experience of being asked by a plaintiff
after several hours of mediation if a one-on-one meeting with the mediator
was possible, and counsel agreed. After telling the mediator that she
reminded her of a former boss who had been an important mentor, the
plaintiff talked about how upset the case had made her. She also talked about
how much the negotiations over dollars were leaving her feeling disassoci-
ated from the process, and from what she was personally looking to accomplish. The mediator was able to help the plaintiff identify her feelings, think
through what she really wanted out of a resolution, and work within the process to accomplish that result. The case settled shortly after their caucus.

Confidentiality

The privacy and confidentiality that mediation affords may be important
to employees and employers alike. For example, in many of the cases involving sexual harassment claims we mediate, a primary focus of claimants is to

have an unpleasant situation stop, stop quickly, and stop permanently. Individual respondents, too, unless they are looking for vindication, may want to get on with their lives and put the incident behind them. Most employees are concerned about their reputations and want their careers to continue uninterrupted. Employers, for their part, are almost always interested in confidentiality. This is particularly true in discrimination cases since publicity can affect the employer's reputation in the marketplace. Employers are also concerned that without confidentiality, settlements will create precedents or "benchmarks" for future complainants, or encourage "me-too" complaints.

Creativity of Outcomes

Mediation's creativity is particularly important in employment disputes, where the impact of the controversy can have profound effects on the parties' lives. We find that in many of the litigated disputes we mediate non-legal and non-monetary issues are barriers as significant to resolution as the financial and legal aspects of the case. For example, in one age discrimination claim we mediated, the settlement called for the employee to retain his employment status without pay for a two-year period, so as to vest certain benefits afforded retirees. In a gender discrimination case, the terms involved keeping the employee on the payroll for a period of time with a new title to assist her in securing alternative employment. In a breach of contract case involving a senior executive, part of the settlement involved a guaranteed loan to invest in a new business.

Cost Savings

Practical considerations also make mediation of employment disputes an attractive alternative to litigation. The process is likely to be much less expensive than litigation, or even arbitration. One attorney who frequently represents plaintiffs in discrimination cases observed that, as of the mid-2000s, the litigation cost of a discrimination claim to individual claimants was roughly $50,000, as compared to $2,000 to $4,000 for mediation. A study in the early 1990s estimated the cost to defend a single discrimination claim at $81,000, a figure that is now almost certainly much higher.

Note also that the monetary cost of litigation does not take into account the indirect, personal, and emotional costs to all parties of a court proceeding. All workplaces have informal information channels; we often hear from individual mediation participants about the disruptive effects of the case on fellow employees. For instance, at one company with which we worked speculation was rampant about who would be let go or reassigned in the event the case resulted in the reinstatement of a discharged employee.

Speed

Mediation is also likely to be significantly faster than litigation. This is of particular importance in the employment context, given the dramatic increase in antidiscrimination claims. In our experience, mediation of a routine employment case involving an individual claimant generally can be concluded in one or sometimes two days. Although some parties are unable to reach complete closure in the mediation sessions, often additional follow-up telephone conferences with one or both parties will bring about a settlement. An evaluation of the EEOC's pilot mediation program, for instance, showed that mediation resolved charges of discrimination less expensively and more quickly than traditional methods, with closure in an average of 67 days as opposed to 294 in the regular charge process.

Questions

Are there disadvantages to mediation in the context of employment disputes? Of course there are, although we believe that some of the "dangers" are often overemphasized. Some employers are concerned that the availability of mediation will encourage frivolous complaints. Others are concerned that mediation simply adds a layer of time and expense when a case does not settle. Certain attorneys have also expressed a concern that an opposing party might merely be using mediation as a form of discovery. There are, of course, specific cases that are inappropriate for mediation, cases that upon analysis are without any apparent merit and call for the employer to take a firm stance.

Challenges for the Mediator

There are some distinctive characteristics of employment cases that can challenge a mediator and require special approaches.

Disparity in Resources

While parties in other kinds of cases may have unequal resources, in employment disputes a lack of parity can make it difficult even to get the parties to the table. Employment claimants are often out of work, or face an uncertain employment future. They may balk at the added expense of a mediator, particularly when the outcome is uncertain. While some employers will agree to pay the entire mediation bill as an inducement to a plaintiff to participate, others are concerned that without some financial investment a plaintiff will not participate in the process wholeheartedly. In these circumstances, we have found several approaches effective. If, for example, the employer is worried about the employee's investment in the process, the mediator can explore the nature of that concern and whether verbal representations by the claimant or claimant's lawyer might allay them. As an alternative, a mediator can suggest having the employer assume most of the cost, while requiring the employee to pay something.

Timing

The timing of mediation can affect both the process and its outcome. Where it is attempted shortly after a claim has been raised, the claimant may need extra help in getting beyond feelings of anger or outrage, while an individual manager or subject of a claim may feel betrayed. If little or no discovery has occurred the lack of information about the facts on the part of one or both parties can hamper productive negotiations. At the other extreme, when a case has already been in litigation for an extended period of time, positions can become hardened and the parties even more determined to stop at nothing short of what they perceive to be "justice."

For instance, in one case we handled, an age discrimination claim referred by the court, the plaintiff's attorney had done little investigation prior to the mediation and thus was unaware of circumstances that called into question the plaintiff's integrity during his final year of employment. Assisting the attorney to become more realistic about the chances for a recovery at trial became the challenge of this mediation. In another case that involved a sexual harassment claim, outside counsel for the employer, who had recommended mediation, was unaware of some of the conduct of the individual manager who was the subject of the allegations. That case required us to mediate between the employer and the manager, the individual manager and the claimant, and the claimant and the corporate entity as well.

Imbalances of Power

In certain employment disputes, such as those involving sexual harassment claims, a perceived or real imbalance in the power relationship between the parties may itself constitute an impediment to settlement. We have found that as a general proposition, particularly in dealing with an individual who feels at a power disadvantage in mediation, movement is better accomplished by pulling rather than by pushing. For example, in one case where the facts underlying the claim were perhaps unconscionable but not legally actionable, helping the claimant to recognize the benefits of moving forward with her life was more effective than trying to convince her that she had a weak case.

When an issue of power imbalance is articulated or apparent, it is helpful to take the time to consult with the parties before the "real" mediation begins in order to structure the process. We typically discuss, for example, whether the complainant or the attorney wants to make an opening statement. We have observed that complainants who prepare a statement for the initial joint session tend to feel a degree of participation that engenders a sense of control and dignity in the process that is not otherwise possible. At times, having a family member or close friend attend a session is helpful. We also attempt to establish in advance whether will be necessary to keep the complainant and individual respondent apart at least initially. We routinely schedule pre-mediation conference calls with all persons involved in the case to work through these kinds of issues.

Desire for Revenge

Complainants who feel they have been wronged will sometimes look for a way to make the employer or the individual charged with harassing or discriminatory behavior "pay." Such a focus on revenge can present a major obstacle to settlement. There is no simple way to deal with this in mediation. Sometimes, particularly in cases where the complaint has already prompted the employer to take preventive measures, explaining the full impact that the complaint has already had on workplace policies or on the careers of others can help the complainant recognize and change to a posture more conducive to resolution. Another approach may be to have the individual respondent contribute out of his or her own pocket to a financial settlement.

Negotiation by Numbers

In some employment mediations one or both parties may become fixed on a settlement figure and refuse to budge. Finding a new framework for analysis that appears objectively fair can help parties stuck on numbers save face and ultimately agree on a different figure to settle the case.

Non-Legal and Personal Issues

At times both parties will fail to realize that a non-legal problem is the root cause of an employment dispute. For example, in one case we handled a personality conflict between the head of accounting and his most senior employee had festered for years. The working relationship between the two had deteriorated to the point that they routinely hurled racial and sexual epithets at one another. At that point, management could see no alternative to dismissing one or both of them. With the mediator's assistance, each party was able to shift focus from placing blame on the other to recognizing their mutual interest in continuing to be employed, and mutually-acceptable procedures for personal interaction in the office were identified and reduced to writing. During the mediation the parties also came to recognize that a contributing, if not overriding, cause of the deterioration of their relationship was an outstanding loan from the department head to the bookkeeper. While the department head had treated the loan as forgiven years ago, in reality the bookkeeper's failure to repay it had continued to bother the department head. The resolution between the parties included a repayment schedule for the loan.

In some employment cases, the real barrier to resolution may be an individual who is not a direct party to the dispute. For instance, in one case we mediated involving a disability claim by an airline manager it became clear that his spouse, who was also present, was so angered by what she perceived as unconscionable treatment that she urged rejection of all settlement offers as insulting. The mediator dealt with this situation by recognizing the spouse's feelings and helping her understand that her anger was fueled at least in part by resentment over the amount of time her spouse had spent on his job rather than with his family. The spouse was also given an opportunity to air her position directly to the corporate representatives. Once she had done this, she was able to reorient her focus from the past to the future and the elements of a mutually acceptable package fell into place.

"Outside" Barriers to Resolution

In some employment cases the real barrier to resolution may be an individual who is not a direct party to the dispute. In one case we mediated involving a disability claim by an airline manager with over 25 years of service, the claimant was moving toward resolution. However, as the mediation progressed, it became clear that his spouse, who was also present, was so angered by what she perceived as unconscionable treatment by the employer that she considered all offers of settlement by the employer insulting. Egged on by his spouse, the claimant became more obstinate and refused to budge from his initial position. The mediator dealt with this situation by giving recognition to the wife's feelings, and by helping her understand that her anger was fueled at least in part by resentment over the amount of time her spouse had spent on his job rather than with his family over the years. The spouse was also afforded an opportunity to air her position directly to the corporate representatives who were present. Once she had communicated her feelings, she was able to reorient her focus from the past to the future, and to consider the potential impact of lengthy litigation on her husband's deteriorating health and well-being. Both she and the complainant were then able to focus on what could be accomplished in mediation, and the elements of a mutually acceptable package fell into place.

Questions

4. What style would you look for in an employment mediator?
5. Would a caucus or no-caucus model be more likely to be effective in such cases?
6. The U.S. Postal Service has used a form of transformative mediation in employee disputes (see Bingham, 2002). Why do you think that two styles as different as conventional commercial and transformative mediation have each enjoyed success in this area?
7. The U.S. Equal Employment Opportunity Commission (EEOC), in an effort to address lengthy delays in processing complaints, has adopted a policy of active and early promotion of mediation of all employment claims filed with the Commission. Do you see any dangers in the EEOC policy? Any advantages for parties?

C. Public and Environmental Controversies

Public and environmental controversies differ from traditional legal disputes in several ways. For one thing, even if public disputes are the subject of a lawsuit they are often not confined to court proceedings. Instead such controversies may be spread among several forums, some political and driven by dynamics other than court calendars and the customs of lawyers. The issues in these disputes are often vague and overlapping, without the precision provided by rules of pleading. Public controversies also often involve complex issues, requiring difficult scientific inquiries.

Another unique aspect of public controversies is that it is often difficult to identify all the parties to the dispute. The conflict may simmer in the community at large for months or years, becoming visible only through discussions in community organizations, city council meetings, and the news media involving a changing cast of characters. In such situations, a mediator's first task is to identify the key participants in the dispute and develop a framework in which they can communicate and bargain effectively. This task is known as "convening."

The goal in public controversies is also not always to reach a global agreement. These processes are sometimes referred to as "consensus-building," because success consists not of reaching agreement among every possible stakeholder, but rather in identifying a solution agreed to or tolerated by enough disputants to make it possible to implement. The following reading discusses this process.

❖ **Chris Carlson,** *Convening*
────────────────────────────────
In The Consensus Building Handbook, 169 (2000)

When someone *convenes* a meeting, he or she typically finds appropriate meeting space, invites people to attend, and perhaps drafts an agenda. In a consensus building process, however, which may involve multiple meetings over the course of weeks, months, or years, convening is a more complex task. In this context, convening typically involves

- assessing a situation to determine whether or not a consensus-based approach is feasible;
- identifying and inviting participants to ensure that all key interests (i.e., stakeholders) are represented;
- locating the necessary resources to help convene, conduct, and support the process; and
- planning and organizing the process with participants or working with a facilitator or mediator to do so.

It may be helpful to think of convening as Phase 1 in a consensus building process, which is followed by Phase 2, the actual negotiating or consensus building phase. . . .

The Importance of Convening: Two Examples

How the convening steps are carried out, and who carries them out, can have an impact on whether or not a consensus process will be successful. The parties who serve as convenors, whether they are government agencies, private corporations, nonprofit organizations, or individuals, need to be viewed as credible and fair-minded, especially in those cases in which issues are contentious or parties are distrustful of each other. At the community level, consensus processes are often sponsored and convened by a local leader, an organization, or a steering committee made up of representatives of different groups. At the state and federal levels, government agencies or officials often serve as sponsors, and sometimes as convenors. Let us look at two examples illustrating the importance of effective convening — one convened by an individual, the other by a federal agency.

A Community Collaboration Gets Off on the Right Foot

In the first example, a diverse conflict over logging practices and their impact on endangered species was under way in a rural community in southern Oregon. By the early 1990s, there had been numerous skirmishes between environmental interests and timber industry supporters over logging in the Applegate Valley. In 1992, the listing of the northern spotted owl on the federal endangered species list led to an injunction prohibiting logging on federal lands. There were bitter and sometimes violent protests. Yet, in the midst of the crisis, some representatives of industry and environmental groups were able to negotiate land exchanges and timber sales. These agreements seemed to signal the possibility that a consensus building approach might be useful for developing a longer-range plan for the watershed.

A local environmentalist who had been one of the architects of the earlier cooperative effort served as the sponsor and convener. He put together a proposal to use a consensus building approach to develop a comprehensive ecosystem management plan. He distributed his proposal to all the involved and affected stakeholders. He then shuttled back and forth among them, discussing and revising the proposal, and got their agreement to start meeting. The participants included most of the major interests: government agency staff, environmentalists, timber industry representatives, farmers and ranchers, and a variety of other local residents.

The convener decided that rather than begin with a formal meeting, complete with flip charts and facilitators, he would host a potluck at his home. The first meeting was spent reaching agreement about how the process would be organized and developing ground rules. The partnership rapidly took shape, and after several months of meetings, the group arrived at an agreement on basic objectives.

After a promising beginning, the Applegate Partnership got swept up in the national politics surrounding the spotted owl issue in Oregon. All the outside attention and publicity caused the partnership to founder, but it managed to survive because participants continued to see a need for building consensus on plans and actions to serve the community's interests. The partnership has been able to develop consensus on projects to restore watersheds, improve agricultural irrigation practices, and initiate economic development projects in the community. By almost any assessment, this convening led to successful outcomes.

A Federal Agency Convenes a Similar Process That Fails

Our second example came about as a result of the Applegate experience. Word spread quickly about the success of the Applegate Partnership. Federal officials caught wind of Applegate's success, and Interior Secretary Bruce Babbitt dropped in on one of the partnership meetings. What he saw fit nicely into the administration's plans for resolving the spotted owl issue: Getting communities involved in working out how federal policies could be implemented locally. The federal government decided that there were 10 communities in which it wanted to stimulate similar partnership efforts.

However, when the federal agency tried to convene local groups and get them to form partnerships, it failed. In each case, stakeholders attended one or two meetings, but were not willing to commit to a longer-term, consensus building process. One probable reason for the failure was that the agency's attempts were made unilaterally, without consulting local stakeholders about what should be discussed and what it would take to make the discussions "safe" for participants, among other things. When the federal government organized meetings, stakeholders came, but they participated only grudgingly. They felt compelled to be there to protect their interests.

When asked, the participants revealed a variety of concerns about how the process had been planned and convened by the federal government. They were concerned, for example, about the federal government's motives, the balance of power at the table, and the availability of resources to enable all groups to participate on an equal footing. Because these questions were not addressed during the convening stage, the groups were ultimately unable and unwilling to form partnerships to work toward consensus on watershed management. . . .

What made the difference in these two cases? The difference was not in *who* carried out the convening role. Federal agencies can convene processes just as successfully as individual community members. The difference in this case lay in how the convening role was handled. . . .

Questions

8.   What qualities would you look for in selecting a mediator for an environmental dispute, as compared with an employment case?
9.   In what ways would the basic strategy described in Chapter 9 need to be modified to deal with an environmental controversy?

D.   Intellectual Property Disputes

❖ **Technology Mediation Services,** *High Tech and*
Intellectual Property Disputes

www.technologymediation.com/hightech (2004)

Mediation is not just for simple contractual disputes. Indeed, complex intellectual property matters may be resolved best through mediation. An intellectual property dispute may be especially ripe for mediation if any of the following factors exist.

One or Both Parties May Have an Interest in Cost Control

Most intellectual property matters are expensive to litigate. It is not unusual for a patent infringement dispute to cost each side well over $1 million through trial, and such cases are often appealed, adding more to the cost. Moreover, they often are settled via business agreements. Much of the cost of extensive discovery, trial preparation, voluminous exhibits, expert witness testimony, and diverted executive time can be spared by using mediation at an early stage to craft an appropriate settlement.

A Business Resolution May Solve the Legal Dispute

A mediator can help the parties craft a variety of business arrangements, such as licensing (or cross-licensing) agreements, joint ventures, distributor agreements, usage phase-out agreements, etc., which may lay the groundwork for future business. A mediated agreement may extend well beyond the subject matter of the pending lawsuit and accommodate larger business interests.

The Decisionmaker May Misunderstand the Law or Technology

If the judge, jury or arbitrator may have trouble understanding intellectual property law issues such as prior art or doctrine of equivalents, or the underlying technology, it may be best to avoid the possibility of being handed a "poor" decision. The parties can keep control of the outcome by mediating, rather than relinquishing the decision to a third party.

The Defendant May Feel Disadvantaged in the Forum Chosen by the Plaintiff

In complex intellectual property matters, a defendant may need lots of time (and money) to prepare its defense and cross-claims alleging invalidity of the patent, trademark, or copyright. If time is short, such as in investigations before the U.S. International Trade Commission, or in federal courts such as the "rocket docket" of the Eastern District of Virginia, it may be better to settle a dispute than to defend under such constraints. Similarly, a defendant may prefer not to defend in a jury trial in the plaintiff's "home" court, or in a jurisdiction with precedent favorable to the plaintiff. Mediation offers a sensible way to end the dispute before it's too late.

The Useful Life of the Subject Matter May Be Depleted Before the Litigation Is Over

Any "hot" products or technologies are covered by patents, trademarks or copyrights, and by virtue of their appeal become subject to infringement. But how good is a favorable judicial decision if the patented technology already has been superseded by another patent, or if last season's most popular toy now sits on the shelf, or if some other copyrighted software game now heads the "top 10" sales list? Mediation can resolve the dispute quickly, while the product is still commercially viable.

One or Both Parties Are Concerned About the Disclosure of Confidential Information

Many intellectual property disputes, particularly alleged trade secret misappropriation, involve confidential business and technical information. Mediation avoids disclosure of such sensitive information, to the public and to your adversary. Everything said in mediation is protected as confidential settlement discussions, and cannot be introduced in litigation or disclosed in public. Additionally, a party can disclose certain information in confidence to the mediator, who will not transmit it to the opponent.

Why Use a Technology Mediator Instead of a General Mediator?

Disputes that involve specialized industries or complex technology benefit from having a mediator that understands the context in which the dispute arose, and/or the technology involved. A mediator knowledgeable about high tech businesses and their problems can delve right into the issues, without expending a lot of time learning about them. In patent, trademark or copyright disputes, it is useful to use a mediator experienced in intellectual property law, who will be familiar with the legal and factual issues related to, e.g., prior art, doctrine of equivalents, and likelihood of confusion. The mediator will know who needs to be included in the mediated settlement. The mediator will have a real-world context for the parties' positions, and won't be easily persuaded by a party's legal bluster or alleged inability to comply with a standard request. Moreover, prior experience will enable the mediator to make suggestions to facilitate resolution, or to offer a realistic evaluation of the parties' chances of success outside of mediation.

Questions

10. Given the advantages of mediation in this area, why do you suppose every high-technology dispute that cannot be directly negotiated is not mediated?

11.   If you were counsel to a company that had a claim against a competitor for infringement of a biotech patent and wished to try mediation, but the only available mediators had either strong process skills or extensive technical knowledge but not both, which type of mediator would you choose? Is there a way to obtain the presence of both qualities?

E.   Criminal Matters

The use of mediation is expanding in the criminal justice system, raising both exciting possibilities and troubling issues.

1.   Victim-Offender Cases

Mediation appears to be taking root at the post-sentencing stage of the process, involving encounters between victims and offenders. The issue at this point is not the defendant's guilt, but rather how he and the victim will deal with what has happened. We have seen that mediation can be used to help people change perspectives and restore ruptured relationships, but in the criminal context such efforts are much more controversial. As you read the following excerpt, ask yourself these questions.

Questions

12.   For what purposes is mediation being used here?
13.   If you were designing a victim-offender program, would you make all types of criminal cases eligible for it or exclude some categories of cases? If so, which ones?

❖ **Marty Price,** PERSONALIZING CRIME: MEDIATION
PRODUCES RESTORATIVE JUSTICE FOR VICTIMS AND OFFENDERS

7 Disp. Resol. Mag. 8 (Fall 2000)

Our traditional criminal justice system is a system of retributive justice — a system of institutionalized vengeance. The system is based on the belief that justice is accomplished by assigning blame and administering pain. If you do the crime, you do the time, then you've paid your debt to society and justice has been done. But justice for whom? . . .

Because our society defines justice in terms of guilt and punishment, crime victims often seek the most severe possible punishment for their offenders. Victims believe this will bring them justice, but it often leaves them feeling empty and unsatisfied. Retribution cannot restore their losses, answer their questions, relieve their fears, help them make sense of their tragedy or heal their wounds. And punishment cannot mend the torn fabric of the community that has been violated. . . .

Focus on Individuals, Healing

Restorative justice has emerged as a social movement for justice reform. Virtually every state is implementing restorative justice at state, regional and/or local levels. . . . Instead of viewing crime as a violation of law, restorative justice emphasizes one fundamental fact: crime damages people, communities, and relationships.

Retributive justice asks three questions: who did it, what laws were broken and what should be done to punish or treat the offender? Contrast a restorative justice inquiry, in which three very different questions receive primary emphasis. First, what is the nature of the harm resulting from the crime? Second, what needs to be done to "make it right" or repair the harm? Third, who is responsible for the repair? . . .

As the most common application of restorative justice principles, VOM [victim-offender mediation] programs warrant examination in detail. These programs bring offenders face to face with the victims of their crimes with the assistance of a trained mediator, usually a community volunteer. Victim participation is voluntary in most programs.

In mediation, crime is personalized as offenders learn the human consequences of their actions, and victims have the opportunity to speak their minds and their feelings to the one who most ought to hear them, contributing to the victim's healing. Victims get answers to haunting questions that only the offender can answer. The most commonly asked questions are "Why did you do this to me? Was this my fault? Could I have prevented this? Were you stalking or watching me?" Victims commonly report a new peace of mind, even when the answers to their questions were worse than they had feared.

Offenders take meaningful responsibility for their actions by mediating a restitution agreement with the victim to restore the victim's losses in whatever [way is] possible. Restitution may be monetary or symbolic; it may consist of work for the victim, community service, or other actions that contribute to a sense of justice between the victim and offender.

Fulfilling Restitution

. . . There are now more than 300 programs in the United States and Canada and more than 700 in England, Germany, Scandinavia, Eastern Europe, Australia, and New Zealand. Remarkably consistent statistics from a cross-section of the North American programs show that about two-thirds of the cases referred resulted in a face-to-face mediation. More than 95 percent of the cases mediated resulted in a written restitution agreement. More than 90 percent of those restitution agreements are completed within one year. In contrast, the rate of payment of court-ordered restitution is typically only from 20 to 30 percent. Recent research has shown that juvenile offenders who participate in VOM subsequently commit fewer and less serious offenses than their counterparts in the traditional juvenile justice system. . . .

Careful Preparation Required

Mediation is not appropriate for every crime, every victim, or every offender, Individual, preliminary meetings between mediator and victim, mediator and offender permit careful screening and assessment according to established criteria. . . . At their best, mediation sessions focus upon dialogue rather than the restitution agreement (or settlement), facilitating empathy and understanding between victim and offender. Ground rules help assure safety and respect. Victims typically speak first, explaining the impact of the crime and asking questions of the offender. Offenders acknowledge and describe their participation in the offense, usually offering an explanation and/or apology. The victim's losses are discussed. Surprisingly, a dialogue-focused (rather than settlement-driven) approach produces the highest rates of agreement and compliance.

Agreements that the victim and offender make together reflect justice that is meaningful to them, not limited by narrow legal definitions. [T]he overwhelming majority of participants — both victims and offenders — have reported in post-mediation interviews and questionnaires that they obtained a just and satisfying result. Victims who feared re-victimization by the offender before the mediation typically report that this fear is now gone.

Forgiveness is not a focus of VOM, but the process provides an open space in which participants may address issues of forgiveness if they wish. Forgiveness is a process, not a goal, and it must occur according to the victim's own timing, if at all. For some victims, forgiveness may never be appropriate. Restorative justice requires an offender who is willing to admit responsibility and remorse to the victim. . . .

Different Concept of Neutrality

Neutrality, as understood in the mediation of civil disputes, requires that the mediator not take sides with either party. Judgments of right and wrong are not within the mediator's role. The mediation of most crime situations, however, presents a unique set of circumstances for a mediator and the concept of neutrality must be different. In the majority of criminal cases, the parties come to VOM as a wronged person and a wrongdoer, with a power imbalance that is appropriate to this relationship. The mediator balances power only to ensure full and meaningful participation by all parties. . . . The mediator is neutral toward the individuals, respecting both as valuable human beings and favoring neither, but the mediator is not neutral regarding the wrong. . . .

Most victim-offender programs limit their service to juvenile offenses, crimes against property, and minor assaults, but a growing number of experienced programs have found that a face-to-face encounter can be invaluable even in heinous crimes. A number of programs have now mediated violent assaults, including rapes, and mediations have taken place between murderers and the families of their victims. Mediation has been helpful in repairing the lives of surviving family members and the offender in drunk-driving fatalities. In severe crime mediations, case development may take a year or more before the mediation can take place. . . . In cases of severely violent crime, VOM has not been a substitute for a prison sentence, and prison terms have seldom been reduced following mediation. . . .

What Can We Learn?

What can attorneys and other dispute resolution professionals learn from the philosophy and successes of restorative justice? Our system, which settles most cases without trial, does so with adversarial assumptions as its foundation. Each attorney is expected to maximize her client's win at the expense of the other attorney's client's loss. In the majority of cases, the clients of both attorneys (and often the attorneys, as well) feel like losers in the settlement. . . .

Our system of money damages and financial settlements for losses and injuries has a faulty assumption at its core. We give lip service to the truth that "no amount of money can right this wrong," then we conclude that the only available measure of amends is the dollar! In contrast, a basic principle of restorative justice is that a wrong creates a singular kind of relationship — an obligation to personally right that wrong. . . . The most important lesson learned from restorative justice practice may be the realization that the key to justice is found not in laws but in the recognition and honoring of human relationships.

Questions

14. Criminal prosecutions serve important public functions. Which of these functions may not be fulfilled when cases go into a VOM program?
15. Does VOM serve functions not met by the traditional criminal justice system?

F.   Deal Mediation

You now understand, as many practicing lawyers do, the potentially significant role that a mediator can play in resolving disputes, enhancing communication, and even repairing relationships. It should therefore come as no surprise that some have theorized about — and in some cases implemented — efforts to apply the same principles at points "upstream" from active disputes.

Chapter 9 gave an example of a situation in which a mediator, Stephen Goldberg, who had been hired to act as bargaining advisor to one side in a business negotiation, became both advisor to his own team and an informal "mediator to the deal" for both sides. The next section describes an international commercial negotiation in which a Hollywood agent performed a similar function. Could "true" mediators — impartial, rather than retained by one side — be helpful in creating deals? The following reading, mentioned earlier in the context of negotiation, explores this question.

❖ **Scott R. Peppet,** *Contract Formation in Imperfect Markets: Should We Use Mediators in Deals?*

38 Ohio St. J. on Disp. Resol. 283 (2004)

[M]any of the same barriers to negotiation that plague litigation settlement exist in commercial transactions, particularly during the closing stage of a deal when lawyers attempt to negotiate terms and conditions. [A] transactional mediator could help lawyers and clients to overcome such barriers.

[O]ccasionally transacting parties fail to "close the deal" because of strategic posturing. [Moreover] . . . empirical analysis of contracts shows that parties often do not trade risk in complex — yet value-creating — ways. Instead, in many domains contracts are simpler than one might expect . . . . [One possible] explanation is that the threat of strategic behavior prevents parties from complex contracting. To create a tailored term requires disclosing information about one's interests and preferences. This again permits exploitation. In the absence of trust, parties may resort to a standard term to minimize this risk.

A mediator might . . . solicit and compare information from each side, potentially finding value-creating trades. The mediator might test the viability of various packages . . . , asking each side in confidence which of several sets of terms the party would accept, but not revealing the origin of the various packages. . . .

[Besides helping the parties to overcome strategic barriers to transactions, mediators can also help them to overcome psychological barriers.] A neutral is in an ideal position to identify self-serving assessments by one or both parties. At a substantive level, if the neutral has sufficient expertise she can check each side's assumptions about "what's fair" and keep the parties from locking in to diverging stories about how a transaction should be priced or closed. Moreover, the mediator may be able to offer a neutral assessment or fair proposal that the parties will adopt. . . .

Negotiating parties must constantly assess information received from the other side. [A] neutral can help parties to overcome reactive devaluation in transactional bargaining by either adding noise to [that is, disguising the source of] the parties' communication or proposing solutions of her own. Adding noise may be as simple as raising Party A's proposed solution privately with Party B without telling B that the idea came from Party A. If B assumes that the idea originated with the neutral, B may be more willing to consider it on the merits.

A neutral may be less susceptible to the endowment effect than a partisan agent, and therefore able to help parties to overcome it. For example, a neutral may be able to provide both sides with market information against which they can test their (biased) evaluations. . . .

In strategic situations it is easy to assume that when the other bargainer "starts high" or "holds out," they do so because they intend to harm you or to treat you unfairly. Bargainers are less likely to attribute such actions to the exigencies of circumstance. By screening some overly opportunistic offers and at times sending fuzzy rather than clear information between the parties, a mediator can blunt such emotions and thereby keep the negotiations on track. Over time, avoiding emotional disagreements may help the parties to establish trust. This not only leads to more amiable negotiations, but also has serious substantive benefits. If the parties trust each other they may be better positioned to find value-creating solutions to their substantive differences. They may be able to rely more on informal agreements rather than contractual obligations and may be more flexible in the face of unexpected bumps in the road. Perhaps most importantly, they may avoid the destructive cycle of misattributions that can lead parties to "blow up" a deal or reach [an inefficient] agreement.

❖ **David A. Hoffman,** *Microsoft and Yahoo: Where Were The Mediators? They Help Countries and Couples. Why Not Businesses?*

Christian Science Monitor (May 12, 2008)

When Microsoft CEO Steve Ballmer met with Yahoo CEO Jerry Yang earlier this month, what kept them from making a deal? With Microsoft offering $33 per share for Yahoo's stock, and Yahoo willing to take $37, was there truly an unbridgeable gulf? The $4 gap seems trivial in comparison to the potential value of the deal. So did Microsoft and Yahoo walk away from a deal that would have made both sides better off? This type of bargaining failure is hardly rare — businesspeople frequently report deals that have come within inches of closing, only to slip away at the last moment, costing their companies plenty.

In the world of litigation, settlement gaps are routinely bridged with the help of mediators. In the world of foreign policy, mediation — sometimes called "shuttle diplomacy" — is used extensively to resolve conflict. Why, then, are business transactions rarely mediated?

One theory is that the functions that mediators perform are already handled by transactional lawyers and investment bankers who work hard — and are handsomely rewarded — to close deals. The problem with this theory is that the lawyers and investment bankers often approach the negotiation from a partisan perspective in order to prove their loyalty to their respective clients.

A more promising explanation is that when conflicts arise — as in a potential hostile takeover situation such as the Microsoft-Yahoo negotiations — the parties reject compromise because they see the world through a distorted lens. Conflict can cause "reactive devaluation" (a negative assessment of a proposal because it comes from an opponent). Neuroscientists tell us that conflict triggers some of our most primitive reactions — a fight-or-flight response — as opposed to the collaborative impulse required for deal-making.

It's not surprising, then, that people — especially in business settings, where egos, competition, and high stakes collide — are unlikely to opt for mediation unless they are forced, or strongly urged, to do so. In the world of diplomacy, it is often the superpowers that intervene when smaller nations quarrel, and court cases are often mediated because a judge insists on it. Indeed, Microsoft mediated its antitrust dispute with the Justice Department only when the court ordered it. In the setting of mergers and acquisitions, however, the key difference is that there is no outside power that can insist on mediation. Accordingly, it is often up to boards of directors or shareholders to push management to mediation.

Dealmaking mediation has been used for years to create collective-bargaining agreements and to resolve impasses in the negotiation of major league sports contracts. . . . In the Microsoft-Yahoo negotiations, a mediator could have helped in several concrete ways.

First, since disagreements about the price of a company usually turn on financial predictions, mediators can help the parties structure creative options for mitigating their risks. Acquisition agreements often contain "earn-out" provisions that award benefits to the seller if the deal turns out to be a winner for the buyer. Without any investment in the outcome, mediators become "honest brokers" who can advance such ideas without the perception that they are seeking an advantage based on secret knowledge.

Second, a mediator can help the parties obtain neutral and independent opinions — as opposed to the potentially partisan opinions of the parties' hired experts, lawyers, and investment bankers.

Third, a "mediator's proposal" can test the waters of compromise. Let's say the mediator asks each side to tell the mediator — on a confidential basis — whether they would accept a deal at $35 per share. This protocol means the mediator will report the answers only if both sides say "yes." Thus, each side can take the risk of saying yes because the other side will never know unless they, too, have said yes.

When deals collapse, conflict often migrates to another venue. Yahoo is already defending lawsuits from disgruntled shareholders, angered by management's failure to accept Microsoft's offer. However, even if there were no possible zone of agreement in the Microsoft-Yahoo case, business managers in other deal negotiations might consider whether calling in mediators, when needed, might save them from bargaining failures and make both sides better off.

> Questions
>
> 16.   Why do you think Microsoft and Yahoo did not use mediation?
> 17.   What problems might an inside counsel who suggested mediation in that situation have encountered?

G.   International Mediation

Until now we have discussed mediation as an almost entirely American phenomenon. In fact, however, people across the world and throughout recorded history have turned to third parties to assist them in resolving disputes. International mediation is best known in the context of disputes involving nation-states. Theodore Roosevelt, for example, won the Nobel Peace Prize for his work as mediator of peace talks between Russia and Japan, Jimmy Carter is remembered for facilitating the Camp David accords between Egypt and Israel, and former Senator George Mitchell played a key role in bringing peace to Northern Ireland.

Mediation can also be used, of course, in private disputes. There are two types of "international" private mediation, "domestic" and "cross-border." "Domestic" refers to use of mediation *within* another country, for example to resolve a lawsuit pending in a British court between two English companies, or in India between Indian landowners. "Cross-border" mediation involves disputes between citizens of *different* countries, for example between a U.S. and an Asian company over commercial contracts. We first focus on the use of mediation domestically within other countries, then on its use in cases arising from international transactions.

1.   Mediation Within Foreign Legal Systems

The use of mediation varies greatly from country to country and no single statement is possible about its prevalence. In countries with common-law legal systems, particularly Canada, Great Britain, and Australia, mediation has become relatively well known. In the civil-law countries of continental Europe, by contrast, it has not been applied broadly except in specialized areas such as family law, and the same is true of most of the rest of the world.

Michael McIlwrath, a manager of litigation for GE Power Systems and former Chair of the International Mediation Institute in the Hague, offers the following assessment of the use of mediation outside the United States.

❖ **Michael McIlwrath,** *Can Mediation Evolve
into a Global Profession?*

www.mediate.com **(2009)**

In many places around the world [commercial] mediation is struggling to
gain any traction at all. It has gained a strong foothold in a few countries,
such as Canada, the UK and the Netherlands, but in most places it is virtually unknown. It is rarely promoted and often misunderstood, causing lack
of respect and acceptance.

In many legal environments, mediation has found itself in a bit of a rut,
experiencing only very marginal growth. Where mediators are plentiful,
they tend to be in chronic over-supply. In the view of many consumers of dispute services, this is not a problem of mediation but of the way it is presented
within these particular markets.

Take the UK for example. Having developed initial techniques and training from the US, there are now thousands of trained mediators. However, it
is claimed that only about 20 people practice as full time mediators, with
perhaps 50 conducting 80% of the country's mediations. Thousands of others struggle to gain experience and practical skills. And this is in the one
place in Europe where mediation is sometimes claimed to be "mature". . . .

Given that so many of us believe mediation represents a generally superior form of dispute resolution, we are bound to ask why it has not become
more popular around the world. There may be many factors preventing a
more rapid spread of the practice of mediation beyond its core jurisdictions.

One possibility is that the cost of litigation in North America, the UK, and
Australia makes the search for an alternative that leads to settlement more
pressing. That may certainly be the case, but it is not a completely satisfying
explanation. [I]n Italy where I live, for example, court proceedings may cost
the typical litigant a fraction of what a similar action would cost in the US,
but the case will still take some years to work its way through the courts. Parties want resolution sooner rather than later, and one would think that inef-
ficiency of dispute resolution would be a fertile environment for mediation.
Yet it is little practiced here, despite efforts over the past decade to promote
it, including legislation imposing an obligation to mediate certain types of
disputes. And there are countries like India that make Italy a shining
example of judicial efficiency, and where mediation is even less known and
practiced.

So there must be other factors stalling the growth of mediation. One in
particular appears to be variability in the quality of the services that are
called "mediation" in different places. [McIlwrath goes on to argue that an
essential prerequisite to the spread of mediation in other countries is a consistent method to certify the competence of mediators across borders.]

2.   *Use in Cross-Border Disputes*

Mediation can also be used to resolve disputes between citizens of different countries. Parties to international contracts are understandably reluctant to litigate in a foreign court system, and typically specify that disputes will be resolved by arbitration. In 2004 the European Commission issued a Directive endorsing the use of mediation in certain civil and commercial disputes, and advocates hope that this will spur its use in the European Union.

Although international business contracts rarely refer to mediation, international arbitrators have long followed the custom of seeking to "conciliate" cases. The following readings explore the different forms that these processes can take and what they mean when implemented by neutrals of different cultures.

❖ **Jeswald Salacuse,** MEDIATION IN INTERNATIONAL BUSINESS

In J. Bercovitch, Studies in International Mediation 213 (2002)

The International Deal: A Continuing Negotiation

All international transactions are the product of negotiation — the result of *deal-making* — among the parties. Although lawyers like to think that negotiations end when the participants agree on all the details and sign the contract, this view hardly ever reflects reality. In truth, an international deal is a *continuing negotiation* between the parties to the transaction as they seek to adjust their relationship to the rapidly changing international environment . . . in which they must work. . . . In the life of any international deal, one may therefore identify three distinct stages when conflict may arise and the parties rely on negotiation and conflict resolution to achieve their goals: *deal-making, deal-managing*, and *deal-mending*. Within the context of each of these three kinds of negotiation, one should ask to what extent third parties, whether called mediators or something else, may assist the parties to make, manage, and mend productive international business relationships. . . .

Deal-Making Mediation

The usual model of an international business negotiation is that of representatives of two companies from different countries sitting across a table in face-to-face discussions to shape the terms of a commercial contract. While many transactions take place in that manner, many others require the services of one or more third parties to facilitate the deal-making process. These individuals are not usually referred to as "mediators." They instead carry a variety of other labels: consultant, adviser, agent, broker, investment banker, among others. . . .

Although it could be argued that consultants and advisors should not be considered mediators since they are not independent of the parties, a close examination of their roles . . . reveals that they exercise a mediator's functions . . . [I]n most cases, one of the principal assets of deal-making mediators is the fact that they are known and accepted by the other side in the deal.

Deal-Making Mediation in Hollywood

The acquisition in 1991 by Matsushita Electric Industrial Company of Japan, one of the world's largest electronics manufacturers, of MCA, one of the United States' biggest entertainment companies, for over $6 billion illustrates the use of mediators in the deal-making process. Matsushita had determined that its future growth was dependent upon obtaining a source of films, television programs, and music — what it termed "software" — to complement its consumer electronic "hardware" products. Matsushita knew that it could find such a source of software within the U.S. entertainment industry, but it also recognized that it was virtually ignorant of that industry and its practices. For Matsushita executives, embarking on their Hollywood expedition may have felt almost interplanetary. . . . They therefore engaged Michael Ovitz, the founder and head of Creative Artists Agency, one of the most powerful talent agencies in Hollywood, to guide them on their journey.

After forming a team to assist in the task, Ovitz . . . first extensively briefed the Japanese over several months, sometimes in secret meetings in Hawaii, on the nature of the U.S. entertainment industry, and he then proceeded to propose three possible candidates for acquisition, one of which was MCA. Ultimately, Matsushita chose MCA, but it was Ovitz, not Matsushita executives, who initiated conversations with the MCA leadership, men whom Ovitz knew well. Indeed, Ovitz assumed the task of actually conducting the negotiations for Matsushita. At one point in the discussions, he moved constantly between the Japanese team of executives in one suite of offices in New York City and the MCA team in another building, a process which one observer described as "shuttle diplomacy". . . . Although Matsushita may have considered Ovitz to be their agent in the talks, Ovitz seems to have considered himself to be both a representative of Matsushita and a mediator between the two sides.

Because of the vast cultural and temperamental differences between the Japanese and American companies, Ovitz's strategy was to limit the actual interactions of the two parties to a bare minimum. . . . He was not only concerned by the vast differences in culture between the two companies but also by the greatly differing personalities in their top managements. The Japanese executives, reserved and somewhat self-effacing, placed a high value on the appearance if not the reality of modesty, while MCA's president was an extremely assertive and volatile personality. Like any mediator, Ovitz's own interests may also have influenced his choice of strategy. His status in the entertainment industry would only be heightened by making a giant new entrant into Hollywood dependent on him and by the public image that he had been the key to arranging one of the biggest deals in the industry's history. . . .

Eventually the talks stalled over the issue of price, and meetings between the two sides ceased. At this point, a second deal-making mediator entered the scene to make a crucial contribution. At the start of the negotiation, Matsushita and Sony together had engaged Robert Strauss, a politically powerful Washington lawyer who had been at various times U.S. Ambassador to the Soviet Union and U.S. Trade Representative, as "counselor to the transaction." Strauss, a member of the MCA board of directors and a close friend of its chairman, was also friendly with the Matsushita leadership and did legal and lobbying work in Washington for the Japanese company. . . . Strauss' close relationship to the two sides allowed him to act as a trusted conduit of communication who facilitated a meeting between the top MCA and Matsushita executives . . . [H]e apparently gained an understanding of the pricing parameters acceptable to each side and then communicated them to the other party. . . . In the end, as a result of that meeting, the two sides reached an agreement by which Matsushita acquired MCA.

[A]lthough Matsushita did succeed in purchasing MCA, the acquisition proved to be troubling and ultimately a disastrous financial loss for the Japanese company. One may ask whether Ovitz' strategy of keeping the two sides apart during negotiations so that they did not come to know one another contributed to this unfortunate result. It prevented the two sides from truly understanding the vast gulf which separated them and therefore from realizing the enormity and perhaps impossibility of the task of merging two such different organizations into a single coordinated and profitable enterprise.

Other Deal-Making Mediators

An opposite mediating approach from that employed by Ovitz is the use of consultants to begin building a relationship between the parties *before* they have signed a contract and indeed before they have actually begun negotiations. When some companies contemplate long-term relationships . . . they may hire a consultant to develop and guide a program of relationship building, which might include joint workshops, get-acquainted sessions, and retreats, all of which take place before the parties actually sit down to negotiate the terms of their contract. . . .

. . . Sometimes persons involved in the negotiation because of their technical expertise or specialized knowledge may assume a mediating function and thus help the parties reach agreement. For example . . . local lawyers or accountants engaged by a foreign party to advise on law or accounting practices in connection with an international negotiation may assume a mediating role in the deal-making process by serving as a conduit between the parties, by suggesting approaches that meet the other side's cultural practices [or] by explaining why one party is behaving in a particular way. . . .

Deal-Managing Mediation

Once the deal has been signed, consultants, lawyers, and advisers may continue their association with one or both parties and informally assist as mediators in managing conflict that may arise in the execution of the transaction. . . . Once top management of the two sides have reached an understanding, they may have to serve as mediators with their subordinates to get them to change behavior and attitudes with respect to interactions at the operational level. . . .

Deal-Mending Mediation

The parties to an international business relationship may encounter a wide variety of conflicts that seem irreconcilable. . . . A poor developing country may stop paying its loan to a foreign bank. Partners in an international joint venture may disagree violently over the use of accumulated profits and therefore plunge their enterprise into a state of paralysis. Here then would seem ideal situations in which mediation by a third party could help in settling conflict. In fact, mediation is relatively uncommon once severe international business conflicts break out. To understand why, one must first understand the basic structure of international business dispute settlement.

International Commercial Arbitration

Nearly all international business contracts today provide that any disputes that may arise in the future between the parties are to be resolved by international commercial arbitration. . . . Thus in the background of virtually all international business disputes is the prospect of binding arbitration if the parties, alone or with the help of a third person, are unable to resolve the conflict themselves.

Arbitrating a dispute is not, however, a painless, inexpensive, quick solution. Like litigation in the courts, it is costly, may take years to conclude, and invariably results in a final rupture of the parties' business relationship. . . . [Arbitrators sometimes seek to play a mediating role. Their usual strategy] is to give the parties a realistic evaluation of what they will receive or be required to pay in any final arbitration award.

Mediation in International Business Disputes

Traditionally, companies engaged in an international business dispute have not actively sought the help of mediators. . . . With increasing recognition of the disadvantages of arbitration, some companies are beginning to turn to more explicit forms of mediation to resolve business disputes.

Conciliation

One type of deal-mending mediation used occasionally in international business is *conciliation*. . . . While the conciliator has broad discretion to conduct the process, in practice he or she will invite both sides to state their views of the dispute and will then make a report proposing an appropriate settlement. The parties may reject the report and proceed to arbitration, or they may accept it.

In many cases, they will use it as a basis for a negotiated settlement. Conciliation is thus a kind of non-binding arbitration. Its function is predictive. It tends to be rights-based. . . . Conciliators do not usually adopt a problem-solving or relationship-building approach. . . . The process is confidential and completely voluntary. . . . Thus far few disputants in international business avail themselves of conciliation. . . .

❖ **M. Scott Donahey,** *The Asian Concept of Conciliator/Arbitrator: Is It Translatable to the Western World?*

10 Foreign Investment L. J. 120 (1995)

In various Asian countries, there is a profound societal and philosophical preference for agreed solutions.[1] Nevertheless, such generalizations are often necessary when comparing one cultural system to another. Rather than a cultural bias toward "equality" in relationships, there exists an intellectual and social predisposition towards a natural hierarchy which governs conduct in interpersonal relations. Asian cultures frequently seek a "harmonious" solution, one which tends to preserve the relationship, rather than one which, while arguably factually and legally "correct," may severely damage the relationship of the parties involved.

Where the Westerner will segregate the function of facilitator from that of decision-maker, the Asian will make no clear distinction. The Westerner seeks an arbiter that is unconnected to the parties to the dispute, one whose mind has not been predisposed by previous knowledge of the dispute or the facts which underlie it, a judge who is prepared to "let the chips fall where they may." On the other hand, many Asians seek a moderator who is familiar with the parties and their dispute, who will not only end their state of disputation but assist the parties in reaching an agreed solution, or, failing that, will find a position which will not only be one that terminates their dispute, but one that will allow the parties to resume their relationship with as little loss of "face" as possible. Thus, the distinction between the function of the arbitrator and that of the conciliator is blurred.

Clearly, as there is increased interaction in the forms of tourism and trade between the Western world and Asia, differences between the two cultures have diminished and will continue to diminish. We in the West tend to view this process as one in which the Asian countries are influenced by our economic and political systems and become more "Westernized." Our western pride and predispositions often do not permit us to recognize the degree to which we have been influenced and changed by the Asian cultures with which we have come in closer contact. . . .

---

1. [Footnote by the article's author] The author recognizes that the generalizations in which he engages tend to explain away the complexities and vast difference that exist in any nation or culture[,] and [thus those generalizations] are inherently suspect.

Within the Confucian tradition, there is a concept known as "li," which concerns the social norms of behavior within the five natural status relationships: emperor and subject, father and son, husband and wife, brother and brother, or friend and friend. *Li* is intended to be persuasive, not compulsive and legalistic, a concept which governs good conduct and is above legal concepts in societal importance. The governing legal concept, "fa," is compulsive and punitive. While having the advantage of legal enforceability, *fa* is traditionally below *li* in importance. The Chinese have always considered the resort to litigation as the last step, signifying that the relationship between the disputing parties can no longer be harmonized. Resort to litigation results in loss of face, and discussion and compromise are always to be preferred. Over time the concepts of *fa* and *li* have become fused, and the concept of maintaining the relationship and, therefore, face, has become part of the Chinese legal system. . . .

Adjudication is an act-oriented process. . . . In contrast, since conciliation/mediation is a "person-oriented" one, it is non-adversarial and set in a warm and friendly air of informality unbound by technical rules of procedure. Furthermore, while the nature of the adjudicative process requires that evidence and arguments presented by one party be made in the presence of the adverse litigant, separate conferences with the parties have been found to be an effective tool of conciliation. It is less important, in conciliation proceedings, to be accurate in finding the truth of the issues than to know what values are held by the parties so that a "trade-off" may be effected that will restore the disrupted harmonious relationship.

In Japan, as well, permitting a relationship to fall into a state of disharmony is culturally unacceptable: In Japan . . . the existence of a dispute may itself cause a loss of "face," and submission of a dispute to a third party may carry with it some sense of failure. . . . Thus, if there is one principle which can be said to lead to the combining of the role of arbitrator with that of conciliator it is that of preserving the harmonious relationship between the parties to the dispute. This principle is one that is frequently cited by Western arbitral institutions in promoting the use of commercial arbitration over litigation. . . .

Perhaps the foremost proponent of the practice of combining the role of conciliator and arbitrator . . . is the People's Republic of China. While no written rules have ever sanctioned or even described the practice, Chinese arbitrators and practitioners both practice and espouse the combination of mediation and conciliation: Arbitration and conciliation are interrelated and complementary with one another. They are not antagonistic and do not exclude each other. . . .

It is important to understand that the Chinese combination of arbitration and conciliation occurs during the ongoing process of arbitration. The arbitrator, after taking some evidence and hearing some witnesses, might attempt to conciliate the differences and, if efforts at conciliation fail, return to the receipt of evidence and the hearing of witnesses, ready to attempt conciliation again at an opportune time during the course of the proceedings. [I]t is unclear whether parties convey information to the arbitrators/ conciliators in confidence during the conciliation phase, and, if so, how it is maintained.... This is different from the way that other Asian nations combine the functions of arbitrator and conciliator....

The traditional Western view is that the conciliation process should be separate from the arbitration process and that the same persons who act as conciliators should not act as arbitrators in the same dispute.... However, the traditional Western view is changing, largely due to the influence of Asian cultures.... A combined conciliation and arbitration process offers significant advantages in reaching an agreed settlement and in preserving existing commercial relations between the parties. It is a system that apparently has worked well in Asia, and we in the West should not shrink from its use....

Questions

18. What approach would you expect in general from an Asian conciliator: facilitative or evaluative? Narrow or broad?

19. You are involved in an arbitration of a business contract dispute on behalf of a U.S. computer manufacturer who contracted with a Chinese firm to produce silicon chips, paid for and installed the chips in its products, and has since found out that they are unreliable, leading to serious repair costs and lost profits. Your client believes that the Chinese partner failed to comply with the quality requirements because it overstated its expertise in the area and simply did not understand them. The contract gives you the right to recover your damages, but it is not clear how you would enforce an award in arbitration against the supplier. If you know that the chair of the arbitration panel is a Chinese attorney,

    a. What, if anything, would you say to the neutral about the possibility of conciliation before the process begins?

    b. What instructions would you give your client about how to act during conciliation?

H.   Online Mediation

One development in mediation does not involve a new subject area, but rather the use of technology to enhance its impact; it is online dispute resolution (ODR). ODR has two meanings. One is as a *method of communication*, as in negotiation or mediation conducted by email. The other is as a *process managed electronically*, such as a program to manage monetary bidding.

ODR as a method of communication is a familiar concept. Lawyers have used electronic methods to negotiate since the invention of the telegraph and telephone, and email and other electronic means are conceptually not very different from a phone. Using a telephone provided bargainers greater efficiency but reduced their ability to observe and interact; email and other electronic forms of communication have similar advantages and shortcomings. Technological developments are constantly changing how mediation can be conducted — video, for example, is now available to anyone with a laptop.

ODR as a process managed electronically, however, is different. For one thing, it is asynchronous: Parties generally do not talk in "real time," as with cell phones and instant messaging, but rather exchange messages at their own pace as with email. Equally important, disputants do not meet face-to-face or even see each other by video. There are advantages and disadvantages to such methods. As a practical matter, however, parties to business disputes appear still to conduct almost all mediations through face-to-face meetings. It may be that the very cost of meeting someone in person — traveling to a site and remaining there for hours — demonstrates a mutual commitment to compromise and signals that the occasion is a "settlement event." It is also possible that lawyers and parties will become so comfortable with electronic media that they no longer feel a need to mediate in person, or in real time.

As of now, ODR is not regularly used to conduct mediation except in disputes too small to justify the cost of meeting in person. For instance, eBay provides a system of computerized dispute resolution that permits buyers and sellers both to negotiate and mediate disputes. Companies that provide ODR services have sprung up and disappeared at a rapid pace in recent years, however, and customs of disputing may change rapidly.

Questions

20. A client bought an old mandolin on eBay for $250. On receiving the instrument she found that it was in much poorer condition than the seller had represented. She wants to return the mandolin and get her money back. Check eBay's website (*www.ebay.com*): What mediation options does eBay appear to provide for resolving her problem?

21. You are consulted by a business client who purchased a computer server system from an out-of-state supplier in a private transaction for $75,000. The system is dysfunctional, and the client believes that the seller defrauded him by not revealing that the system would function only with customized software, which would require an additional $15,000 to $20,000 to create. Even with this

software, the client says, the system will not handle the volume of data that he has to process, contrary to assurances given during the sales process. He wishes to revoke the transaction. He has heard about the Cybersettle system (see *www.cybersettle.com*) and wonders if it would make sense to use it. What would you advise your client and why?

22. More generally, what seem to be the pluses and minuses of mediating through a computerized system using asynchronous communication conducted by email?

CHAPTER

14

Court-Connected Mediation and Fairness Concerns

A. Court-Connected Mediation

Much of the early impetus for applying ADR in legal disputes came from judges concerned about overloaded dockets. It is not surprising, therefore, that courts throughout the United States have established dispute resolution programs and legislators have supported court-connected ADR. Modern ADR programs cover both general litigation and special categories such as divorce and small claims cases. Programs are most common at the trial level, but exist in appellate courts as well.

Congress required in the ADR Act of 1998, 28 U.S.C. § 651(b), that every federal district court in the nation implement a dispute resolution program. Most federal courts allow litigants to choose among ADR processes, and mediation is the most popular option. A study of 49 federal district courts that received special ADR funding showed the following pattern (Stienstra, 2005):

Federal Court Cases Referred to ADR Processes

Mediation	15,555
N.D. CA multi-option program (largely mediations)	3,317
Arbitration	2,588
Settlement conferences	1,608
Early neutral evaluation	1,332
Settlement week	296
Summary trials	6
Other	133
Total	24,835

The primary reason that state and federal courts have embraced mediation is to relieve their dockets of unwanted cases. In the words of one Texas judge, "I am interested in mediation because the cases settle earlier, and that gives me more time to be a judge, to spend that time I can gain improving the quality of justice in my court" (Bergman and Bickerman, 1998).

Although their primary motivation is usually to reduce backlogs, courts divert cases to mediation for other reasons as well. Some cases involve continuing relationships, such as disputes between parents over visitation rights to their children. Adjudication is often ineffective to resolve such disputes, and litigation is beyond the financial means of many individuals. Court personnel also find some cases frustrating and personally demanding; family and neighborhood disputes, for example, often provoke raw emotions that defy rational analysis. Along with small claims and prisoners' rights suits, they also frequently involve pro se litigants who place extra burdens on court staff.

Court-connected mediation raises important policy issues, which involve designing programs not simply to yield the greatest benefit to the system but also to ensure fairness to participants. This section describes how court-connected programs are structured and explores the process issues they present.

B.   Issues of Program Design

1.   What Goals Should a Program Seek to Achieve?

What should be the purpose of a court-connected mediation program? Although many judges have embraced mediation as a means to reduce delay, the evidence that it accomplishes this is conflicting. For example, a study of six federal court programs that used mediation as one option did not find statistically significant evidence that the programs affected the duration of cases (Kakalik et al., 1996). On the other hand, studies of one federal and a group of state courts found that mediation programs did significantly reduce the length of cases, and a California study found similar results (Stienstra et al., 1997; Stipanowich, 2004). (Summaries of numerous studies of court-related programs appear at *http://courtadr.org/files/MedStudyBiblio2ndEd2.pdf*.)

The differences in study results may owe to the great variations in how individual courts design and implement programs. Some courts, for example, do not send cases to mediation until after discovery is complete, greatly reducing their ability to cut cost or delay, and some courts have initial time frames for mediation as short as one or two hours, too little time to apply most of the techniques described in this book. Given these variations it is not surprising that results are mixed. But whether or not court-sponsored mediation consistently reduces delay, there may be reasons to support its use.

As a U.S. Magistrate Judge in California, Wayne Brazil has directed one of the nation's most innovative court-connected ADR programs. In this article he presents the rationale for a multifaceted approach.

❖ **Wayne D. Brazil,** *Why Should Courts Offer Non-Binding ADR Services?*
16 Alternatives 65 (1998)

[T]here is no one method of procedure that works best for resolving . . . every kind of dispute. . . . In some cases, the parties' dominating concern will be with trying to establish the truth. They will want to use the process that is most likely to generate historically accurate factfinding, regardless of other considerations. . . . Traditional adversarial litigation may well best meet the needs of such parties.

But for parties to whom other values or interests loom larger, other processes are likely to deliver more valued service — and are more likely to result in consensual disposition. . . . To some parties, relationship-building . . . may be of prime importance. . . . In some cases, what the parties care most about are feelings. . . . In some disputes, it is the quality and character of communication that matters most — or that holds the most promise of delivering constructive solutions. . . . It follows that if our judicial system is to be responsive to the full range of interests and needs that cases filed in our courts implicate, then the system cannot offer only one dispute resolution method. . . .

One role of public courts in a democratic society is to try to assure that it is not only the wealthy or the big case litigants who have access to appropriate and effective dispute resolution processes. Poor litigants, and parties to cases without substantial economic value, should not be relegated by our judicial system to the often-slow and disproportionately expensive procedures of traditional adversarial litigation. To force poor people and small cases into that system can be tantamount to denying them access to any system at all. . . .

A related consideration supporting court sponsorship of ADR begins with the observation that some litigants and lawyers might have greater confidence in the integrity of an ADR process and the neutral when the ADR services are provided or sponsored by a court than when they are provided in a wholly private setting. When the service provider is a public court, for example, there is no occasion for the concerns that have surfaced about the possible influence . . . of large companies that are current or potential sources of considerable repeat business. . . .

[In addition,] active participation in designing and implementing ADR programs provides courts with opportunities to gain insight that they can use to improve their handling of traditional litigation. [A] thoughtfully monitored ADR program can develop . . . insights into negotiation dynamics that can be shared with judges who host settlement conferences, enhancing the skills . . . that judges can bring to their work as settlement facilitators. . . .

Unhappily, there is a risk that courts could be tempted to permit institutional selfishness to infect the thinking that drives their program design. Some judges and judicial administrators, for example, might be attracted to ADR only or primarily as a docket reduction tool, [posing] serious threats to fairness or other values that ADR should be promoting. There also is a risk that some judges and administrators could try to use ADR programs as dumping grounds for categories of cases that are deemed unpopular, unimportant, annoying, or difficult.

Questions

1. Would a traditional, trial-oriented judge disagree with the arguments that Judge Brazil makes for court-connected mediation? Which ones?
2. Brazil promotes mediation as a means of securing justice for poor people. We will see that other commentators argue that ADR provides second-class justice to the disadvantaged. On what aspects of the process does each side focus?
3. One study found that attorneys permitted to choose from among several ADR processes were more likely than attorneys who did not have a choice to report that the ADR process lowered litigation costs, reduced the amount of discovery and number of motions, was fair, resulted in settlement, and had benefits that outweighed the costs (Stienstra et al., 1997). What downside might there be to permitting attorneys to choose among court ADR processes?

Professor Nancy Welsh has delved into some of the fairness concerns raised by Judge Brazil, focusing on what ordinary people mean by "justice" and whether court-connected ADR programs deliver it. In doing so, she distinguishes between "procedural" justice, which refers to disputants' feelings about process, and "distributive" justice, which focuses on their assessment of outcomes.

❖ **Nancy A. Welsh,** *Making Deals in Court-Connected Mediation: What's Justice Got to Do with It?*

79 Wash. U. L. Q. 787 (2001)

Researchers have found that procedural justice matters profoundly. Disputants' perceptions of the justice provided by a procedure affect their judgments of the distributive justice provided by the outcome, their compliance with that outcome, and their faith in the legitimacy of the institution that offered the procedure. Disputants use the following indicia to assess procedural justice:

- whether the procedure provided them with the opportunity to tell their stories,
- whether the third party considered their stories, and
- whether the third party treated them in an even-handed and dignified manner.

The procedures used in socially-sanctioned dispute resolution processes assume such significance because disputants seek personal and pragmatic reassurance. Disputants need to believe that they are valued members of society and that the final outcome of a dispute resolution process will be based on full information. . . .

The Effects of Procedural Justice

Although issues of procedural justice often do not attract as much public attention as concerns about distributive justice, research has shown that when people experience dispute resolution and decision-making procedures, they pay a great deal of attention to the way things are done [i.e., how decisions are made] and the nuances of their treatment by others. . . .

Research has repeatedly confirmed that . . . [d]isputants who believe that they have been treated in a procedurally fair manner are more likely to conclude that the resulting outcome is substantively fair. In effect, a disputant's perception of procedural justice anchors general fairness impressions or serves as a fairness heuristic [heuristic is a social science term for a mental shortcut]. Further, research has indicated that disputants who have participated in a procedure that they evaluated as fair do not change their evaluation even if the procedure produces a poor or unfair outcome.

The perception of procedural justice also serves as a shortcut means of determining whether to accept or reject a legal decision or procedure. Disputants who believe that they were treated fairly in a dispute resolution procedure are more likely to comply with the outcome of that procedure. This effect will occur even if outcomes do not favor the disputants or they are actually unhappy with the outcomes . . . .

Process Characteristics That Enhance Perceptions of Procedural Justice

Several rather specific process characteristics enhance perceptions of procedural justice. First, perceptions of procedural justice are enhanced to the extent that disputants perceive that they had the opportunity to present their views, concerns, and evidence to a third party and had control over this presentation ("opportunity for voice"). Second, disputants are more likely to perceive procedural justice if they perceive that the third party considered their views, concerns, and evidence. Third, disputants' judgments about procedural justice are affected by the perception that the third party treated them in a dignified, respectful manner and that the procedure itself was dignified. Although it seems that a disputants' perceptions regarding a fourth factor — the impartiality of the third party decision maker — also ought to affect procedural justice judgments, it appears that disputants are influenced more strongly by their observations regarding the third party's even-handedness and attempts at fairness.

. . . Concerns regarding the opportunity for voice apply in a variety of settings, including the courtroom, arbitration proceedings, contacts with the police, political decision making, and decision making in work organizations. Even in countries where the judicial systems typically use non-adversarial procedures, citizens often prefer procedures that allow a full opportunity for voice. Perhaps most surprisingly, both field and laboratory studies have demonstrated that the opportunity for voice heightens disputants' judgments of procedural justice even when they know that their voice will not and cannot influence the final outcome. . . .

Disputants' perceptions of procedural justice also are influenced by how the third party interacts with them on an interpersonal level. . . . For example, in one study comparing litigants' reactions to the third-party processes of trial, arbitration, and judicial settlement conferences, the litigants gave much higher procedural justice rankings to trial and arbitration, even though these proceedings required the litigants to surrender decision-making control. Most litigants perceived trial and arbitration as dignified and careful. In contrast, settlement conferences were more likely to strike litigants as undignified and contrary to the litigants' sense of procedural fairness.

Significantly, several studies have shown that disputants value these process characteristics as much as, or even more than, control over the final decision (also termed "decision control"). . . .

Ultimately, the procedural justice literature highlights the need to focus not solely on the fairness of outcomes, but also on the fairness of procedures. Further, the literature suggests that disputants are less concerned about receiving formal due process during their experiences with the courts than they are about being treated in a manner that is consistent with their everyday expectations regarding social relations and norms.

Questions

You are an advisor to a court seeking to design a mediation program for disputes in which only about half of the participants will be represented by a lawyer.

4. What do the procedural justice findings suggest about how the program should be designed in terms of structure — format, length of sessions, and physical facilities — and the selection and training of mediators?
5. Can you suggest specific problems the program should try to avoid?

2. How Should Services Be Provided?

The goals of promoting settlement and satisfying litigants' interests are not necessarily contradictory, but varying goals are likely to lead to different program designs. A program focused on stimulating settlements at minimal cost, on the one hand, might encourage participants to "cut to the chase." A program with a goal of addressing parties' underlying interests, by contrast, would be more likely to require longer sessions, probably increasing cost.

One key issue is who will mediate such cases. Most court programs rely on panels made up of neutrals with limited training and experience, usually practicing attorneys who often serve on a volunteer basis. This approach allows courts to offer ADR services at low cost and build support for mediation in the private bar. The services themselves, however, vary widely in quality. A second option is to create a roster of professional neutrals. Such panels are more consistently competent, but professionals are likely to require payment for their services. Some courts seek to achieve both goals by using professionals but requiring them to contribute some initial time without charge or to work at reduced rates. Finally, some courts, particularly in the federal and family court systems, use full-time employees as mediators, either exclusively or in combination with an outside panel. These neutrals may be lawyers, magistrates, senior judges, or lay personnel. Some have the advantage of receiving training and being able to devote substantial time to each case. However, the "full-time employee" model requires the court to bear most or all of the cost of providing neutrals and may make it difficult for litigants to avoid a mediator whom they consider ineffective.

Cases may be sent to court-connected programs by litigants, judges, or court screeners. Courts vary widely as to when they order or permit cases to go into mediation. Empirical research has not resolved whether earlier or later mediation is more effective in terms of settlement rate, but the general trend is to mediate disputes earlier in their lives.

Courts that offer mediation services face the following issues:

1. Will participation in the program be voluntary or mandatory?
   - If mandatory, will the mandate apply to all cases or only a subset of them?
   - If a subset, will it be defined by the type of case, the parties (e.g., pro se versus represented litigants), the amount in controversy, or some other criterion?

- If voluntary, will they enter by referral only, or will litigants be allowed to opt in?
2. How will neutrals be selected?
3. How much time will be allowed for the process? Can the time be extended?
4. How will program costs be covered?
   - Will neutrals be paid?
   - Will participants be charged? On what basis?
   - Will waivers be available to indigents?
5. What level of attendance will be required?
   - Will individual parties be required to attend in person?
   - Will corporate parties be required to send a representative with a specific level of authority (e.g., "full authority")?
6. What level of participation will be required?
   - Will parties be either required or permitted to file written materials?
   - Will disputants be required to adhere to a standard of conduct (e.g., to "mediate in good faith")?

These questions trigger others. If, for instance, parties are required to mediate in "good faith," what does this mean in practice? Should a court invade mediation confidentiality to gather evidence about what happened in the process? These and other legal questions are explored in Chapter 15.

Problem 1

Investigate a mediation program offered by your local courts. How does the program deal with the issues listed above?

Questions

6. A court has been requiring parties to participate in ADR for several years, and as a result the local bar has become very familiar with how mediation can be used to resolve disputes. The court has asked you whether as a matter of policy it should now drop its requirement and allow parties and lawyers to decide voluntarily whether to use ADR. What would you recommend? What factors or data might be important to your decision?
7. What are the potential pluses and minuses of using full-time court employees or judges, rather than a panel of trained lawyers, as the neutrals in a court-affiliated program?

C. Policy Issues Regarding the Use of Mediation

An unstated assumption of the readings to this point is that settlement is desirable, and that because mediation assists parties to settle it is a good thing. But is this always true?

1. Should Some Cases Not Be Settled?

❖ **Owen M. Fiss,** AGAINST SETTLEMENT
93 Yale L.J. 1073 (1984)

In a recent report to the Harvard Overseers, Derek Bok called for a new direction in legal education. He decried "the familiar tilt in the law curriculum toward preparing students for legal combat," and asked instead that law schools train their students "for the gentler arts of reconciliation and accommodation." He sought to turn our attention from the courts to "new voluntary mechanisms" for resolving disputes. In doing so, Bok echoed themes that have long been associated with the Chief Justice and that have become a rallying point for the organized bar and the source of a new movement in the law. . . .

The movement promises to reduce the amount of litigation initiated, and accordingly the bulk of its proposals are devoted to negotiation and mediation prior to suit. But the interest in the so-called "gentler arts" has not been so confined. It extends to ongoing litigation as well, and the advocates of ADR have sought new ways to facilitate and perhaps even pressure parties into settling pending cases. . . .

The advocates of ADR are led to support such measures and to exalt the idea of settlement more generally because they view adjudication as a process to resolve disputes. They act as though courts arose to resolve quarrels between neighbors who had reached an impasse and turned to a stranger for help.

Courts are seen as an institutionalization of the stranger and adjudication is viewed as the process by which the stranger exercises power. The very fact that the neighbors have turned to someone else to resolve their dispute signifies a breakdown in their social relations; the advocates of ADR acknowledge this, but nonetheless hope that the neighbors will be able to reach agreement before the stranger renders judgment. Settlement is that agreement. It is a truce more than a true reconciliation, but it seems preferable to judgment because it rests on the consent of both parties and avoids the cost of a lengthy trial.

In my view, however, this account of adjudication and the case for settlement rest on questionable premises. I do not believe that settlement as a generic practice is preferable to judgment or should be institutionalized on a wholesale and indiscriminate basis. It should be treated instead as a highly problematic technique for streamlining dockets. Settlement is for me the civil analogue of plea bargaining: Consent is often coerced; the bargain may be struck by someone without authority; the absence of a trial and judgment renders subsequent judicial involvement troublesome; and although dockets are trimmed, justice may not be done. Like plea bargaining, settlement is a capitulation to the conditions of mass society and should be neither encouraged nor praised.

The Imbalance of Power

By viewing the lawsuit as a quarrel between two neighbors, the dispute-resolution story that underlies ADR implicitly asks us to assume a rough equality between the contending parties. It treats settlement as the anticipation of the outcome of trial and assumes that the terms of settlement are simply a product of the parties' predictions of that outcome. In truth, however, settlement is also a function of the resources available to each party to finance the litigation, and those resources are frequently distributed unequally. Many lawsuits do not involve a property dispute between two neighbors, or between [a major corporation] and the government . . . , but rather concern a struggle between a member of a racial minority and a municipal police department over alleged brutality, or a claim by a worker against a large corporation over work-related injuries. In these cases, the distribution of financial resources, or the ability of one party to pass along its costs, will invariably infect the bargaining process, and the settlement will be at odds with a conception of justice that seeks to make the wealth of the parties irrelevant.

The disparities in resources between the parties can influence the settlement in three ways. First, the poorer party may be less able to amass and analyze the information needed to predict the outcome of the litigation, and thus be disadvantaged in the bargaining process. Second, he may need the damages he seeks immediately and thus be induced to settle as a way of accelerating payment, even though he realizes he would get less now than he might if he awaited judgment. . . . Third, the poorer party might be forced to settle because he does not have the resources to finance the litigation, to cover either his own projected expenses, such as his lawyer's time, or the expenses his opponent can impose through the manipulation of procedural mechanisms such as discovery. It might seem that settlement benefits the plaintiff by allowing him to avoid the costs of litigation, but this is not so. The defendant can anticipate the plaintiff's costs if the case were to be tried fully and decrease his offer by that amount. The indigent plaintiff is a victim of the costs of litigation even if he settles.

There are exceptions. Seemingly rich defendants may sometimes be subject to financial pressures that make them as anxious to settle as indigent plaintiffs. But I doubt that these circumstances occur with any great frequency. I also doubt that institutional arrangements such as contingent fees or the provision of legal services to the poor will in fact equalize resources between contending parties....

Of course, imbalances of power can distort judgment as well: Resources influence the quality of presentation, which in turn has an important bearing on who wins and the terms of victory. We count, however, on the guiding presence of the judge, who can employ a number of measures to lessen the impact of distributional inequalities. He can, for example, supplement the parties' presentations by asking questions, calling his own witnesses, and inviting other persons and institutions to participate as amici. These measures are likely to make only a small contribution toward moderating the influence of distributional inequalities, but should not be ignored for that reason. Not even these small steps are possible with settlement. There is, moreover, a critical difference between a process like settlement, which is based on bargaining and accepts inequalities of wealth as an integral and legitimate component of the process, and a process like judgment, which knowingly struggles against those inequalities. Judgment aspires to autonomy from distributional inequalities, and it gathers much of its appeal from this aspiration....

The Lack of a Foundation for Continuing Judicial Involvement

The dispute-resolution story trivializes the remedial dimensions of lawsuits and mistakenly assumes judgment to be the end of the process. It supposes that the judge's duty is to declare which neighbor is right and which wrong, and that this declaration will end the judge's involvement.... Under these assumptions, settlement appears as an almost perfect substitute for judgment, for it too can declare the parties' rights. Often, however, judgment is not the end of a lawsuit but only the beginning. The involvement of the court may continue almost indefinitely. In these cases, settlement cannot provide an adequate basis for that necessary continuing involvement, and thus is no substitute for judgment.

The parties may sometimes be locked in combat with one another and view the lawsuit as only one phase in a long continuing struggle.... This often occurs in domestic-relations cases, where the divorce decree represents only the opening salvo in an endless series of skirmishes over custody and support.

The structural reform cases that play such a prominent role on the federal docket provide another occasion for continuing judicial involvement. In these cases, courts seek to safeguard public values by restructuring large-scale bureaucratic organizations....

The drive for settlement knows no bounds and can result in a consent decree even in the kinds of cases I have just mentioned, that is, even when a court finds itself embroiled in a continuing struggle between the parties or must reform a bureaucratic organization. The parties may be ignorant of the difficulties ahead or optimistic about the future, or they may simply believe that they can get more favorable terms through a bargained-for agreement.

Soon, however, the inevitable happens: One party returns to court and asks the judge to modify the decree, either to make it more effective or less stringent. But the judge is at a loss: He has no basis for assessing the request. He cannot, to use Cardozo's somewhat melodramatic formula, easily decide whether the "dangers, once substantial, have become attenuated to a shadow," because, by definition, he never knew the dangers....

Justice Rather Than Peace

The dispute-resolution story makes settlement appear as a perfect substitute for judgment, as we just saw, by trivializing the remedial dimensions of a lawsuit, and also by reducing the social function of the lawsuit to one of resolving private disputes. In that story, settlement appears to achieve exactly the same purpose as judgment — peace between the parties — but at considerably less expense to society. The two quarreling neighbors turn to a court in order to resolve their dispute, and society makes courts available because it wants to aid in the achievement of their private ends or to secure the peace.

In my view, however, the purpose of adjudication should be understood in broader terms. Adjudication uses public resources, and employs not strangers chosen by the parties but officials chosen by a process in which the public participates. These officials, like members of the legislative and executive branches, possess a power that has been defined and conferred by public law, not by private agreement. Their job is not to maximize the ends of private parties, nor simply to secure the peace, but to explicate and give force to the values embodied in authoritative texts such as the Constitution and statutes; to interpret those values and to bring reality into accord with them. This duty is not discharged when the parties settle.

In our political system, courts are reactive institutions. They do not search out interpretive occasions, but instead wait for others to bring matters to their attention. They also rely for the most part on others to investigate and present the law and facts. A settlement will thereby deprive a court of the occasion, and perhaps even the ability, to render an interpretation. A court cannot proceed (or not proceed very far) in the face of a settlement. To be against settlement is not to urge that parties be "forced" to litigate.... To be against settlement is only to suggest that when the parties settle, society gets less than what appears, and for a price it does not know it is paying....

The Real Divide

To all this, one can readily imagine a simple response by way of confession and avoidance: We are not talking about *those* lawsuits. Advocates of ADR might insist that my account of adjudication, in contrast to the one implied by the dispute-resolution story, focuses on a rather narrow category of lawsuits. They could argue that while settlement may have only the most limited appeal with respect to those cases, I have not spoken to the "typical" case. My response is twofold.

First, even as a purely quantitative matter, I doubt that the number of cases I am referring to is trivial. . . .

Second, it demands a certain kind of myopia to be concerned only with the number of cases, as though all cases are equal simply because the clerk of the court assigns each a single docket number. All cases are not equal. The Los Angeles desegregation case, to take one example, is not equal to the allegedly more typical suit involving a property dispute or an automobile accident. The desegregation suit consumes more resources, affects more people, and provokes far greater challenges to the judicial power. The settlement movement must introduce a qualitative perspective; it must speak to these more "significant" cases, and demonstrate the propriety of settling them. . . .

[In] fact, most ADR advocates make no effort to distinguish between different types of cases or to suggest that "the gentler arts of reconciliation and accommodation" might be particularly appropriate for one type of case but not for another. They lump all cases together. This suggests that what divides me from the partisans of ADR is not that we are concerned with different universes of cases — that Derek Bok, for example, focuses on boundary quarrels while I see only desegregation suits. I suspect instead that what divides us is much deeper and stems from our understanding of the purpose of the civil lawsuit and its place in society. It is a difference in outlook.

Someone like Bok sees adjudication in essentially private terms: The purpose of lawsuits and the civil courts is to resolve disputes, and the amount of litigation we encounter is evidence of the needlessly combative and quarrelsome character of Americans. Or as Bok put it, using a more diplomatic idiom: "At bottom, ours is a society built on individualism, competition, and success." I, on the other hand, see adjudication in more public terms: Civil litigation is an institutional arrangement for using state power to bring a recalcitrant reality closer to our chosen ideals. We turn to the courts because we need to, not because of some quirk in our personalities. We train our students in the tougher arts so that they may help secure all that the law promises, not because we want them to become gladiators or because we take a special pleasure in combat.

To conceive of the civil lawsuit in public terms as America does might be unique. I am willing to assume that no other country — including Japan, Bok's new paradigm — has a case like Brown v. Board of Education in which the judicial power is used to eradicate the caste structure. I am willing to assume that no other country conceives of law and uses law in quite the way we do. But this should be a source of pride rather than shame. What is unique is not the problem that we live short of our ideals, but that we alone among the nations of the world seem willing to do something about it. Adjudication American-style is not a reflection of our combativeness but rather a tribute to our inventiveness and perhaps even more to our commitment.

Questions

8. Based on what you have learned, how would ADR advocates criticize Professor Fiss's arguments?
9. What kinds of cases does Professor Fiss think are especially inappropriate for ADR? Would you carve out certain areas, or types of disputes, as inappropriate for mediation?
10. If you would allow mediation in certain types of cases only if it is subject to special conditions, what conditions would you impose?

❖ **Richard Delgado,** *ADR and the Dispossessed: Recent Books About the Deformalization Movement*

13 Law & Soc. Inquiry 145 (1988)

There are only a handful of basic ways in which our society responds to insoluble social problems — ones that, like blacks' demands for justice, women's claims for comparable worth, consumers' demands for well-made, reasonably priced goods, workers' demands for a larger share of the industrial pie, and everyone's desire for a safe, nonpolluted environment, cannot be solved at an acceptable cost.

If those agitating for reform are aroused and united, we cannot dismiss their problem as a nonproblem or the claimants as nonpersons (as we once did with slaves or do today with children and the insane). That would simply inflame them further. The only solution is to seem to be addressing the problem, but without doing anything that threatens the status quo too drastically. . . .

[One] approach is to enlarge the problem — to concede its existence but insist that it is much broader than most realize, that its solution entails expanding the context and taking account of a multitude of factors. . . . When "the problem" is transformed into something so complex and multifaceted that no simple legal formula can encompass it, it is also likely that no single remedy — such as an injunction or damages — can solve it. Instead, we must strive to avoid simplistic win-lose thinking and look for creative solutions that maximize many variables at once. Equally important, . . . [s]ince dozens, perhaps hundreds, of details are relevant to a case's resolution, the likelihood that identical cases will recur is remote. Therefore, we can dispense with stare decisis, the rule of law, written opinions, and judicial review. . . .

The movement toward alternative dispute resolution illustrates [this] approach. . . . It is an excellent way of seeming to be doing something about intractable social problems while actually doing relatively little . . . [P]roblems are not faced, responsibility is diffused, grievants are cooled out, while everyone leaves thinking something positive has been done.

Some grievances will not succumb to burial. They will retain their sharp edges despite being embedded in a mass of extraneous detail. The grievant will decline ADR's demand for peace, for compromise, and insist that his or her problem be dealt with in accord with justice. In disputes of this type — ones that retain their initial polarity — a second problem with ADR emerges. . . .

Formal adjudication contains a multitude of rules and practices the effect, and sometimes intent, of which is to constrain bias and prejudice. These range from rules dealing with disqualification of judges and jurors for bias, to rules that protect the jury from prejudicial influence. . . . Moreover, studies indicate that simply becoming a member of a jury has a fairness-inducing effect on jurors, causing them to display a greater degree of impartiality and fairness than they ordinarily do in daily life. . . .

[P]rejudice is widespread in American society — surveys and polls indicate that most Americans harbor some degree of prejudice toward members of groups other than their own. . . . The expression of prejudice is far from simple, however, and certainly not automatic. . . . The formalities of a court trial are calculated to check prejudice. . . . [They] also encourage minority-race persons to press their claims more forthrightly. . . .

ADR can, by expanding disputes beyond recognition, cause them to lose their urgency and sharp edges. When ADR cannot avoid dealing with sharply contested claims, its structureless setting and absence of formal rules increase the likelihood of an outcome colored by prejudice, with the result that the haves once again come out ahead. . . .

Questions

11. In what types of cases is it most likely that the concerns set out by Professor Delgado would arise? Why?
12. Could mediation procedures be modified to take account of these concerns without losing the essential character of the process? How might this be done?

---

2. Should Some Disputes Not Be Mediated?

a. Issues of Gender, Ethnicity, and Culture

❖ **Michele Hermann,** NEW MEXICO RESEARCH EXAMINES IMPACT OF GENDER AND ETHNICITY IN MEDIATION

1 Disp. Resol. Mag. 10 (Fall 1994)

Professors and students from the University of New Mexico Schools of Law and Sociology are collaborating on a research project . . . to study the effects of race and gender on mediation and adjudication of cases in Albuquerque's small claims court. This court, the Bernalillo County Metropolitan Court, is a non-record court with jurisdiction to hear civil cases in which the amount in controversy is $5,000 or less. All three judges are male; one is African American, one is Hispanic American, and one is European American. . . . The court contracts with a local mediation center to operate the court's mediation program, under which all civil filings are screened . . . and about one-third of the cases are referred to mediation.

The research project randomly assigned more than 600 cases to either adjudication or mediation, and tracked both the case results and the participants' reactions. . . . The study sought to evaluate results in mediation and adjudication by using two measures: (1) an objective formula for outcome . . . and (2) subjective measures of satisfaction. . . . Perhaps the most startling finding is that in the objective outcomes of both adjudicated and mediated cases, disputants of color fared worse than did white disputants. These disparate results were more extreme in mediated than in adjudicated cases. An ethnic-minority plaintiff could be predicted to receive eighteen cents on the dollar less than a white plaintiff in mediation, while an ethnic-minority respondent could be predicted to pay twenty cents on the dollar more.

When examining how the ethnicity of the co-mediators affected outcomes, the study found that when there were two mediators of color, the negative impact of the disputant's ethnicity disappeared. The ethnicity of the mediators did not change the objective outcomes of white disputants' cases.

The negative outcomes found for ethnic minority participants were not replicated when the data were analyzed for gender. For the most part, neither the gender of the claimant nor that of the respondent had a statistically significant effect on monetary outcomes in either adjudicated or mediated cases, except that female respondents did better in mediation than male respondents, paying less than their male counterparts.

The examination of procedural and substantive satisfaction produced interesting contrasts to the objective outcome analysis. Despite their disparately poorer outcomes, ethnic minority disputants were more likely to express satisfaction with mediation than were white disputants. Female disputants, on the other hand, were more likely to express satisfaction with adjudication. Indeed, white female respondents, who had the most favorable objective outcomes in mediation, reported the lowest level of satisfaction. Furthermore, compared to other mediation respondents, white women were less likely to see the mediation process as fair and unbiased. Women of color, on the other hand, reported the highest level of satisfaction with mediation, despite their tendency to fare the worst in objective outcomes as either claimants or respondents.

The evidence that disputants of color fare significantly worse in mediation than do white participants raises important questions about whether the traditional mediation process is appropriate in disputes involving ethnic minorities, as well as members of other groups who are traditionally disempowered in American society. . . .

It is far from clear, however, that bias, prejudice, and cultural blindness are the only explanation for the results of the UNM study. The underlying effects may be considerably more complex. . . . Similarly, the fact that white women fare well in small claims mediation does not dispel the concerns raised by scholars. . . about gender bias in other forums, such as family court. . . . In the meantime, mediation and other dispute resolution programs need to pay serious attention to the potential impact of power imbalances between and among parties who are in dispute, and should not assume that mediator neutrality will guarantee fairness.

Questions

13. If the conclusions of the New Mexico study are correct, can you think of safeguards that might reduce the risk of disparate results in small claims mediation? In mediation of family disputes?
14. Why do you think Latino disputants might be more satisfied with mediation than Anglo disputants, despite receiving less favorable results?
15. The federal courts for the District of Columbia and the Northern District of California have created panels of lawyers to represent pro se parties in ADR (Stienstra et al., 2001).
    a. Would providing legal representation in mediation resolve any of the issues identified by Delgado?
    b. Would it resolve the problems suggested in the New Mexico study?
16. Some courts will not refer pro se parties to mediation in situations in which the other side is represented by counsel. Do you agree with this policy? What are its advantages and disadvantages?

❖ **Sina Bahadoran,** *A Red Flag: Mediator Cultural Bias in Divorce Mediation*

18 Mass. Fam. L.J. 69 (2000)

Scenario One: An American wife and her Albanian husband are participating in divorce mediation. The couple shares a four-year-old daughter. During mediation, the wife alleges that her husband sometimes acts inappropriately with their daughter — one time fondling her genitalia. The mediator asks the husband about the wife's allegation and the husband responds that it is true.

Scenario Two: An American man and his Danish wife are involved in a divorce mediation. The couple shares a 14-month-old son. During mediation, the husband alleges that on several occasions his wife left their son outside in his stroller, while she went into diners to have lunch.

Scenario Three: An American woman and her Iraqi husband are participating in divorce mediation. The couple shares a nine-year-old daughter. During mediation, the wife accuses the husband of being violent and aggressive with their daughter. The wife also expresses fear over her husband's renewed interest in Islam.

In each of the above scenarios a mediator, as currently trained, would be unprepared to adequately handle these situations. In other words, mediation would be inappropriate. Scenario One is based on the incident involving Sadri Krasniqi of Plano, Texas. After fondling his daughter during a basketball match, Krasniqi was charged with sexual abuse and lost custody of his daughter. Eventually, five years later, charges against him were dropped after the prosecutors became aware that the idea of parent-child sex is so unimaginable in Albania that parental fondling is acceptable behavior.

Scenario Two is based on the case of Annette Sorenson, a Danish woman who left her 14-month-old daughter outside while she went into a diner to have lunch. Sorensen was jailed and charged with child endangerment. Only later was she freed after authorities learned that "parking," or leaving children in their strollers outside of stores, is common behavior in Denmark.

Scenario Three is a fictitious situation in which the foreign spouse would be just as disadvantaged as in the first two scenarios, not because of actual cultural differences, but rather because of perceived cultural stereotypes. . . .

American Collective Unconscious: Cultural Myths and Stereotypes

. . . A non-American spouse entering divorce mediation will face a great many cultural myths and stereotypes. . . . The cultural myths that surround people of various ethnicity and nationality vary greatly, but all are unified by a common theme: cultural inferiority.

. . . Parent-child suicide, religious fanaticism, barbarity, laziness, wife beating, forced marriage, and female genital mutilation are just some of the images associated with non-European immigrants. . . . Arab Muslims are seen as irrational beings, incapable of achieving cultural or intellectual success . . . . With Asian cultures, the myths take on a different quality. Asians are often seen as the "model minority." . . . Although intended to be complimentary to Asian-Americans, the "praise" can go too far. Most Asians are seen as being fungible . . . . In contrast to the "model" minority status associated with Asians, Latinos are often relegated to the bottom of the minority hierarchy: laziness, alcoholism, criminality, and gang culture are just a few of the myths. . . . [G]iven the cultural myths and stereotypes that pervade the American collective unconscious, the informal nature of mediation creates an atmosphere that is particularly prone to bias. . . .

Power and Danger of Narrative in Mediation

Much of the power of mediation comes from its opportunity for divorcing spouses to tell their own stories. Each spouse is the director, producer, and actor . . . . Despite the benefits of the narrative style, it is also at the center of the problems with mediation. Mediation is essentially a struggle between two opposing narratives. The prevailing narrative sets the context for all of the subsequent descriptions. Minority spouses will have more negative cultural myths aligned against them and will be disadvantaged in their ability to compete for narrative preeminence. . . .

Imagine a scenario where the Iraqi husband and his American wife are seeking mediation for their divorce. The couple has a nine-year-old daughter and is in a heated disagreement as to custody. One portion of the mediation revolves around an incident where the husband smacked their daughter's hand for misbehaving. In the wife's description, she will assign her husband the role of the violent, strict middle-easterner and herself and her daughter as the innocent victims of his rage. The husband will try and reconfigure the wife's "primary narrative." He will explain that the young girl had repeatedly misbehaved and that he lightly slapped her hand after several previous admonitions. In his narrative, the husband will assign himself the role of the "good" loving father and his wife as the unresponsive, distant mother who allows their daughter to be spoiled.

. . . Each spouse will attempt to manipulate the conversation by relying on as many positive cultural stereotypes about their identity group and negative ones about their spouse as possible. . . . The mediator sits in the middle of the competing stories as they circle around her. She must choose one . . . . Her choice will not be explicit, but she will offer more credence to one narrative over the other. The mediator enters mediation with his or her own selected conscious and unconscious cultural stereotypes. As the mediator listens to each spouse's perception of reality, she filters all of the narratives through her own individual (experiential) and cultural (identity group) filter. The effects of the narratives will be greater if they are of a subliminal rather than overt nature. . . .

Questions

17.   Do you think that cultural myths are widespread enough to pose a serious problem in mediation? In what areas are problems most likely to occur?

18.   You are the lawyer for a client from an Arabic culture who is involved in a parenting dispute that is going to mediation. How might you monitor whether your mediator is allowing stereotypes to influence her approach to the case? What could you do about it if she were?

b.   Mandatory Mediation of Family Disputes

Many state court systems now require litigants to go through mediation before obtaining access to a judge, and the most popular area for mandatory mediation has been family disputes. Mandatory mediation raises special questions, however, particularly when intimate relationships are involved and the participants do not have lawyers. The following reading argues against the use of mandatory mediation in such situations. As you read it, ask yourself these questions.

Questions

19. To what extent do the concerns raised by Professor Grillo exist if mediation is voluntary?
20. To what extent do they exist if the parties have access to lawyers?
21. If parties to domestic relations cases are not required to mediate, what is likely to happen to them?

❖ **Trina Grillo,** THE MEDIATION ALTERNATIVE: PROCESS DANGERS FOR WOMEN

100 Yale L.J. 1545 (1991)

There is little doubt that divorce procedure needs to be reformed, but reformed how? Presumably, any alternative should be at least as just, and at least as humane, as the current system, particularly for those who are least powerful in society. Mediation has been put forward, with much fanfare, as such an alternative. The impetus of the mediation movement has been so strong that in some states couples disputing custody are required by statute or local rule to undergo a mandatory mediation process if they are unable to reach an agreement on their own. . . .

[S]tudies have shown that mediation clients are more satisfied with their divorce outcomes than persons using the adversary system. Although there are significant methodological problems with each of these studies, the existence of substantial client satisfaction with some models of mediation cannot be completely discounted.

Nonetheless, I conclude that mandatory mediation provides neither a more just nor a more humane alternative to the adversarial system of adjudication of custody, and, therefore, does not fulfill its promises. In particular, quite apart from whether an acceptable result is reached, mandatory mediation can be destructive to many women and some men. . . .

The Rise of Mandatory Custody Mediation in California

The movement for voluntary mediation of divorce disputes began several decades ago as lawyers and therapists offered to help their clients settle their cases in a nonadversarial manner. . . . As mediation caught on, it began to be heralded as the cure for the various ills of adversary divorce. . . . Consumers, however, were not embracing the mediation cure. . . . In order to bypass this consumer resistance, some state legislatures established court-annexed mediation programs, requiring that couples disputing custody mediate prior to going to court. . . .

Local courts [in California] have the option of requiring mediators to make a recommendation to the court regarding custody or visitation. If the parties do not reach an agreement, the mediator may also make a recommendation that an investigation be conducted or mutual restraining orders be issued. More than half of California counties have opted to require mediators to make such recommendations . . . .

The Betrayal of Mediation's Promises: The Informal Law of Mediation

The good woman: She comes into mediation ready to be cooperative. She does not deny her feelings, but does not shift them onto her children. She realizes her problems are her problems, that she should not use the children as a way of solving them, and that it is critically important that her husband stay involved in the lives of the children. She does not play victim, but realizes what she is entitled to and insists on it calmly. She is rational, not bitter or vengeful, and certainly not interested in hurting her husband. She understands that she played a role in whatever harms he inflicted on her, since in a family no one person is ever at fault.

The bad woman: She is bitter and wants revenge for things that have happened to her in the past. She fights over the most trivial, petty things. She is greedy and ready to sacrifice her children as a tool against her husband. She is irrational and unwilling to compromise. When a specific, focused response is called for, she responds by bringing up a completely unrelated matter. It is hard to keep her on track. She keeps venting her anger instead of negotiating constructively.

In even the most mundane settings there develops a type of informal law, shared expectations that there is a right way of acting, that departures from this way are wrong, and that an offender should be sanctioned. . . . The norms that govern microlegal systems are unwritten and often not consciously perceived, but they are always present. . . . Persons in the midst of a divorce often experience what seems to them a threat to their very survival. Their self-concepts, financial well-being, moral values, confidence in their parenting abilities, and feelings of being worthy of love are all at risk. . . . They are especially vulnerable to the responses they receive from any professional with whom they must deal. Against this backdrop, mediation must be seen as a relatively high-risk process. [T]he parties are extremely sensitive to cues as to how they are supposed to act; they will look to the mediator to provide these cues. Mediators are often quite willing to give such cues, to establish the normative components of the mediation, and to sanction departures from the unwritten rules. . . .

The Promise to Contextualize Decisionmaking: Principles and Fault in Mediation

. . . The informal law of the mediation setting requires that discussion of principles, blame, and rights, as these terms are used in the adversarial context, be deemphasized or avoided. Mediators use informal sanctions to encourage the parties to replace the rhetoric of fault, principles, and values with the rhetoric of compromise and relationship. For example, mediators typically suggest that the parties eschew the language of individual rights in favor of the language of interdependent relationships. They orient the parties toward reasonableness and compromise, rather than moral vindication. The conflict may be styled as a personal quarrel, in which there is no right and wrong, but simply two different, and equally true or untrue, views of the world. . . .

. . . It is typical for mediators to insist that parties waste no time complaining about past conduct of their spouse, eschew blaming each other, and focus only on the future. For example, one of the two essential ground rules mediator Donald Saposnek suggests a mediator give to the parties is the following:

> There is little value in talking about the past, since it only leads to fighting and arguing, as I'm sure you both know. . . . Our focus will be on your children's needs for the future and on how you two can satisfy those needs. . . . [U]nless I specifically request it, we will talk about plans for the future. . . .

Mandatory Mediation and the Promise of Self-Determination

Often, the time allotted to a mandatory mediation is short. Frequently, an entire mediation is expected to take place in an hour or less. Some take place in the hallways of the courthouse. Given these conditions, it is impossible for the state to ensure that an adequate process is being offered even in cases in which people have chosen it. Where the process is inadequate, its imposition is even more troubling.

Moreover, a person married to a liar or con artist knows that that person is often more persuasive than someone telling the truth. In a relationship in which the wife has been abused, for example, the abuser will often appear dominant, charming, agreeable, and socially facile in comparison to his less assertive wife. . . .

A substantial proportion of women who file for divorce state that they do so, at least in part, because they have been the victims of domestic violence. . . . Mediation where abuse has occurred is troubling even when mediation is voluntary. Mandatory mediation programs, however, do not always permit abused parties to opt out. Moreover, even where such an exception to the mediation requirement exists, the abused spouse might have trouble showing she is entitled to it. . . .

Choice of Mediator: Partiality and Unacknowledged Perspective

Typically in mandatory mediation, the participants cannot choose their mediator or, at best, have a very limited choice of mediators.... Mediators, however, exert a great deal of power....

Exclusion of Lawyers

In California, lawyers typically are excluded from mediation sessions, and the parties are required to speak for themselves, whether or not they wish to do so. Some argue that exclusion of lawyers contributes to client empowerment. In evaluating whether their exclusion actually furthers client empowerment, it is useful to consider the reasons why a person engaged in a divorce might want the services of a lawyer....

Lawyers as Protectors of Rights

A lawyer who is excluded from the mediation sessions may be hampered in protecting her client's rights, particularly if custody is ultimately to be litigated in court....

Lawyers as Providers of Insulation

Lawyers serve another function in the divorce process, that of insulating the parties from the hand-to-hand combat and self-help that the rule of law is intended to avoid. The presence of a lawyer means that a party does not have to face his adversary directly if he does not wish to do so. Mediation is often put forward as a method of empowering the parties to a dispute, but the words "Don't call me, call my lawyer" are sometimes the most empowering words imaginable....

There are, then, many good reasons why a party might choose not to mediate.... If the state were committed only to making sure that disputants become familiar with mediation, something less than mandatory mediation — such as viewing a videotaped mediation or attending an orientation program — could be required, and mediators would certainly not be permitted to make recommendations to the court.... The legislative choice to make mediation mandatory has been a mistake....

The only reason to prefer mediation to other, more obvious alternatives is that the parties may, through the mediation process, ultimately benefit themselves and their children by learning how to communicate and work together. Whether this will happen in the context of a particular mediation is something only the parties can judge....

Questions

22. Your local family court has decided that it should impose protective rules to ensure that litigants are not subject to undue pressure to settle in its mandatory mediation program. It has asked you for advice:
    a. In what situations should the rules apply?
    b. What specific protections would you suggest?
23. Under California law, a divorce settlement that "advantages one spouse" gives rise to a presumption of undue influence. However a California appellate court has ruled that such a presumption does not apply when settlements are reached through mediation. *In re Kieturakis*, 31 Cal.Rptr.3d 119, 141 (Cal. App. 2006). Why might the court have ruled this way? Do you agree with the holding?

The issues raised by the use of mandatory mediation in domestic relations cases do not necessarily apply to other types of civil litigation. Thus Professor Roselle Wissler, for example, found in a study of two state court mediation programs that "the manner in which the case entered mediation produced few differences in parties' assessments of the mediator, the mediation process, and the outcome" (Wissler, 1997). See, to the same effect, Stienstra et al. (1997).

c. Domestic Violence Cases

Mediation, especially when mandated by a court, is particularly controversial when a case involves possible spousal abuse. Many, like Professor Grillo in the earlier reading, would object even to "voluntary" mediation in such cases. In the following reading, an experienced mediator presents a contrarian view.

❖ **Ann L. Milne**, *Mediation and Domestic Abuse*

In Divorce and Family Mediation, 304
(J. Folberg et al. eds., 2004)

There are nearly 6 million incidents of physical assault against women reported every year, and 76% of these are perpetrated by current or former husbands, cohabiting partners, or dates.... Changes in the law and the increased media attention given to domestic abuse have sensitized the public to this formerly private issue. In contrast, the use of mediation has increased significantly as a less-public forum to resolve disputes between former spouses. Courts in at least 38 states have mandated that parents be referred to mediation when they are disputing custody or parental access schedules.

... The juxtaposition of strengthened court and legal interventions in domestic abuse cases with the expanded use of mediation has resulted in considerable controversy. . . . Current arguments about the use of mediation in domestic abuse cases . . . do not focus so much on the mediation process itself, but rather on the nature of domestic abuse and the concerns endemic to these cases. Mediators should take these public policy concerns seriously. . . .

Most mediation proponents agree with the following guidelines:

- Some cases involving domestic abuse are inappropriate for mediation.
- Screening is necessary to determine which cases are appropriate.
- Mediators must be well trained in the dynamics of domestic abuse.
- Participation in the mediation process must be safe, fair, and voluntary.
- Victims of abuse should not be required to mediate.

Given these guidelines, proponents of making mediation available in cases of domestic abuse generally start with the argument of the "BATMA": What is the couple's "best alternative to a *mediated* agreement"? . . . In short, if mediation is not used, then what? It is argued by both social science experts and legal scholars that mediation is more appropriate and effective than the adversarial process, even in cases of domestic abuse. Some have said that the adversarial process exacerbates the dynamics between partners when abuse is a factor by escalating the conflict and reinforcing the power and control differential and the win/lose aspects of the relationship. . . . Few judges and lawyers have expertise in the subject of domestic abuse, whereas many mediators have had training in it. . . .

Reframing the Debate

. . . As in any conflict, the framing of the issues is critical. . . . Rather than framing the question, Should mediation be used in cases involving domestic abuse?, a more useful framing of the issue would be: What process can we develop that will best help individuals who have been involved in an abusive relationship address the issues between them, so that they can move on with their lives without violence and without the need for ongoing court and legal interventions? . . .

When providing mediation to batterers and victims, the following are excluded from the list of topics to be addressed:

- We are not mediating whether or not the abuse occurred. . . .
- We are not mediating reconciliation. . . .
- We are not mediating fault and blame. . . .
- We are not mediating punishment and consequences. . . .
- We are not mediating dropping of charges, protective orders, or restraining orders ("Do this, then she will drop the abuse charges.").
- We are not mediating contingencies or leveraging of issues. . . .

- We are not mediating court orders.
- We are not mediating threshold issues.

With the above procedural ground rules in place, the following areas can be effectively mediated:

Terms of Living Apart

Matters such as establishing a date for moving out, determining who is going to live where, division of household accessories, establishing a parenting schedule, and payment of household expenses are all day-to-day living arrangements that parties may need to address. The judge often does not have the time to take up each of these individual issues, and paying lawyers to negotiate them can be too costly for many. . . .

Property Division

Mediation can be a very helpful process for dividing up personal possessions such as furnishings, household supplies, photographs, books, tools, and all the other sundry things that family members need to manage their daily lives.

Financial Support . . . Use of Clothing and Toys . . . Activities with the Children

Mediation can be a very useful forum in which to share information about what activities the children would enjoy as well as to resolve disputes regarding activities of which a parent disapproves. Is it OK to take the children hunting? To a friend's home? To the corner tavern? . . .

School Contact

Is it OK for a parent to stop by the school to say hello to a child or to chat with the teacher? . . . Will both parents participate in children's sporting and other school events? . . .

Child-Care Arrangements

How will child-care decisions be made? . . . If a parent is called away from home, will the other parent be given the first opportunity to babysit? . . .

Research Findings

Quantitative longitudinal research on the impact of mediation in cases of domestic abuse is lacking. [S]tudies found that mediation was associated with a greater reduction in physical, verbal, and emotional abuse than lawyer-assisted settlement. . . . For the growing unrepresented or pro se population of litigants, mediation may be the only consumer support available, short of litigation. Outcome studies on the impact of precluding mediation would be very illuminating.

"Confessions of a Mediator"

I have been a mediator for more than 30 years and have worked in both a court-connected setting and a private practice. Over time I have come to several personal conclusions and observations about my own practices when mediating cases involving allegations or instances of domestic abuse:

I Am Far More Controlling of the Process

Whereas I normally espouse a mildly directive, facilitative style, when I am mediating in a case known to me to include allegations or instances of domestic abuse, I often find that I must be far more controlling of the process. . . . At the same time, I need to avoid becoming enmeshed in an arm-wrestling contest with the batterer, who may attempt to take over the process. . . .

Judgment Is Important

The role of the mediator is typically described as that of a nonjudgmental neutral party. . . . However, when mediating in cases of possible or known domestic abuse, . . . [t]he mediator must continually reevaluate whether this case is appropriate for mediation and whether he or she has the skills needed to work effectively with this couple.

Forget the Balancing Act

Terms such as maintaining balance, power balancing, and level playing field are often used when describing the mediation process. However, when mediating in a case involving issues of domestic abuse, I find that I am "off-balance" much of the time because I am challenged to keep control of the process.

The Process Is Less Collaborative and More of a Facilitated Negotiation

. . . The parties focus more on their separate interests and solutions rather than the mutual interests that I tend to focus on when abuse is not a factor.

Short-Term Agreements

One of the incentives to using mediation in cases involving concerns about domestic abuse is the ability to put in place agreements of a short-term nature and revisit and revise them as needs dictate. Predictability and steadfastness are not often present with these couples. Putting together agreements or court orders that apply over the long haul is often counterproductive. . . .

Need for Reliable Resources

The need to establish a scaffolding of support can be very important when mediating in domestic abuse cases. The support of the parties' attorneys, victim and batterer advocates, counselors, and a safety plan can all work together to facilitate the success of the mediation process.

Watch Your Language

Colloquialisms that I use in everyday speech can often take on unintended meanings with domestic abuse partners. Using expressions such as "Can you live with that?," "It strikes me that . . . ," or "Please cut that out," would be insensitive and inappropriate with couples who have abuse issues. . . .

Sweat Equity Is a Fact of Life

I usually tell my mediation students that I know something is wrong when I am working harder than the clients. I have found that, when mediating in cases where abuse concerns have been raised, my skills are challenged, there is a level of stress not found with non-abuse cases, and I work hard to ensure that the mediation process is serving the interests and safety of both parties.

Conclusions

The question of whether or not mediation is appropriate in cases of domestic abuse must be reframed to focus on finding an answer to the question of what kind of system we could design that would provide a safe and secure decision-making process for spouses and parents in dispute. Although a traditional mediation process may not offer the protection necessary in domestic abuse cases, dismissing mediation outright may also be a mistake. The development of hybrid mediation models that embody the self-determination principles of the mediation process while also addressing power, control, coercion, and safety issues must be the goal.

Questions

24. Does Ms. Milne's model accommodate Professor Grillo's concerns? Overall, which approach seems most appropriate?
25. Assuming Ms. Milne's model could work in the right circumstances, is it practical to implement in court programs, even on a voluntary basis? What assurances would you need to support such a program in your local family court?
26. If you favor excluding cases involving allegations of abuse from court programs, would you also favor barring such cases from going to private mediation on a voluntary basis?

A Case Example: A Student Mediates Access to Her Child[1]

Just after my eighteenth birthday I discovered I was pregnant with my daughter Emily. After carefully considering my options as an unwed, single mother without a college degree, I knew I could never provide Emily with

---

1. This is an account of an actual dispute; identifying information has been changed to protect the privacy of the participants.

the life I felt she deserved. In time, I accepted that I needed to explore alternatives to parenting and I chose to look at adoption. Through my research I learned about open adoption. Open adoption is an arrangement that allows for the birthmother to choose the couple who will parent her child and to work with them to design a plan for meaningful, ongoing contact throughout the child's life. Although it was the most painful choice I have ever made, I knew that choosing open adoption was in my daughter's best interest.

After almost five months of searching, I met my daughter's parents through an adoption agency in New York. At six months pregnant, I had reviewed countless profiles of prospective adoptive parents and was becoming discouraged by my inability to find the right couple. Clearly, this was not a situation where I could compromise — the "right couple" needed to have all of my predetermined qualifications. So after months of searching, I was overjoyed when I found David and Maureen, the couple that eventually became my daughter's parents.

For the remaining three months of my pregnancy, David, Maureen, and I essentially dated. We went out to dinner. I stayed over at their house. David called me every day to check in and demonstrated genuine concern for both me and the baby. In time, we agreed to maintain an extended family-type relationship after Emily's birth and pledged to always respect, value, and honor each other and the commitments that we had made. Unfortunately, everything changed as soon as Emily left the hospital with them.

The first year of her life was torturous for me. Despite what we had agreed upon, I never knew when I was going to see her, if I would hear from them, or whether or not it was even OK to contact them. When we did have visits, Maureen made it clear that I was not welcome and that this was simply something she "had" to do but certainly not something she wanted. Early on, I was not allowed to hold her for any extended period of time. After five minutes, she would always find a reason to take her back. Needless to say, this is not what I agreed to in the pre-birth discussions.

I felt devastated by the change in David and Maureen and eventually sought counsel to explore my rights. I thought very seriously about petitioning the court to overturn Emily's adoption based on fraud. However, the attorney I consulted (who I later learned was an adoptive parent of five children) told me the courts would never respect our agreement and that my only option was to work it out with them if I ever hoped to see my daughter. (I have since learned that that is not true.) Eventually, I requested that we enter mediation with the counselors at the agency that handled our adoption, and David and Maureen agreed.

At the time I entered mediation I knew nothing about the process. I had never been involved in anything like it before and I had serious doubts about the prospect of a positive result. I felt betrayed by both the agency and David and Maureen, and I wasn't confident that the agency-provided mediator would help us come to an agreement that was binding. However, I didn't have any other options so I decided I had to try it.

Power played a huge part in our mediation. Neither side was represented by counsel, but David and Maureen are almost 20 years older than me, have advanced degrees, and are well-respected professionals in their respective fields. As an uneducated, single 19-year-old, I felt disadvantaged. Beyond the educational differences, I was plainly outnumbered. But most importantly, they had Emily, the seminal piece of the power puzzle. Because of that, I always felt like I was in a poor bargaining position. As the professional, our mediator should have done more to recognize and work around that imbalance of power. For example, by caucusing she could have buffered some of their posturing and helped diffuse a lot of the insecurity I felt as a (seemingly) powerless 19-year-old.

The mediator did not use caucusing. Rather, we had five 1-2 hour sessions together as a group. The first sessions were essentially extended opening statements, followed by the final sessions in which we attempted to talk to each other and develop a suitable visitation agreement.

I learned a lot about what not to do as a mediator through my experience. The mediator often cried, rubbed her chest in a circular motion, and expressed her desire to "honor our difficult work." I understand that she was attempting to be supportive but at the time, I thought she was ridiculous and inappropriate. Also, I couldn't stand it when I could express the incredible hurt, betrayal, and anger I felt about the situation and she would respond with "That sounds like it was really hard." Frequently, I wanted to scream "*No shit!*" because it felt so incredibly patronizing and condescending to me.

Finally, she never advised me to consult an attorney. I think that was because the agency had its own agenda for our sessions. It was in the agency's best interest to not have litigation spring from our troubled relationship. Therefore, I think the mediator's lack of neutrality affected the counsel she provided to all of us.

After almost 15 years, I am happy to report that I have a wonderful relationship with my daughter. The irony of our mediation result was that I left the state almost immediately after it was finalized because it was too painful to be so close to them, both physically and psychologically. However, after over a decade of living apart and seeing my daughter a couple of times per year, I am now back in Boston and visiting with her on a schedule that is based on our mediated agreement from so long ago. Thus, despite the problems with the process that I encountered, I still left with a legally enforceable agreement that protected my rights.

Questions

27. Should this dispute have gone to mediation at all? If it had not, what do you think would have happened?

28. Should it have gone ahead only with safeguards? What ground rules or procedures might have protected everyone's interests without overly burdening the process?

CHAPTER
15

The Law and Ethics of Mediation

A. Confidentiality

One of the key attractions of mediation for both parties and lawyers is that the process is confidential. Participants in mediation regularly sign agreements in which they commit not to disclose to outsiders anything communicated during the process. In addition, states and the federal government have given mediation varying levels of confidentiality protection. Sometimes, however, participants in mediation seek to disclose, or outsiders attempt to discover, what occurred during the process.

Disputes over mediation confidentiality arise in three basic ways.

- Litigants sometimes attempt to take confidential information from the mediation process and use it in another context, usually in court. ("Isn't it true that in mediation you admitted that . . . ?"). We refer to these as *litigation* breaches.
- Disputants sometimes allege that the mediation process itself went awry ("Your Honor, I signed the agreement at 2 a.m. and wasn't thinking clearly. The mediator just wouldn't let me go home!"). This latter category can be thought of as *supervisory* intrusions, because confidentiality is being invaded allegedly to protect the mediation process itself.
- Parties may disagree about whether they reached agreement during mediation and if so what the terms were, and call each other or the mediator to testify. This is an *enforcement* intrusion.

To understand how confidentiality issues arise consider the following problems.

Problem 1

You represent a St. Louis company, Bates, Inc. Bates is a "headhunter" firm that fills executive positions for corporations. A year ago Bates contracted with a Chicago software consultant, Alpha Websites, to develop a website for Bates. A key goal for Bates was that its clients

---

be able to advertise openings without revealing their identity, and that candidates be able to input personal data online in confidence. One important function of the new software was to screen out conflicting requests (e.g., an executive applying for an opening at a company where he is currently working). The site was to be developed over six months for a total fee of $150,000.

Bates reports that the transaction was a disaster. The developer took nearly a year to deliver the site, and the security provisions proved to be porous. Clients complained that candidates could determine who was advertising, and some found themselves applying to their current employer, causing embarrassment for all concerned. Bates estimates that it lost at least a million dollars in business as a result of the website problems.

You filed suit against Alpha in federal court and a few months later accepted an invitation from Alpha's counsel to go to mediation. The mediation was governed by a confidentiality agreement. After several hours of mediation you deadlocked, with your client at $350,000 and Alpha at $50,000. In an effort to break the impasse, the mediator offered both sides a tentative opinion that while Bates had a good case on the contract, the site was now up and running fairly smoothly, and that given the language of the contract he did not think the court would grant a recovery on the lost profits claim. He recommended a settlement at $125,000. You declined this proposal, feeling that the evaluation was unrealistic and that the neutral was "bending" his evaluation to produce a number that Alpha would accept.

Three months later, you are called into a status conference with the judge presiding over the case. He asks both sides if they have explored settlement. You mention the unsuccessful mediation. The judge asks if the mediator gave an evaluation of the case. You say that the discussions were confidential, but the Alpha lawyer says, "Yes, Judge. Do you want to know what it was?" The judge nods affirmatively.

a. What should you do?
b. Is there anything you could have done in advance to prevent this situation?

Problem 2

Assume that at a settlement conference in the Bates-Alpha case, the presiding judge suggests that the litigants participate in mediation. Bates is willing, but Alpha declines. The judge says that in his experience mediation is often beneficial, and exercises his authority to order the parties to mediate. Rules of the court's mediation program require that participants mediate "in good faith" and bring with them "full settlement authority." Three weeks later Bates and Alpha appear before a court-appointed mediator. Bates is represented by its CFO and outside counsel, Alpha by an associate from its outside law firm. In its opening statement Bates indicates that while it believes strongly in its case, it is willing to consider a reasonable compromise. Alpha argues that there is no basis for liability and that Bates's damage claims are wildly inflated.

After four hours of mediation, Bates, which entered the mediation demanding $750,000, has dropped to $450,000. Alpha, which had made no offer before the mediation, offers $5,000, then $10,000, and then refuses to move further. In a caucus discussion with the mediator, Alpha's counsel reveals that she has no authority to go beyond $15,000, and that any offer above $100,000 would have to be approved by the defendant's board of directors. Bates does not know about this conversation, but tells the neutral that it strongly suspects that Alpha never gave its negotiator "real" settlement authority.

A week later, Bates files a motion for sanctions with the judge, charging that Alpha's conduct at mediation violated the court's ADR program rules. Bates subpoenas the mediator to testify at the hearing on its motion.

a. How should Alpha respond to Bates's claim that it violated program rules?

b. How should it respond to the mediator subpoena?

1. How Important Is Confidentiality to Mediation?

❖ **Frances Leary & others v. Father John J. Geoghan & others**

(Single Justice, Mass. App. Ct. 2002)

Note: People who had been sexually abused as children sued the priest who abused them and the Roman Catholic Archbishop of Boston, who they argued had failed to use reasonable care to prevent the abuse. After years of litigation the parties agreed to mediate and eventually announced a settlement. A dispute soon arose, however, over its terms. The defendants argued that the settlement, which required the Church to sell real estate, was subject to review by the Archdiocese's financial council. The plaintiffs, however, maintained that the agreement was not subject to any such condition and called the mediator as a witness. The mediator objected and moved for a protective order barring him from testifying.

Cohen, Single Justice [The plaintiffs] have represented . . . that their sole purpose in calling the mediator is to ask him whether a document that was drafted at the conclusion of the mediation contained all of the terms that the parties wished to include in an agreement to settle. . . .

. . . The [trial] judge construed the [state confidentiality] statute as not establishing an absolute bar to disclosure, but as creating a waivable privilege, belonging solely to the parties to the mediation and capable of being waived explicitly or by conduct. Because she found that the privilege was waived by both the plaintiffs and the supervisory defendants, she concluded that the statute created no impediment to the mediator's testimony. . . .

. . . As mediation has gained popularity . . . virtually all states have promulgated statutes or court rules providing for varying degrees of confidentiality in mediation. . . . The underlying rationale of these statutes and rules is that confidentiality is crucial to the effectiveness of mediation. As one commentator has explained:

> The willingness of mediation parties to "open up" is essential to the success of the process. The mediation process is purposefully informal to encourage a broad ranging discussion of facts, feelings, issues, underlying interests and possible solutions to the parties' conflict. Mediation's private setting invites parties to speak openly, with complete candor. In addition, mediators often hold private meetings — "caucuses" — with each of the parties. . . . Under such circumstances, mediation parties often reveal personal and business secrets, share deep-seated feelings about others, and make admissions of fact and law. Without adequate legal protection, a party's candor in mediation might well be "rewarded" by a discovery request or the revelation of mediation information at trial. . . . Participation will diminish if perceptions of confidentiality are not matched by reality. Another critical purpose of the privilege is to maintain the public's perception that individual mediators and the mediation process and neutral and unbiased. . . .

[Kirtley 1995]

. . . There are those who have suggested that the need for strict confidentiality may be overstated. . . . However, our legislature has enacted a statute that plainly reflects a policy judgment in favor of confidentiality, and it is that statute and that policy judgment that dictates the result here. . . .

. . . I conclude that whether or not the parties have chosen to maintain the confidentiality of the mediation, [state law] does not permit a party to compel the mediator to testify, when to do so would require the mediator to reveal communications made in the course of and relating to the subject matter of the mediation. Compelling such testimony, even if potentially helpful to the motion judge's decision on the merits of the parties' dispute, would conflict with the plain intent of the statute to protect the mediation process and to preserve mediator effectiveness and neutrality. . . .

Questions

1. What kind of breach would this have been: litigation, supervisory, or enforcement?
2. How would you have ruled on the issue?

There is a consensus that some degree of confidentiality in the process is appropriate, but commentators do not agree on how strong the protection should be. In particular, some question whether mediation requires a formal legal privilege, whereas others argue that confidentiality protection should be stronger than a legal privilege, which is waivable. Consider the following article by a scholar who is skeptical of the need for confidentiality.

❖ **Scott H. Hughes,** *A Closer Look: The Case for a Mediation Confidentiality Privilege Still Has Not Been Made*

5 Disp. Resol. Mag. 14 (Winter 1998)

Consider the case of the manipulating minister: At a small women's college, a minister with the campus ministry seduces a naive young coed into a sexual relationship. When she attempts to break off the relationship, the minister responds with harassment. She subsequently sinks into a deep depression and drops out after her first semester. Several months later, she confides in her sister, who promptly relays the sordid tale to their mother.

The family's attorney files suit and commences discovery, from which she learns about an earlier incident involving the same minister while at the college's sister institution. Finding that the previous dispute had been settled through mediation, the attorney issues a subpoena for the mediator and his notes. During a caucus with the mediator, it seems, the minister stated that his supervisors had been aware of his illicit urges for some time. The mediator, joined by the church and the minister, seeks to quash the subpoena by asserting the privilege contained in the state mediation act. Does the need to encourage settlement outweigh the victim's rights to this information? I think not.

[Or] consider the case of the disputant in duress: During a mediation, one party complains of chest pains and fatigue, only to be told by the mediator that he cannot leave the mediation session until a settlement has been reached. The disputant subsequently signs a settlement, but tries to have it set aside during a subsequent action for specific performance. The adverse party contends that the mediation privilege prohibits an examination of the communications that took place during mediation, preventing the assertion of such a defense. Mediation privileges would foreclose disputants from raising this or many other contract defenses. . . .

Over the past two decades we have witnessed a vast proliferation of mediation statutes throughout the United States, many of which contain privileges shielding the mediator and/or the parties from the disclosure of events that take place during mediation, thus shrouding mediation proceedings in a veil of secrecy. . . . Before rushing to create another privilege that may preclude the law's traditional right to "every person's evidence," we should take at least one more close look at the social and legal cost of such a privilege. If that important step is taken, it will become apparent that the benefit of the mediation privilege does not justify its cost.

To begin with, it should be noted that there is almost no empirical support for mediation privileges. For example, no data exists to show a difference in growth rates or overall use of mediation services between jurisdictions with privileges and those without such protections, or from within any jurisdiction before and after the creation of a privilege. . . . Moreover, there is no empirical work to demonstrate a connection between privileges and the ultimate success of mediation. Although parties may have an expectation of privacy, no showing has been made that fulfilling this expectation is crucial to the outcome of mediation. . . .

[T]o assess the overall value of mediation privileges, it is important to weigh any gains that would be attributable to mediation against their cost. Privileges sacrifice potentially important evidence for subsequent legal proceedings and restrict public access to information that may be necessary to a democratic society. Of course, finely detailed exceptions to a mediation privilege could be crafted that would help overcome many problems. However, numerous exceptions could well lead to an unpredictable privilege that would be more detrimental than no privilege at all.

Until [an] empirical connection can be made, the arguments in favor of mediation privileges should not overcome the historical presumption favoring the availability of "every person's evidence."

Questions

3. Who do you find more persuasive — Professor Kirtley, whose views are quoted in the *Leary* opinion, or Professor Hughes?
4. In the absence of a legal privilege, what can a lawyer do to increase the likelihood that mediation communications will be kept confidential?
5. Chapter 9 lists several ways in which a mediator can facilitate settlement, including:
   * Helping to ensure the presence of key decision makers at the table.
   * Allowing disputants to present arguments, interests, and feelings directly to their opponent.
   * Moderating negotiations, coaching bargainers, and reframing positions.
   * Assisting each side to reassess its litigation option.
   * Helping participants to focus on their underlying interests.
   For which of these functions is the assurance of confidentiality most significant?

2. *Sources of Mediation Confidentiality*

There are five primary sources of rules governing confidentiality in mediation:

*   Rules of evidence
*   Privileges
*   Confidentiality statutes and rules
*   Mediation agreements
*   Disclosure statutes and rules

a. **Rules of Evidence**

Virtually every jurisdiction has adopted a rule of evidence to protect the confidentiality of settlement discussions. The key federal provision is Federal Rule of Evidence (FRE) 408.[1] Most states have evidentiary rules patterned on FRE 408 (Cole et al., 2008). The first point to note about FRE 408 is that it is a rule of evidence, not a guarantee of confidentiality. FRE 408 is intended to limit what litigants can offer in evidence in a court proceeding, not what parties or observers can disclose in any other context. The rule does not, for example, apply to discovery depositions, nor does it limit what a person can say in a conversation or a media interview. In addition, FRE 408 and its counterparts typically apply only to court proceedings, and may therefore not be effective in less formal forums such as administrative hearings and arbitrations; whether a mediation conversation will be admissible in another forum will depend on its rules and the philosophy of the presiding officer.

Even in court FRE 408 may not prevent information about settlement discussions from being disclosed. The rule and its state counterparts cover only evidence that a person offered or agreed to accept "valuable consideration" to compromise a claim, not everything said in settlement discussions. Thus, for example, the rule does not protect a trade secret disclosed in mediation from being introduced into evidence unless it formed part of an offer to settle.

Indeed, even an offer of compromise is not necessarily sacrosanct under FRE 408, because the rule has many exceptions. The rule applies only if an

---

1. The text of the rule is as follows:

Rule 408. Compromise and Offers to Compromise. Evidence of (1) furnishing or offering or promising to furnish, or (2) accepting or offering or promising to accept, a valuable consideration in compromising or attempting to compromise a claim which was disputed as to either validity or amount, is not admissible to prove liability for or invalidity of the claim or its amount. Evidence of conduct or statements made in compromise negotiations is likewise not admissible. This rule does not require the exclusion of any evidence otherwise discoverable merely because it is presented in the course of compromise negotiations. This rule also does not require exclusion when the evidence is offered for another purpose, such as proving bias or prejudice of a witness, negativing a contention of undue delay, or proving an effort to obstruct a criminal investigation or prosecution.

offer of compromise is introduced for the purpose of proving "liability for or invalidity of the claim or its amount." Confidential information offered, for example, to show that a witness is biased or that a party did not bargain in good faith is not protected by the rule.

Other uncertainties arise from the fact that only the person against whom evidence is being offered can make an FRE 408 objection. The rule, in other words, is designed to prevent a party from being shot in court with a "gun" it provided to the other side during settlement discussions, not to help non-parties or mediators keep discussions confidential. Finally, a rule of evidence can often be hard to enforce, as parties who evade it ordinarily risk at most a judicial reprimand.

b. Privileges

Roughly half the states now have statutes that apply generally to mediation, and every state has a law covering the use of mediation in specific types of cases or settings, such as environmental disputes or court-connected programs. Of the states with general statutes, most have created formal legal privileges. It is important to bear in mind the following distinction: Although a privilege bars evidence from being admitted in adjudication, it does not bar persons from disclosing the same information outside of court. A privilege alone, therefore, is not necessarily a guarantee of complete confidentiality. By contrast, a statute providing "confidentiality" would ordinarily bar the release of information in all contexts. The terminology can be confusing, however: The lawyer-client privilege, for example, bars disclosures in all circumstances, unless waived by the client, who is the "holder" of the privilege.

A privilege is less subject to evasion than an evidentiary rule such as FRE 408 because privileges bar the admission of evidence regardless of the purpose for which it is offered. Violations of privileges may also give rise to a cause of action for damages.

To understand the level of protection offered by a privilege in any particular setting, consider the following issues:

- What privilege applies to the process?
- What does it cover? Testimony in litigation only, or disclosure in any context?
- In what phases of the process does the privilege apply?
- Who can invoke it?
- Is it subject to exceptions or exclusions?

What Privilege Applies?

Courts almost always apply their own rules of evidence, but this is not true of privileges. Thus, if a mediation takes place in State A but the case later goes to trial in State B, which state's privilege will be applied will depend on choice-of-law principles, making the outcome hard to predict. As Professor Ellen Deason has commented, "Mediation confidentiality would make an ideal poster child for the shortcomings of choice-of-law" (Deason, 2002b).

A few federal courts have recognized a mediation privilege as a matter of federal common law, but there is no general mediation privilege in federal proceedings. FRE 501 authorizes courts to apply either state or federal privilege rules in a federal case, making it difficult to predict how confidential communications will be treated in federal court.

What Is Covered? In What Phases of the Process?

As we have noted, some privileges apply only to testimony given during litigation, whereas other privileges impose confidentiality in non-court settings as well. A particular privilege may, for example, apply only to the mediation session itself, but not to conversations and e-mails between counsel and the neutral before and afterward. The rule on what phases of the mediation process are covered by privilege varies from state to state and is sometimes poorly defined.

Who "Holds" the Privilege?

Only persons designated as "holders" of a privilege are entitled to invoke it. Typically the parties to a case hold a mediation privilege and thus can prevent disclosures. The mediator, however, may not be entitled to use the privilege as a shield, just as lawyers are not usually permitted to invoke the attorney-client privilege unless their client elects to do so. Thus, if a neutral is called to testify about what occurred during a mediation he may have to ask a party to protect him from testifying. In *Hauzinger v. Hauzinger*, 892 N.E.2d 849 (N.Y. App. 2008), for example, a New York appellate court ruled that when both parties in a divorce case waive a right to confidentiality granted by state law, and the mediation agreement contemplates possible disclosure, a court can order the mediator to testify.

By contrast, in the *Leary* sex abuse case, the judge barred the mediator's testimony even though both sides had waived their objections. The Uniform Mediation Act (UMA), discussed below, similarly grants mediators the right to prevent disclosure of their own mediation communications (UMA § 4). California's law is even stronger: The consent of the mediator and the parties is needed for anyone to testify as to the content of a mediation and mediators may not testify at all (Cal. Evid. Code §§ 1122, 703.5).

Is the Privilege Qualified or Absolute? What Exceptions Apply?

Some states have adopted mediation privileges that are absolute, meaning that they contain no exceptions. The UMA allows disclosure and other statutes require disclosure in certain situations, for example, to report evidence of a felony, threats of harm to children, perjury, and other matters. Even when a privilege is absolute on its face, courts sometimes create exceptions as a matter of common law.

c.   Confidentiality Statutes and Rules

As noted, roughly half of the states have enacted statutes governing mediation. Many of these go beyond establishing an evidentiary privilege to make the entire mediation process confidential. A Massachusetts statute, for instance, states that any communication during a mediation, as well as the mediator's work product, "shall be confidential," as well as inadmissible in adjudication, and California statutes similarly provide that the mediation process shall be "confidential." (See Mass. Gen. Laws ch. 233, § 23C; Cal. Code §§ 1115-1128.)

Neither Congress nor the federal courts have provided any general guarantee of confidentiality to mediation. Confidentiality provisions exist, however, in specific federal statutes, such as the Administrative Dispute Resolution (ADR) Act of 1996, 5 U.S.C. § 574, which provides that neutrals and parties in mediations of administrative cases "shall not voluntarily disclose or through discovery or compulsory process be required to disclose any dispute resolution communication." The ADR Act of 1998, 28 U.S.C. § 652(d), requires that federal district courts adopt local rules to provide for the confidentiality of ADR processes that occur within their court-connected programs. As a result, parties are more likely to find confidentiality protected in federal cases if they mediate under the aegis of a court ADR program than if they go to a private mediator.

State court and private mediation programs also typically provide that mediations held under their auspices will be confidential. The rules of such programs often do not specify, however, what is meant by confidentiality. In one sense a party's incentive to comply with the rules of a court-affiliated program is strong, because litigants may be concerned that if they violate a rule, they will incur the wrath of the judge who will hear their case. This is not to say, however, that a party will have a legal cause of action or other remedy if an opponent violates a confidentiality rule.

d.   Mediation Agreements

Mediation agreements offer the best opportunity for a lawyer to tailor confidentiality protections to the needs of particular clients. A mediation agreement is a contract, however, and thus is subject to the limitations inherent in any contractual undertaking. First, agreements bind only those who enter into them, not nonparties. In the case of mediation, this means that outsiders to the process, such as third-party litigants, are not bound by agreements between parties to maintain confidentiality. Second, if a breach does occur, the only remedy is usually to sue for monetary damages, which rarely can be proved. Even in the unusual situation in which a litigant knows of an impending violation and is able to seek a court order to prevent it, a judge may refuse to act out of concern that a contract not to provide evidence in court violates public policy. This said, however, practicing neutrals report few complaints from parties to commercial mediation that an opponent agreed to confidentiality and then violated it.

Parties also often contract for confidentiality as part of settlement agreements. Such agreements typically provide that the terms of settlement shall remain confidential and sometimes specify liquidated damages for any breach.

e. Disclosure Statutes and Rules

Public policy sometimes weighs against secrecy concerning settlement negotiations. Many states, concerned that secret settlements have operated to hide serious social problems from officials and society, have considered statutes that would bar courts from ordering certain kinds of settlements sealed.

Some states also have decisional law or statutes that require persons who become aware of certain offenses to report them to authorities. Thus, for example, some jurisdictions require therapists to report potential physical harm that they learn about from clients (see *Tarasoff v. Regents of Univ. of Cal.*, 17 Cal. 3d 425 (1976)), and many states require mediators to report instances of child abuse.

Finally, individual states and the federal government have enacted "sunshine laws," which require that certain meetings involving government officials be open to the public. As a result when government officials participate, the mediation process may have to be open to outside observers.

3. Examples from Practice

As we have discussed, most attempts to penetrate the confidentiality of mediation occur because a litigant is seeking to use information revealed in mediation to bolster its case, because a participant is alleging that the process itself was defective, or as proof of what was agreed to. We consider each category in turn.

a. Use of Mediation Information in Litigation

❖ Rojas v. Superior Court of Los Angeles County
33 Cal. 4th 407 (2004)

CHIN, J.:

We granted review in this case to consider the scope of Evidence Code Sec. 1119(b), which provides: "No writing . . . that is prepared for the purpose of, in the course of, or pursuant to, a mediation . . . is admissible or subject to discovery. . . ."

Factual Background

Julie Coffin is the owner of an apartment complex in Los Angeles that includes three buildings and a total of 192 units. In 1996, Coffin sued the contractors and subcontractors who built the complex . . . alleging that water leakage due to construction defects had produced toxic molds and other microbes on the property. . . . In April 1999, the litigation settled as a result of mediation. . . .

In August 1999, several hundred tenants of the apartment complex filed the action now before us against [Coffin and] numerous . . . entities that participated in development or construction of the complex. Tenants alleged that defective construction had allowed water to circulate and microbes to infest the complex, causing numerous health problems. They also alleged that all defendants had conspired to conceal the defects and that they (Tenants) had not become aware of the defects until April 1999. Tenants served [a] request for production of all photographs . . . taken . . . during the underlying action. . . . Coffin asserted that, under section 1119, the requested documents were not discoverable. . . .

[The trial judge] denied Tenants' motion . . . explaining: "The plaintiffs say that they need these photos and there's no other evidence of the conditions as they were at that time and in those places, and defendants are saying these photographs were created for mediation purposes. . . . They're clearly protected by the mediation privilege. This is a very difficult decision . . . because it could well be that there's no other way for the plaintiffs to get this particular material. On the other hand, the mediation privilege is an important one, . . . and if courts start dispensing with it by using the . . . test governing the work product privilege, . . . you may have people less willing to mediate."

[The intermediate court of appeal reversed the trial court.]

Discussion

As we recently explained, implementing alternatives to judicial dispute resolution has been a strong legislative policy since at least 1986. Mediation is one of the alternatives the Legislature has sought to implement. . . . One of the fundamental ways the Legislature has sought to encourage mediation is by enacting several mediation confidentiality provisions. [C]onfidentiality is essential to effective mediation because it promotes a candid and informal exchange regarding events in the past. This frank exchange is achieved only if participants know that what is said in the mediation will not be used to their detriment through later court proceedings and other adjudicatory processes.

The particular confidentiality provision at issue here is section 1119(b) [of the California Code], which provides: "No writing . . . that is prepared for the purpose of, in the course of, or pursuant to, a mediation or a mediation consultation, is admissible or subject to discovery, and disclosure of the writing shall not be compelled, in any . . . noncriminal proceeding. . . ." The Court of Appeal's holding directly conflicts with the plain language of these provisions. . . .

[Section 1120 of the Code] does not, as the Court of Appeal held, support a contrary conclusion. As noted above, section 1120(a), provides that "[e]vidence otherwise admissible or subject to discovery outside of a mediation . . . shall not be or become inadmissible or protected from disclosure solely by reason of its introduction or use in a mediation. . . ." Read together, sections 1119 and 1120 establish that a party cannot secure protection for a writing — including a photograph, a witness statement, or an analysis of a test sample — that was not "prepared for the purpose of, in the course of, or pursuant to, a mediation" simply by using or introducing it in a mediation. [The statutory scheme] prevents parties from using a mediation as a pretext to shield materials from disclosure.

. . . More broadly, the Court of Appeal's construction is inconsistent with the overall purpose of the mediation confidentiality provisions. . . .

For all of the above reasons, we conclude that the Court of Appeal erred in holding that photographs, videotapes, witness statements, and "raw test data" from physical samples collected at the complex — such as reports describing the existence or amount of mold spores in a sample — that were "prepared for the purpose of, in the course of, or pursuant to, [the] mediation" in the underlying action are . . . discoverable "upon a showing of good cause." . . .

Questions

6. The California Supreme Court in *Rojas* refused to allow judicially created exceptions to the state's mediation privilege statute. Suppose, however, that you were a legislator considering the issue. Would you support a law giving materials prepared for mediation absolute protection, or the narrower protection available under the "work product doctrine" that governs materials lawyers create in preparation for trial? Why?

7. Can you think of other situations in which the interest in mediation confidentiality should give way to the needs of the justice system or other social needs?

8. Is the effect of the *Rojas* decision that the defendant Coffin, having created the photographs, can use them but the plaintiffs cannot? If so, is that fair? If not, should she be permitted to do so? Why?

9. If you conclude that *Rojas* bars all parties to a case from introducing data created for a mediation in court, how would you handle this situation: The plaintiff lawyer in a California personal injury case creates a video that shows a "day in the life" of his seriously handicapped client to dramatize the extent of the plaintiff's injuries to the insurer and the neutral in a mediation process. The mediation, however, is not successful. The plaintiff later seeks to introduce the same video at trial. The defense objects, citing the statute at issue in *Rojas*. Assuming that a video is a "writing" for purposes of the statute, how should the court rule? Is your result fair? Can you suggest any changes to the statute to deal with this issue?

10. In the mediation of more than 500 civil cases alleging priest abuse, the Archdiocese of Los Angeles offered to prepare written summaries or proffers of the personnel files of more than 100 priests who had been identified by private plaintiffs as molesters, to deal with the issue of whether the Archdiocese had notice of an accused priest's propensities before the alleged misconduct took place. After the Archdiocese indicated its intention to make the proffers public, 26 priests named in the proffers objected. An appellate court ruled that under the *Rojas* rule the proffers could not be made public, although nothing prevented the Archdiocese from releasing the underlying information from which they were prepared. *Doe 1 et al v. Superior Court*, 34 Cal. Rptr. 3d 248 (2005).

11. An insurance company mediated a Delaware medical malpractice case in which liability was conceded. It settled the case for $945,000, based on the plaintiff's representations that the medical error had left her with "immediate, chronic and unrelenting nerve pain in her right neck, jaw, shoulder, and arm [and an inability to] employ her arm for lifting even light objects. For example she is unable to hold a can of soda. . . ." The plaintiff talked at her deposition of having "good days" when she had "a lot of energy and I try to do some stuff . . . a little laundry . . . and then I tend to end up paying for that for the next two or three days."

    The day after the mediation, the defendant's lawyer saw the plaintiff dancing at a fundraiser for local cheerleaders while holding a beer with her injured arm. He got a video camera and secretly videotaped her. The insurer then moved to rescind the settlement alleging fraud, and in support of its request asked the court to allow the mediator to testify that the video was inconsistent with his understanding of the plaintiff's claims, or his statement to the

> defense during the mediation that he thought the plaintiff would
> be a good witness. The court denied the motion. *Princeton Ins.
> Co. v. Vergano*, 883 A.2d 33 (Del. Ch. 2005).
>
> Was *Vergano* a stronger or weaker case for disclosure than *Rojas*
> or *Doe*? Why?

For a discussion of cases and principles concerning mediation confidentiality, see Widman (2008).

One of the strongest arguments for allowing a party to disclose information revealed in mediation in a subsequent proceeding involves criminal law enforcement. The following case illustrates one way that the issue can arise.

❖ Byrd v. The State

367 S.E.2d 300 (Ga. App. 1988)

[Byrd was accused of stealing property from Graddy. He participated in pretrial mediation and agreed to pay $800 in restitution. Byrd failed to make the payments required by the mediated settlement, criminal charges were reinstated, and he was convicted. Byrd appealed on the ground that statements he had made during mediation were introduced against him at trial.]

BEASLEY, J. . . . Appellant alleges error [by the trial court] in allowing evidence concerning a mediation proceeding. . . . [T]he parties were directed to the Neighborhood Justice Center of Atlanta, Inc., by the state court before which the criminal charge was first pending. The purpose was to facilitate a civil settlement for the dispute by way of the mediation process provided by that agency. The criminal charge, brought by warrant, remained pending, to await the outcome of the settlement efforts. If they were successful, the state court would entertain dismissal of the criminal charges. If not, the latter would proceed. After about eight months elapsed without appellant's compliance with the mediated agreement, he was indicted and bound over to superior court for trial.

By allowing this alternative dispute resolution effort to be evidenced in the subsequent criminal trial, the trial court's ruling eliminates its usefulness. For no criminal defendant will agree to "work things out" and compromise his position if he knows that any inference of responsibility arising from what he says and does in the mediation process will be admissible as an admission of guilt in the criminal proceeding which will eventualize if mediation fails . . . Federal Rule of Criminal Procedure 11(e)(6) . . . protects statements and conduct made in negotiations and plea bargains in criminal cases except in very limited circumstances. . . .

In the instant case, as is standard in these referrals, defendant's mediation-related statements and actions were not made with any warning of rights against self-incrimination, and yet they were prompted by court action, itself creating a close procedural tie. A serious Fifth and Fourteenth Amendments *Miranda* problem is created by the admission of the objected-to evidence. This differs from the situation in *Williams v. State*, 342 S.E.2d 703 (Ga. App. 1986), in which a privately-negotiated agreement, not insti-gated at court direction during criminal proceedings, was ruled admissible.

Just as a withdrawn plea of guilty "shall not be admissible as evidence against [a defendant] at his trial," so too must be the words and actions which defendant undertakes in an effort to comply with the court's direction that mediation be pursued to resolve the pending criminal matter.

A new trial is required because we cannot conclude that the inadmissible evidence did not contribute to reaching the verdict. . . . Judgment reversed.

SOGNIER, J., dissenting:

I respectfully dissent. "Any statement or conduct of a person, indicating a consciousness of guilt, where such person is, at the time or thereafter, charged with or suspected of the crime, is admissible against him upon his trial for committing it." . . . The mediation proceedings in this case occurred while appellant was under criminal charges, and his conduct in signing a mediation agreement acknowledging his liability is conduct indicating a consciousness of guilt. Hence, under the rule . . . the evidence was admis-sible as bearing on appellant's guilt or innocence. Accordingly, I would affirm appellant's conviction. . . .

Questions

12. Do you agree with the majority or the dissent in *Byrd*? Does it make a difference that Byrd failed to comply with the agreement he made in mediation?

13. Would it be better policy to give a *Miranda*-type warning to all defendants in such mediations, then to permit the use of any state-ments that they make?

14. The court says that an admission by someone in Byrd's situation presents different issues from one made by a party in a private mediation process. Should a defendant's admissions during a non–court-sponsored process be admissible?

15. If a defendant cannot be "hoist with his own petard" by using state-ments he makes in mediation against him, is it also improper to invade confidentiality when it is the defendant who asks for disclo-sure? In one case a defendant charged with attempted murder claimed that he had acted in self-defense. To support his defense he sought to introduce into evidence threatening statements made by the alleged victim during the mediation of an earlier alterca-tion between them. Should defendants be barred from using such evidence? (See *State v. Castellano*, 400 So. 2d 480 (Fla. App. 1984).)

Problem 3

Assume that you are counsel for the defendant Alpha in the Alpha-Bates case mentioned at the start of this chapter. In the course of mediation you argued that Bates should accept a reasonable settlement, because as a practical matter your client could never pay a six-figure judgment. In response to a request for substantiation, you provided the mediator with an asset-liability statement for Alpha. The mediation failed and the parties returned to court. Two days later Bates moves for a $250,000 attachment against Alpha's bank account, including with its motion copies of the asset-liability statement that your client provided in mediation.

1. How should you respond on behalf of Alpha?
2. Is there anything that you could have done, before or during the process, to make admission less likely?

Problem 4

Seven years ago you represented a young man, James Connor, who said that he had been sexually abused ten years before by the minister of his church. The abuse occurred when your client was 12 years old, during outings of the church's youth group. It appeared to be a difficult case to prove because of the absence of objective evidence and the time that had elapsed since the incidents, but you gave notice of your intent to sue the minister and the church official who oversaw his work. Shortly afterward the church agreed to mediate the matter. In the course of the mediation, the supervisory official offered your client a heartfelt apology and swore that this kind of abuse would never happen again. The church made what you thought was a good monetary offer; however, it was conditional on Connor signing a confidentiality clause that barred him from ever discussing the case. Connor decided to accept the offer, and the settlement was finalized.

Over the past month your local newspaper has published a series of dramatic stories alleging a widespread pattern of sexual abuse by clergy. One of the stories said that the same minister who abused your client had been sued several other times, and that two months after the settlement in your case the church had transferred him to a different community, where he continued his pattern of abuse. Connor has just called you. He is outraged by the stories, and even more so by the church's violation of its promise to him. He wants to talk to a reporter about what happened in his case, including the promise he was given in mediation.

a. What advice should you give to Connor? What are the potential consequences of his talking with the reporter?

b. Assume that your client has said nothing yet, but that a lawyer has subpoenaed him to testify at a deposition in another case brought against the same minister. The lawyer plans to ask about what occurred during Connor's mediation. What advice should you give Connor?

c. If Connor refuses to answer questions at the deposition and the lawyer seeks a court order compelling him to testify, how should the court rule?

b. Supervisory Intrusions into the Process

To this point we have focused on the confidentiality issues that arise when a litigant discloses confidential mediation information for an ulterior purpose — usually to support a position in court. Another major category of confidentiality disputes involves claims that the mediation process itself went awry. In these situations a litigant is typically alleging either that mediation was thwarted because an opponent did not participate in good faith or the process itself was badly flawed. This kind of claim poses a conflict between a court's need to gather evidence to supervise the process and the interest in preserving confidentiality. In the following case, Judge Brazil, known for his commitment to ADR, grapples with these issues.

As you read the *Olam* case, consider these questions:

Questions

16. Are you persuaded by the decision? What factors seem most significant to it?

17. If you were a lawyer practicing in the court that decided *Olam*, would the decision affect the advice you gave to clients about what to say or do during mediation?

18. Would the decision affect your willingness to recommend that a client enter the court's mediation program?

❖ Olam v. Congress Mortgage Co.
68 F. Supp. 2d 1110 (N.D. Cal. 1999)

BRAZIL, UNITED STATES MAGISTRATE JUDGE:

The court addresses in this opinion several difficult issues about the relationship between a court-sponsored voluntary mediation and subsequent proceedings whose purpose is to determine whether the parties entered an enforceable agreement at the close of the mediation session. As we explain below, the parties participated in a lengthy mediation that was hosted by this court's ADR Program Counsel — an employee of the court who is both a lawyer and an ADR professional. At the end of the mediation (after midnight), the parties signed a "Memorandum of Understanding" (MOU) that states that it is "intended as a binding document itself. . . ." Contending that the consent she apparently gave was not legally valid, plaintiff has taken the position that the MOU is not enforceable. She has not complied with its terms. Defendants have filed a motion to enforce the MOU as a binding contract. One of the principal issues with which the court wrestles, below, is whether evidence about what occurred during the mediation proceedings, including testimony from the mediator, may be used to help resolve this dispute. . . .

Facts

The events in the real world out of which the current dispute arises began unfolding in 1992, when Ms. Olam applied for and received a loan from Congress Mortgage in the amount of $187,000. The 1992 loan is secured by two single-family homes located in San Francisco and owned by Ms. Olam. Eventually she defaulted. Thereafter, Congress Mortgage initiated foreclosure proceedings. [Mrs. Olam later sued the mortgage company, alleging violations of state and federal consumer laws, and the case went through discovery.]

At the final pretrial conference, the court asked plaintiff's counsel whether there was any meaningful possibility that a mediation would be useful. [Both sides subsequently agreed to mediate.] The mediation continued throughout the day and well into the evening. Sometime around 10:00 P.M. [the mediator and counsel went into another room] to type up what they believed were the essential terms of a binding settlement agreement. At approximately 1:00 A.M., when the mediation concluded, Ms. Olam and her lawyer, and [the defendant] signed the MOU.

[Later on the same day, counsel confirmed the settlement with the court.] At approximately 1:45 P.M. [that day], plaintiff telephoned my chambers. She was referred to the mediator. . . . [M]ore than seven months after the mediation, defendants filed a Motion to Enforce the Original Settlement. . . . Ms. Olam, through [a] new attorney, filed her "Opposition" to the defendants' motion to enforce. [One ground] for opposition was that at the time she affixed her name to the MOU (at the end of the mediation) the plaintiff was incapable (intellectually, emotionally, and physically) of giving legally viable consent. Specifically, Ms. Olam contended that at the time she gave her apparent consent she was subjected to "undue influence" as that term is defined by California law.

[P]laintiff alleges that at the time she signed the MOU she was suffering from physical pain and emotional distress that rendered her incapable of exercising her own free will. She alleges that after the mediation began during the morning of September 9, she was left *alone* in a room *all* day and into the early hours of September 10, while all the other mediation participants conversed in a nearby room. She claims that she did not understand the mediation process. In addition, she asserts that she felt pressured to sign the MOU — and that her physical and emotional distress rendered her unduly susceptible to this pressure. As a result, she says, she signed the MOU against her will and without reading and/or understanding its terms.

[The court determined that California law, rather than federal law, governed the issue of mediation confidentiality.] California has offered for some time a set of strong statutory protections for mediation communications. If anything, those state law protections might be stronger than the [federal] protections offered through the relevant local rule of the Northern District of California or through any federal common law mediation privilege that might have been emerging when the mediation took place in this case.

As we noted earlier, the plaintiff and the defendants have expressly waived confidentiality protections conferred by [California law.] Both the plaintiff and the defendants have indicated, clearly and on advice of counsel, that they want the court to consider evidence about what occurred during the mediation, including testimony directly from the mediator. . . .

The Mediator's Privilege

[U]nder California law, a waiver of the mediation privilege by the parties is not a sufficient basis for a court to permit or order a mediator to testify. Rather, an independent determination must be made before testimony from a mediator should be permitted or ordered.

. . . First, I acknowledge squarely that a decision to require a mediator to give evidence, even *in camera* or under seal, about what occurred during a mediation threatens values underlying the mediation privileges. [T]he California legislature adopted these privileges in the belief that without the promise of confidentiality it would be appreciably more difficult to achieve the goals of mediation programs. While this court has no occasion or power to quarrel with these generally applicable pronouncements of state policy, we observe that they appear to have appreciably less force when, as here, the parties to the mediation have waived confidentiality protections, indeed have asked the court to compel the mediator to testify — so that justice can be done.

. . . [O]rdering mediators to participate in proceedings arising out of mediations imposes economic and psychic burdens that could make some people reluctant to agree to serve as a mediator, especially in programs where that service is pro bono or poorly compensated. This is not a matter of time and money only. Good mediators are likely to feel violated by being compelled to give evidence that could be used against a party with whom they tried to establish a relationship of trust during a mediation. . . . These are not inconsequential matters.

. . . But the level of harm to that interest likely varies, at least in some measure, with the perception within the community of mediators and litigants about how likely it is that any given mediation will be followed at some point by an order compelling the neutral to offer evidence about what occurred during the session. . . . [T]his case represents the first time that I have been called upon to address these kinds of questions in the more than fifteen years that I have been responsible for ADR programs in this court. [M]y partially educated guess is that the likelihood that a mediator or the parties in any given case need fear that the mediator would later be constrained to testify is extraordinarily small.

The magnitude of the risk to values underlying the mediation privilege that can be created by ordering a mediator to testify also can vary with the nature of the testimony that is sought. [E]vidence about what words a party to the mediation uttered, what statements or admissions that party made . . . could be particularly threatening to the spirit and methods that some people believe are important both to the philosophy and the success of some mediation processes.

[W]e turn to the other side of the balance. The interests that are likely to be advanced by compelling the mediator to testify in this case are of considerable importance. Moreover, as we shall see, some of those interests parallel and reinforce the objectives the legislature sought to advance by providing for confidentiality in mediation. The first interest we identify is the interest in doing justice. Here is what we mean. For reasons described below, the mediator is positioned in this case to offer what could be crucial, certainly very probative, evidence about the central factual issues in this matter. There is a strong possibility that his testimony will greatly improve the court's ability to determine reliably what the pertinent historical facts actually were [and to do justice.]

. . . In sum, it is clear that refusing even to determine what the mediator's testimony would be, in the circumstances here presented, threatens values of great significance.

[The Court decided that the mediator's testimony might be sufficiently important to justify an *in camera* exploration of what he would say. After the hearing, the Court decided] that testimony from the mediator would be crucial to the court's capacity to do its job.

The Evidentiary Hearing

The court held the evidentiary hearing. We heard testimony and considered documentary evidence about Ms. Olam's medical conditions, the events of September 9–10 . . . and various post-mediation events related to the purported settlement. All the participants in the mediation testified, as did the physician who was treating plaintiff during the pertinent period. We took [the mediator's] testimony.

Conclusion

Because plaintiff has failed to prove either of the necessary elements of undue influence, and because she has established no other grounds to escape the contract she signed . . . the court GRANTS defendants' Motion to Enforce the settlement contract that is memorialized in the MOU.

Questions

Recall that in *Rojas v. Superior Court*, the California Supreme Court rejected a litigant's effort to intrude into the mediation process for purposes of discovery.

19. Which do you think is more likely to promote effective mediation, the approach adopted by the court in *Rojas* or the one favored by the *Olam* judge?
20. Would the *Olam* decision make you, as a California lawyer, more or less likely to advise clients to participate in mediation?
21. Other courts have, like *Olam*, invaded mediation confidentiality to determine whether participants were competent to make settlement decisions. See, e.g., *Wilson v. Wilson*, 282 Ga. 728 (2007) (court may call mediator to testify concerning his general impression of competence of unrepresented party who claimed he lacked the capacity to agree to a divorce settlement due to depression, exhaustion, and effect of medication).

---

c.   Enforcement of Mediated Agreements

The third category of dispute over confidentiality occurs when parties disagree about whether they reached agreement, or what they agreed to do. A few states bar the introduction even of some signed agreements. A California statute, for instance, requires that for evidence of a mediated agreement to be admissible over objection, the document must either state that it is admissible or intended to be enforceable or binding, or words to that effect, or be offered to show illegality (Cal. Evid. Code § 1123(b)).

The issue of invading confidentiality to establish an agreement arises most often, however, when one party alleges that disputants reached an oral meeting of the minds. An example is the *Leary* sexual abuse case at the start of this chapter. Some laws contain exceptions to permit introduction of evidence of oral settlements, and other statutes, although absolute on their face, have been interpreted to permit such testimony. In many states, however, it is not clear whether disputants may testify about the existence of an oral settlement, or whether the mediator can be called as a witness on the issue.

Sections 4(a) and 6(a) of the UMA, discussed below, prevent participants from testifying about agreements reached in mediation, but allow the introduction into evidence of accords that are signed and in writing or electronically recorded. The effect of the UMA is to bar enforcement of purely oral settlements, but permit enforcement of written or recorded ones.

Questions

22. Is the UMA provision allowing the introduction of evidence about written or recorded settlements, but not oral ones, justified? Why or why not?
23. Do you agree with the California rule on admission of mediated agreements?

---

4. Confidentiality in Caucusing

So far we have discussed confidentiality in terms of disclosures that are made to persons outside the mediation process or the courts. In caucus-based mediation, however, there is an additional layer of privacy: Mediators typically assure disputants that if they request that information disclosed in a caucus be held in confidence, the mediator will not disclose it to their opponent. As we have seen, however, one of a mediator's key functions is to facilitate communication between parties to a dispute. What is the appropriate balance between confidentiality and communication in caucus-based mediation? Consider how you would respond to the following situations, drawn by Professor Marjorie Aaron from actual cases.

Problem 5

You are plaintiff's counsel in the mediation of a commercial contract case. After hours of bargaining, the parties are stuck, with the plaintiff at $240,000 and the defendant at $90,000. The mediator proposes to play "confidential listener," and asks for the absolute lowest dollar number that you would accept to settle the case. The mediator also asks you for a "public" offer that he can convey to the other side. You tell the mediator that your client will never accept less than $150,000 to settle, and authorize him to communicate to the other side a new demand of $225,000.

When the mediator conveys the $225,000 figure, the other side expresses frustration. "They've hardly moved at all," says counsel. "It looks like they won't go any lower than $200,000 to settle, and we're just not going to go that high. The very most this case is worth is 150. We'd be prepared to go to $100,000 at this point, but it's probably a waste of time. I hate playing games — what will it take? Should we just pack up and leave?"

a.   The mediator says to the defense, "I think I can get them to 150, if I can tell them that that will truly settle it — Are you saying that 150 would do it?" Has he broken his pledge of confidentiality to you?

b.   Suppose you had told the mediator that your bottom line was $175,000, but the mediator suspects from observations of your client's body language that he would in fact go as low as $150,000. Can the mediator say, "They're hanging tough at 225, but I think I can get them to 150. If I can do that, will it settle the case?" Does it depend on whether the mediator "read" your client's intentions correctly?

Problem 6

You are representing the complainant in the mediation of a discrimination case. After the legal arguments have been aired in joint session, the mediator moves both sides into private caucusing. The mediator spends a great deal of time with you and your client, who is decidedly "dug in" and unwilling to see any weakness in his case or the need to lower her settlement expectations. Although you are well known as a zealous advocate, in this case you see reasons to reach a reasonable settlement. In a hallway conversation you indicate to the mediator that you are aware of the problems in the case and support his efforts to bring your client into a zone of reality.

In the mediator's caucus with the defense side, counsel expresses frustration at the lack of progress. "I bet the problem is the lawyer here. I've litigated with her before," he complains. "She is just hell-bent on getting a high number. This is a political cause for her, but we're not going to cave to meet her agenda." His anger toward you seems to be driving his resistance to further movement.

What, if anything, can the mediator appropriately say about your or your client's attitude toward the case?

5.   A Movement Toward Consistency: The Uniform Mediation Act

The Current State of Protection

How serious is the problem of mediation confidentiality in practice? From the discussion above and the varying responses of courts, it is plain that many gaps and ambiguities exist in mediation's "confidentiality safety net," and there is disagreement about how much confidentiality protection the process needs. Although court cases over confidentiality issues exist, they appear to represent only a tiny fraction of all disputes mediated. Commercial mediators report, for instance, that they rarely hear parties complain about breaches of confidentiality, and the judge in *Olam* commented that he had never before encountered a case in which parties sought a mediator's testimony.

Confidentiality cases do arise, however: Over a seven-year period between 1999 and 2005, for example, researchers at Hamline University identified nearly 250 reported decisions that dealt with mediation confidentiality. See *www.law.hamline.edu/adr/mediation-case-law-database*. Some scholars cite this as evidence that "misuse of mediation communications is common" (Cole et al., 2008). At the same time, such a number amounts to less than one reported case per year per state, in an environment where courts in states such as Florida send more than 100,000 cases a year to mediation (Press, 1998).

Why do disputes over confidentiality not arise more often? For one thing, a large majority of mediated cases reach agreement, and even those that do not settle in mediation are very unlikely ever to go to trial. If a case is never adjudicated, the parties have less reason to breach confidentiality. It also appears that when people enter into a clear commitment to keep information confidential, they honor their agreement. And, as we have seen, when the mediation process focuses on distributive bargaining, disputants are less likely to reveal sensitive information in the first place. Finally, we should bear in mind that to the extent that mediation brings a sense of peace to a situation, the process itself may induce participants to treat rules with respect. Whatever the cause, parties' compliance with confidentiality obligations appears to be higher than a purely tactical analysis would suggest.

Reported cases involving confidentiality arise largely in the context of court-connected mediation. This may be because parties are often compelled to participate in court programs, whereas they usually enter private mediation voluntarily. A person unhappy to be in a process is probably less likely to respect its rules. Also, litigants are probably more apt to complain, and judges to impose sanctions, when a problem arises in a court-affiliated setting. That said, "courts rarely punish parties who misuse mediation communications" (Cole et al., 2008). It is rare for parties complaining about confidentiality abuses to sue for damages, perhaps because it is so difficult to prove that an ascertainable monetary loss resulted from the alleged breach (Moffit, 2003b).

A Response

What level of protection should be given to confidentiality in mediation? Assuming that confidentiality is necessary, the lack of uniformity among jurisdictions, and the resulting uncertainty about what rule will apply to a given mediation, is troublesome. One possibility is for states to adopt a uniform confidentiality statute. To this end the National Conference of Commissioners on Uniform State Laws has proposed a Uniform Mediation Act. (For the complete text of the UMA, see the Web Appendix.)

The Act states that communications made during mediation are not "subject to discovery or admissible in evidence" in a legal proceeding (§ 4(a)). The UMA thus prevents parties from using mediation communications in adjudicatory proceedings. It leaves them free, however, to make disclosures outside litigation, for example in conversations or media interviews, unless they agree not to do so. (See comments to UMA § 8.) Disputants in UMA jurisdictions who wish mediation communications to remain confidential in all circumstances must therefore enter into confidentiality agreements. Samples of such agreements appear in the Web Appendix.

The UMA contains exceptions to its bar on disclosure in legal proceedings. Sections 5 and 6(a) of the Act permit a court to order disclosure of mediation communications about:

*   Agreements signed by all parties.
*   Documents required to be kept open to the public.
*   Threats to commit bodily injury or crimes of violence.
*   Plans to commit or conceal an ongoing crime.
*   Information needed for a mediator to respond to claims or charges against him.
*   Situations involving child abuse and neglect.

Section 6(b) of the UMA creates an additional exception to confidentiality in situations where a tribunal finds that a party has shown that:

*   Evidence is not otherwise available,
*   There is a need for the evidence that substantially outweighs the interest in protecting confidentiality, and
*   The mediation communication is sought or offered in a court proceeding involving a felony or litigation over a contract reached in mediation (but in the latter situation the mediator cannot be compelled to testify).

The UMA has provoked disagreement within the mediation community. Some commentators argue that its provisions are inadequate because they do not cover out-of-court disclosures, and others consider the UMA's restrictions excessive. In addition, some mediators and lawyers who practice in states with stronger confidentiality rules object to "watering down" their protections in the interest of national uniformity. If the UMA is enacted on a widespread basis, confidentiality rules will become more uniform from one state to another, and the likelihood that federal courts will develop a uniform rule may also increase. As of this writing ten states have adopted the UMA, but it is not yet clear whether it will achieve nationwide acceptance.

B.   Enforcement of Participation in Mediation

1.   Agreements to Mediate

Parties entering into relationships, particularly ones that are lengthy or complex, are increasingly likely to include in contracts a clause obligating them to mediate any disputes that may arise in their interactions. Businesses entering into commercial supply agreements or divorcing parents with young children, for instance, can expect to encounter changes in circumstances over the term of their agreement and would benefit from a process to address such changes. Commitments to mediate are also required by law in some states; Arizona and Washington, for example, require divorcing couples who seek court approval of joint custody or other parenting arrangements to include an ADR provision in their plan (Cole et al., 2008).

The first question raised by a mediation clause is whether a court will enforce it. In early cases defendants objected successfully to enforcement, arguing that it would impossible to determine whether a party was in compliance or to supervise participation. "Until the mid-1980s, courts refused to enforce mediation . . . agreements on the theory that a court would not use its equity powers to order a 'futile gesture' . . . [but] enforcement is gradually becoming routine, and little is heard today about futile acts, vain orders, or the problem of adequate remedies" (Katz, 2008a).

California residential real estate purchase contracts, for example, permit the prevailing party in litigation to recover attorneys' fees, but deny recovery to parties who fail to mediate before suit. Applying this language, courts have refused to grant fees to prevailing parties who refused to mediate. *Frei v. Davey,* 124 Cal. App. 4th 1506 (2004). Another enforcement option is to dismiss complaints filed by parties who have failed to comply with an obligation to mediate. See *Halcomb v. Office of the Senate Sergeant-at-Arms of the U.S. Senate,* 205 F.Supp. 2d 175 (D.D.C. 2002).

Parties who have the right to compel mediation may decide not to enforce it, on the theory that a forced process would be meaningless. At the same time, a party who is opposed to mediation but subject to a requirement may decide that it is easier to go through a mediation session than to litigate over it. Still, between 1999 and 2005 the Hamline mediation case law project identified nearly 500 reported court decisions that dealt with parties' duty to mediate.

One commentator has suggested the following guidelines for drafting an enforceable obligation to mediate:

* Keep the language simple,
* Avoid ambiguity; in particular keep commitments to mediate separate from obligations to arbitrate,

- Include specific reference to sanctions and other consequences for breach, for example, dismissal of the claim or imposition of attorneys fees, and
- Make the process fair, given the context of the contract (Katz, 2008b).

Questions

In the early 1990s, a large California bank instituted a multistep ADR program for many of its customers, which required consumers to mediate any dispute they might have with the bank. Under the program, professional mediators would be provided through either of two prominent ADR organizations. Many of these mediators charged hundreds of dollars per hour for their time. Consumers were obligated to pay half of the cost of mediation, although the program allowed them to apply for an exemption from the obligation to pay. The plan also stated that neither party could leave mediation until the mediator had made a finding that there was "no possibility of resolution without pursuing the adjudicatory phase."

24. If you were a customer with a claim against the bank, would you challenge this program? What grounds might there be to do so?
25. Is the program likely to create practical problems for the mediators?
26. Two parties mediate, sign a term sheet with the expectation of drafting a formal settlement document later, and send emails informing the court that the matter has been settled. They then fall into disagreement over what terms should appear in the final document. Are the parties bound by their emails? What factors should determine the outcome? Compare *Delyanis v. Dyna-Empire, Inc.*, 465 F.Supp.2d 170 (E.D.N.Y. 2006), with *DeVita v. Macy's East, Inc.*, 828 N.Y.S.2d 531 (2d Dept. 2007).

Problem 7

An owner of land and a general contractor enter into a contract to build a shopping center. The contract includes a clause requiring the parties to mediate all disputes that arise during the project, to come to mediation with "full settlement authority," and to mediate "in good faith." The project is seriously delayed by the discovery of bedrock during excavation and a dispute arises over who should bear the cost of the delay and extra work. One side seeks mediation and the other objects, saying that mediating would be a waste of time and money. How could a supervising court determine whether the parties:

a.   Participated in mediation?
b.   Came with full settlement authority?
c.   Mediated in good faith?

2.   Mandates to Mediate

a.   Issues of Court Authority

Many court systems, impressed with the potential of mediation, have decided to make participation in the process mandatory. Courts sometimes do so in the belief that disputants and counsel are unfamiliar with the benefits of mediation and need to be compelled to "try some." Or they may impose mediation out of concern that the very parties most in need of the process, or most likely to consume judicial resources unnecessarily, will not enter mediation voluntarily. Thus, for example, many states require parents involved in child visitation or custody disputes to mediate before seeking a court order.

Early in the development of court-connected mediation commentators were concerned that for a court to order parties into ADR might be unconstitutional — for instance that such requirements might interfere with state constitutional provisions that give citizens a right to free access to justice. Courts have upheld mediation mandates against arguments that they violate constitutional guarantees, probably because participation is inherently no more burdensome than other steps in the litigation process, such as compelled appearance at depositions (Golann, 1989).

The fact that mandatory ADR is constitutional, however, does not mean that a particular court has the authority to order it. Courts ordinarily derive their authority from specific statutes and rules. Many federal courts, for example, base orders compelling litigants to mediate on plans and rules adopted pursuant to the Civil Justice Reform Act of 1990 or the ADR Act of 1998. The 1998 Act, in particular, bars federal courts from forcing parties to arbitrate but says nothing about whether disputants can be required to mediate, which some courts have interpreted to mean that they can adopt rules requiring mandatory mediation.

Can a federal court that has not adopted a rule nevertheless order parties to mediate as a matter of "inherent judicial power"? The Court of Appeals in *In re Atlantic Pipe Corp.*, 304 F.3d 135 (1st Cir. 2002), confronted the issue in a complex construction dispute with many parties. It confirmed the inherent power of a trial judge to order mediation over a party's objection, to require the objector to pay part of the cost, and to name as a mediator a private neutral nominated by one of the parties. The court nevertheless expressed concern over the lack of any conditions on the appointment, particularly in light of the fact that the mediator charged $9,000 per day. It remanded the case to the trial court to enter additional orders.

Courts in other jurisdictions have reached contrary results. In *Jeld-Wen v. Superior Court*, 146 Cal. App. 4th 536 (2007), for example, an appellate court found that although California courts have the statutory power to order smaller civil cases to mediation processes whose cost is paid for by the state, they could not order parties to attend and pay for private mediation.

> Question
>
> 27.   Assume you are a law clerk to the trial judge in *Atlantic Pipe*. What conditions might you add to the mediation order to meet the First Circuit's concerns?

b.   Good-Faith Bargaining Requirements

If a court has the power to order disputants to mediate, should it require them to satisfy any minimum standard of conduct? If the adoption of rules is any guide, the answer is plainly yes. Professor John Lande found that at least 22 states have "good-faith bargaining" requirements for mediation, and that many federal district and state trial courts have local rules imposing such duties on disputants, usually in connection with a court-related ADR program. The problem is that virtually none of these rules defines what "good faith" means. According to Professor Lande, the reported cases on good-faith obligations break down as follows:

- Failure to attend mediation at all.
- Failure to send a representative with adequate settlement authority.
- Failure to submit required memoranda or documents.
- Failure to make a suitable offer or otherwise participate in bargaining.
- Failure to sign an agreement.

In practice courts have found it easiest to sanction objective acts, such as a party's failure to appear or file a statement. They have found it much more difficult to assess subjective matters, such as whether a party's offer was adequate in the circumstances. Apart from having to define amorphous concepts such as good faith, courts would usually have to take evidence about what occurred in the mediation process, raising confidentiality concerns. Only a few decisions to impose sanctions based on a trial judge's subjective conclusions about mediation misconduct have been upheld on appeal (Lande, 2002).

Even if enforcement is feasible, good-faith bargaining requirements arguably conflict with a key value of mediation, self-determination. The first principle in the Model Standards of Conduct for Mediators states that "Parties may exercise self-determination at any stage of a mediation, including . . . participation in or withdrawal from the process." Under this standard, can a court order parties into mediation or compel and specific level of participation? Suppose, however, that one party in a compelled process expends substantial resources to participate — should an adversary be permitted to frustrate the effort by failing to prepare or refusing to bargain? The following questions illustrate the issue.

Questions

28. Consider again the problem at the start of this section, in which Alpha's counsel offered $10,000 in response to the plaintiff lowering its demand from $750,000 to $450,000.
    a. If applicable rules require that the parties "bargain in good faith," has Alpha complied?
    b. Does anything else that Alpha did or failed to do in that process strike you as "bad faith"?
29. Consider the situation of defense counsel in the following case: A court-appointed master ordered the parties to engage in a five-day mediation of a complex construction defect claim. Knowing that such claims necessarily involve expert testimony, the neutral instructed each side to bring its experts to the process. The neutral's charges and the plaintiff's cost for assembling its experts for mediation totaled nearly $25,000. Defense counsel, however, arrived 30 minutes late for the first session and appeared alone. Asked about his failure to bring his client or his experts, he said, "I'm here, you can talk to me." See *Foxgate Homeowner's Association, Inc., v. Bramlea California, Inc., et al.*, 25 P.3d 1117 (Cal. 2001).
    a. Did the defense counsel's actions constitute bad faith? Why, exactly?
    b. The mediator in *Foxgate* reported to the court that defense counsel took this approach because he believed that his pending motion for partial summary judgment would substantially reduce the value of the plaintiff's claims. Does this justify the lawyer's strategy?
    c. The neutral also reported that in his opinion, the defendant had sufficient time to present the motion before the mediation but had not done so. How relevant is the mediator's opinion on this issue? Should the mediator have offered it?

The fact that mediation often leads people to change their minds makes it particularly important that the persons who attend have the authority to adopt new positions. If a negotiator ultimately decides that a difficult compromise is appropriate, for example, he needs the authority to implement his judgment. Recognizing this, mediation agreements and program rules usually require that if a party does not appear personally — which is not possible for a corporation — it must send a representative who has "full" or "adequate" settlement authority. This raises similar issues to the problem of defining good faith. As you read the following case, ask yourself these questions.

Questions

30. If the authority that the defendant brought to this mediation was not adequate, what would have been sufficient?
31. If you were counsel to a corporation whose business required it to mediate cases around the country, what practical problems might the court's ruling present for you?

❖ Nick v. Morgan's Foods of Missouri, Inc.
270 F. 3d 590 (8th Cir. 2001)

Gee Gee Nick, a Kentucky Fried Chicken employee, filed a district court complaint against her employer, Morgan's Foods, alleging sexual harassment. Following a scheduling conference, the parties were ordered to participate in the federal court's Alternative Dispute Resolution ("ADR") process pursuant to its local rules, which provided in part: "Duty to Attend and Participate: All parties, counsel of record, and corporate representatives or claims professionals having authority to settle claims shall attend all mediation conferences and participate in good faith." (Court rules also required that each side file a memorandum with the mediator in advance, but Morgan's Foods's lawyer did not do so because, the court said, he "believed it was unnecessary and a waste of time.")

The mediation conference was attended by Nick, her court-appointed counsel, Morgan's Foods's outside counsel, and the local regional manager. The manager's settlement authority was limited to $500. Any decision to change the company's settlement position had to be made by its general counsel, . . . who was in Connecticut and only available by telephone. During the mediation, Nick twice made offers of settlement that were rejected without counteroffers. The mediation was terminated shortly thereafter. The neutral informed the district court of the minimal level of Morgan's Foods's participation in the ADR process. In response, the trial court . . . sanctioned Morgan's Foods $1,390 [in costs], . . . its outside counsel $1,390 [as well, and] ordered the company to pay a $1,500 fine. . . . In its Memorandum and Order, the Court explained why personal attendance at a mediation session is a sine qua non:

"For ADR to work, the corporate representative must have the authority and discretion to change her opinion in light of the statements and arguments made by the neutral and opposing party. Meaningful negotiations cannot occur if the only person with authority to actually change their mind and negotiate is not present. Availability by telephone is insufficient because the absent decision-maker does not have the full benefit of the ADR proceedings, the opposing party's arguments, and the neutral's input. The absent decision-maker needs to be present and hear first-hand the good facts and the bad facts about their case."

"Instead, the absent decision-maker learns only what his or her attorney chooses to relate over the phone. This can be expected to be largely a recitation of what has been conveyed in previous discussions. Even when the attorney attempts to summarize the strengths of the other side's position, there are problems. First, the attorney has a credibility problem: the absent decision-maker wants to know why the attorney's confident opinion expressed earlier has now eroded. Second, the new information most likely is too much to absorb and analyze in a matter of minutes. Under this dynamic it becomes all too easy for the absent decision-maker to reject the attorney's new advice, reject the new information, and reject any effort to engage in meaningful negotiations."

It is quite likely that the telephone call is viewed as a distraction from other business being conducted by the absent decision-maker. . . . [The] easiest decision is to summarily reject any offer and get back to the business on her desk. . . .

"Morgan's Foods's lack of good faith participation in the ADR process was calculated to save Morgan's Foods a few hours of time in preparing the mediation memorandum and to save its general counsel the expense and inconvenience of a trip to attend the mediation. The consequence of Morgan's Foods's lack of good faith participation in the ADR process, however, was the wasted expense of time and energy of the Court, the neutral, Nick, and her court-appointed counsel. If Morgan's Foods did not feel that ADR could be fruitful and had no intention of participating in good faith, it had a duty to report its position to the Court and to request appropriate relief. Morgan's Foods did not do so and sanctions are appropriate to remedy the resulting waste of time and money."

[The court affirmed the sanctions ordered by the trial judge.]

Questions

32.   You are counsel to Morgan's Foods. Another employee has filed a claim similar to Nick's, and it has been referred to the same mediation program. What do you need to do to comply with the court's rule?

33.   In a case involving an East Coast computer company's claim that a Silicon Valley firm had improperly "stolen" its development team, the defendant's general counsel refused to travel to a mediation session in New York. At the mediator's request, however, she did agree to be present on a conference call during all of the joint

meetings and throughout each caucus that the mediator held with her side. Does that level of presence meet the objections of the *Nick* court? What are the potential drawbacks to such an arrangement?

34.   Florida, one of the most active states in promoting court-related ADR, requires litigants to appear at mediation, and defines appearance to mean that: "[The] party or a representative with full settlement authority is present along with the party's counsel, if any, and a representative of the insurance carrier with full authority to settle up to the plaintiff's last demand or policy limits, whichever is less. . . ." Assume that you are the national litigation counsel for a Fortune 500 company with operations in Florida that occasionally result in cases being filed against your company, and you are required to mediate under this rule.

   a.   Could your local outside counsel appear at a court-connected mediation in Florida without a company representative, if he had full authority to bind your company?

   b.   What practical problems would this rule create for you? Can you think of any steps that would lessen them?

In response to the difficulty of defining and enforcing "good-faith" requirements, some have argued that such rules should be discarded entirely. Professor Lande, for example, warns that

> Sanctioning bad faith in mediation actually may stimulate adversarial and dishonest conduct. . . . [It] might also encourage surface bargaining. . . . Because mediators are not supposed to force people to settle, participants who are determined not to settle can wait until the mediator gives up. . . . Similarly, tough mediation participants could use good-faith requirements offensively to intimidate opposing parties. . . . [Innocent] participants may have legitimate fears about risking sanctions when they face an aggressive opponent. . . . [In addition, a] good-faith requirement gives mediators too much authority . . . to direct the outcome in mediation.

He has proposed that litigants instead be given education about the value of interest-based processes, and that courts limit themselves to enforcing objective standards of conduct, for example that parties appear at mediation for a minimum period of time (Lande 2002).

Problem 8

Two companies are in mediation. In the underlying lawsuit, the plaintiff has alleged that the defendant knowingly violated a franchise agreement. The "hard" damages in the case, computed on the basis of the franchisee's minimum purchase requirements, are about $100,000. However, the plaintiff has also claimed $500,000 in lost profits and made an initial settlement demand of $600,000. It appears to the franchisee's lawyer that her client has about a 50-50 chance of being found liable under the contract and having to pay the hard damages, but that the risk that her client will be liable for lost profits is virtually nil. Applying the 50-percent risk factor to the hard damages, the defense therefore assesses the value of the case at $50,000. The parties agree to mediate.

In a first caucus meeting with the mediator, the plaintiff's lawyer says that while its demand is "negotiable," it will not make any concessions until the defense puts a "significant offer" on the table. The defense lawyer informs the neutral that he will not make any offer at this point because the plaintiff is "on another planet." He tells the mediator that it's his job first to bring the plaintiff into a zone of reality, and $600K is not it. The mediation agreement commits the parties to "engage in good-faith bargaining." Is either the plaintiff or the defendant violating its obligation? If so, why?

3. Enforcement of Mediated Settlements

Mediation is a voluntary process, but if it is successful then the parties usually enter into a binding contract — a settlement agreement. Even settlements, however, may provoke new controversies over issues such as the following:

- Did the parties actually reach a final agreement? If so, what were its terms?
- Should the agreement be invalidated on grounds such as duress, mistake, unconscionability, or lack of authority?

We have seen that such issues provoke disputes over confidentiality, as courts are asked to take testimony about what occurred in the process. Apart from confidentiality concerns, however, there are substantive questions: What is required to make a settlement binding? And how much deviation should courts permit from an "ideal" process before overturning its result?

a. The Existence of an Agreement

Good practice calls for parties who settle in mediation to memorialize their agreements in writing. To ensure that this occurs, mediation texts counsel neutrals, however late the hour or strong the settling parties' wish to depart, to push the disputants to sign a memorandum that summarizes the settlement before they leave. Sometimes, however, the parties do not execute an agreement, or it is attacked as, or alleged to be, incomplete.

Most courts test mediated settlements by the standards that apply to contracts generally. If an agreement is oral, the first issue is whether it complies with the applicable statute of frauds. Courts in several states have held oral mediated settlements to be enforceable contracts, and although there are few reported cases it appears that federal common law also permits enforcement of oral settlements. Where a court has refused to enforce an oral agreement reached in mediation, it has usually been because state law imposes procedural rules more severe than the requirements of the common law of contracts. Florida and Texas, for example, mandate that pending court cases may be settled only through a written document signed by the parties or their counsel (Cole et al., 2008).

Another possibility is that the parties sign an agreement but one side later argues that the writing is incomplete, as in the *Leary* case at the start of this chapter. Such claims raise issues under the Parol Evidence Rule and other evidentiary standards, as well as concerns about invading confidentiality.

b. Grounds for Invalidation

Suppose, following a successful mediation process, the lawyers draw up an agreement and the parties sign it. Is that enough to ensure that a settlement will be enforced? Generally the answer is yes, but not always. Again there are potential concerns. Some of these are formal in nature. First, settlement agreements must contain the essential terms of the parties' bargain. If, for example, a settlement provided that "the parties shall exchange mutual releases," a court would probably find the language sufficient to form a binding agreement. If, however, a settlement stated that a defendant would make payments "in installments" but did not specify a schedule, a challenge would be more likely to succeed. A few jurisdictions also require that mediated settlements of pending litigation be approved by a court.

The most serious basis for invalidating a mediated settlement is a substantive one: that the process of mediation itself was so deficient that any resulting agreement is invalid. On the one hand, the presence of a neutral person would seem to make it less likely that a "bad" settlement would result. On the other hand, aspects of the process that are intended to push litigants to confront unpleasant realities can also create stress that inhibits good decision making. An example is the *Olam* case, above, in which an individual who agreed to a settlement in the early morning hours later claimed that she did so under duress.

Questions

35. Are there particular circumstances in which a mediated settlement should be subject to special scrutiny? When, for example, might this be true?

36. When a mediated agreement is challenged on grounds such as duress or misrepresentation, should the court apply a different

standard than it would to a settlement reached through direct negotiation? Why or why not?

❖ Christian Cooper v. Melodie Austin

750 So. 2d 711-715 (Fla. App. 2000)

HARRIS, J.:

Cooper appeals a final judgment which adopted a mediation agreement Cooper alleges was obtained by extortion and was the basis for [a] contempt citation. . . . During the course of a lengthy mediation, it is undisputed that the wife sent Cooper the following note:

> If you can't agree to this, the kids will take what information they have to whomever to have you arrested, etc. Although I would get no money if you were in jail — you wouldn't also be living freely as if you did nothing wrong.‡

Relatively soon thereafter, the parties "settled" their property matters. . . . In the midst of extended negotiations before the mediator, the wife sent the husband a note that constituted classic extortion. However, the wife convinced the [trial] judge that the note was merely a "wake-up" call and did not influence the agreement subsequently reached. The court relied on two established facts to reach this conclusion. First, the husband did not immediately accede to the wife's demands but continued to negotiate for a period thereafter. Second, the husband did not seek relief from the extortionate agreement until after his efforts to reconcile with the wife failed. Even accepting these facts as true, we cannot agree that they negate the effect of extortion when reviewing the remainder of the record.

The husband testified, without contradiction, that the result of the mediated agreement was that the wife received $128,000 in marital assets while the husband received $10,000. . . . This grossly unequal distribution speaks volumes about the effect of the extortionate note sent by the wife. . . .

In this case, the wife's "wake-up call," which demanded the husband either give in to her demands or go to jail, was clearly extortionate and her presentation of the extorted agreement to the court was a fraud on the court making the trial court an instrument of her extortion. Mrs. Cooper should not profit from her actions. Nor should this Court, or any court, ignore them.

---

‡ [Footnote to court opinion] The crime threatened to be reported by the wife was Cooper's photographing a nude, underage girl. Cooper, who had experienced firsthand the law's disapproval of this practice on an earlier occasion, was aware that in going through his property, the wife's children had found a photograph taken by him of a young woman who indeed looked under age. It was not until shortly before this action for relief from judgment was filed that Cooper tracked down the woman and verified she was "of age" at the time the photograph was taken.

GRIFFIN, J., dissenting:

This is not the first time an appellate court has been unable to overcome the urge to trump factual findings of a trial judge with which the panel violently disagrees, nor will it be the last. But it is awkward when it happens. . . . *How*, the majority asks incredulously, could the trial judge have allowed himself to be hoodwinked in this fashion? After reading the transcript of the hearing, it is clear to me that Judge Hammond simply did not believe Mr. Cooper. This is important because there are only three items of evidence to support Mr. Cooper's claim of duress: (1) the threat; (2) the apparent uneven distribution of assets; and (3) Mr. Cooper's testimony that the reason he entered into the agreement was because of the threat.

The lower court so much as said it did not find Mr. Cooper to be credible. First of all, Mr. Cooper, who has a bachelor's degree and a master's degree in business, both from Duke University . . . testified repeatedly that he had no idea of the value of the marital assets. [T]he evidence, in fact, showed that he had a very good idea of what the marital assets were. . . .

There was direct conflict between Mr. and Mrs. Cooper concerning Mr. Cooper's response to her threat. She testified that his response was that he was not scared, that the kids did not "have anything" and that he knew that he "owed it to her to put her through school." . . . As the lower court succinctly said: "The former husband knew that the photographs in his possession were not illegal."

There is also the fact that Mr. Cooper, his free will forborne due to his "fear of arrest," continued to negotiate the agreement for another two and one-half hours[, securing substantial changes in the terms of a promissory note to the wife]. . . . The fact that he received all of the benefits of the mediation agreement as adopted by the Final Judgment, made all alimony payments . . . , received back all of the personal property he was concerned about, [and] continued his pursuit of the Former Wife are not the actions of a man who was subject to extortion, coercion or duress. . . . We should affirm.

Question

37. If Mr. Cooper's counsel thought that his client was feeling extorted during the mediation, what should he have done?

C. Certification

It might surprise you to hear that mediators, unlike many professionals, do not need a license to practice — there is no equivalent to bar membership, or even a driver's license, for mediators. A child can act as a mediator, and in fact some schools have programs in which students mediate peer disputes. This reflects the history of modern mediation, which was fueled in large measure by frustration with the litigation system and peoples' wish to find new ways to approach disputes. The idea of creating a licensing system for mediators, with the need for an official body to define and test "good" practices and exclude and perhaps sanction those who do not qualify, strikes many in the field as antithetical to its basic values.

There is more of a debate over whether mediators should be certified. Certification is less centralized and has less restrictive impact than licensing and is carried out by a variety of private and public organizations rather than a single government agency. While lack of certification prevents people from working in situations in which it is required, it does not foreclose them from mediating generally.

Certification does, however, allow mediators to indicate that they have been "certified by" a particular organization. Professional associations of mediators, for instance, have established membership requirements and certification schemes to encourage quality mediation and allow members to indicate that they have been "certified" by the organization. In 2008 the International Mediation Institute, based in the Hague and supported by international companies, embarked on a project to certify a panel of mediators qualified to handle private international disputes. In the domestic relations field, Family Mediation Canada has created a private certification scheme that includes videotaped mediations observed and evaluated by experienced mediators and a written examination; those who pass the test can advertise that they are "certified" by the organization.

Another form of certification involves imposing requirements on mediators who wish to participate in a program. Thus professionals who want to be listed on court-connected mediation panels are often required to meet specific criteria, reflecting the view that a court, as a branch of government, should take responsibility for the quality of those who practice under its aegis. Florida was the first state to establish qualifications for court-connected panelists and other states have followed; in 2009, for example, California had pending "Model Qualification Standards" for mediators recommended, appointed, or compensated by its courts. There is no uniformity in the standards applied by court mediation programs, however, and admission to a court's program does not ordinarily authorize a mediator to say that she has been "certified" by the court.

The absence of any general system of state regulation or certification of mediation is not for lack of proposals. In California alone, hundreds of bills have been introduced to control or regulate mediation, and the American Bar Association and many state bar associations have worked to formulate policy proposals on the issue.

Why have these efforts met resistance? George Bernard Shaw is credited with saying that any effort to professionalize services is a conspiracy against the public, and this cynical note may have relevance to efforts to certify mediators. Although mediation is now widespread in the United States, consumers have not come forward to register frequent complaints or make claims of being damaged by non-certified mediators. This may reflect the fact that in commercial cases at least, parties are usually represented by counsel who are well-positioned to select, assess, and — through their control over hiring — exclude neutrals who are ineffective. Indeed most of the push for certification and licensing has come from mediators wanting the field to have the status of a distinct profession rather than from parties or lawyers.

Even assuming some public benefit in certifying mediators, the question remains whether it would create more problems than it resolved. Certification raises questions about diversity and exclusion, defining competence, squelching creativity, increasing costs, encouraging misplaced reliance, and deciding who to make the gatekeeper. One example of the divisiveness that can be created by the issue is the debate regarding what is "real" mediation. If, for example, a gatekeeper believed that mediation must be facilitative, then mediators who help parties evaluate outcomes would be disqualified and consumers deprived of a choice of styles. If, on the other hand, evaluative mediators dominated the process, purely facilitative approaches might be excluded.

The following article, part of the ongoing debate, suggests how certification might be implemented.

❖ **James E. McGuire,** CERTIFICATION: AN IDEA WHOSE TIME HAS COME
10 Disp. Resol. Mag. 22 (Summer 2004)

Is mediation a profession? If it is, what are the requirements to be a professional mediator? Who should do the certifying? These seemingly simple questions have been part of the mediation dialogue in the United States for more than 25 years. . . .

Why Certify Any Mediator?

Mediators not only want to be competent, they want to be perceived as competent. Currently, mediators do so by collecting credentials: training programs taken, panels joined, articles written, and for those with actual experience, number of cases mediated. While not ensuring competence, credentialing creates a competitive advantage for a mediator.

In order to secure the credential of participating on a panel, taking the sponsor's training course is often a prerequisite. Training programs can be a major source of revenue for the sponsor and a significant burden for potential mediators. Moreover, multiple, repetitive, mandatory entry-level training programs exist within most states and practice areas. Certification may provide an answer to the frustration these duplicative requirements present. . . .

As legislators begin to codify mediation confidentiality . . . some are asking the basic hard questions: Who are these mediators? How do they get trained? What safeguards exist to ensure that the mediators are trustworthy?

An additional reason for considering voluntary mediator certification is recognition that if mediators do not create a certification process, others will and it may not be as voluntary or nuanced and flexible as the field would desire. . . .

How to Become Certified

. . . A likely model is [a] two-step process . . . : preparation and submission of a "portfolio". . . . The portfolio is a paper submission documenting . . . hours of training and relevant course work [and experience] as an active mediator. . . . Letters of recommendation, evidence of professional liability insurance, and disclosure of disciplinary matters complete the portfolio requirements.

A candidate with an acceptable portfolio would then take a written examination. . . . The exam is intended to test awareness of mediation principles, approaches, and relevant techniques. [T]here is likely to be no provision for reviewing an actual demonstration of mediation skills. Such live evaluations are difficult to develop and expensive to administer. This is especially true where the goal is to avoid having certification itself become an economic barrier to entry into the mediation field.

Who Certifies?

The development and successful implementation of certification standards is most likely to succeed if it is a multi-organizational effort. . . . [N]either lawyers nor the ABA "own" the mediator certification process. . . . Though there can be no guarantee of success, any other approach may well be a guarantee of failure.

Questions

38. Assume that you wish to become a mediator and can meet the qualifications described by Mr. McGuire. Would you prefer to have your state adopt a credentialing program like the one he outlines, or take a "hands-off" approach?

39. What is gained or lost if regulation of mediators is limited to certification, rather than a licensing system like bar membership?

D. Ethics Issues for Advocates and Neutrals

Lawyers may engage in mediation either as advocates or as neutrals. Some attorneys play both roles, maintaining an active law practice and also acting as a mediator. The ethical issues for each role are different and we discuss them in turn.

1. Advocates in Mediation

We have seen that advocates in mediation act primarily as negotiators. The rule that governs lawyers as negotiators is ABA Model Rule 4.1, which does not mention mediation at all. Several years ago the ABA proposed changes to the Model Rules through its Ethics 2000 (E2K) Commission. The E2K recommendations changed lawyers' obligations in the arbitration process by defining an arbitrator as a "tribunal" to which counsel owe a heightened duty of candor. (See E2K Report, Rules 1.0(m), 3.3, in the Web Appendix.)

The proposed changes did not, however, grant similar tribunal status to mediators. Neither current ethical rules nor the E2K revisions require attorneys to be more truthful with mediators than with opponents in direct negotiation. See Formal Opinion 06-439, ABA Standing Committee on Ethics and Professional Responsibility ("the same standards that apply to lawyers engaged in negotiations must apply to them in the context of caucused mediation"). In the view of Dean James Alfini, the effect of the E2K changes is that mediation

> would appear to fall into a gap (or black hole) between the formal proceedings contemplated by Rule 3.3 [Candor Toward the Tribunal] and the informal settings contemplated by Rule 4.1 [Truthfulness in Statements to Others]. . . . Thus, lawyering activities in mediation would appear to be governed by the permissive Rule 4.1 . . . which provides an inadequate ethics infrastructure to support the settlement culture that has developed over the past 20 years. . . . The rules should be redrafted to hold lawyers to a higher standard of conduct [in mediation]. . . . (Alfini, 2001)

Professor Cooley similarly has written that "As long as there are not uniform ethical standards defining truthfulness in mediation, lawyer-mediators and mediation advocates will have the unfettered capacity to practice their showmanship and produce their 'magic' effects by any method they wish" (Cooley, 1997).

Although the Model Rules do not impose any special standards on mediation, other rules may. For one thing, many court-connected ADR programs impose standards of conduct on participants such as the obligation to mediate in good faith, and lawyers who engage in private mediation often sign agreements that commit them to similar conduct. Finally, advocates may voluntarily observe standards higher than the minimum imposed by law, either because of their personal values or for practical reasons we explore below. Special issues do arise, however, when advocates bargain in the context of mediation, and are discussed below.

a. Candor Toward the Mediator

We saw in Chapter 12 that bargaining in mediation is unique because it is often three-sided. At times disputants are negotiating directly with their opponent, using the mediator simply as a channel of communication ("Tell them that we won't move into six figures until . . . "), but attorneys adopting a competitive approach also negotiate with the neutral. Here are two examples:

Mediator: "I understand that your current offer is $10,000, but can you give me a private indication of where you'd be willing to go if the plaintiff dropped its demand?"
Lawyer: "Well, if they drop to six figures, I would recommend. . . ."

Mediator: "I am going to ask each side to tell me confidentially how far they would go to get a final settlement in this matter. . . ."
Lawyer: "The bottom dollar we can take is. . . ."

Should lawyers be more candid with a mediator than with an adverse party? Although there is no legal obligation to bargain differently, there are practical reasons to do so. To begin with, an attorney, sensing that a mediator is acting in an impartial and cooperative manner, might feel a natural inclination to reciprocate. A lawyer might also opt to treat a mediator well in the hope that she would reciprocate by exercising influence over the process to the attorney's benefit.

Problem 9

   You represent the employer in a bitterly contested case involving an executive fired from a Silicon Valley company. The parties have bargained fiercely for several hours. For the past hour they have been at an impasse. The mediator now makes a mediator's proposal in an effort to break the deadlock. You ask for a few minutes to confer privately with your client, the company's CEO. After batting the proposed number back and forth, the CEO says, "I don't think we can live with that, but let's say 'yes' and see if the plaintiff bites. Nothing's final until it's signed anyway." You fear that the CEO is simply testing the waters and will renege if the employee accepts the deal.

   a.   Can you indicate that your client assents to the proposal? Would doing so violate the Model Rules?
   b.   Suppose that the CEO's tactic will achieve her goal, but will impair your credibility with the mediator in future cases. Does this change the analysis?
   c.   Under the law of confidentiality in your jurisdiction, can anyone be compelled to testify concerning your client's response to the mediator's proposal?

Problem 10

Assume the same facts, except that the CEO thinks that the plaintiff's entire case is bogus. She does not authorize you to make any settlement offer, and tells you to go to mediation "just to see where they're coming from." The president has given no indication that she will authorize you to make a settlement offer, but it is possible.

a.   If the mediation agreement commits the parties to bargain "in good faith," is your client violating it?
b.   Do you owe the mediator or the other party any obligation to disclose your situation?
c.   If you disagree with this approach, how would you explain your viewpoint to the client?

b.   Obligations to Other Parties

We have seen that the Model Rules of Professional Conduct impose few obligations on a lawyer vis-à-vis an adversary when negotiating, and that an attorney's obligations are no higher in mediation than in direct bargaining. Still, the structure of the process can create unique issues for lawyers. Consider these problems.

Problem 11

You are a lawyer preparing for mediation with mediator Alvarez, who began her practice as a neutral about a year ago, after a long career as a civil litigator. She had an excellent reputation as a lawyer and did well with a small personal injury case that you mediated with her six months ago. You ran into Alvarez on the street a few weeks ago, and she mentioned her interest in doing another case with you. A long-term client, a casualty insurer, has asked you to mediate a major tort case. You recommended Alvarez as a possibility, and it appears that she would be acceptable to the plaintiff's counsel. As you are preparing to call the mediator to make final arrangements, your contact at the insurer calls and says, "Tell her we're a major player in the market. If she gets a good result on this one, we'll think strongly about sending her more cases."

a.   Under the Model Rules, the sample commercial mediation agreement in the Web Appendix, or any other applicable standard, is it improper for you to pass along this comment to Alvarez? Why or why not?
b.   If you say something to the mediator, how will you phrase it? If not, what if anything will you say to the adjuster?

> Problem 12
>
> You practice as a litigator in a small firm and are representing a plaintiff in an automobile tort case. The defendant is insured by a major insurance company. Given the market power of the insurer, you are concerned that the mediator might be less than fully neutral. Is there anything that you can do to alleviate your concern? Is there any risk to your proposed course of action?

c.   The Duty to Advise Clients About ADR

An increasing number of jurisdictions require lawyers to advise clients about the nature of alternative dispute resolution and the potential for using it in their dispute. For example, Colorado (via the bar association), Arkansas (by statute), and Ohio, New Jersey, and Massachusetts (through court rules), each require attorneys to give such advice. Several federal and state courts have adopted similar rules. Comments to the ABA's Ethics E2K proposals also mention ADR, stating that, "In general, a lawyer is not expected to give advice until asked by the client, . . . " but going on to say that "[W]hen a matter is likely to involve litigation, it may be necessary . . . to inform the client of forms of dispute resolution that might constitute reasonable alternatives to litigation . . . " (E2K Report, Comments to Rule 2.1).

> Questions
>
> 39.   The Colorado Bar's Code of Ethics states that lawyers should "advise the client of alternative forms of dispute resolution that might reasonably be pursued to attempt to resolve the legal dispute or to reach the legal objective sought." Draft the key points you would mention about ADR if you were meeting with a secretary at a local manufacturing company who had just retained you to sue the company for sexual harassment that created a hostile work environment, forcing her to leave her job.
> 40.   What, in practical terms, does the Colorado rule require an attorney to do? Could a lawyer comply with the rule by giving a one-sentence definition of mediation and saying that it would be a waste of time in this particular case? If so, does the rule have any value?

2.   *Concerns for Mediators*

There is no empirical evidence that mediators often engage in misconduct. Professor Michael Moffit conducted a survey of cases filed against mediators and concluded that: "Despite the thousands, if not millions of disputants who have received mediation services, instances of legal complaints against mediators are extraordinarily rare" (Moffit, 2003b). His survey yielded only one reported case in the past quarter-century in which a verdict had been entered against a mediator for improper conduct, and that result was overturned on appeal. The cost of mediator malpractice insurance is also very low. As of 2009, for example, a leading insurer of mediators was offering a malpractice liability policy in most states that provided $300,000 in coverage for a premium of less than $300 per year. Such rates could not be offered if there were a significant number of claims requiring a defense, much less a money payment.

The rarity of lawsuits against mediators does not necessarily mean that they do not commit misconduct, however. Many neutrals operate under immunity conferred by court-sponsored programs or mediation agreements and even if a mediator is not immune from suit, a plaintiff would find it very difficult as a practical matter to prove a causal connection between a mediator's misconduct and an ascertainable monetary loss (Moffit, 2003b). How could a complainant show, for example, that a mediator's misconduct caused it to settle for a specific amount more or less than if the mediator had acted competently?

Even allegations of mediator misconduct are relatively unusual. In Florida during the late 1990s, for example, state courts were sending more than 100,000 cases per year to mediation. Although Florida maintains a board to investigate complaints against court-certified mediators, over its first eight years of operation it received an average of only six complaints per year (Bergman and Bickerman, 1998). Formal complaints against mediators thus appear to be infrequent — although this is admittedly only a minimal measure of ethical behavior.

The absence of any system of licensing means that mediators are not subject to any binding system of rules akin to the canons of ethics for lawyers. Nor do the Model Rules for Professional Conduct impose a higher duty on lawyers when they act as mediators. For example, the ABA Standing Committee on Ethics and Professional Responsibility has opined Model Rule 8.4(c), which bars lawyers from engaging in dishonesty or misrepresentation, does not impose higher obligations on lawyers acting as mediators than their obligations under Model Rule 4.1 (ABA Formal Opinion 06-439, at 6 n. 19).

In the interest of advancing the field and recognizing the value of self-regulation, however, three organizations — the American Arbitration Association, American Bar Association, and Association for Conflict Resolution — have jointly promulgated an ethical code known as the Standards of Conduct for Mediators (Model Standards). Specialty organizations have created similar ethical codes for mediators in fields such as family mediation. In addition, the UMA contains a requirement that mediators disclose conflicts of interest, and both courts and private ADR organizations like JAMS and CPR impose ethical rules on mediators on their panels.

The American Bar Association maintains a clearinghouse with a searchable database of state and local opinions on mediation ethics at *www.abanet.org/dispute/clearinghouse.html* and the ABA Section on Dispute Resolution has a Mediator Ethical Guidance Committee that issues opinions in response to requests. The Model Standards, the UMA, and other prominent ethical standards for mediators appear on the companion website to this book.

Excerpts from the some of the most important ethical standards appear below. They are followed by problems drawn from actual practice.

❖ Excerpts from the Model Standards of Conduct for Mediators (2005)

Standard I: Self Determination

A. A mediator shall conduct a mediation based on the principle of party self-determination. Self-determination is the act of coming to a voluntary, uncoerced decision in which each party makes free and informed choices as to process and outcome. Parties may exercise self-determination at any stage of a mediation, including mediator selection, process design, participation in or withdrawal from the process, and outcomes. . . .

B. A mediator shall not undermine party self-determination by any party for reasons such as higher settlement rates, egos, increased fees, or outside pressures from court personnel, program administrators, provider organizations, the media or others.

Standard II: Impartiality

A. A mediator shall decline a mediation if the mediator cannot conduct it in an impartial manner. Impartiality means freedom from favoritism, bias or prejudice.

B. A mediator shall conduct a mediation in an impartial manner and avoid conduct that gives the appearance of partiality. . . .

Standard III: Conflicts of Interest

A. A mediator shall avoid a conflict of interest or the appearance of a conflict of interest during and after a mediation. A conflict of interest can arise from involvement by a mediator with the subject matter of the dispute or from any relationship between a mediator and any mediation participant, whether past or present, personal or professional, that reasonably raises a question of a mediator's impartiality. . . .

Standard IV: Competence

A. A mediator shall mediate only when the mediator has the necessary competence to satisfy the reasonable expectations of the parties. . . .

Standard V: Confidentiality

A. A mediator shall maintain the confidentiality of all information obtained by the mediator in mediation, unless otherwise agreed to by the parties or required by applicable law.

B. A mediator who meets with any persons in private session during a mediation shall not convey directly or indirectly to any other person, any information that was obtained during that private session without the consent of the disclosing person. . . .

Standard VI: Quality of the Process

A. A mediator shall conduct a mediation in accordance with these Standards and in a manner that promotes diligence, timeliness, safety, presence of the appropriate participants, party participation, procedural fairness, party competency and mutual respect among all participants. . . .

Standard VII: Advertising and Solicitation

A. A mediator shall be truthful and not misleading when advertising, soliciting or otherwise communicating the mediator's qualifications, experience, services and fees. . . .

Standard VIII: Fees and Other Charges

A. A mediator shall provide each party or each party's representative true and complete information about mediation fees, expenses and any other actual or potential charges that may be incurred in connection with a mediation. . . .

B. . . . A mediator should not enter into a fee agreement which is contingent upon the result of the mediation or the amount of the settlement. . . .

Standard IX: Advancement of Mediation Practice

A mediator should act in a manner that advances the practice of mediation. . . .

❖ Excerpt from the Uniform Mediation Act

Section 9. Mediator's Disclosure of Conflicts of Interest, Background

(a) Before accepting a mediation, an individual who is requested to serve as a mediator shall:

   (1) make an inquiry that is reasonable under the circumstances to determine whether there are any known facts that a reasonable individual would consider likely to affect the impartiality of the mediator . . . and

   (2) disclose any such known fact to the mediation parties as soon as is practical before accepting a mediation.

(b) If a mediator learns any fact described in subsection (a)(1) after accepting a mediation, the mediator shall disclose it as soon as is practicable.

(c) At the request of a mediation party, an individual who is requested to serve as a mediator shall disclose the mediator's qualifications to mediate a dispute. . . .

Note: UMA Sections 4–8 contain substantive prohibitions on a mediator disclosing confidential information, violation of which would be an ethical breach.

❖ Excerpt from ABA Model Rules of Professional Conduct
(2004)

Excerpt from Rule 1.12 Former . . . Mediator or Other Third-Party Neutral

(a) Except as stated in paragraph (d), a lawyer shall not represent anyone in connection with a matter in which the lawyer participated personally and substantially as a . . . mediator . . . unless all parties to the proceeding give <u>informed consent</u>, <u>confirmed in writing</u>.

(b) A lawyer shall not negotiate for employment with any person who is involved as a party or as lawyer for a party in a matter in which the lawyer is participating personally and substantially as a judge or other adjudicative officer or as an arbitrator, mediator or other third-party neutral. . . .

(c) If a lawyer is disqualified by paragraph (a), no lawyer in a <u>firm</u> with which that lawyer is associated may <u>knowingly</u> undertake or continue representation in the matter unless:

(1) the disqualified lawyer is <u>screened</u> from any participation in the matter and is apportioned no part of the fee therefrom; and

(2) <u>written</u> notice is promptly given to the parties and any appropriate <u>tribunal</u> to enable them to ascertain compliance with the provisions of this rule . . . [emphasis in original].

Questions

41. Any standard of conduct embodies a vision of what the mediation process should be. Can you classify the vision implicit in the Model Standards in terms of mediator styles — broad or narrow? Facilitative or evaluative/directive?

42. Do the Model Standards appear to discourage any particular approach to mediation?

The Model Standards embody core values of mediation and for that reason are fairly noncontroversial. This does not mean, however, that they are easy to apply in practice. Ethical codes are clear about what a mediator must do in egregious situations, such as when she discovers that a case involves a close friend. Good mediators, however, have little difficulty deciding how to handle such situations. The more difficult problems arise when two ethical principles, each valid in itself, come into conflict and there appears to be no way to satisfy both of them. To understand how this can occur consider the following problems.

a.　Issues of Fairness

Among the most serious problems are issues of fairness. They arise most often in cases in which the disputants are proceeding pro se. Such situations present a tension between Sections I, II, and VI of the Model Standards.

Problem 13

In a private mediation of a divorce case, the husband appears without a lawyer and the wife has counsel. As the process goes forward, the husband becomes progressively more upset, sometimes making illogical arguments and reversing decisions that he had previously made. The mediator suggests to the husband that the mediation be adjourned so that he can rest and consult a lawyer, but the husband expresses a strong wish to "get it over with." He tells the mediator privately that "outside factors" make it important that he resolve the case quickly. The husband will not explain what they are, but the mediator suspects that he has formed a new relationship and is anxious to get out of his old one. The wife's counsel, sensing this, drives a very hard bargain, demanding that she receive 50 percent more alimony than court guidelines would suggest and three-fourths of the marital estate. The process continues for several hours. The husband becomes increasingly upset but refuses to stop. At one point, late in the afternoon during a private caucus, he says to the mediator in an agitated tone, "This can't go on any longer! I guess I've got to take their offer."

a.　What provisions of the Model Standards apply to this situation?
b.　How should the mediator respond? What problems could arise if the husband signs an agreement?

Problem 14

Professor Timothy Hedeen has noted numerous cases in which parties later sought to overturn mediated settlements on the ground that they were incompetent to bargain. He cites a case in which a plaintiff "who was on heart medicine tried to set aside a mediation settlement agreement by claiming that despite chest pains and fatigue he was told that he would have to continue in the mediation session until he was willing to reach agreement." [*Wilson v. Wilson*, 282 Ga. 728, 731-32 (2007)] Given the experiences of disputants in this case and cases such as *Olam*, he asks whether mediation requires advisory packaging such as

> Warning: This dispute resolution process may involve long hours, many in small rooms alone (while the mediator meets with other parties) and without obvious opportunity to obtain food, drink or even necessary medications. (Hedeen, 2009)

The suggestion was delivered with tongue in cheek, but what should a mediator who uses such techniques tell an unrepresented party? Draft a short disclosure or explanation.

Problem 15

A volunteer mediator is handling landlord-tenant cases in a community mediation program. A case is referred over by a court clerk. The defendant is a tenant facing eviction who is proceeding pro se. The landlord is a corporation represented by counsel. The tenant seems to have little understanding of what will happen in court if he does not settle. At one point shortly before lunch, the landlord offers a "final deal": He will allow the tenant two more months' occupancy, provided that all past rent is paid, the future rent is put into escrow, and the tenant agrees now to the entry of judgment for eviction at the end of the two months. The landlord's representative states that if the plaintiff does not accept the offer by 2 p.m., he will go back to court and ask the judge to rule on his request that the tenant be ordered to vacate the premises within seven days.

The tenant is unsure what to do, and in a private caucus asks the mediator, "Are they right about the law here? What do you recommend?" The mediator privately believes that if the tenant offers to pay rent into escrow, it is very likely that the court will give him at least six months to move, although for a judge to grant the landlord's request is not inconceivable.

a. Which of the Model Standards apply? What do they counsel the mediator to do?
b. Does it make a difference that this case was referred to mediation by a court? Why?

b. Questions of Competence

Mediators sometimes encounter cases in areas in which they have not practiced or previously mediated — indeed if their practices expand, then such situations are quite likely. What obligation does a mediator have to disclose her lack of expertise to disputants? Article IV of the Model Standards and § 9 of the UMA each deal with this issue.

Problem 16

You are a litigator with ten years' experience who occasionally acts as a mediator. You have handled a total of 15 mediations as a neutral and participated in dozens more as an advocate. You have been asked to mediate a bitter employment dispute involving an employee who says that she was sexually harassed by her supervisor and that management knew of the problem but "swept it under the rug." You do not handle employment cases and have never mediated one, but you do read summaries of decided cases that are printed in your local legal newspaper, and these include court decisions in employment cases, among others.

a.   Do the Model Standards or the UMA require you to make any disclosure?
b.   Draft an outline of what you would tell the parties if you do make a disclosure.
c.   Does it make a difference if the parties are represented by counsel?

---

c. Repeat-Player Concerns

To be successful as a mediator one must have clients, and busy neutrals rely on repeat business. One national organization of mediators estimates, for example, that two thirds of the revenue of their successful panelists comes from cases involving lawyers who have mediated with that neutral at least three times during the past year. When does repeat business create unhealthy dependence? Sections II and III of the Model Standards and § 9 of the UMA may apply to a mediator in such situations; other standards may apply to advocates.

Problem 17

Assume that you are a mediator and have mediated three cases involving Attorney Okawa. In each case the result was a settlement satisfactory to both sides, and at least one of the opposing lawyers in those other cases has selected you as a neutral again. Okawa now calls and asks you to mediate another case. He says that he has just about persuaded the other party to use you, but has not mentioned to them that he has previously mediated with you because it would require discussing the earlier cases, which his clients strongly want to be kept confidential. He asks that you not mention the prior mediations to the other party.

a.   What do the Model Standards require?
b.   What should you do?

d.   Differences Between Attorney and Client

At times a mediator is dealing with people who are on the same side of a dispute but have widely divergent viewpoints. An attorney, for example, may not appear to be "on the same page" as her client about the risks of litigation or whether to take an offer. Ethical standards for both lawyers and mediators state that in such situations the client's wishes govern. However, parties often hire lawyers in part because they have more experience and are thought to have better judgment in highly charged situations, and many lawyers feel that clients sometimes become too emotional to make good decisions. And, it should be noted, commercial mediators know that attorneys, not clients, are their primary source of referrals. Sections I, III, and VI of the Model Standards for Mediators and § 1.2 of the Model Rules for lawyers may apply to such situations.

Problem 18

Two parties have gone through nine hours of difficult mediation in a product liability case. The plaintiffs have alleged that their infant daughter died because of defects in a baby carriage manufactured by the defendant. The plaintiff couple is represented by experienced counsel and has held up well to the stress of the process. The maker of the carriage is represented by its CFO and outside counsel. The mediator's impression is that the CFO is being unrealistic about the company's legal exposure. The mediator has tried to bring other company officials into the case, but without success.

At 6 p.m. the mediator brings another offer to the defense, which is promptly rejected. At this point the neutral says to the defense team that although she's willing to keep talking, they appear to be close to deadlock and it may make sense to adjourn for the day. As the neutral leaves the room, defense counsel says she's going to the restroom. In a private conversation in the hallway, she asks the mediator to "get tough" with her client. The CFO, she says, has a visceral dislike of the plaintiff's lawyer. He is letting his determination to beat the other guy lead him into a position that is against the company's best interests. This is her firm's first case with this client, and she does not have the clout to make him listen to advice herself.

The neutral respects counsel's reputation as an advocate and privately agrees with her assessment of the situation. On her return she asks the defense team if it would be helpful for her to give her impressions of how a court would view the case if it had to be tried. The defense lawyer promptly responds that they would welcome her thoughts. The mediator delivers a hard-hitting evaluation that represents her honest assessment, emphasizing some jury sympathy factors that she believes the CFO is ignoring. The CFO does not respond to the mediator's comments, but appears to be a bit taken aback. The bargaining process resumes, and the disputants continue without a dinner break, munching on fast food. At 9:30 p.m., after several lengthy caucuses, the CFO agrees to essentially the same proposal that the mediator had brought to him at 6 p.m.

a.   Did the lawyer act unethically in saying what she did to the mediator?
b.   Did the mediator act improperly in her response? Why or why not?

Problem 19

Assume the same situation as in the prior problem, but that the reason for the CFO's refusal, in counsel's judgment, is that he is seriously overconfident about the company's chances of prevailing in litigation. The lawyer again meets the mediator in the hallway. She says that she selected the neutral, a retired judge, primarily for her credibility on legal issues and asks her to "bring out your gavel" and give her client a "hard" evaluation of the company's chances of success in court. It is clear to the mediator that the counsel wants her to give a reasoned evaluation, but also to strongly emphasize the risks of continuing in litigation. Would such a request be more or less troublesome than the prior problem?

---

e.   Improper Conduct by Litigants

Ethical standards instruct mediators to support the parties' right to self-determination. But what should a mediator do if she learns that one party is acting improperly vis-à-vis another party, or that both parties are considering terms that appear likely to harm the interests of a person not represented in the process? Family mediators may find, for instance, that parents seek to satisfy other goals by agreeing to a visitation arrangement likely to create serious difficulties for their children. In commercial mediation the problem is more likely to arise when disputants create value for themselves by cheating an outsider — often the Internal Revenue Service. Mediators may not be asked to contribute ideas in such situations, but they are typically called on to carry proposals back and forth, advocate their acceptance, and act as scribes to memorialize dubious arrangements.

Problem 20

You are mediating a divorce case in which the parents are negotiating over custody and visitation of their two young children. As is common in family mediation, the process is occurring entirely in joint session, and lawyers are not present. You have stated that you will not talk with a party unless the other is present. However, after one session the wife returns to pick up a hat that she had left behind and, as she is leaving, mentions, "You know, I've just gotten a really attractive job offer, so I'm going to move out of state in two months. But I can't tell Jim — we've almost agreed on everything. If he knows I'm moving 2,000 miles away it'll blow everything up. Let's just work out the custody and visitation and all, and then I'll deal with it."

Your impression is that the husband is conceding much more than he otherwise would on issues such as support, and has agreed to grant the wife sole legal custody of the children, in return for her agreement to generous visitation arrangements.

a. What should you do in this situation?
b. Does it matter if the mediation is being conducted under the auspices of a court-connected ADR program?

Problem 21

You are mediating a family dispute in which one of the spouses is self-employed. As part of the process the parties are mediating alimony, support for their seven-year-old child, and a division of assets. You have asked each spouse to prepare a financial statement, which they have exchanged. As the mediation goes forward, stray comments by the husband make you strongly suspect that he is hiding substantial cash income that is not reflected on his financial statement. What should you do?

Problem 22

A terminated executive has been mediating with his former employer for ten hours. After fierce bargaining in which the mediator has used her entire "bag of tricks," the defense has come painfully to a final offer of $180,000, but the plaintiff refuses to accept less than $200,000. A key issue, from the plaintiff's perspective, is that he needs to come out of the process with $100,000 in the bank, net of his attorney's one-third contingency fee. Because the primary claim is for lost pay, however, any settlement will be treated by the company as back pay and therefore will be subject to payroll withholding. The effect is that the plaintiff would net only about $70,000, well below his minimum requirement. The plaintiff also has asserted a vague claim for emotional distress, but federal law bars plaintiffs from receiving settlement money tax-free unless an injury is physical in nature. "Mere" emotional distress is not sufficient to avoid a tax bite.

Suddenly the plaintiff attorney asks the mediator to take an idea to the defense: In a spell of depression caused by the firing, the plaintiff now remembers, he suffered from erectile dysfunction. Counsel didn't make it an explicit part of the claim because of the embarrassment factor, but it's there and it was a physical injury. The lawyer, with her client's approval, proposes allocating most of the settlement to this injury, allowing the plaintiff to receive his $100,000.

a. Is there a problem for the mediator in presenting this idea to the defense?

b. Assume that the mediator does so. Defense counsel laughs and says that this is the first she's heard about this malady, but if the plaintiff says he's dysfunctional, that's his problem. She says the proposal is OK with her client, as long as the plaintiff certifies the condition and assumes any risk that the IRS will contest it. The lawyers ask you to write down the terms they dictate summarizing the deal. Does this pose a problem?

c. Model Rule of Professional Conduct for Lawyers 8.3 states that "a lawyer who knows that another lawyer has committed a violation of the Rules of Professional Conduct that raises a substantial question as to that lawyer's honesty . . . shall inform the appropriate professional authority. . . ." Is it a violation of Rule 8.3 for a lawyer-mediator in the circumstances of Problem 21 not to report an apparent tax violation? For an argument that it is, see Rubin and Spector (2008).

3. Combining Practice as an Advocate and a Mediator

Experienced lawyers increasingly seek to combine their practices as litigators with work as mediators. Experienced attorneys find it refreshing to take on new roles and if a lawyer is thinking of changing careers, this allows her to explore being a neutral without "quitting her day job." Even if an attorney decides to continue to practice law, experience as a mediator is likely to enhance her effectiveness as an advocate in the process.

a.   Conflicts of Interest

One major issue for lawyers who alternate between the roles of advocate and neutral is the potential for conflicts of interest — the possibility that a party in a mediated case will be a past or future legal client of the mediator-lawyer or his firm. This is a particular concern in large law firms, where a single modestly compensated mediation can disqualify the entire firm from representing a party in a much more lucrative litigation matter.

Standards for neutrals call for disclosure in such situations. Model Standard III requires disclosure of "all actual and potential conflicts that are reasonably known to the mediator and could reasonably be seen as raising a question about the mediator's impartiality." If the conflict "might reasonably be viewed as undermining the integrity of the mediation," the Standards require a mediator to recuse himself.

The UMA also relies on disclosure: Section 9(a) requires a neutral "to make an inquiry . . . to determine whether there are any known facts that a reasonable individual would consider likely to affect the impartiality of the mediator [including] an existing or past relationship with a mediation party or foreseeable participant. . . ." If such facts exist, the UMA requires the neutral to disclose them. The UMA does not impose disqualification on the lawyer or his firm for violating this rule, but § 9(d) does bar violators from asserting the mediation privilege.

The ABA's E2K Report deals explicitly with conflicts between roles, stating that "a lawyer shall not represent anyone in connection with a matter in which the lawyer participated personally and substantially as a . . . mediator. . . ." The rule goes on to provide that "If a lawyer is disqualified . . . no lawyer in a firm with which that [lawyer-mediator] is associated may knowingly undertake or continue representation in that matter." However, the firm may represent a mediator's client if the lawyer-mediator is screened from knowledge or fees associated with the case, and the parties to the mediation are notified of the situation (E2K Report, § 1.12 [a, c]). The issue is also addressed by other codes of ethics, in particular the CPR-Georgetown Rule (on the companion website to this book).

Question

43.   A lawyer-mediator has no current or past attorney-client relationship with the parties in a case she is mediating, but she knows that lawyers in another department of her firm have approached the defendant in the case about serving as outside counsel. The firm has never received a case from the defendant, but hopes to represent it in the future.

a.   What do the above standards require of the lawyer?
b.   Must she disqualify herself as mediator?
c.   If she mediates the case, is her firm disqualified from representing the party as counsel?

b.   Role Confusion

The very fact that a mediator is an attorney may lead pro se litigants to believe that the neutral will provide them with legal advice. The E2K report proposed the following rule to deal with this issue:

Rule 2.4(b) . . . A lawyer serving as a third-party neutral shall inform unrepresented parties that the lawyer is not representing them. When the lawyer knows or reasonably should know that a party does not understand the lawyer's role in the matter, the lawyer shall explain the difference between the lawyer's role as a third-party neutral and a lawyer's role as one who represents a client.
   Comment: . . . Where appropriate, the lawyer should inform unrepresented parties of the important differences between the lawyer's role as third-party neutral and a lawyer's role as a client representative, including the inapplicability of the attorney-client evidentiary privilege. . . .

Questions

44.   In what types of disputes is the danger of confusion between the role of counsel and mediator likely to be greatest?

45.   Assume that you are a lawyer who has agreed to mediate a dispute between a quarry and neighbors who are complaining about noise and dust from its operations. The company is represented by its business manager, the neighbors by a committee of three laypeople.
   a.   Draft a statement that you could make to the participants to explain your role.
   b.   When and how would you deliver it?

46.   Consider these situations:
   a.   Lawyer-mediator Garcia successfully mediates a case in which Allen sued Thompson. A month later, Allen approaches Garcia and asks her to represent her in a matter not related to the dispute that was mediated. Can Garcia accept the case? Must she follow any special procedure? Does it matter whether the matter, although unrelated in terms of subject matter, involves Thompson in any way?
   b.   Suppose that Allen instead approaches Garcia's law partner, Black, to represent her in the new case. What, if anything, is required then?

c. What if Thompson asks Garcia to represent her in pursuing a third-party defendant in the *Allen v. Thompson* dispute? The activities of the third party were discussed during the mediation, but the third party was not involved in the mediation process. Does Allen have to consent? If so, why?

d. Lawyer-mediator Horwitz conducts a one-hour orientation session about the mediation process for a couple who are considering divorce, but they decide not to go ahead with the mediation. Two months later the wife asks one of Horwitz's partners to represent her in the divorce, which is contested. Is the lawyer disqualified from doing so? Should she be? (See *Bauerle v. Bauerle*, 615 N.Y.S.2d 954 (1994), *later opinion* 616 N.Y.S.2d 275 [1994].)

The role of a mediator is inherently somewhat ambiguous, in that she has obligations toward both sides in disputes as well as to the process itself, and ethical standards for mediators tend to be quite general. This leaves even conscientious neutrals in doubt about what to do in particular situations. We hope to have convinced you that being an ethical mediator or lawyer is a process of continuing self-examination rather than simply a matter of learning a set of rules, and that you will continue to explore these issues for the rest of your professional life.

This completes our analysis of mediation. We now move to a third form of ADR, arbitration. Arbitration differs from negotiation and mediation in many ways, the most important of which is that it is binding — participants cannot reject the outcome of arbitration, as they can offers in negotiation or mediation. This gives rise to a variety of issues that we explore in the chapters that follow.

PART
III

Arbitration

CHAPTER
16

Arbitration — The Big Picture

Knowledgeable attorneys understand the term "arbitration" to refer to any process in which a private third party neutral renders a judgment, or "award," regarding a dispute after hearing evidence and argument, like a judge. "Arbitration" comprehends a wide variety of procedures, similar in varying degrees to litigation and usually intended as a partial or complete substitute for court trial.

Look again at the "Dispute Resolution Spectrum" on page 6 in Chapter 1. Several forms of arbitration are referenced in the chart — but most types are listed on the right side of the spectrum, among "Adjudicative Processes/ Binding." This arrangement emphasizes two essential characteristics of most arbitration procedures: they are adversary *adjudicative* procedures analogous to court trial, and they result in a judgment that is *binding*.

When lawyers are involved in arbitration, they act as advocates for parties in arbitration in much the same way they do in court trial. They make oral arguments at hearings, present documentary and testimonial evidence, and prepare briefs for the arbitrators, who act as neutral decision makers. When the lawyers' work is done, the parties and lawyers await an award from the arbitrators. Arbitration awards are generally more difficult to overturn than court judgments. Although arbitration procedures and practice vary in detail and may differ significantly from court trial, arbitration processes are of a fundamentally different character from negotiation, mediation, and other processes on the left side of the Dispute Resolution Spectrum.

One form of arbitration, "Advisory Arbitration," is included on the left side of the Dispute Resolution Spectrum. This refers to a kind of process used in some federal and state court programs where an arbitration panel is employed to render a non-binding advisory award prior to trial of a case. The advisory award is not enforceable in court, but it may stimulate voluntary settlement of a dispute before trial. Advisory arbitration is not, however, the primary focus of the next four chapters. Instead, we will concentrate on binding arbitration pursuant to agreement of the parties.

In the United States, lawyers are most often involved with arbitration pursuant to a private agreement between two or more parties. The agreement usually provides that the arbitration award will be mutually binding and enforceable in a court of law. An extensive body of rules, practices, case decisions, and ethical standards has grown up around forms of contract-based, binding arbitration. This will be the chief emphasis of Chapters 16 through 19.

What kinds of disputes may find their way into binding arbitration under the terms of an agreement? The answer may surprise you. Consider the following examples of disputes that have been the subject of arbitration:

- A dispute involving the design and construction of a Major League Baseball stadium;
- A controversy between U.S financial institutions and the government of Iran;
- A claim for employment discrimination and intentional infliction of emotional distress by an employee against his employer;
- A claim of fraud by an investor against her securities broker;
- A controversy between a bank issuing a credit card and a customer;
- A fight over the valuation and distribution of assets among entities and individuals in the wake of a corporate dissolution;
- A disagreement over the quality of textiles manufactured by one company for another;
- A dispute over liability and damages resulting from delays in the arrival of a cargo ship in San Francisco;
- The controversy over the disqualification of an Olympic skater;
- A dispute aired on TV as entertainment, like The People's Court.

For a compendium of arbitration and dispute resolution approaches, see Stipanowich (2001).

A. A Brief History of Arbitration

Arbitration has a long and venerable history, having been used by many cultures in a variety of contexts over the centuries. In Biblical times, King Solomon was famous for his wisdom as an arbitrator. Archaeologists have found papyrus documenting arbitration among Phoenician grain traders. In England, arbitration was recognized as part of the judicial system as early as 1281. Many Native American tribes turned to wise elders to resolve disputes.

Binding arbitration has long been an attractive alternative for commercial parties, for whom courts were often too slow and cumbersome, too expensive, too inflexible in remedy-making, and lacking in familiarity with business practices. In medieval times, merchant courts dispensed speedy justice for traders at commercial fairs. In the American colonies, arbitration among merchants was common, since it proved more efficient and effective than the courts. Our first president, George Washington, served as an arbiter of private disputes before the Revolution, and incorporated the following provision in his will:

I hope and trust, that no disputes will arise concerning [the devises in this will]; but if, contrary to expectation, of the usual technical terms, or because too much or too little has been said on any of the Devises to be consonant with law, My Will and direction expressly is, that

- all disputes (if unhappily any should arise) shall be decided by three impartial and intelligent men, known for their probity and understanding.
- two to be chosen by the disputants — each having a choice of one — and the third by those two.
- Which three men thus chosen, shall, unfettered by Law, or legal constructions; declare their Sense of the Testator's intention;
- and such decision is, to all intents and purposes to be as binding on the Parties as if it had been given in the Supreme Court of the United States (Nordham, 1982).

The New York Chamber of Commerce has provided for the use of arbitration beginning with its inception in 1768, and the New York Stock Exchange established arbitration as a dispute resolution mechanism in its 1817 constitution. By the middle of the twentieth century, dozens of industry and trade associations were sponsoring private arbitration programs for business-to-business disputes. Binding arbitration also became a fixture in arbitration of rights and interests under collective bargaining agreements between unions and employers.

Today, arbitration remains an important alternative to court litigation of business disputes. Use of arbitration is widespread among Fortune 1000 corporations (PERC, 1997). In international business relationships, binding arbitration provides a critical substitute for litigation in national courts.

In recent years, binding arbitration agreements have become a feature of many contracts between employers and individual employees, as well as contracts for consumer goods and services. These developments reflected, among other things, an important shift in prevailing judicial attitudes toward arbitration, as courts that were once skeptical of binding arbitration have tended to embrace it as an effective dispute resolution option. The United States Supreme Court has spearheaded this evolution by liberally interpreting the Federal Arbitration Act, which provides for the enforcement of arbitration agreements.

As you will see in our survey of arbitration practice in Chapter 17, arbitration procedures are in many respects analogous to litigation, and have become even more similar as a result of the dramatic expansion of arbitration into what has been called an "all-purpose surrogate" for court trial. A substantial body of case law has grown up around arbitration, as explored in Chapter 18. Not surprisingly, business users of arbitration often complain that their experiences have become more and more like going to court. Paradoxically, concerns about the relative non-reviewability of arbitration awards have led some attorneys to draft contract provisions for judicial review of the legal or factual merits of arbitration awards — in other words, trying to erase one of the primary distinctions between arbitration and court.

Meanwhile, the appearance of provisions for binding arbitration in credit card agreements and other consumer contracts, and also in individual employment contracts, have raised legitimate and strong concerns regarding the fairness of particular arbitration procedures and outcomes in these settings. These concerns have produced a variety of responses — including the creation of special protocols and standards, judicial decisions, and state and federal legislation. These concerns and related responses are the subject of Chapter 19.

B. Arbitration vs. Litigation

According to one much-publicized study of conflict resolution among leading corporations, business lawyers choose arbitration over litigation in a public forum for a variety of reasons: to achieve a speedy resolution; to avoid the costs and delays of litigation; to forego extensive discovery; to escape the glare of a public proceeding; to avoid the publication of a legal precedent; to choose a decision maker with pertinent business or legal expertise; or to achieve a more satisfactory or more durable resolution. Arbitration may or may not achieve these anticipated benefits. Much hinges on key choices made by attorneys at the time of drafting and during the course of the arbitration process — choices that should be informed by the particular needs and goals of their clients.

1. Relative Speed and Economy

As compared to litigation, arbitration has traditionally been touted as a more efficient, speedy, and inexpensive path to justice. There is no question that in certain jurisdictions, private arbitration may be a welcome alternative to waiting one's turn on a crowded civil docket. There is empirical evidence indicating that in some categories of cases, especially those that do not involve high stakes, arbitration is often speedier than court trial. *See, e.g.,* Stipanowich (1988) (summarizing survey of U.S. construction lawyers). Arbitration sometimes avoids, and often limits, time-consuming (and costly) procedural steps such as pretrial motion practice and discovery. And due to relatively strict limits on judicial review of arbitration awards, the likelihood of lengthy post-arbitration appellate practice is relatively low.

However, depending on the scope or complexity of the issues, the nature of agreed-upon procedures, and the process management skills of the arbitrator(s), arbitration may end up being just as lengthy or as costly as litigation. High stakes may induce lawyers to introduce more extensive procedural elements into the process, including discovery and motion practice analogous to that available in court, and to require the services of multiple arbitrators whose often busy schedules must be coordinated. In some cases, lawyers have even tried to establish procedures for expanded judicial review of arbitration awards — sometimes with disastrous results. Indeed, many business attorneys now say that arbitration is often too much like litigation; a 2002 survey of leading commercial arbitrators supports the same conclusion (Phillips, 2002).

2. *Privacy and the Avoidance of Precedent*

Arbitration typically involves proceedings that are not open to the public, and privacy is a major concern for many parties who utilize the arbitration process. Extremely sensitive business and personal documents, including those detailing financial information, are foreclosed from the public, and witnesses are also shielded from public scrutiny during arbitration. In a case where special protection is desired, however, for financial data, intellectual property, or other proprietary information, the normal confidentiality provisions in arbitration agreements may not be sufficient, and special arrangements may be necessary. Arbitration awards are not normally made public (although there are significant exceptions). Moreover, the law places major obstacles in the way of parties seeking court testimony by arbitrators regarding the process or their decision.

Additionally, arbitration awards do not establish precedent in most circumstances. In most arbitral proceedings, the absence of a public award and published reasoning accompanying awards ensures that awards in one dispute are not used as precedent in similar situations. As discussed below, arbitrators traditionally have issued written decisions that are publically available only in special areas such as labor law and domain name disputes. Even there, the awards do not function as a strict form of precedent. Thus, arbitration is a desirable dispute resolution option if one party wants to avoid a precedent. If, on the other hand, a client seeks to establish a new precedent affecting other pending or future disputes, arbitration may be less attractive.

Finally, because one is usually not bound to participate in arbitration or to accept the legal consequences of an arbitration award unless one is a party to an agreement to arbitrate, lawyers who craft business arrangements involving several parties and multiple contracts need to pay particular attention to the functioning of arbitration in multiparty disputes. Otherwise a client may find itself engaged in multiple proceedings, facing the prospect of inconsistent results.

3.   Choice of Expert Decision Maker(s)

Arbitration allows parties to select their own decision makers; they have the freedom to choose an expert in pertinent fields including law, business and finance, accounting, engineering, technology, and other areas. In some cases, a panel of arbitrators may bring to the table complementary knowledge, skill, and experience. For example, an arbitration panel selected to resolve a complex construction dispute might consist of a lawyer familiar with construction contracts and disputes, an architect or engineer, and a contractor or construction manager. Moreover, the ability of an arbitrator (or chair of an arbitration panel) to manage a dispute resolution process may be of paramount significance — especially in large or complex cases.

Of course, the practice of choosing decision makers with related professional background and expertise enhances the likelihood that those chosen will have connections to the parties or will already have formed perspectives on issues at the heart of the dispute. While some arbitrating parties may view such relationships as positive qualifications for arbitrators, others may take the opposite view. The important thing is for parties to have sufficient information to make an informed judgment about the background and connections of prospective arbitrators. For this reason, as explored later, arbitration agreements, statutes, and ethical codes routinely require arbitrators to disclose relationships to the parties and their counsel, as well as other information that might indicate a conflict of interest.

4.   Informality, Arbitral Flexibility, Finality

Another trademark of arbitration is its informality. The atmosphere tends to be less formal and intimidating than a court proceeding; arbitrations frequently take place in an attorney's conference room or other suitable meeting space. Moreover, the rules of evidence and procedure are usually somewhat flexible, allowing the parties to submit certain kinds of evidence that would not be considered in court. For clients frustrated by the sometimes technical constraints of formal rules of evidence and the cost of formal procedures, this can be a benefit. However, an attorney must make her client aware that this relaxation of the rules also means that parties in an arbitration process may not receive all of the formal procedural opportunities and protections of litigation. For example, hearsay may be more widely admitted than in court, even if arbitrators give it less weight. On the one hand, proceedings may be truncated, foreclosing certain avenues of evidence or testimony (although an arbitrator's refusal to hear material evidence is grounds for reversal of award under federal and state law). On the other hand, some arbitrators tend to be very expansive in their admission of evidence, leading to the complaint that the proceeding resembles a "fishing expedition." Again, much hinges on the choice of arbitrator(s) and other decisions made by attorneys in defining the process.

In arriving at a final decision, arbitrators typically have broad flexibility. The law recognizes that their awards will not be measured against judicial precedent, and courts have sometimes spoken of the ability of arbitrators to rely on their own notions of fairness and equity to tailor a remedy appropriate to the circumstances. On the one hand, in some forms of arbitration, including many forms of commercial and labor arbitration, the emphasis was and is on "fact-dominated rough justice. Equity, not law, is the order of the day . . ." (Brunet, 2002). In high-stakes commercial cases, on the other hand, lawyers often dominate the process; advocates and arbitrators often place considerable emphasis on legal issues and legal precedents. Nevertheless, based on the principle that in choosing arbitration parties bargain for the determination of the arbitrator, and not the court, modern law places stringent limits on judicial review of arbitral awards, and restricts the ability of parties to overturn awards on the basis of errors of fact or law.

Arbitration awards are, in fact, more ironclad than jury verdicts or trial court judgments, since appeal is limited to very narrow grounds. Courts give great deference to arbitrators and allow very few avenues of redress. This finality may be one of the greatest advantages of arbitration for many clients who want to get a dispute behind them and move on with new business. It can, however, be a serious disadvantage for parties that are displeased with a ruling or believe that the integrity of the process was compromised, or where a dispute presents important or novel legal issues. Lawyers sometimes express concern about the possibility that arbitral awards will be undisciplined by legal or other norms, resulting in unpredictable and unforeseeable outcomes. The complaint is often made, with some justification, that some arbitrators "split the baby" to avoid hard decisions on the merits. But in modern, lawyer-dominated arbitration practice, law is increasingly likely to play an important role throughout the arbitration proceeding — and an award of 40 to 60 percent of the amount claimed may be fully justified on legal or factual grounds.

Concerns regarding rigorous application of precedent and the danger of an extreme or seemingly irrational award may cause counsel to conclude that arbitration is an unacceptable option for a particular dispute. Alternatively, attorneys may use arbitrator selection; guidelines, standards, or limits for decision making; or other means to reduce the risk of a "knucklehead" award. A more extreme and controversial "solution" is a term in the arbitration agreement providing that courts may overturn arbitration awards for errors of law or fact; besides raising serious legal questions, such arrangements present a minefield of procedural issues.

5. Flexibility and Choice

When all is said and done, it may be that the greatest potential benefit of arbitration is the flexibility afforded participants in crafting a private system of justice tailored to fit the needs of their specific dispute. However, this places a premium on the ability of counsel to provide effective guidance in making process choices. Parties often choose an administered process where arbitral institutions help with the various stages of arbitration. Forms of administrative support include selection of arbitrators, scheduling, and handling fees and expenses. Some parties forego administrative support, opting instead for a non-administered arbitration to minimize costs.

6.   *Fairness Concerns*

Finally, serious issues of fairness and unequal bargaining power arise in disputes involving those who find themselves bound by predispute arbitration provisions in contracts for consumer goods and services. There are concerns over the elimination of an aggrieved party's right to a trial by jury as well as arbitration's impact on class action disputes. Fairness issues also arise in employment disputes, when employees find they are bound to assert any claims against an employer through arbitration because of the individual employment agreement they signed before any disputes arose. Consumers or employees may find themselves in a "take it or leave it" position because all jobs in a given industry or all similar products can only be obtained by signing nearly identical arbitration clauses. In such circumstances, the secrecy provided by the arbitral process, plus participants' real or perceived lack of control over designing the dispute resolution process and choosing the arbitration provider or arbitrators, can foster suspicion, anger, and less incentive to comply with an arbitral award. Besides inspiring a number of efforts by stakeholders to create due process standards for consumer or employment arbitration, these concerns have prompted some courts to more carefully scrutinize arbitration agreements and awards. State legislatures have also sought to place restrictions on arbitration agreements in adhesion settings — efforts that have often faltered in the face of strong federal pro-arbitration policy. It appears increasingly likely, however, that Congress will pass laws dramatically restricting the use of arbitration in consumer and employment transactions. These subjects will be explored in more detail in Chapter 19.

Problem 1

Choosing Arbitration: A Digital Download Contract

Your client, MDM, is an entertainment production company based in Los Angeles. One of the many television shows the company produces is a popular series entitled *Starscape*. The series is shown exclusively on a cable network, which airs the show in an expanding number of U.S. markets. *Starscape* has enjoyed relatively high ratings and has a strong following of loyal and enthusiastic fans.

The Fandom Company (Fandom) of Chicago, Illinois owns and administers a website called "ScapePlace.com." On this site, visitors can find transcripts of interviews with *Starscape* cast members as well as airdates and other things of interest to fans of the show. Users can log on to the site after a brief, and free, registration process.

Now that *Starscape* is about to enter its third season, MDM is negotiating a contract with Fandom allowing Fandom to host video files of *Starscape* episodes on its "ScapePlace" site. Fandom is interested in hosting the files, as it would mean a huge increase in traffic to the Scape-Place site. ScapePlace, like many other such sites, makes its profit by providing advertising space. The more visitors, the more money advertisers will be willing to pay to place their banners on the site.

MDM also anticipates benefits from the arrangement. Its marketing people believe that allowing Fandom to distribute episodes of *Starscape* to people who access the ScapePlace site would increase the show's following beyond that which the limited cable market could provide. MDM hopes the increased interest in the show will put pressure on the network to expand the number of markets airing the series, as well as increase the interest in the season boxed DVD sets of *Starscape* MDM plans on releasing early next year.

MDM plans to include in the contract numerous limitations and conditions relating to the quality of the video files Fandom can provide. For example, the contract will prohibit Fandom from hosting video captures of seasons one and two of *Starscape* that are larger than 80 MB. The clarity of an 80 MB video file would be enough for a viewer to enjoy the episode in a two-inch box on their computer monitor, but would not be of a high enough quality to compete with the soon-to-be-released DVDs.

Suppose you are discussing with your client MDM the possibility of including an arbitration provision in the dispute resolution clause of the proposed contract with Fandom. What, if any, aspects of this scenario suggest that MDM may want to propose an arbitration provision? What aspects might make arbitration less appealing than litigation? Use the following "Suitability Screen" to help you evaluate your answers.

❖ A "Suitability Screen" for Arbitration

(Copyright 2004, The International Institute for Conflict Prevention & Resolution, reprinted with permission, with adaptations)

The International Institute for Conflict Prevention & Resolution (CPR), a New York-based non-profit organization, published an ADR Suitability Screen for the guidance of lawyers and clients considering the use of mediation, arbitration, and other ADR options. The following set of questions, adapted from that document, provides a starting point for counsel advising clients about whether to arbitrate or to litigate. A "Yes" answer to a question would tend to support a choice of arbitration, while a "No" answer would support using traditional litigation.

A.   Is the selection of the decision maker an important objective for either party?
____ Yes
____ No

B.   Will the dispute(s) require an understanding of complex or technical factual issues?
— Yes
— No

C.   Is the ability to have some degree of control over case-scheduling issues an important objective?
— Yes
— No

D.   Is there little or no concern regarding the establishment of precedent or articulation of public policy?
— Yes
— No

E.   Will it be satisfactory to employ something less than the full discovery procedures contemplated by court rules?
— Yes
— No

F.   Is there unlikely to be a vital corporate interest or "bet the company" dispute that will require the full panoply of procedural protections afforded by a court, including full appellate rights?
— Yes
— No

Questions

1.   Note that the decision to include arbitration in a business agreement is usually made at the outset, before conflict actually arises. Moreover, the parties to a contract may have different priorities, goals, and expectations that will affect their view of the utility of arbitration. How do you suppose that lawyers and developers of arbitration procedures address these realities?

2.   Does the Suitability Screen take account of the fact that parties may choose among a wide array of different arbitration procedures, and modify them to reflect their particular needs regarding, say, discovery?

C. Arbitration vs. Negotiation and Mediation

If you have read the prior parts of this book you have become familiar with the role negotiation and mediation may play in resolving disputes outside the courtroom. Parties have the opportunity to forge their own paths to a resolution in ways that take into account personal or business priorities and interests that no court judgment can address, and tailoring solutions beyond the scope of judicial relief. Party-centered, informal, and flexible approaches can enhance the possibility of preserving important continuing relationships and improving communication and understanding among participants.

While binding arbitration is often perceived as preferable to going to court, it is nearly always more formal, time consuming, and expensive than unassisted negotiation or mediation — and cedes final decision-making authority to a third party. And although it is sometimes said that arbitration may help to reduce friction between the parties and lay the groundwork for future relations, its impact is often as negative as litigation. Arbitration processes are, after all, typically backward-looking, adversarial proceedings in which the parties often take a back seat to their lawyers and to a third-party decision maker who will impose a judgment.

For these reasons, sophisticated lawyers and parties increasingly view arbitration as a last resort among ADR processes, to be employed only after negotiation and/or mediation have failed. Today, business lawyers often advise clients to attempt negotiation and mediation even after they have agreed to arbitrate, and, if appropriate, to continue such settlement attempts during the arbitral process. Where other methods are unavailing, of course, binding arbitration may be the most appropriate "backstop" form of third party adjudication.

Question

3. Take another look at the facts set out in Problem 1. If you were proposing a dispute resolution provision for a contract between MDM and Fandom, would you include terms calling for the parties to negotiate or mediate before turning to arbitration? Why or why not?

D. The Many Faces of Arbitration

To make the most of the opportunities afforded by arbitration, you will need to appreciate the wide diversity of arbitration processes and the range of choices available to parties in arbitration. The following summaries provide a glimpse into a spectrum of different applications of arbitration and to encourage you to think about underlying process choices and policy questions.

After reading each summary, consider the following general questions, along with any other questions posed:

1. How would you briefly characterize the arbitration procedure(s) discussed? (Court-like or informal? Law-oriented or focused on something else? Lengthy or expedited?)
2. What policies or practical concerns do you suppose led responsible decision makers to develop the current system? What are the pros and cons of the approach(es), and why was the balance struck in the way it was?
3. Who are the arbitrators and what kind of background or experience do they bring to the table?

1. Construction/Commercial Arbitration

As a lawyer, you are most likely to have an experience with arbitration in the course of disputes arising under a commercial or construction contract. The construction industry is an example of a commercial sector that places strong emphasis on resolving grievances and disputes informally, efficiently, and outside the court system. Motivated by the desire to achieve a profit and to maintain good working relations with clients and other project participants, most successful design and construction businesses generally seek to avoid trial if at all possible. Going to court can ruin business relationships, destroy morale, and derail a construction project.

Arbitration has long been a favored alternative to going to court to resolve engineering and construction disputes. A mid-1980s survey of construction attorneys demonstrated that arbitration was generally perceived as a fair alternative to trial before a judge or jury. On average, moreover, arbitration was a speedier means of dispute resolution than either jury trial or bench trial, and somewhat less costly overall. Perceptions and experiences varied significantly, however, and there was a strong impetus for trying to improve arbitration.

In the late 1990s the American Arbitration Association (AAA), which for most of the twentieth century was virtually the only major organization in the field of commercial and construction dispute resolution, developed new Construction Industry Arbitration Rules that provided three clear alternative paths for cases of different sizes. These included a "Fast Track" scheme for cases involving claims under $50,000; a "Standard Track" aimed at cases involving claims up to $1 million; and a "Large and Complex Track" for cases involving more than $1 million. Each scheme represents a different prioritization of various process attributes. Fast Track procedures emphasize speed and simplicity: Procedures include abbreviated timetables, limited extensions of time, expedited arbitrator appointment, limited information exchange, and streamlined hearings.

Standard Track procedures represent an updating of traditional arbitration procedures aimed at more competent arbitrators, clarified arbitrator authority, and enhanced speed. Revisions to standard forms permit parties' input regarding desired arbitrator qualifications. The new rules made clear the arbitrator's authority to control discovery "consistent with the expedited nature of arbitration"; a more explicit statement of arbitral authority to control hearings and to take interim protective measures, "including measures for the conservation of property." The new rules also admonish arbitrators to provide a "concise, written breakdown of the award" and a "written explanation" if requested by all parties or if the arbitrator believes it to be appropriate.

Large and Complex Track procedures feature an elite panel of neutrals and special supplementary prehearing procedures, including arbitrator-supervised discovery; they may be further tailored to the specific needs of the case by agreement of the parties. The process commences with an administrative conference with an AAA officer to discuss the parties' needs, including views on arbitrator qualifications, and to consider the use of mediation. A later "preliminary conference" is conducted by the arbitrators to discuss discovery and other preparations for arbitration and, once again, to explore the possibility of mediation and other alternatives. In addition to directing the production of documents, the rules make clear that arbitrators may order depositions or interrogatories for good cause and may place limits on discovery in accordance with the expedited nature of arbitration.

The AAA thus sought to maximize the flexibility of its arbitration procedures and permit a tailoring of the process to the particular needs of different cases. Ultimately, however, the best-crafted procedures mean little in comparison to the capabilities of arbitrators in whom so much discretion is placed. For this reason, the AAA's most important reform was to pare down its large national rosters of construction arbitrators in an attempt to enhance the quality of neutrals. The AAA has made a major effort to develop and maintain a multidisciplinary list of potential arbitrators comprised of legal, design/engineering, and construction professionals, and to ensure that all receive regular skills training.

The AAA's reforms in the construction arbitration arena paved the way for almost identical changes to the AAA Commercial Arbitration Rules and commercial arbitration panels. The "three-track" approach, pared-down panels, and enhanced training are therefore common elements of AAA administration.

More recently, competition for commercial arbitration business has arisen in other organizations such as JAMS (for "Judicial Arbitration and Mediation Services") and various other national and regional provider organizations. They do not, however, follow the "three-track" approach of the AAA; some only list lawyers on their panel of prospective arbitrators. Administrative options for arbitration will be discussed in Chapter 17.

Questions

4. What do you think of the AAA's response to concerns about construction arbitration? Does it surprise you to learn that the same multitiered system was later adopted for broader commercial use? Would you prefer to use an arbitration panel comprised of three lawyers or a multidisciplinary panel for a construction or business dispute? Explain.
5. Although arbitration is still an important option for resolving construction disputes, in the last decade standard construction industry contract documents have been modified to place greater emphasis on mediation and at processes aimed at resolving disputes in early stages. Why do you suppose this is true? See Stipanowich (2010).

2. *Labor Arbitration Under Collective Bargaining Agreements*

Labor arbitration arises under the collective bargaining agreements between employers and the unions representing employees. This area of the law is one in which the federal government predominates due to a history of congressional involvement designed to keep the economy running as smoothly as possible while parties to labor agreements resolve disputes. Additionally, both management and union leaders sought systems for addressing inevitable disputes safely and efficiently. Labor disputes were among the most common subjects for arbitration for much of the twentieth century, and arbitration has played a central role in the sphere of labor-management relations. Labor arbitration is statutorily mandated, chiefly under § 301(a) of the Labor Management Relations Act. Procedures for dispute resolution are set out in federal law and contractual agreements between unionized employees and management.

Arbitration procedures under collective bargaining agreements vary with needs and circumstances. Some parties agree to conduct labor arbitration under the pertinent rules of an institution such as the AAA, while others use an ad hoc process. Parties usually employ a single arbitrator selected by mutual agreement; however, depending on the industry and the nature of the dispute, a three-member "tripartite" arbitration board may be appointed. In this instance the board will consist of one member chosen by management, one selected by the labor or union, and a neutral who will serve as chairman (Ruben, 2003). It is up to the parties to decide what qualifications they want in arbitrators. Generally speaking, an arbitrator of labor disputes need not be a specialist in the subject matter but a background in social or economic study is desirable; labor arbitrators are frequently non-lawyers. Labor arbitrators are typically required to issue published awards, although the awards are not regarded as binding precedents.

Labor cases under collective bargaining agreements tend to divide into two modes of adjudication: rights-based arbitration and interest arbitration. In a rights-based arbitration parties are looking for an interpretation or application of the laws, agreements, and practices that exist within the "four-corners" of the collective bargaining agreement. A party may dispute the meaning or application of one or more of the provisions that are already in existence. In an interest arbitration, the arbitrator must determine what *should* or *could* have been in the terms and conditions of employment; the arbitrator must look outside of the pre-existing contract, considering fairness, policy, and expediency to make a determination (Ruben, 2003).

Question

6. Why do you suppose management and labor often use "tripartite" arbitration panels?

---

3. Arbitration of Investor/Broker Disputes

Ever since the seminal Supreme Court decision in *Shearson/American Express v. McMahon*, 482 U.S. 270 (1987) (holding that claims under the Racketeer Influenced Corrupt Organizations Act and the Securities and Exchange Act of 1934 are subject to arbitration), investors have been required by contract to arbitrate their disputes with brokerage firms. With the Securities and Exchange Commission's oversight and approval, a quasi-governmental but essentially private administrative body now known as The Financial Industry Regulatory Association, Inc. (FINRA) was established to administer the arbitrations. As a result of the recent economic downturn, securities arbitration case filings with FINRA have spiked dramatically; as of July 2009 there were a total of 4,481 filings as compared to 2,614 filings in the whole of 2008. See *http://www.finra.org/ArbitrationMediation*.

Judicial encouragement of securities arbitration is founded in part on the perceived benefits of the alternative for both industry members and customers, including reduced costs and speedier results (Perino, 2002). The arbitration system has made it possible to try smaller cases that might never have seen the inside of a courtroom. At the same time, the costs associated with arbitration hearings, including administrative costs and arbitrator fees, can in some cases be an obstacle.

A securities arbitration panel typically consists of three arbitrators, traditionally including a public chairperson, a public non-chairperson, and a representative of the securities industry, typically a broker or manager. Because there has been a significant amount of controversy about the requirement that an investor be compelled to arbitrate his dispute and thereby give up his right to trial by jury in court, critics have further complained that fairness in the process is compromised when a member of the securities industry has the authority to pass judgment on peers in the industry. Therefore, several large brokerage firms recently agreed to a pilot program whereby a limited number of cases could be heard by three public arbitrators, although the investor still has the right to choose two public and one industry arbitrators.

In a typical case, a party receives a list of 24 arbitrators divided into three groups; each party may strike up to four of the eight in each group, and rank the remaining arbitrators. In connection with this rank and strike procedure, FINRA provides each party with an arbitrator disclosure report that briefly summarizes the arbitrators' educational and work background, any accounts each have with any broker dealer, and a listing of every securities arbitration in which the arbitrator has participated. The arbitrations listed in the arbitration disclosure report are available for review by the parties.

Securities arbitration procedures vary to some extent with the size of the claim, but they have become increasingly similar to court procedures to ensure fundamental due process for investors. There is, for example, document discovery in securities arbitration, and arbitrators have the authority to award punitive or exemplary damages in appropriate cases. On the other hand, there are usually no pre-hearing depositions, pre-hearing substantive motions, contention interrogatories, or requests for admissions.

Investor/broker arbitration and mediation are regulated more extensively than any other form of out-of-court dispute resolution. The Securities and Exchange Commission oversees the practices and policies of all Supplemental Relief Order arbitration programs, conducting audits and passing upon changes to arbitration procedures; the General Accounting Office also conducts occasional reviews. There is also a well-established body of experienced lawyers who regularly represent investors in arbitration.

Despite all the regulation, there is a significant movement in Congress to prevent contract terms requiring arbitration of securities brokerage disputes along with other kinds of consumer contract disputes. Should this occur, it is possible that investors will have a choice of whether to have their disputes decided in arbitration or in court. Some argue that this approach would preserve the right of investors with smaller financial losses to prosecute efficiently in arbitration cases that otherwise they and their lawyers could not afford to pursue in civil court with its significantly greater time and attendant costs.

Questions

7. Why is investor/broker arbitration subject to government agency regulation, unlike construction industry and commercial arbitration?

8. If you were an investor, would you prefer to go to arbitration or to court? Does your answer depend on the circumstances? Explain.

4.   Arbitration at the Olympics

The Court of Arbitration for Sport (CAS) was established to address international sporting disputes of many kinds. The CAS created a special ad hoc program for arbitration of disputes at Olympic Games.

During the 2002 Olympic Winter Games in Salt Lake City, Utah, a major controversy erupted in the final of the men's 1,500-meter short track speed-skating race. Many Americans cheered for Apolo Anton Ohno, an aggressive young skater who had qualified for the final despite sustaining an injury requiring six stitches in an earlier race during the games. He competed against a strong field, including Korea's most acclaimed short-track skater, Kim Dong-Sung. The skaters raced around the track at incredible speeds. Heading into the final lap, Kim was the only skater Ohno needed to pass to win gold. Kim cut off Ohno and crossed the finish line just ahead of him. The referee ruled immediately, however, that Kim was disqualified because he had illegally blocked Ohno during the final lap. While many American fans rejoiced and the Salt Lake City crowd cheered, a "firestorm of protest" was set off around the globe. Ohno received death threats, and an Italian skater declared he should be shot. The U.S. Olympic Committee's server crashed after it received over 16,000 e-mails protesting the disqualification.

Korean officials immediately protested, but Chief Referee James Hewish of Australia refused to overturn the disqualification. The next day, Korean officials pursued their claims within speed-skating's governing body. When that group confirmed the referee's decision as final, the Korean Olympic Committee appealed to the CAS, the final and exclusive dispute resolution board for the Olympic Games. As a condition of participating in the games, all athletes and organizations must sign entry forms agreeing to binding arbitration before the CAS. Two days after the race, the CAS held a hearing. Judge R. S. Pathak of India headed the Salt Lake arbitral pool, which involved nine arbitrators, each from a different country. The International Council of Arbitration for Sport had selected the arbitrators before the start of the games for their expertise in arbitration and sports law. Each arbitrator signed a declaration attesting to his independence before the games began.

Late that evening, Kim's disqualification appeal was heard by a panel of three arbitrators; a British lawyer served as president and the other members were from Switzerland and Finland. During the arbitration proceeding, panelists called the referee and his four assistants as witnesses. Other interested parties were summoned, including the Korean Skating Union and the Olympic Committees of the United States, Canada, China, Italy, and France. An American attorney represented the Korean committee, which had to establish that the referees acted with bad faith or arbitrarily. All parties agreed that the panelists could not attempt to "second guess" decisions made by referees on technical "field of play" issues. The grievant's attorney cited the controversy surrounding the earlier men's 1,000-meter race when

Ohno, who was leading, wiped out in the final turn and brought down three other skaters with him. Additionally, counsel argued that U.S. media pressure and local audience pressure in Ohno's favor influenced the referees.

The arbitrators could review a videotape of the race, even though the head referee did not have instant replay review at the time of the race, but declined to do so because this would be closer to a technical "field of play" review than an examination of bad faith or illegitimate decision making. Instead, the arbitrators heard from three assistant referees (from the United States, Norway, and England) that they had independently observed the Korean skater's "cross-tracking" infraction, noted that disqualification was the appropriate penalty, and reported this to the head referee at the conclusion of the race. The arbitrators, finding the witnesses honest and straightforward, ruled in favor of Ohno retaining the gold medal. On February 23, only three days after the race, the arbitrators issued a nine-page "Final Award" upholding the disqualification.

Questions

9.   Is the fact that we are dealing with an *international* sporting event relevant to the discussion?
10.   Why do you suppose this kind of expedited arbitration process was selected for the Olympics? If arbitration was not an available alternative, how would problems of this kind be resolved?

---

5.   *Writers Guild Arbitration*

The matter of who gets credit for writing a screenplay is of critical importance to the reputation and economic well-being of writers (whose residual income from long-term exploitation of a film usually depends on being credited), and the question is often laden with controversy. In the U.S. the Writers Guild of America, East or the Writers Guild of America, West determines who receives credit for writing screenplays or developing an original story or character(s) on which a screenplay is based. Any production company that has signed the Guild Basic Agreement is bound by the Guild rules, including the procedure for determining credit. When a film is completed, the producer is required to present proposed credits for screenwriting to the Guild and send copies of the final script to all writers who worked on the script. Upon objection by any writer to the producer's proposal, the matter is submitted to arbitration. Arbitration is also required in any circumstance where a director or producer of the film is proposed for credit. The arbitration process is frequently triggered; between 1993 and 1997, for example, there were 415 Guild arbitrations representing around one-third of all films whose credits were submitted.

During arbitration, members of the Guild review all drafts of the screenplay by each writer and follow a set of arcane formulae for determining the credits. For example, an "original writer" must contribute at least one-third of the final screenplay to receive credit. Subsequent "script doctors" must author more than half of the final screenplay to receive credit, as must a production executive. A maximum of three writers may receive screenplay credit if they worked in collaboration, and a maximum of three teams of three writers may be credited, no matter how many actually worked on it. Often, many more individuals are actually involved; for example, it is said that the film adaptation of *The Flintstones* (1994) had more than 60 writers.

Arbitrators may also be required to address the permissible use of requested pseudonyms. One memorable case involved a writer who was so angry over changes made to his work by the production company that he sought to take his name off the credits and substitute "Eiben Scrood" in protest. His request was denied.

In screenwriting credit arbitration the identities of the arbitrators are secret, and parties sometimes complain about the fact that they have no opportunity to object to the lack of qualifications or the possible lack of impartiality of their judges. Moreover, parties are not given the opportunity for an oral hearing, nor is a rationale provided for the decision of the arbitrators. (While there is a panel to address appeals from arbitration, it is limited to considering procedural objections.) The secrecy of the arbitration process and the formulae governing decisions have led to strong criticisms by some Guild members. For example, after arbitrating credits for the 1998 film adaptation of Hunter Thompson's *Fear and Loathing in Las Vegas*, Terry Gilliam resigned from the Guild in protest. He described the arbitration process as a "Star Chamber" and claimed he spent more effort on the credit battle than he did on the screenplay itself. However, the Writers Guild of America, West membership upheld the arbitration procedures in 2002.

> ### Question
>
> 11. Can a process that does not involve a face-to-face hearing be "arbitration"? (In Chapter 18 we will see that whether something qualifies as "arbitration" under applicable statutes may make a difference.)

6. National Advertising Division Arbitration

A high-profile program of non-binding evaluation is sponsored by the National Advertising Division of the Council of Better Business Bureaus, better known as the NAD. The NAD was created in 1971 "to help sustain high standards of truth and accuracy in national advertising" by monitoring the media and acting upon complaints by consumers, competitors, and others. The NAD conducts investigations into the truth of advertising, and its National Advertising Review Board issues decisions.

If a competitor, a consumer, or the NAD believes an advertisement to be false or misleading they can initiate a challenge by a "challenge letter." The NAD's alternative dispute resolution panel will then review the claim, and if they decide to pursue the allegations, the letter is forwarded to the offending advertiser who then has 15 business days to respond. The NAD's panel "work[s] closely with in-house counsel, marketing executives, research and development departments and outside consultants to decide whether claims have been substantiated."[2] The parties are given the opportunity to offer further submissions in a confidential setting, and have the option to meet in person with representatives of the NAD before a decision is rendered. Although the NAD has no power to demand change or withdrawal of an advertisement, its challenges have a compliance rate of over 95 percent and parties often comply to avoid referrals to the Federal Trade Commission or other government agencies. These referrals can result in far stronger sanctions than the NAD's "recommendations," including fines, demanded compliance, and consent decrees (Bernstein, 2002). *See also AMF v. Brunswick Corp.*, 621 F. Supp. 456, 457-58 (S.D.N.Y. 1985).

> Question
>
> 12.   Why do you suppose the NAD uses an arbitration process that results in a decision or award that is not legally binding? What factors make it so effective in terms of "compliance rate"?

7.   *Court-Connected Arbitration*

In recent decades, court-connected pretrial arbitration became popular as a perceived remedy for backlogs and delays experienced in some court systems. Hence, court rules or statutes sometimes require advisory arbitration or non-binding arbitration of certain types of disputes, such as lawsuits involving medical malpractice claims and civil claims filed in courts of a lesser monetary amount (e.g., suits involving less than $25,000 or $50,000 in damages). See Chapter 13. Typically, volunteer lawyers serve as neutrals in these proceedings. The arbitrations are "mandatory" only in the sense that arbitration is a precondition to litigation. The arbitral awards issued are usually not binding in such situations, and indeed they often cannot be since both the United States and most state constitutions guarantee access to the courts and juries for most civil controversies. However, the systems of states

---

2. See *http://www.nadreview.org*.

such as California and Michigan provide that if the party insisting on litigation does not improve on the arbitration award at trial, that party may be required to pay the opponent's expenses. Keep in mind that court-annexed arbitration tends to be quite different from private arbitration pursuant to party agreement. Indeed, one of the key benefits of binding arbitration — relative finality — does not apply to advisory or non-binding arbitration. Court-connected arbitration programs have become much less popular in recent years, eclipsed by court-connected mediation.

Question

13.   Note that parties may be required to participate in court-connected arbitration even if they have not agreed to arbitrate. What value would arbitration have in this context?

E.   The Framework of Arbitration: Contractual and Legal Standards

Arbitration practice involves a lot of rules, and effective counselors, advocates, and arbitrators need to have a working knowledge of all of them. They reflect both the private contractual foundation of arbitration as well as public laws, and include:

1.   The Agreement to Arbitrate

Because binding arbitration is usually a creature of contract, the clauses by which parties bind themselves to arbitrate are usually the primary source of rules for the process. The arbitration clause will probably identify the arbitration procedures and administrative framework, if any, that will apply. It may also indicate what law should control the arbitration agreement and any resulting award, as well as the separate issue of what law should be applied by the arbitrators.

2.   Arbitration Procedural Rules

Agreements to arbitrate frequently incorporate procedural rules covering everything from the filing of an arbitration demand and the selection of arbitrators to the rendition of an arbitration award. (E.g., "All disputes arising under the contract . . . shall be resolved under the ACME Commercial Arbitration Procedures.") Such rules are often developed and published by organizations that provide services to arbitrating parties in the form of administrative support for arbitration and lists of prospective arbitrators.

3.   Arbitration Statutes

Today, federal and state statutes, along with a vast and growing body of related case law, play an important role in U.S. arbitration practice. The most important source of public law governing arbitration is the Federal Arbitration Act, 9 U.S.C. §§ 1-16 (2000). State arbitration laws may also figure prominently in some circumstances. Although these statutes are mainly addressed to courts enforcing arbitration agreements and awards, they may have a direct or indirect impact on arbitration proceedings.

4.   International Conventions

Arbitration plays an indispensable role in international business transactions, in part because the great majority of sovereign nations have signed key conventions that provide for arbitration of private disputes. The leading international convention is the 1958 New York Convention on the Recognition and Enforcement of Arbitral Awards, also known as the "New York Convention."

5.   Substantive Law Applicable to the Merits of an Arbitrated Dispute

Although it will be discussed only briefly in this volume, it is common for contracting parties to provide that their agreement will be interpreted in accordance with the law of a particular jurisdiction. Such provisions are likely to control the law that arbitrators apply in the course of deciding issues before them.

6.   Ethics Rules

The parties' agreement or organizations providing arbitration services may require arbitrators to abide by certain ethical standards in the course of their service. In the United States the most widely used set of arbitrator ethics standards is the Code of Ethics for Arbitrators in Commercial Disputes.

F.   Overview of Part III

Chapter 17 provides an introduction, or "roadmap" to the fundamentals of arbitration practice in its most prevalent form: business-to-business arbitration. We will explore, among other things, the various routes by which parties arrive at arbitration; basic considerations for attorneys drafting arbitration agreements; the selection of qualified arbitrators; arbitration procedures, including the management of information exchange and discovery; and arbitral awards and remedies.

Chapter 18 will treat the expanding legal framework of American arbitration and address current legal issues confronting practitioners, including the scope and functions of arbitration statutes, judicial enforcement and facilitation of arbitration agreements, and judicial treatment of arbitration awards.

Chapter 19 will examine the special concerns associated with arbitration under the terms of standardized contracts, including transactions involving consumer goods and services and individual employment contracts.

CHAPTER
17

Arbitration Agreements, Procedures, and Awards

A. Introduction

In the modern environment arbitration deals with a much broader range of conflict, including big cases involving complex legal issues. While parties may see the virtues of a private substitute for court trial in many different kinds of cases, the nature of that private alternative will vary with the circumstances. Arbitration may mean anything from a rudimentary, expedited, non-lawyered process involving a quality determination by a technical expert to a much more formal proceeding with many of the trappings of court trial.

As an attorney you will need to carefully tailor arbitration processes to the varying needs and expectations of users — and legal counselors and advocates must be well informed regarding the many choices that arbitration presents. By introducing you to key issues surrounding arbitration, we hope to provide you with the knowledge and skills you will need to fulfill the promise and avoid the pitfalls of arbitration for your clients. We will place considerable emphasis on various standards that govern or provide guidance for arbitration proceedings, arbitrators, and advocates. These include procedures, policies, and guidelines of national and international institutions supporting or sponsoring arbitration.

Arbitration is generally a creature of contract, and businesses often participate in private arbitration processes and comply with the decisions of arbitrators without any resort to courts of law; indeed, avoidance of court processes is often an important goal of parties choosing arbitration. We devote this chapter to a start-to-finish consideration of arbitration processes and procedures and defer extensive treatment of the legal "backdrop" to Chapter 18.

Nevertheless, it is critical to have a framework for the judicial enforcement of agreements to arbitrate and of arbitration awards. In the last three decades this legal framework has assumed an ever-increasing role in the practice of arbitration, directly or indirectly affecting virtually every aspect of arbitration. Lawyers must therefore understand the interplay of federal arbitration law and state statutes on arbitration in the United States, and the role of international treaties in arbitration of cross-border disputes. Hence, while the legal framework of arbitration will be primarily addressed in Chapter 18, we will make brief references to the impact of arbitration law throughout this chapter.

B.   The Contractual Foundations of Arbitration

Parties usually end up in arbitration because they have entered into a contractual agreement to arbitrate. Occasionally, parties agree to submit a dispute to arbitration after it has arisen. These post-dispute agreements are called *submission agreements*. Much more commonly, however, parties commit themselves to arbitrate long before any dispute arises through a clause that binds them to arbitrate some or all future disputes that arise out of the relationship. Such clauses, known as *executory agreements to arbitrate*, have long been a standard feature of collective bargaining agreements between unions and employers, as well as construction and other kinds of commercial contracts. In recent years they have been included in contracts relating to employment, insurance, health care, retail sales, banking, professional services (including legal services), real estate agreements, repair services, utility services, and myriad other transactions.

You may be the attorney responsible for considering whether to incorporate an arbitration provision in a client's contract. That decision is often complicated by the fact that no disputes have actually arisen, and decisions about arbitration must be based on prior experience and educated guesses. Today, a contract drafter should also consider whether arbitration should be preceded by other strategies for resolving disputes, such as stepped negotiation or mediation. These options, and the growing use of multistep or "hybrid" approaches, will be explored in Sections P and Q below. Other choices remain. How broad should the arbitration agreement be? Is it necessary to have the administrative support (including arbitration procedures, a list of arbitrators and case managers) of a third-party institution? How should arbitrators be selected? What level of "due process" — discovery, prehearing practice, evidentiary rules — is appropriate? What remedies may an arbitrator grant? Will the award include findings of fact or conclusions of law, or will it be a "bare" award? These and other considerations for drafters will be treated in the following pages, as will issues confronting lawyers who serve as advocates for parties in the arbitration process.

Increasingly, businesses are placing arbitration clauses in "boilerplate" contracts with employees and consumers. (Do you have a credit card? A cell phone? Are you required to arbitrate with anyone?) Because such terms are not usually subject to negotiation and typically purport to waive the right to go to court, they raise legitimate concerns about the fairness of the alternative system. We return to these intriguing issues in Chapter 19. First, however, it is important to gain an appreciation of how arbitration works, and how it may be most effectively employed, in the broad run of business-to-business arrangements.

Questions

1. *Basic Executory Provisions.* Arbitration provisions come in all shapes and sizes. Most, however, tend to be relatively concise and straightforward. Consider the following model arbitration clause, which is recommended by a major provider of arbitration services for inclusion in contracts:

    > Any controversy or claim arising out of or relating to this contract, or the breach thereof, shall be settled by arbitration administered by the American Arbitration Association in accordance with its [insert type of rules] Arbitration Rules [including the Emergency Interim Relief Procedures], and judgment on the award rendered by the arbitrator(s) may be entered in any court having jurisdiction thereof.

    Can you identify five functions served by this provision? Notice that the parties can select from arbitration rules for various types of disputes (e.g., commercial, construction, labor, patent, financial planning, and wireless Internet).

2. *Submission Agreements.* As noted above, sometimes parties agree to submit existing disputes to arbitration. A basic template for such an agreement would look something like this:

    > We, the undersigned parties, hereby agree to submit to arbitration the following controversy:_____.
    >   We agree that the arbitration will be conducted in accordance with the Commercial Arbitration Procedures of the ACME Dispute Resolution Association, as modified below.
    >   We further agree that a judgment of any court having jurisdiction may be entered upon the award.

    What are the potential advantages of making the decision to arbitrate after disputes have arisen? Why do you suppose that many fewer arbitrations are conducted pursuant to the terms of submission agreements than predispute executory agreements in contracts?

C.   Making Effective Choices Regarding Arbitration

Because users seek different things from arbitration, and because business goals and needs vary by company, by transaction, and by dispute, no one form of arbitration is always appropriate. For this reason, the central value of arbitration is not speed, or economy, or privacy, or neutral expertise, but rather the ability of users to make key process choices to suit their particular needs.

A 2009 report of the American College of Trial Lawyers links the disappearance of civil trials with high cost and delay; the report calls for an end to the "one-size-fits-all" approach of current federal and state litigation procedures and for the development of alternatives that offer quicker, less expensive resolution. Such choices are readily available in arbitration, as it is based on the agreement of those involved. If parties truly desire an expedited procedure in which speed and economy are the preeminent goals, it is possible to structure and implement a "lean" arbitration. If, on the other hand, cost savings and a quick result are much less important than having a controlled, private version of litigation with extensive legal due process and a tribunal comprised of three high-profile decision makers that results in a highly "authoritative" decision, that, too, is an option. The key is fitting the process to the problem.

Unfortunately, contract planners and drafters usually drop arbitration and dispute resolution provisions into commercial contracts without much reflection or discussion. While effective arbitrators and thoughtful advocates may function effectively within this kind of framework, all too often, arbitration under standard one-size-fits-all procedures takes on many of the trappings of litigation, with commensurate costs and delays. The result is frustration and disappointment for those coming to arbitration expecting it to be more efficient and economical than trial.

If you have the opportunity to counsel clients regarding arbitration and dispute resolution, therefore, the following are a few key practice pointers.

1.   Don't Wait Until You Are in the Middle of Negotiating to Consider and Discuss Dispute Resolution Options

Beforehand, discuss your client's goals and priorities in managing conflict in a particular contractual relationship, including (1) flexibility; (2) low cost or cost efficiencies; (3) a speedy outcome; avoidance of undue delay; (4) "fairness" and "justice"; (5) legal due process; (6) results comporting with commercial, technical, or professional standards; (7) predictability and consistency in result; (8) a final and binding resolution; (9) privacy and confidentiality; and (10) preservation of a relationship; continuing performance. The identified goals and priorities become touchstones for process selection.

2. *Employ Arbitration as Part of a Conscientiously Developed Program for Managing Conflict*

As discussed in Chapter 16, arbitration is rarely the appropriate starting point for resolving disputes. More and more contractual dispute resolution provisions include arbitration as the final stage in (and backdrop for) other approaches to resolve disputes such as negotiation and mediation. See Sections P and Q below.

3. *Make Sure the Arbitration Procedures (and Administering Organizations) You Choose Support Your Client's Goals*

Don't simply drop in the same old arbitration boilerplate. Today, arbitration counsel should know about choices in the arbitration marketplace, and make a knowledgeable selection among procedures and among organizations sponsoring arbitration. For example, you should be aware that some organizations publish or emphasize a single one-size-fits-all set of arbitration rules, whereas others offer a range of procedures designed for different kinds of cases or disputes of different sizes. Some institutions specialize in arbitrators who are lawyers or retired judges, and others offer a choice among arbitrators with different professional backgrounds. Some organizations have rules that offer much more protection for confidential information.

4. *Choose Outside Counsel and Arbitrators on the Basis of Client Goals*

There are two other key "choice points" for users of arbitration — the selection of legal counsel to represent one's interests in the resolution of disputes, and the selection of arbitrators to resolve those disputes. In both cases, the choices parties make are just as critical as process choices, if not more so. Indeed, effective advocates and arbitrators may overcome the deficiencies of inadequate procedures; ineffective advocates and arbitrators may undermine the best-crafted procedural program.

Thoughtful and sophisticated lawyers may navigate through the arbitration process in a way that most effectively promotes client goals, and may find it possible to collaborate with opposing counsel to develop integrative process solutions that promote mutual benefits. Similarly, well-equipped arbitrators may make effective use of their discretion to strike an appropriate balance between efficiency and fairness — or, as necessary, to address other user needs such as confidentiality.

> Questions
>
> 3. Based on the reading and your own experience, what are the practical barriers to thoughtful consideration of and planning for arbitration in business contracts?
> 4. Under what circumstances might business persons be most likely to devote time and attention to planning and drafting such provisions?

The remainder of this chapter is intended to provide you with basic guidance regarding choices made by lawyers and clients during the course of arbitration, and to help develop the skills you will need to provide effective counseling and advocacy in arbitration.

D. Drafting Arbitration Agreements: Arbitration Procedures, Arbitration Institutions

1. Standard Institutional Procedures

Today, arbitrations are commonly conducted under stipulated rules or procedures that regulate the process in roughly the same way that judicial rules of procedure regulate litigation in court. The following discussion will remind you in some ways of your first-year course in civil procedure.

Arbitration rules and procedures are developed and published by various for-profit or non-profit institutions that provide guidance or support for arbitration proceedings. Leading institutions in the U.S. include the non-profit American Arbitration Association (AAA), the for-profit Judicial Arbitration and Mediation Services (JAMS), the non-profit International Institute for Conflict Prevention & Resolution (CPR), and other national and regional organizations. Global arbitration institutions include the International Chamber of Commerce (ICC), the London Court of International Arbitration (LCIA), the AAA's International Dispute Resolution Center (IDRC), and many other national or regional bodies.

These institutions have developed arbitration rules that often are lengthy and thus are typically incorporated only by reference in the agreement to arbitrate. Arbitration procedures vary among institutions, and by subject matter. In the United States there are a wide variety of arbitration rules for different trade groups or practice areas, including securities disputes, construction matters, commercial disputes, and intellectual property disputes. Some organizations publish different sets of rules to handle cases of varying size or complexity. You can find examples on organization websites.

Arbitration procedures usually address most or all of the following: the filing of an arbitration demand (or joint submission) and other pleadings, what constitutes "notice" for procedural purposes, methods of choosing arbitrators (including procedures for challenging appointees), prehearing conferences, elements of the hearing, arbitral awards and remedies, and procedures for publication or clarification of awards.

Even if parties elect not to adopt any organization's arbitration procedures and instead follow an "ad hoc" approach to arbitration, drafters who fail to consult institutional rules or other models for guidance do so at their peril. In addition to publishing arbitration procedures, "arbitration institutions" also (1) maintain lists or panels of arbitrators, (2) provide administrative support for arbitration proceedings, and (3) in some cases, support mediation and other processes as well as arbitration. When it comes to arbitration, therefore, familiarity with applicable rules, and with the organizations that publish them, is as essential for drafters and advocates as familiarity with the procedural and evidentiary rules in court trial.

2. Panels of Arbitrators: Ethical Standards

By incorporating an institution's arbitral procedures in their agreement, parties have probably indicated their mutual intent to utilize certain services of the "provider" institution (although they usually can alter provider rules by agreement). These services include, among other things, help in appointing arbitrators. For this purpose most providers sponsor "panels" or lists of prospective arbitrators. The makeup of these lists varies considerably from institution to institution, and offers a critical point of comparison.

In a particular case, the institutional role may involve providing names of candidates from which the parties may choose arbitrators, helping with the appointment process, administering a process for determining and resolving conflicts of interest, and replacing arbitrators if necessary. Some arbitration organizations collect and distribute arbitrator fees; a few share fees with the arbitrators.

Some arbitral institutions also publish or adhere to ethical rules for the guidance of arbitrators. The leading U.S. standard is the *Code of Ethics for Arbitrators in Commercial Disputes*. Originally developed in 1977, the Code was updated by a joint effort of the American Bar Association, the AAA, and CPR and reissued in 2004. The Code of Ethics is used extensively by commercial arbitrators in the United States, and has been adopted as a standard of practice by the AAA, CPR and other institutions for arbitrators operating under their rules. Some ethical precepts, including principles governing arbitrator disclosure of conflicts of interest, may parallel legal principles under federal and state arbitration law or provisions of institutional arbitration procedures. However, the Code is not intended to have legal consequences, but only to guide the behavior of the arbitrator. And, unlike rules of professional conduct for lawyers, there is no general mechanism for policing infractions of the Code by arbitrators (Sabin, 2002).

3. Administrative Support; Other Services

There are considerable differences in the level of administrative support provided by arbitral institutions, and in related administrative costs. Some procedures provide only limited institutional support — such as helping parties with the selection of arbitrators. Many rules, however, envision a higher level of institutional involvement; this may include transmitting communications between parties and arbitrators, handling fees and expenses, scheduling and setting locations for hearings, putting arbitration awards in final form, and even conducting a substantive review of the award before publication.

Some institutions sponsoring arbitration services also provide mediation and other services. Because arbitration is less and less likely to "stand alone" as a dispute resolution approach, multifaceted institutional support may be critical in situations involving multistep ADR processes such as the ones discussed in Section P.

4. Ad Hoc Arbitration vs. Arbitration Supported by an Institution

The AAA and JAMS are two of the most visible arbitration "provider" institutions in the United States. Although there are important differences between the two organizations, both publish a variety of arbitration procedures, sponsor lists of individuals who may act as arbitrators, and offer administrative support for arbitrations. Both assess fees for these services.

By way of contrast, the CPR offers a system aimed at non-administered or "minimally administered" arbitration. The CPR Rules for Non-Administered Arbitration of Business Disputes are designed to allow parties to arbitrate with no administrative support from an outside organization; "administrative" functions are instead performed by the parties and/or the arbitrator(s). Under the CPR Rules, CPR's only potential role is to help with arbitrator selection upon the request of the parties; then and only then does CPR charge an administrative fee.

Should attorneys incorporate institutional rules or develop ad hoc arrangements under which the parties conduct arbitration without institutional support? The answer depends on the circumstances.

Using established procedures reduces the possibility that disputes will arise regarding *the procedures themselves*. An experienced, independent organization may be able to help the parties avoid common problems that they did not anticipate when drafting an arbitration agreement. In cases where counsel or clients lack experience with the arbitration process, an administrative structure may provide comfort and guidance. Where hostility or lack of trust hinders the working relationship between parties or between counsel, the administrative structure may be necessary to promote a smoother and more efficient process. For example, it is important in most cases to have a default procedure for arbitrator selection and other functions in the event that a party fails to comply with procedures. Finally, consistent with the consensual character of arbitration, institutional procedures may be modified in important ways by agreement of the parties where necessary.

However, institutional involvement usually entails costs that should be weighed against benefits provided. In some cases, moreover, there may be questions about the quality of an institution's administrative services, or delays resulting from institutional efforts.

A non-administered or "self-administered" arbitration avoids or minimizes the administrative fees and offers great potential flexibility in the structuring and management of the arbitration process, but must be approached with care. The sophistication and working relationship of parties and their counsel are the primary factors to consider in choosing administered or non-administered arbitration. Parties with more experience may choose little or no administration on the grounds that some or all of those functions may be unnecessary, or will be assumed by the arbitrators. Parties opting for non-administered arbitration need to put great importance on selecting an experienced arbitrator or chair (for a panel) because this individual will often assume administrative responsibilities. Thus, one factor in deciding whether to use non-administered arbitration is the availability to the parties of an experienced, efficient arbitrator who can shepherd the parties through the process. Parties should also depend on appropriate models in structuring their rules, such as the CPR Rules (either U.S. or international versions) or the UNCITRAL Model Rules in the international sphere.

Problem 1

Selecting Arbitration Procedures and Arbitration Institutions

Review the hypothetical scenario of Problem 1 in Chapter 16, which involves a planned contractual arrangement between your client, Los Angeles-based entertainment company MDM, and Chicago-based "dot-com" Fandom for the Internet posting of video files. Assume that after discussing the matter with your client (MDM), there is a strong inclination to incorporate an arbitration agreement in the contract currently being negotiated between MDM and Fandom. Your client informs you that the parties have no prior relationship, and that the Fandom people are, in the opinion of your client's business people, "really smart but typical dot-com types, crossed with obsessive TV fan types" — not your typical business partners. Their lawyer is a relatively sophisticated corporate lawyer, but probably knows little about arbitration or other forms of ADR. If disputes arise under the agreement, they are most likely to involve questions of contract interpretation and breach, intellectual property law (copyright, licensing, etc.), as well as technical factual issues involving software and electronic transmission.

To help you in rendering advice to the client, your senior partner has encouraged you to engage in some online research. She says you can learn a lot by carefully examining the websites of arbitration provider organizations, looking carefully at their arbitration rules, and reviewing their administrative services and fee structures. She asks you to look at the website of either (a) the AAA or (b) JAMS. She suggests that you attempt to answer each of the following questions with respect to the organization you chose.

a. Taking into account the nature of the contract and the parties, does the organization publish arbitration rules, including specialized rules, which might be useful in resolving disputes between MDM and Fandom? Are there different procedures for cases of different size or complexity?

b. What kinds of administrative services does the organization provide? What are the administrative fees, if any?

c. Does the organization list arbitrators with pertinent backgrounds or expertise? Where are they located? What are their fees?

d. Where are the organization's administrative offices? Can arbitration hearings be held at convenient locations?

e. Compare and contrast the rules and services of AAA or JAMS with CPR, which publishes "non-administered" procedures. Which organization or rules do you believe are most appropriate to use in the MDM/Fandom contract, and why?

E. Scope of the Arbitration Agreement and Other Drafting Issues

1. Scope of the Arbitration Agreement

An important issue for every drafter is the *scope* of the arbitration agreement — in other words, what disputes related to the contract and the parties' relationship will be subject to arbitration? This question is key because, as will be explained more fully in Chapter 18, parties are legally required to arbitrate only those disputes that are contemplated by their arbitration agreement. One of the most common grounds for setting aside an arbitration award — and the ground most likely to result in an over-turned award — is that the arbitrators "exceeded their power" under the arbitration agreement.

As noted earlier, it is the common practice of drafters to use language of extreme breadth in describing the scope of the agreement. Broad provisions can minimize the likelihood of court disputes over what is "arbitrable," especially since courts enforcing arbitration agreements under the Federal Arbitration Act (FAA) and similar state statutes interpret these now-familiar, essentially ubiquitous terms with a presumption in favor of arbitration.

Sometimes, however, attorneys may believe they have sound reasons for limiting what is arbitrable to specific issues. They may wish to reserve issues of particular size, complexity, or subject matter for the public forum, either because they are uncomfortable with the perceived risks of arbitration or because they believe a court may provide more suitable relief, such as a preliminary injunction or temporary restraining order. Attorneys must be aware that great care is required in the drafting of arbitration provisions, since they may result in controversies about whether the dispute that has arisen is arbitrable.

2. Other Drafting Issues

❖ **John Townsend,** *Drafting Arbitration Clauses: Avoiding the 7 Deadly Sins*

58 Dispute Resolution J. 28 (Feb.-Apr. 2003)

From time to time, someone tries to define what a perfect arbitration clause would look like. Efforts to do so usually founder on one of the strengths of arbitration, which is its adaptability to the particular circumstances of the parties and the dispute. Therefore, while it is difficult to generalize about what would make a "perfect" clause, it is not nearly as difficult to identify some of the features that make for a bad one. This article identifies seven of the most damning "sins" that plague arbitration clauses and offers suggestions for addressing the most important issues drafters face.

Equivocation

... The essence of this sin is the failure to state clearly that the parties have agreed to binding arbitration. Because arbitration is a creature of contract, if there is no contract, there is no agreement to arbitrate. ... [The author offers the following example]

> In case of dispute, the parties undertake to submit to arbitration, but in case of litigation the Tribunal de la Seine shall have exclusive jurisdiction.

What this clause commits the parties to is nothing other than years of litigation about how to resolve any dispute that may arise. That is the sulfur and brimstone that threatens the drafter who puts such a clause in the client's contract: The client will spend what will seem like an eternity, and a great deal of money, trying to resolve the dispute.

The overriding goal of the drafter of an arbitration clause should be to draft a provision that, if a dispute arises, will help the parties obtain an arbitration award without a detour through the court system. First and foremost, that means that the drafter must produce an enforceable agreement to arbitrate. For an American lawyer drafting an agreement that will involve a transaction in interstate commerce, that means an agreement that a court will recognize as coming within the meaning of Section 2 of the Federal Arbitration Act. This provision states:

> A written provision in . . . a contract evidencing a transaction involving commerce to settle by arbitration a controversy thereafter arising out of such contract or transaction, or the refusal to perform the whole or any part thereof, . . . shall be valid, irrevocable, and enforceable, save upon such grounds as exist at law or in equity for the revocation of any contract. . . .

Inattention

Anyone who regularly deals with arbitration has no doubt heard someone say, "No one really paid any attention to the arbitration clause," explaining that the drafters decided at around 2:00 a.m. on the morning on the day of the closing that they should provide for arbitration and pasted in a copy of the nearest clause available.

What this describes is the sin of inattention: drafting an arbitration clause with insufficient attention to the transaction to which it relates. This is far from the ideal approach. An arbitration clause should be designed to fit the circumstances of the transaction and the parties' needs. The drafter may well select a standard "off-the-shelf" clause prepared by one of the well-known arbitration institutions — one can do far worse — but the off-the-shelf clause should only be selected because it is right for the deal. "The key is to pay sufficient attention to the underlying transaction so that the arbitration clause can be tailored to the client's particular requirements and to possible disputes that may reasonably be anticipated."

When advising a client about dispute resolution options and deciding on the type of clause to use, the drafter, at a minimum, should ask the following questions:

- *What type of dispute resolution process is best suited to the client and the transaction?*

Arbitration is not the only option. There are many alternative dispute resolution processes and there is always litigation. In particular circumstances it may be preferable to litigate in court, provided that the parties can agree on which court to designate and whether that court will have jurisdiction. Litigation, however, may not be an option in an international agreement.

- *If arbitration is selected, does the client understand that the arbitration clause will commit the client to a binding process that involves certain trade-offs?*

Arbitration has advantages, prominent among them privacy, as well as the possibility of crafting a process that will be speedier and more economical than litigation. It also provides the opportunity for the parties to choose a fair and neutral forum — and to participate in the selection of the decision maker and the rules that will be applied.

On the trade-off side, the client should understand that it is giving up some rights provided by law to litigants. These may include the right to a jury trial, the right to an appeal and, under certain [mainly international] institutional arbitration rules . . . the right to claim punitive damages, unless the contract provides otherwise.

The drafter should be especially cautious about giving in to the temptation to advise the client to agree to arbitrate some types of disputes and go to court for others. This may be inevitable in some countries that do not allow certain types of disputes to be arbitrated (e.g., patent disputes) — but dividing jurisdiction should be the subject of an advanced course in drafting. Do not try it at home.

- *Have the parties considered providing for steps preceding arbitration, especially if the relationship between the parties is an ongoing one?*

It may be that, in light of their prior relationship, the parties should agree to mediate or negotiate before heading into arbitration. They can always arbitrate if less adversarial techniques are unsuccessful. A "step clause" can be drafted with as many steps preceding arbitration as the parties desire.

Omission

A drafter who omits a crucial (or even a useful) element from an arbitration clause commits the sin of omission. This can result in a clause that expresses an agreement to arbitrate, but fails to provide guidance as to how or where to do so. Here is an extreme example:

Any disputes arising out of this Agreement will be finally resolved by binding arbitration.

This clause is probably enforceable because it clearly requires the parties to arbitrate disputes. However, it does not achieve the goal of an arbitration clause, which is to stay out of court. Unless the parties can agree on the details concerning their arbitration, they will have to go to court to have an arbitrator or arbitral institution selected for them.

. . .

In the arbitration, the parties will still have to resolve disputes about when, where and how to conduct the arbitration. It is far better to provide in the arbitration clause for the minimum fundamentals needed to get an arbitration under way without the intervention of a court. . . .

Over-Specificity

The opposite of the sin of omission is the sin of over-specificity. Rather than providing insufficient detail, the drafter provides too much. Drafters occasionally take the job of crafting an arbitration clause as a challenge to show how many terms they can invent. This can produce a clause that is extremely difficult to put into practice. For example:

> *The Arbitration shall be conducted by three arbitrators, each of whom shall be fluent in Hungarian and shall have twenty or more years of experience in the design of buggy whips, and one of whom, who shall act as chairman, shall be an expert on the law of the Hapsburg Empire.*

This may seem like a comic exaggeration, but if you substitute computer chips for buggy whips, with appropriate adjustment of the language and law in question, you will find this example chillingly similar to many that make their way to arbitration.

Basically, it is a big mistake to over-draft an arbitration clause. When the arbitration clause is excessively detailed, those layers of detail can make it difficult or impossible to arbitrate a dispute when one arises. The standard clauses recommended by the major arbitral institutions are used by many knowledgeable people because they have been tested by the courts and they do the job.

Unrealistic Expectations

A companion sin to over-specificity is the sin of unrealistic expectations. We have all encountered arbitration clauses along the following lines:

> *The claimant will name its arbitrator when it commences the proceeding. The respondent will then name its arbitrator within seven (7) days, and the two so named will name the third arbitrator, who will act as chair, within seven (7) days of the selection of the second arbitrator. Hearings will commence within fifteen (15) days of the selection of the third arbitrator, and will conclude no more than three (3) days later. The arbitrators will issue their award within seven (7) days of the conclusion of the hearings.*

There are circumstances that may justify, indeed even require, tight time limits. It may be reasonable to provide for accelerated resolution of an urgent matter, such as the need for provisional relief of a dispute involving the use of a trademark or one that would delay a major construction project. But most commercial arbitration proceeds at a more stately pace. While clients and their attorneys understandably become impatient with that pace, they should be aware that too tight a timeframe for an arbitration can cripple the process before it gets started. The risk is, as usual, collateral litigation. American courts have been less rigid than their European counterparts in finding that a failure to meet a deadline in an arbitration agreement deprives an arbitrator of jurisdiction to proceed with the arbitration. However, drafters should not invite a challenge on that basis by imposing unrealistic deadlines on the parties, the case administrator, or the arbitrator.

Litigation Envy

Sometimes the drafter of an arbitration clause cannot be reconciled to the thought of letting go of the familiar security blanket of litigation. What sometimes results is a clause that calls for the arbitration to follow court rules. This is the sin of litigation envy. Take the following clause, which the author once had to deal with as the chair of an ad hoc arbitration panel:

> *The arbitration will be conducted in accordance with the Federal Rules of Civil Procedure applicable in the United States District Court for the Southern District of New York, and the arbitrators shall follow the Federal Rules of Evidence.*

Trying to conduct the arbitration under rules designed for an entirely different kind of proceeding produced predictable and needlessly expensive wheel-spinning. The arbitrators had to decide whether and how to apply the local rules of the Southern District, whether a pre-trial order was required, whether the parties were obligated to make the mandatory disclosures required by the Federal Rules, and other controversies about discovery of the sort that people resort to arbitration to escape.

Whether administered or non-administered arbitration is desired, there are many good sets of procedural rules available that can be incorporated in an arbitration clause. Any one of them is preferable to requiring an arbitration to be conducted according to the rules governing litigation.

. . .

Overreaching

Sometimes the drafter of an arbitration clause cannot resist the temptation to tilt the arbitration process in favor of his or her client. This is the sin of overreaching. . . . The temptation to overreach in drafting the arbitration clause should be strongly resisted. It is not only wrong, but it is also counterproductive. [The author uses as an example the notorious arbitration provision included in Hooters' individual employment contracts, which we will read about in Chapter 19.]

. . .

Doing it Right

If one knows what to avoid in drafting the arbitration clause, how does the drafter go about drafting it correctly? . . . The beginning drafter is well advised to begin with a standard clause by one of the many respected arbitral institutions. The websites of the principal arbitral institutions provide recommended provisions for both administered and non-administered arbitration that have been tested by the courts and that work . . . . [It is wise to begin with the following steps.:]

Step 1: Define what is arbitrable.
Step 2: Commit the parties to arbitration.
Step 3: Pick a set of rules (and, in this case, an arbitration institution to administer the case).
Step 4: Provide for entry of judgment. This is essential to enforcement in the United States.

Problem 2

How Not to Draft an Arbitration Clause!

Building on the fact pattern set out in Problem 1 in Chapter 16, assume MDM and Fandom included in their contract the following arbitration provision:

> Any controversy arising out of any of the terms or conditions of the contract and involving more than $1,000,000 may be submitted to arbitration administered by the AAA. Said arbitration will commence within five days of the dispute arising and will be completed within ten days.

Once the contract was in place, Fandom began uploading 80 MB video files of seasons one and two *Starscape* episodes on ScapePlace.com. Six months into the contract, MDM discovered that Fandom had begun uploading high-quality 450 MB videos of season three episodes to ScapePlace.com. In total, seven such video files of *Starscape* had been made available on the site. Outraged, MDM asked you, its attorney, to initiate immediate legal action.

You immediately notified Fandom of MDM's intention to arbitrate. One week later you filed a demand with the AAA on behalf of MDM, alleging that Fandom had frustrated the contract's purpose, and that Fandom had distributed the season three video files without MDM's permission and in violation of MDM's copyright as well as the specific terms of the parties' contract. On behalf of MDM, you requested compensatory damages for copyright violations and breach of contract totaling $900,000 for each third season episode of *Starscape* uploaded to ScapePlace.com, as well as $5 million in punitive damages. You also sought interim relief in the form of a preliminary injunction to prevent Fandom from continuing to display the season three episodes.

a.   Do you see any potential procedural defenses that Fandom might raise in response to your arbitration demand? If you were counseling MDM with regard to other contracts, would you advise your client to use different language in its arbitration clauses? If so, what language would you suggest adding or removing?

b.   Assume for the sake of discussion that the agreement called for the application of the AAA Commercial Arbitration Rules and Mediation Procedures (including Procedures for Large, Complex Commercial Disputes). (Reminder: These rules may be found on the AAA website.) If Fandom decides not to submit voluntarily to arbitration, what do these Rules say about who would decide the question of whether certain issues are within the scope of the arbitration clause — the court or the arbitrator(s)?

F.   Selecting the Arbitrator(s)

1.   *Key Attributes of Arbitrators*

It has been said that the selection of the arbitrator(s) is the single most important decision confronting parties in arbitration, since in many respects "the arbitrator *is* the process." The choice of arbitrators is critical for two reasons: arbitrators have primary control over the arbitration proceedings, and their decisions on the merits of a case are unlikely to be disturbed since, as we will see in Chapter 18.E, judicial review of arbitral awards tends to be extremely limited.

The necessary attributes of arbitrators will vary according to particular circumstances and a party's interests, needs, and priorities. In selecting their own decision maker(s), parties to arbitration frequently seek out those with specialized commercial, legal, or technical knowledge, training, and experience. The assumption is that such grounding reduces the amount of time that will be required to explain issues in dispute to the arbitrators and enhances the likelihood that the outcomes will be more in keeping with pertinent business, legal, or technical standards. This approach contrasts with the realities of most public tribunals: Judges tend to be generalists, steeped in legal traditions and focused on application of legal standards; jurors may be chosen precisely because they *lack* pertinent expertise.

Fairness and open-mindedness are deemed critical to the reality and perception of due process, and standard arbitration procedures are designed from the vantage point of promoting even-handedness in the process. Of course, there is frequently a tension between expertise and impartiality. Besides the fact that arbitrators may bring to the hearing room a point of view that is conditioned by their experience, they are often of the same business or professional community as the parties. While this may only enhance their acceptability as arbitrators, such relationships might also give rise to potential conflicts of interest. For this reason, standard arbitration procedures provide a mechanism for disclosure of potential conflicts of interest by prospective and sitting arbitrators. See Section G below.

Particularly in large or complex cases, arbitrators must have strong case management skills. They, or at least the designated chair of the tribunal, should be able to run arbitration proceedings efficiently and attentively, and act decisively when necessary. Foresight, planning, diligence, and dedication are normally required to achieve a quick and efficient resolution — which is what arbitrating parties should expect in the absence of a mutual agreement to the contrary. Unfortunately, judging by the experiences of arbitrating parties, such expectations are often frustrated in big arbitrations. One of the authors of this text was counsel in commercial arbitrations involving complex disputes that extended over several years, with months elapsing between hearings. The length of the processes and delays between hearings were in large part the fault of the arbitrators, who failed to maintain control of the timetable.

2.   Sources of Information about Arbitrators

It is imperative for counsel to conduct a thorough, independent investigation of potential arbitrators; this may mean examining their professional qualifications, education, training, arbitration experience, fees, and even published awards and writings. Most sponsoring organizations offer updated arbitrators' biographies, as well as information on the identification, training, and evaluation of listed arbitrators. They may also provide information on potential arbitrators' possible conflicts of interest, availability, and fee schedules.

In important cases, counsel sometimes seek to arrange a joint interview with the arbitrator in which both sides ask questions of the arbitrator in person or by telephone. Candidates may be asked about their background, relevant professional experience, including experience with the issues of the particular dispute, the availability of the candidate to oversee the dispute, and what the candidate's personal expertise and style is in handling disputes. Moreover, the parties and their counsel often clear up potential conflicts of interest during this interview.

One fast and efficient means of accumulating information about candidates is through the use of the Internet. Some professional, trade, and Internet groups provide arbitrator biographies and links to their publications. Public, private, and governmental ADR organizations and alternative dispute resolution resources can also be accessed. In some cases, awards that have been written by arbitrators may be found by using an arbitrator's name, company, or firm using LexisNexis, Westlaw, and other search engines.

3.   The Number of Arbitrators

Another consideration for parties is the number of arbitrators who will be employed to adjudicate the dispute. The most common scenarios involve using a single arbitrator or a panel of three arbitrators to issue a decision.

Generally, arbitration procedures establish guidelines for the use of arbitration panels. As a rule, for relatively low-dollar disputes, or where it is vital to limit the cost of the arbitration, a single arbitrator is preferable. If cost is less of a factor, then a panel of three arbitrators can offer distinct advantages. Some lawyers advance the rationale that the decision of a three-member panel is more authoritative, especially if the award is unanimous. Further, it is thought, a panel of three arbitrators is less likely to hand down irrational or arbitrary awards because the arbitrators can "check" each other. Finally, a three-member panel can provide a unique mix of experience and perspectives. Differing expertise may be complementary: for instance, an arbitrator familiar with construction disputes states,

> I've appreciated the way arbitrators with different backgrounds complement each other. Construction professionals understand the way things go together, the dynamics of the job site, and relevant cost implications. Experienced construction lawyers place these realities in the legal framework of statute, common law and contract. In the best case, each arbitrator brings something to the table, and relies on the other arbitrators.

When choosing a panel, measures must be taken to identify the panel's chair. Sometimes the panel chair is selected by the arbitration organization; other times, the arbitrators agree on a chair. The chair normally acts as the panel's voice and is primarily responsible for managing the arbitration proceedings. Chairs may have to arrange the meeting times and locations for the parties. Sometimes, they solely run several or all of the prehearing conferences. They should be counted on to facilitate a sense of teamwork and effective communication among panel members. In addition to supervising the work of the panelists, the chair is expected to keep in close contact with the appropriate arbitration organization. Under AAA rules, for instance, the chair should coordinate with the AAA case administrator regarding issues such as fee deposits, scheduling, hearing location, physical surroundings, availability of equipment, and storage of documents. Under the Code of Ethics for Arbitrators in Commercial Disputes, the chair is also responsible for reassuring the arbitration organization that all panelists are conforming their behavior to the Code.

4.   Selection Processes

There are several different methods of selecting arbitrators. In some cases the parties identify an arbitrator or arbitrators by name in the agreement, or set forth experiential or professional qualifications in the arbitration provision. Most commonly, however, selection occurs after a dispute has arisen. The parties may jointly agree on the arbitrator(s), or delegate an arbitration institution or other third party to make the selection(s) for them. Many institutional arbitration procedures contemplate a "list selection" process, in which parties identify and rank suitable candidates from lists provided by the institution; the latter selects those mutually acceptable candidates based on highest overall rankings. In some cases, the failure of the parties to agree upon one or more arbitrators requires the institution to select an arbitrator. One popular approach in the United States and in international arbitration is the "tripartite panel" — a panel of three arbitrators in which each party designates one panelist, and the two party-designees (or "party arbitrators") agree upon a third, who then chairs the panel. This seemingly straightforward and balanced approach appears to have much to recommend it. As we will see, however, there has been considerable concern regarding the role of party arbitrators and their relationships with those who appointed them. In U.S. practice, party arbitrators are sometimes expected to forsake independence and impartiality and instead advocate the cause of the party that appointed them; such expectations conflict with conventional international practice and may produce confusion and disarray.

Problem 3

Arbitrator Selection Methods

Suppose you are representing ECOPLAZA, an owner/developer that intends to construct a vast new "green" (environmentally sustainable) shopping center/office complex. You are negotiating a contract with Biggtel, Inc., one of the world's largest engineering and construction companies, to design and build the project. You expect the project to take at least two and perhaps as many as three years to complete, and believe it may cost $500 million or more.

a. Consider the pros and cons of each of the following approaches:
    i.   Identifying a mutually acceptable retired judge (by name) as the sole arbitrator of disputes under the ECOPLAZA/Biggtel contract;
    ii. Identifying some other mutually acceptable person (by name) as the sole arbitrator;
    iii. Setting out experiential or professional qualifications for one or more arbitrators in the contract;
    iv. Agreeing to have each party pick an arbitrator after a dispute arises, resulting in a two-member arbitration tribunal;
    v.   The same as the last approach, except that the panel has three members; the party-appointed arbitrators (or the parties themselves) pick the third arbitrator.

b.   Suppose the parties elected to arbitrate under the auspices of the most relevant AAA arbitration rules and did not specify any method for selecting arbitrators. (Does the AAA have rules specifically designed for construction disputes? If you can't recall, check the website.)

    i.   Would there be a single arbitrator or arbitration panel? (Does the answer depend on the circumstances?)

    ii.   How would the selection process work, assuming the parties had no other selection agreement?

    iii.   How are the arbitrators' fees paid, and how are communications between the parties and the arbitrators handled?

    iv.   What are the relative merits or demerits of the AAA "list selection" process as compared to the alternatives set out in Question a? Could you agree to use the AAA lists of arbitrators but utilize a different arbitrator selection process?

G.   Arbitrator Disclosure and Challenges

As discussed above, the selection of private decision makers with ties to the same business or professional community as the parties or their counsel involves a tension between two principles: party autonomy in selecting arbitrators of their choice, on the one hand, and concepts of judicial fairness, independence, and impartiality, on the other. To reconcile the potential conflict between these principles, arbitrators are expected to make a timely disclosure of facts that may raise conflict-of-interest concerns, including relationships with counsel, the parties, witnesses, or the issues in dispute. Armed with this information, parties may make a knowledgeable choice about a candidate's suitability for the role of arbitrator, and accede to or, alternatively, deny or challenge their appointment. The concept of arbitrator disclosure — and related guidelines for arbitrators, parties and counsel, arbitral institutions, and courts — are embodied in institutional arbitration procedures, ethical guidelines for arbitrators, and federal and state arbitration law. We will emphasize institutional procedures and ethical standards below, and address the legal issues in Chapter 18.E.

1.   Institutional Procedures for Disclosure and Challenge

A key element of most institutional arbitration procedures is the procedure for arbitrator disclosure and challenge. Under the AAA Commercial Arbitration Rules, for example, upon appointment arbitrators must "disclose to the AAA any circumstance likely to affect impartiality or independence, including bias or any financial or personal interest in the result of the arbitration or any past or present relationship with the parties or their representatives." Upon a showing of arbitrator partiality, the AAA will inform the parties of the situation, and conclusively rule on any objections the parties make to the continued appointment of the allegedly biased arbitrator. Under the CPR Rules, "[a]ny arbitrator may be challenged if circumstances exist or arise that give rise to justifiable doubt regarding that arbitrator's independence or impartiality... If neither agreed disqualification nor voluntary withdrawal occurs, the challenge shall be decided by CPR."

2.   *Ethical Standards*

The *Code of Ethics for Arbitrators in Commercial Disputes* (2004) contains numerous admonitions to arbitrators regarding the fairness and integrity of the arbitration process. (Note: The Code of Ethics may be found on the AAA and CPR websites, among other places.) Among other things, Canon II requires arbitrators, before they accept appointment, to "disclose any interest or relationship likely to affect impartiality or which might create an appearance of partiality or bias." The obligation is a continuing one, and requires disclosure to all parties and to other appointed arbitrators. The Canon proceeds to identify courses of action for an arbitrator, including withdrawal in appropriate circumstances (Cole, 2004).

Problem 4A

Arbitrator Disclosure and Challenge — Ethical Issues

a.   You represent the Carmin Co., a manufacturer of high-tech GPS units used in automobiles, in a dispute with SamCo, Inc., a national "buying club" with stores all over the country. The parties have a long-term contract under which SamCo is obligated to buy certain amounts of various Carmin products each month. In recent months SamCo has refused to accept the required number of various Carmin products, citing various alleged defects. After efforts to negotiate were unavailing, Carmin demanded arbitration under the terms of the contract, and three arbitrators were mutually selected for the arbitration panel through a list selection process. The parties have been preparing for hearings for several months, and have just exchanged lists of the witnesses they plan to present in the arbitration hearing. The chair of the arbitration panel now reveals that she has current business dealings with a key witness for SamCo. You and your client are very concerned about the connection. Please select a set of published commercial arbitration procedures (e.g., AAA, JAMS, CPR) and ascertain what your client should expect to happen, and what course of action it should pursue, under those procedures. Be prepared to cite pertinent sections.

b. If, instead, you are the chair of the arbitration panel in this proceeding and have just become aware that one of the key witnesses will be an individual with whom you have business dealings, what would your ethical responsibilities be under the current version of the Code of Ethics for Arbitrators in Commercial Disputes?

    i. What if, instead of a current business connection, your relationship with the witness was common membership in a state bar association committee? A country club?

    ii. What if a partner in your law firm represents the witness's company in a separate legal action?

Note on Arbitration Law

As discussed in Chapter 18.E, disclosure standards under arbitration procedures and ethical rules are reinforced by case law applying federal and state arbitration statutes. Strong policies supporting the finality of arbitration awards make courts hesitant to allow parties who are disappointed by an award to use a claim of bias as a way to undermine an award. An arbitrator's failure to disclose real or perceived conflicts of interest is often the basis for a motion to vacate an arbitration award, although relatively few court decisions have resulted in awards being vacated on such grounds (Mills et al., 2004).

3. "Party Arbitrators" on Tripartite Panels

Tripartite arbitration panels are a common feature of the landscape. The concept — each party picking an arbitrator, and the two "party arbitrators" agreeing on a third arbitrator — is seemingly straightforward and inherently fair. Such arrangements, however, often bring unanticipated results and not a little litigation.

Problem 4B

Arbitrator Disclosure and Challenge — "Party Arbitrators"

As in Problem 4A, you represent Carmin Co. in arbitration proceedings with SamCo., Inc. Now, however, assume that their arbitration agreement called for a tripartite arbitration panel. Accordingly, Carmin appointed Craft as its arbitrator and SamCo appointed Silver; Craft and Silver jointly selected Professor Perfect as the third arbitrator. You and your client have been very careful not to communicate with arbitratorCraft, but now, midway through the hearings, you find out that arbitrator Silver has been actively working with and assisting SamCoin the preparation of its case. You and your client are truly alarmed and are considering your next steps.

a. What procedural options does your client possess if the parties agreed to arbitrate under the JAMS Comprehensive Arbitration Rules? Would the result be the same under the AAA Commercial Arbitration Rules?
b. Would it make any difference if the parties incorporated the JAMS Rules in their agreement but specified that the arbitrators would not be independent and impartial but could be "predisposed toward the party that appointed them"?
c. What procedural options does your client possess if the parties did not specify any arbitration rules and did not specify what role the arbitrators would play under this arrangement? *See, e.g., Delta Mine Holding Co. v. AFC Coal Properties, Inc.*, 280 F.3d 815 (8th Cir. 2001), cert. denied, 123 S. Ct. 87 (2002). See Chapter 18.E.
d. What does the Code of Ethics for Arbitrators in Commercial Disputes (2004) provide with respect to the standards applicable to "party arbitrators"?

H. Overview of the Arbitration Process

1. Stages of Arbitration

Arbitration typically involves several procedural stages, although specific features will depend on the parties' agreement and incorporated arbitration rules. The process nearly always begins with the filing of a demand and other pleadings and the appointment of arbitrators. Arbitrators usually begin preliminary planning for the process by means of a prehearing conference or phone call to develop a tentative timetable, flesh out procedures, and set the stage for all that follows.

What follows depends on the nature and complexity of the case, but modern commercial arbitration usually involves weeks or months of prehearing preparation. Counsel may be engaged in filing and arguing motions, exchanging information and engaging in discovery, identifying and preparing witnesses (including experts), assembling documents to be presented at the hearing, and preparing prehearing briefs. During this stage, arbitrators often play an active oversight role, addressing motions, discovery disputes, and other procedural issues.

Then comes some form of hearing. Although in some cases arbitration hearings may be a far cry from a court trial, they typically embody basic rudiments of due process; commercial cases involving lawyers may bear a number of the earmarks of a court trial — with some important differences. See Section M below.

Arbitration concludes with arbitrator deliberations leading to the rendition of an award. The form of the award will vary depending on the parties' agreement and applicable rules; there may or may not be a published rationale or opinion along with the award. The issuance of a "bare" award, limited to a straightforward declaration of the panel's grant or denial of relief, has long been viewed as a bulwark against judicial intrusion into the realm of the arbitrator. However, especially in larger cases, parties usually require arbitrators to provide a statement of reasons for their decisions.

2.   Roles of Attorneys

The attorney's role during the arbitration process is similar in many respects to preparing and presenting a case in litigation. There are analogues to the familiar incidents of trial process, including the filing of pleadings, interviewing and preparing witnesses, the development of a direct case (including the preparation of exhibits, demonstrative evidence, a trial notebook, etc.), and some, perhaps extensive, information exchange and discovery. As an attorney in arbitration you should normally be prepared to make opening and closing arguments, to prepare briefs on factual or legal issues, and perhaps to file a dispositive motion or even a motion to vacate an arbitration award.

This is not to say, however, that arbitration advocacy is the same as trial advocacy. Prehearing practice in arbitration — motion practice and discovery — tends to be much more abbreviated and attenuated than in litigation. Experienced lawyers and arbitrators warn that arbitration before experienced arbitrators is not a forum for the strutting and posturing employed by some lawyers in civil trials. Moreover, attorneys should remember that because their panel of adjudicators may bring significant expertise to the table, they may find extensive explication or foundation-laying unnecessary or even offensive. Arbitrators may also engage in extensive interrogation of witnesses.

Problem 5

The Arbitration Process

Assume you have been appointed chair of a panel of three arbitrators to arbitrate the dispute involving Carmin Co., manufacturer of the "Nügi" high-tech GPS units used in automobiles, and SamCo, Inc., a national "buying club" with stores all over the country. The parties have a long-term contract under which SamCo is obligated to buy certain amounts of various Carmin products each month. In recent months SamCo has refused to accept the required number of various Carmin products, citing various alleged defects. Carmin's demand for arbitration includes a claim for more than $5 million in damages. For the purpose of answering the questions below and in the following sections (I–L), assume the AAA Commercial Arbitration Rules are applicable.

Questions

a.   Just after the arbitrators have been appointed, the defendant, SamCo, seeks to file a counterclaim for damages against Carmin. Who determines whether the counterclaim should be heard?

b.   After reviewing the initial pleadings of the parties, you realize that you have very little information on the factual and legal issues. How might you go about getting more information about the parties' positions? What other information might you seek, how and when?

c.   If you were an attorney for one of the parties in this arbitration, how might you make the most of the arbitration process? In what ways might your preparation and presentation be different from your efforts in litigation?

I.   Laying the Groundwork: The Prehearing Conference

No set of commercial arbitration procedures, however comprehensive, provides a precise blueprint for conducting an arbitration. Even if such detail were possible, it would not be desirable in light of the wide range of claims, controversies, and circumstances with which arbitrators are presented. It is during the prehearing process that the often sketchy procedural framework established by the arbitration agreement is refined. It is here that the participants often determine the precise character of their arbitration experience.

In "fleshing out" the bare bones of the arbitration agreement, arbitrators typically enjoy considerable leeway. Leading commercial arbitration rules reinforce the well-recognized broad discretion of arbitrators to manage virtually all aspects of the arbitration. At the same time, effective arbitrators recognize that all participants usually are best served by striving for party consensus, and by reserving unilateral arbitrator rulings for when consensus cannot be achieved.

In the simplest commercial arbitrations, there may be little or no need for active prehearing management by the arbitrator. Standard "fast-track" rules place a premium on getting the dispute resolved with minimal process. (See, e.g., AAA Commercial Dispute Resolution Rules, Expedited Procedures.) As the stakes grow or the issues become more complex, it becomes increasingly important for the arbitrator to take a more active role in managing the process with the involvement, and, hopefully, the cooperation of the parties.

In light of the variety of management issues that may arise in the course of arbitration, participants are well advised to consult appropriate guidelines. Applicable arbitration procedures may provide guidelines for the prehearing stage. For example, the CPR Non-Administered Arbitration Rules direct arbitrators to hold a "pre-hearing conference for the planning and scheduling of the proceeding." The purpose of the conference is "to discuss all elements of the arbitration with a view to planning for its future conduct." The prehearing conference (or in AAA parlance, "preliminary hearing") provides an opportunity to address the full range of procedural matters, including (1) clarifying the contractual basis of the arbitration and the issues presented, the rules governing arbitration, and the location of hearings; (2) specifying approved methods of communication; (3) identifying jurisdictional issues; (4) establishing a framework for addressing motions for interim or provisional relief, and for dispositive motions; (5) establishing a timetable or schedule for the process; (6) developing a framework for information exchange and discovery; (7) setting specific ground rules for the hearings; (8) considering protections for confidential information; and (9) setting parameters for the arbitration award. Additional conferences may be scheduled from time to time as the arbitrators deem necessary for effective management of the process.

The prehearing conference often results in the issuance of an initial procedural order by the arbitrators. This document, which sets forth a timetable and many other elements of the "arbitration plan," is usually submitted to the parties for their review and comment before final issuance.

Questions

5. As chair of the arbitration tribunal for the Carmin/SamCo arbitration in Problem 5, what kinds of things would you hope to accomplish at an initial prehearing conference? Can you find one or more useful templates for subjects to be addressed in a prehearing conference? Some arbitration procedures offer lists of potential topics. An excellent example designed for use in international proceedings is the UNCITRAL Notes on Organizing Arbitral Proceedings (1996); it is sometimes used as a set of guidelines in U.S. commercial arbitration.

6. Might it make sense to have the parties' representatives try to see what procedural matters they can agree on before the prehearing conference? Should business executives representing Carmin and SamCo be present in the prehearing conference? Why or why not?

7. If you were the attorney for Carmin in this arbitration, what things should you do in preparation for, during, and after the preliminary hearing?

J.   Jurisdictional Issues

Because arbitration is a creature of contract, a valid and enforceable agreement to arbitrate is a fundamental prerequisite to an arbitrator's jurisdiction. Usually, there is no question that the parties have agreed to arbitrate the issues, and there is no threshold question of jurisdiction. When, however, a party challenges an arbitrator's jurisdiction on the basis that it is not bound by a valid arbitration agreement, or that the arbitration agreement does not cover the matters at issue, there may be a question as to whether the jurisdictional issue should be resolved by the arbitrator or by a court. The answer depends on the agreement of the parties.

If the parties have agreed that arbitration shall be governed by any of the leading standard arbitration procedures, the authority of arbitrators to decide jurisdictional issues will probably be clear. For example, the JAMS Comprehensive Arbitration Rules provide:

> Once appointed, the Arbitrator shall resolve disputes about the interpretation and applicability of these Rules and conduct of the Arbitration hearing. . . . Jurisdictional and arbitrability disputes, including disputes over the existence, validity, interpretation or scope of the agreement under which Arbitration is sought, and who are proper Parties to the Arbitration, shall be submitted to and ruled on by the Arbitrator. The Arbitrator has the authority to determine jurisdiction and arbitrability issues as a preliminary matter.

Under the foregoing provision, a party to a contract that incorporates the JAMS procedures (or other procedures with similar language) has agreed to consign virtually all questions touching upon the arbitrator's authority to the arbitrator. The policy behind such provisions is to discourage resort to the courts and avoid related delays and disruptions to the arbitration process.

The goals of speed and efficiency are further served by provisions that require those asserting jurisdictional challenges to act promptly or run the risk of being deemed to have waived the right to challenge. For example, the AAA Commercial Arbitration Rules provide:

> A party must object to the jurisdiction of the arbitrator or to the arbitrability of a claim or counterclaim no later than the filing of the answering statement to the claim or counterclaim that gives rise to the objection.

Note on arbitration law. As we will see, in the absence of a clear agreement that gives the arbitrator power to decide whether an agreement to arbitrate is valid or whether a controversy is within the jurisdiction of the arbitrators, federal arbitration law and prevailing state arbitration law put those matters in the hands of the courts. However, an arbitration provision that incorporates language such as that above provides "clear and unmistakable" evidence that the parties want the arbitrators to determine jurisdictional questions and overcomes the usual presumption in favor of having a court do so. See Chapter 18.C.

> Question
>
> 8. Suppose Carmin's arbitration demand includes a request that the arbitrators render a decision declaring its rights under the contract with SamCo — what is commonly referred to as a "declaratory judgment." In its answering statement, SamCo states that Carmin's claim is outside the jurisdiction of the arbitrators under the AAA Commercial Arbitration Rules. As chair of the arbitration panel, your fellow arbitrators look to you to offer guidance on a course of action. Based on your reading of the AAA Rules, how should the arbitrators handle this matter?

K. Dispositive Motions

Arbitration usually begins with very general pleadings offering little detail regarding the issues in dispute or the positions of the parties. As a rule, therefore, dismissal of claims on the pleadings will be inappropriate in arbitration. As the parties exchange information and develop more detailed positions, however, there may be some point at which issues have ripened sufficiently for arbitrators to act knowledgeably upon a motion for summary disposition — that is, the equivalent of a motion for summary judgment in court. It may then be possible to determine that a party will be unable to bear the burden of proving a case in the arbitration hearing, and render an award in favor of the opposing party.

The AAA Commercial Rules, while not addressing dispositive motions specifically, permit arbitrators to "direct the parties to focus their presentations on issues the decision of which could dispose of all or part of the case." Coupled with other provisions of the AAA Rules, such language probably implicitly authorizes arbitrators to rule on dispositive motions (Ferris & Biddle, 2007). The JAMS Comprehensive Arbitration Rules and Procedures are more direct, stating that

> [t]he Arbitrator(s) may hear and determine a Motion for Summary Disposition of a particular claim or issue, either by agreement of all interested Parties or at the request of one Party, provided other interested Parties have reasonable notice to respond to the Request.

The JAMS rule sets parameters for the establishment of a briefing schedule and record, stating that "[o]rdinarily, oral argument will not be allowed, unless all Parties or the Arbitrator(s) so request."

Note on arbitration law. Some arbitrators are reluctant to make preliminary rulings that will dispose of all or part of the case because they are fearful of having their award vacated by a court on the basis that they failed to hear material or relevant evidence. See Chapter 18.E. However, by carefully tailoring an appropriate process for the submission of evidence and argument, arbitrators may be able render an early decision and avoid vacatur. *See, e.g., Schlessinger v. Rosenfeld, Meyer & Susman,* 47 Cal. Rptr. 2d 650 (Cal. Ct. App. 1995).

Question

9.   Suppose SamCo moves to dismiss Carmin's claim on the basis that the contract provides:

> No claim may be brought more than one (1) year after the transaction, occurrence, or event on which it is based.

SamCo argues that Carmin did not file its original demand for arbitration until 14 months after SamCo first refused to take some of Carmin's goods, and therefore Carmin's claim should be barred by this contractual "statute of limitations." How should you as an arbitrator respond to this motion? What information might be relevant to resolving this on a preliminary basis?

L.   Information Exchange and Discovery

For many years, a popular understanding was that there was "no discovery in arbitration." In recent years, however, that has changed. Counsel for parties in arbitration often agree to mutual information exchange, with or without arbitrator supervision. Moreover, leading arbitration procedures, some state statutes and judicial decisions constructing the FAA, and state law have made clear that some form of arbitrator-supervised discovery is often a feature of arbitration processes. In private proceedings as in court trial, fundamental fairness often requires a sharing of information, and it is generally fairer and more efficient to have a consensual or supervised information exchange prior to hearings. Indeed, in large, complex commercial cases, discovery is very likely.

However, discovery in arbitration is usually more limited than that contemplated by civil procedural rules. This reflects the normal expectation that arbitration offers a speedier and more efficient path to resolution, and that cost/benefit considerations will temper the normal broad relevance standard in litigation. For example, the CPR Rules state that the Tribunal may require and facilitate such discovery as it shall determine is appropriate in the circumstances, taking into account the needs of the parties and the desirability of making discovery expeditious and cost-effective.

The accompanying commentary explains that as contemplated by the CPR procedures, "[a]rbitration is not for the litigator who will 'leave no stone unturned'." Most often, arbitrators will seek to restrict discovery to categories of information, such as documents, that speak to the primary issues in dispute. Requests for admission and interrogatories are relatively rare, and, unless the parties have otherwise agreed, arbitrators often demand justification for the taking of depositions. For example, the AAA Procedures for Large, Complex Commercial Disputes (a part of the AAA Commercial Arbitration Procedures) provide that arbitrators can

> upon good cause shown and consistent with the expedited nature of arbitration, . . . order the depositions of, or the propounding of interrogatories to, such persons who may possess information determined by the arbitrators to be necessary to the determination of the matter.

Arbitrators in larger or high-stakes disputes often permit depositions to preserve testimony or save time at the hearing.

Often, experienced arbitrators initially seek to facilitate agreement among the parties regarding the nature and scope of discovery rather than adjudicate multiple discovery disputes. Competent arbitrators help set and enforce strict time limits for information exchange, which can expedite the discovery process. An arbitrator may draw an adverse inference if a party refuses to comply with a discovery order.

Note on arbitration law. The FAA and most state arbitration statutes do not specifically address the subject of arbitration-related discovery. However, the FAA and corresponding state laws give arbitrators authority to issue summons or subpoenas to parties or nonparties, and provide for their judicial enforcement. FAA § 7, for example, states that arbitrators may "summon in writing any person to attend before them or any of them as a witness and in a proper case to bring with him or them any book, record, document, or paper which may be deemed material as evidence in the case." As we will see in Chapter 18.D, however, courts have reached different conclusions about whether the FAA language supports judicial enforcement of subpoenas for a deposition. Recent revisions to the Uniform Arbitration Act (UAA) have attempted to directly address these and other concerns through specific provisions for arbitrator-supervised discovery, including depositions.

Question

10. Again returning to the Carmin/SamCo scenario described in earlier problems, suppose that at the time Carmin filed an arbitration demand, it was discovered that SamCo's CEO, Gates, is severely ill.

> If Mr. Gates's testimony is considered essential to Carmin's case, what steps might be undertaken to preserve Mr. Gates's testimony in arbitration? Assume the AAA rules apply.

M. The Hearing

1. General Structure of Hearings

Arbitration hearings are usually less formal than court trial, and may be held around a conference table. However, commercial arbitrations typically feature some of the basic elements of trial. Usually each side will present an opening statement, followed by introductory evidence, examination and cross-examination of witnesses, testimony under oath, and closing statements and arguments. Unless otherwise agreed, the formal rules of evidence and civil procedure do not apply, and thus hearsay or other testimony inadmissible in court may be considered by arbitrators. Arbitrators normally have plenary authority over all aspects of the hearing; leading institutional arbitration procedures give arbitrators wide discretion on whether to allow in various evidence.

Depending on the complexity of the matter and number of parties involved, a hearing could last less than a day or could extend over a long period of time, at the convenience of parties and arbitrators. Scheduling hearings in complex cases can sometimes delay arbitral proceedings, particularly with a panel of highly sought-after neutrals.

Note on arbitration law. Many arbitrators err on the side of admitting evidence, at least partly because they are aware that an award may be overturned (vacated) by a court where an arbitrator is "guilty of misconduct... in refusing to hear evidence pertinent and material to the controversy" or "guilty of misconduct in refusing to postpone the hearing, upon sufficient cause shown." Federal Arbitration Act, 9 U.S.C. § 10(a)(3) (West Supp. 1994). See Chapter 18.E.

Questions

Please refer to the AAA Commercial Rules in addressing these questions.

11. Suppose one party to arbitration seeks to avoid the expense and inconvenience of an oral hearing, and rely entirely on submissions of written documents, briefs, and so on. Is it within the arbitrators' authority to direct a "paper hearing"?

12. You would like to have the statements of several witnesses that are redundant of other testimony to be introduced by affidavit. Is this permissible?

13. The night before the first day of four consecutive days of scheduled hearings, an attorney for one of the parties sends a fax and e-mail to inform opposing counsel and the arbitrators that she and her client will be unable to attend the proceedings that week. The explanation is that the client has been called away "on personal business." You learn of the communication the following morning, right before the hearing is scheduled to begin. Meanwhile, the other party has appeared for the hearing. What is the appropriate course of action for the arbitrators?

14. The case centers on a valuation question, and each of the parties has hired an accountant to address the key issues. Can the arbitrators put them on the stand at the same time, ask them questions simultaneously, and even permit them to question one another? Can the arbitrators appoint their own expert and have the parties pay the cost?

15. After several days of hearings, the plaintiff announces that it has concluded the presentation of its case. It is fairly clear that the plaintiff has not proved its case, but the arbitrators believe that it is likely that the information exists to support its case. Is it appropriate, and within the arbitrators' authority, to direct the parties to provide additional information on the key issues?

2. Confidentiality

Arbitration hearings offer a greater degree of privacy and confidentiality than does the courthouse. There is often no stenographer present to take a record, and arbitrators have authority to bar nonessential persons from the hearing room. In some cases, additional confidentiality protections are established by the agreement of the parties or by arbitral order.

However, neither standard procedures nor applicable laws provide a cloak of confidentiality for arbitration-related communications or events (Buys, 2003). While arbitrators and arbitral institutions have obligations to preserve the privacy of the process under applicable procedural rules and ethical standards, public policies protect arbitrators from having to testify.

But absent a specific agreement, parties and their agents have no obligation to preserve the confidentiality of exchanged documents or arbitration-related communications or events. In fact, the latter may be disclosed to third parties (including the media). This lesson was brought home in one memorable case involving the Los Angeles-based J. Paul Getty Museum and its former curator of European drawings, Nicholas Turner. Turner had sued the Getty Museum for fraud on the basis of allegations that the Museum had failed to reveal that several drawings in its collection were forged, and the matter was submitted to arbitration. Getty lawyers filed a motion with the arbitrator for an order preventing Turner from sharing any information discovered during the case; their argument was that arbitration is an "inherently confidential proceeding." Denying the motion, the arbitrator is reported to have observed, "Erin Brockovich was an arbitration" (Landesman, 2001). Thus, parties must take special additional steps to protect confidentiality if they want to ensure that arbitration proceedings remain confidential.

Information shared in arbitration may also be sought by third parties who are engaged in legal action against one of the parties to the arbitration, and they may be able to get that information through discovery in the absence of some means of establishing its confidential status. Therefore, parties seeking to protect sensitive or proprietary information usually request that the arbitrators issue appropriate protective orders or, if mutually acceptable, enter into a post-dispute confidentiality agreement. In transactions involving key intellectual property or other sensitive proprietary information, however, the best course is to take specific affirmative steps to ensure confidentiality in arbitration as a part of initial contract planning (Stipanowich, 2009).

Problem 6

Guidance to a Client on Confidentiality

You just received the following memo from a valued client who seeks guidance on confidentiality in arbitration. Please prepare responses to each of his questions. (Note to students: If your teacher assigns you to prepare a written memo in response to your client's questions, you should plan on devoting two to three single-spaced pages to your answers.)

PRIVILEGED AND CONFIDENTIAL MEMORANDUM

FROM: **Wilma O. Wiggins, Vice President & General Counsel Wee Willie's Waffelhaus, Inc.**

TO: **Outside Counsel**

Re: *Concerns about confidentiality in pending arbitration*

I thank you for taking the time to speak with me about our upcoming arbitration with International House of Crepes (IHOC). I appreciate your agreeing to represent us; your experience in arbitration will serve us well, I am sure. It occurred to me that there were one or two things I needed to get clarified before we get into this proceeding.

As I explained, this arbitration proceeding was brought by IHOC under a licensing agreement under which they are permitted to use Wee Willie's proprietary batter and boysenberry syrup in their U.S. outlets. The license agreement provides that only Wee Willie's franchises and IHOC may use these products in their outlets (restaurants). In their demand they accuse us of licensing the same batter to Pancake Kastle, Inc. As I explained, nothing could be further from the truth. However, the batter we are licensing to Pancake Kastle is somewhat similar to the untrained palate.

The problem is, I anticipate that they will seek revelation in the arbitration proceeding of the secret proprietary formula that we license to Pancake Kastle. I am very worried about them seeing it, and moreover I am worried about the formula getting out to third parties. (We are in a very competitive industry, as you know.)

Please give me a brief explanation of one or two pages about some of these issues.

a. What kind of confidentiality protection I can expect in arbitration under the AAA Rules? Can I count on total privacy there?

b. We have been in mediation before, and I know it is a very confidential process. Is arbitration as confidential as mediation? Please explain. Would we be wise to try to mediate this before arbitrating?

c. One of my colleagues told me not to worry; the other side won't be able to get access to the formula because there is no discovery in arbitration. Is that correct?

d. Is there anything we can do beyond the basic protections to protect our information and our product, both in terms of (A) limiting what IHOC sees in the present arbitration and (B) any future litigation in which other competitors might try to obtain information from this proceeding? (I should mention that we also have proprietary information on IHOC's Western Crepes, and I might be able to do a little negotiating with them about agreeing to protections.)

Anything you can offer will be appreciated.

[Some helpful hints to students: See *A.T. v. State Farm Mut. Auto. Ins. Co.*, 989 P.2d 219 (Colo. Ct. App. 1999) (holding that records disclosed at an arbitration hearing were permitted to be used at a later, unrelated trial because the party did not request a protective order and did not enter into a confidentiality agreement with insurance company); but see *Group Health Plan, Inc. v. BJC Health Systems, Inc.*, 30 S.W.3d 198 (Mo. Ct. App. 2000) (holding that confidentiality agreement signed by parties in an earlier arbitration proceeding was enough to prevent documents from being disclosed in a new arbitration proceeding). You should take a careful look at the International Institute for Conflict Prevention & Resolution (CPR), Rules for Non-Administered Arbitration of Patent & Trade Secret Disputes (2005 Revision) (which may be found through the CPR website). Does it provide a useful template here?]

N.   Remedies in Arbitration

One reason many parties choose arbitration is to avoid the risk of facing a large, unpredictable, or unreasonable jury award. They repose trust instead in the decision-making abilities of an arbitrator who may be a former judge, a legal professional, or a subject matter expert that they personally selected.

Under typical arbitration rules, the arbitrator has great freedom in determining awards and damage amounts. For example, the AAA Rules allow for "any remedy or relief that the arbitrator deems just and equitable and within the scope of the agreement, including, but not limited to, specific performance of a contract." This freedom from the limited remedies a trial court can offer is certainly one of the hallmarks of arbitration. Although experienced attorneys know that arbitrators in commercial cases tend not to produce unconventional remedies, it is important to keep in mind that they have considerable discretion.

1.   *Provisional Remedies*

In some instances, irreparable injury will occur to one or more parties if the arbitrator does not act quickly to address a situation and render a final award. Many providers' rules allow the arbitrator equitable discretion to grant interim remedies equivalent to a preliminary injunction from a court, such as preserving the condition of perishable goods or taking appropriate security measures or even monetary relief. In some circumstances, institutions such as the AAA allow for the appointment of a single emergency arbitrator, a quick hearing, and emergency monetary relief, pending the formation of an arbitration panel. Additionally, the FAA and state arbitration statutes grant implied power to arbitrators to provide interim remedies. Most broad-form commercial arbitration agreements allow arbitrators the authority, for instance, to direct a posting of a bond as security for claims, or order the creation of an escrow account.

Courts may also grant limited provisional relief to parties in certain situations. If the need for an immediate order for relief must be satisfied before an arbitrator can be appointed, a court may order relief. Courts, however, are hesitant to interfere if the parties have an arbitral agreement. Only a court is able to exercise a contempt power to enforce the preservation of assets or to ensure continuing performance. Arbitrators lack such a contempt power, even though they are able to issue sanctions against one or more parties. Therefore, if a party secures interim relief, an arbitrator's order may be given to the court as an interim award subject to confirmation under the relevant state or federal arbitration law. These court powers are also reflected in the revisions to the UAA. The relationship between the arbitral forum and courts is explored in more detail in Chapter 18.

2.   Punitive or Exemplary Damages

Notes on arbitration law. As we will see in Chapter 18.C, the authority of arbitrators to entertain and to honor claims for punitive or exemplary damages under the broad provisions of standard arbitration procedures is well established under federal arbitration law and the law of most states. Thus, arbitrators have considered and on occasion awarded relief in the nature of "common law" punitive damages as well as exemplary damages pursuant to statutes like the Racketeer Influenced Corrupt Organizations Act. This in turn raises questions regarding the ability of courts to police punitive arbitral awards under limited standards for judicial vacatur of award. See Chapter 18.E.

Questions

16.   If you were drafting an arbitration provision in a commercial contract, would you favor or disfavor denying arbitrators the authority to award punitive and exemplary damages? Why or why not?

17.   Should parties be able to entirely avoid punitive or exemplary damages by contract? Because it is generally within the power of the parties to arbitration agreements to include or exclude particular claims or controversies as they see fit, isn't it possible to structure an arbitration provision that functions as a partial or complete predispute waiver of claims for punitive damages? One commentator suggests that remedy-stripping arbitration clauses may be limited as a practical matter because they raise preclusion problems. See Schwartz (2003). Could the parties agree to exclude an arbitral award of punitive damages after a dispute has arisen? What are the difficulties of securing such an agreement? See Stipanowich (1997).

3.   Final Offer Arbitration

Options exist for parties to create their own arbitration rules, and to limit the scope of arbitral remedies. One popular variant parties have adopted is "final offer arbitration," often termed "baseball arbitration" because of its importance in Major League Baseball salary dispute resolution. It is also used in commercial cases and can be adapted for other disputes. Final offer arbitration requires that each party submit its "final offer" to the arbitrator after making appropriate submissions on the merits of the dispute. The arbitrator then chooses the most fair and reasonable offer, considering all of the facts and arguments presented. The arbitrator is not permitted to compromise, to split the difference, or compose what he regards as a better or more just solution. He must choose one party's final offer. In contrast, with conventional arbitration, an arbitrator can select either party's position on some or all of the pending issues or adopt another approach (as, for example, where an arbitrator awards a measure of damages different from that requested). In final offer arbitration, the arbitrator's discretion is limited because the parties themselves create the only two possible awards.

A "final offer arbitration" procedure has been used in Major League Baseball salary arbitrations with great success for nearly 25 years and has become a familiar example of arbitration for baseball fans (Abrams, 1998). The hope in "final offer arbitration" is that the parties will partake in good faith negotiations to facilitate a reasonable settlement. The risk of a complete loss if the arbitrator chooses the other party's offer encourages both parties to engage in prearbitration negotiations and to produce final offers closer to the other party's final offer. "Under baseball's salary arbitration scheme, a neutral arbitrator selects either the final demand of the eligible player or the final offer of the employing [baseball team]. . . . A greedy player who sets his demand too high or a stingy club that makes an offer too low is likely to lose. . . . *Pennsylvania Environmental Defense Foundation (P.E.D.F.) v. Canon-McMillan School Dist.*, 152 F.3d 228, 239 (3d Cir. 1998) (Garth, J. dissenting), citing Abrams (1998).

Questions

18.   Consider the following conclusion:

"Baseball's salary arbitration saves time and money over conventional negotiations by providing structure to salary negotiations and imposing strict timing requirements for filing, submission of final offers, the hearing, and the arbitrator's decision. Because the arbitrator does not issue a written decision, further costs are eliminated." (Meth, 1998)

Do you tend to agree or disagree with this conclusion? Why?

19.   Can you think of a situation where you would use final offer arbitration? Why do you suppose it is not more widely used?

4.   *Bracketed Arbitration*

Other variants designed to encourage reasonableness and minimize exposure on awards include "bracketed (high-low)" and "incentive" arbitration. In bracketed (high-low) arbitration, parties agree in advance to limit the amount of recovery and loss by placing specific upper and lower limits on authority of the arbitrator to render a monetary award. (For example, "The arbitrator shall render a monetary award in favor of A that shall be no greater than $2,000,000 and no less than $1,000,000.") (*The ABCs of ADR: A Dispute Resolution Glossary*, 1995).

Questions

20.   When might you propose to opposing counsel that you agree to a "bracketed" arbitration award? How would you come up with an agreement regarding upper and lower limits for the award?

21.   Could you agree to a "bracketed" approach with the other party but not tell the arbitrator? Would you ever want to do so? Consider the following example: Parties A and B agree to abide by the monetary award of the arbitrator, but Party A will pay no more than $2,000,000 and no less than $1,000,000. They agree that if the arbitrator renders an award higher or lower than the bracketed amount, the award will be limited by the agreement of the parties. Thus, if the arbitrator renders an award of $1,200,000, Party A would pay that amount. If the arbitrator awards $3,000,000, Party A would pay $2,000,000. If the arbitrator awards $500,000, Party A would pay $1,000,000.

O.   Arbitration Awards

1.   *Forms of Award*

Traditionally, arbitration awards have tended to be issued without an accompanying rationale or explanation. Under this approach, an arbitrator in the case of Carmin, Inc. and SamCo., Inc. (Problem 5) might review papers and hold hearings over several days, and a few weeks later issue a single-sentence award:

> SamCo shall pay Carmin $125,000 in damages.
>
> /s/ Arbitrator

As Carmin's lawyer, you might be terribly disappointed in the amount of the award, reasoning that if the arbitrator ruled in Carmin's favor, damages so far below the amount claimed make no sense as a matter of contract law or in terms of fairness. SamCo's lawyer might also be upset because the award does not acknowledge its counterclaims. Nevertheless, both parties have little recourse. Even if courts were willing to scrutinize arbitral awards closely, the lack of explanation leaves little to scrutinize.

The AAA traditionally advised commercial arbitrators not to explain their awards because written reasoning gives parties possible grounds for appeal based on their dissatisfaction with the outcome, undermining the advantage of arbitration as a prompt and final method of dispute resolution. Writing a rationale may also take time and complicate the deliberation process, especially when there are three arbitrators. The process may also be more difficult for non-lawyer arbitrators.

If parties to a dispute agree that some statement of explanation is appropriate, however, it is their prerogative to so direct the arbitrators. Written awards explaining in detail the rationale behind an arbitrator's decision have been standard for many years in the areas of labor relations and international commercial arbitration. Today, commercial arbitration agreements in business contracts often call for arbitrators to reveal their reasoning. Under AAA Rules, the arbitrator(s) are advised to accommodate such a request, and the CPR Rules make written opinion the default option for arbitrators, unless the parties agree otherwise. While the drawbacks to written, reasoned awards mentioned above are valid, their benefits are becoming more apparent — especially in high-stakes cases. For one thing, obvious errors can be brought to the arbitrator's attention rapidly. Moreover, requiring arbitrators to write out their thought process can lead to a more complete analysis of the issues involved. Parties are more likely to feel that they were, if not "victorious," at least heard on the matter. While written opinions by arbitrators do not function as broad judicial precedent, they may in some cases provide insight into an arbitrator's leanings, experience, and qualifications. Of course, the outcome and reasoning in one arbitral decision might be limited by the factual circumstances and evidence presented, providing little indication of how that arbitrator would rule in the next situation, or with a different panel of arbitrators.

Although it is becoming more common for parties and administering organizations to require written opinions, lawyers are less likely to advise clients to seek written opinions in disputes where the stakes are smaller because parties usually will bear the expense of the additional time arbitrators devote to rendering more detailed written opinions. Written opinions may be most valuable where a novel issue is presented, where a case is quite complex or where significant amounts of money are at stake, or where there is a special need for the adjudicator's rationale — such as, for example, a dispute where an award may serve as a basis for damages in a separate adjudication involving a third party.

2. *Finality of Arbitration Awards*

To ensure the finality of arbitral awards, consistent with the agreement of the parties, while promoting fundamental fairness of process, the FAA and corresponding state arbitration statutes contemplate very limited avenues of appeal and forms of redress from arbitral awards. Judicial scrutiny is generally restricted to due process considerations. As a rule, the fact that a court disagrees with the outcome — that is, believes the arbitrator "got it wrong" — is not a ground for reversal. There is no provision authorizing vacatur of award for errors of law or fact, leading at least one court to suggest that the process under the FAA "ought not to be called review at all." *UHC Management Co. v. Computer Services Corp.*, 148 F.3d 992 (1998). Over time, however, federal and state courts have enunciated additional standards for review and vacatur of arbitration awards. These "non-statutory" grounds — "manifest disregard of the law," "irrationality," "arbitrariness and capriciousness," "public policy" — vary from jurisdiction to jurisdiction, but in one way or the other they all open the door, however slightly, to some judicial review or oversight of the subject matter or the merits of the case.

In recent years, a few lawyers have assisted in the drafting of contractual provisions for expanded judicial review of arbitrators' factual or legal determinations. Besides inspiring a fundamental legal debate resulting in conflicting federal and state court decisions, such arrangements raise a host of serious practical concerns. These and other issues associated with judicial review will be explored in Chapter 18.E.

3. *Private Appellate Processes*

In light of concerns regarding the lack of oversight of arbitration awards, some attorneys have counseled clients to opt for an appellate arbitration process. Some providers offer an optional appellate procedure within the arbitration process; the CPR Institute, for example, not only offers appellate rules, but also an appellate arbitration panel of former federal judges. The JAMS appellate procedure is adopted as a part of consensual arbitration procedures in a small percentage of filed cases, although it is seldom actually used. Those favoring private appeal may view it as a salutary alternative to judicial review, both in terms of cost- and time-saving, while providing meaningful oversight of the arbitral award. Some believe private procedures can alleviate the need to challenge an award in court, while enhancing confidence in the arbitration process. Others argue that appeal to a private panel may only add to the time and expense of finally resolving a dispute. Better, some say, to concentrate on the first arbitral proceeding and "getting it right the first time around."

Questions

22.   Suppose your business client, Micron, is in the process of forming
      a contract with Dall Computers to install Micron 2005 software in
      every computer Dall makes. Micron is inclined to include an arbi-
      tration provision in the contract, but is concerned about the risk of
      an extreme or irrational award in arbitration. This contract is of
      critical importance to Micron's business and there could well be a
      dispute with "bet-the-company" stakes. Advise Micron regarding
      the pros and cons of each of the following options:

      a.   Employ a panel of three arbitrators for disputes involving
           larger stakes;
      b.   Direct the arbitrators to follow certain legal standards in
           reaching a decision;
      c.   Direct the arbitrators to provide a written rationale for their
           award;
      d.   Agree that the parties will attempt to establish a range (a mini-
           mum and a maximum) for the arbitrators' award;
      e.   Agree that the arbitrators will not be empowered to consider
           claims for punitive or exemplary damages, or to make such
           awards;
      f.   Agree to expanded judicial review of arbitration awards;
      g.   Agree to appellate arbitration.

P.   Arbitration in Multistep Agreements

In seeking to fulfill client goals and priorities through effective conflict management, arbitration should not be considered in isolation. Binding arbitration is often a favorable alternative to the litigation process, but it is ill suited
to be the primary process option for serving the day-to-day needs of businesses. Rather, the logical, normal first step is negotiation, followed in many
commercial dispute resolution procedures by mediation. Although opinions
may vary regarding the desirability of a contractual provision for mediation,
the option should normally be considered (Stipanowich, 2010).

     Once the decision is made to incorporate multiple steps or stages, how-
ever, a good deal of care must be given to the practical efficacy of the provisions to be employed. Careless drafting can result in confusion and
unintended consequences — including the intervention of a court.

Q.   When an Arbitrator Wears Multiple Hats

1.   Formats in Which Neutrals "Change Hats"

Disputing parties have experimented with formats in which a single person plays more than one neutral role in a dispute. Typically the neutral plays these roles in succession, but in some formats the roles are mixed. In a common format known as "Med-Arb," a single individual acts as mediator and, if the negotiations fail to achieve settlement, assumes the role of arbitrator. The following account describes an early, notable example of how appointed arbitrators "changed hats" to help craft a remarkable resolution to a complex, high-profile intellectual property dispute.

❖ **Francis Flaherty,** Neutrals Deployed Several Kinds of ADR to Solve IBM-Fujitsu Copyright Dispute

5 Alternatives 187 (November 1987)

During the late 1970s and early 1980s, a dispute arose between IBM and Fujitsu over software copyright. Prior to 1980, the year that Congress passed the Computer Software Act, few thought that copyright protection extended to this intellectual property. The right to protection confirmed, IBM lodged a formal complaint against Fujitsu in October 1982, necessitating a settlement agreement between the companies that took eight months to negotiate. Unfortunately, the 1983 accord was poorly drafted and collapsed not long after its adoption.

IBM and Fujitsu continued to negotiate for a solution to the dispute, but no resolution was forthcoming. The parties at last turned to the ADR clause in the 1983 accord, which mandated a two-part ADR procedure: negotiation and arbitration. Basically, the parties agreed to attempt negotiation between themselves and, should that fail to resolve the issue in 60 days, then submit the dispute to binding arbitration. Each side nominated an arbitrator — IBM choosing retired railroad executive and computer expert John Jones and Fujitsu nominating Stanford Law Professor Robert Mnookin. A third arbitrator, Donald A. MacDonald, was nominated by these two.

Although the neutrals began the case in conventional arbitration fashion, they soon resolved to conduct a mini-trial. [The mini-trial is a process in which counsel for each party makes an abbreviated "best case" presentation before senior executives of both parties and a neutral; thereafter the executives seek to reach a negotiated resolution and, if necessary, call upon the neutral for an opinion or for other assistance.] Arbitrators *and* executives from both parties listened to arguments from both sides relating to Fujitsu's alleged violation of IBM's rights under the 1983 agreement, following the recitations with negotiations. The mini-trial took place between June and July 1986; it was unsuccessful.

At this point in time, MacDonald resigned, leaving Jones and Mnookin to resolve the case. They decided to engage the parties in mediation, with themselves acting as mediators. Unlike the mini-trial, the mediation attempt was successful at reaching a solution to the dispute. Two documents resulted from the mediation strategy, the "1986 Agreement," settling all IBM's intellectual property claims with respect to Fujitsu programs, and the "Washington Agreement," a framework for the resolution of all other issues. This agreement provided the foundation for the Order detailing the neutrals' two-fold solution to the dispute.

First, the neutrals called for Fujitsu to pay a sum for the past and future use of an agreed-upon list of software items. The second part of the solution, a "Secured Facility Regime," dictates a process by which each of the two companies may, under elaborate safeguards and for a fee, observe the software of the other and make use of the technology in their own products. This agreement makes use of another ADR approach: preventative law. Professor Mnookin summarized the benefits of this scheme:

> "The Secured Facility regime provides a unique advantage as a means of settling complicated issues in evolving technological and legal fields. In the past, IBM could never know exactly how Fujitsu was using IBM programming material. In order to determine if some violation of its rights may have occurred, IBM had to wait until after the public release of a Fujitsu program and then conduct an elaborate technical examination of the program. Then, if it chose to pursue a claim, it was extremely expensive and time-consuming.
>
> "Meanwhile, of course, the Fujitsu program at issue was already in the marketplace. Even the threat that IBM might at some point pursue a claim would create a potential problem for both Fujitsu and for the Fujitsu customers using a new Fujitsu program.
>
> "The Secured Facility exposes and resolves disagreements before public release of software. The determination made in the facility as to what goes on the survey sheet is the final word on what material of one company can be used by the other company. Once that sheet leaves the facility, the issue is settled. IBM can be assured that only the material allowed by the instructions is being shared. Fujitsu can be assured that IBM will not make a claim with respect to the use of that material at some date in the future. And customers who license Fujitsu operating system software can be assured that no future controversy will disrupt their use of these programs."

Mini-trial, arbitration, mediation, and preventative law were not the only ADR approaches utilized by the neutrals. They described in their award a Secured Facility supervisor, "an experienced, unbiased, and qualified person or firm ... with relevant programming experience," to serve as an expert factfinder under the direction of the neutrals. The neutrals themselves were to serve as monitors or "special masters," overseeing the resolution of the dispute and aiding the parties in resolving further disputes.

2.   "Med-Arb"

Although ADR institutions and commentators have expressed concerns about neutrals wearing "multiple hats," the reality is that a significant percentage of active arbitrators and mediators sometimes end up serving roles very different from the one to which they were initially appointed. Some years ago a group of 128 commercial and employment mediators were queried about how frequently they end up changing hats. They responded as follows:

When initially appointed as a mediator, I have arbitrated issues at the request of the parties when mediation failed resolve them:

Always	Often	About half the time	Occasionally	Never
1	3	0	45	78

I have mediated issues at the request of the parties even though I was initially appointed as arbitrator:

Always	Often	About half the time	Occasionally	Never
1	3	3	46	69

Attorneys representing clients in mediation or arbitration are likely to be confronted with the option of employing a neutral in multiple roles, either as a matter of initial planning or midway through the course of an ADR process. Therefore, it is critical to understand relevant practical, legal, and ethical concerns. See Stipanowich (2001).

Some neutrals regularly employ Med-Arb — that is, a stepped process in which a single person serves as mediator and, failing agreement through that process, changes roles and proceeds to arbitrate the dispute; some institutional sponsors of ADR are now offering Med-Arb procedures. Advocates of such approaches argue that having a single neutral serve in both roles avoids the necessity of having to educate two separate neutrals, saving time and money. They also reason that if the parties are aware that their mediator will render a final and binding decision if disputes are not settled, they may be encouraged to resolve the issues in mediation.

Despite the arguments put forward in favor of Med-Arb, many generally disfavor a mixing of such roles, for the following reasons:

First, it is argued that the roles of mediator and arbitrator are fundamentally incompatible: The arbitrator's interaction with the parties is confined to adversary hearings in which parties present evidence and contest opposing evidence, while mediation usually involves extensive confidential ex parte communications with individual parties. Parties who know their mediator will decide should mediation fail may be less candid in communicating with the mediator, undermining a primary goal of the mediation process. Moreover, there is always the possibility that the mediator-turned-arbitrator's view of the issues has been affected by information imparted confidentially in ex parte discussions — information that may not be directly relevant to the issues contested in arbitration, and never subjected to cross-examination or rebuttal. Another concern is that the "big stick" wielded by a mediator-arbitrator will undermine party self-determination and prevent a negotiated settlement from expressing the free will of the parties — especially if the intervener "telegraphs" her own views of the issues in dispute. Finally, many mediators have little or no experience conducting an arbitration hearing, and may not be competent to take on the other role or to address the foregoing concerns. In any event, parties who want a neutral to serve in mixed roles must be very clear about the resolution of these issues and should address pertinent waiver issues (such as parties' waiver of the right to challenge any resulting arbitration award on grounds of ex parte contact). Otherwise, the arrangement may set the stage for a motion to disqualify an arbitrator or vacate a resulting arbitration award.

The problem is exemplified by *Township of Aberdeen v. Patrolmen's Benevolent Ass'n*, 669 A.2d 291 (N.J. S. Ct., App. Div. 1996), a decision under New Jersey law regarding a Med/Arb arrangement in a public employment contract. When negotiations over a new collective bargaining agreement between the township and the police officers' union reached an impasse, the union petitioned for the initiation of arbitration under the state's Compulsory Interest Arbitration Act. Prior to the start of hearings, the parties agreed to have the arbitrator attempt to mediate the dispute. When mediated settlement negotiations fell apart, the case went to arbitration. The arbitrator rendered an award in favor of the union, largely on the basis of the township's shifting positions during mediation. Although the interest arbitration statute and implementing regulations permitted Med-Arb, the court struck down the award on the basis that the arbitrator had improperly relied on information gained during the course of mediation and not presented in the arbitration hearing. The court reasoned that "parties should feel free to negotiate without fear that what they say and do will later be used against them," and that "[m]ediation would be a hollow practice if the parties' negotiating tactics could be used against them by the arbitrator in rendering the final decision." For the same reason that "it would be unthinkable for a trial court to base its decision on information disclosed in pretrial settlement negotiations," mediated negotiations preceding arbitration should be protected.

With these concerns in mind, consider your approach to the following scenarios based on real cases.

Questions

23. ExGen Corporation, a major multinational corporation, filed suit in federal court against Sosumi, Inc., a supplier of components for ExGen's new manufacturing process, alleging $8 million in damages resulting from delays in the delivery of components. Liability

was not contested, but there was a dispute as to damages. When discovery was nearly concluded and the parties were on the verge of going to trial, they were persuaded by the court to mediate the disputes.

You are selected to be the mediator. After two lengthy days of bargaining, including extensive ex parte discussions with both parties, you have engendered some movement on both sides. The parties are still about $1.8 million apart — ExGen demands about $4.8 million and Sosumi is offering $3.0 million. There does not appear to be an opportunity for avoiding impasse by expanding the pie through collateral business arrangements, and so on.

a.   Faced with the possibility that there will be no settlement, you are considering a recommendation to the parties to consider submitting the dispute to an abbreviated "baseball arbitration" process in which the arbitrator picks between the final numbers. How should you handle this situation?

b.   Suppose you go ahead and invite the parties to discuss whether or not to use this process and jointly advise you as to their mutual decision. You are somewhat surprised when the parties' attorneys notify you that they have agreed to such a process, and want *you* to be the arbitrator. What will you do?

c.   What if the parties also tell you that after discussing the matter, they want you to decide the matter without a hearing, but on the basis of memoranda that each party will submit to you in confidence?

24.   Assume you have resolved some but not all the issues in a complex commercial dispute between ExGen and Sosumi. The parties indicate that they desire to arbitrate, but have reached no agreement on the nature of the agreement or the selection of arbitrators. Can you help design an arbitration process?

25.   You are designated as chair of a panel of arbitrators in a significant commercial case involving ACME Corporation and Green Solutions. During a break in the initial prehearing conference with the parties, all three arbitrators share the sense that the circumstances might lend themselves to mediated negotiation.

a.   Should you raise the issue with the parties? If so, how?

b.   What if the parties discuss the matter and ask that you mediate the dispute?

26.   You have been appointed to arbitrate various issues associated with a corporate "divorce." The parties have agreed that the proceeding will be bifurcated. The initial series of sessions will address the valuation of assets; after the rendition of the initial partial award, a second set of sessions will consider allegations of breach of contract, fraud, and so forth, among the parties. After several

> sessions, the parties jointly inform you that they have discussed settlement of the valuation issue and believe it would be productive to mediate. Given your familiarity with the issues and their comfort with you as a neutral, they seek your participation as mediator. What will you do?
>
> 27. Would you consider incorporating a Med-Arb arrangement in a contractual dispute resolution provision? If so, what if any provisions would you employ to address concerns expressed above?

3. "Arb-Med"

Although not as popular as Med-Arb, another process involves neutrals acting as arbitrators and then switching to the mediator's hat. In "Arb-Med," a neutral initially acts as sole arbitrator, or as a member of an arbitration panel, avoiding all ex parte contact with the parties during hearings, deliberations, and rendition of a final award. Once the award is signed by the arbitrator(s), it is sealed pending mediation of the dispute. The arbitrator-turned-mediator is free to engage in ex parte discussions with the parties and to help them settle the case, but may not disclose the contents of the award. The parties, meanwhile, know that the award will be published in the event mediation fails to produce a settlement.

> Questions
>
> 28. Does Arb-Med avoid any of the practical, legal, and ethical issues raised by Med-Arb?
> 29. Does it lack any of the potential advantages of Med-Arb?

4. The Need for Precision in Structuring Neutral Roles

Efforts to structure a suitable, workable, and enforceable ADR agreement are sometimes undermined by a lack of precision. Such an issue may be particularly acute when a single individual is assigned multiple roles, or where the neutral's role may be characterized in more than one way.

These concerns are illustrated by *Ex parte Industrial Technologies*, 707 So. 2d 234 (Ala. 1997), a case in which a bank filed suit on a promissory note, and the defendants counterclaimed for conversion of certain equipment taken by the bank during collection efforts. Prior to trial, the parties agreed to refer the matter to out-of-court process (described as "mediation or arbitration") with a retired circuit judge, Snodgrass, as "mediator/arbitrator." After a period of settlement negotiations supervised by the latter, the parties announced to Snodgrass their "stipulation of agreement" acknowledging the conversion of the equipment, calling for appraisers to determine fair market value of the detained property, and for Snodgrass to determine the interest factor to be used in computing the rental value of the property during the detention period.

Snodgrass subsequently issued an "order" directing the bank to pay both rental value during the detention and the value of the equipment at the time of detention, less salvage value at the time of return. The defendants/counterclaimants sought to enforce the outcome, which they termed a "binding arbitration order," but the bank responded that the proceeding was merely mediation without binding results. The Alabama Supreme Court determined that both the parties' agreement and the subsequent process were fatally flawed. First of all, it was impossible to determine the precise character of the process agreed to by the parties, but rather only that the parties apparently intended for the judge to determine damages based on a mutually agreeable formula. Unfortunately, the court concluded, there was never a meeting of the minds as to whether Snodgrass was empowered to award damages over and above the rental value. While the lack of precision in tailoring the original ADR agreement might have been overcome by the participants during the subsequent negotiation and drafting of the "stipulation of agreement," they merely exacerbated their earlier mistakes.

Question

30.   The borrower in the *Snodgrass* case has approached you. He/she wants to know how in the future it should draft an ADR clause so as to avoid the problems identified by the court. What suggestions can you offer?

CHAPTER

18

The Legal Framework Supporting Arbitration

A. Introduction: Historical Shifts in Judicial and Legislative Support for Arbitration

As discussed in Chapter 16, arbitration has been a popular dispute resolution choice throughout history in many cultures. But its use has waxed and waned over time in the United States, reflecting power struggles between advocates of arbitration and those who were suspicious of its potential to supplant court adjudication and interfere with the law governing contractual relations. On the one hand, English and American colonial courts guarded their power "jealously" and were quite hostile to arbitration agreements, readily allowing parties to evade their agreements to arbitrate or, if they had to proceed to arbitration, get unsatisfactory awards revoked. On the other hand, merchants favored arbitration because they could select their own decision makers and rules. At the behest of increasingly powerful business interests, state legislatures actively attempted to reverse judicial hostility and encourage arbitration in the twentieth century. In 1925 Congress enacted the Federal Arbitration Act (FAA) — a "modern" arbitration statute in the sense that it provided for the specific enforcement of predispute arbitration provisions in contracts. Business-to-business disputes were a most common subject of arbitration in the decades following enactment of the FAA; after World War II, arbitration became an increasingly popular method of resolving labor disputes, an arena for which Congress had developed a specified framework for arbitration to prevent violence, delayed resolution of problems, and the resultant disruption of business.

Until the 1980s, however, the use of arbitration was limited by judicial decisions refusing to allow statute-based claims to be arbitrated. Judges were suspicious that arbitration would be too different from court adjudication and arbitrators less willing to follow or capable of following the law. They recalled, perhaps, that Aristotle once explained that "the arbitrator sees equity, the juror the law; indeed that is why an arbitrator is found — that equity might prevail" (Stipanowich, 2001). Moreover, the Supreme Court viewed public judgments rendered by federal trial courts as desirable mechanisms of social regulation on statutory matters, emphasizing their effect in shaping the conduct of nonparties. Moreover, judges were skeptical that parties had knowingly and voluntarily waived their rights to the judicial forum for statutory claims like those under federal securities laws. See, e.g., *Wilko v. Swan*, 346 U.S. 427 (1953); see also Resnik (1995).

During the 1980s, however, the Supreme Court reinterpreted congressional intent, finding that the FAA created a broad national policy favoring arbitration when parties choose it. In a number of cases, the Court emphasized that, "[b]y agreeing to arbitrate a statutory claim, a party does not forgo the substantive rights afforded by the statute; it only submits to their resolution in an arbitral, rather than judicial, forum." *Mitsubishi Motors Corp. v. Solar Chrysler-Plymouth, Inc.*, 473 U.S. 614, 628 (1985). The Court reasoned that the arbitral forum provided distinct advantages for many parties: in the words of the Court, "[Arbitration] trades the procedures and opportunity for review of the courtroom for the simplicity, informality, and expedition of arbitration."

Following the Supreme Court's lead, many other federal and state courts have been highly respectful of arbitration as a dispute resolution option, even for statutory claims founded on alleged employment discrimination, consumer fraud, or securities law violations. Although fairness concerns surrounding the use of predispute arbitration agreements in standardized consumer and employment contracts have generated great controversy, as discussed in Chapter 19, most courts have heartily endorsed arbitration as a general alternative to litigation of civil disputes; they have also shown great deference to arbitrators and their decisions (awards). One federal judge's remarks about why courts should welcome arbitration rather than be suspicious of it typified the tone and sentiments of many American jurists at the close of the twentieth century:

> Access to the courts now is neither affordable nor expeditious. In many federal district courts and state courts, years pass before an aggrieved party can even have the proverbial day in court. In the meantime, the process grinds along, inflicting staggering legal expenses on the parties. Except for the very rich (and very poor, in some circumstances), we have simply priced the court system beyond the reach of most citizens, because the cost of litigation far exceeds the value of the decision itself. Indeed, even the most resourceful parties often decline to pursue legal rights, simply because quickly accepting or paying a sum of money in settlement of any claim often costs far less than determining in court the merit of that claim. In short, our current legal system for resolving disputes is losing the respect of the public and is rapidly approaching failure.

Bright v. Norshipco & Norfolk Shipbuilding & Drydock Corp., 951 F. Supp. 95, 98 (E.D. Va. 1997). See also *Gilmer v. Interstate/Johnson Lane Corp.*, 500 U.S. 20 (1991).

This chapter traces the evolution and expansion of arbitration under court decisions during the past three decades. It details the legal framework developed by courts as they interpret federal and state statutes governing arbitration. In general, modern courts, relying in large part on the FAA, have developed a legal framework that respects and undergirds the role of arbitrators as decision makers and honors the apparent mutual intent of parties to use arbitration rather than the courts. These decisions also tend to give effect to important arbitration attributes, including efficiency and finality. (Not until Chapter 19 do we directly address the fairness concerns that have caused courts, legislatures, and other groups to seek to limit the use of arbitration clauses in consumer and employment contracts and other "adhesion contract" settings.)

B.   Elements of Modern Arbitration Law

1.   *The Federal Arbitration Act*

Common law developed in England and early colonial practice in the United States supplied two doctrines that courts used frequently to undermine parties' agreements to arbitrate: revocation and unenforceability. Although arbitration has been used throughout American history (Abraham Lincoln occasionally acted as an arbitrator or advocate in arbitration on the Illinois frontier in the 1840s and 1850s), courts might, for example, allow a party to revoke its earlier consent to arbitration once a dispute arose. To counter these doctrines when parties had clearly agreed to arbitration, Congress in the FAA instructed judges to treat written agreements to arbitrate like other valid contracts — and to provide for their specific enforcement. Although this bare-bones act is short and straightforward, it has become a powerful tool to support agreements to arbitrate, allowing courts to compel parties to proceed with arbitration and stay (i.e., put on hold) related litigation, enforce subpoenas issued by arbitrators, and enforce arbitration awards. After Congress adopted the FAA, most states also adopted statutes giving courts specific authority to support arbitration agreements and enforce arbitral awards. Because the Supreme Court has construed the FAA so broadly in recent decades, however, the role of state arbitration statutes has been minimized to some extent in comparison to the role of the FAA. This will become clear as you read Section C.5, which explains how the law regarding enforcement of arbitration agreements under the FAA *preempts* contrary state law. Today, judicial decisions under the FAA make agreements to arbitrate fully enforceable in both federal and state courts. As the Second Circuit recently observed, "it is difficult to overstate the strong federal policy in favor of arbitration, and it is a policy we 'have often and emphatically applied.'" *Arciniaga v. Gen. Motors Corp.*, 460 F.3d 231, 234 (2d Cir. 2006) (*quoting Leadertex, Inc. v. Morganton Dyeing & Finishing Corp.*, 67 F.3d 20, 25 (2d Cir. 1995)). These policies are pragmatically reinforced by commensurate restrictions on the role of courts in the management and disposition of issues covered by arbitration agreements.

The FAA is relatively brief, and it's worth reading in its entirety. The following road map examines its major provisions and illustrates the different ways courts are called on to enforce and facilitate arbitration agreements and awards. Courts must assist parties by enforcing agreements to arbitrate, support the arbitrators in exercising the powers granted to them by Congress and the parties' agreements, and enforce duly issued arbitration awards.

❖ A Quick Tour of the Federal Arbitration Act

- **Section 1** provides that the FAA applies to:
  . . . all contracts affecting commerce (as well as certain other contracts),
  . . . but NOT to employment contracts for certain categories of workers engaged in interstate commerce.

The Supreme Court has broadly construed "commerce" — or, to be more explicit, "interstate commerce" — to include most economic transactions in our modern national (and global) economy. For this reason it is not at all difficult to find some interstate elements in a transaction, and therefore a predicate for the application of the FAA. Several decisions exploring the breadth of this provision are included in Section C.5 below. *See, e.g., Citizens Bank v. Alafabco, Inc.*, 123 S. Ct. 2037 (2003); *Allied-Bruce Terminix Companies v. Dobson*, 513 U.S. 265 (1995).

In *Circuit City Stores v. Adams*, 532 U.S. 105 (2001), the Court held that Section 1 exempts from the FAA only employment contracts of transportation workers. The FAA therefore applies to employees generally, even if their work involves interstate commerce. Thus, the FAA has been construed to provide a broad umbrella for enforcement of arbitration agreements.

- **Section 2** of the FAA states that written contracts to arbitrate are:
  . . . valid, irrevocable, and enforceable
  . . . except on "such grounds as exist at law or in equity for the revocation of any contract."

This section expressly counters the common law's hostility toward arbitration, reversing the court precedents making predispute arbitration agreements unenforceable and putting arbitration contracts on equal footing with other types of contracts. It also makes clear that parties can raise standard state law contract defenses to challenge an arbitration clause. Courts must enforce arbitration agreements unless a valid defense is raised to the arbitration clause. We will canvas some of the most commonly raised defenses in Chapter 19.D.

- **Section 3** of the FAA provides that if one party to an arbitration contract sues, the court *shall*, upon a finding that there is a valid, applicable arbitration agreement, stay the trial [i.e., court proceedings on the same controversy] until the arbitration is completed.

This language has been broadly construed so that courts are required to *stay*, or stop, all court proceedings, including pretrial phases, until arbitration proceedings are concluded. Courts also have been deemed to have discretion to stay other, non-arbitrable disputes in the same court proceeding. FAA thus tries to avoid duplicative proceedings and the potentially conflicting outcomes that might occur if arbitrators and courts both conducted proceedings on the same matter simultaneously.

- **Section 4** provides that if a party refuses to arbitrate, the opposing side can sue in federal court for an order to compel the party to participate in arbitration. **Section 6** states that any application to compel arbitration shall be heard as a motion, and the court shall proceed summarily to determine whether a written agreement to arbitrate affecting commerce exists.

This section attempts to ensure expeditious resolution of the question by mandating that courts issue orders to compel arbitration if an agreement to arbitrate is present. Its provisions make it relatively easy for a lawyer to go to federal or state court, file a petition, and get a fairly speedy resolution of the issue, backed by the contempt power of the court.

To underscore the presumption in favor of courts not interfering with the progress of arbitration if any arbitration agreement is found, the FAA provides that appellate courts can conduct interlocutory review of certain anti-arbitration rulings by a trial court (e.g., orders enjoining or stopping arbitration proceedings). Such interlocutory review is extremely rare; appellate courts generally try not to interfere with ongoing trial court proceedings and parties must normally await a final judgment before appealing. Consistent with this view the FAA declares that appellate courts are not allowed to review orders of trial courts *upholding* arbitration (e.g., orders directing parties to arbitrate or staying related litigation) on an interlocutory basis. The latter underscores the idea that courts should strive hard to avoid interfering with arbitral proceedings — another important policy that underpins case law in this chapter.

Sections 2, 3, and 4 will be prominently featured in the cases and materials in Section C below.

- **Section 5** of the FAA provides that if the parties fail to agree on an arbitrator, the court may appoint one.

The court's power to appoint an arbitrator is rarely exercised, as parties usually agree to other methods for selecting arbitrators and overcoming impasse or unforeseen difficulties. As explained in Chapter 17, many parties agree to employ arbitration procedures that include rules for selecting arbitrators, including default mechanisms if one or both parties fail to cooperate. Other parties incorporate their own ad hoc procedures for selection. Nevertheless, Section 5 is an important fallback option for a party in those cases where a party attempts to evade or slow arbitration proceedings by refusing to cooperate in selecting arbitrators and there is no specified default mechanism, or where an agreed method for appointing arbitrators fails for some other reason. We touch briefly on this topic in Section D below.

- **Section 7** recognizes the power of arbitrators to issue "summonses" (subpoenas) for witnesses to appear before them and to bring material evidence. If a witness refuses, a court may compel attendance in accordance with the subpoena or hold the person in contempt of court.

Arbitrators, like courts, have the ability to summon (or subpoena) individuals (including nonparties) to provide critical evidence in arbitral proceedings. This power, like the subpoena power trial courts possess under the Federal Rules of Civil Procedure and state court counterparts, make arbitration and litigation good alternatives to negotiation and mediation when a party is dependent on securing material evidence from the opposing party or nonparty witnesses to prove its claims. Curiously, the language of the FAA speaks of witnesses coming before the arbitrator(s), and, moreover, makes no reference to subpoenas for prehearing discovery. Therefore, as discussed in Section D.2 below, some courts have interpreted the FAA to provide only for the enforcement of subpoenas to witnesses to attend hearings, and not to empower courts to enforce so-called "discovery subpoenas."

- **Section 9** provides that a victorious party in arbitration may petition a court to enter the arbitration award as a court judgment, if the parties have provided for this option in their agreement. If such a petition is filed within a year of the award being issued, the court *must* grant judgment unless it modifies or vacates the award (on the limited grounds described in Sections 10-11 of the FAA). Once a party secures a court judgment, it can execute on that judgment just as if it had won a victory in court.

While most students do not learn much about enforcing judgments during law school, this provision can make a great deal of practical difference. With a negotiated settlement or mediation agreement, enforcing compliance is sometimes difficult. On the other hand, a party who secures an arbitral award and has it entered as a judgment has access to the court's authority and processes for enforcement, including garnishing of wages, post-judgment discovery of assets, and so on. Thus, although most arbitration clauses are brief, it is common to include language providing for entry of judgment in court of any arbitral award rendered. (Indeed, as we discussed in Chapter 17, it is highly advisable to provide for court enforcement of arbitration awards in an agreement to arbitrate to avoid any question about the enforceability of an award.)

- Finally, **Section 10** of the FAA provides narrow grounds for judicial vacatur (or setting aside) of arbitral awards.

As you might imagine, the grounds for vacating or setting aside an arbitration award are of great interest to lawyers. In Section E we explore the statutory grounds for vacatur in some detail. For now, the main thing to keep in mind is that judicial review of arbitral rulings and awards is *extremely limited*, buttressing arbitration as a final, efficient, cost-effective dispute resolution option. However, the picture is complicated by the fact that some courts have appeared to enunciate additional grounds for judicial review of awards. Moreover, some parties have attempted to expand judicial scrutiny of awards by contract — with mixed, and sometimes unfortunate, results.

To sum up, the FAA is aimed at regulating the interface between the private forum of arbitration and the courts, with primary emphasis on the judicial enforcement of agreements to arbitrate and of resulting arbitration awards. It promotes the autonomy of parties by enforcing their agreements to arbitrate. It also serves channeling, evidentiary, and cautionary functions by judicially enforcing only those agreements evidenced by a writing or record, and against which no valid defense can be asserted. Finally, it establishes supplementary or default terms for different aspects of arbitration processes.

2.   *State Arbitration Laws — Another "Layer" of Arbitration Law*

It is not enough for lawyers to be familiar with the FAA; they must also be aware of analogous arbitration statutes passed by the legislatures of U.S. states and territories. Although the FAA usually governs arbitration-related procedures in federal courts and also governs some "arbitrability" issues in state court proceedings, it does not completely preempt the application of state law, as we will see in Section C.5. Of course, in most situations it will not matter which body of law is applicable, for the result will be the same. There are, however, important exceptions.

Two leading commercial states, New York and California, have unique arbitration statutes. N.Y. CPLR § 7501 et seq (West 1998); Cal. Civ. Proc. Code §§ 1280-1294.2 (West 2007). The overwhelming majority of states, however, have adopted some version of the Uniform Arbitration Act, which was originally approved by the National Conference of Commissioners on Uniform State Laws (NCCUSL) in 1955. Although the original UAA was a bare-bones statute like the FAA, recent revisions to that uniform law have produced a much lengthier, more detailed, and more prescriptive statutory framework for arbitration (RUAA). These include a number of provisions setting forth default procedural elements — some of which are non-waivable by parties. At least a dozen states have thus far adopted the RUAA, which is discussed in Chapter 19.F. Another very detailed statute is the California Arbitration Act, which among other things contains very specific disclosure requirements as "ethical standards" for arbitrators.

Questions

1.   Can you list at least five functions performed by the FAA?
2.   Take a look at the RUAA and compare it to the FAA in terms of the overall length, number of sections, and the subjects covered. What are some of the key differences? As you read the rest of this chapter, you may want to look back to see how the RUAA addresses many of the issues covered. See *www.law.upenn.edu/bll/ulc/uarba/arbitrat1213.htm*.

3.   What Is "Arbitration" for the Purposes of Applying Federal or State Law?

What is "arbitration"? Curiously, neither the FAA nor state statutes define the term! Therefore it is up to courts to reach their own conclusions about the applicability of arbitration law to different kinds of dispute resolution agreements.

The fulfillment of parties' intent as expressed in their arbitration agreement is the dominant theme of American arbitration (Rau, 2005). Arbitration law gives parties a lot of flexibility to structure processes as they see fit. The principle of freedom to choose among procedural options has resulted in a very rich and diverse array of arbitration procedures. Arbitration law views legal enforcement within broad bounds of agreements about the nature and scope of arbitration, the precise breadth of the arbitrator's jurisdiction/authority, the selection of the tribunal, the character of the hearing, and pre-and post-hearing procedure. Additional flexibility inheres in the ability of parties to agree to modify or unilaterally waive elements of an agreed-upon process, even to the extent of forgoing participation in a hearing. Parties may even agree to have an arbitrator enter the arbitral equivalent of a consent order — an award based on terms of settlement crafted by the parties.

A Tenth Circuit panel went so far as to say that "[p]arties need not establish quasi-judicial proceedings resolving their disputes to gain the protections of the FAA, but may choose from a broad range of procedures and tailor arbitration to suit their peculiar circumstances." *Salt Lake Tribune Publ'g Co. v. Mgmt. Planning, Inc.*, 390 F.3d 684, 690 (10th Cir. 2004). This however, begs the essential question: What, for the purposes of arbitration law, is "arbitration"? Put another way, when does arbitration law apply?

A determination that a particular dispute resolution procedure is not "arbitration" means that a number of questions, including the ability of courts to require participation in the process, to facilitate its implementation, or to enforce its results, must be decided on grounds other than arbitration law. These may be questions of first impression for courts, as may be questions about the confidentiality of related communications, the immunity of the third party interveners or "neutrals" from legal process and their obligation to make disclosures about potential conflicts of interest. "When one of these powers or duties is important," in the words of Judge Easterbrook, "the choice between 'arbitration' and other forms of private dispute resolution matters." *Omni Tech Corp. v. MPC Solutions Sales, LLC*, 432 F.3d 797, 799 (7th Cir. 2005). Some courts, moreover, have concluded that if a procedure is not "arbitration," there is no basis for judicial enforcement.

So what kinds of dispute resolution agreements are covered by arbitration law? There are certainly strong clues in the overall form and content of the statutes. Viewed in full, both the FAA and the UAA appear to contemplate a process in which disputes are submitted to a hearing before a third party, who renders a binding decision that fully and finally addresses the disputes presented. Moreover, standards for vacatur of arbitral decisions, or awards, envision some form of hearing before an impartial tribunal, as do provisions authorizing the issuance of summonses or subpoenas. From these indicators, reinforced by long custom and practice, some courts have identified at least four "signifying elements" of procedures that, when framed in an agreement, fall within the scope of arbitration law: (a) a process to settle disputes between parties; (b) a neutral third party; (c) an opportunity for the parties to be heard; and (d) a final, binding decision, or award, by the third party after the hearing. See, e.g., *Fit Tech, Inc. v. Bally Total Fitness Holding Corp.*, 374 F.3d 1, 7 (1st Cir. 2004). These elements denote what we will refer to as *"classic" arbitration* for the purposes of comparison.

Some federal and state courts, however, have applied arbitration law to agreed procedures that in one way or another fail to conform to the "classic" model, including processes in which there is no legally enforceable final award or no hearing. These determinations are often made without explanation or on the basis of questionable, vague, and/or unreliable tests.

Given what has been characterized as the irresistible "gravitational force" of arbitration law — a body of well-established precedent according legitimacy, strong protection, and expedited enforcement to arrangements for resolving conflict — it is no wonder that many courts have swept aside "definitional niceties" and used arbitration law as a convenient hook for enforcement of other kinds of dispute resolution agreements — including mediation and non-binding arbitration. Indeed, at least one thoughtful scholar forcefully argues that the strong policies supporting party autonomy require courts to apply arbitration law very liberally, affording breathing room for the evolution of various forms of private ordering. (Rau, 2005). But there are counterarguments supporting a more restrained application of arbitration law and the promotion of appropriate alternative grounds for the enforcement of non-binding arbitration, mediation, and other alternatives to "classic" arbitration (Stipanowich, 2007).

Questions

3. Suppose your client enters into a contract that includes a provision requiring the parties to submit disputes to mediation before filing suit. If one party files suit without trying to mediate, should the other party be able to file for a judicial stay of litigation pending mediation under the FAA? See, e.g., *Advanced Bodycare Solutions, LLC v. Thione Int'l, Inc.,* 524 F.3d 1235 (11th Cir. 2008).
4. Would your answer be different if the contract called for the parties to enter into non-binding arbitration — that is, arbitration culminating in a non-binding, advisory award — before suit? See, e.g., *AMF, Inc. v. Brunswick Corp.,* 621 F.Supp. 456, 460 (E.D.N.Y.1985).

C.   Arbitrability

The first and most prominent function of the FAA and other arbitration statutes is to require courts to specifically enforce agreements to arbitrate. For example, the FAA calls upon U.S. courts to enforce written agreements to arbitrate unless they are presented with "grounds as exist at law or in equity for the revocation of any contract." If a particular dispute is within the scope of an enforceable arbitration agreement, courts have authority to stay pending litigation on the same issues and grant a motion to compel arbitration proceedings. Threshold jurisdictional questions — (a) whether there was an enforceable agreement to arbitrate and (b) what topics the agreement covers — are termed "arbitrability" issues.

Given the clarity and breadth of many standard contractual arbitration provisions in use today, "arbitrability" questions (Have the parties agreed to arbitrate? Does the agreement cover the issues in dispute?) are less likely to arise. Moreover, prominent arbitration procedures now usually include language that purports to give *arbitrators* the authority to resolve these same kinds of questions. For example, the American Arbitration Association (AAA) Commercial Arbitration Rules state:

> The arbitrator shall have the power to rule on his or her own jurisdiction, including any objections with respect to the existence, scope or validity of the arbitration agreement.

AAA Commercial Arbitration Rules R-7(a) (Amended and effective Sept. 1, 2007.)

The Supreme Court decision below gives direction as to the division of functions between arbitrators and courts regarding arbitrability issues.

❖ First Options of Chicago, Inc. v. Kaplan
514 U.S. 938 (1995)

[First Options of Chicago, Inc., a firm that clears stock trades on the Philadelphia Stock Exchange, entered into a "workout" agreement, embodied in four documents, that governed the "working out" of debts owed by Manuel Kaplan, Carol Kaplan, and their investment company ("MKI"). The Kaplans and MKI lost money in the October 1987 stock market crash and in 1989. First Options sought arbitration after its demands for payment were not satisfied. MKI, which had signed the only workout document containing an arbitration agreement, submitted to arbitration, but the Kaplans, who had not signed that document, objected. The arbitrators ruled in First Options' favor. The District Court confirmed the award, but the Court of Appeals reversed, finding that the dispute was not arbitrable.]

Justice Breyer delivered the opinion for a unanimous Court.

. . . The first question — the standard of review applied to an arbitrator's decision about arbitrability — is a narrow one. To understand just how narrow, consider three types of disagreements present in this case. First, the Kaplans and First Options disagree about whether the Kaplans are personally liable for MKI's debt to First Options. That disagreement makes up the *merits* of the dispute. Second, they disagree about whether they agreed to arbitrate the merits. That disagreement is about the *arbitrability* of the dispute. Third, they disagree about *who should have the primary power to decide the second matter*. Does that power belong primarily to the arbitrators (because the court reviews their arbitrability decision deferentially) or to the court (because the court makes up its mind about arbitrability independently)? We consider here only this third question.

Although the question is a narrow one, it has a certain practical importance. That is because a party who has not agreed to arbitrate will normally have a right to a court's decision about the merits of its dispute (say, as here, its obligation under a contract). But, where the party has agreed to arbitrate, he or she, in effect, has relinquished much of that right's practical value. The party still can ask a court to review the arbitrator's decision, but the court will set that decision aside only in very unusual circumstances. . . . Hence, who — court or arbitrator — has the primary authority to decide whether a party has agreed to arbitrate can make a critical difference to a party resisting arbitration.

We believe the answer to the "who" question (i.e., the standard-of-review question) is fairly simple. Just as the arbitrability of the merits of a dispute depends upon whether the parties agreed to arbitrate that dispute . . . so the question "who has the primary power to decide arbitrability" turns upon what the parties agreed about *that* matter. Did the parties agree to submit the arbitrability question itself to arbitration? If so, then the court's standard for reviewing the arbitrator's decision about *that* matter should not differ from the standard courts apply when they review any other matter that parties have agreed to arbitrate.... That is to say, the court should give considerable leeway to the arbitrator, setting aside his or her decision only in certain narrow circumstances.... If, on the other hand, the parties did *not* agree to submit the arbitrability question itself to arbitration, then the court should decide that question just as it would decide any other question that the parties did not submit to arbitration, namely, independently. These two answers flow inexorably from the fact that arbitration is simply a matter of contract between the parties; it is a way to resolve those disputes — but only those disputes — that the parties have agreed to submit to arbitration....

We agree with First Options, therefore, that a court must defer to an arbitrator's arbitrability decision when the parties submitted that matter to arbitration. Nevertheless, that conclusion does not help First Options win this case. That is because a fair and complete answer to the standard-of-review question requires a word about how a court should decide whether the parties have agreed to submit the arbitrability issue to arbitration....

When deciding whether the parties agreed to arbitrate a certain matter (including arbitrability), courts generally (though with a qualification we discuss below) should apply ordinary state-law principles that govern the formation of contracts.... The relevant state law here, for example, would require the court to see whether the parties objectively revealed an intent to submit the arbitrability issue to arbitration ...

This Court, however, has ... added an important qualification ... : Courts should not assume that the parties agreed to arbitrate arbitrability unless there is "clear and unmistakable" evidence that they did so.... In this manner the law treats silence or ambiguity about the question "*who* (primarily) should decide arbitrability" differently from the way it treats silence or ambiguity about the question "*whether* a particular merits-related dispute is arbitrable because it is within the scope of a valid arbitration agreement" — for in respect to this latter question the law reverses the presumption.... [With respect to the pro-arbitration presumption that applies to a court's determination of whether a particular dispute is arbitrable, the Court cites *Mitsubishi Motors Corp. v. Soler Chrysler Plymouth, Inc.*, 473 U.S. 614, 626 (1985) ("'[A]ny doubts concerning the scope of arbitrable issues should be resolved in favor of arbitration'") (quoting *Moses H. Cone Memorial Hospital* v. *Mercury Constr. Corp.*, 460 U.S. 1, 24-25 (1983)); *Warrior & Gulf, supra*, at 582-583.] ...

The latter question arises when the parties have a contract that provides for arbitration of some issues. In such circumstances, the parties likely gave at least some thought to the scope of arbitration. And, given the law's permissive policies in respect to arbitration ... one can understand why the law would insist upon clarity before concluding that the parties did *not* want to arbitrate a related matter. ... On the other hand, the former question — the "who (primarily) should decide arbitrability" question — is rather arcane. A party often might not focus upon that question or upon the significance of having arbitrators decide the scope of their own powers. . . . And, given the principle that a party can be forced to arbitrate only those issues it specifically has agreed to submit to arbitration, one can understand why courts might hesitate to interpret silence or ambiguity on the "who should decide arbitrability" point as giving the arbitrators that power, for doing so might too often force unwilling parties to arbitrate a matter they reasonably would have thought a judge, not an arbitrator, would decide. . . .

On the record before us, First Options cannot show that the Kaplans clearly agreed to have the arbitrators decide (i.e., to arbitrate) the question of arbitrability. . . . We conclude that, because the Kaplans did not clearly agree to submit the question of arbitrability to arbitration, the Court of Appeals was correct in finding that the arbitrability of the Kaplan/First Options dispute was subject to independent review by the courts. The judgment of the Court of Appeals is *affirmed*.

Questions

5. As the Court indicates, the law's "permissive policies" respecting arbitration mean that courts are supposed to interpret arbitration provisions liberally. In *Moses H. Cone Memorial Hosp. v. Mercury Constr. Corp.*, 460 U.S. 1, 24-25 (1983), in what proved to be the first in a long series of pro-arbitration pronouncements, the Court observed:

   > Although our holding in *Prima Paint* extended only to the specific issue resented, the courts of appeals have since consistently concluded that questions of arbitrability must be addressed with a healthy regard for the federal policy favoring arbitration. We agree. The [Federal] Arbitration Act establishes that, as a matter of federal law, any doubts concerning the scope of arbitrable issues should be resolved in favor of arbitration, whether the problem at hand is the construction of the contract language itself or an allegation of waiver, delay, or like a defense to arbitrability.

   Given its generally favorable attitude toward arbitrability, why does the Court insist that a district court should itself decide whether a particular matter is arbitrable unless there is "clear and unmistakable" evidence that the parties intend such decisions to be made by arbitrators?

6. Would the AAA provision quoted in the paragraph prior to the decision qualify as the kind of "clear and unmistakable" evidence to which the Court referred?

Note: Arbitration Agreements and the "Battle of the Forms"

You may recall from your Contracts course that the process of determining the terms of an agreement is not always a simple one, especially when parties have exchanged standardized contract forms. In this regard you may remember (perhaps not fondly) U.C.C. § 2-207, which was the drafters' effort to address the so-called "battle of the forms" that often occurs in sales of goods between merchants. One of the aims of § 2-207 was to avoid the perceived unfairness and surprise that may result when the terms of the contract are determined by the provisions of the last form sent by either party — the usual result under the old common law "last shot" rule.

U.C.C. § 2-207 provides, among other things, that if a response to an offer contains a term that materially alters the contract, then that term will not be included in the contract. In a much-cited 1978 decision, the New York Court of Appeals, applying U.C.C. § 2-207(2)(b), ruled that where an offer did not include an arbitration provision but the form sent in response to that offer did include an arbitration provision, the latter provision would materially alter the contract and therefore would not become part of the contract. *In re* arbitration between *Marlene Indus. v. Carnac Textiles*, 380 N.E.2d 239 (N.Y. 1978).

Question

7. Why do you suppose the New York Court of Appeals concluded that the inclusion of an arbitration agreement would "materially alter" the contract? Recall our comparison of arbitration and litigation in Chapter 16.B.

1. *Procedural Questions*

The Supreme Court has enunciated a "liberal federal policy favoring arbitration agreements" under the FAA. *Moses H. Cone Memorial Hosp. v. Mercury Constr. Corp.*, 460 U.S. 1, 24-25 (1983). This policy is manifested in several ways. As discussed above, it is reflected in the liberality with which courts handle questions about whether issues in disputes are "arbitrable" under particular arbitration provisions, resolving doubts in favor of sending the disputes to arbitration. It is also illustrated by a long line of cases standing for the proposition that "procedural" questions that grow out of a dispute, even if they bear on its final disposition, are presumptively for the arbitrator, *not* for the judge, to decide. Almost four decades ago the Supreme Court stated:

> Once it is determined, as we have, that the parties are obliged to submit the subject matter of a dispute to arbitration, "procedural" questions which grow out of the dispute and bear on its final disposition should be left to the arbitrator.

John Wiley & Sons, Inc. v. Livingston, 376 U.S. 543, 557 (1964). Since that time the concept that arbitrators should have authority to resolve "procedural" issues associated with arbitration has been reaffirmed again and again. It has sometimes proven difficult, however, for courts to define the line between procedural issues growing out of a dispute and issues that should be reserved by the court in determining whether to enforce an arbitration clause.

In *Howsam v. Dean Witter Reynolds, Inc.*, 123 S. Ct. 588, 592 (2003), the Supreme Court noted that "one might call any potentially dispositive gateway question a 'question of arbitrability,' for its answer will determine whether the underlying controversy will proceed to arbitration on the merits." The Court's unanimous opinion concluded, however, that it has defined arbitrability much more narrowly, finding the "phrase applicable in the kind of narrow circumstance where contracting parties would likely have expected a court to have decided the gateway matter." This rather circular inquiry into parties' intent after a dispute has arisen can generate confusion, but the *Howsam* Court gave a few examples. A court should decide whether an arbitration contract binds parties who did not sign the agreement and whether an arbitration agreement survives a corporate merger to bind the resulting entity. However, the Court did not find procedural matters such as whether required grievance procedures were completed prior to arbitration, or whether a party had waived its right to arbitrate, to be questions of arbitrability, but rather procedural questions relating to the dispute and within the authority of arbitrators to address.

In *Howsam*, for example, Karen Howsam chose to arbitrate a dispute that arose with her brokerage firm under the National Association of Securities Dealers' (NASD) Code of Arbitration Procedure. The Code provides that a dispute must be submitted to arbitration within six years of the occurrence or event giving rise to the dispute. The Supreme Court held that an NASD arbitrator, not a court, should apply the six-year limit to the underlying dispute to see if Ms. Howsam's arbitration submission was timely. Although the federal circuit courts were divided on the question of whether an arbitrator or court should determine this issue, the Court reasoned that what constitutes a question of arbitrability — presumed to be within the court's control absent party agreement to the contrary — should be narrowly construed. The Court emphasized the comparative expertise of the NASD arbitrators in construing their own time limits, and expressed hope that this outcome would advance goals of both arbitration systems and judicial systems by "secur[ing] a fair and expeditious resolution of the underlying controversy."

Parties can always agree expressly that arbitrators should handle certain types of threshold questions. But even if they do not vest such authority explicitly, courts that apply the FAA and state arbitration laws will normally defer such decisions to arbitrators. Under a typical, broadly framed arbitration provision (e.g., covering "all disputes arising under or relating to the contract or the breach thereof"), arbitrators will determine any procedural questions that arise in connection with an arbitration agreement. There remain, however, gray areas about what is "procedural" and what is a matter of arbitrability.

Questions

8.   Suppose you desire to include an arbitration agreement in your contract but you want a court, not arbitrators, to handle any determinations regarding the effect of a failure to file a claim within a certain period of time (e.g., a statute of limitations). Would you need to state that intent "clearly and unmistakably" because arbitrators are typically deemed to have authority over such determinations under the FAA?

The growing use of contractual dispute resolution clauses has confronted federal and state courts with a number of issues of first impression, including whether arbitration governs the enforceability of provisions for mediation or non-binding arbitration. *See supra* Section B.3. Another set of issues has to do with questions relating to a party's failure to comply with a contractual obligation to participate in negotiation or mediation prior to arbitration. Should such questions be handled by courts, or are they within the authority of arbitrators to handle procedural questions associated with an arbitrable dispute? Judicial responses vary.

Problem 1

Who Should Determine the Consequences of a Failure to Negotiate or Mediate Under a Stepped Dispute Resolution Provision?

Kalua Company entered into a long-term agreement to provide syrup to Rise 'n' Shine, a coffee shop chain. The parties' agreement included a stepped dispute resolution clause that stated in pertinent part:

It is mutually agreed that the parties shall be free to bring any and all such matters to the attention of the other at any time without prejudicing their harmonious relationship and operations hereunder, and that the offices of either party shall be available at all times for the prompt and effective adjustment of any and all such differences, either by mail, telephone, or personal meeting under friendly and courteous circumstances.

> In the event that a dispute cannot be settled between the parties, the matter shall be mediated within fifteen (15) days after receipt of notice by either party that the other party requests the mediation of a dispute pursuant to this paragraph. If the parties are unable to select a mediator, the See You Out of Court! Mediation Group shall select a mediator. The parties agree to use their best efforts to mediate a dispute.
>
> In the event that the dispute cannot be settled through mediation, the parties shall submit the matter to arbitration within ten (10) days after receipt of notice by either party. The arbitration shall be conducted in accordance with the Commercial Arbitration Rules of the American Arbitration Association then in effect. The parties shall each select an arbitrator and the two arbitrators thus selected shall select a third arbitrator. These three arbitrators shall constitute the arbitration panel. It is understood that a judgment or award rendered, which may include an award of damages, may be entered in any court having jurisdiction thereof.

Sadly, things did not go well under the contract. In May, Kalua made a demand on Rise 'n' Shine for payment of three months of unpaid invoices. On June 15, Rise 'n' Shine sent Kalua a notice acknowledging that it owed some of the money, but not all. A payment was not included with the notice. Kalua presented Rise 'n' Shine with another demand on June 28. Rise 'n' Shine did not respond. Kalua terminated the Agreement with Rise 'n' Shine on August 3.

On August 15, Kalua then brought this suit. On September 20, Rise 'n' Shine filed a motion to stay the proceeding pending arbitration pursuant to FAA § 3. Kalua seeks to defeat the motion and insists that the right to arbitrate has been waived because there was no effort by Rise 'n' Shine to negotiate or mediate.

a. If you are the federal district court judge charged with deciding how to address the motion to stay the proceeding pending arbitration, would you (1) grant the stay and let the arbitrators address the impact of the failure to negotiate and mediate, or (2) deny the stay and have the parties stay in court? See *Welborn Clinic v. Medquist, Inc.*, 301 F.3d 634 (7th Cir. 2002); *Kemiron Atlantic, Inc. v. Aguakem Int'l.*, 290 F.3d 1287 (11th Cir. 2002).

b. Might your answer be in any way affected by the provisions of the AAA Commercial Arbitration Rules?

2. Separability (Severability)

In *Prima Paint Corp. v. Flood & Conklin Mfg. Co.*, 388 U.S. 395 (1967), a party who had signed a contract containing a broad arbitration clause claimed that the entire contract was induced by fraud. The Supreme Court had to determine whether the arbitration clause should be considered separately from the underlying contract for the purpose of enforcement. The Court's decision — founded on the principle of separability (severability) of arbitration agreements — established an important limit on the authority of courts considering the enforceability of arbitration agreements. The separability doctrine has become one of the cornerstones of modern arbitration law.

❖ **Prima Paint Corp. v. Flood & Conklin Mfg. Co.**

388 U.S. 395 (1967)

[In 1964, Prima Paint purchased Flood & Conklin's ("F&C") paint business and entered into a consulting agreement with the chairman of F&C. Soon Prima Paint stopped making payments under the agreements, charging that F&C had breached both agreements by fraudulently representing that it was solvent when it intended to file for bankruptcy. F&C served a notice of intent to arbitrate. Three days before its answer to the notice was due, Prima Paint filed a lawsuit in the federal court in New York, seeking to rescind the consulting agreement as fraudulently induced. The court had subject matter jurisdiction because the parties were from New Jersey and Maryland and the dispute met the amount in controversy requirement of the diversity statute.] Justice FORTAS delivered the opinion of the Court.

This case presents the question whether the federal court or an arbitrator is to resolve a claim of "fraud in the inducement," under a contract governed by the [FAA] where there is no evidence that the contracting parties intended to withhold that issue from arbitration.

. . . [T]he parties agreed to a broad arbitration clause, which read in part: "Any controversy or claim arising out of or relating to this Agreement, or the breach thereof, shall be settled by arbitration in the City of New York, in accordance with the rules then obtaining of the American Arbitration Association. . . ."

Having determined that the contract in question is within the coverage of the Arbitration Act [because the underlying transaction involved interstate commerce], we turn to the central issue in this case: whether a claim of fraud in the inducement of the entire contract is to be resolved by the federal court, or whether the matter is to be referred to the arbitrators. The courts of appeals have differed in their approach to this question. The view of the Court of Appeals for the Second Circuit . . . is that — *except where the parties otherwise intend* — arbitration clauses as a matter of federal law are "separable" from the contracts in which they are embedded, and that where no claim is made that fraud was directed to the arbitration clause itself, a broad arbitration clause will be held to encompass arbitration of the claim that the contract itself was induced by fraud. . . . The Court of Appeals for the First Circuit, on the other hand, has taken the view that the question of "severability" is one of state law, and that where a State regards such a clause as inseparable a claim of fraud in the inducement must be decided by the court . . . [Under the FAA], we think that Congress has provided an explicit answer. That answer is to be found in § 4 of the Act, which provides a remedy to a party seeking to compel compliance with an arbitration agreement. Under § 4 . . . , the federal court is instructed to order arbitration to proceed once it is satisfied that "the making of the agreement for arbitration or the failure to comply [with the arbitration agreement] is not in issue." Accordingly, if the claim is fraud in the inducement of the arbitration clause itself — an issue which goes to the "making" of the agreement to arbitrate — the federal court may proceed to adjudicate it. But the statutory language does not permit the federal court to consider claims of fraud in the inducement of the contract generally. . . . We hold, therefore . . . that a federal court may consider only issues relating to the making and performance of the agreement to arbitrate. In so concluding, we not only honor the plain meaning of the statute but also the unmistakably clear congressional purpose that the arbitration procedure, when selected by the parties to a contract, be speedy and not subject to delay and obstruction in the courts.

[The Court further concluded that such a rule was constitutionally permissible.]

. . . Accordingly, the decision below dismissing Prima Paint's appeal is *affirmed*.

Justice BLACK, with whom Justice DOUGLAS and STEWART join, dissenting:

The Court here holds that the [FAA] . . . compels a party to a contract containing a written arbitration provision to carry out his "arbitration agreement" even though a court might, after a fair trial, hold the entire contract — including the arbitration agreement — void because of fraud in the inducement. The Court holds, what is to me fantastic, that the legal issue of a contract's voidness because of fraud is to be decided by persons designated to arbitrate factual controversies arising out of a valid contract between the parties. And the arbitrators who the Court holds are to adjudicate the legal validity of the contract need not even be lawyers, and in all probability will be nonlawyers, wholly unqualified to decide legal issues, and even if qualified to apply the law, not bound to do so. I am by no means sure that thus forcing a person to forgo his opportunity to try his legal issues in the courts where, unlike the situation in arbitration, he may have a jury trial and right to appeal, is not a denial of due process of law. I am satisfied, however, that Congress did not impose any such procedures in the [FAA]. And I am fully satisfied that a reasonable and fair reading of that Act's language and history shows that both Congress and the framers of the Act were at great pains to emphasize that nonlawyers designated to adjust and arbitrate factual controversies arising out of valid contracts would not trespass upon the courts' prerogative to decide the legal question of whether any legal contract exists upon which to base an arbitration. . . .

Notes and Questions

9. What, practically speaking, is the effect of the holding and doctrine announced in *Prima Paint*? Consider the following excerpt:

> There was a time not so long ago when courts would single out a clause of a business contract calling for arbitration of any disputes under that contract for the specific purpose of striking the arbitration clause down. Now, the tables have effectively turned: Courts will enforce a commercial arbitration agreement under federal or state law even if there are allegations that the contract of which it is a part is unenforceable, so long as there are no valid defenses to the arbitration agreement itself (such as a misrepresentation of the nature or content of that arbitration agreement, or unconscionable arbitration procedures). That's a relatively rare case in the commercial world.
>
> Under the typical broadly framed arbitration provision . . . virtually any defense relating to the overall contract — material breach, mutual mistake, fraud — you name it — is a matter for the arbitrators to decide. Some people have problems with the separability concept because it means that arbitrators determine the viability and enforceability of the contract under which they are empowered. On the other hand, the separability principle substantially reduces the likelihood of a party running to court to challenge an arbitration agreement on the eve of arbitration. Stipanowich and Kaskell (2001).

What practical or policy arguments support the separability doctrine? What, if any, concerns does it raise?

10. Recall that most prominent arbitration procedures give arbitrators authority to resolve all jurisdictional issues. *See, e.g.,* AAA Commercial Arbitration Rules R-7(a). Do such provisions reinforce the doctrine of *Prima Paint*? Explain.

11. Should the doctrine of *Prima Paint* extend to circumstances where a party seeks to assert that the contract containing the arbitration clause was not just voidable, but illegal? The matter was addressed directly in *Buckeye Check Cashing, Inc. v. Cardegna*, 126 S. Ct. 1204 (2006) (holding that issue of illegality of contract is arbitrable under broad-form arbitration agreement), discussed below in Section C.6.

12. Should *Prima Paint* apply with equal vigor in a situation involving a standardized consumer or employment contract? See *Buckeye, supra*; see also generally Chapter 19, discussing the use of arbitration provisions in standardized "adhesion" contracts and related fairness issues.

3. *Public Policy Limitations*

Until relatively recently, courts routinely recognized significant public policy limitations on the enforcement of arbitration agreements. In particular, arbitration was not deemed amenable to the resolution of "public law" issues (i.e., rights created by the legislature, including federal antitrust or civil rights claims). "Less than twenty years ago, the concept of arbitrating federally created rights...was virtually unthinkable" (Offenkrantz, 1997). Traditionally many arbitrators were not lawyers, and it was thought inappropriate to have them consider complex statutory claims, particularly when any legal decision they reached was not subject to a more public court process and appellate review. There were also concerns that arbitrators might prove insufficiently rigorous in upholding statutory protections and policing business peers.

An illustration of judicial unwillingness to allow arbitration of statutory claims is *Wilko v. Swan*, 346 U.S. 427 (1953). Although the FAA had been in existence since 1925, the *Wilko* Court held that an agreement to arbitrate disputes arising under the Securities Act of 1933 was unenforceable, because the Act prohibited waiver of "compliance with any provision of this title," which the court interpreted as including the right to a judicial forum to resolve any disputes. The Court noted that arbitrators do not receive "judicial instruction on the law," "their award may be made without explanation of their reasons and without a complete record," and "the arbitrators' conception of the legal meaning of... statutory requirements" is not subject to judicial review. As Professor Judith Resnik summarizes:

> Three assumptions, central to *Wilko*, were key to its intellectual framework. First, arbitration was assumed to be something *different* from and less loyal to law than adjudication. Second, public judgments rendered by federal trial courts on factual questions, such as the claim of fraudulent inducement of a client by a firm to purchase stock, in individual cases, were viewed as desirable *mechanisms* of social regulation. Third, the judiciary viewed with skepticism the agreements of parties; parties' agreements were *insufficient*, in and of themselves, to valorize all the decisions embodied in those agreements. Resnik (1995)

For many years, "public policy" considerations served as a barrier to the arbitration of statutory claims. However, the attitude of the Supreme Court toward arbitration of statute-based claims shifted dramatically in the mid-1980s. Consider the following decisions.

❖ Mitsubishi Motors Corp. v. Soler Chrysler-Plymouth, Inc.
473 U.S. 614 (1985)

[Mitsubishi, an auto manufacturer, brought an action in federal court against one of its dealers (Soler), to compel arbitration of a variety of claims for breach of contract. The contract contained a clause requiring arbitration by the Japan Commercial Arbitration Association of all disputes arising under the contract. Soler filed an answer and counterclaim alleging violation of the Sherman Antitrust Act as well as other causes of action. The district court ordered arbitration of most of the claims, including the federal antitrust issues. The Court of Appeals reversed the order compelling arbitration of the antitrust claim, relying on *American Safety Equipment Corp. v. J.P. Maguire & Co.*, 391 F.2d 821 (2d Cir. 1968), which held that rights conferred by the antitrust laws are inappropriate for arbitration.]

Justice BLACKMUN delivered the opinion of the Court.

. . . [W]e find no warrant in the Arbitration Act for implying in every contract within its ken a presumption against arbitration of statutory claims. . . .

By agreeing to arbitrate a statutory claim, a party does not forgo the substantive rights afforded by the statute; it only submits to their resolution in an arbitral, rather than a judicial, forum. It trades the procedures and opportunity for review of the courtroom for the simplicity, informality, and expedition of arbitration (emphasis added). We must assume that if Congress intended the substantive protection afforded by a given statute to include protection against waiver of the right to a judicial forum, that intention will be deducible from text or legislative history. Having made the bargain to arbitrate, the party should be held to it unless Congress itself has evinced an intention to preclude a waiver of judicial remedies for the statutory rights at issue. Nothing, in the meantime, prevents a party from excluding statutory claims from the scope of an agreement to arbitrate. . . .

We now turn to consider whether Soler's antitrust claims are nonarbitrable even though it has agreed to arbitrate them. In holding that they are not, the Court of Appeals followed the decision of the Second Circuit in *American Safety Equipment Corp. v. J.P. Maguire & Co.*, 391 F.2d 821 (1968). Notwithstanding the absence of any explicit support for such an exception in either the Sherman Act or the Federal Arbitration Act, the Second Circuit there reasoned that "the pervasive public interest in enforcement of the antitrust laws, and the nature of the claims that arise in such cases, combine to make . . . antitrust claims . . . inappropriate for arbitration." . . .

At the outset, we confess to some skepticism of certain aspects of the *American Safety* doctrine. As distilled by the First Circuit, the doctrine comprises four ingredients. First, private parties play a pivotal role in aiding governmental enforcement of the antitrust laws by means of the private action for treble damages. Second, "the strong possibility that contracts which generate antitrust disputes may be contracts of adhesion militates against automatic forum determination by contract." Third, antitrust issues, prone to complication, require sophisticated legal and economic analysis, and thus are "ill-adapted to strengths of the arbitral process, i.e., expedition, minimal requirements of written rationale, simplicity, resort to basic concepts of common sense and simple equity." Finally, just as "issues of war and peace are too important to be vested in the generals, . . . decisions as to antitrust regulation of business are too important to be lodged in arbitrators chosen from the business community — particularly those from a foreign community that has had no experience with or exposure to our law and values."

Initially, we find the second concern unjustified. The mere appearance of an antitrust dispute does not alone warrant invalidation of the selected forum on the undemonstrated assumption that the arbitration clause is tainted. A party resisting arbitration of course may attack directly the validity of the agreement to arbitrate . . . But absent such a showing — and none was attempted here — there is no basis for assuming the forum inadequate or its selection unfair.

Next, potential complexity should not suffice to ward off arbitration. We might well have some doubt that even the courts following *American Safety* subscribe fully to the view that antitrust matters are inherently insusceptible to resolution by arbitration, as these same courts have agreed that an undertaking to arbitrate antitrust claims entered into *after* the dispute arises is acceptable. And the vertical restraints which most frequently give birth to antitrust claims covered by an arbitration agreement will not often occasion the monstrous proceedings that have given antitrust litigation an image of intractability. In any event, adaptability and access to expertise are hallmarks of arbitration. The anticipated subject matter of the dispute may be taken into account when the arbitrators are appointed, and arbitral rules typically provide for the participation of experts either employed by the parties or appointed by the tribunal. Moreover, it is often a judgment that streamlined proceedings and expeditious results will best serve their needs that causes parties to agree to arbitrate their disputes; it is typically a desire to keep the effort and expense required to resolve a dispute within manageable bounds that prompts them mutually to forgo access to judicial remedies. In sum, the factor of potential complexity alone does not persuade us that an arbitral tribunal could not properly handle an antitrust matter. . . .

For similar reasons, we also reject the proposition that an arbitration panel will pose too great a danger of innate hostility to the constraints on business conduct that antitrust law imposes. International arbitrators frequently are drawn from the legal as well as the business community; where the dispute has an important legal component, the parties and the arbitral body with whose assistance they have agreed to settle their dispute can be expected to select arbitrators accordingly. We decline to indulge the presumption that the parties and arbitral body conducting a proceeding will be unable or unwilling to retain competent, conscientious, and impartial arbitrators. . . .

We are left, then, with the core of the *American Safety* doctrine — the fundamental importance to American democratic capitalism of the regime of the antitrust laws. As the Court of Appeals pointed out:

" 'A claim under the antitrust laws is not merely a private matter. The Sherman Act is designed to promote the national interest in a competitive economy; thus, the plaintiff asserting his rights under the Act has been likened to a private attorney-general who protects the public's interest." ' 723 F.2d at 168, quoting *American Safety*, 391 F.2d at 826.

The treble-damages provision wielded by the private litigant is a chief tool in the antitrust enforcement scheme, posing a crucial deterrent to potential violators.

The importance of the private damages remedy, however, does not compel the conclusion that it may not be sought outside an American court. . . . Having permitted the arbitration to go forward, the national courts of the United States will have the opportunity at the award-enforcement stage to ensure that the legitimate interest in the enforcement of the antitrust laws has been addressed. . . .

The judgment of the Court of Appeals is affirmed in part and reversed in part, and the cases are remanded for further proceedings consistent with this opinion.

Justice STEVENS filed a dissenting opinion.

. . . This Court agrees with the Court of Appeals' interpretation of the scope of the arbitration clause, but disagrees with its conclusion that the clause is unenforceable insofar as it purports to cover an antitrust claim against a Japanese company. This Court's holding rests almost exclusively on the federal policy favoring arbitration of commercial disputes and vague notions of international comity arising from the fact that the automobiles involved here were manufactured in Japan. . . . The plain language [of the FAA] encompasses Soler's claims that arise out of its contract with Mitsubishi, but does not encompass a claim arising under federal law, or indeed one that arises under its distributor agreement with Chrysler. Nothing in the text of the 1925 Act, nor its legislative history, suggests that Congress intended to authorize the arbitration of any statutory claims. . . .

Until today all of our cases enforcing agreements to arbitrate under the [FAA] have involved contract claims . . . [T]his is the first time the Court has considered the question whether a standard arbitration clause referring to claims arising out of or relating to a contract should be construed to cover statutory claims that have only an indirect relationship to the contract. In my opinion, neither the Congress that enacted the Arbitration Act in 1925, nor the many parties who have agreed to such standard clauses, could have anticipated the Court's answer to that question. . . .

"Arbitral procedures, while well suited to the resolution of contractual disputes, make arbitration a comparatively inappropriate forum for the final resolution of rights created by [statute]. This conclusion rests first on the special role of the arbitrator, whose task is to effectuate the intent of the parties rather than the requirements of enacted legislation . . . [T]he specialized competence of arbitrators pertains to the law of the shop, not the law of the land . . . " (quoting *Alexander v. Gardner-Denver*, 415 U.S. 36, 56–57 (1974)).

[T]he informal procedures which make arbitration so desirable in the context of contractual disputes are inadequate to develop a record for appellate review of statutory questions. Such review is essential on matters of statutory interpretation in order to assure consistent application of important public rights.[14] . . . "Finally, not only are arbitral procedures less protective of individual statutory rights than are judicial procedures, but arbitrators very often are powerless to grant the aggrieved employees as broad a range of relief." . . .

The Sherman and Clayton Acts reflect Congress' appraisal of the value of economic freedom; they guarantee the vitality of the entrepreneurial spirit. Questions arising under these Acts are among the most important in public law. . . . The provision for mandatory treble damages — unique in federal law when the statute was enacted — provides a special incentive to the private enforcement of the statute. . . .

There are . . . several unusual features of the antitrust enforcement scheme that unequivocally require rejection of any thought that Congress would tolerate private arbitration of antitrust claims in lieu of the statutory remedies that it fashioned. . . .

In view of the history of antitrust enforcement in the United States, it is not surprising that all of the federal courts that have considered the question have uniformly and unhesitatingly concluded that agreements to arbitrate federal antitrust issues are not enforceable. . . .

This Court would be well advised to endorse the collective wisdom of the distinguished judges of the Courts of Appeals who have unanimously concluded that the statutory remedies fashioned by Congress for the enforcement of the antitrust laws render an agreement to arbitrate antitrust disputes unenforceable . . . Despotic decision making of this kind is fine for parties who are willing to agree in advance to settle for a best approximation of the correct result in order to resolve quickly and inexpensively any contractual dispute that may arise in an ongoing commercial relationship. Such informality, however, is simply unacceptable when every error may have devastating consequences for important businesses in our national economy and may undermine their ability to compete in world markets. Instead of "muffling a grievance in the cloakroom of arbitration," the public interest in free competitive markets would be better served by having the issues resolved "in the light of impartial public court adjudication."

Notes and Questions

13. This case involved an antitrust claim arising in the international context. How do you think the increasingly global nature of commerce influenced the assumptions of the Justices in *Mitsubishi*? Would the result be different if the case had involved a wholly

14. "Moreover, the factfinding process in arbitration usually is not equivalent to judicial factfinding. The record of the arbitration proceedings is not as complete; the usual rules of evidence do not apply; and rights and procedures common to civil trials, such as discovery, compulsory process, cross-examination, and testimony under oath, are often severely limited or unavailable."

domestic dispute where a party sought to compel arbitration of an antitrust claim? Is the *American Safety* doctrine, which holds that domestic antitrust claims are not subject to arbitration, still good law? *See, e.g., Coors Brewing Company v. Molson Breweries*, 51 F.3d 1511 (10th Cir. 1995).

14. In this particular case the arbitrators would likely be Japanese. They *might* be lawyers. How familiar would they be with, and how supportive of, U.S. antitrust law? If the parties agreed in advance to use what Justice Stevens termed "despotic" decision makers (arbitrators), why should U.S. courts be concerned? If this dispute arose today, and it was understood that all civil claims, including antitrust issues, would be arbitrable, do you believe it would influence the choice of arbitrators? Explain.

15. Writing for the majority, Justice Blackmun stated that "the national courts of the United States will have the opportunity at the award-enforcement stage to ensure that the legitimate interest in the enforcement of the antitrust laws has been addressed." Is this conclusion realistic? Keep this statement in mind as you read the decisions regarding judicial vacatur of arbitration awards in Section E below.

16. Two years after *Mitsubishi* the Court held that statutory claims arising under the Racketeer Influenced and Corrupt Organizations Act (RICO) are subject to mandatory arbitration. See *Shearson/American Express, Inc. v. McMahon*, 482 U.S. 220 (1987) (finding no basis for concluding that Congress intended to prevent enforcement of agreements to arbitrate RICO claims and concluding that a RICO claim can be effectively vindicated in an arbitral forum).

17. *Shearson/American Express v. McMahon* also held that claims under the Securities Act of 1934 are subject to binding arbitration, rejecting the reasoning of *Wilko v. Swan*, 346 U.S. 427 (1953), which held that claims arising under the Securities Act of 1933 were not subject to binding arbitration. Not surprisingly, the Court overruled *Wilko* two years later in *Rodriguez de Quijas v. Shearson/American Express, Inc.*, 490 U.S. 477 (1989). *Gilmer v. Interstate/Johnson Lane Corp.*, 500 U.S. 20 (1991), supporting the arbitrability of statutory employment discrimination claims, narrowed the so-called "public policy" limitation even further. These developments are treated further in Chapter 19.

4.   *Preemption of State Law by the Federal Arbitration Act*

Another critical aspect of the evolution of modern arbitration law is the concept of preemption of state law by a "substantive law of arbitrability" — that is, a body of law supporting enforcement of arbitration agreements — under the FAA. In the 1980s and 1990s, as evidenced by the decisions cited in the previous sections, the Supreme Court spent a significant portion of its time and effort determining controversies about the scope and force of the FAA. It construed the FAA broadly to cover arbitration of statutory claims. In doing so, it displaced the traditional role of state law in this arena.

These decisions conflict with what the Court has done during the same period in many other areas of law, as it delegated more power to States and reined in the role of federal law (Kloppenberg, 2001; Noonan, 2002). Two commentators explain why the Court, in this series of "bold" decisions, rewrote the law governing arbitration:

> The Court's aggression has been the product of two worthy but overindulged impulses. One impulse has been to encourage international trade by enforcing dispute resolution provisions in international commercial contracts. The second has been to conserve scarce judicial resources by encouraging citizens to resolve disputes by private means.

Carrington and Haagen (1996).

With some important exceptions, the Court came to express unanimity in a number of these rulings, and frequently issued *per curiam* decisions. The agreement among the Justices in interpreting the FAA contrasts sharply with its 5-4 rulings in many areas of constitutional law, including other federalism decisions. The Court may reason that, in interpreting congressional intent, it can rely on Congress to revise the FAA if the Court misconstrues its scope and import.

As noted above, most States adopted versions of the UAA after Congress enacted the FAA. However, the operational scope of these statutes is now significantly qualified — at least in the fundamental area of enforcement of arbitration agreements — by the following Supreme Court decision and its progeny.

❖ Southland Corp. v. Keating
465 U.S. 1 (1984)

[The Southland Corporation, which is the franchisor of 7-Eleven convenience stores, had an arbitration clause in its standard franchise agreements requiring arbitration of "any controversy or claim arising out of or relating to this agreement." Keating, a franchisee, filed a class action against Southland on behalf of approximately 800 California franchisees alleging fraud, oral misrepresentations, breach of contract, breach of fiduciary duty, and violation of the disclosure requirements of the California Franchise Investment Law. Southland petitioned the Superior Court to compel arbitration of all claims. The trial court granted the petition and compelled arbitration, except with respect to claims based on the California Franchise Investment Law, which provided as follows: "Any condition, stipulation or provision purporting to bind any person acquiring any franchise to waive compliance with any provision of this law or any rule or order hereunder is void." The California Supreme Court agreed with the trial court that the claims under the state statute were not arbitrable, and the decision was appealed to the United States Supreme Court.]

Chief Justice BURGER delivered the opinion of the Court.

[We noted probable jurisdiction to consider] (a) whether the California Franchise Investment Law, which invalidates certain arbitration agreements covered by the Federal Arbitration Act, violates the Supremacy Clause. . . .

In enacting § 2 of the federal Act, Congress declared a national policy favoring arbitration and withdrew the power of the states to require a judicial forum for the resolution of claims which the contracting parties agreed to resolve by arbitration. The Federal Arbitration Act provides:

> "A written provision in any maritime transaction or a contract evidencing a transaction involving commerce to settle by arbitration a controversy thereafter arising out of such contract or transaction, or the refusal to perform the whole or any part thereof, or an agreement in writing to submit to arbitration an existing controversy arising out of such a contract, transaction, or refusal, shall be valid, irrevocable, and enforceable, save upon such grounds as exist at law or in equity for the revocation of any contract." 9 U.S.C. § 2 (1976).

Congress has thus mandated the enforcement of arbitration agreements.

We discern only two limitations on the enforceability of arbitration provisions governed by the Federal Arbitration Act: they must be part of a written maritime contract or a contract "evidencing a transaction involving commerce" and such clauses may be revoked upon "grounds as exist at law or in equity for the revocation of any contract." We see nothing in the Act indicating that the broad principle of enforceability is subject to any additional limitations under State law. . . .

At least since 1824 Congress' authority under the Commerce Clause has been held plenary. *Gibbons v. Ogden*, 22 U.S. 1 (1824). In the words of Chief Justice Marshall, the authority of Congress is "the power to regulate; that is, to prescribe the rule by which commerce is to be governed." Id. The statements of the Court in *Prima Paint* (388 U.S. 420) that the Arbitration Act was an exercise of the Commerce Clause power clearly implied that the substantive rules of the Act were to apply in state as well as federal courts. . . .

Although the legislative history is not without ambiguities, there are strong indications that Congress had in mind something more than making arbitration agreements enforceable only in the federal courts. The House Report plainly suggests the more comprehensive objectives:

> "The purpose of this bill is to make valid and enforceable agreements for arbitration contained *in contracts involving interstate commerce* or within the jurisdiction or admiralty, *or* which may be the subject of litigation in the Federal courts." H.R. Rep. No. 96, 68th Cong., 1st Sess. 1 (1924) (Emphasis added.).

This broader purpose can also be inferred from the reality that Congress would be less likely to address a problem whose impact was confined to federal courts than a problem of large significance in the field of commerce. The Arbitration Act sought to "overcome the rule of equity, that equity will not specifically enforce any arbitration agreement." Hearing on S. 4214 Before a Subcomm. of the Senate Comm. on the Judiciary, 67th Cong., 4th Sess. 6 (1923) ("Senate Hearing") (remarks of Sen. Walsh). The House Report accompanying the bill stated:

> "[t]he need for the law arises from . . . the jealousy of the English courts for their own jurisdiction. . . . This jealousy survived for so [long] a period that the principle became firmly embedded in the English common law and was adopted with it by the American courts. The courts have felt that the precedent was too strongly fixed to be overturned without legislative enactment. . . ." H.R. Rep. No. 96, *supra*, 1-2 (1924).

Surely this makes clear that the House Report contemplated a broad reach of the Act, unencumbered by state law constraints. . . .

The problems Congress faced were therefore twofold: the old common law hostility toward arbitration, and the failure of state arbitration statutes to mandate enforcement of arbitration agreements. To confine the scope of the Act to arbitrations sought to be enforced in federal courts would frustrate what we believe Congress intended to be a broad enactment appropriate in scope to meet the large problems Congress was addressing. . . .

In creating a substantive rule applicable in state as well as federal courts, Congress intended to foreclose state legislative attempts to undercut the enforceability of arbitration agreements. We hold that § 31512 of the California Franchise Investment Law violates the Supremacy Clause. . . . The judgment of the California Supreme Court denying enforcement of the arbitration agreement is reversed. . . .

Justice O'CONNOR with whom Justice REHNQUIST joins, dissenting.

Section 2 of the Federal Arbitration Act (FAA) provides that a written arbitration agreement "shall be valid, irrevocable, and enforceable, save upon such grounds as exist at law or in equity for the revocation of any contract." Section 2 does not, on its face, identify which judicial forums are bound by its requirements or what procedures govern its enforcement. The FAA deals with these matters in §§ 3 and 4. Section 3 provides:

> "If any suit or proceeding be brought *in any of the courts of the United States* upon any issue referable to arbitration . . . the court . . . shall on application of one of the parties stay the trial of the action until such arbitration has been had in accordance with the terms of the agreement . . . "

Section 4 specifies that a party aggrieved by another's refusal to arbitrate "may petition *any United States district court* which, save for such agreement, would have jurisdiction under Title 28 . . . for an order directing that such arbitration proceed in the manner provided for in such agreement. . . ."

Today, the Court takes the facial silence of § 2 as a license to declare that state as well as federal courts must apply § 2. In addition, though this is not spelled out in the opinion, the Court holds that in enforcing this newly discovered federal right state courts must follow procedures specified in § 3. The Court's decision is impelled by an understandable desire to encourage the use of arbitration, but it utterly fails to recognize the clear congressional intent underlying the FAA. Congress intended to require federal, not state, courts to respect arbitration agreements. . . . One rarely finds a legislative history as unambiguous as the FAA's. That history establishes conclusively that the 1925 Congress viewed the FAA as a procedural statute, applicable only in federal courts, derived, Congress believed, largely from the federal power to control the jurisdiction of the federal courts. . . .

If characterizing the FAA as procedural was not enough, the draftsmen of the Act, the House Report, and the early commentators all flatly stated that the Act was intended to affect only federal court proceedings. Mr. Cohen, the American Bar Association member who drafted the bill, assured two congressional subcommittees in joint hearings:

> "Nor can it be said that the Congress of the United States, *directing its own courts* . . . , would infringe upon the provinces or prerogatives of the States. . . . [T]he question of the enforcement relates to the law of remedies and not to substantive law. The rule must be changed for the jurisdiction in which the agreement is sought to be enforced. . . . There is no disposition therefore by means of the Federal bludgeon to force an individual State into an unwilling submission to arbitration enforcement." [Additional discussion of legislative history is omitted.]

Today's decision is unfaithful to congressional intent, unnecessary, and, in light of the FAA's antecedents and the intervening contraction of federal power, inexplicable. Although arbitration is a worthy alternative to litigation, today's exercise in judicial revisionism goes too far. I respectfully dissent.

Notes and Questions

18. The majority opinion concludes that the FAA is a source of substantive law governing the enforcement of arbitration agreements — a law based on the power of Congress under the Commerce Clause to regulate interstate commerce. It therefore applies in both federal and state courts. The dissent argues that it is a procedural statute based upon congressional power under Article III to establish and regulate federal courts and therefore applies only in federal proceedings. Who has the better of the argument? This is a complicated area of constitutional and statutory law; if these issues intrigue you, we recommend *Constitutional Law* by Erwin Chemerinsky (3rd ed., 2009).

19. In another part of its opinion, the majority expressed concern that interpreting the FAA to apply only in federal courts and not state courts would "encourage and reward forum shopping." Justice O'Connor responded to this concern as follows:

> Because the FAA makes the federal courts equally accessible to both parties to a dispute, no forum shopping would be possible even if we gave the FAA a construction faithful to the congressional intent. In controversies involving incomplete diversity of citizenship there is simply no access to federal court and therefore no possibility of forum shopping. In controversies *with* complete diversity of citizenship the FAA grants federal court access equally to both parties; no party can gain any advantage by forum shopping. Even when the party resisting arbitration initiates an action in state court, the opposing party can invoke FAA § 4 and promptly secure a federal court order to compel arbitration.

20. Assume the majority is right that § 2 of the FAA, which makes arbitration clauses "valid, irrevocable and enforceable," creates a substantive right which state courts must enforce. Does this mean state courts are required to apply the enforcement mechanisms of the FAA, which include compelling arbitration and staying judicial proceedings? The majority apparently concluded the answer was "yes," but Justice O'Connor thought not:

> [A]bsent specific direction from Congress the state courts have always been permitted to apply their own reasonable procedures when enforcing federal rights. Before we undertake to read a set of complex and mandatory procedures into § 2's brief and general language, we should at a minimum allow state courts and legislatures a chance to develop their own methods for enforcing the new federal rights. Some might choose to award compensatory or punitive damages for the violation of an arbitration agreement; some might award litigation costs to the party who remained willing to arbitrate; some might affirm the "validity and enforceability" of arbitration agreements in other ways. Any of these approaches could vindicate § 2 rights in a manner fully consonant with the language and background of that provision.

Southland concludes that the enactment of the FAA was an exercise of congressional power under the Commerce Clause. How broad an exercise of that power was intended? Consider the following case, in which the preemptive power of the FAA was tested against a state statute purporting to make predispute arbitration agreements unenforceable.

❖ Allied-Bruce Terminix Companies v. Dobson

513 U.S. 265 (1995)

[The plaintiffs, Mr. and Mrs. G. William Dobson, purchased a house which had been subject to a lifetime "Termite Protection Plan" provided by Allied-Bruce Terminix. After the purchase they found the house to be severely infested with termites. They filed a lawsuit against defendant Allied-Bruce in Alabama state court. Defendant asked the court for a stay, citing the fact that the "Termite Protection Plan" contained an arbitration clause providing for arbitration of "any controversy or claim . . . arising out of or relating to the interpretation, performance or breach of any provision of this agreement." The Alabama court refused to grant the stay on the basis of a state statute making predispute arbitration agreements invalid and unenforceable. The Alabama court found the FAA inapplicable because the connection between the termite contract and interstate commerce was too slight. Despite some interstate activities (e.g., Allied-Bruce was a multistate firm and shipped treatment and repair material from out of state), the court found that the parties "contemplated" a transaction that was primarily local and not "substantially" interstate. . . . The court took the view that the FAA applied only if at the time the parties entered a contract they "contemplated substantial interstate activity."]

Justice Breyer delivered the opinion of the Court.

This case concerns the reach of § 2 of the Federal Arbitration Act. That section makes enforceable a written arbitration provision in "a contract *evidencing* a transaction *involving* commerce."9 U.S.C. § 2 (emphasis added). Should we read this phrase broadly, extending the Act's reach to the limits of Congress' Commerce Clause power? Or, do the two italicized words — "involving" and "evidencing" — significantly restrict the Act's application? We conclude that the broader reading of the Act is the correct one, and we reverse a State Supreme Court judgment to the contrary. . . .

After examining the statute's language, background, and structure, we conclude that the word "involving" is broad and is indeed the functional equivalent of "affecting." For one thing, such an interpretation, linguistically speaking, is permissible. The dictionary finds instances in which "involve" and "affect" sometimes can mean about the same thing. For another, the Act's legislative history, to the extent that it is informative, indicates an expansive congressional intent. . . . Further, this Court has previously described the Act's reach expansively as coinciding with that of the Commerce Clause. . . .

Finally, a broad interpretation of this language is consistent with the Act's basic purpose, to put arbitration provisions on "'the same footing'" as a contract's other terms. Conversely, a narrower interpretation is not consistent with the Act's purpose, for (unless unreasonably narrowed to the flow of commerce) such an interpretation would create a new, unfamiliar test lying somewhere in a no man's land between "in commerce" and "affecting commerce," thereby unnecessarily complicating the law and breeding litigation from a statute that seeks to avoid it. We recognize arguments to the contrary: The pre-New Deal Congress that passed the Act in 1925 might well have thought the Commerce Clause did not stretch as far as has turned out to be the case. But, it is not unusual for this Court in similar circumstances to ask whether the scope of a statute should expand along with the expansion of the Commerce Clause power itself, and to answer the question affirmatively — as, for the reasons set forth above, we do here. . . .

Section 2 applies where there is "a contract *evidencing a transaction* involving commerce." The second interpretive question focuses on the italicized words. Does "evidencing a transaction" mean only that the transaction (that the contract "evidences") must turn out, *in fact,* to have involved interstate commerce? Or, does it mean more?

Many years ago, Second Circuit Chief Judge Lumbard said that the phrase meant considerably more. He wrote:

> "The significant question . . . is not whether, in carrying out the terms of the contract, the parties *did* cross state lines, but whether, *at the time they entered into it* and accepted the arbitration clause, they *contemplated* substantial interstate activity. Cogent evidence regarding their state of mind at the time would be the terms of the contract, and if it, on its face, evidences interstate traffic . . . , the contract should come within § 2. In addition, evidence as to how the parties expected the contract to be performed and how it was performed is relevant to whether substantial interstate activity was contemplated." *Metro Industrial Painting Corp. v. Terminal Constr. Co.,* 287 F.2d 382, 387 (CA2 1961) (concurring opinion).

The Supreme Court of Alabama and several other courts have followed this view, known as the "contemplation of the parties" test.

We find the interpretive choice difficult, but for several reasons we conclude that the first interpretation ("commerce in fact") is more faithful to the statute than the second ("contemplation of the parties"). First, the "contemplation of the parties" interpretation, when viewed in terms of the statute's basic purpose, seems anomalous. That interpretation invites litigation about what was, or was not, "contemplated." Why would Congress intend a test that risks the very kind of costs and delay through litigation (about the circumstances of contract formation) that Congress wrote the Act to help the parties avoid?

Moreover, that interpretation too often would turn the validity of an arbitration clause on what, from the perspective of the statute's basic purpose, seems happenstance, namely, whether the parties happened to think to insert a reference to interstate commerce in the document or happened to mention it in an initial conversation. After all, parties to a sales contract with an arbitration clause might naturally think about the goods sold, or about arbitration, but why should they naturally think about an interstate commerce connection?

Further, that interpretation fits awkwardly with the rest of § 2. That section, for example, permits parties to agree to submit to arbitration "an existing controversy arising out of" a contract made earlier. Why would Congress want to risk nonenforceability of this *later* arbitration agreement (even if fully connected with interstate commerce) simply because the parties did not properly "contemplate" (or write about) the interstate aspects of the earlier contract? The first interpretation, requiring only that the "transaction" *in fact* involve interstate commerce, avoids this anomaly, as it avoids the other anomalous effects growing out of the "contemplation of the parties" test.

Second, the statute's language permits the "commerce in fact" interpretation. . . .

Third, the basic practical argument underlying the "contemplation of the parties" test was, in Chief Judge Lumbard's words, the need to "be cautious in construing the act lest we excessively encroach on the powers which Congressional policy, if not the Constitution, would reserve to the states." The practical force of this argument has diminished in light of this Court's later holdings that the Act does displace state law to the contrary. See *Southland Corp. v. Keating*. . . .

The parties do not contest that the transaction in this case, in fact, involved interstate commerce. In addition to the multistate nature of Terminix and Allied-Bruce, the termite-treating and house-repairing material used by Allied-Bruce in its (allegedly inadequate) efforts to carry out the terms of the Plan, came from outside Alabama. Consequently, the judgment of the Supreme Court of Alabama is reversed, and the case is remanded for further proceedings not inconsistent with this opinion.

Justice O'CONNOR, concurring.

I agree with the Court's construction of § 2 of the Federal Arbitration Act. As applied in federal courts, the Court's interpretation comports fully with my understanding of congressional intent. A more restrictive definition of "evidencing" and "involving" would doubtless foster prearbitration litigation that would frustrate the very purpose of the statute. As applied in state courts, however, the effect of a broad formulation of § 2 is more troublesome. The reading of § 2 adopted today will displace many state statutes carefully calibrated to protect consumers, see, e.g., Mont. Code Ann. § 27-5-114(2)(b) (1993) (refusing to enforce arbitration clauses in consumer contracts where the consideration is $5,000 or less), and state procedural requirements aimed at ensuring knowing and voluntary consent, see, e.g., S.C. Code Ann. § 15-48-10(a) (Supp. 1993) (requiring that notice of arbitration provision be prominently placed on first page of contract). I have long adhered to the view, discussed below, that Congress designed the Federal Arbitration Act to apply only in federal courts. But if we are to apply the Act in state courts, it makes little sense to read § 2 differently in that context. In the end, my agreement with the Court's construction of § 2 rests largely on the wisdom of maintaining a uniform standard.

I continue to believe that Congress never intended the Federal Arbitration Act to apply in state courts, and that this Court has strayed far afield in giving the Act so broad a compass . . . Yet, over the past decade, the Court has abandoned all pretense of ascertaining congressional intent with respect to the Federal Arbitration Act, building instead, case by case, an edifice of its own creation. I have no doubt that Congress could enact, in the first instance, a federal arbitration statute that displaces most state arbitration laws. But I also have no doubt that, in 1925, Congress enacted no such statute.

Were we writing on a clean slate, I would adhere to that view and affirm the Alabama court's decision. But, as the Court points out, more than 10 years have passed since *Southland*, several subsequent cases have built upon its reasoning, and parties have undoubtedly made contracts in reliance on the Court's interpretation of the Act in the interim. After reflection, I am persuaded by considerations of *stare decisis*, which we have said "have special force in the area of statutory interpretation," to acquiesce in today's judgment. Though wrong, *Southland* has not proved unworkable, and, as always, "Congress remains free to alter what we have done."

Today's decision caps this Court's effort to expand the Federal Arbitration Act. Although each decision has built logically upon the decisions preceding it, the initial building block in *Southland* laid a faulty foundation. I acquiesce in today's judgment because there is no "special justification" to overrule *Southland*. It remains now for Congress to correct this interpretation if it wishes to preserve state autonomy in state courts.

Notes and Questions

21. Justice Breyer gives the FAA the broadest possible interpretation, holding that it can extend to any contracts involving matters "affecting" interstate commerce. How broad a scope is that? *See Wickard v. Filburn*, 317 U.S. 111 (1942) (giving an expansive interpretation to Commerce Clause); but *see United States v. Lopez*, 514 U.S. 549 (1995) (holding unconstitutional a federal statute prohibiting carrying of a gun within 1,000 feet of a school on grounds that it exceeded congressional authority under the Commerce Clause).

22. In *Citizen's Bank v. Alafabco, Inc.*, 123 S. Ct. 2037 (2003), the Court again construed the "commerce" requirement in the FAA broadly. There, residents of Alabama entered into debt restructuring agreements providing for arbitration. Although all parties were Alabama residents, one of the parties had engaged in business throughout the southeastern United States using loans related to the agreements. The debt was secured by goods that contained out-of-state parts and raw materials. After *Allied Bruce* and *Citizen's Bank*, what scope of operation is left for state arbitration statutes? What disputes can be viewed as involving matters that are purely intrastate?

In her concurring opinion, Justice O'Connor points out that the Court's broad interpretation of the FAA means that it will override statutory protections that have been enacted by state legislatures to protect their citizens from unknowing waiver of their rights by signing arbitration clauses. Consider the following case.

❖ Doctor's Associates, Inc. v. Casarotto
517 U.S. 681 (1996)

Justice GINSBURG delivered the opinion of the Court.

This case concerns a standard form franchise agreement for the operation of a Subway sandwich shop in Montana. When a dispute arose between parties to the agreement, franchisee Paul Casarotto sued franchisor Doctor's Associates, Inc. (DAI), and DAI's Montana development agent, Nick Lombardi, in a Montana state court. DAI and Lombardi sought to stop the litigation pending arbitration pursuant to the arbitration clause set out on page nine of the franchise agreement.

The Federal Arbitration Act (FAA or Act) declares written provisions for arbitration "valid, irrevocable, and enforceable, save upon such grounds as exist at law or in equity for the revocation of any contract." 9 U.S.C. § 2. Montana law, however, declares an arbitration clause unenforceable unless "[n]otice that [the] contract is subject to arbitration" is "typed in underlined capital letters on the first page of the contract." Mont. Code Ann. § 27-5-114(4) (1995). The question here presented is whether Montana's law is compatible with the federal Act. We hold that Montana's first-page notice requirement, which governs not "any contract," but specifically and solely contracts "subject to arbitration," conflicts with the FAA and is therefore displaced by the federal measure. . . .

Section 2 of the FAA provides that written arbitration agreements "shall be valid, irrevocable, and enforceable, save upon such grounds as exist at law or in equity for the revocation of *any* contract." 9 U.S.C. § 2 (emphasis added). . . . [S]tate law may be applied "*if* that law arose to govern issues concerning the validity, revocability, and enforceability of contracts generally." Thus, generally applicable contract defenses, such as fraud, duress, or unconscionability, may be applied to invalidate arbitration agreements without contravening § 2.

Courts may not, however, invalidate arbitration agreements under state laws applicable *only* to arbitration provisions. By enacting § 2, we have several times said, Congress precluded States from singling out arbitration provisions for suspect status, requiring instead that such provisions be placed "upon the same footing as other contracts." Montana's § 27-5-114(4) directly conflicts with § 2 of the FAA because the State's law conditions the enforceability of arbitration agreements on compliance with a specialnotice requirement not applicable to contracts generally. The FAA thus displaces the Montana statute with respect to arbitration agreements covered by the Act. . . .

For the reasons stated, the judgment of the Supreme Court of Montana is *reversed*, and the case is remanded for further proceedings not inconsistent with this opinion.

Notes and Questions

23. Do you think decisions such as *Doctor's Associates* might create occasional tensions between state judges and federal judges, at least in states that have developed special protections for consumers with respect to arbitration clauses? Consider the specially concurring opinion of Justice Trieweiler in the decision below of the Montana Supreme Court:

> To those federal judges who consider forced arbitration as the panacea for their "heavy case loads" and who consider the reluctance of state courts to buy into the arbitration program as a sign of intellectual inadequacy, I would like to explain a few things.
>
> In Montana, we are reasonably civilized and have a sophisticated system of justice which has evolved over time and which we continue to develop for the primary purpose of assuring fairness to those people who are subject to its authority. . . .
>
> What I would like the people in the federal judiciary, especially at the appellate level, to understand is that due to their misinterpretation of congressional intent when it enacted the Federal Arbitration Act, and due to their naive assumption that arbitration provisions and choice of law provisions are knowingly bargained for, all of these procedural safeguards and substantive laws are easily avoided by any party with enough leverage to stick a choice of law and an arbitration provision in its preprinted contract and require the party with inferior bargaining power to sign it. . . .
>
> [I]f the Federal Arbitration Act is to be interpreted as broadly as some of the decisions from our federal courts would suggest, then it presents a serious issue regarding separation of powers. What these interpretations do, in effect, is permit a few major corporations to draft contracts regarding their relationship with others that immunizes them from accountability under the laws of the states where they do business, and by the courts in those states.
>
> These insidious erosions of state authority and the judicial process threaten to undermine the rule of law as we know it.
>
> Nothing in our jurisprudence appears more intellectually detached from reality and arrogant than the lament of federal judges who see this system of imposed arbitration as "therapy for their crowded dockets." These decisions have perverted the purpose of the FAA from one to accomplish judicial neutrality, to one of open hostility to any legislative effort to assure that unsophisticated parties to contracts of adhesion at least understand the rights they are giving up.

24. Would the result in *Doctor's Associates* be different if the franchise agreement had provided that the agreement was to be governed by Montana law? See *Volt Information Sciences, Inc. v. Stanford*, 489 U.S. 468 (1989) (holding that where an arbitration agreement contained a choice-of-law clause providing that the contract was to be governed by the law of California, it was proper for a federal district judge to apply a California statute authorizing a stay of the arbitration proceeding pending resolution of related litigation between a party to the arbitration agreement and third parties not bound by it; even though such a state statute conflicts with the FAA, it is proper to apply state law where the parties have specified that state law controls). The majority in *Doctor's Associates* suggested that *Volt* is limited to state procedural rules regulating arbitration. The majority distinguished *Volt* as follows:

> *Volt* involved an arbitration agreement that incorporated state procedural rules, one of which, on the facts of that case, called for arbitration to be stayed pending the resolution of a related judicial proceeding. The state rule examined in *Volt* determined only the efficient order of proceedings; it did not affect the enforceability of the arbitration agreement itself. . . . Applying [the Montana notice requirement], in contrast, would not enforce the arbitration clause in the contract between DAI and Casarotto; instead, Montana's first-page notice requirement would invalidate the clause. (517 U.S. at 688.)

5.   *Recent Decisions on Arbitrability and the Federal Arbitration Act*

All of the foregoing decisions demonstrate the strong and abiding Supreme Court jurisprudence strengthening arbitration provisions under the FAA and the authority of arbitrators to address questions of procedure and interpretation related to arbitrable disputes.

We conclude this section with two fairly recent decisions, both of which involve consumer transactions and the application of state consumer protection statutes. Both cases came to the Court on writs of certiorari from state supreme courts, and both decisions generated a good deal of controversy.

The *Green Tree* decision, focused on the concept of "class action arbitration," contained surprises for everyone when it was published. As you read it, ask yourself whether you buy Justice Breyer's rationale that the issue here is a procedural one and not a threshold "arbitrability" issue for a court to handle.

❖ **Green Tree Financial Corp. v. Bazzle**
123 S. Ct. 2402 (2003)

[Five homeowners brought class actions in South Carolina state courts against Green Tree Financial Corp. ("Green Tree") in connection with a home improvement loan and loans for mobile homes. State appellate courts affirmed class certification and awards in two separate actions against Green Tree. The South Carolina Supreme Court consolidated the appeals and affirmed that the class action arbitration was legally permissible.]

Justice BREYER announced the judgment of the Court and delivered an opinion, in which Justices SCALIA, SOUTER, and GINSBURG join.

This case concerns contracts between a commercial lender and its customers, each of which contains a clause providing for arbitration of all contract-related disputes. The Supreme Court of South Carolina held (1) that the arbitration clauses are silent as to whether arbitration might take the form of class arbitration, and (2) that, in that circumstance, South Carolina law interprets the contracts as permitting class arbitration . . . We granted certiorari to determine whether this holding is consistent with the Federal Arbitration Act . . .

We are faced at the outset with a problem concerning the contracts' silence. Are the contracts in fact silent, or do they forbid class arbitration as petitioner Green Tree Financial Corp. contends? Given the South Carolina Supreme Court's holding, it is important to resolve that question. But we cannot do so, not simply because it is a matter of state law, but also because it is a matter for the arbitrator to decide.

[Lynn and Burt Bazzle and Green Tree entered into a contract providing that]:

> "All disputes, claims, or controversies arising from or relating to this contract or the relationships which result from this contract . . . *shall be resolved by binding arbitration by one arbitrator selected by us with consent of you.* This arbitration contract is made pursuant to a transaction in interstate commerce, and shall be governed by the Federal Arbitration Act. . . . THE PARTIES VOLUNTARILY AND KNOWINGLY WAIVE ANY RIGHT THEY HAVE TO A JURY TRIAL, EITHER PURSUANT TO ARBITRATION UNDER THIS CLAUSE OR PURSUANT TO COURT ACTION BY US (AS PROVIDED HEREIN). . . . The parties agree and understand that the arbitrator shall have all powers provided by the law and the contract. These powers shall include all legal and equitable remedies, including, but not limited to, money damages, declaratory relief, and injunctive relief." . . .

[Other class members signed similar agreements with Green Tree.]

In April 1997, the Bazzles asked the court to certify their claims as a class action. Green Tree sought to stay the court proceedings and compel arbitration. On January 5, 1998, the court both (1) certified a class action and (2) entered an order compelling arbitration. . . . Green Tree then selected an arbitrator with the Bazzles' consent. And the arbitrator, administering the proceeding as a class arbitration, eventually awarded the class $10,935,000 in statutory damages, along with attorney's fees. The trial court confirmed the award . . . and Green Tree appealed to the South Carolina Court of Appeals claiming, among other things, that class arbitration was legally impermissible. . . .

The South Carolina Supreme Court's determination that the contracts are silent in respect to class arbitration raises a preliminary question. Green Tree argued . . . that the contracts are not silent — that they forbid class arbitration. . . . Whether Green Tree is right about the contracts themselves presents a disputed issue of contract interpretation. . . . [Three of the dissenting Justices argue] that the contracts say that disputes "shall be resolved . . . by one arbitrator selected by us [Green Tree] with consent of you [Green Tree's customer]." . . . [and they conclude] that class arbitration is clearly inconsistent with this requirement. After all, class arbitration involves an arbitration, not simply between Green Tree and a *named customer*, but also between Green Tree and *other* (represented) customers, all taking place before the arbitrator chosen to arbitrate the initial, *named customer*'s dispute.

We do not believe, however, that the contracts' language is as clear . . . The class arbitrator *was* "selected by" Green Tree "with consent of" Green Tree's customers, the named plaintiffs. And insofar as the other class members agreed to proceed in class arbitration, they consented as well. Of course, Green Tree did *not* independently select *this* arbitrator to arbitrate its disputes with the *other* class members. But whether the contracts contain this additional requirement is a question that the literal terms of the contracts do not decide . . . Do the contracts forbid class arbitration? Given the broad authority the contracts elsewhere bestow upon the arbitrator, (. . . "all powers," including certain equitable powers "provided by the law and the contract"), the answer to this question is not completely obvious.

At the same time, we cannot automatically accept the South Carolina Supreme Court's resolution of this contract-interpretation question. Under the terms of the parties' contracts, the question — whether the agreement forbids class arbitration — is for the arbitrator to decide. The parties agreed to submit to the arbitrator "*all* disputes, claims, or controversies arising from or relating to this contract or the relationships which result from this contract." . . . And the dispute about what the arbitration contract in each case means . . . is a dispute "relating to this contract" and the resulting "relationships." Hence the parties seem to have agreed that an arbitrator, not a judge, would answer the relevant question. . . . And if there is doubt about that matter — about the " 'scope of arbitrable issues' " — we should resolve that doubt " 'in favor of arbitration.' " . . .

In certain limited circumstances, courts assume that the parties intended courts, not arbitrators, to decide a particular arbitration-related matter (in the absence of "clear and unmistakable" evidence to the contrary). . . . These limited instances typically involve matters of a kind that "contracting parties would likely have expected a court" to decide. . . . The question here — whether the contracts forbid class arbitration — does not fall into this narrow exception. It concerns neither the validity of the arbitration clause nor its applicability to the underlying dispute between the parties. Unlike *First Options*, the question is not whether the parties wanted a judge or an arbitrator to decide *whether they agreed to arbitrate a matter*. . . . Rather the relevant question here is what *kind of arbitration proceeding* the parties agreed to. . . . It concerns contract interpretation and arbitration procedures. Arbitrators are well situated to answer that question. Given these considerations, along with the arbitration contracts' sweeping language concerning the scope of the questions committed to arbitration, this matter of contract interpretation should be for the arbitrator, not the courts, to decide. . . .

The judgment of the South Carolina Supreme Court is *vacated*, and the case is *remanded* [to the arbitrator] for further proceedings.

Justice STEVENS, concurring in the judgment and dissenting in part.

The parties agreed that South Carolina law would govern their arbitration agreement. The Supreme Court of South Carolina has held as a matter of state law that class-action arbitrations are permissible if not prohibited by the applicable arbitration agreement, and that the agreement between these parties is silent on the issue. . . . There is nothing in the [FAA] that precludes either of these determinations by the Supreme Court of South Carolina. Arguably the interpretation of the parties' agreement should have been made in the first instance by the arbitrator, rather than the court. . . . Because the decision to conduct a class-action arbitration was correct as a matter of law, and because petitioner has merely challenged the merits of that decision without claiming that it was made by the wrong decision maker, there is no need to remand the case to correct that possible error.

Chief Justice REHNQUIST, with whom Justices O'CONNOR and KENNEDY join, dissenting:

The parties entered into a contract with an arbitration clause that is governed by the Federal Arbitration Act . . . The Supreme Court of South Carolina held that arbitration under the contract could proceed as a class action even though the contract does not by its terms permit class-action arbitration. . . . This determination is one for the courts, not for the arbitrator, and the holding of the Supreme Court of South Carolina contravenes the terms of the contract and is therefore pre-empted by the FAA. . . .

While the observation of the Supreme Court of South Carolina that the agreement of the parties was silent as to the availability of class-wide arbitration is literally true, the imposition of class-wide arbitration contravenes [the contract's provision about the consent of each party to the arbitrator selected]. . . . [P]etitioner had the contractual right to choose an arbitrator for each dispute with the other 3,734 individual class members . . . Petitioner may well have chosen different arbitrators for some or all of these other disputes; indeed, it would have been reasonable for petitioner to do so, in order to avoid concentrating all of the risk of substantial damages awards in the hands of a single arbitrator. . . . [T]he FAA does not prohibit parties from choosing to proceed on a class-wide basis. Here, however, the parties simply did not so choose. . . .

Notes and Questions

25. Chief Justice Rehnquist's opinion, on behalf of four members of the Court, finds that the parties did not agree to authorize a class-wide arbitration through individual arbitration contracts. Which interpretation most likely evidences the parties' intent? What do you draw on to support your conclusion? Were you surprised that the Supreme Court sent the case back to the arbitrator?

26. As is sometimes the case in Supreme Court jurisprudence, Justice Stevens provides the critical fifth vote, but concurs only in the judgment. He refuses to join in the plurality's reasoning. How does his approach diverge from that of the plurality opinion?

27. Although the three dissenting Justices conclude that the FAA pre-empts (or bars) the conclusion of the South Carolina court, they do so merely because they view the judgment as conflicting with their interpretation of the contract. They do not state that the FAA prohibits class-wide arbitration if permitted by state law. Instead, they expressly leave that option open for contracting parties. "[T]he FAA does not prohibit parties from choosing to proceed on a class-wide basis. Here, however, the parties simply did not so choose." What are some potential advantages and disadvantages of class-wide arbitration in these circumstances?

28. Justice Thomas separately dissented and did not join the Chief Justice's opinion. He would have affirmed the South Carolina Supreme Court's judgment because he does not believe that the FAA applies to state court proceedings. Thus, it cannot be a ground for preempting South Carolina's interpretation of a private arbitration agreement. (See *infra*, Section E, for cases on FAA preemption of state law.) Other Justices have espoused this view in earlier decisions, but most have now agreed (albeit reluctantly) with Court precedents applying the FAA to both state and federal courts. *See, e.g., Allied-Bruce Terminix Companies v. Dobson*, 513 U.S. 265, 283 (1995) (O'Connor, J., concurring) ("I continue to believe that Congress never intended the [FAA] to apply to state courts. . . . Were we writing on a clean slate, I would adhere to that view . . . But . . . more than 10 years have passed since [precedent establishing otherwise] and parties have undoubtedly made contracts in reliance on the Court's interpretation. . . . After reflection, I am persuaded by considerations of *stare decisis* . . .").

29. If you were a lawyer advising Green Tree Financial Corporation and they asked you to help them enforce arbitration agreements without the possibility of consumers joining together in a class action, what would you suggest they do?

As you may recall from other courses, federal courts, including the Supreme Court, are restricted in construing state law. Federal courts must defer to state court interpretation of state substantive law. *See Erie v. Tompkins*, 58 S. Ct. 817 (1938). Because much of what arbitrators do is construe state contract law, federal judges have two reasons to be very deferential in reviewing arbitral decisions: for the general reasons supporting deference to arbitrators discussed earlier, and to honor the *Erie* principle.

Should the doctrine of *Prima Paint* extend to a scenario where a contract is allegedly void because it is illegal — even criminal — under state law? That was the issue in the following case.

❖ Buckeye Check Cashing, Inc. v. Cardegna
126 S. Ct. 1204 (2006)

Justice SCALIA delivered the opinion of the Court.

We decide whether a court or an arbitrator should consider the claim that a contract containing an arbitration provision is void for illegality.

I

Respondents John Cardegna and Donna Reuter entered into various deferred-payment transactions with petitioner Buckeye Check Cashing (Buckeye), in which they received cash in exchange for a personal check in the amount of the cash plus a finance charge. For each separate transaction they signed a "Deferred Deposit and Disclosure Agreement" (Agreement), which included the following arbitration provisions:

> "1. *Arbitration Disclosure* By signing this Agreement, you agree that i[f] a dispute of any kind arises out of this Agreement or your application therefore or any instrument relating thereto, th[e]n either you or we or third-parties involved can choose to have that dispute resolved by binding arbitration as set forth in Paragraph 2 below . . . .
>
> "2. *Arbitration Provisions* Any claim, dispute, or controversy . . . arising from or relating to this Agreement . . . or the validity, enforceability, or scope of this Arbitration Provision or the entire Agreement (collectively 'Claim'), shall be resolved, upon the election of you or us or said third-parties, by binding arbitration. . . . This arbitration Agreement is made pursuant to a transaction involving interstate commerce, and shall be governed by the Federal Arbitration Act. ('FAA'), 9 U.S.C. Sections 1-16. The arbitrator shall apply applicable substantive law constraint [sic] with the FAA and applicable statu[t]es of limitations and shall honor claims of privilege recognized by law. . . ."

Respondents brought this putative class action in Florida state court, alleging that Buckeye charged usurious interest rates and that the Agreement violated various Florida lending and consumer-protection laws, rendering it criminal on its face. Buckeye moved to compel arbitration. The trial court denied the motion, holding that a court rather than an arbitrator should resolve a claim that a contract is illegal and void *ab initio*. The District Court of Appeal of Florida for the Fourth District reversed, holding that because respondents did not challenge the arbitration provision itself, but instead claimed that the entire contract was void, the agreement to arbitrate was enforceable, and the question of the contract's legality should go to the arbitrator.

Respondents appealed, and the Florida Supreme Court reversed, reasoning that to enforce an agreement to arbitrate in a contract challenged as unlawful "'could breathe life into a contract that not only violates state law, but also is criminal in nature . . . .' "

II

A

To overcome judicial resistance to arbitration, Congress enacted the Federal Arbitration Act (FAA), 9 U.S.C. §§ 1-16. Section 2 embodies the national policy favoring arbitration and places arbitration agreements on equal footing with all other contracts:

> "A written provision in . . . a contract . . . to settle by arbitration a controversy thereafter arising out of such contract . . . or an agreement in writing to submit to arbitration an existing controversy arising out of such a contract . . . shall be valid, irrevocable, and enforceable, save upon such grounds as exist at law or in equity for the revocation of any contract."

Challenges to the validity of arbitration agreements "upon such grounds as exist at law or in equity for the revocation of any contract" can be divided into two types. One type challenges specifically the validity of the agreement to arbitrate. The other challenges the contract as a whole, either on a ground that directly affects the entire agreement (*e.g.*, the agreement was fraudulently induced), or on the ground that the illegality of one of the contract's provisions renders the whole contract invalid Respondents' claim is of this second type. The crux of the complaint is that the contract as a whole (including its arbitration provision) is rendered invalid by the usurious finance charge.

In *Prima Paint Corp. v. Flood & Conklin Mfg. Co.*, we addressed the question of who — court or arbitrator — decides these two types of challenges. The issue in the case was "whether a claim of fraud in the inducement of the entire contract is to be resolved by the federal court, or whether the matter is to be referred to the arbitrators." Guided by § 4 of the FAA, . . . we held that "if the claim is fraud in the inducement of the arbitration clause itself — an issue which goes to the making of the agreement to arbitrate — the federal court may proceed to adjudicate it. But the statutory language does not permit the federal court to consider claims of fraud in the inducement of the contract generally." We rejected the view that the question of "severability" was one of state law, so that if state law held the arbitration provision not to be severable a challenge to the contract as a whole would be decided by the court.

Subsequently, in *Southland Corp.,* we held that the FAA "create[d] a body of federal substantive law," which was "applicable in state and federal courts." We rejected the view that state law could bar enforcement of § 2, even in the context of state-law claims brought in state court.

B

Prima Paint and *Southland* answer the question presented here by establishing three propositions. First, as a matter of substantive federal arbitration law, an arbitration provision is severable from the remainder of the contract. Second, unless the challenge is to the arbitration clause itself, the issue of the contract's validity is considered by the arbitrator in the first instance. Third, this arbitration law applies in state as well as federal courts. The parties have not requested, and we do not undertake, reconsideration of those holdings. Applying them to this case, we conclude that because respondents challenge the Agreement, but not specifically its arbitration provisions, those provisions are enforceable apart from the remainder of the contract. The challenge should therefore be considered by an arbitrator, not a court.

In declining to apply *Prima Paint's* rule of severability, the Florida Supreme Court relied on the distinction between void and voidable contracts. "Florida public policy and contract law," it concluded, permit "no severable, or salvageable, parts of a contract found illegal and void under Florida law." *Prima Paint* makes this conclusion irrelevant. That case rejected application of state severability rules to the arbitration agreement *without discussing* whether the challenge at issue would have rendered the contract void or voidable. Indeed, the opinion expressly disclaimed any need to decide what state-law remedy was available, Likewise in *Southland,* which arose in state court, we did not ask whether the several challenges made there — fraud, misrepresentation, breach of contract, breach of fiduciary duty, and violation of the California Franchise Investment Law — would render the contract void or voidable. We simply rejected the proposition that the enforceability of the arbitration agreement turned on the state legislature's judgment concerning the forum for enforcement of the state-law cause of action. So also here, we cannot accept the Florida Supreme Court's conclusion that enforceability of the arbitration agreement should turn on "Florida public policy and contract law."

Respondents assert that *Prima Paint's* rule of severability does not apply in state court. . . . *Southland* itself refused to "believe Congress intended to limit the Arbitration Act to disputes subject only to *federal*-court jurisdiction."

Respondents point to the language of § 2, which renders "valid, irrevocable, and enforceable" "a written provision in" or "an agreement in writing to submit to arbitration an existing controversy arising out of" a "contract." Since, respondents argue, the only arbitration agreements to which § 2 applies are those involving a "contract," and since an agreement void *ab initio* under state law is not a "contract," there is no "written provision" in or "controversy arising out of" a "contract," to which § 2 can apply. We do not read "contract" so narrowly. The word appears four times in § 2. Its last appearance is in the final clause, which allows a challenge to an arbitration provision "upon such grounds as exist at law or in equity for the revocation of any *contract*." There can be no doubt that "contract" as used this last time must include contracts that later prove to be void. Otherwise, the grounds for revocation would be limited to those that rendered a contract voidable — which would mean (implausibly) that an arbitration agreement could be challenged as voidable but not as void. Because the sentence's final use of "contract" so obviously includes putative contracts, we will not read the same word earlier in the same sentence to have a more narrow meaning.

* * *

We reaffirm today that, regardless of whether the challenge is brought in federal or state court, a challenge to the validity of the contract as a whole, and not specifically to the arbitration clause, must go to the arbitrator.

The judgment of the Florida Supreme Court is reversed, and the case is remanded for further proceedings not inconsistent with this opinion.

It is so ordered.

Notes and Questions

30. Do you see any potential concerns associated with giving arbitrators authority to address questions such as those at the heart of *Buckeye Check Cashing*? Consider, also, that many arbitration rules now give arbitrators plenary authority over all questions relating to and challenges to their jurisdiction. For a discussion of potential limitations on arbitral authority and a role for courts in the context of adhesion contracts, see Chapter 19.D.

31. A contract between Ferrer, who appears on television as "Judge Alex," and Preston, an entertainment lawyer, required arbitration of "any dispute . . . relating to the [contract] terms . . . or the breach, validity, or legality thereof . . . in accordance with the [AAA] Rules." When Preston demanded arbitration, seeking fees allegedly due under the contract, Ferrer petitioned the California Labor Commissioner for a determination that the contract was invalid and unenforceable under the California Talent Agencies Act because Preston had failed to acquire a license as a talent agent. Should a court enforce the arbitration agreement or direct the parties to proceed before the Labor Commissioner? See *Preston v. Ferrer*, 128 S. Ct. 978 (2008).

D. Other Forms of Preaward Judicial Support of Arbitration Proceedings

1. *Judicial Appointment of Arbitrators*

Where parties follow the common practice of incorporating standard arbitration procedures by reference in their agreement, such procedures normally include specific provisions setting forth an administrative procedure for the timely filling of vacancies on the arbitration tribunal and related procedural questions. *See, e.g.,* American Arbitration Association, Commercial Arbitration Rules and Mediation Procedures R-19 "Vacancies" (Amended and Effective September 1, 2007). Where, however, the parties neglect to incorporate such provisions by reference in their agreement, the death, incapacity, or resignation of an arbitrator during proceedings and prior to the rendition of an award may produce confusion and disagreement about the proper method of addressing the vacancy — and may even lead to a stalemate. In such circumstances a party may seek judicial intervention under FAA § 5, which states:

> If in the agreement provision be made for a method of naming or appointing an arbitrator or arbitrators or an umpire, such method shall be followed; but if no method be provided therein, or if a method be provided and any party thereto shall fail to avail himself of such method, or if for any other reason there shall be a lapse in the naming of an arbitrator or arbitrators or umpire, or in filling a vacancy, then upon the application of either party to the controversy the court shall designate and appoint an arbitrator or arbitrators or umpire, as the case may require. . . .

Consider how this provision might be applied in the following scenario.

Problem 2

Court Assistance in Filling a Vacancy

A significant dispute arises under a contract for the chartering of a ship. The parties, Marine and Globe, have a contract that includes a provision calling for arbitration of disputes before a three-member panel consisting of one party-selected arbitrator nominated by each party and a third arbitrator selected jointly by the party arbitrators. During the course of arbitration hearings and prior to the making of an award, Globe's arbitrator dies. Neither the arbitration agreement in the Globe–Marine charterage contract nor the parties' submission to arbitration made any provision for the filling of vacancies on the panel. As the lawyer for Globe, you are concerned about what to do.

a. What options are open to you, and how specifically might a court, utilizing FAA § 5, assist if you and Marine's counsel are unable to find a collaborative solution to this problem? Could a court, for example, direct the parties to essentially start the whole arbitration process over again? See *Marine Products Export Corp v. M.T. Corp. Galaxy*, 977 F.2d 66 (2d Cir. 1992).

b. What is to prevent a party from having a party-appointed arbitrator resign late in the process to disrupt or delay an arbitration that does not seem to be going its way? See *Insurance Co. of N. Am v. Public Serv. Mutual Ins. Co.*, No. 08CV7003 (HB), U.S. Dist. LEXIS 101788 (S.D.N.Y. Dec. 10, 2008).

2. *Judicial Enforcement of Arbitral Summonses and Subpoenas*

The FAA and most state arbitration statutes do not specifically address the subject of arbitration-related discovery. However, the FAA and corresponding state laws give arbitrators authority to issue summons or subpoenas to parties or nonparties, and provide for their judicial enforcement. FAA § 7, for example, states that arbitrators may "summon in writing any person to attend before them or any of them as a witness and in a proper case to bring with him or them any book, record, document, or paper which may be deemed material as evidence in the case." This language, with its reference to "attend[ing] before [one or more arbitrators]" fails to establish a clear predicate for ordering a party to appear at a deposition. Indeed, the section goes on to require subpoenas issued by arbitrators to be directed and served "in the same manner as subpoenas to appear and testify before the court." While some courts have interpreted the section to permit deposition subpoenas, others have held to the contrary. *Compare Meadows Indemnity Co. v. Nutmeg Insur. Co.*, 157 F.R.D. 45 (M.D. Tenn. 1994) *with COMSAT Corp. v. National Science Foundation*, 190 F.3d 269 (4th Cir. 1999).

Some courts question whether a party's agreement gives arbitrators subpoena power over nonparty witnesses. Generally, the subpoena power of arbitrators is supported by court enforcement as long as information being requested is relevant and material, and subject to territorial limits on the arbitral subpoena power. The RUAA, which is now law in several states, includes provisions that directly address these and other concerns through specific provisions for arbitrator-supervised discovery, including depositions. See *www.law.upenn.edu/bll/archives/ulc/uarba/arbitrat1213.pdf.*

> Question
>
> 32. You are representing a client in arbitration and intend to conduct depositions of several witnesses. You are concerned that you may need judicial help to compel their attendance by enforcing arbitrator subpoenas. If you have a choice of going to federal court and applying for court assistance under FAA § 5 or going to a state court and utilizing state arbitration law, which would you prefer? Why? (You may assume for the sake of this question that the state is one of those jurisdictions that have adopted the RUAA.)

3.   Other Preaward Judicial Intervention

Aside from the specific ways set forth in the FAA and state arbitration statutes, should parties be able to seek the intervention of courts to address issues that arise during the arbitration process? For example, should parties be able to go to court to challenge a procedural ruling by an arbitrator prior to the rendering of an award, or try to have an arbitrator replaced by a court in the middle of hearings because the arbitrator made prejudicial remarks? Why do you suppose courts nearly always resist such requests?

E.   Judicial Treatment of Arbitral Awards

1.   Overview of Statutory Standards for Confirmation, Vacation, and Modification

If a claim or controversy proceeds to arbitration and the arbitrators render an award, one likely result is that the parties will comply with the award and no judicial action will be necessary or appropriate. On the other hand, a party may seek to confirm the award, thereby converting it into a judgment of the court. The FAA provides:

§ 9. Award of arbitrators; confirmation; jurisdiction; procedure

If the parties in their agreement have agreed that a judgment of the court shall be entered upon the award made pursuant to the arbitration, and shall specify the court, then at any time within one year after the award is made any party to the arbitration may apply to the court so specified for an order confirming the award, and thereupon the court must grant such an order unless the award is vacated, modified, or corrected as prescribed in sections 10 and 11 of this title. If no court is specified in the agreement of the parties, then such application may be made to the

United States court in and for the district within which such award was made. . . .

Confirmation of an award may be needed to harness the coercive authority of the court to locate and move against funds or property of a party against whom a monetary award was rendered.

It is also possible that one or both parties will seek a judicial order vacating (that is, overturning or setting aside) all or some part of the award. In addition or in the alternative, a motion might be made to the court to modify or correct the award. A careful study of Sections 10 and 11 of the FAA helps one to appreciate the very narrow scope of judicial scrutiny contemplated by arbitration statutes.

§ 10. Same; vacation; grounds; rehearing

(a) In any of the following cases the United States court in and for the district wherein the award was made may make an order vacating the award upon the application of any party to the arbitration —

(1) where the award was procured by corruption, fraud, or undue means;

(2) where there was evident partiality or corruption in the arbitrators, or either of them;

(3) where the arbitrators were guilty of misconduct in refusing to postpone the hearing, upon sufficient cause shown, or in refusing to hear evidence pertinent and material to the controversy; or of any other misbehavior by which the rights of any party have been prejudiced; or

(4) where the arbitrators exceeded their powers, or so imperfectly executed them that a mutual, final, and definite award upon the subject matter submitted was not made.

(b) If an award is vacated and the time within which the agreement required the award to be made has not expired, the court may, in its discretion, direct a rehearing by the arbitrators.

(c) The United States district court for the district wherein an award was made that was issued pursuant to section 580 of title 5 may make an order vacating the award upon the application of a person, other than a party to the arbitration, who is adversely affected or aggrieved by the award, if the use of arbitration or the award is clearly inconsistent with the factors set forth in section 572 of title 5.

§ 11. Same; modification or correction; grounds; order

In either of the following cases the United States court in and for the district wherein the award was made may make an order modifying or correcting the award upon the application of any party to the arbitration —

(a) Where there was an evident material miscalculation of figures or an evident material mistake in the description of any person, thing, or property referred to in the award.

(b) Where the arbitrators have awarded upon a matter not submitted to them, unless it is a matter not affecting the merits of the decision upon the matter submitted.

(c) Where the award is imperfect in matter of form not affecting the merits of the controversy.

The order may modify and correct the award, so as to effect the intent thereof and promote justice between the parties.

Both of the foregoing sections establish fairly clear boundaries for judicial action. Notable by its absence is any reference to judicial vacation or correction based upon arbitrator errors of law or fact, save clerical or mathematical mistakes evident on the face of the award.

On the following pages we take a closer look at court decisions addressing various grounds for vacatur under FAA § 10. Courts have tended to construe these grounds narrowly, reinforcing the finality of arbitral awards. Thus, courts are generally much more deferential to arbitral awards and less likely to overturn them than the judgment of a lower court. Appellate courts typically review trial courts' findings on legal issues *de novo*, but they overturn trial courts' factual findings only if they are clearly erroneous and revise procedural choices only if the lower court abused its discretion. When it comes to arbitration awards, the deference is even greater, and extends to legal as well as factual determinations. As one prominent jurist summarized:

> [T]he question for decision by a federal court asked to set aside an arbitration award . . . is not whether the arbitrator or arbitrators erred in interpreting the contract; it is not whether they clearly erred in interpreting the contract; it is not whether they grossly erred in interpreting the contract; it is whether they interpreted the contract.

Hill v. Norfolk and Western Ry. Co., 814 F.2d 1192, 1194 (7th Cir. 1987) (Hon. Richard Posner). Thus, even if a judge would have reached a different conclusion on the merits, she is not supposed to substitute her judgment for that of the arbitrator(s).

Moreover, as a practical matter, a court is hampered in reviewing the merits of an arbitrator's ruling because written reasoning to support the decision is sometimes withheld, making it quite difficult to review an arbitrator's rulings pertaining to the making of the agreement to arbitrate or the merits of the underlying dispute. In international commercial arbitration and labor relations arbitration, however, arbitrators typically do provide reasoning to support their decisions, and the practice has probably become the norm in large commercial cases. While these rulings are not used as precedent in the same fashion as judicial precedent, they nevertheless provide a basis for parties to familiarize themselves with an arbitrator's work and give a court more assurance that the award was supported by actual contractual interpretation.

Thus, it is not surprising that arbitration awards are very likely to be upheld. There are indications, however, that some courts are much less deferential to arbitration awards than others. A survey of published federal and state court decisions on motions to vacate arbitration awards during a ten-month period in 2004, although far from conclusive, suggests that the much-vaunted "finality" of arbitration awards varies considerably among jurisdictions. In particular, it appears that reversal, or vacatur, may be much more likely in the courts of key commercial states. While federal courts granted only about one tenth of the motions to vacate that were considered during the survey period, the courts of California, New York, and Connecticut collectively honored motions to vacate awards nearly one-third of the time! Although one must take care in drawing final conclusions from such a small sample, the numbers suggest that at least in some states arbitration awards challenged in court may be as vulnerable to reversal as trial court judgments (Mills et al., 2005).

In the following sections we explore individual grounds for vacation of awards, and exemplary decisions. For the most part, these grounds are focused on procedural irregularities in arbitration proceedings. To justify vacatur, generally speaking, the procedural problem must affect the fundamental fairness of the process.

2. Was the Award Procured by Corruption, Fraud, or Undue Means?

Awards are seldom vacated on the basis of "corruption, fraud, or undue means," but there are notable exceptions. One court vacated an arbitral award under the FAA when it found that an expert witness whose testimony influenced an arbitral award had committed perjury. The circumstances were unusual in that there was very clear evidence of perjury with respect to a central issue in the case, and the aggrieved party was not in a position to discover the evidence until after the arbitration proceedings ended. *Bonar v. Dean Witter Reynolds, Inc.*, 835 F.2d 1378 (Fla. 1988).

In most cases where claims of perjury or improper evidence are raised after arbitrators have ruled, courts find that they do not need to "reopen" proceedings and hear such "new" evidence. *See, e.g., Terk Technologies Corp. v. Dockery*, E.D. Mich. 2000, 86 F. Supp. 2d. 706, *aff'd* 3 Fed. Appx. 459, 2001 WL 128317 (arbitration award was not procured by fraud, even if party agreed to arbitration only after witness gave perjured testimony, where witness's testimony was not considered by arbitrators). Instead, they emphasize finality, giving parties and lawyers incentives to present all evidentiary problems, including claims of perjured testimony, to the arbitrators themselves.

3.   Was There Evident Partiality or Corruption in the Arbitrators?

Disclosure standards under arbitration procedures and ethical rules are reinforced by case law interpreting federal and state arbitration statutes. In light of strong policies supporting the finality of arbitration awards, courts are hesitant to allow parties who are disappointed by an award to use a claim of bias as a way to undermine the finality of arbitration. It is unusual to find decisions in which the statements or acts of arbitrators during arbitration demonstrate actual partiality or bias.

However, an arbitrator's failure to disclose actual or perceived conflicts of interest may result in judicial overturning, or vacation, of a subsequent arbitration award. In *Commonwealth Coatings Corp. v. Casualty Co.*, 393 U.S. 145 (1968), the Supreme Court established that an arbitrator's failure to disclose a business relationship with one of the parties was sufficient to support judicial vacation of an arbitration award on the ground of "evident partiality." The case involved an arbitration tribunal made up of two arbitrators chosen by each of the parties and a third "neutral" arbitrator who had previously had a business relationship with one of the parties to the arbitration. The neutral arbitrator voted with the panel for an award in favor of the party with whom he had done business. Thereafter, the party that lost the arbitration challenged the award, claiming that the failure of the arbitrator to disclose his significant business relationship with the winning party amounted to "evident partiality" under 9 U.S.C. § 10, warranting vacatur of the award. A majority of the Court reached the conclusion that vacatur was warranted even though there was no proof of actual bias or partiality on the part of the arbitrator and no proof that the undisclosed connection had any direct impact on the deliberations leading to the award. The mere fact that the relationship had not been disclosed on a timely basis was sufficient to warrant the finding of "evident partiality" and to strike down the award.

Justice Black, writing for a four-member plurality, offered the following rationale for the holding:

> It is true that arbitrators cannot sever all their ties with the business world, since they are not expected to get all their income from their work deciding cases, but we should, if anything, be even more scrupulous to safeguard the impartiality of arbitrators than judges, since the former have completely free rein to decide the law as well as the facts and are not subject to appellate review. We can perceive no way in which the effectiveness of the arbitration process will be hampered by the simple requirement that arbitrators disclose to the parties any dealings that might create an impression of possible bias.

Justice White and Justice Marshall joined in the holding, but Justice White's concurring opinion arguably reflects a more restrained view of what kinds of undisclosed relationships may justify vacatur of a subsequent award:

> [A]rbitrators are not automatically disqualified by a business relationship with the parties before them if both parties are informed of the relationship in advance, or

if they are unaware of the facts but the relationship is trivial. I see no reason automatically to disqualify the best informed and most capable potential arbitrators.

The arbitration process functions best when an amicable and trusting atmosphere is preserved and there is voluntary compliance with the decree, without need for judicial enforcement. This end is best served by establishing an atmosphere of frankness at the outset, through disclosure by the arbitrator of any financial transactions which he has had or is negotiating with either of the parties. In many cases the arbitrator might believe the business relationship to be so insubstantial that to make a point of revealing it would suggest he is indeed easily swayed, and perhaps a partisan of that party. But if the law requires the disclosure, no such imputation can arise. And it is far better that the relationship be disclosed at the outset, when the parties are free to reject the arbitrator or accept him with knowledge of the relationship and continuing faith in his objectivity, than to have the relationship come to light after the arbitration, when a suspicious or disgruntled party can seize on it as a pretext for invalidating the award. The judiciary should minimize its role in arbitration as judge of the arbitrator's impartiality. That role is best consigned to the parties, who are the architects of their own arbitration process, and are far better informed of the prevailing ethical standards and reputations within their business.

Alleged "evident partiality" based on arbitrator nondisclosure is one of the most common grounds for a motion to vacate an arbitration award. Yet, despite the outcome in *Commonwealth Coatings*, relatively few court decisions have overturned awards on the basis of undisclosed relationships or facts. Moreover, as explained in the following decision, the difference of opinion apparently reflected in the Black and White opinions have been reflected in variations in the rigor with which courts police undisclosed relationships.

❖ Positive Software Solutions, Inc. v. New Century Mortgage Corp.
476 F.3d 278 (5th Cir. 2007)

Appeal from the United States District Court for the Northern District Texas.

. . .

Jones, Chief Judge, joined by Jolly, Higginbotham, Davis, Smith, Barksdale, DeMoss, Clement, Prado and Owen, Circuit Judges:

The court reconsidered this case en banc in order to determine whether an arbitration award must be vacated for "evident partiality," 9 U.S.C. § 10(a)(2), where an arbitrator failed to disclose a prior professional association with a member of one of the law firms that engaged him. We conclude that the Federal Arbitration Act ("FAA") does not mandate the extreme remedy of vacatur for nondisclosure of a trivial past association, and we reverse the district court's contrary judgment, but it is necessary to remand for consideration of appellee's other objections to the arbitral award. . . .

[New Century Mortgage Corporation ("New Century") licensed a software program from Positive Software Solutions, Inc. ("Positive Software") in 2001. Later, Positive Software alleged that New Century copied the program in violation of the parties' contract and applicable copyright law. Positive

Software sued New Century in the Northern District of Texas alleging numerous causes of action. The district court later submitted the matter to arbitration under American Arbitration Association ("AAA") rules as provided for in the parties' contract.]

[T]he AAA provided the parties with a list of potential arbitrators and asked the parties to rank the candidates. After reviewing biographical information, the parties selected Peter Shurn to arbitrate the case.... The AAA contacted Shurn about serving as an arbitrator, and he agreed, after stating that he had nothing to disclose regarding past relationships with either party or their counsel.

After a seven-day hearing, Shurn issued an eighty-six page written ruling, concluding that New Century did not infringe Positive Software's copyrights, did not misappropriate trade secrets, did not breach the contract, and did not defraud or conspire against Positive Software. He ordered that Positive Software take nothing on its claims and granted New Century $11,500 on its counterclaims and $1.5 million in attorney's fees.

Upon losing the arbitration, Positive Software conducted a detailed investigation of Shurn's background. It discovered that several years earlier, Shurn and his former law firm, Arnold, White, & Durkee ("Arnold White"), had represented the same party as New Century's counsel, Susman Godfrey, L.L.P., in a patent litigation between Intel Corporation and Cyrix Corporation ("the Intel litigation"). One of Susman Godfrey's attorneys in the New Century arbitration, Ophelia Camiña, had been involved in the Intel litigation.

The Intel litigation involved six different lawsuits in the early 1990s. Intel was represented by seven law firms and at least thirty-four lawyers, including Shurn and Camiña. The dispute involved none of the parties to the arbitration. Camiña participated in representing Intel in three of the lawsuits from August 1991 until July 1992, although her name remained on the pleadings in one of the cases until June 1993. In September 1992, Shurn, along with twelve other Arnold White attorneys, entered an appearance in two of the three cases on which Camiña worked. Although their names appeared together on pleadings, Shurn and Camiña never attended or participated in any meetings, telephone calls, hearings, depositions, or trials together.

Positive Software filed a motion to vacate the arbitration award, alleging [among other things that] ... despite the lack of contact between Shurn and Camiña, Shurn had been biased, as evidenced by his failure to disclose his past connection to Camiña. In September 2004, the district court granted Positive Software's motion and vacated the award, finding that Shurn failed to disclose "a significant prior relationship with New Century's counsel," thus creating an appearance of partiality requiring vacatur.... New Century appealed, and a panel of this court affirmed the district court's vacatur on the ground that the prior relationship "might have conveyed an impression of possible partiality to a reasonable person." ... Neither the district court nor the appellate panel found that Shurn was actually biased toward New Century. This court granted New Century's petition for rehearing en banc.

Discussion

To assure that arbitration serves as an efficient and cost-effective alternative to litigation, and to hold parties to their agreements to arbitrate, the FAA narrowly restricts judicial review of arbitrators' awards. The ground of vacatur alleged here is that "there was evident partiality" in the arbitrator.... The meaning of evident partiality is discernible definitionally and as construed by the Supreme Court and a number of our sister circuits.

On its face, "evident partiality" conveys a stern standard. Partiality means bias, while "evident" is defined as "clear to the vision or understanding" and is synonymous with manifest, obvious, and apparent. *Webster's Ninth New Collegiate Dictionary* 430 (1985). The statutory language, with which we always begin, seems to require upholding arbitral awards unless bias was clearly evident in the decisionmakers.

The panel decision here disagreed with the straightforward interpretation, however, and concluded that, in "a nondisclosure case in which the parties chose the arbitrator," the "arbitrator selected by the parties displays evident partiality by the very failure to disclose facts that might create a reasonable impression of the arbitrator's partiality." ... The panel acknowledged a lack of any actual bias in this award even as it substituted a reasonable impression of partiality standard for "evident" partiality in cases of an arbitrator's nondisclosure to the parties. The panel believed this different standard to be required by the Supreme Court's decision in *Commonwealth Coatings Corp. v. Continental Cas. Co.* ...

How *Commonwealth Coatings* guides this court is a critical issue. Reasonable minds can agree that *Commonwealth Coatings*, like many plurality-plus Supreme Court decisions, is not pellucid. Justice Black delivered the opinion of the Court and imposed "the simple requirement that arbitrators disclose to the parties any dealings that might create an impression of possible bias." ... He noted that, while arbitrators are not expected to sever all ties with the business world, courts must be scrupulous in safeguarding the impartiality of arbitrators, who are given the ability to decide both the facts and the law and whose decisions are not subject to appellate review.... Thus, arbitrators "not only must be unbiased but also must avoid even the appearance of bias," ... in order to maintain confidence in the arbitration system.

Justice White, the fifth vote in the case, together with Justice Marshall, purported to be "glad to join" Justice Black's opinion, but he wrote to make "additional remarks." ... Justice White emphasized that "[t]he Court does not decide today that arbitrators are to be held to the standards of judicial decorum of Article III judges, or indeed of any judges." ... Indeed, Justice White wrote that arbitrators are not "automatically disqualified by a business relationship with the parties before them if ... [the parties] are unaware of the facts but the relationship is trivial." ... While supporting a policy of disclosure by arbitrators to enhance the selection process, Justice White also concluded, in a practical vein, that an arbitrator "cannot be expected to provide the parties with his complete and unexpurgated business biography." . . . His opinion fully envisions upholding awards when arbitrators fail to disclose insubstantial relationships. . . .

A majority of circuit courts have concluded that Justice White's opinion did not lend majority status to the plurality opinion. . . . While these courts' interpretations of *Commonwealth Coatings* may differ in particulars, they all agree that nondisclosure alone does not require vacatur of an arbitral award for evident partiality. An arbitrator's failure to disclose must involve a significant compromising connection to the parties.

This court's prior caselaw is also consistent with a narrow reading of *Commonwealth Coatings*. In *Bernstein Seawell & Kove v. Bosarge*, 813 F.2d 726 (5th Cir. 1987), the losing party in the arbitration challenged the award because of the alleged evident partiality of one of the arbitrators. The arbitrator owned a fractional share of the disputed property and had received commissions on the sale of certain interests. The court held the party had waived his objection to the composition of the panel. Nevertheless, "[e]ven assuming no waiver," he had not produced evidence of evident partiality, . . . because "[t]he appearance of impropriety, standing alone, is insufficient." . . . The court also noted that "[e]vident partiality means more than a mere appearance of bias." . . .

Only the Ninth Circuit has interpreted *Commonwealth Coatings*, as the panel majority did, to de-emphasize Justice White's narrowing language. See *Schmitz v. Zilveti*, 20 F.3d 1043 (9th Cir. 1994). In *Schmitz*, the court criticized case law suggesting "that an impression of bias is sufficient while an appearance [of bias] is not." . . . *Commonwealth Coatings*, it held, does not merit such a "hairline distinction." . . .

As we have concluded, the better interpretation of *Commonwealth Coatings* is that which reads Justice White's opinion holistically. The resulting standard is that in nondisclosure cases, an award may not be vacated because of a trivial or insubstantial prior relationship between the arbitrator and the parties to the proceeding. The "reasonable impression of bias" standard is thus interpreted practically rather than with utmost rigor.

According to this interpretation of *Commonwealth Coatings,* the outcome of this case is clear: Shurn's failure to disclose a trivial former business relationship does not require vacatur of the award. The essential charge of bias is that the arbitrator, Peter Shurn, worked on the same litigation as did Ophelia Camiña, counsel for one of the parties. They represented Intel in protracted patent litigation that lasted from 1990 to 1996. Camiña and Shurn each signed the same ten pleadings, but they never met or spoke to each other before the arbitration. They were two of thirty-four lawyers, and from two of seven firms, that represented Intel during the lawsuit, which ended at least seven years before the instant arbitration.

No case we have discovered in research or briefs has come close to vacating an arbitration award for nondisclosure of such a slender connection between the arbitrator and a party's counsel. In fact, courts have refused vacatur where the undisclosed connections are much stronger. . . .

The relationship in this case pales in comparison to those in which courts have granted vacatur. *See, e.g., Commonwealth Coatings*, 393 U.S. at 146, 89 S.Ct. at 338 (business relationship between arbitrator and party was "repeated and significant"; the party to the arbitration was one of the arbitrator's "regular customers"; "the relationship even went so far as to include the rendering of services on the very projects involved in this lawsuit"); *Olson v. Merrill Lynch, Pierce, Fenner & Smith, Inc.*, 51 F.3d 157, 159 (8th Cir. 1995) (arbitrator was a high-ranking officer in a company that had a substantial ongoing business relationship with one of the parties); *Schmitz*, 20 F.3d at 1044 (arbitrator's law firm represented parent company of a party for decades, including within two years of the arbitration); [*Morelite Constr. Corp. v. New York City Dist. Council Carpenters Benefit Funds*, 748 F.2d 79, 83 n. 3 (2d Cir. 1984) (arbitrator's father was General President of the union involved in the arbitrated dispute).

Finally, even if Justice White's "joinder" is not read as a limitation on Justice Black's opinion in *Commonwealth Coatings*, and the controlling opinion emphatically requires arbitrators to "disclose to the parties any dealings that might create an impression of possible bias," . . . we cannot find the standard breached in this case. The facts of *Commonwealth Coatings* are easily distinguishable. In *Commonwealth Coatings*, the arbitrator and a party had a "repeated and significant" business relationship. . . . The relationship involved fees of about $12,000 paid to the arbitrator by the party, extended over a period of four or five years, ended only one year before the arbitration, and even included the rendering of services on the very projects involved in the arbitration before him. . . . Such a relationship bears little resemblance to the tangential, limited, and stale contacts between Shurn and Camiña. Nothing in *Commonwealth Coatings* requires vacatur for the undisclosed relationship in this case.

Conclusion

Awarding vacatur in situations such as this would seriously jeopardize the finality of arbitration. Just as happened here, losing parties would have an incentive to conduct intensive, after-the-fact investigations to discover the most trivial of relationships, most of which they likely would not have objected to if disclosure had been made. Expensive satellite litigation over nondisclosure of an arbitrator's "complete and unexpurgated business biography" will proliferate. Ironically, the "mere appearance" standard would make it easier for a losing party to challenge an arbitration award for nondisclosure than for actual bias.

Moreover, requiring vacatur based on a mere appearance of bias for nondisclosure would hold arbitrators to a higher ethical standard than federal Article III judges. In his concurrence, Justice White noted that the Court did not decide whether "arbitrators are to be held to the standards of judicial decorum of Article III judges, or indeed of any judges." . . . This cannot mean that arbitrators are held to a higher standard than Article III judges. Had this same relationship occurred between an Article III judge and the same lawyer, neither disclosure nor disqualification would have been forced or even suggested. . . . While it is true that disclosure of prior significant contacts and business dealings between a prospective arbitrator and the parties furthers informed selection,[1] it is not true, as Justice White's opinion perceptively explains, that "the best informed and most capable potential arbitrators" should be automatically disqualified (and their awards nullified) by failure to inform the parties of trivial relationships. . . . .

Finally, requiring vacatur on these attenuated facts would rob arbitration of one of its most attractive features apart from speed and finality — expertise. Arbitration would lose the benefit of specialized knowledge, because the best lawyers and professionals, who normally have the longest lists of potential connections to disclose, have no need to risk blemishes on their reputations from post-arbitration lawsuits attacking them as biased.

Neither the FAA nor the Supreme Court, nor predominant case law, nor sound policy countenances vacatur of FAA arbitral awards for nondisclosure by an arbitrator unless it creates a concrete, not speculative impression of bias. Arbitration may have flaws, but this is not one of them. The draconian remedy of vacatur is only warranted upon nondisclosure that involves a significant compromising relationship. This case does not come close to meeting this standard.

The judgment of the district court is REVERSED, and the case is REMANDED FOR FURTHER PROCEEDINGS.

REAVLEY, Circuit Judge, dissenting, joined by WIENER, GARZA, BENAVIDES and STEWART, Circuit Judges:

In 1968 the Supreme Court held that an arbitral award could not stand where the arbitrator had failed to disclose a past relationship that might give the impression of possible partiality. . . . The Court has never changed that holding; it is the law that rules us today. . . .

The majority opinion manages to substitute actual bias, or the reasonable impression of bias, or concrete impression of bias for the Supreme Court's ruling that dealings that might create only an impression of possible bias must be disclosed. And it purports to join other circuits to hold that nondisclosure alone does not require vacatur of an arbitral award. If the circuit courts could overrule the Supreme Court, the majority might be on a bit firmer ground, because the *Commonwealth Coatings* ruling has not been well received by some of the circuit courts. . . .

---

1. The American Arbitration Association ("AAA"), whose rules governed this proceeding, requires broad prophylactic disclosure of "any circumstance likely to affect impartiality or create an appearance of partiality," so that parties may rely on the integrity of the selection process for arbitrators. Whether Shurn's nondisclosure ran afoul of the AAA rules, however, is not before us and plays no role in applying the federal standard embodied in the FAA.

While I can understand the desire to protect the finality of arbitration awards and avoid a return to extended court expense and delay, this does not justify evading the law of the Supreme Court by misstating it or by avoiding it by bleaching the evidence of possible partiality. Nor should we miss the need to promote the impartiality of arbitrators in this time when that is the favored method of dispute resolution. Influence can so easily corrupt the decision-making process even when it is not recognized by the magistrate or arbitrator himself. And to prove bias or improper influence is rarely possible. It is imperative that we not allow even the good faith or memory of the potential arbitrator to control the disclosure decision for, as the Justices made clear in *Commonwealth Coatings*, it is the protection and reassurance of the party that matters most. . . .

[The dissent discusses the instant action and the efforts of the federal district court to assist Positive Software in getting its software back from New Century, and the court's issuance of an injunction and protective order "based on a finding that New Century had copied Positive Software's material and enjoining New Century from use of Loan Force software, its database, or the software New Century was claiming to be its own products." Later, the district court "found that its orders had been violated in an order telling the disturbing story."]

Meanwhile the dispute had gone to arbitration where the award favored New Century completely. The award found that there had been no infringement or breach of the licensing contract and charged Positive Software with several million dollars of damages, fees, and costs.

At the outset of his ruling the arbitrator ridiculed Positive Software's claim and wrote: "It involves a saga of how failure to renew an $86,100 software license has led to a claim for $500,000,000 in damages in this arbitration, and for $38,000,000,000 in Federal Court." The district court expressed curiosity about the explanation for this statement of the arbitrator's disdain. . . . .

Positive Software searched for an answer to this award and found a prior relationship between counsel for New Century, the Susman Godfrey law firm, and the arbitrator, Peter J. Shurn, a member of the Arnold White & Durkee firm. These two prominent law firms in Houston both represented Intel in its protracted patent litigation with Cyrix. . . . [The dissent discusses the fact that Shurn and Susman Godfrey lawyers' names appeared together on multiple pleadings and motions, and that various questions remained about the extent of the relationship.] The district court said that the fact that Camiña's name remained on pleadings and court records, for years after she claimed to have ended her participation, itself gives the appearance of impropriety. . . .

When Shurn was being considered to arbitrate this dispute, he was told the names of counsel and told of the importance of disclosing any relationship with them. He signed a disclosure for the American Arbitration Association saying that he had nothing to disclose of past relationship with the parties or their counsel, "direct or indirect, whether financial, professional, social or of any other kind." He was further instructed: "If any relationship arises during the course of the arbitration, or if there is any change . . . it must also be disclosed." When Shurn was appointed he was asked: "Have you had any professional or social relationship with counsel for any party in this proceeding or the firms for which they work?" He checked: "I have nothing to disclose." And he signed an oath that he would act in accord with the rules of the American Arbitration Association.

The majority opinion portrays this relationship as trivial by reducing the record to Camiña's statement that she did no work with Shurn. The district court had a different picture of the relationship, one that would have been remembered if Shurn or the other lawyers had given any thought to it, and certainly would have prevented Positive Software from resting its case with Peter Shurn.

Positive Software asked the district court for more discovery of the relationship between the arbitrator and the Susman Godfrey firm, but this request was not granted because the record had already established a failure to disclose a relationship requiring vacatur under the rule of *Commonwealth Coatings*. . . .

[The dissent concludes that the district court judgment vacating the arbitration award should be affirmed.]

WIENER, Circuit Judge, Specially Concurring in Circuit Judge REAVLEY's dissent, joined by REAVLEY, Circuit Judge:

As I wholeheartedly concur in Judge Reavley's dissent, I write separately only to add a perspective that I find helpful in analyzing this case and demonstrating that Judge Reavley has gotten it right. I refer in general to the key differences between arbitration under the FAA and litigation in federal court. . . .

The tradeoffs attendant on the dispute-resolution choice between litigation and arbitration are well and widely known: The principal benefits usually ascribed to arbitration are speed, informality, cost-savings, confidentiality, and services of a decision-maker with expertise and familiarity with the subject matter of the dispute. These "pluses," however, are not without offsetting "minuses." The informalities attendant on proceedings in arbitration come at the cost of the protections automatically afforded to parties in court, which reside in such venerable institutions as the rules of evidence and civil procedure. Likewise sacrificed at the altar of quick and economical finality is virtually the entire system of appellate review . . . . By dispensing with such basic standards of review as clearly erroneous, de novo, and abuse of discretion, there remain to parties in arbitration only the narrowest of appellate recourse. . . .

A less frequently encountered and less frequently discussed distinction and its tradeoffs is the one implicated here: the vital difference between the method by which a federal judge is selected to hear a case in litigation vis-à-vis the method by which arbitrators are selected — a distinction hinted at by Justice White but frequently overlooked or misinterpreted. All know that trial judges in the federal system are nominated and confirmed only after a rigorous testing of their capabilities, experience, and integrity. In contrast, arbitrators are quickly selected by the parties alone, who frequently have unequal knowledge of or familiarity with the full history of potential arbitrators. Federal trial judges are full-time dispute resolvers; the experience of arbitrators falls all along the experience spectrum, from those who might serve but once or twice in a lifetime to those who conduct arbitration with increasing regularity. The trial judge who is to hear a case is almost never "selected" by or agreed on by the parties; rather, such judge is "selected" or designated by objectively random or blind assignment through long established court procedures (except in the rare case of a party's successful forum shopping in a single-judge district, or consenting to try a case to a known magistrate judge). In stark contrast, it is the parties to arbitration themselves who have sole responsibility for the selection of their arbitrator or arbitrators.

It follows then that because they alone do the selecting, the parties to arbitration must be able to depend almost entirely on the potential arbitrator's good faith, sensitivity, understanding, and compliance with the rules of disclosure by candidates for the post. And, even then, appellate relief is an avis rara when it comes to questions of bias, prejudice, or non-disclosure in arbitration. Consequently, except for such background checks that the parties might be able to conduct, the only shield available to the parties against favoritism, prejudice, and bias is full and frank disclosure, "up front," by each potential arbitrator. And even that is far less efficacious than the safeguards that are afforded to parties in litigation through the elaborate rules of professional conduct, disqualification, and recusal, and the body of law and procedure thereon developed in the crucible of the very formal and extensive judicial system.

The point that I belabor here is that, because parties to arbitration have virtually none of the protections against prejudice and bias (or the appearances thereof) that are automatically and routinely afforded to litigants in federal court, the single arrow remaining in the otherwise-empty quiver of protection afforded to parties in arbitration — full, unredacted disclosure of every prior relationship — must be rigorously adhered to and strenuously enforced. Indeed, it is these very differences in the disclosure standards — not disqualification standards — to which judges are held vis-à-vis those to which arbitrators are held that demand unyielding fealty to both the letter and spirit of the disclosure requirement: With such a slim safeguard against bias or the appearance of bias in arbitration, the reason is obvious why such mandated disclosure of every relationship, without self-abridgment by the potential arbitrator, must be assiduously enforced. . . .

Notes and Questions

33.   *Positive Software* reflects the key policy and practical concerns that
      underlie judicial interpretation of the "evident partiality" stan-
      dard of the FAA. The majority correctly notes that courts tend to
      be loathe to overturn awards on the basis of undisclosed relation-
      ships. Why do you suppose this is the case? In *Merit Insurance Com-
      pany v. Leatherby Insurance Company*, 714 F.2d 763 (7th Cir. 1983),
      the court refused to find grounds for vacatur on the basis of an
      undisclosed prior business relationship with a party that had
      ended 14 years before the dispute. The court stated that it "d[id]
      not want to encourage the losing party to every arbitration to con-
      duct a background investigation of each of the arbitrators in an
      effort to uncover evidence of a former relationship with the adver-
      sary. This would only increase the cost and undermine the finality
      of arbitration."

34.   Consider the opinions of the dissenting judges in *Positive Software*.
      What is their apparent perception of what was going on in the arbi-
      tration? What other arguments did they advance?

35.   What was the standard of disclosure required of Arbitrator Shurn
      under the AAA Commercial Arbitration Rules? Should the par-
      ticular disclosure standard applicable under the parties' arbitra-
      tion agreement have an impact on a judicial finding of "evident
      partiality." Why or why not?

Problem 3A

Arbitrator Nondisclosure and Vacatur of Award

[Before doing this exercise you may wish to refer back to Problem 4A on
Arbitrator Disclosure in Chapter 17 for purposes of comparison. This
earlier exercise deals with disclosure and challenge procedures under
standard arbitration rules.]
You are attorney for the Carmin Co., a manufacturer of high-tech GPS
units used in automobiles, in a dispute with SamCo, Inc., a national
"buying club" with stores all over the country. The parties have a contract containing an arbitration provision that incorporates the AAA
Commercial Arbitration Rules. A dispute arises between the parties and
Carmin demands arbitration. Arbitration proceedings are conducted
before a single arbitrator under the AAA Rules; the arbitrator renders
an award in favor of SamCo.

a.   Shortly after the award is rendered, you discover that the arbitrator
      failed to disclose that she had approached SamCo. about serving as

an attorney for them in a series of cases unrelated to the present action. The contact had occurred about two months before the arbitration. What are your options? Will a court vacate the award on grounds of "evident partiality" under the FAA? *See, e.g., University Commons-Urbana, Ltd. v. Universal Constructors Inc.*, 304 F.3d 1331 (11th Cir. 2002).

b. In Section B.2 above you were introduced to the Uniform Arbitration Act and its relatively recent revised version, the RUAA. Among other things, the RUAA sets forth affirmative guidelines for arbitrator disclosure and more specific guidance on the impact of nondisclosure on judicial action. Suppose you were seeking to vacate the award in a state court proceeding in which the RUAA was applicable. How, if at all, does Section 12 of the RUAA affect your analysis in this problem? Under the RUAA, could Carmin Co. sue the arbitrator for failing to disclose the relationship?

c. Suppose instead that you are seeking to vacate the award in a California state court, and California arbitration law applies. Consider the effect of the California Ethics Standards for Neutral Arbitrators in Contractual Arbitration of the California Rules of Court, Cal. Civ. Prac. Code § 1281.85 (West Supp. 2002).

Problem 3B

Nondisclosure by a "Party Arbitrator" and Vacatur

You will recall from Chapter 17 that tripartite arbitration panels are a common feature of the landscape. The concept — each party picking an arbitrator, and the two "party arbitrators" agreeing on a third arbitrator — is seemingly straightforward and fair. Such arrangements, however, often bring unanticipated results and not a little litigation. The issue inevitably comes down to the precise role of party arbitrators and their obligation of disclosure. We saw that under current leading arbitration rules and the revised Code of Ethics for Arbitrators in Commercial Disputes, arbitrators appointed by a single party are subject to disclosure requirements similar to other arbitrators, and rules make them subject to similar administrative challenge procedures. Now we consider the impact of a "party arbitrator's" failure to disclose, and the possibility of judicial vacation of award on grounds of "evident impartiality."

[Before doing this exercise you may wish to refer back to Problem 4B on Disclosure by Party Arbitrators in Chapter 17 for purposes of comparison. This earlier exercise deals with disclosure and challenge procedures under standard arbitration rules.]

Again, assume you represent Carmin Co. in arbitration proceedings with SamCo, Inc. In this scenario, however, the proceeding is ad hoc — that is, there is no administering organization and, moreover, the parties have *not* incorporated any arbitration procedures (e.g., AAA, JAMS, etc.) by reference in their agreement. Each party selected an arbitrator, and the party arbitrators selected a third individual to serve as chair of the panel. After the arbitration tribunal renders a binding award in favor of SamCo, you find out for the first time that the arbitrator appointed by SamCo worked directly with SamCo before and during the proceedings on virtually every aspect of SamCo's case. You and your client are horrified by the situation.

a. Are these circumstances grounds for judicial vacatur of award under the FAA on grounds of "evident partiality"? *See Delta Mine Holding Co. v. AFC Coal Properties, Inc.,* 280 F.3d 815 (8th Cir. 2001), *cert. denied,* 123 S. Ct. 87 (2002) (overturning district court order vacating award). In describing standards for party arbitrators, in what specific ways does the Eighth Circuit part ways with standards established under *Commonwealth Coatings* and its progeny? To what extent does *Delta Mine Holding* reinforce — or undermine — the following policies associated with arbitration: party autonomy, finality of award, and respect for the integrity of the arbitration as an adjudication process?

b. Would your analysis be the same or different under Section 12 of the RUAA?

c. What if the arbitration proceedings had been governed by standard arbitration procedures such as the current AAA Commercial Arbitration Rules or the JAMS Comprehensive Arbitration Rules? Would that have an impact on your analysis under the FAA?

4. *Was There Arbitral Misconduct (a Failure to Postpone the Hearing or Refusing to Hear Pertinent and Material Evidence, etc.)?*

Arbitrator misconduct such as a failure to postpone a hearing for cause or refusing to hear pertinent material evidence is not often a basis for vacation. Arbitrators generally understand that such mistakes should be avoided and they tend to err on the side of allowing evidence to be heard. Moreover, arbitrators enjoy broad discretion regarding the management of hearings and the receipt of evidence under the law of arbitration, and such discretion is reinforced by standard arbitration rules. Most courts are therefore very deferential to arbitrators' evidentiary determinations and other rulings.

Occasionally, however, a court will vacate an arbitral award when an evidentiary ruling was deemed prejudicial. For example, one court found that an employer's administrative assistant was a crucial witness for the employer/party, but the arbitrator refused to postpone hearings after the assistant was hospitalized. This was no fake claim of illness; the court noted that she was noticeably ill in the presence of the arbitrators. *Tempo Shain Corp. v. Bertek, Incorp.*, 120 F.3d 16 (2d Cir. 1997).

5.   Did the Arbitrators "Exceed Their Powers"?

It appears that, generally speaking, the most successful of the grounds for judicial vacatur of arbitration awards is a finding that arbitrators "exceeded their powers" (Mills et al., 2005). Such a finding usually employs as its touchstone the agreement of the parties; vacation is warranted when an arbitrator's action is clearly beyond the scope of her authority as set forth in the agreement, or in contravention of that agreement. Of course, as illustrated by the following decision, the breadth of most arbitration provisions and the liberality with which courts tend to interpret arbitration agreements often cut against vacation on such grounds.

❖ David Company v. Jim Miller Construction, Inc.
444 N.W.2d 836 (Minn. 1989)

[Miller Construction Co. contracted with David Co. to construct townhouses in two phases on property owned by David Co. After phase one was complete, a dispute between the parties regarding defective workmanship arose. Following arbitration of the dispute, the arbitrators, as part of their award, ordered the general contractor (Miller) to purchase the real property on which the subject buildings had been erected. The issue presented to the court is whether in so doing the arbitrators exceeded their powers. A divided court of appeals panel affirmed a district court order which had affirmed the award. The Minnesota Supreme Court now hears Miller's appeal.]

KELLEY, Justice.

The construction contract at issue was entitled "General Conditions of the Contract for Construction." It included an arbitration clause by which the parties agreed that "[a]ll claims, disputes and other matters in question . . . arising out of, or relating to, the contract documents or the breach thereof . . ." would be subject to arbitration with the exception of claims waived by the making of final payment. . . .

Shortly after the commencement of construction on Phase I of the project, construction problems began to surface and thereafter continued throughout construction. David Company attributed the recurrence of these problems to Miller's inadequate supervision of subcontractors and its tolerance of poor workmanship by them. Primarily because of those problems, completion of construction on Phase I was delayed beyond the contract completion date of May 1984 to October of that year. David Company claimed this delay not only caused it to lose sales of the units and to incur additional interest and other expense, but, in addition, left it with shoddily constructed units which were unmarketable as the luxury-type units originally contemplated by the project.

David Company was aware of numerous construction deficiencies, knew they had not been rectified, and that Phase I completion had been delayed for months, when it made final payment to Miller on Phase I in November 1984. Miller argues that the final payment constituted waiver under subparagraphs 9.9.4 and 9.9.5 of the contract. In response, David Company claims it made the payment reluctantly and only after it had been induced to do so by Miller's reaffirmation of its contractual and other legal obligations to remedy all construction deficiencies in its work.

Shortly after making final payment, David Company learned of additional previously unknown extensive and serious construction defects. Moreover, further nonconformities with contract requirements and building code violations emerged. After Miller refused to correct the newly discovered deficiencies, David Company filed its Demand for Arbitration with the American Arbitration Association. In its Demand it alleged breach of contract, negligence and misrepresentation. For relief it requested "compensation for damages in excess of $250,000, including damages which continue to accrue, plus costs, disbursements, attorney fees and interest." It likewise expressly reserved the right to later amend the demand.

A building contractor and two professional engineers were selected by the parties to arbitrate the dispute. The arbitrators heard evidence presented by the parties over a span of three days, heard submissions of counsel for each party, and physically visited the project site to inspect and evaluate the quality of construction. Evidence presented to the arbitrators revealed numerous and serious construction defects and deficiencies...resulting in rescission demands from owners to whom David had sold units prior to completion, and [rendering] the unsold units, in a practical sense, unmarketable absent extensive and costly repairs.

During the course of his closing argument before the arbitration panel, one of David Company's attorneys, while highlighting the numerous and substantial items of shabby workmanship, observed that his client, and, perhaps as well, vendees who had purchased the units, might be saddled with contingent future liabilities under statutory warranties. He noted that Miller was not only a building contractor, but, as well a developer and owner of real estate thereby implying that, as such, Miller might well better bear that risk than could the respondents. Thereupon, the arbitrators suggested to the parties that they might consider an award resulting in Miller ending up with the project and the property on which it was located in exchange for a cash payment to David Company. Miller's counsel promptly objected on the ground that to so structure an award, the arbitrators would exceed the power granted to them. Nonetheless, David Company's lawyers prepared an itemized "sell back" option claiming $884,476 in damages.... The arbitrators' award incorporated the "sell back" option. Alternatively, in the event David Company was unable to convey the property free of liens within 45 days, the award provided for a monetary damages award of $497,925 to be paid to

David Company. David Company chose to exercise the "sell back" option, and pursuant thereto, made timely tender of performance. When Miller refused to perform by making the payment as required by the arbitrators' award, David Company commenced an action in district court to confirm the award. . . .

Before this court Miller contends that the arbitrators exceeded their powers within the meaning of Minn. Stat. § 572.19.1(3) (1988) when they ordered it to purchase real property from David Company when an alternative damage award was likewise made because: (a) the compelled purchase violated strong public policy as codified by the statute of frauds, and, (b) the order for compelled purchase of real estate was not authorized by either the contract between the parties nor the submittal. Miller further asserts that the arbitrators exceeded their powers by inclusion in the purchase figure that was part of the ultimate award, certain claims which, pursuant to the contract documents, Miller claims had been waived by David Company when it made final payment of Phase I of the project in October 1984.

We first address the claim that the arbitrators did exceed their powers. Because David Company's Demand for Arbitration claimed relief for negligence, breach of contract and misrepresentation, all of which arose out of, or were relevant to, the contract documents, the issue raised here relates not to the question of arbitrability, but rather to the question of whether the arbitrators exceeded their powers in structuring a remedy. If they did, of course, their award may be vacated (Minn. Stat. § 572.19, subd. 1(3)). While the parties, either by contract or by written submission circumscribing the arbitrator's authority, may limit the arbitrator's authority, absent such consensual limitations, the arbitrators are the final judges of both the facts and the law concerning the merits. *State v. Berthiaume*, 259 N.W.2d 904, 910 (Minn. 1977). Moreover, an award will not be vacated merely because the court may believe the arbitrators erred.

The innovative and unique remedy structured by the arbitrators in the instant case, unlike the customary award ordering payment of monetary damages, may be considered equitable in nature. However, merely because the relief granted is equitable in nature does not, by itself, preclude arbitrators from employing it when otherwise appropriate. Indeed, it appears that our statute contemplates "equitable" as well as "legal" remedies in that it provides that upon confirmation of an award, a "judgment or *decree*" shall be entered. Minn. Stat. § 572.21 (1988). No prior holdings of this court which involved comparable types of awards in construction disputes have been brought to our attention. However, in the area of labor relations although an agreement itself contained no provision relative to the scope of the authority of the arbitrators to structure a remedy, we observed that "we defer to the arbitrator's discretion, preserving the flexibility which commends arbitration as an effective means of resolving labor disputes." *Children's Hosp. v. Minnesota Nurses Ass'n*, 265 N.W.2d 649 (Minn. 1978) (a case where arbitrators "mandated" collective bargaining — arguably an equitable remedy — as an alternative in their award). . . .

Our cases as well as those from other jurisdictions . . . reveal the emergence of a general trend of courts, in the absence of limiting language in the contract itself, to accord judicial deference and afford flexibility to arbitrators to fashion awards comporting with the circumstances out of which the disputes arose. Recognition by us in this case that arbitration awards of an equitable nature may be appropriately fashioned would be entirely consistent with this court's long tradition of favoring the use of arbitration in dispute resolution and rejecting challenges to its employment, which, if granted, would limit, rather than expand, its utility. Thus, we hold that merely because the novel relief structured by the arbitrators in this case may have been equitable in nature does not support appellant's claim that they thereby exceeded their authority. Nonetheless, the power exercised in fashioning the award must have its genesis either from the underlying contract, the arbitration clause itself, or the submission. . . .

In the instant case the basis for the award cannot be found in the submission. The original demand sought "compensation for damages in excess of $250,000" (later increased to $598,622.45). Prior to the close of the final arguments before the arbitrators, never did David amend its submission demand to seek relief of the nature provided in the award. Rather, it was one of the arbitrators who, after argument, suggested the "sell back" option. When he did so, appellant promptly voiced its objection. Neither expressly nor tacitly did Miller agree that the submission be expanded to authorize a remedy of this type. Nor, with the exception of the arbitration clause itself in the "General Conditions of the Contract for Construction," does the underlying contract provide any basis for the remedy formulated by the arbitrators. Accordingly, the basis, if any, for the award which was fashioned must depend upon construction of the contract's arbitration clause. . . .

The scope of the arbitration clause is extremely broad. It authorizes arbitrators to decide "[a]ll claims, disputes and other matters in question . . . relating to, the Contract . . . or the breach thereof. . . . " No provision in the arbitration clause expressly or implicitly limits the arbitrators to structuring only a remedy calling for the payment of a monetary award nor does any provision expressly authorize, or prohibit, arbitrators from formulating remedies that are equitable in nature. However, in conformity with our long established policy favoring expansion of the arbitration remedy, we conclude that implicit in the exceedingly broad powers which were granted by the parties to the arbitrators to decide "[a]ll claims, disputes, and other matters in question" is a grant of authority to structure an award which is commensurate with the extent, the pervasiveness, and nature of the poor workmanship resulting in construction deficiencies of such patent magnitude which existed. The appellant, and the dissenter in the court of appeals' opinion, argue that the arbitration clause should be more restrictively construed to limit the type of relief to the more traditional monetary award. While it may be correct to surmise that initially neither party specifically contemplated that in case of dispute between them this type of an equitable award might ensue from arbitration, yet both, neither of whom were inexperienced in construction projects of this nature, knew that the project involved the construction of luxury style residential townhomes for immediate resale to third parties, and each were undoubtedly aware of the potential future warranty liability to vendees and subvendees. Nonetheless, the parties executed a contract containing an arbitration clause affording to arbitrators wide and virtually unlimited latitude to fashion a remedy. By their agreement, either initially or in the submission, the parties could have limited the arbitrators' authority. . . . They failed to do so. We decline to judicially restrict the powers of the arbitrators which the parties themselves have so broadly granted to them. Nor, in our opinion, does the fact that the arbitrators were able to make an alternative monetary award have relevance to the determination of the scope of the powers delegated to them. By fashioning the award, the arbitrators not only acted within the scope of the broad grant of authority in fashioning the "sell back" option, but also placed the obligation on Miller, the party responsible for the gross construction deficiencies, to remedy them and bear the risk of potential future warranty liabilities . . .

[The court then went on to address Miller's claims that the arbitration award violated the Statute of Frauds, and that David Co. had waived its right to collect damages by rendering final payment to Miller.]

Accordingly, because we hold that the award structured by the arbitrators was within the powers granted to them by the arbitration clause of the general contract; that the award did not do violence to the underlying policy of the Statute of Frauds; and that the award did not include items which were "waived" by final payment, we *affirm*.

Questions

36. How does the remedy-making power of arbitrators as described by the Minnesota Supreme Court in *David Co.* differ from that of a civil court? Would a court have been able to render similar relief had the case been brought in court?

37. Why is the court so deferential to the arbitrators?

38. What specific elements of the arbitration agreement reinforced the court's conclusion regarding the breadth of the arbitrators' authority? Could the parties have limited the scope of their remedial power by a specific statement in the agreement?

39. Do you believe the makeup of the panel of arbitrators had anything to do with the nature of the final arbitration award? What if the panel had consisted of three attorneys? Three laypersons without pertinent knowledge or experience?

Notes and Questions on Punitive Damages in Arbitration

Should arbitrators have the authority to consider and render awards for punitive or exemplary damages? U.S. courts make such awards in some civil actions under the authority of common law or statutes; their fundamental purpose is to punish those who engage in certain proscribed behavior and to deter others from engaging in the similar behavior. A generation ago, in a decision by Chief Judge Charles Breitel, the New York Court of Appeals vacated an arbitration award of punitive damages on the basis that arbitrators had no business considering or awarding "socially exemplary remedies." *Garrity v. Lyle Stuart, Inc.*, 40 N.Y.2d 354 (N.Y. 1976). Among other things, Breitel's opinion reflected a highly skeptical view of arbitrator's abilities and motivations, and a concern that punitive damage might become an instrument of oppression in private hands.

Given the subsequent evolution of arbitration into a highly favored alternative under judicial interpretations of the FAA, you may not be surprised to learn that the New York Court's strong stance against arbitration of punitive damages under New York law did not hold sway in decisions governed by the FAA. *See, e.g., Willoughby Roofing v. Kajima Int'l*, 598 F. Supp. 353 (N.D. Ala. 1984), *aff'd*, 76 F.2d 269 (11th Cir. 1985). *Willoughby* and similar decisions built on *Southland* and other precedents defining a "substantive law of arbitrability" under the FAA (discussed in Section C.5 above) since the question of whether arbitrators had authority to award punitive damages also raised the question of whether claims for punitive damages were arbitrable. In *Mastrobuono v. Shearson Lehman Hutton, Inc.*, 115 S. Ct. 1212 (1995), the Supreme Court concluded that where a broad-form arbitration agreement was governed by the FAA, the agreement should be read to permit arbitral awards of punitive damages in the absence of specific terms to the contrary. Although punitive or exemplary damages are very rarely awarded in commercial arbitration cases, they are frequently sought in employment and securities brokerage disputes.

40. Judge Breitel's specter of unbridled, oppressive awards does not appear to have been borne out by experience with punitive damage. On the other hand, what happens if a seemingly extreme punitive award is rendered? What, if any, oversight should courts have of arbitral awards of punitive damages? *See Sawtelle v. Waddell & Reed*, No. 2330 (N.Y. App. Div. 1st Dep't. 2003) (overturning judgment affirming $25 million punitive damages award against brokerage firm on the ground that it was grossly disproportionate to the harm suffered by the plaintiff, a mutual funds broker, and thus "arbitrary and irrational" under New York law).

41. Should parties be able to avoid punitive or exemplary damages by contract? Since it is generally within the power of the parties to arbitration agreements to include or exclude particular claims or controversies as they see fit, isn't it possible to structure an arbitration provision that functions as a partial or complete predispute waiver of claims for punitive damages? One commentator suggests that remedy-stripping arbitration clauses may be limited as a practical matter because they raise preclusion problems. See Schwartz (2003). Could the parties agree to exclude an arbitral award of punitive damages after a dispute has arisen? What are the difficulties of securing such an agreement? See Stipanowich (1997). As we will see in Chapter 19, your answer may be different in the context of a standardized contract of adhesion, such as an individual employment contract or a consumer contract.

6. *Contractual Provisions Attempting to Expand or Narrow Grounds for Vacatur of Award*

In recent years some parties have attempted to expand the grounds of judicial review of arbitral awards by contract. For example, in *Lapine Technology Corp. v. Kyocera Corp.*, 130 F.3d 884, 887 (9th Cir. 1997), the parties expressly provided grounds for judicial review beyond those available under the FAA, including court modification or vacatur if arbitrators made findings not supported by substantial evidence or made erroneous legal conclusions. The federal circuits divided on whether to permit this expansion of judicial review by contract, with some honoring contractual autonomy and others finding that expansion of review would undercut the pro-arbitration policy of the FAA, as interpreted by the Court in recent decades (Moses, 2004). Then the Supreme Court stepped in.

❖ Hall Street Associates, L.L.C. v. Mattel, Inc.
128 S. Ct. 1396 (2008)

Justice SOUTER delivered the opinion of the Court. . . .

The Federal Arbitration Act (FAA or Act), 9 U.S.C. § 1 *et seq.*, provides for expedited judicial review to confirm, vacate, or modify arbitration awards. §§ 9-11. The question here is whether statutory grounds for prompt vacatur and modification may be supplemented by contract. We hold that the statutory grounds are exclusive.

I

This case began as a lease dispute between landlord, petitioner Hall Street Associates, L.L.C., and tenant, respondent Mattel, Inc. The property was used for many years as a manufacturing site, and the leases provided that the tenant would indemnify the landlord for any costs resulting from the failure of the tenant or its predecessor lessees to follow environmental laws while using the premises.

Tests of the property's well water in 1998 showed high levels of trichloro-ethylene (TCE), the apparent residue of manufacturing discharges by Mattel's predecessors between 1951 and 1980. After the Oregon Department of Environmental Quality (DEQ) discovered even more pollutants, Mattel stopped drawing from the well and, along with one of its predecessors, signed a consent order with the DEQ providing for cleanup of the site.

After Mattel gave notice of intent to terminate the lease in 2001, Hall Street filed this suit, contesting Mattel's right to vacate on the date it gave, and claiming that the lease obliged Mattel to indemnify Hall Street for costs of cleaning up the TCE, among other things. Following a bench trial before the United States District Court for the District of Oregon, Mattel won on the termination issue, and after an unsuccessful try at mediating the indem-nification claim, the parties proposed to submit to arbitration. The District Court was amenable, and the parties drew up an arbitration agreement, which the court approved and entered as an order. One paragraph of the agreement provided that

> "[t]he United States District Court for the District of Oregon may enter judgment upon any award, either by confirming the award or by vacating, modifying or cor-recting the award. The Court shall vacate, modify or correct any award: (i) where the arbitrator's findings of facts are not supported by substantial evidence, or (ii) where the arbitrator's conclusions of law are erroneous."

Arbitration took place, and the arbitrator decided for Mattel. In particu-lar, he held that no indemnification was due, because the lease obligation to follow all applicable federal, state, and local environmental laws did not require compliance with the testing requirements of the Oregon Drinking Water Quality Act (Oregon Act); that Act the arbitrator characterized as dealing with human health as distinct from environmental contamination.

Hall Street then filed a District Court Motion for Order Vacating, Modi-fying And/Or Correcting the arbitration decision on the ground that failing to treat the Oregon Act as an applicable environmental law under the terms of the lease was legal error. The District Court agreed, vacated the award, and remanded for further consideration by the arbitrator. The court expressly invoked the standard of review chosen by the parties in the arbi-tration agreement, which included review for legal error, and cited *LaPine Technology Corp. v. Kyocera Corp.* for the proposition that the FAA leaves the parties "free . . . to draft a contract that sets rules for arbitration and dictates an alternative standard of review."

On remand, the arbitrator followed the District Court's ruling that the Oregon Act was an applicable environmental law and amended the decision to favor Hall Street. This time, each party sought modification, and again the District Court applied the parties' stipulated standard of review for legal error, correcting the arbitrator's calculation of interest but otherwise upholding the award. Each party then appealed to the Court of Appeals for the Ninth Circuit, where Mattel switched horses and contended that the Ninth Circuit's recent en banc action overruling *LaPine* in *Kyocera Corp. v. Prudential-Bache Trade Servs., Inc.* left the arbitration agreement's provision for judicial review of legal error unenforceable. Hall Street countered that *Kyocera* (the later one) was distinguishable, and that the agreement's judicial review provision was not severable from the submission to arbitration.

The Ninth Circuit reversed in favor of Mattel in holding that, "[u]nder *Kyocera* the terms of the arbitration agreement controlling the mode of judicial review are unenforceable and severable." The Circuit instructed the District Court on remand to

> "return to the application to confirm the original arbitration award (not the subsequent award revised after reversal), and . . . confirm that award, unless . . . the award should be vacated on the grounds allowable under 9 U.S.C. § 10, or modified or corrected under the grounds allowable under 9 U.S.C. § 11."

After the District Court again held for Hall Street and the Ninth Circuit again reversed, we granted certiorari to decide whether the grounds for vacatur and modification provided by §§ 10 and 11 of the FAA are exclusive. We agree with the Ninth Circuit that they are, but vacate and remand for consideration of independent issues.

II

Congress enacted the FAA to replace judicial indisposition to arbitration with a "national policy favoring [it] and plac[ing] arbitration agreements on equal footing with all other contracts." As for jurisdiction over controversies touching arbitration, the Act does nothing, being "something of an anomaly in the field of federal-court jurisdiction" in bestowing no federal jurisdiction but rather requiring an independent jurisdictional basis. But in cases falling within a court's jurisdiction, the Act makes contracts to arbitrate "valid, irrevocable, and enforceable," so long as their subject involves "commerce." § 2. And this is so whether an agreement has a broad reach or goes just to one dispute, and whether enforcement be sought in state court or federal.

The Act also supplies mechanisms for enforcing arbitration awards: a judicial decree confirming an award, an order vacating it, or an order modifying or correcting it. §§ 9-11. An application for any of these orders will get streamlined treatment as a motion, obviating the separate contract action that would usually be necessary to enforce or tinker with an arbitral award in court § 6. Under the terms of § 9, a court "must" confirm an arbitration award "unless" it is vacated, modified, or corrected "as prescribed" in §§ 10 and 11. Section 10 lists grounds for vacating an award, while § 11 names those for modifying or correcting one. . . .

The Courts of Appeals have split over the exclusiveness of these statutory grounds when parties take the FAA shortcut to confirm, vacate, or modify an award, with some saying the recitations are exclusive, and others regarding them as mere threshold provisions open to expansion by agreement. As mentioned already, when this litigation started, the Ninth Circuit was on the threshold side of the split, see *LaPine,* 130 F.3d, at 889, from which it later departed en banc in favor of the exclusivity view, see *Kyocera,* 341 F.3d, at 1000, which it followed in this case. We now hold that §§ 10 and 11 respectively provide the FAA's exclusive grounds for expedited vacatur and modification.

III

Hall Street makes two main efforts to show that the grounds set out for vacating or modifying an award are not exclusive, taking the position, first, that expandable judicial review authority has been accepted as the law since *Wilko v. Swan,* 346 U.S. 427, 74 S. Ct. 182, 98 L.Ed. 168 (1953). This, however, was not what *Wilko* decided, which was that § 14 of the Securities Act of 1933 voided any agreement to arbitrate claims of violations of that Act, see *id.,* at 437-438, 74 S. Ct. 182, a holding since overruled by *Rodriguez de Quijas v. Shearson/American Express, Inc.,* 490 U.S. 477, 484, 109 S. Ct. 1917, 104 L.Ed.2d 526 (1989). Although it is true that the Court's discussion includes some language arguably favoring Hall Street's position, arguable is as far as it goes.

The *Wilko* Court was explaining that arbitration would undercut the Securities Act's buyer protections when it remarked (citing FAA § 10) that "[p]ower to vacate an [arbitration] award is limited," 346 U.S., at 436, 74 S. Ct. 182, and went on to say that "the interpretations of the law by the arbitrators in contrast to manifest disregard [of the law] are not subject, in the federal courts, to judicial review for error in interpretation," *id.,* at 436-437, 74 S. Ct. 182. Hall Street reads this statement as recognizing "manifest disregard of the law" as a further ground for vacatur on top of those listed in § 10, and some Circuits have read it the same way. . . . Hall Street sees this supposed addition to § 10 as the camel's nose: if judges can add grounds to vacate (or modify), so can contracting parties.

But this is too much for *Wilko* to bear. Quite apart from its leap from a supposed judicial expansion by interpretation to a private expansion by contract, Hall Street overlooks the fact that the statement it relies on expressly rejects just what Hall Street asks for here, general review for an arbitrator's legal errors. Then there is the vagueness of *Wilko*'s phrasing. Maybe the term "manifest disregard" was meant to name a new ground for review, but maybe it merely referred to the § 10 grounds collectively, rather than adding to them. . . . Or, as some courts have thought, "manifest disregard" may have been shorthand for § 10(a)(3) or § 10(a)(4), the subsections authorizing vacatur when the arbitrators were "guilty of misconduct" or "exceeded their powers." . . . We, when speaking as a Court, have merely taken the *Wilko* language as we found it, without embellishment, . . . and now that its meaning is implicated, we see no reason to accord it the significance that Hall Street urges.

Second, Hall Street says that the agreement to review for legal error ought to prevail simply because arbitration is a creature of contract, and the FAA is "motivated, first and foremost, by a congressional desire to enforce agreements into which parties ha[ve] entered." *Dean Witter Reynolds Inc. v. Byrd*, 470 U.S. 213, 220, 105 S. Ct. 1238, 84 L.Ed.2d 158 (1985). But, again, we think the argument comes up short. Hall Street is certainly right that the FAA lets parties tailor some, even many features of arbitration by contract, including the way arbitrators are chosen, what their qualifications should be, which issues are arbitrable, along with procedure and choice of substantive law. But to rest this case on the general policy of treating arbitration agreements as enforceable as such would be to beg the question, which is whether the FAA has textual features at odds with enforcing a contract to expand judicial review following the arbitration.

To that particular question we think the answer is yes, that the text compels a reading of the §§ 10 and 11 categories as exclusive. To begin with, even if we assumed §§ 10 and 11 could be supplemented to some extent, it would stretch basic interpretive principles to expand the stated grounds to the point of evidentiary and legal review generally. Sections 10 and 11, after all, address egregious departures from the parties' agreed-upon arbitration: "corruption," "fraud," "evident partiality," "misconduct," "misbehavior," "exceed[ing] . . . powers," "evident material miscalculation," "evident material mistake," "award[s] upon a matter not submitted;" the only ground with any softer focus is "imperfect[ions]," and a court may correct those only if they go to "[a] matter of form not affecting the merits." Given this emphasis on extreme arbitral conduct, the old rule of *ejusdem generis* has an implicit lesson to teach here. Under that rule, when a statute sets out a series of specific items ending with a general term, that general term is confined to covering subjects comparable to the specifics it follows. Since a general term included in the text is normally so limited, then surely a statute with no textual hook for expansion cannot authorize contracting parties to supplement review for specific instances of outrageous conduct with review for just any legal error. "Fraud" and a mistake of law are not cut from the same cloth.

That aside, expanding the detailed categories would rub too much against the grain of the § 9 language, where provision for judicial confirmation carries no hint of flexibility. On application for an order confirming the arbitration award, the court "must grant" the order "unless the award is vacated, modified, or corrected as prescribed in sections 10 and 11 of this title." There is nothing malleable about "must grant," which unequivocally tells courts to grant confirmation in all cases, except when one of the "prescribed" exceptions applies. This does not sound remotely like a provision meant to tell a court what to do just in case the parties say nothing else. . . .

Instead of fighting the text, it makes more sense to see the three provisions, §§ 9-11, as substantiating a national policy favoring arbitration with just the limited review needed to maintain arbitration's essential virtue of resolving disputes straightaway. Any other reading opens the door to the full-bore legal and evidentiary appeals that can "rende[r] informal arbitration merely a prelude to a more cumbersome and time-consuming judicial review process," and bring arbitration theory to grief in post-arbitration process.

When all these arguments based on prior legal authority are done with, Hall Street and Mattel remain at odds over what happens next. Hall Street and its *amici* say parties will flee from arbitration if expanded review is not open to them. One of Mattel's *amici* foresees flight from the courts if it is. We do not know who, if anyone, is right, and so cannot say whether the exclusivity reading of the statute is more of a threat to the popularity of arbitrators or to that of courts. But whatever the consequences of our holding, the statutory text gives us no business to expand the statutory grounds.

IV

In holding that §§ 10 and 11 provide exclusive regimes for the review provided by the statute, we do not purport to say that they exclude more searching review based on authority outside the statute as well. The FAA is not the only way into court for parties wanting review of arbitration awards: they may contemplate enforcement under state statutory or common law, for example, where judicial review of different scope is arguable. But here we speak only to the scope of the expeditious judicial review under §§ 9, 10, and 11, deciding nothing about other possible avenues for judicial enforcement of arbitration awards. . . .

We express no opinion on these matters beyond leaving them open for Hall Street to press on remand. . . .

Although we agree with the Ninth Circuit that the FAA confines its expedited judicial review to the grounds listed in 9 U.S.C. §§ 10 and 11, we vacate the judgment and remand the case for proceedings consistent with this opinion.

It is so ordered.

Notes and Questions

The Supreme Court's pronouncement in *Hall Street* failed to fully resolve questions surrounding the enforcement of contractual provisions for expanded judicial scrutiny of arbitration awards. The majority concluded that agreements for expanded review were inconsistent with the specific language of FAA §§ 10 and 11, which "substantiat[e] a national policy favoring arbitration with just the limited review needed to maintain arbitration's essential virtue of resolving disputes straightaway." But the Court proceeded to invite consideration of other avenues to the same ends, as where parties "contemplate enforcement under state statutory or common law . . . where judicial review of different scope is arguable." Although it may be some time before the full import of this invitation is clarified, it is likely that state statutes or controlling judicial decisions promoting contractually expanded review will become "safe harbors" for such activity. New Jersey is perhaps the sole example of a statutory template for parties that wish to "opt in" to the legislative framework for elevated scrutiny of awards. See N.J. Stat. Ann., § 2A:23A-12 (West 1999). In *Cable Connection, Inc. v. DIRECTV, Inc.*, 190 P.3d 586 (Cal. 2008), California's highest court recognized a more general "safe harbor" for contractually expanded judicial review under that state's law.

42. *Cable Connection* appears to be a rational interpretation of California arbitration law (which is virtually identical in pertinent part to the FAA). However, even if your client had a legal right to contract for expanded judicial review of arbitration awards (e.g., provide that a reviewing court could vacate awards for errors of fact or law) is it something that you would want to include in your contract? Recall that effective judicial review requires a variety of implementing steps including the creation of a record and the preparation of a rationale to accompany the award. Such elements are more common in current arbitration practice as reflected in leading commercial procedures.

43. *Manifest disregard of the law.* In addition to the statutory grounds for vacation of award included in the FAA and state analogs, courts have infrequently recognized non-statutory grounds for vacating arbitral awards. In unusual circumstances, courts might vacate awards as being "arbitrary and capricious" or irrational. See, e.g., *Ainsworth v. Skurnick*, 960 F.2d 939 (11th Cir. 1992) (district court upheld the decision of an arbitration panel finding Skurnick negligent, but vacated the arbitration judgment as being in manifest disregard of the law for failing to provide for mandatory damages under Florida law, rendering the panel's denial of damages arbitrary or capricious). The most prominent of these judicially declared grounds for vacatur, however, is "manifest disregard of the law." As explained in *Hall Street*, the notion that courts might vacate an award on such grounds sprang from dicta by Justice Black in a 1953 decision, *Wilko v. Swan*. Yet while parties often move to vacate an award on the basis that the arbitrators acted in "manifest disregard of the law," such motions seldom succeed. The Second Circuit described the basic contours of the doctrine as follows:

> The party seeking to vacate an award on the basis of the arbitrator's alleged "manifest disregard" of the law bears a "heavy burden." Our review under the [judicially constructed] doctrine of manifest

disregard is "severely limited." . . . "It is highly deferential to the arbitral award and obtaining judicial relief for arbitrators' manifest disregard of the law is rare." . . .

In this light, "manifest disregard" has been interpreted "clearly [to] mean more than error or misunderstanding with respect to the law." . . . A federal court cannot vacate an arbitral award merely because it is convinced that the arbitration panel made the wrong call on the law. On the contrary, the award should be enforced, despite a court's disagreement with it on the merits, if there is a barely colorable justification for the outcome reached.

In the context of contract interpretation, we are required to confirm arbitration awards despite "serious reservations about the soundness of the arbitrator's reading of th[e] contract." . . .

The concept of "manifest disregard" is well illustrated by *New York Telephone Co. v. Communication Workers*. There the arbitrator recognized binding Second Circuit case but deliberately refused to apply it, saying — no doubt to the astonishment of the parties — "Perhaps it is time for a new court decision." Because the arbitrator explicitly rejected controlling precedent, we concluded that the arbitral decision was rendered in manifest disregard of the law. . . .

[We doubt it is] necessary for arbitrators to state that they are deliberately ignoring the law. If the arbitrator's decision "strains credulity" or "does not rise to the standard of barely colorable," a court may conclude that the arbitrator "willfully flouted the governing law by refusing to apply it. . . ."

There are three components to our application of the "manifest disregard" standard. First, we must consider whether the law that was allegedly ignored was clear, and in fact explicitly applicable to the matter before the arbitrators. An arbitrator obviously cannot be said to disregard a law that is unclear or not clearly applicable. Thus, misapplication of an ambiguous law does not constitute manifest disregard.

Second, once it is determined that the law is clear and plainly applicable, we must find that the law was in fact improperly applied, leading to an erroneous outcome. We will, of course, not vacate an arbitral award for an erroneous application of the law if a proper application of law would have yielded the same result. In the same vein, where an arbitral award contains more than one plausible reading, manifest disregard cannot be found if at least one of the readings yields a legally correct justification for the outcome. Even where explanation for an award is deficient or non-existent, we will confirm it if a justifiable ground for decision can be inferred from the facts of the case.

Third, once the first two inquiries are satisfied, we look to a subjective element, that is, the knowledge actually possessed by the arbitrators. In order to intentionally disregard the law, the arbitrator must have known of its existence, and its applicability to the problem before him. In determining an arbitrator's awareness of the law, we impute only knowledge of governing law identified by the parties to the arbitration. Absent this we will infer knowledge and intentionality on the part of the arbitrator only if we find an error that is so obvious that it would be instantly perceived as such by the average person qualified to serve as an arbitrator.

Stolt-Nielsen SA v. Animalfeeds Int'l Corp., 548 F.3d 85 (2d Cir. 2008), cert. granted, 129 S.Ct. 2793 (2009).

Based on your reading of *Hall Street*, do you believe the Supreme Court in that decision affected the "scope or vitality" of the doctrine of "manifest disregard"? The courts are split on its implications. In *Stolt-Nielsen, supra*, the Second Circuit observed:

> In the short time since *Hall Street* was decided, . . . [some courts] have concluded or suggested that the doctrine simply does not survive. Others think that "manifest disregard," reconceptualized as a judicial gloss on the specific grounds for vacatur . . . in the FAA, remains a valid ground for vacating arbitration awards. The *Hall Street* Court . . . did not, we think, abrogate the "manifest disregard" doctrine altogether.

44.   Some arbitration institutions (including JAMS and the International Institute for Conflict Prevention & Resolution) have established processes that are private counterparts of appellate courts. See, e.g., JAMS Optional Arbitration Appeal Procedure. *www.jamsadr.com/rules/optional*. What are the features of these appellate arbitration procedures? Would you consider such an alternative in place of a contractual provision for expanded judicial review?

This chapter has charted the dramatic evolution of arbitration as a strongly favored alternative to litigation under the broad aegis of the FAA. It has shown how the U.S. Supreme Court has promoted broad enforcement of agreements to arbitrate through a body of substantive federal law applicable in both federal and state courts. It has examined the gradual expansion of arbitration into a full-blown court surrogate, given responsibility to address statute-based claims as well as common law actions, and even "socially exemplary remedies" such as punitive damages.

We have also seen the expansion of arbitration provisions into the realm of employment and consumer contracts — standardized documents that are often presented to individuals seeking a job, or consumer goods or services, on a "take it or leave it" basis. As we will see in Chapter 19, these sorts of situations have given rise to a host of fairness concerns that have stimulated a variety of responses. A growing body of judicial decisions and significant legislative efforts aim to limit party autonomy or police unfairness in arbitration provisions in adhesion contracts.

CHAPTER
19

Fairness in Arbitration: Developments in Employment, Consumer, and "Adhesion" Contexts

A. Introduction

A couple of decades ago consumers usually encountered arbitration in the form of short procedures for determining whether a motor vehicle was a "lemon" under state statutes. A decision in the buyer's favor would require the manufacturer to pay damages, give a refund, or provide a replacement vehicle. If the buyer lost, however, she could still sue in court. Such systems are skewed toward the consumer, and, overseen by state attorney generals, appear to work fairly well.

Beginning in the mid-1980s, however, the Supreme Court began dramatically expanding the reach of arbitration agreements under the Federal Arbitration Act (FAA) — a series of developments charted in Chapter 18. These developments encouraged companies to begin incorporating predispute binding arbitration clauses in all kinds of consumer contracts and individual employment contracts. Because individuals could suddenly be bound by private arbitration awards, they began raising questions about the fairness of different aspects of these procedures.

In the last two decades binding arbitration became a fact of everyday life. Binding arbitration clauses became commonplace in transactions such as banking, credit card agreements, insurance policies, and sales of consumer goods. Very often people sign contracts that contain boilerplate arbitration clauses without focusing on those clauses. They might enter into a contract without being aware, or with only vague awareness, of what they were agreeing to by consenting to binding arbitration.

A private arbitration process may well provide individuals with a fundamentally fair, inexpensive, and relatively speedy alternative to going to court. However, it all depends on the details — and the suitability of defined procedures to the circumstances. Some arbitration procedures will fall short of parties' reasonable expectations of fairness and have a dramatic impact on consumers' or employees' substantive rights and remedies. Concerns are magnified where such provisions are presented as part of a "take it or leave it" deal — forcing an individual to accept the terms or seek other alternatives for goods or employment. The presence of arbitration provisions in so-called contracts of "adhesion" prepared and presented by companies to consumers, employees, and others have generated considerable debate and provoked a variety of responses.

This chapter is chiefly devoted to the wide range of fairness concerns raised by binding predispute arbitration agreements in consumer or employment transactions. It explores *concerns surrounding the making of the agreement*, including lack of awareness of the arbitration provision and of waiver of the right to trial; as well as lack of access to information about the arbitration program and related rules and procedures. It also looks at key *process-related concerns* including the independence and impartiality of decision makers, and of the administering institution, if any; the quality of the process and the competence of arbitrators; the cost, location, and time frame of arbitration; the ability to present a claim as part of a class action; the right to representation; the ability to secure needed information (discovery); and the fundamental fairness of hearings. Also relevant are *outcome-related concerns*: the nature of arbitral remedies, including the availability of punitive damages in cases where they would be available in court; the scope of judicial review of arbitration awards; and the availability of binding precedents for the future guidance of actors in various arenas (Stipanowich, 2001).

Not surprisingly, such concerns have given rise to almost incessant litigation over the enforcement of arbitration agreements in adhesion contracts, or resulting arbitration awards. Although federal and state courts have tended to reinforce the ability of companies to require their employees or customers to arbitrate, they have, to varying degrees, established limits on the contracting process and the kinds of procedures companies can impose. To some extent these judicial efforts have been supplemented or reinforced by state or federal legislation governing arbitration, and by the efforts of organizational or collective efforts to create minimum due process standards — or protocols — for arbitration in these settings. However, the debate continued to rage (now centered on the ability of companies to cause employees or customers to waive their right to bring claims as a class action), and the stage was set for passage of the Arbitration Fairness Act, a statute designed to outlaw predispute arbitration agreements in consumer, employment, and other adhesive contracts that was pending at the time this book went to press.

B. Pro-Consumer Dispute Resolution: State Lemon Laws and the Magnuson-Moss Warranty Act

1. State Lemon Laws

If you buy a car and it appears to have fundamental defects, you probably have rights and remedies under a state lemon law. Consider the following summary of the terms of the Massachusetts New Car Lemon Law:

- A consumer (purchaser of a new car) may file for arbitration under the "lemon law" within 18 months of taking delivery of a new car.
- The arbitrators are appointed by the Secretary of Consumer Affairs.
- The arbitrators must render a decision within 45 days of the consumer's demand for arbitration.
- If the consumer loses, the consumer may still sue in court.
- If the manufacturer loses . . .
  - It must give the consumer a refund, replace the car, or appeal to Superior Court within 21 days.
  - The manufacturer's appeal must be accompanied by a bond for the full arbitration award plus $2,500 attorney's fees.
  - If the court decides the "manufacturer did not have any reasonable basis for its appeal or that the appeal was frivolous" then the "court shall double the amount" of the arbitration award.

Mass. Gen. Laws ch. 90, § 7N1/2 (2009).

Lemon laws like the Massachusetts law summarized above are still in place throughout the country; they vary in detail, but all are aimed at an abbreviated, speedy, out-of-court remedy for disgruntled buyers with some level of state supervision. Maine's lemon law, for example, provides that all manufacturers submit to state-certified new car arbitration if arbitration is requested by the consumer within two years from the date of original delivery of a new car to the consumer or during the first 18,000 miles, whichever comes first. This state-certified arbitration panel consists of one or more neutral arbitrators selected by the Department of the Attorney General. The Attorney General's office is responsible for administering the proceedings under such rules as will "promote fairness and efficiency." Me. Rev. Stat. Ann. 10, § 1169 (West 1997).

Question

1. Does the state regulation of arbitration promote confidence in the process? How do you view the pro-consumer orientation of these processes?

2. *Magnuson-Moss Warranty Act*

An analogous attempt by the federal government to encourage the use of ADR in the consumer setting can be seen in the Magnuson-Moss Warranty Act (MMWA), enacted in 1975 in response to increasing consumer protection concerns. 15 U.S.C. §§ 2301-2312 (2004). The Act allows warrantors to require that consumers enter into ADR if a dispute arises, but it specifies that the ADR be non-binding, and that the consumer be able to assert claims in court if ADR is unsuccessful. The Act attempts to provide common ground and fair process for resolving certain types of consumer disputes, as can be seen from the floor remarks of the Act's sponsor:

> First, the bill provides the consumer with an economically feasible private right of action so that when a warrantor breaches his warranty or service contract obligations, the consumer can have effective redress. Reasonable attorney's fees and expenses are provided for the successful consumer litigant, and the bill is further refined so as to place minimum extra burden on the courts by requiring as a prerequisite to suit that the purchaser give the [warrantor] reasonable opportunity to settle the dispute out of court, including the use of a fair and formal dispute settlement mechanism. . . . (119 Cong. Rec. 972 (1973) (statement of Rep. Moss)).

After the enactment of the MMWA, every federal court that had a Magnuson-Moss case come before it concluded that the Act vested a non-waivable right of court access and thus that the Act precluded binding arbitration. One of the first and most prominent cases dealing with the Act was *Wilson v. Waverlee Homes Inc.*, in which a federal district court held that the Act makes clear that the "informal dispute resolution procedures" allowed by the Act "are a prerequisite, not a bar, to relief in court." 954 F. Supp. 1530, 1537 (M.D. Ala. 1997), *aff'd* 127 F.3d 40 (11th Cir. 1997). This holding was followed by many other courts in the years that followed. As late as 2000, in *Pitchford v. Oakwood Mobile Homes, Inc.*, a federal district court in Virginia held that the clear intent behind the implementation of Magnuson-Moss was to encourage ADR without stripping parties of their access to the judicial system. 124 F. Supp. 2d 958 (W.D. Va. 2000).

In light of Supreme Court decisions in the 1980s and 1990s expanding the scope of the FAA, however, the validity of that interpretation of the MMWA was questioned. In *Davis v. Southern Energy Homes, Inc.*, 305 F.3d 1268 (11th Cir. 2002), a federal circuit that had previously ruled that the Act prevented binding arbitration in warranty agreements held that homeowners who signed a predispute arbitration agreement must arbitrate their claims against the builder, including their MMWA claim. The Eleventh Circuit reasoned that the MMWA does not expressly preclude arbitration and the Act's "legislative history only addresses internal dispute settlement procedures"; it never directly addresses the role of binding arbitration or the FAA." The court added that the purposes of the MMWA — "to improve the adequacy of information available to consumers, prevent deception, and improve competition in the marketing of consumer products" — do not conflict with the FAA.

Questions

2.   Almost all federal cases interpreting the MMWA prior to *Davis* held that the Act precluded binding arbitration. Frequently, those courts relied on the Act's distinction between "more formal" binding arbitration and the informal dispute resolution that the Act explicitly regulates. In contrast, the Michigan Supreme Court reached the same outcome as the *Davis* court, finding that the MMWA does not preclude enforcement of binding arbitration agreements in *Abela v. General Motors*, 469 Mich. 603, 677 N.W.2d 325 (2004). Which approach do you believe is appropriate? Why?

3.   The MMWA fails to mention binding arbitration or the FAA directly — probably because it was passed at a time before the pro-arbitration judicial activism of the 1980s and 1990s. However, Congress did not amend the MMWA during the 1980s or 1990s to address the Supreme Court's precedents favoring arbitration. Did the Eleventh Circuit approach this statutory ambiguity correctly? The court was constrained in part by the Supreme Court's test for determining congressional intent set out in *Shearson/American Express, Inc. v. McMahon*, 482 U.S. 220 (1987). In reviewing the text, legislative history, and the existence of any "inherent conflict between arbitration" and the statute's purpose, the Supreme Court warned that courts must be mindful of the federal policy favoring arbitration, and that the party opposing arbitration bears the burden of showing that Congress intended to preclude arbitration. *Id.* at 226-227.

C.   Predispute Arbitration Clauses in Consumer and Employment Contracts and Related Fairness Concerns

1.   *Expansion of Predispute Binding Arbitration Agreements into Consumer and Employment Realms*

As discussed in Chapter 17 and alluded to above, the U.S. Supreme Court's broad, pro-arbitration interpretations of the FAA ushered in a sea of change in judicial attitudes toward binding arbitration and the role of arbitrators in administering civil justice in the 1980s and 1990s. *Southland Corp. v. Keating*, 465 U.S. 1 (1984) and progeny reinforced strong pro-arbitration policies under the FAA and recognized a body of substantive law governing the enforcement of arbitration agreements applicable in state as well as federal courts in cases regarding transactions involving interstate commerce — a truly broad rubric. *See, e.g., Terminix v. Allied Bruce,* 513 U.S. 265 (1995). State laws designed to single out arbitration clauses from other contractual clauses, even if meant to protect consumers from arbitral abuses, are preempted by national pro-arbitration policies of the FAA. *See, e.g., Cassarotto v. Doctor's Associates,* 517 U.S. 861 (1996). Decisions such as *Mitsubishi Motors Corp. v. Soler Chrysler-Plymouth, Inc.,* 473 U.S. 614 (1985), and *Shearson/ American Express, Inc. v. McMahon,* 482 U.S. 220 (1987), were among the early precedents promoting expansive views of the authority of arbitrators to resolve various kinds of statutory claims. None was more significant than the decision below, which opened the door to widespread use of predispute arbitration agreements in employment contracts.

❖ Gilmer v. Interstate/Johnson Lane Corp.
500 U.S. 20 (1991)

[Robert Gilmer was employed by defendant as a Manager of Financial Services, which required him to register as a securities representative with the New York Stock Exchange (NYSE). His registration application provided that he agreed to arbitrate "any dispute, claim or controversy" arising between him and his employer. After Interstate terminated Gilmer's employment in 1987, at which time Gilmer was 62 years of age, he filed an action in federal court under the Age Discrimination in Employment Act (ADEA). Interstate filed a motion to compel arbitration pursuant to the NYSE rules. The Fourth Circuit ruled in favor of Interstate that the dispute should be resolved by arbitration.]

Justice WHITE delivered the opinion of the Court.
...Congress enacted the ADEA in 1967 "to promote employment of older persons based on their ability rather than age; to prohibit arbitrary age discrimination in employment; [and] to help employers and workers find ways of meeting problems arising from the impact of age on employment." To achieve those goals, the ADEA, among other things, makes it unlawful for an employer "to fail or refuse to hire or to discharge any individual or otherwise discriminate against any individual with respect to his compensation, terms, conditions, or privileges of employment, because of such individual's age."...

As Gilmer contends, the ADEA is designed not only to address individual grievances, but also to further important social policies. We do not perceive any inherent inconsistency between those policies, however, and enforcing agreements to arbitrate age discrimination claims. It is true that arbitration focuses on specific disputes between the parties involved. The same can be said, however, of judicial resolution of claims. Both of these dispute resolution mechanisms nevertheless also can further broader social purposes....

We also are unpersuaded by the argument that arbitration will undermine the role of the EEOC in enforcing the ADEA. An individual ADEA claimant subject to an arbitration agreement will still be free to file a charge with the

EEOC, even though the claimant is not able to institute a private judicial action. . . .

Gilmer also argues that compulsory arbitration is improper because it deprives claimants of the judicial forum provided for by the ADEA. Congress, however, did not explicitly preclude arbitration or other nonjudicial resolution of claims, even in its recent amendments to the ADEA. . . . Moreover, Gilmer's argument ignores the ADEA's flexible approach to resolution of claims. The EEOC, for example, is directed to pursue "informal methods of conciliation, conference, and persuasion," which suggests that out-of-court dispute resolution, such as arbitration, is consistent with the statutory scheme established by Congress. . . .

In arguing that arbitration is inconsistent with the ADEA, Gilmer also raises a host of challenges to the adequacy of arbitration procedures. Initially, we note that in our recent arbitration cases we have already rejected most of these arguments as insufficient to preclude arbitration of statutory claims. . . .

Gilmer first speculates that arbitration panels will be biased. However, "[w]e decline to indulge the presumption that the parties and arbitral body conducting a proceeding will be unable or unwilling to retain competent, conscientious and impartial arbitrators." . . .

Gilmer also complains that the discovery allowed in arbitration is more limited than in the federal courts, which he contends will make it difficult to prove discrimination. It is unlikely, however, that age discrimination claims require more extensive discovery than other claims that we have found to be arbitrable, such as RICO and antitrust claims. . . .

A further alleged deficiency of arbitration is that arbitrators often will not issue written opinions, resulting, Gilmer contends, in a lack of public knowledge of employers' discriminatory policies, an inability to obtain effective appellate review, and a stifling of the development of the law. The NYSE rules, however, do require that all arbitration awards be in writing, and that the awards contain the names of the parties, a summary of the issues in controversy, and a description of the award issued. In addition, the award decisions are made available to the public. Furthermore, judicial decisions addressing ADEA claims will continue to be issued because it is unlikely that all or even most ADEA claimants will be subject to arbitration agreements. Finally, Gilmer's concerns apply equally to settlements of ADEA claims, which, as noted above, are clearly allowed. . . .

It is also argued that arbitration procedures cannot adequately further the purposes of the ADEA because they do not provide for broad equitable relief and class actions. As the court below noted, however, arbitrators do have the power to fashion equitable relief. Indeed, the NYSE rules applicable here do not restrict the types of relief an arbitrator may award, but merely refer to "damages and/or other relief." But "even if the arbitration could not go forward as a class action or class relief could not be granted by the arbitrator, the fact that the [ADEA] provides for the possibility of bringing a collective action does not mean that individual attempts at conciliation were intended to be barred." *Nicholson v. CPC Int'l Inc.*, 877 F.2d 221, 241 (CA3 1989) (Becker, J., dissenting). Finally, it should be remembered that arbitration agreements will not preclude the EEOC from bringing actions seeking class-wide and equitable relief.

An additional reason advanced by Gilmer for refusing to enforce arbitration agreements relating to ADEA claims is his contention that there often will be unequal bargaining power between employers and employees. Mere inequality in bargaining power, however, is not a sufficient reason to hold that arbitration agreements are never enforceable in the employment context. Relationships between securities dealers and investors, for example, may involve unequal bargaining power, but we nevertheless held in *Rodriguez de Quijas* and *McMahon* that agreements to arbitrate in that context are enforceable. As discussed above, the FAA's purpose was to place arbitration agreements on the same footing as other contracts. Thus, arbitration agreements are enforceable "save upon such grounds as exist at law or in equity for the revocation of any contract." 9 U.S.C. § 2. "Of course, courts should remain attuned to well-supported claims that the agreement to arbitrate resulted from the sort of fraud or overwhelming economic power that would provide grounds 'for the revocation of any contract.'" *Mitsubishi*, 473 U.S. at 627, 105 S. Ct. at 3354. There is no indication in this case, however, that Gilmer, an experienced businessman, was coerced or defrauded into agreeing to the arbitration clause in his registration application. As with the claimed procedural inadequacies discussed above, this claim of unequal bargaining power is best left for resolution in specific cases. . . .

We conclude that Gilmer has not met his burden of showing that Congress, in enacting the ADEA, intended to preclude arbitration of claims under that Act. Accordingly, the judgment of the Court of Appeals is *Affirmed*.

Justice STEVENS filed a dissenting opinion.

. . . There is little dispute that the primary concern animating the FAA was the perceived need by the business community to overturn the common-law rule that denied specific enforcement of agreements to arbitrate in contracts between business entities. . . . At the [legislative hearing regarding the FAA], Senator Walsh stated:

> "The trouble about the matter is that a great many of these contracts that are entered into are really not [voluntary] things at all. Take an insurance policy; there is a blank in it. You can take that or you can leave it. . . . It is the same with a good many contracts of employment. A man says, 'These are our terms. All right, take it or leave it.' Well, there is nothing for the man to do except to sign it; and then he surrenders his right to have his case tried by the court, and has to have it tried before a tribunal in which he has no confidence at all.". . .

Not only would I find that the FAA does not apply to employment-related disputes between employers and employees in general [based on construction of section 1 of the Act], but also I would hold that compulsory arbitration conflicts with the congressional purpose animating the ADEA. . .

[A]uthorizing the courts to issue broad injunctive relief is the cornerstone to eliminating discrimination in society. . . . Because commercial arbitration is typically limited to a specific dispute between the particular parties and because the available remedies in arbitral forums do not provide for class-wide injunctive relief, . . . an essential purpose of the ADEA is frustrated by compulsory arbitration of employment discrimination claims. Moreover, as Chief Justice Burger explained:

> "Plainly, it would not comport with the congressional objectives behind a statute seeking to enforce civil rights protected by Title VII to allow the very forces that had practiced discrimination to contract away the right to enforce civil rights in the courts. For federal courts to defer to arbitral decisions reached by the same combination of forces that had long perpetuated discrimination would have made the foxes guardians of the chickens."

Notes and Questions

4. Did Congress intend the FAA to apply to employment disputes such as Gilmer's ADEA claim? The FAA provides in Section 1 that "nothing herein contained shall apply to contracts of seamen, railroad employees, or any other class of workers engaged in foreign or interstate commerce." Doesn't this mean that arbitration clauses cannot bind employees whose work involves interstate commerce, as Gilmer's surely did? The Court refused to address the question in *Gilmer* but resolved it ten years later in *Circuit City Stores v. Adams*, 532 U.S. 105 (2001). There, the Court held that section 1 exempts from the FAA only employment contracts of transportation workers, not contracts of employees generally even though their work may involve interstate commerce.

5. Doesn't the *Gilmer* decision conflict with *Alexander v. Gardner-Denver Co.*, 415 U.S. 36 (1974), which held that even though an employment dispute has been arbitrated pursuant to a collective bargaining agreement the employee is not precluded from filing a subsequent lawsuit for employment discrimination under Title VII? The Court in *Gilmer* distinguished the *Alexander* case on three grounds: (1) The arbitration clause in *Alexander* authorized arbitration only of claims under the collective bargaining agreement, not statutory claims; (2) the claimant in *Alexander* was represented by his union in the arbitration proceeding rather than proceeding individually; and (3) *Alexander* was not decided under the FAA.

6. What role does the Equal Employment Opportunity Commission (EEOC) have in pursuing employment discrimination claims inlight of the *Gilmer* decision? See *EEOC v. Wright*, 534 U.S. 279 (2002) (agreement between employer and employee to arbitrate specific employment-related disputes does not bar the EEOC

from pursuing judicial relief (including back pay, reinstatement, and damages, in an Americans with Disabilities Act of 1990 (ADA) enforcement action) on behalf of the victim).

7. Which do you find more persuasive — the arguments of the majority or those of the dissent in *Gilmer*? Would it make any difference to know that Mr. Gilmer eventually was awarded $200,000 in arbitration — essentially a victory on the merits?

2.   *Fairness in Entering into Arbitration Agreements*

A decision by the U.S. Fifth Circuit Court of Appeals is exemplary of recent judicial approaches to the enforcement of arbitration provisions in standardized consumer and employment contracts. The court found that life insurance purchasers had agreed to submit to arbitration because they signed a document that contained the following clause, located just above the signature lines:

THE PARTIES UNDERSTAND THAT BY SIGNING THIS ARBITRATION AGREEMENT, THEY ARE LIMITING ANY RIGHT TO PUNITIVE DAMAGES AND GIVING UP THE RIGHT TO A TRIAL IN COURT, BOTH WITH AND WITHOUT A JURY.

The court found that the consumers had thereby waived their right to a judicial forum and "their corresponding right to a jury trial." *American Heritage Life Ins. Co. v. Orr*, 294 F.3d 702 (5th Cir. 2002). Other court decisions have enforced "agreements" to arbitrate based on a consumer's indication of assent by "clicking" a box in an online website. *Hill v. Gateway 2000, Inc.*, 105 F.3d 1147 (7th Cir. 1997); *Davis v. Dell, Inc.*, 2007 U.S. Dist. Lexis 94767 (D. N.J. 2007); *Hauenstein v. Softwrap Limited*, 2007 U.S. Dist. Lexis 60618 (D.W. Wa. 2007).

Many consumers were unaware that by entering into agreements with arbitration clauses, they were agreeing to forego rights to trial, including jury trial, with its procedural protections including judicial review (Schwartz, 1997). Concerns about fairness in arbitration may also arise due to a lack of transparency in the arbitration process and a lack of understanding about how the process works. As you have come to understand by reading Chapters 16 to 18, even a relatively sophisticated attorney may not have more than a general idea of how arbitration will proceed without knowing what particular arbitration rules are governing the process. Modern dispute resolution procedures often run to dozens of provisions covering many pages, similar to rules of procedure in the courts. The governing documents and provisions are usually only incorporated by reference in the contract, and are not always easy to locate. With the advent of the Internet, arbitration procedures and other relevant information is often available online.

Concerns about how consumers and employees become bound to arbitrate and how arbitration procedures are set up have stimulated considerable academic commentary, state legislative measures, and court decisions addressing the enforceability, formation, and contents of arbitration agreements. Courts and legislatures have been attempting to make arbitration a more "user-friendly" process — an effort supplemented by initiatives of the American Arbitration Association (AAA) and some other dispute resolution organizations and groups. The economic problems engulfing banks, including the foreclosure crisis and bank bailout, have spurred some legislators to pay close attention to arbitration in the consumer context.

Notes and Questions

8. *Contract law and arbitration.* You may remember from your Contracts course that one of the key principles to forming a valid contract is mutual assent; this principle is often an important issue for courts examining the validity of arbitration clauses. Under classic contract theory mutual assent is often found through the "objective manifestations" of parties, including acts that somehow signify that one is entering into a bargain. Do you see how classic contract theory comes into play in cases like *American Heritage* and others cited above? In Section D below we examine various doctrines that have come into play in judicial efforts to police arbitration agreements, including unconscionability, fraud, and breach of contract.

9. *Critical commentary.* Commentators have explored a wide variety of concerns about the growth of predispute arbitration clauses, including the foreclosure of access to juries and judges, restriction of remedies (e.g., class-wide relief), and process failures (arbitral bias, cost, etc.). Most scholarly commentary has been quite critical of consumer and employment arbitration. See, e.g., Bingham (2003), Sternlight (1996, 2002), and Stone (1996). Despite the concerns fostered by predispute arbitration clauses, many courts uphold such arbitration agreements. What value might they yield for the contracting parties and court systems (Ware, 2003)?

10. *Punitive damages.* The note above alludes to the enforcement of an arbitration agreement that purports to "waive" punitive damages. Should such a limitation in an adhesion contract be enforced (Stipanowich, 1997)? There are a number of court decisions striking down such "waiver" provisions on grounds of unconscionability. See, e.g., *Armendariz v. Foundation Health Psychcare Service, Inc.*, 24 Cal. 4th 83 (Cal. S. Ct. 2000); *Cole v. Burns International Security Systems* 105 F.3d 1465 (D.C. Cir. 1997).

11. *Arbitration and surprise in commercial transactions.* It is somewhat ironic that protections against being "surprised" by an arbitration

provision evolved first in the commercial realm. As discussed in Chapter 18, the New York Court of Appeals, applying U.C.C. 2-207(2)(b), ruled that an inclusion of an arbitration agreement without the consent of all parties materially alters a contract for the sale of goods and therefore does not become part of the contract. *In re* arbitration between *Marlene Indus. v. Carnac Textiles*, 380 N.E.2d 239 (N.Y. 1978). Of course, that provision of the U.C.C. did not apply to consumer transactions but only to transactions between merchants.

Problem 1

You are interested in buying a new computer. You go online and make the purchase through the TZ Computer ("TZC") website. The terms and conditions include the following provision:

Arbitration

13.   ANY CLAIM, DISPUTE, OR CONTROVERSY (WHETHER IN CONTRACT, TORT, OR OTHERWISE, WHETHER PREEXISTING, PRESENT OR FUTURE, AND INCLUDING STATUTORY, COMMON LAW, INTENTIONAL TORT AND EQUITABLE CLAIMS) BETWEEN YOU AND TZC arising from or relating to this Agreement, its interpretation, or the breach, termination or validity thereof, the relationships which result from this Agreement (including, to the full extent permitted by applicable law, relationships with third parties who are not signatories to this Agreement), TZC's advertising, or any related purchase SHALL BE RESOLVED EXCLUSIVELY AND FINALLY BY BINDING ARBITRATION ADMINISTERED BY THE NATIONAL ARBITRATION FORUM (NAF) under its Code of Procedure then in effect (available via the Internet at http://www.arb-forum.com, or via telephone at 1-800-474-2371). In the event of any inconsistency or conflict between NAF Code of Procedure and this Agreement, this Agreement shall control. The arbitration will be limited solely to the dispute or controversy between you and TZC. NEITHER YOU NOR TCZ SHALL BE ENTITLED TO JOIN OR CONSOLIDATE CLAIMS BY OR AGAINST OTHER CUSTOMERS, OR ARBITRATE ANY CLAIM AS A REPRESENTATIVE OR CLASS ACTION OR IN A PRIVATE ATTORNEY GENERAL CAPACITY. The individual (non-class) nature of this dispute provision goes to the essence of the parties' arbitration agreement, and if found unenforceable, the entire arbitration provision shall not be enforced. This transaction involves interstate commerce, and this provision shall be governed by the Federal Arbitration Act 9 U.S.C. sec. 1-16 (FAA). Any award of the arbitrator(s) shall be final and binding on each of the parties, and may be entered as a judgment in any court of competent jurisdiction. TZC will be responsible for paying any arbitration fees to the extent such fees exceed the amount of the filing fee for initiating a claim in the small claims or similar court in the state in which you reside. Each party shall pay for its own costs and attorneys' fees, if any. However, if you prevail on any claim that affords the prevailing party attorneys' fees, or if there is a written agreement providing for fees, the Arbitrator may award reasonable fees to the prevailing party, under the standards for fee

shifting provided by law. Information may be obtained and claims may be filed with the NAF at P.O. Box 50191, Minneapolis, MN 55405.

a.   In real life, would you bother to read these contents before signifying your acceptance by "clicking" on the "accept" button? (Remember, under U.S. contract law, generally a failure to read terms and conditions will not operate as a defense against their enforcement!)

b.   Read the provision above with care. What are its key features? Would you agree to the terms stated? What more would you like to know? Suppose you go on the National Arbitration Forum (NAF) website, referenced above, and you find the following provisions in the referenced NAF Code of Procedure:

- arbitration is confidential unless all parties agree otherwise or the law requires otherwise;

- arbitrators are to follow applicable substantive law and may grant any legal, equitable, or other remedy or relief provided by law;

- parties are required to cooperate in the exchange of documents and information, and arbitrators can issue subpoenas against non-parties to provide documents and information or to appear as witnesses; and

- arbitrators have the power to sanction for failure to comply with NAF rules or for asserting an unsupportable claim or defense.

Are you comfortable with these procedures? What relative advantages or disadvantages do they present in comparison to going to court?

You might be interested to know that the NAF is an actual company based in Minnesota. It specializes in and focuses on consumer debt actions — something that distinguishes it from some other national arbitration institutions that we have discussed. In the summer of 2009 NAF ceased its consumer arbitration program as part of a settlement with the Minnesota Attorney General. The latter had sued over its management of debt actions involving consumers and credit card companies. NAF was accused of violating state consumer fraud, deceptive trade practices, and false advertising laws by hiding financial connections to collection agencies and credit card companies. "Firm Agrees to End Role in Arbitrating Card Debt," *New York Times* B8 (July 20, 2009).

The NAF saga is one of the more colorful (and troubling) episodes in the recent history of consumer arbitration. The 2009 NAF Code of Procedure mentioned above reflects some of the due process protections that came about partly as a result of judicial decisions like some of those discussed in the following pages. The Minnesota Attorney General alleged that the NAF had handled more than 214,000 collection claims in 2006, 60 percent of which were filed by law firms with ties to the collection industry. The NAF denied the allegations. Under the settlement, the NAF can continue to arbitrate certain types of claims performed under supervision of government entities or non-government organizations (e.g., Internet domain name, cargo, personal injury protection suits, etc.) In August 2009, Bank of America Corporation said that it will stop requiring that disputes with its credit card holders and banking and lending customers be settled by binding arbitration. Joshua Freed, "Bank of America drops arbitration requirement" (August 13, 2009), *http://www.forbes.com/feeds/ap/2009/08/13/ap6777903.html.*

The NAF story — that of a provider with an apparent deep-seated conflict of interest — resonates with concerns long expressed by some scholars that consumers and employees cannot find equitable treatment in justice systems set up by companies who are "repeat players" in the system. In the following excerpt, Professor Sarah Rudolph Cole articulates some of these concerns in the context of employment agreements.

❖ **Sarah Rudolph Cole,** INCENTIVES AND ARBITRATION: THE CASE
AGAINST ENFORCEMENT OF EXECUTORY ARBITRATION AGREEMENTS
BETWEEN EMPLOYERS AND EMPLOYEES

64 UMKC L. Rev. 449 (Spring 1996)

... To ensure the continued success and viability of the alternative dispute resolution (ADR) movement, courts confronted with challenged executory arbitration agreements must learn to separate those cases where it is appropriate to enforce an executory agreement to arbitrate from those where the agreement should be overridden and the dispute resolved using alternative methods. Failure to limit the types of disputes that may be arbitrated is likely to discredit arbitration as a legitimate means for resolving disputes. As challenges to the fairness of arbitral proceedings increase, litigants who might otherwise welcome the use of arbitration may reject it as ill-advised because they are fearful that arbitration will result in a restriction of their basic rights.

This increasing suspicion of arbitration may be traced to the courts' willingness to enforce executory arbitration agreements without regard to the parties' disparate negotiating incentives. . . . In such a setting, the arbitral agreement is suspect because the employer, like a merchant or a labor union, is a "repeat player." The employee, by contrast, is a one-shot player. An analysis of the interactions between these types of people and entities demonstrates that repeat players will have a distinct and systematic advantage in interactions with one-shot players. As a result, agreements between one-shot and repeat players should only be enforced where the incentives and ability of the parties to negotiate is similar.

A repeat player is an individual or organization who repeatedly interacts with a particular institution or engages in certain behaviors, for example, commercial transactions or dispute resolution. Representative repeat players include merchants as well as large organizations such as securities firms or insurance companies. By contrast, a lack of organization and sophistication characterizes the one-shot player. The one-shot player will usually have few opportunities to negotiate agreements and even fewer opportunities to litigate a claim. In essence, the one-shot player's limited exposure to contracts and the legal system are the defining aspects of his nature.

Typically, a repeat player will have greater experience and expertise in both contract negotiation and dispute resolution than will a one-shot player. Because the repeat player more frequently engages in these activities, he will have a greater understanding of both processes. Moreover, economies of scale favor the repeat player over the one-shot player; the repeat player typically has lower start-up costs in each separate negotiation and is in a better position to draft the agreement. While this, in itself, may not be problematic — the repeat player may be able to structure an agreement that provides benefits to both parties — it does provide the opportunity for abuse. In drafting the agreement, the repeat player may attempt to garner the lion's share of the potential benefits for himself. . . .

Further aggravating circumstances increase the repeat player's opportunity for undetected exploitation of his superior position. One-shot players, such as employees, improperly value the inclusion of an arbitration agreement in their employment agreement. Employees suffer from judgmental bias as a result of their personal experiences. That is, they systematically ignore or deemphasize the likelihood that a low probability event will occur because the event has never affected them. In the employment context, this judgmental bias causes employees to misapprehend the risk that they will engage in litigation with their employer. This informational problem leads employees to demand lower wages and fewer benefits than they might if they were fully cognizant of the risks present in the proposed arbitral agreement.

Obviously, many of these problems could be eliminated if employees could make fully-informed job choices. Unfortunately, imperfect information and constraints on employee mobility prevent this outcome. In the employment setting, neither the employer nor the employee need suffer. There are a number of legitimate ways in which employers can reduce their litigation expenses and, at the same time, avoid placing their employees in a disadvantageous position. For example, the employer could describe arbitration at the time the dispute arises and allow the employee to choose to proceed with arbitration or litigation at that time. Alternatively, the employer could continue to include the arbitration agreement in the employment contract, but permit a disgruntled employee to opt out of the process at the time the dispute arises. Both alternatives would allow employers to reduce costs while avoiding inequity.

Notes and Questions

Repeat Player Concept. Note carefully the distinction between a "one-shot" and "repeat" player. One of the "findings" in the Senate's version of the proposed Arbitration Fairness Act of 2009, H.R. 1020, 111th Cong. (2009) is that "[p]rivate arbitration companies are sometimes under great pressure to devise systems that favor the corporate repeat players who decide whether those companies will receive their lucrative business."

13.   How might a company that wanted to continue to use arbitration prevent such bias or mitigate perceptions of bias?

14.   Do the data support the repeat player concept? The quantitative underpinning of the concept is primarily the work of Professor Lisa Bingham. Thus far, extensive research conducted by Professor Bingham on issues in employment arbitration has not produced clear evidence to reinforce such concerns, although the author concludes that "superior bargaining power is affecting the outcomes of arbitration" (Bingham, 1998). One researcher has suggested that the data do not clearly support the concept that repeated experiences with a single arbitrator are a critical factor in outcomes (Hill, 2004). Of course, it is easy to imagine scenarios in which repeat players reap advantages over their opponents through superior information about procedures and neutrals, personal familiarity, perceived economic leverage, or other factors. In a well-established arena such as securities arbitration, on the other hand, the existence of a relatively well-informed and influential plaintiff's bar, the presence of Securities Industry Conference on Arbitration, SEC and GAO oversight, and case reporting have helped establish a relatively level playing field (Stipanowich, 2004).

15.   *Due Process Protocols.* In Section E below you will read about the development of the Employment and Consumer Due Process Protocols promulgated by the AAA in collaboration with other representatives of other national bodies. The Protocols were intended to establish minimum due process standards for arbitration under standardized employment or consumer contracts. If you review the text of the Protocols, consider whether they represent meaningful responses to the repeat player concerns. As noted in Section E, recent empirical studies indicate that some categories of individual employees actually do better in arbitration than trial. Moreover, there are data supporting the conclusion that the AAA's reformation of its employment rules to bring them into

> conformance with the Employment Due Process Protocol has improved the results of arbitration for employees. This is reinforced by Professor Bingham's research (Bingham & Sharaf, 2004).

3.   *Procedural and "Outcome" Fairness in Arbitration*

The most pointed criticisms of predispute arbitration provisions in consumer, employment, and other potentially "adhesive" contracts usually stem from perceived unfairness in arbitration procedures and remedies. It is worth reviewing some of the advantages of arbitration you have learned throughout these chapters and attempting to compare and contrast the consumer and employment contexts from the business-to-business and international agreements in which arbitration has long been popular. Rational consumers and employees, like business counterparts, may very well conclude that in some cases arbitration procedures provide a speedier and less expensive alternative to going to court, as well as a greater likelihood of getting to a hearing.

However, where one party is a company that "sets the stage" for binding arbitration by putting arbitration provisions in its contracts with consumers or employees, some of the attributes of arbitration that would be perceived as favorable in a commercial contract may appear to be one-sided advantages.

An individual forced to submit to arbitration may be unfamiliar with the process, while the party who drafted the arbitration clause may be a repeat player who is familiar with the process and with particular arbitrators. Although in one sense an arbitrator is like a judge without a robe, that lack of a robe can sometimes be a cause for concern. In the judicial system a party is not able to choose the person who adjudicates her case, as parties can in arbitration. Thus, while businesses may look for commercial or technical expertise in an arbitrator, consumers may be wary of the perceived bias borne of experience as an "insider." This becomes a special cause for concern when certain companies continue to give repeat business to the same arbitrators, and it is those very same companies that provide all or a large part of the arbitrators' fees. While the FAA provides that a court may overturn an arbitration award if an arbitrator engages in "evident partiality," this is not easy to prove and is rarely found. 9 U.S.C. § 10(a)(2); see Chapter 18. Clearly, these concerns are real and call into question the viability of arbitration when significant gaps in bargaining power exist between parties entering arbitral agreements.

The choice of decision maker is only one of a number of key procedural choices that may present opportunities to "tilt" the playing field. These include choices governing the scope of information exchange and discovery, the location of proceedings, the confidentiality of the process, the nature of hearings, the availability of remedies (including punitive damages and attorney fees), the scope and format of awards, and the ability to challenge awards.

Finally, arbitration may be a mechanism to shield the company from consolidated consumer efforts (e.g., class action lawsuits). Since the Supreme Court tacitly acknowledged the authority of arbitrators to direct and supervise class-wide arbitration in *Green Tree v. Bazzle*, 123 S. Ct. 2402 (2003), many companies have responded by including terms in their predispute consumer and employment arbitration provisions to the effect that arbitration is to be restricted to the company and the individual consumer or employee. In this way, companies hope to handle each claim on a case-by-case basis in the relative privacy of an arbitral proceeding. If such terms are enforced it may be difficult for an individual consumer or employee to expend time and resources pursuing justice in these situations. And many may choose not to pursue redress if the prospect of a large damages award is removed.

As we will see in the following section, courts have been moved to intervene to protect consumers and employees from egregious unfairness in arbitration, both by striking down specific terms in the arbitration agreement or by denying enforcement to the whole arbitration provision. They have used a variety of defenses to contract, including fraud and misrepresentation, breach of contract, and unconscionability. These efforts, however, must be seen in the context of the broader pro-arbitration policy that has led most courts to enforce arbitration agreements in all kinds of contracts, even standardized agreements. *See, e.g., Gilmer v. Interstate/Johnson Lane Corp.*, 500 U.S. 20 (1991), *supra* C.1. Judges find themselves trying to strike the right balance between upholding the federal and state laws promoting arbitration and reining in some of the more egregious examples of unfairness — with varied and conflicting results.

D. Judicial Policing of Arbitration Agreements in Consumer and Employment Contracts

As you read each of the decisions below, note the different approaches the courts used to establish limits on arbitration agreements in the interest of promoting fairness. Consider, also, the array of procedural concerns that gave rise to and were addressed by these decisions.

❖ Engalla v. Permanente Medical Group, Inc.
15 Cal. 4th 951 (1997)

[Plaintiffs in this case were the surviving family of Wilfredo Engalla, who through his employer was enrolled in Kaiser's health maintenance organization. Part of the standard insurance agreement contained an arbitration clause providing for binding arbitration of disputes related to Kaiser's services. Alleging that Kaiser had lost X-rays, failed to follow its physician's recommendations, and otherwise negligently failed to diagnose his cancer until it was inoperable, Mr. Engalla initiated arbitration. Although Kaiser represented that an arbitration within its self-administered program would reach a hearing within several months' time, the final arbitrator was not even selected until more than five months after the service of Mr. Engalla's claim. Mr. Engalla died before an arbitral hearing could be held. After his death, his family initiated a medical malpractice action in superior court.]

MOSK, J.:

. . . The arbitration clause contained in the Service Agreement . . . provides that each side "shall" designate a party arbitrator within 30 days of service of the claim and that the 2 party arbitrators "shall" designate a third, neutral arbitrator within 30 days thereafter. . . . The arbitration program is designed, written, mandated, and administered by Kaiser. It does not . . . employ or contract with any independent person or entity to provide such administrative services, or any oversight or evaluation of the arbitration program or its performance. Rather, administrative functions are performed by outside counsel retained to defend Kaiser in an adversarial capacity. . . . The fact that Kaiser has designed and administers its arbitration program from an adversarial perspective is not disclosed to Kaiser members or subscribers . . . [In materials distributed to Kaiser members,] Kaiser represented that an arbitration in its program would reach a hearing within several months' time, and that its members would find the arbitration process to be a fair approach to protecting their rights. [The opinion recounts in detail multiple requests from Mr. Engalla's counsel for expeditious processing of the claim due to his terminal condition. It details delays on the part of the lawyers for Kaiser in the selection of arbitrators so that the final, neutral arbitrator was not appointed until more than five months after the service of Mr. Engalla's claim, well beyond the representations made by Kaiser, and shortly before his death.]. . .

The Engallas claim fraud in the inducement of the arbitration agreement and therefore that "[g]rounds exist for the revocation of the agreement" [under California law]. As has been pointed out . . . "Offers are 'revoked.' . . . Contracts are extinguished by rescission.". . . Fraud is one of the grounds on which a contract can be rescinded. In order to defeat a petition to compel arbitration, the parties opposing a petition to compel must show that the asserted fraud claim goes specifically "'to the "making" of the agreement to arbitrate,'" rather than to the making of the contract in general. . . .

The Engallas claim that Engalla was fraudulently induced to enter the arbitration agreement — in essence a claim of promissory fraud. "'Promissory fraud' is a subspecies of fraud and deceit. A promise to do something necessarily implies the intention to perform; hence, where a promise is made without such intention, there is an implied misrepresentation of fact that may be actionable fraud. . . ."

Here the Engallas claim (1) that Kaiser misrepresented its arbitration agreement in that it entered into the agreement knowing that, at the very least, there was a likelihood its agents would breach the part of the agreement providing for the timely appointment of arbitrators and the expeditious progress towards an arbitration hearing; (2) that Kaiser employed the above misrepresentation in order to induce reliance on the part of Engalla and his employer; (3) that Engalla relied on these misrepresentations to his detriment. The trial court found evidence supporting those claims. . . .

First, evidence of misrepresentation is plain. "[F]alse representations made recklessly and without regard for their truth in order to induce action by another are the equivalent of misrepresentations knowingly and intentionally uttered." As recounted above, section 8.B. of the arbitration agreement provides that party arbitrators "shall" be chosen within 30 days and neutral arbitrators within 60 days, and that the arbitration hearing "shall" be held "within a reasonable time thereafter." Although Kaiser correctly argues that these contractual representations did not bind it to appoint a neutral arbitrator within 60 days, since the appointment of that arbitrator is a bilateral decision that depends on agreements of the parties, Kaiser's contractual representations were at the very least commitments to exercise good faith and reasonable diligence to have the arbitrators appointed within the specified time. This good faith duty is underscored by Kaiser's contractual assumption of the duty to administer the health service plan as a fiduciary.

Here there are facts to support the Engallas' allegation that Kaiser entered into the arbitration agreement with knowledge that it would not comply with its own contractual timelines, or with at least a reckless indifference as to whether its agents would use reasonable diligence and good faith to comply with them. As discussed, a survey of Kaiser arbitrations between 1984 and 1986 submitted into evidence showed that a neutral arbitrator was appointed within 60 days in only 1 percent of the cases, with only 3 percent appointed within 180 days, and that on average the neutral arbitrator was appointed 674 days — almost 2 years — after the demand for arbitration. Regardless of when Kaiser became aware of these precise statistics, which were part of a 1989 study, the depositions of two of Kaiser's in-house attorneys demonstrate that Kaiser was aware soon after it began its arbitration program that its contractual deadlines were not being met, and that severe delay was endemic to the program. Kaiser nonetheless persisted in its contractual promises of expeditiousness.

Kaiser now argues that most of these delays were caused by the claimants themselves and their attorneys, who procrastinated in the selection of a neutral arbitrator. But Kaiser's counterexplanation is without any statistical support, and is based solely on anecdotal evidence related by Kaiser officials. Moreover, the explanation appears implausible in view of the sheer pervasiveness of the delays. While it is theoretically possible that 99 percent of plaintiffs' attorneys did not seek a rapid arbitration, a more reasonable inference, in light of common experience, is that in at least some cases Kaiser's defense attorneys were partly or wholly responsible for the delays, and

Kaiser's former general counsel conceded as much in deposition testimony. It is, after all, the defense which often benefits from delay, thereby preserving the status quo to its advantage until the time when memories fade and claims are abandoned. Indeed, the present case illustrates why Kaiser's counsel may sometimes find it advantageous to delay the selection of a neutral arbitrator. There is also evidence that Kaiser kept extensive records on the arbitrators it had used, and may have delayed the selection process in order to ensure that it would obtain the arbitrators it thought would best serve its interests. Thus, it is a reasonable inference from the documentary record before us that Kaiser's contractual representations of expeditiousness were made with knowledge of their likely falsity, and in fact concealed an unofficial policy or practice of delay.

The systemwide nature of Kaiser's delay comes into clearer focus when it is contrasted with other arbitration systems. As the Engallas point out, many large institutional users of arbitration, including most health maintenance organizations (HMO's), avoid the potential problems of delay in the selection of arbitrators by contracting with neutral third party organizations, such as the American Arbitration Association (AAA). These organizations will then assume responsibility for administering the claim from the time the arbitration demand is filed, and will ensure the arbitrator or arbitrators are chosen in a timely manner. Though Kaiser is not obliged by law to adopt any particular form of arbitration, the record shows that it did not attempt to create within its own organization any office that would neutrally administer the arbitration program, but instead entrusted such administration to outside counsel retained to act as advocates on its behalf. In other words, there is evidence that Kaiser established a self-administered arbitration system in which delay for its own benefit and convenience was an inherent part, despite express and implied contractual representations to the contrary. . . .

We turn then to the Engallas' unconscionability argument. We have required that "contractual arrangement[s] for the nonjudicial resolution of disputes" must possess "'minimum levels of integrity.'" Thus, in *Graham v. Scissor-Tail, Inc.*, we held that an arbitration agreement that called for the selection of an arbitrator affiliated with one of the parties to the contract was unconscionable. . . . In addition to the general doctrine of unconscionability derived from contract law, HMO's such as Kaiser are regulated by the Knox-Keene Health Care Service Plan Act, which provides among other things that all contracts made in connection with a health service plan be "fair, reasonable, and consistent with the objectives" of that statute. HMO's are therefore especially obligated not to impose contracts on their subscribers that are one-sided and lacking in fundamental fairness.

In determining whether a contract term is unconscionable, we first consider whether the contract between Kaiser and Engalla was one of adhesion. In [*Madden*], we held that an agreement between Kaiser and a state employee was not a true contract of adhesion, although Kaiser's health plan was offered to state employees "on a 'take it or leave it' basis without opportunity for individual bargaining." We reasoned that the Kaiser contract was not adhesive because (1) it "represents the product of negotiation between two parties, Kaiser and the [State Employees Retirement System], possessing parity of bargaining strength" and (2) the state employee could choose from among a number of different health plans, and thus was not confronted with the choice typical of a contract of adhesion of "either adher[ing] to the standardized agreement or forego[ing] the needed service." We also found that the arbitration clause in question was not, unlike the unconscionable clauses in adhesion contracts, a term that limits the liability or obligations of a stronger party, but rather "could prove helpful to all parties."

The present agreement, which was also offered to Engalla on a "take it or leave it" basis, has more of the characteristics of an adhesion contract than the one considered in *Madden*. First, although Oliver Tire [Engalla's employer] is a corporation of considerable size, it has had only a small number of employees enrolled in Kaiser, and did not have the strength to bargain with Kaiser to alter the terms of the contract. Second, Engalla did have one other health plan from which to choose, but not several plans as was the case in *Madden*. Finally, unlike in *Madden*, the Engallas do not claim that the arbitration clause itself is unconscionable, but that the arbitration program Kaiser established was biased against them.

Nonetheless, although the present contract has some of the attributes of adhesion, it did not, *on its face*, lack "'minimum levels of integrity.'" The unfairness that is the substance of the Engallas' unconscionability argument comes essentially to this: The Engallas contend that Kaiser has established a system of arbitration inherently unfair to claimants, because the method of selecting neutral arbitrators is biased. They claim that Kaiser has an unfair advantage as a "repeat player" in arbitration, possessing information on arbitrators that the Engallas themselves lacked. They also argue that Kaiser, under its arbitration system, has sought to maximize this advantage by reserving for itself an unlimited right to veto arbitrators proposed by the other party. This method is in contrast to arbitration programs run by neutral, third party arbitration organizations such as the AAA, which give parties a very limited ability to veto arbitrators from its preselected panels.

Yet none of these features of Kaiser's arbitration program renders the arbitration agreement per se unconscionable. . . . The alleged problem with Kaiser's arbitration in this case was not any defect or one-sidedness in its contractual provisions, but rather in the gap between its contractual representations and the actual workings of its arbitration program. It is the doctrines of fraud and waiver, rather than of unconscionability, that most appropriately address this discrepancy between the contractual representation and the reality. Thus, viewing the arbitration agreement on its face, we cannot say it is unconscionable.

[REVERSED and REMANDED to the trial court for a determination of the Engalla's waiver claim. The Engallas argued that arbitration should not be compelled because of Kaiser's conduct.]

BROWN, J., dissenting:

. . . Almost lost in the majority's exhaustive procedural summary is one key fact — namely, the arbitration process was already underway by the time the plaintiffs unilaterally withdrew . . . The reason the Engallas withdrew from the arbitration was that Kaiser declined to stipulate that Mrs. Engalla's separate loss of consortium claim survived her husband's death. It is this unilateral withdrawal from a pending arbitration that the majority's decision validates. . . .

In evaluating both the Engallas' fraudulent inducement claim and their waiver claim, the majority focuses on Kaiser's *performance* during the course of the aborted private arbitration. According to the majority, the sine qua non of successful fraudulent inducement and waiver claims is unreasonable or bad faith delay by Kaiser. . . .

Although the majority's desire to penalize Kaiser's obduracy is understandable, the consequences of validating a party's unilateral withdrawal from a pending arbitration based on the conduct of its arbitration adversary will reverberate far beyond the bad facts of the instant case. In stark contrast to the legislative response, which enhances the procedures for *keeping* a case in private arbitration, . . . the majority expands the procedures for *removing* a case from arbitration. . . .

In this case, having previously submitted their dispute to private arbitration and having already completed the arbitrator selection process, the Engallas should have sought relief for Kaiser's dilatory conduct in the pending arbitration. For example, the Engallas could have presented their fraud and waiver claims directly to the arbitrators and requested that they not enforce the arbitration provision. Likewise, the Engallas could have requested that the arbitrators sanction Kaiser's dilatory conduct by deeming Mrs. Engalla's separate loss of consortium claim to have survived her husband's death [describing broad remedial powers of arbitrators]. In fact, at oral argument, the Engallas' counsel conceded that this case could likely have remained in private arbitration if Mrs. Engalla's economic loss had been ameliorated.

The one thing the Engallas should not be permitted to do, however, is to circumvent the arbitrators altogether. The consequences of validating a party's unilateral withdrawal from a pending arbitration will be dramatic. Jurisdictional disputes will inevitably arise. Suppose, for example, that following the Engallas' unilateral withdrawal, Kaiser had elected to continue to pursue the pending arbitration and that the arbitrators had ultimately entered a default judgment in favor of Kaiser. Would that default judgment have been valid? Would the same have been true if the trial court had simultaneously entered a default judgment in favor of the Engallas in the pending litigation?

In addition, . . . other parties to pending arbitrations will doubtlessly engage in the same conduct. Counsel's answer to this dilemma was that this court should "trust the trial courts." The majority's answer is to "emphasize . . . that the delay must be substantial, unreasonable, and in spite of the claimant's own reasonable diligence" and not "the result of reasonable and good faith disagreements between the parties."

Neither answer is satisfactory. Under the majority's holding, which has all the precision of a "SCUD" missile, the resolution of fraudulent inducement and waiver claims will necessarily entail fact-intensive, case-by-case determinations. The disruptive, time-consuming nature of these determinations is well illustrated by the facts of the present case, in which "[t]he Engallas ultimately had five months to complete discovery [on the petition to compel arbitration], during which time thirteen motions were filed and more than a dozen depositions were taken." Even assuming that the trial courts ultimately resolve all future claims correctly, the interim disruption to pending arbitrations will be simply intolerable.

Great cases like hard cases make bad law. For great cases are called great, not by reason of their real importance in shaping the law of the future, but because of some accident of immediate overwhelming interest which appeals to the feelings and distorts the judgment. These immediate interests exercise a kind of hydraulic pressure which makes what previously was clear seem doubtful, and before which even well settled principles of law will bend. Although legislators, practitioners, and courts have all expressed concern that disparities in bargaining power may affect the procedural fairness of consumer arbitration agreements, this case amply demonstrates why any solutions should come from the Legislature, whose ability to craft precise exceptions is far superior to that of this court.

However well-intentioned the majority and however deserving its intended target, today's holding pokes a hole in the barrier separating private arbitrations and the courts. Unfortunately, like any such breach, this hole will eventually cause the dam to burst. Ironically, the tool the majority uses to puncture its hole is the observation that "those who enter into arbitration agreements expect that their dispute will be resolved without necessity for any contact with the courts." Because I suspect that parties to private arbitrations will be having quite a bit more contact with the courts than they ever bargained for, I dissent.

Questions

15. *Role of the arbitrator.* The dissent states that although Kaiser's process did have unreasonable delays, the issues regarding delay should have been first brought up with the arbitrator because the arbitration had already begun. Judge Brown believes that the majority has essentially created more problems than it solved because now parties will find it easier to circumvent arbitrators in favor of the courts during the arbitral proceeding. Can you think of better solutions to address the delay problem?

16.   After this ruling, Kaiser formed a "Blue Ribbon Panel" of outside experts to suggest reforms to its arbitration process designed tospeed the process and ensure greater fairness.

17.   *Health Care Due Process Protocol.* In the 1990s a group of national organizations developed due process standards for arbitration in the health care field and jointly proposed some limits on predispute arbitration provisions. See Section E. Would the Kaiser approach pass muster under the Health Care Due Process Protocol?

Note: The Use of Unconscionability Doctrine in Policing Arbitration Agreements

The *Engalla* majority declined to find the Kaiser arbitration provision unconscionable. Although the agreement had certain "adhesive" characteristics (that is, the consumer's relevant options were limited and Kaiser's control was great), the procedures spelled out in the agreement did not fail to meet "minimum levels of integrity" because, on their face, they did not appear to be unfair. Rather, the court reasoned, Kaiser misled the public as to its ability to meet the promised schedule.

Although unconscionability is the legal doctrine that is most often used to police fairness in arbitration agreements, what constitutes an unconscionable arbitration clause varies widely from state to state and court to court. The California courts have been especially active in using unconscionability as a basis for striking down arbitration agreements in whole or in part. In *Armendariz v. Foundation Health Psychcare Service, Inc.*, 24 Cal. 4th 83 (Cal. S. Ct. 2000), for example, the California Supreme Court used unconscionability doctrine as the basis for considering what procedural protections would be essential requisites for the arbitration of statutory discrimination claims under an employment agreement. Such elements included an independent and impartial arbitrator, an opportunity for the employee to have adequate discovery, limits on the cost of arbitration, remedies akin to those available in court, a written decision allowing limited judicial review, and procedural "bilaterality." Because not all of these requirements were met, the court struck down the entire agreement as unconscionable. Of course, the strong presumption in favor of enforcing agreements to arbitrate might lead other courts to take a more tailored approach and reform the arbitration agreement to address fairness concerns.

In any event, an arbitration clause will not be unconscionable solely because it is contained in a preprinted sales agreement that was prepared by the seller and that the buyer may not have fully read. In *Harper v. J.D. Byrider of Canton*, 772 N.E.2d 190 (Ohio App. 9th Dist. 2002), for example, the court explained that a used car buyer who believed that the car he purchased had a false odometer reading was bound to arbitrate his dispute with the car dealer: "Preprinted forms are a fact of commercial life and do not serve to demonstrate prima facie unconscionability with regard to arbitration clauses." Normally, unconscionability comes into play when significant disparities in bargaining power are coupled with terms unreasonably favorable to the stronger, drafting party.

Courts have a good deal of flexibility in how to address perceived unconscionability, and this is another point of potential variation among courts. They might strike down individual provisions, modify ("blue pencil") those provisions, or deny enforcement to the entire arbitration agreement, as the California Court did in *Armendariz*. As a general rule, of course, the more suspect terms an arbitration agreement contains, the more likely it that the whole arbitration agreement will be struck down. See, e.g, *Geiger v. Ryan's Family Steakhouses, Inc.*, 134 F. Supp. 2d 985 (S.D. Ind. 2001) (refusing enforcement to arbitration agreement that allowed the employer to select the arbitration panel, forced the employees to pay half or more of the cost of arbitration, and limited discovery to one deposition).

Interestingly, concerns about arbitration provisions in consumer and employment contracts may be said to have "reinvigorated" the doctrine of unconscionability. Most first-year Contracts casebooks now introduce the doctrine of unconscionability with a case about arbitration. Did your casebook do so? How did your authors, and your teacher, characterize arbitration?

Note and Question

18. *Arbitrators deciding arbitrability issues, including unconscionability and other fairness-based defenses to arbitration provisions.* As explained in Chapter 18, the Supreme Court in *First Options of Chicago, Inc. v. Kaplan,* 514 U.S. 938 (1995), indicated that although issues regarding the enforceability of an arbitration agreements are normally for the courts, the parties may agree that such arbitrability issues may be submitted to the determination of arbitrators if the parties' agreement to that effect is "clear and unmistakable." Moreover, if such issues are to be handled by the arbitrator, courts should give great leeway to the arbitrator's determination on issues of arbitrability. What if you have an arbitration agreement in a standardized consumer contract that contains numerous terms, including terms regarding arbitrator selection, that a consumer alleges to be grossly unfair? The arbitration agreement "clearly

and unmistakably" states that all arbitrability issues, including allegations of unconscionability, should be handled by the arbitrator. Should courts, following the guidance of *First Options*, enforce the provision?

❖ Hooters of America, Inc. v. Phillips
173 F.3d 933 (4th Cir. 1999)

[Annette R. Phillips alleges that she was sexually harassed while working as a bartender at a Hooters restaurant in Myrtle Beach, South Carolina. After quitting her job, Phillips threatened to bring a suit against Hooters ("HOMB") under Title VII. Arguing that Phillips had agreed to arbitrate employment-related disputes, Hooters preemptively filed suit to compel arbitration under section 9 of the FAA. She responded, asserting individual and class counterclaims against HOMB. The federal district court refused to compel arbitration, finding the agreement unconscionable and void for reasons of public policy.]

WILKINSON, Chief Judge:

... This agreement arose in 1994 during the implementation of Hooters' alternative dispute resolution program. As part of that program, the company conditioned eligibility for raises, transfers, and promotions upon an employee signing an "Agreement to arbitrate employment-related disputes." The agreement provides that Hooters and the employee each agree to arbitrate all disputes arising out of employment, including "any claim of discrimination, sexual harassment, retaliation, or wrongful discharge, whether arising under federal or state law." The agreement further states that:

> The employee and the company agree to resolve any claims pursuant to the company's rules and procedures for alternative resolution of employment-related disputes, as promulgated by the company from time to time ("the rules"). Company will make available or provide a copy of the rules upon written request of the employee.

The employees of HOMB were initially given a copy of this agreement at an all-staff meeting held on November 20, 1994. HOMB's general manager, Gene Fulcher, told the employees to review the agreement for five days and that they would then be asked to accept or reject the agreement. No employee, however, was given a copy of Hooters' arbitration rules and procedures. Phillips signed the agreement on November 25, 1994. When her personnel file was updated in April 1995, Phillips again signed the agreement. . . .

Pre-dispute agreements to arbitrate Title VII claims are thus valid and enforceable. The question remains whether a binding arbitration agreement between Phillips and Hooters exists and compels Phillips to submit her Title VII claims to arbitration. . . . "It [i]s for the court, not the arbitrator, to decide in the first instance whether the dispute [i]s to be resolved through arbitration.". . . In so deciding, we "'engage in a limited review to ensure that the dispute is arbitral — i.e., that a valid agreement to arbitrate exists between the parties and that the specific dispute falls within the substantive scope of that agreement.'". . .

. . . The judicial inquiry, while highly circumscribed, is not focused solely on an examination for contractual formation defects such as lack of mutual assent and want of consideration. . . . Courts also can investigate the existence of "such grounds as exist at law or in equity for the revocation of any contract." 9 U.S.C. § 2. . . . In this case, the challenge goes to the validity of the arbitration agreement itself. Hooters materially breached the arbitration agreement by promulgating rules so egregiously unfair as to constitute a complete default of its contractual obligation to draft arbitration rules and to do so in good faith. . . .

The Hooters rules when taken as a whole . . . are so one-sided that their only possible purpose is to undermine the neutrality of the proceeding. The rules require the employee to provide the company notice of her claim at the outset, including "the nature of the Claim" and "the specific act(s) or omissions(s) which are the basis of the Claim." Rule 6-2(1), (2). Hooters, on the other hand, is not required to file any responsive pleadings or to notice its defenses. Additionally, at the time of filing this notice, the employee must provide the company with a list of all fact witnesses with a brief summary of the facts known to each. Rule 6-2(5). The company, however, is not required to reciprocate.

The Hooters rules also provide a mechanism for selecting a panel of three arbitrators that is crafted to ensure a biased decision maker. Rule 8. The employee and Hooters each select an arbitrator, and the two arbitrators in turn select a third. Good enough, except that the employee's arbitrator and the third arbitrator must be selected from a list of arbitrators created exclusively by Hooters. This gives Hooters control over the entire panel and places no limits whatsoever on whom Hooters can put on the list. Under the rules, Hooters is free to devise lists of partial arbitrators who have existing relationships, financial or familial, with Hooters and its management. In fact, the rules do not even prohibit Hooters from placing its managers themselves on the list. Further, nothing in the rules restricts Hooters from punishing arbitrators who rule against the company by removing them from the list. Given the unrestricted control that one party (Hooters) has over the panel, the selection of an impartial decision maker would be a surprising result.

Nor is fairness to be found once the proceedings are begun. Although Hooters may expand the scope of arbitration to any matter, "whether related or not to the Employee's Claim," the employee cannot raise "any matter not included in the Notice of Claim." Rules 4-2, 8-9. Similarly, Hooters is permitted to move for summary dismissal of employee claims before a hearing is held whereas the employee is not permitted to seek summary judgment.

Rule 14-4. Hooters, but not the employee, may record the arbitration hearing "by audio or videotaping or by verbatim transcription." Rule 18-1. The rules also grant Hooters the right to bring suit in court to vacate or modify an arbitral award when it can show, by a preponderance of the evidence, that the panel exceeded its authority. Rule 21-4. No such right is granted to the employee.

In addition, the rules provide that upon 30 days notice Hooters, but not the employee, may cancel the agreement to arbitrate. Rule 23-1. Moreover, Hooters reserves the right to modify the rules, "in whole or in part," whenever it wishes and "without notice" to the employee. Rule 24-1. Nothing in the rules even prohibits Hooters from changing the rules in the middle of an arbitration proceeding.

If by odd chance the unfairness of these rules were not apparent on their face, leading arbitration experts have decried their one-sidedness. George Friedman, senior vice president of the American Arbitration Association (AAA), testified that the system established by the Hooters rules so deviated from minimum due process standards that the Association would refuse to arbitrate under those rules. [other expert testimony omitted] . . . In a similar vein, two major arbitration associations have filed amicus briefs with this court. The National Academy of Arbitrators stated that the Hooters rules "violate fundamental concepts of fairness . . . and the integrity of the arbitration process." Likewise, the Society of Professionals in Dispute Resolution noted that "[i]t would be hard to imagine a more unfair method of selecting a panel of arbitrators." It characterized the Hooters arbitration system as "deficient to the point of illegitimacy" and "so one-sided, it is hard to believe that it was even intended to be fair."

We hold that the promulgation of so many biased rules — especially the scheme whereby one party to the proceeding so controls the arbitral panel — breaches the contract entered into by the parties. The parties agreed to submit their claims to arbitration — a system whereby disputes are fairly resolved by an impartial third party. Hooters by contract took on the obligation of establishing such a system. By creating a sham system unworthy even of the name of arbitration, Hooters completely failed in performing its contractual duty.

Moreover, Hooters had a duty to perform its obligations in good faith. . . . Good faith "emphasizes faithfulness to an agreed common purpose and consistency with the justified expectations of the other party." Restatement (Second) of Contracts § 205 cmt. a. Bad faith includes the "evasion of the spirit of the bargain" and an "abuse of a power to specify terms." *Id.* § 205 cmt. d. By agreeing to settle disputes in arbitration, Phillips agreed to the prompt and economical resolution of her claims. She could legitimately expect that arbitration would not entail procedures so wholly one-sided as to present a stacked deck. Thus we conclude that the Hooters rules also violate the contractual obligation of good faith.

Given Hooters' breaches of the arbitration agreement and Phillips' desire not to be bound by it, we hold that rescission is the proper remedy.

Generally, "rescission will not be granted for a minor or casual breach of a contract, but only for those breaches which defeat the object of the contracting parties."... As we have explained, Hooters' breach is by no means insubstantial; its performance under the contract was so egregious that the result was hardly recognizable as arbitration at all. We therefore permit Phillips to cancel the agreement and thus Hooters' suit to compel arbitration must fail....

We respect fully the Supreme Court's pronouncement that "questions of arbitrability must be addressed with a healthy regard for the federal policy favoring arbitration." *Moses H. Cone*, 460 U.S. at 24. Our decision should not be misread: We are not holding that the agreement before us is unenforceable because the arbitral proceedings are too abbreviated. An arbitral forum need not replicate the judicial forum. "[W]e are well past the time when judicial suspicion of the desirability of arbitration and of the competence of arbitral tribunals inhibited the development of arbitration as an alternative means of dispute resolution."... Nor should our decision be misunderstood as permitting a full-scale assault on the fairness of proceedings before the matter is submitted to arbitration. Generally, objections to the nature of arbitral proceedings are for the arbitrator to decide in the first instance. Only after arbitration may a party then raise such challenges if they meet the narrow grounds set out in 9 U.S.C. § 10 for vacating an arbitral award. In the case before us, we only reach the content of the arbitration rules because their promulgation was the duty of one party under the contract. The material breach of this duty warranting rescission is an issue of substantive arbitrability and thus is reviewable before arbitration.... This case, however, is the exception that proves the rule: fairness objections should generally be made to the arbitrator, subject only to limited post-arbitration judicial review as set forth in section 10 of the FAA.

By promulgating this system of warped rules, Hooters so skewed the process in its favor that Phillips has been denied arbitration in any meaningful sense of the word. To uphold the promulgation of this aberrational scheme under the heading of arbitration would undermine, not advance, the federal policy favoring alternative dispute resolution. This we refuse to do....

AFFIRMED and REMANDED.

Note and Questions

19. Are there other possible grounds on which the court could have held that Ms. Phillips should not be required to arbitrate? Might another court have used unconscionability doctrine?

20. If you were advising a restaurant chain, what advice would you give if it sought to establish a process for settling disputes between the chain and its employees? We will explore some alternatives in Section E below.

The following excerpt from *Cole v. Burns International Security Services*, written by Judge Harry Edwards, should help you reflect on these controversies. The case involved the enforcement of an arbitration claim of employment discrimination pursuant to Title VII of the Civil Rights Act of 1964 under the AAA Employment Rules. Accepting the Supreme Court's decision in *Gilmer v. Interstate/Johnson Lane Corp.*, 500 U.S. 20 (1991), as a qualified mandate for arbitration as a condition of employment, Judge Edwards set forth a number of "minimal standards of procedural fairness" for employees entering into binding arbitration of statutory discrimination claims. In the conclusion of the ruling, excerpted below, he offers a thoughtful discourse on binding employment arbitration.

❖ Cole v. Burns International Security Services
105 F.3d 1465 (D.C. Cir. 1997)

HARRY T. EDWARDS, Chief Judge:

. . . We acknowledge the concerns that have been raised regarding arbitration's ability to vindicate employees' statutory rights. However, for all of arbitration's shortcomings, the process, if fairly conducted, is not necessarily inferior to litigation as a mechanism for the resolution of employment disputes. As the Dunlop Commission recognized:

> [L]itigation has become a less-than-ideal method of resolving employees' public law claims. . . . employees bringing public law claims in court must endure long waiting periods as governing agencies and the overburdened court system struggle to find time to properly investigate and hear the complaint. Moreover, the average profile of employee litigants . . . indicates that lower-wage workers may not fare as well as higher-wage professionals in the litigation system; lower-wage workers are less able to afford the time required to pursue a court complaint, and are less likely to receive large monetary relief from juries. Finally, the litigation model of dispute resolution seems to be dominated by "ex-employee" complainants, indicating that the litigation system is less useful to employees who need redress for legitimate complaints, but also wish to remain in their current jobs. . . .

Arbitration also offers employees a guarantee that there will be a hearing on the merits of their claims; no such guarantee exists in litigation where relatively few employees survive the procedural hurdles necessary to take a case to trial in the federal courts.

As a result, it is perhaps misguided to mourn the Supreme Court's endorsement of the arbitration of complex and important public law claims. Arbitrators, however, must be mindful that the Court's endorsement has been based on the assumption that "competent, conscientious, and impartial arbitrators" will be available to decide these cases. . . . Therefore, arbitrators must step up to the challenges presented by the resolution of statutory issues and must be vigilant to protect the important rights embodied in the laws entrusted to their care.

Greater reliance on private process to protect public rights imposes a professional obligation on arbitrators to handle statutory issues only if they are prepared to fully protect the rights of statutory grievants. . . . To meet that obligation, arbitrators must educate themselves about the law. . . . They must follow precedent and must adopt an attitude of judicial restraint when entering undefined areas of the law. . . . Arbitrators must actively ensure that the record is adequately developed and that procedural fairness is provided. . . . And appointing agencies like AAA must be certain that only persons who are able to satisfy these criteria are added to arbitrator-panel lists. For if arbitrators and agencies do not meet these obligations, the courts will have no choice but to intercede.

Note on Cole v. Burns International

Judge Edwards's opinion in *Cole* was notable in that it drew upon the 1994 recommendations of the Presidential Commission on the Future of Worker-Management Relations, chaired by Harvard economist and former Labor Secretary John T. Dunlop. His intent was to give these standards — including (1) a neutral arbitrator schooled in the relevant law; (2) a fair method for securing information necessary to present a claim; (3) affordable access to arbitration; (4) the right to independent representation; (5) a range of remedies equal to those available in court; (6) a written opinion explaining the reasons for the award; and (7) sufficient judicial review to ensure compliance with governing laws. While *Cole* has undoubtedly had some influence, no other court has gone quite so far as the *Cole* decision.

As we will see in Section E, the desire to systematically establish minimum due process standards also prompted a number of efforts in the mid- and late 1990s. These standards have had some influence on the evolution of employment and consumer arbitration procedures.

Note on Class Action Waivers and Differing Judicial Treatment

While it may be said that judicial decisions like those above, coupled with private responses such as those in Section E below, have tended to produced fairer arbitration procedures for many consumers and employees, some key procedural issues remain flashpoints for debate. Among these no issue is more hotly contested than the enforceability of terms in arbitration agreements purporting to prevent employees or consumers from presenting their claims as part of a class action. The issue has resulted in conflicting decisions in the courts. The U.S. Supreme Court has left the decision of whether a particular arbitration agreement provides for or prohibits class-wide arbitration to the arbitrators rather than the courts, as noted in the discussion of *Green Tree Fin. Corp v. Bazzle,* 539 U.S. 444, 453 (2003), discussed in Chapter 18. That, in turn, has led financial services companies and other organizations to include provisions in consumer or employment contracts purporting to reflect the intent of the parties not to participate in class actions. Challenges to such provisions have produced conflicting responses in the courts. The issue of whether parties can waive the right to proceed as a class was a major contributor to efforts to pass bills in Congress to outlaw predispute arbitration agreements in adhesion contracts.

E. Organizational and "Community" Responses to Fairness Issues: Due Process Protocols and Standards

Even as courts have intervened for the purpose of policing fairness in consumer and employment arbitration, leading dispute resolution organizations have taken their own initiatives. The AAA has sponsored or co-sponsored several national efforts to establish due process standards — all of which have underpinned changes to its own rules and procedures while encouraging the development of analogous rules by some other provider organizations.

1. The Employment Due Process Protocol

A Due Process Protocol for Mediation and Arbitration of Statutory Disputes Arising Out of the Employment Relationship was one of the first attempts to resolve the problems arising from mandated arbitration of statutory claims. 91 Daily Lab. Rep. (BNA) A-8, E-11 (May 11, 1995). The Protocol, which was adopted by AAA and JAMS, was geared specifically to deal with issues of due process for one-shot disputants in employment arbitration. The Protocol attempted to address these problems by recommending that certain procedural and substantive aspects of litigation be employed in arbitration. For example, the Protocol recommends allowing employees to be represented by an attorney, having the employer reimburse the employee for attorney's fees, encouraging the use of pretrial discovery, and allowing the arbitrator to provide any type of relief that would be similar to that available in a court proceeding. These recommendations would in many situations give an employee a greater sense of fairness, preserving some protections available in litigation and further reducing the cost of arbitration.

2.   Consumer, Health Care Due Process Protocols

The Employment Protocol was the primary model for the 1998 *Due Process Protocol for Mediation and Arbitration of Consumer Disputes*, a statement of 15 principles to "establish clear benchmarks for conflict resolution processes involving consumers," embodying consumers' "fundamental reasonable expectation" of a fair process. The Consumer Protocol is a major step beyond the Employment Protocol in several respects. In addition to requiring an independent administration of ADR if participation is mandated by a predispute agreement, the Protocol sets forth many elements of a "fundamentally fair process," a few of which are: (1) provision of "full and accurate information regarding Consumer ADR programs," (2) independent and impartial neutrals, and (3) the right of parties "to seek relief in a small claims court for disputes or claims within the scope of its jurisdiction."

The principles of the Consumer Protocol address many of the problems observed in the cases above regarding the perceived unfairness sometimes associated with binding arbitration. Providing for a full disclosure of information about consumer arbitration programs means that consumers are aware of what rights they are surrendering by agreeing to submit to the process. This helps to prevent problems with unconscionability of arbitration clauses in contracts, removing a ground of challenge that could, to a great extent, undermine arbitration as a quick and efficient resolution of disputes. The ability to resolve some issues in small claims courts may assuage consumers by allowing them to feel that a public airing of the dispute before an independent judiciary remains an option. Many small claims courts in the United States offer mediation or settlement services for parties (Raitt and Folberg, 1993).

In 1998, a leading group of organizations involved in ADR, law, and medicine issued a special variant of the Consumer Protocol for health care disputes. The Health Care Due Process Protocol encourages the use of ADR to resolve disputes over health care coverage and access arising out of the relationship between patients and private health plans and managed care organizations. The sponsoring organizations agreed, however, that the use of *predispute* arbitration agreements should be limited in the health care arena for disputes involving patients. The drafters sought to promote efficiency as well as fairness and did find mandatory, predispute arbitration appropriate in disputes *not* involving patients.

3.   Impact of the Protocols: The AAA Experience

The Protocols have greatly influenced arbitration because prominent arbitration providers have chosen to abide by them and promulgated corresponding rules. The AAA based its employment and consumer rules on the protocols, and there are indications that there have been tangible positive results. One study compared randomly selected arbitrated cases under the

AAA National Rules for Resolution of Employment Disputes in 1999-2000 with state court trial outcomes reported by the Civil Trial Court Network (see Eisenberg and Hill, 2003-2004). Researchers concluded that higher-paid employees pursuing non-civil-rights employment claims, the group most likely to be able to afford representation to go to court and therefore most represented in state court trials, won more frequently in arbitration than at trial. The authors found no statistically significant difference in median or mean awards in trial and arbitration. Moreover, the evidence indicated that the mean and median times to resolution were much shorter in arbitration than in litigation. They also observed that some pro-employee arbitration awards would probably have ended up as pro-employer summary judgments in litigation, as courts are significantly more likely than arbitrators to dismiss claims prior to trial on the merits. The authors considered it important that the AAA adheres to the Employment Due Process Protocol. Research by Professor Bingham supports the conclusion that the imposition of community due process standards in private arbitration has positive implications for employees (Bingham and Sharaf, 2004).

Critics remain concerned, however, that providers' adherence to the Protocols is voluntary and that the Protocols may be insufficient to guarantee fairness in some circumstances.

> Although the protocols have had an impact on arbitration, they do not have the force of law. They were developed by task forces and advisory committees composed of various groups, including the arbitration industry, interested in the resolution of disputes concerning employment, consumer, and health care issues. The effectiveness of the protocols thus lies in the voluntary agreement by arbitrators and arbitration service providers to require adherence to the procedures called for in the protocols for the administration and conduct of an arbitration proceeding. By voluntarily agreeing to adhere to the requirements of the protocols, those providing arbitration services have essentially agreed to regulate themselves. As a self-regulatory effort, the protocols seek to infuse arbitration with certain due process protections, thereby filling the procedural gap that was created when the United States Supreme Court endorsed the use of arbitration for the resolution of statutory claims. They also seek to encourage and promote the use of alternative dispute resolution for certain disputes. By committing itself to ensuring that due process protections are provided, the arbitration industry's decision to regulate itself may have helped to legitimize the prevalent and growing use of predispute arbitration clauses in contracts of adhesion. It may also have been instrumental in fending off more direct government regulation of the arbitration industry and in maintaining the favored status the Supreme Court has bestowed upon arbitration (Harding, 2004).

Note and Questions

21.   It is worthy of note that while the AAA and some other organizations have been particularly attentive to due process issues and

have actively sought to administer arbitration accordingly, there is no requirement that all providers of arbitration services adopt or adhere to the protocols. Recall, for example, the reported conflicts of interest that undermined the NAF consumer arbitration program (discussed above) that recently demonstrated the potential for abuse of private arbitration. In 2009, in the wake of NAF's withdrawal from the arena of consumer arbitration, the AAA suspended that part of its own consumer arbitration program relating to consumer credit card contracts.

22. Do any of the Protocols, all of which were developed in the 1990s, take a position on provisions purporting to prevent class actions or classwide arbitration of claims?

F. Legislative Intervention

Concerns about the fairness of arbitration under predispute arbitration agreements binding consumers and employees also prompted repeated efforts to pass laws outlawing or limiting such agreements. However, state statutory initiatives were repeatedly blunted by the preemptive effect of the FAA, discussed in Chapter 18. In recent years, however, a revised uniform act and a California law purporting to promote "ethics" among arbitrators and arbitration institution made inroads in this area. More recently, efforts in Congress to outlaw predispute arbitration agreements in adhesion contracts gradually gained steam, culminating in the proposed Arbitration Fairness Act. These developments are discussed in the following pages.

1. The Revised Uniform Arbitration Act

The Revised Uniform Arbitration Act (RUAA) was published by the National Conference of Commissioners on Uniform State Laws (NCCUSL) in 2000 and has been enacted into law in at least 12 states. The NCCUSL drafting committee was warned against any categorical treatment of consumer and employee contracts that might run afoul of the preemptive effect of the FAA; they therefore made do with a commentary regarding the role of unconscionability and other means of policing overreaching in adhesive arbitration agreements. Concerns about mass arbitration involving consumer and employee "outsiders," however, formed a subtext for other, substantive elements of the RUAA. Like its close federal counterpart, the FAA, the original UAA was carefully tailored to provide a "bare-bones" legal framework to facilitate very limited judicial intervention to specifically enforce arbitration agreements and awards, including a limited statute of frauds, key default provisions (including authority for judicial appointment of arbitrators where the stipulated method failed), and severely restrained judicial review challenges to awards. But the RUAA is a much more expansive document incorporating many more procedural default rules and, more important, a number of mandatory (required and non-waivable) procedural elements. These elements represent an effort to channel arbitration agreements and restrict the party autonomy that is a traditional hallmark of arbitration in favor of certain perceived requirements of due process. Arguably superfluous in a statute aimed at traditional business-to-business arbitration agreements incorporating detailed and varied arbitration procedures, these provisions appear to be intended primarily if not entirely for the protection of consumers, employees and other "adhering parties" from overreaching.

These include RUAA Section 16, which states: "A party to an arbitration proceeding may be represented by a lawyer." The right to legal representation is not waivable by a predispute agreement under RUAA section 4(b). Legal representation is taken for granted in most commercial arbitration processes, while in some traditional industry or trade settings lawyers are actually excluded from hearings by the rules. Section 16 works little if any benefit in the former scenarios and may entail undesirable transaction costs if raised in the latter context. The concern of Section 16 must center on the special concerns of individual employees or consumers who find themselves in arbitration.

Also non-waivable by executory agreement are Section 17 (a) and (b) regarding the authority of arbitrators to issue subpoenas and to "permit the deposition of a witness to be taken for use as evidence at the hearing." To say that parties cannot, by predispute agreement, limit the ability of arbitrators to order prehearing depositions is significant turnabout on traditional "no discovery" arbitration, and justifiable primarily on the basis of concerns about employees and consumers and other adhering parties not having access to information and witnesses. One critique describes the RUAA's approach as a "complicated arrangement . . . to balance, on the one hand, providing certain non-waivable protections to consumers, employees, and others who may be 'forced' into arbitration through pre-dispute agreements and, on the other hand, providing flexibility to sophisticated commercial entities and other repeat players who wish to shape the arbitration process in ways they like. Neither group is likely to be entirely happy with the balance struck."

Finally, Section 21 provides that arbitrators "may award punitive damages or other exemplary relief if such an award is authorized by law in a civil action involving the same claim. . . . " Although the provision is waivable under the RUAA, the commentary clarifies that limits or waivers of certain remedies may run afoul of judicial decisions requiring that employees and other parties "[have] the right to obtain the same relief in arbitration as is available in court." While punitive damages are by no means unknown in the commercial arena, it is not uncommon for business parties to limit their arbitration agreement to exclude punitive damages from the arbitral arsenal of remedies, especially in international agreements. Again, this provision is motivated primarily by the concerns of parties in adhesion contract scenarios, a reality reflected in the cases and standards cited in the commentary.

Although each of these statutory elements is likely to be brought to bear most directly in adhesion settings involving consumers or employees, they will undoubtedly have an impact on the law and practice of commercial arbitration. As noted previously, the expansive discovery provisions of the RUAA are already being cited to arbitrators as a standard for practice (Stipanowich, 2010).

Questions

23. The RUAA differs from the Arbitration Fairness Act of 2009, which outlaws categories of disputes for predispute arbitration agreements. Which approach is likely to yield more satisfactory results?
24. What impact, if any, are the quoted provisions of the RUAA likely to have on the practice of business-to-business arbitration?

2. The California "Ethics Standards"

Due to concern about the proliferation of predispute arbitration clauses in consumer, health care, and employment contracts, the California legislature in 2001 directed the California Judicial Council to implement ethics strictures governing private arbitrators in "mandatory" arbitration. The 2002 Standards established a general duty of impartiality and included, among other matters, rules governing arbitrator disclosures, confidentiality, and written fee explanations. "One of the more controversial new disclosure requirements is the arbitrator's policy regarding acceptance of new employment as a neutral from any current party, lawyer or lawyer's firm," designed to address the appearance of favoritism (Folberg, 2003). The California standards are broad because they render any and all disclosures grounds for disqualificaiton upon the motion of any party, even if the disclosures might not be considered material to a finding of evident partiality under traditional arbitration law. They create the potential for cynical manipulation of the arbitration process and dramatically increase the risk that a process will be derailed midstream, with potentially significant transaction costs. By way of illustration, consider the situation in which, months or years into the arbitration of a complex commercial case, a party who fears it will be on the losing end of the arbitrator's award hires new counsel or identifies a witness having some relationship to the arbitrator for the purpose of creating a requirement for the arbitrator to make a supplemental disclosure under the statute. An arbitrator who elects to make a disclosure of the relationship gives the parties an automatic right to have the disclosing arbitrator disqualified no matter how insignificant the relationship. Should the arbitrator fail to make the disclosure and the "aggrieved" party learns of the non-disclosed relationship, the arbitration award may be vacated if the non-disclosure is found to be "a ground for disqualification of which the arbitrator was then aware" (Stipanowich, 2010).

Conflicts between the applicability of the California ethics standards and other federal standards (e.g., the National Association of Securities Dealers and the New York Stock Exchange Standards) soon ensued (Kent, 2004). While federal and state courts have found that federal securities arbitration rules preempt the California Ethics Standards in investor-broker disputes under the SEC-supervised arbitration system, the exact extent of the preemption in many contexts remains uncertain.

3.   *Efforts in Congress; The Arbitration Fairness Act*

In recent years Congress has considered numerous bills intended to outlaw or limit the use of arbitration agreements in standardized contracts, but nearly all have failed to gather sufficient traction to become law. One exception was The Motor Vehicle Franchise Contract Arbitration Fairness Act of 2002, 15 U.S.C.S. § 1226(a)(2), requires that, before car manufacturers and their dealerships settle a dispute through arbitration, all parties must consent in writing after the controversy arises. The bill, which was sponsored by Republican Congressman (and former Cher partner) Sonny Bono and was later championed by his widow, found bi-partisan support. See, e.g., *Volkswagen of Am., Inc. v. Sud's of Peoria, Inc.*, 474 F.3d 966 (7th Cir. 2007).

Given the economic decline of 2008, the foreclosure crisis, and the federal bailouts of the banking and auto industries, pressure on legislators to assist consumers in financial straits is heavy. With changes in the political scene in Washington and the severe economic challenges facing consumers, the stage appears to be set for passage of legislation that will dramatically affect U.S. arbitration law.

The Arbitration Fairness Act of 2009, H.R. 1020, 111th Cong. (2009), introduced in the U.S. Congress, seeks to amend the FAA so that no *predispute* arbitration agreement will be valid if it requires arbitration of an employment, consumer, franchise or civil rights dispute. The law would not apply to arbitration provisions in collective bargaining agreements. If the law is enacted, federal and state courts will face a host of interpretive issues, including what constitutes a "civil rights" claim and what a "consumer" dispute encompasses. Presumably, the broad language is designed to cover state and federal civil rights and anti-discrimination laws of many types, arising under statute or common law, but raises many questions and concerns for the future of arbitration across a broad spectrum of transactions.

This legislation, if enacted, would overturn many significant rulings by the U.S. Supreme Court under the FAA with respect to consumer and individual employment contracts as well as other contracts of adhesion. In addition, the proposed legislation would amend the FAA to require a court, rather than an arbitrator, to determine whether an arbitration agreement is valid or enforceable. Of course, the FAA was created by Congress in 1925 and the Supreme Court's precedent in recent decades is based on the Court's reading of congressional intent. Congress has substantial leeway in setting policies in this area and revising or clarifying its intent.

In addition to heightened legislative scrutiny, other challenges to arbitration are likely to be proposed in this era. For instance, the U.S. Department of the Treasury in 2009 recommended legislation that would give the Securities and Exchange Commission clear authority to prohibit mandatory arbitration clauses in broker-dealer and investment advisory accounts with retail customers. Previously, concerns about the fair administration of the arbitration process prompted the Securities and Exchange Commission to create the Securities Industry Conference on Arbitration (SICA). SEC and SICA have been the primary instruments for the development, implementation, and monitoring of uniform policies and procedures governing securities arbitration.

Looking Ahead: The Future of Employment and Consumer Dispute Resolution

Without the option of binding predispute arbitration agreements, how will companies manage conflict with consumers and employees? Do the lemon law and Magnuson-Moss abbreviated procedures set out above in Section B provide viable models for consumer dispute resolution? Keep in mind that what suffices as adjudicative "due process" hinges heavily on circumstances. As in the court system, small claims may permit — or require — the use of processes that place a premium on efficiency and expedition, even to the point of dispensing with many of the incidents of traditional court proceedings and permitting judges to rule "from the hip." Procedural concerns may be much further attenuated if a consumer retains the option to go to court, as in lemon law programs and other procedures that require consumers to submit to arbitration but permit a de novo hearing in court if they are dissatisfied with the arbitration award.

In the employment arena, organizations have already been experimenting with a variety of sophisticated, multifaceted approaches to the management of conflict. As lawyers become increasingly involved in designing dispute resolution systems, they are often emphasizing full exploration of informal settlement mechanisms before approaching arbitration or litigation. See Chapter 12.B. Open-door policies, employee hotlines, and mediation are frequently used elements of corporate programs. Experience has shown that these approaches resolve the vast majority of employee grievances, claims, and controversies, substantially limiting the need for arbitration or litigation. Many corporate programs permit employees to choose arbitration as a post-dispute option, or to opt out of arbitration if they so choose. A more extensive treatment of such systems is provided in Chapter 21.

PART
IV

Mixing, Matching, and Moving Forward

CHAPTER
20

Matching the Process to the Dispute

The Big Picture

The prior chapters of this book have explored the roles lawyers play in the context of various discrete conflict resolution approaches: negotiation, mediation, and arbitration. The final section offers different forms of synthesis. These include an examination of ways in which multiple conflict resolution approaches have been integrated in multifaceted court programs (Chapter 20) or multistep dispute resolution systems (Chapter 21), and a preview of trends that may represent the future of ADR and conflict management (Chapter 22).

It is not surprising that legal counselors, experiencing the benefits and limitations of various approaches to conflict resolution, have tried to synthesize their experience and find creative ways of matching a given dispute with the process most appropriate to achieving their clients' goals. This chapter briefly examines several ADR processes that evolved alongside mediation to provide multiple "doors" to resolution of disputes in federal and state courts. These include procedures such as minitrial, summary jury trial, and non-binding arbitration, which provide a foretaste of the courtroom through abbreviated best-case presentations by advocates — not for the purpose of adjudication on the merits, but to promote settlement.

Chapter 21 looks at multistep conflict resolution or conflict management programs that offer new opportunities for lawyers to serve as creative problem solvers, but require particularly careful crafting and implementation. These developments began with wide acceptance of "ice breaker" clauses that commit a company or law firm to attempt to resolve problems out of court. Today, more attorneys in the United States and abroad are drafting contractual provisions that incorporate two or three process elements — so-called stepped ADR processes — and advising clients how to implement them. Over the past 20 years, lawyers have increasingly become experts in dispute resolution design, working with clients to design systems to prevent conflict, address inevitable conflict at earlier stages, and manage ongoing conflict. These multistep systems nearly always place primary emphasis on negotiation, mediation, and other approaches that give parties control over the process and permit them to address underlying interests and relationships. If these steps fail, however, stepped ADR clauses typically require the parties to adjudicate their dispute — either through court litigation or through binding arbitration.

Chapter 22, the final chapter, deals with important themes on the cutting edge of ADR and conflict management. We consider changing roles for lawyers as they craft with clients more collaborative processes, requiring the cooperating lawyers to limit their adversarial roles later if no settlement is reached and litigation ensues. We also explore the new frontier of the Internet, which affords disputants unique opportunities to resolve conflicts speedily, economically, and efficiently. We conclude with essays by several leaders in the field — from President Abraham Lincoln's encouragement of problem-solving approaches to U.S. Attorney General Janet Reno's vision of a society transformed by the values inherent in the Quiet Revolution in constructive conflict management.

A. New "Doors" for Resolving Disputes at the Courthouse

In their search for appropriate ways of resolving disputes, modern lawyers have experimented with many different variations on the fundamental process elements (negotiation, mediation, arbitration) described in this book. One primary arena for experimentation is the public justice system.

Many date the modern era of conflict resolution to the 1976 Pound Conference, at which Chief Justice Warren Burger and other leaders of bench and bar sounded a clarion call for more appropriate, less costly alternatives to traditional litigation. No presentation was more influential than that of Professor Frank Sander, who called for "a flexible mechanism that serves to sort out the large general question from the repetitive application of settled principle" (Sander, 1976). Sander's proposed solution was a "multidoor courthouse" incorporating three notions: (1) a choice of several discrete approaches to conflict resolution, (2) a mechanism for channeling disputes into specific processes, and (3) sufficient information about a given dispute to facilitate a rational pairing of problem and process (or, as Sander would say, "fitting the form to the fuss").

In the quarter-century following Sander's call for a multidoor courthouse, the judiciary came to acknowledge the value of programmed third-party intervention in conflict. Federal and state court-connected programs centered on mediated negotiation, non-binding or advisory arbitration, early neutral evaluation, and other processes are now ubiquitous (Plapinger and Stienstra, 1996).

Look once again at the Dispute Resolution Spectrum in Chapter 1. On the left side of the chart, under the heading "Settlement Processes," a number of process alternatives are listed. Nearly all of these except Direct Negotiation evolved in whole or in part through court programs. Some of these — Direct Negotiation, Facilitative Mediation, and Evaluative Mediation — are very familiar to you from prior chapters. Others — Neutral Evaluation, Settlement Conference, Mini-Trial (Minitrial), Summary Jury Trial, and Advisory Arbitration — have not yet been discussed.

On the following pages, we briefly explore some of these latter options; we do not focus on the Settlement Conference, which is a common element of Civil Procedure courses. As you read about these processes, consider why — from the standpoint of degree of party control over process and outcome, degree of formality, place in the "chronology" of litigation or adjudication, or similarity to court trial — we place them in the "spectrum" of nonbinding processes.

B.   Simulating Adjudication and Stimulating Settlement: Early Neutral Evaluation, Minitrial, Summary Jury Trial, and Non-Binding (Advisory) Arbitration

Mediation is far and away the most widely used ADR approach in court-connected programs. However, courts have also employed several other processes with discrete aims, such as providing an objective judgment of matters in controversy and providing a forecast of the result at trial, thereby enhancing the likelihood of settlement and avoiding full-blown adjudication.

❖ **Robert J. Niemic et al.,** DESCRIPTIONS OF THE PRINCIPAL
COURT-BASED ADR PROCESSES

**Guide to Judicial Management of Cases in ADR
(Federal Judicial Center, 2001)**

[This excerpt from a guidebook on federal court ADR summarizes various processes now in use in federal district court ADR programs. The authors' order of discussion reflects the relative frequency of use of different processes, from most widely used to least widely used. References to the most popular court-connected process, mediation, are deleted in light of its extensive treatment in Part II of this book.]

1. Advisory or Non-Binding Arbitration

Unlike mediation, arbitration is an adjudicatory, rights-based process. In federal court-based arbitration, one or three arbitrators hear adversarial presentations, usually in summary form, by each side to the litigation and then issue a nonbinding "award," or decision, on the merits. Witnesses may or may not be called, but exhibits are often submitted to the arbitrators. At a party's request and cost, the hearing may be held on the record. Either party may reject the arbitration award and request a trial de novo in the district court. Arbitration is a fairly formal process, in many ways resembling an expedited court trial. . . .

[Under a 1988 federal statute ten district courts were authorized] to implement arbitration programs where litigant participation is presumptively mandatory. Eligible cases, which are defined by specific objective case characteristics such as nature of suit, are generally automatically referred to arbitration by court order once the suit is filed. Certain types of cases are excluded from mandatory arbitration, such as cases involving violations of constitutional rights or damage claims in excess of a specified dollar amount. In all mandatory arbitration programs, the parties are provided an avenue for seeking exemption from the referral to arbitration. . . .

Several of [the ten courts that were authorized to implement mandatory programs] . . . have amended their processes to make them voluntary; one has dropped the program altogether. . . . The ADR Act [of 1998] authorizes voluntary arbitration for all district courts. Among other provisions, referral to arbitration requires party consent, the action may not be based on alleged violations of constitutional rights, jurisdiction may not be based on an alleged deprivation of civil or elective franchise rights, and the relief sought must consist of money damages not in excess of $150,000. The ADR Act does not alter any arbitration program established under the 1988 Act.

2. Early Neutral Evaluation

Early neutral evaluation (ENE) is a nonbinding process designed to improve case planning and settlement prospects by giving litigants an early advisory evaluation of the case. Like mediation, ENE is thought to be widely applicable to many types of civil cases, including complex disputes.

In ENE, a neutral evaluator, usually a private attorney with expertise in the subject matter of the dispute, holds a confidential session with the parties and counsel early in the litigation — generally before much discovery has taken place — to hear both sides of the case. The evaluator then helps the parties clarify issues and evidence, identifies strengths and weaknesses of the parties' positions, and gives the parties a nonbinding assessment of the values or merits of the case. Depending on the goals of the program, the evaluator also may mediate settlement discussions or offer case management assistance, such as developing a discovery plan.

The process was originally designed to improve attorneys' pretrial practices and knowledge of their cases by forcing them and their clients to conduct core investigative and analytical work early, to communicate directly across party lines, to expose each side to the other's case, and to consider the wisdom of early settlement.

In some district courts with ENE programs, the ENE sessions occur later, rather than earlier, in the case. Although the term "*early* neutral evaluation" is less apt in such circumstances, the key feature of the process — evaluation of the case by a neutral — remains the same.

3. Summary Jury Trial

The summary jury trial is a non-binding ADR process designed to promote settlement in trial-ready cases. A judge presides over the trial, where attorneys for each party present the case to a jury, generally without calling witnesses but relying instead on the submission of exhibits. After this abbreviated trial, the jury deliberates and then delivers an advisory verdict. After receiving the jury's advisory verdict, the parties may use it as a basis for subsequent settlement negotiations or proceed to trial.

A summary jury trial is typically used after discovery is complete. Depending on the structure of the process, it can involve both facilitated negotiations, which can occur throughout the planning, hearing, deliberation, and post-verdict phases, and outcome prediction, that is, an advisory verdict. Part or all of the case may be submitted to the jury. The jurors are chosen from the court's regular venire; some judges tell the jurors at the outset that their role is advisory, but others wait until a verdict has been given.

Some judges use this process only for protracted cases where the predicted length of a full trial justifies the substantial resources required by a summary jury trial. Other judges use it for routine civil litigation where litigants differ significantly about the likely jury outcome. The format of this ADR process is determined by the individual judge more than in most ADR procedures. A variant of the summary jury trial is the summary bench trial, where a judge, rather than a jury, issues the advisory opinion.

4. Minitrial

The minitrial is a flexible, non-binding ADR process used primarily out of court. A few federal judges have developed their own versions of the minitrial, which is generally reserved for large cases.

In a typical court-based minitrial, each side presents a shortened version of its case to party representatives who have settlement authority — for example, the senior executives of corporate parties. The hearing is informal, with no witnesses and with relaxed rules of evidence and procedure. A judge or nonjudicial neutral may preside over the one-day or two-day hearing. Following the hearing, the client representatives meet, with or without the neutral presider, to negotiate a settlement. . . .

***

Although it is difficult to generalize, certain types of cases are usually seen as more suitable than others to particular kinds of ADR processes. Below we identify the types of cases typically viewed as suitable for each of the major types of court-based ADR. . . .

1. Mediation

Mediation is considered appropriate for most kinds of civil cases, and in some district courts, referral to mediation is routine in most general civil cases. In some other courts, use of the process is targeted at specific kinds of disputes or is determined by the judge on a case-by-case basis. Most courts exclude certain categories of cases from mediation, such as cases involving a pro se party, prisoner civil rights cases, and Social Security cases. . . .

2. Non-Binding or Advisory Arbitration

. . . [E]xamples of cases traditionally considered appropriate for voluntary arbitration:

- Cases involving small money damages claims, and
- Cases in which technical or scientific questions are involved and an arbitrator with expertise in the field would be beneficial to resolution and is available to serve as arbitrator.

Cases that are traditionally considered inappropriate for voluntary arbitration include:

- Cases exempted by statute or local rules;
- Cases in which the parties want help in improving communications, finding common ground, or arriving at a creative solution to the dispute;
- Cases in which equitable relief is sought;
- Cases involving complex or novel legal issues;
- Cases where legal issues predominate over factual issues;
- Class actions; and
- Administrative agency appeals . . .

3. Early Neutral Evaluation (ENE)

Like mediation, ENE is generally thought to be applicable to civil cases of varying kinds and complexity. Some courts select cases for ENE according to case type; types of cases targeted include not only routine cases, but also more complex cases, such as fraud, antitrust, banking, environmental, copyright, patent, trademark, and labor/employment cases. . . .

Listed below are examples of kinds of cases generally considered appropriate for ENE:

- Cases in which subject matter expertise may be helpful in narrowing issues or simplifying them at trial;
- Cases in which issues raised in papers filed in the case indicate that one or more of the attorneys in the case are inexperienced or poorly prepared;

- Cases in which a party refuses to confront the weaknesses in its case and has unrealistic expectations regarding the amount of damages involved;
- Cases with complex legal issues;
- Cases involving multiple parties with diverse interests and numerous cross-claims, as opposed to merely multiple defendants with the same or similar interests; and
- Cases in which discovery will be substantial.

Examples of cases generally considered inappropriate for ENE include the following:

- Class actions;
- Cases in which there are significant personal or emotional barriers to settlement that might better be addressed in mediation;
- Cases in which the decision will turn primarily on the credibility of witness testimony; and
- Cases needing substantial discovery before an evaluation can be made.

4. Summary Jury Trial

Because the summary jury trial (SJT) is a resource-intensive ADR process, it is most often used for fairly large cases that would involve long jury trials. Generally, the more complex and potentially protracted a case is, the greater the potential that a summary jury trial will result in reduced costs for the parties when compared with traditional litigation.

Notes and Questions

1. *Benefits, Limitations of Summary Jury Trial.* Based on what you know about summary jury trial, what more might you guess about the cases that are generally considered appropriate for, or inappropriate for, the process? The strongest advocate for the summary jury trial was Judge Thomas Lambros, who successfully utilized the process in a wide range of cases (Lambros, 1984).
2. *The Waxing and Waning of Minitrial.* As noted in the excerpt above, minitrial, or mini-trial, evolved primarily as a private process outside the courts. The process is unique in that it postures key decision makers from each party as members of a panel hearing "best shot" presentations of evidence and arguments by advocates for each party to the controversy — thus potentially laying a foundation for mutual discussions aimed at settlement that would follow immediately upon the conclusion of the "hearing." In the typical minitrial proceeding, principals of each party sit on either side of a neutral

third-party referee or minitrial "judge" who supervises the process. As lawyers for the parties present rigorously abbreviated cases, with summaries of best evidence (including, perhaps, videotapes of key witnesses) and arguments, the principles and the referee act as inquisitors, probing the main elements of each party's case. At the conclusion of the presentations, the principals have the opportunity to negotiate face-to-face, perhaps with the assistance of the neutral. The latter may at some point be called upon to offer a nonbinding advisory opinion regarding a resolution of the controversy. Like summary jury trials, minitrials are not widely used today, largely because the format has often proven to be quite costly. Moreover, where minitrial is not used until the conclusion of discovery, the possibility of deriving significant cost savings is substantially diminished. Today, whether or not they are so-described, abbreviated minitrial formats are sometimes employed in the context of mediation.

3. *Mediation versus Early Neutral Evaluation.* Although mediation is the most popular option in many courts, mediation advocate and federal judge Wayne Brazil urges lawyers to consider the benefits of ENE for certain types of disputes. ENE is particularly apt when a neutral's subject matter expertise is needed. The process focuses on the merits of a dispute, developing sufficient information to predict a litigated outcome. Judge Brazil suggests that ENE can also be useful when extensive group sessions to evaluate the merits would be effective, rather than mediation's oft-used "shuttle diplomacy" (Brazil, 2009).

4. *The Evolution of the Multidoor Courthouse Concept.* A number of federal and state court programs here and abroad have attempted to provide a smorgasbord of ADR choices for parties. However, for a variety of reasons most court programs have tended to emphasize only one or two processes. The last decade has seen a proliferation of settlement programs within the federal appellate courts as well, with a heavy emphasis on mediation in civil cases (Niemic, 2006). As discussed in Chapter 22, the most promising evocations of the spirit of Sander's vision for a dynamic program matching ADR process to the issues at hand are court programs in which magistrates or special masters have been given wide discretion as process architects and case managers (Stipanowich, 1998).

5. *Creative Possibilities.* One federal judge, frustrated by certain parties who regularly enlisted the court's time and resources in pretrial disputes in a particular case, ordered "a new form of alternative dispute resolution." The judge instructed the parties and counsel to meet at a certain place and time and engage in one game of "rock,

paper, scissors." The court ruled that the winner of this engagement would be entitled to select the deposition location! *Avista Management, Inc. v. Wausau Underwriters Ins. Co.,* Case No. 6:05-cv-1430-Orl-31JGG (Mid. Dist. Fla. June 6, 2006). Perhaps this example of protracted (and expensive) pretrial litigation skirmishes among parties illustrates why federal courts have increasingly turned to court-annexed ADR to move civil suits along more expeditiously.

CHAPTER
21

Dispute Resolution Design: Stepped Clauses and Conflict Management Systems

The developments described in Chapter 20 paralleled (and to some extent prefigured) a growing body of experience with approaches incorporating a series of discrete dispute resolution "steps." Such stepped ADR "systems" often begin with simple, straightforward, and informal approaches (such as face-to-face negotiation of a business issue, or a confidential "hotline" for employee grievances). Then, if necessary, the systems provide parties with a series of additional strategies for addressing conflict up to and including arbitration or litigation. Stepped approaches are well established in commercial and employment settings in the United States and are becoming increasingly common in international business transactions. In the past few decades, this has led more lawyers to the creative work of counseling clients on systemic approaches to conflict management extending beyond particular lawsuits. Lawyers have opportunities to work with clients to create effective, cost-efficient systems to prevent conflicts or manage them as they (inevitably) arise among parties with ongoing relationships. Lawyers who are well versed in dispute resolution options and system design issues offer value to clients with the need to minimize conflict or manage it well.

A. General Commitments, "Ice Breaker" Clauses

The first step many organizations took to implement an ADR system was to make a general commitment to employ ADR before litigation by signing what might be called an "ice breaker" clause. Lawyers often voiced concern that if they raised the possibility of settlement, it would be taken by adversaries, and even by their own clients, as a signal that they did not believe in their cases and were overanxious to settle. One way to overcome this barrier, it was thought, would be for corporations and law firms to adopt a uniform policy of exploiting ADR in every dispute. Lawyers could then tell both clients and opposing counsel that they were mentioning settlement as a matter of policy and not because of concern about any particular case.

The first and most influential of such clauses was created by the CPR Institute of Dispute Resolution. The current text is set forth below.

❖ CPR Corporate Policy Statement on Alternatives to Litigation

_____
(COMPANY NAME)

We recognize that for many disputes there is a less expensive, more effective method of resolution than the traditional lawsuit. Alternative dispute resolution (ADR) procedures involve collaborative techniques which can often spare businesses the high costs of litigation.

In recognition of the foregoing, we subscribe to the following statements of principle on behalf of our company and its domestic subsidiaries:*

In the event of a business dispute between our company and another company which has made or will then make a similar statement, we are prepared to explore with that other party resolution of the dispute through negotiation or ADR techniques before pursuing full-scale litigation. If either party believes that the dispute is not suitable for ADR techniques, or if such techniques do not produce results satisfactory to the disputants, either party may proceed with litigation.

_____
CHIEF EXECUTIVE OFFICER

_____
CHIEF LEGAL OFFICER

_____
DATE

Copyright © 2004 by CPR Institute for Dispute Resolution, New York, NY. All rights reserved.

_____

Forms of this Policy Statement, often referred to as the "CPR Pledge," have been adopted by several thousand companies and their subsidiaries. A similar Policy Statement for law firms has been signed on behalf of more than 1,500 of the world's largest law firms and legal practices.

Questions

1. Does the foregoing commitment appear to be legally binding?
2. Why do you suppose so many corporate counsel signed the document on behalf of their companies or law firms? Can you see any potential limitations of this approach?

B. Stepped Dispute Resolution Programs

1. *General Principles for Design and Implementation*

a. Design

❖ **Stephen B. Goldberg, Jeanne M. Brett, & William L. Ury,**
DESIGNING AN EFFECTIVE DISPUTE RESOLUTION SYSTEM

**Adapted from Stephen B. Goldberg et al., in John Wilkinson et al., Donovan
Leisure Newton & Irvine ADR Practice Book 253 (1997 Supp.)**

In 1987, IBM and Fujitsu, in settling a number of disputes arising out of
IBM's charge that Fujitsu had improperly used IBM software, agreed to set
up a technical facility under the direction of a neutral expert. In that facility,
Fujitsu could examine certain categories of IBM software and choose those
it wished to use. IBM was entitled to compensation for any software used by
Fujitsu. Disputes about appropriate use were to be resolved by the neutral
expert; disputes about compensation were to be resolved by arbitration
prior to Fujitsu's use of the software in question.

In 1986, two oil companies that were about to engage in a joint venture
agreed that all disputes arising out of the joint venture would be submitted
to a partnership committee. Disputes not resolved by the partnership committee were to be referred to two senior executives, one from each company,
both uninvolved in the joint venture. The executives' task was to study the
problem and, in consultation with their companies, negotiate a settlement.
If they were unsuccessful, the dispute was to be sent to final and binding arbitration.

Why did the corporations in these two examples set up elaborate dispute
resolution systems? Why didn't Fujitsu and IBM simply agree on a monetary
settlement of their disputes? Why didn't the two oil companies simply provide that any dispute between them would be resolved by arbitration?

The answer is clear. More and more companies are realizing that if they
are involved in a long-term relationship — buyer-seller, client-service provider, joint venture, or market leader-follower (like IBM and Fujitsu)
— disputes between them are inevitable. It is not enough to settle one of
those disputes, as IBM and Fujitsu might have done, because many more are
likely to arise. It is not enough to agree on a single dispute resolution procedure, as the oil companies might have done, because a procedure that is
satisfactory for one dispute may not be satisfactory for all disputes, and a
procedure that is satisfactory at one stage of a dispute may not be satisfactory at another stage of the same dispute.

The task for parties who can reasonably anticipate a stream of disputes
between them is thus to go beyond settling those disputes one at a time and
to go beyond selecting one procedure to resolve all disputes. Their goal
should be to design a comprehensive and effective dispute resolution system

which contains effective procedures arranged in an appropriate sequence. In addition, the people using the system should possess the skills, motivation, and resources they need to make those procedures function effectively.

Interests, Rights, and Power

In seeking to resolve a dispute, parties may focus on their interests, their rights, or their power. *Interests* are the needs, desires, concerns, or fears that underlie what the parties say they want: the positions they take in a dispute. If the parties focus on interests, the procedure they will use, at least initially, is interests-based negotiation, in which a dispute is treated as a problem to be resolved by reconciling the parties' underlying interests...

[For parties with an ongoing relationship, an approach to dispute resolution which focuses on interests is better than one which focuses on rights, which in turn is better than one which focuses on power. What does *better* mean? That is determined by four criteria: satisfaction with outcome, effect on the relationship, recurrence of disputes, and transaction costs.]

Research shows that reconciling interests tends to produce higher satisfaction with outcomes, better relationships, and less recurrence of disputes than does determining who is right or more powerful.... If the parties are more satisfied, their relationship benefits and disputes are less likely to recur. Determining who is right or more powerful, with the emphasis on winning and losing, typically makes the relationship more strained if it does not completely destroy it.... The transaction costs — time, money, and emotional energy — involved in reconciling interests through negotiation can be great.... Still, the transaction costs of interest-based negotiation pale in comparison with those of a rights or power battle.

Despite the general advantages of resolving disputes by procedures that focus on the parties' interests, resolving all disputes in this fashion is not possible. In some disputes, though fewer than is often supposed, interests are so opposed that agreement is not possible. In others, the parties' perceptions of who is right or more powerful are so different that they cannot establish a range within which to negotiate a resolution of their competing interests. A rights procedure may be needed to clarify their rights before an interests-based resolution can be sought....

In sum, the general principle is not that *all* disputes should be resolved by focusing on interests, but that *most* should. The problem is that rights and power procedures are often used when they are not necessary. A procedure that should be the last resort too often becomes the first resort. The task of those designing a dispute resolution system, typically the parties' attorneys, is not to eliminate rights and power procedures but to limit their use to those situations in which they are necessary. It is also to provide low-cost ways to determine rights or power for those disputes that cannot be resolved by focusing on interests alone....

Diagnosis

[The authors explain that dispute systems design may occur when parties are about to enter into a relationship, or midstream, perhaps after efforts to resolve disputes have proved unsuccessful.]

Learning what kinds of disputes occur and with whom is the designers' first diagnostic task.... If the disputes tend to have a strong emotional element, the designer should consider methods to vent emotions. If the disputes involving purely legal or technical issues, such as the extent to which Fujitsu may use IBM software, a low-cost rights procedure may be appropriate.... [T]he designers will also focus on the causes of those disputes. Sometimes identifying causes can suggest ways to prevent similar disputes in the future.

The designers' next diagnostic task is to determine how many disputes are currently being handled and why. If the parties are relying substantially upon rights and power contests, rather than resolving their disputes through interests-based negotiation, there may not be a convenient or well-understood procedure for encouraging negotiations....

Design: Six Principles

Principle 1: Building in Consultation Before, Feedback After

When one party to a relationship is considering action that will affect the other, it should at least notify, and ideally consult, the other before taking that action. (*Notification* refers simply to an announcement in advance of the intended action; *consultation* goes further and offers an opportunity to discuss the proposed action before it takes place.) Notification and consultation can prevent disputes that arise through sheer misunderstanding. They can also reduce the anger and unthinking opposition that often result when decisions are made unilaterally. They further serve to identify points of difference that may be more easily resolved before action is taken than after.

Sophisticated parties seek not only to avoid disputes but also to learn from them. At some manufacturing companies, lawyers, and managers regularly analyze consumer complaints to determine what changes in product design might reduce the likelihood of similar disputes in the future. Wise designers build into the system procedures for postdispute analysis and feedback.

Principle 2: Put the Focus on Interests

In order to encourage the interests-based resolution of disputes, an increasing number of contract clauses explicitly provide for negotiation as the first step in resolving a dispute between competing businesses. These clauses typically designate who will participate in the negotiation, when it must begin and end, and what happens if it is unsuccessful. They often provide for a multistep procedure in which a dispute that is not successfully resolved at one step is then negotiated at a higher step by different negotiators. [The authors also recommend providing negotiation skills training within the organization, including joint negotiations training for parties who will be negotiating with each other in the future.]

Principle 3: Build in "Loop-Backs" to Negotiation

Sometimes interests-based negotiations fail because the parties' perceptions of who is right or who is more powerful are so different that, when interests clash, they cannot establish a range within which to negotiate. At the same time, resort to a full-blown rights or power contest would be costly, not only in financial terms but also in relational terms. Thus, the wise designer will build into the system procedures for providing the parties with information about who would prevail in the event of a contest, without the necessity of their actually engaging in such a contest. Because such procedures are designed to encourage the parties to return to negotiation, they are called *loop-back* procedures. [The authors provide examples such as mediator predictions of the outcome of a case, as well as the use of minitrial and summary jury trial.]

Principle 4: Provide Low-Cost Rights and Power Backups

In some disputes interests are so opposed that agreement is not possible. Still, resort to a full-blown court battle would have damaging financial and relational consequences. Thus, an effective dispute resolution system will contain procedures for final and binding resolution of disputes through low-cost alternatives to litigation. Among these procedures are conventional arbitration, expedited arbitration, final-offer arbitration and Med-Arb....

Principle 5: Arrange Procedures in a Low-to-High Cost Sequence

The first four design principles — consultation before, feedback after; put the focus on interests; build in loop-backs to negotiation; provide low-cost rights and power backups — suggest a fifth. Create a sequence of procedures that is based on these principles. The following is a menu of procedures to draw on in designing such a sequence:

1. Prevention procedures:
    — Notification and consultation
    — Postdispute analysis and feedback
2. Interests-based procedures
    — Negotiation
    — Mediation
3. Loop-back procedures
    — Advisory arbitration
    — Minitrial
    — Summary jury trial
    — Cooling-off period
4. Low-cost backup procedures
    — Conventional arbitration
    — Expedited arbitration

— Med-Arb
— Final offer arbitration

Principle 6: Provide Disputants with the Necessary Motivation, Skills, and Resources

A final principle cuts across all others. Providing appropriate procedures is important, but insufficient if the parties lack the motivation, skills and resources to use those procedures effectively. For example, two companies entering into a long-term buyer-seller relationship set up a three-step negotiation procedure in which the first-step negotiators were the managers involved in any dispute, the second-step negotiators were their immediate supervisors, and the third-step negotiators were vice presidents from each corporation. Although both corporations hoped that most disputes would be resolved at step one, the results were just the opposite. After the first few months, nearly all disputes went to steps two and three for resolution. The reason? Investigation disclosed that the first few settlements reached at step one were carefully scrutinized and strongly criticized by a high-ranking officer at one of the companies. As a result, managers at that company decided that the wisest course of action for them was simply to go through the motions of attempting to negotiate a settlement, rather than to try to reach agreement. They would then blame the resulting impasse on the other party's intransigence. In that way, they were able to avoid the criticism from corporate higher-ups.

The moral is clear: If the goal of the parties is to encourage negotiated settlements, the negotiators must be motivated to settle. At one corporation, this is done by providing positive feedback to all managers who negotiate step-one settlements. The terms of the settlement are discussed with the manager, but all comments that might be viewed as critical are directed toward improving future settlements, not criticizing the subject settlement. Good settlements are reflected in positive evaluations; bad settlements are ignored. Management's philosophy is clear: in the long run, the cost of a few bad step-one settlements will be outweighed by the increased step-one settlement rate resulting from a corps of managers who are genuinely motivated to negotiate settlements at step one. . . .

---

b.   Implementation

Systems design work has now been used in a variety of settings, from commercial relationships to restorative justice work in post-war societies. This work affords many creative opportunities for lawyers.

❖ **Stephanie Smith and Janet Martinez,** *An Analytic Framework for Dispute Systems Design*

14 Harv. Nego. L. Rev. 123 (2009)

Law graduates are . . . called upon to be organizational problem solvers as members of multidisciplinary teams. . . . Attorneys in these broader roles sometimes have the opportunity to help organizations create or improve systems that prevent or address conflicts before and after they evolve into full-fledged disputes. . . .

The fact is, attorneys are rarely faced with the need to design a system from scratch. More often, they must improve existing, flawed systems, or adapt an existing system to a new context. Systems analysis skills may thus be used in situations as diverse as:

- An attorney who must negotiate contracts for joint business ventures as they select and draft language for the processes that will be used to prevent, manage and resolve conflicts that may arise;
- A general counsel or outside counsel who must revamp an employee grievance procedure or design a payout system connected to the settlement of a multi-party class action;
- A legal advisor or diplomat who must counsel a country emerging from conflict on how to create multi-tiered justice systems that address punishment as well as reconciliation in an effort both to achieve justice and prevent future violence;
- A judge or court administrator who is developing multiple settlement and case management processes to better serve litigants;
- A legislator or legislative staff member who must develop new policy and an implementing regulatory scheme.

Two systems design experts urge that lawyers and organizations involved in dispute resolution design use pilot programs in many circumstances to build support for new processes, test systems, and assess their effectiveness. Cathy Constantino and Christina Sickles Merchant emphasize tailoring the processes to specific problems and ensuring that disputants have the knowledge and skills to use the ADR processes. They suggest creating ADR systems that are simple and easily accessible, resolving disputes early and at the lowest bureaucratic level possible. These experts also advise the designers to allow disputants to retain maximum control over the ADR method and choice of neutrals to maximize the effectiveness of a system (Constantino & Sickles Merchant, 1996).

2.   *Examples of Stepped Programs or Systems*

a.   Commercial Relationships

Many companies have created "stepped" dispute resolution programs or systems and written them into their business contracts. Stepped systems have long been in use in the field of construction disputes. A notable example is the program developed by British Columbia Hydro (BC Hydro), which oversees a broad range of construction projects. Frustrated with its inability to handle construction project claims and concerned with expanding contract verbiage, BC Hydro established an ADR program that begins with face-to-face negotiation and progresses, if necessary, through the following formal steps: an initial decision on claims and controversies by a BC Hydro project representative, a review of the initial decision by a "standing neutral" (appointed for the specific purpose of addressing such claims during the life of the construction project), and, ultimately, binding arbitration. In the first three years of operation, BC Hydro used the system in 119 contracts involving $55 million in construction costs. Forty-seven disputed claims were processed through the system; all but 12 were negotiated face-to-face. Only two reached the "standing neutral," and all were settled without the need for binding arbitration (Stipanowich, 1998).

The Boston Central Artery/Tunnel Project, better known as the "Big Dig," is one of the nation's largest construction projects. It is also the premier application of a "real-time" dispute resolution system called the Dispute Review Board (DRB). The typical Artery/Tunnel construction contract calls for a DRB made up of two neutral technical panelists (such as construction engineers with specialties in excavation) and a panel chair with significant dispute resolution experience. Panelists are appointed at project startup, permitting them to become familiar with project personnel, technical aspects, and progress. DRB operating rules minimize formality and attempt to cut out all vestiges of legal hearing process, such as lawyer argument and examination of witnesses, and maximize the flexibility of the panel to control the gathering of information. At the conclusion of the inquisitorial process, the panel deliberates and produces a recommendation, complete with supporting rationale, for the project director. The DRB system has been a great success in getting disputes resolved short of the courthouse.

In some industries, companies have entered into collective agreements embracing the principles set forth above. For example, the American Chemistry Council has created its own stepped dispute resolution system for corporations in the chemical industry. Signatories to the Chemical Industry Dispute Resolution Commitment agree to "commit that any dispute arising hereafter between our company, including its subsidiaries, and another company in the chemical industry which has made a similar commitment, will be resolved in the manner stated below." The document continues:

A. PROCEDURES

1. *Negotiation*

When a dispute has arisen between our company and another signatory and negotiations between the regularly responsible persons have reached an impasse, other executives having authority to settle the matter . . . shall confer in a good faith effort to resolve the dispute. The General Counsel of the companies shall arrange the conference and may participate in it.

2. *Mediation*

If the parties have not resolved the dispute within 30 days of their first contact pursuant to paragraph A.1., they will attempt in good faith to resolve the dispute by mediation in accordance with the CPR Procedure for Chemical Industry Dispute Resolution . . .

3. *Adjudication*

If the mediation procedure fails to result in resolution of the dispute within 60 days of selection of a mediator, any party may unilaterally terminate the procedure and pursue other remedies. Either party may propose submission of the dispute to arbitration . . . or to a private judicial procedure, but no party is obligated to agree to any such procedure. . . .

CONTRACTUAL DISPUTE RESOLUTION PROVISIONS

Signatories are encouraged to include dispute resolution provisions in their contracts. The above procedures notwithstanding, if a dispute relates to a matter which is subject to a contractual dispute resolution provision (including without limitation an agreement among co-defendants in a litigation), and if such provision is in conflict with those set forth above, such contractual provision will govern.

The above commitment is entered into in consideration of similar commitments by other companies in the chemical industry and shall become operative when signed by ten companies. After two years from the date thereof, this commitment may be terminated on 90 days written notice to CPR, without affecting any case then pending.

Questions

3. In what ways does this document differ from the previously discussed CPR Policy Statement?
4. What are the pros and cons of the Chemical Industry approach?
5. What are the potential benefits of a system such as that used in the "Big Dig"? What are the limitations?

---

b. Employment Programs

The first stepped dispute resolution systems were created in the context of collective bargaining agreements between companies and unions. With the rise of protective legislation and the modern labor movement, unions and management recognized that they were in long-term relationships from which they could not escape. Both labor and management saw a need for systems that could handle the inevitable disputes that would arise under collective bargaining agreements efficiently, without triggering retaliatory actions by either side. The solution was to create grievance systems defined by contract. Originally such systems consisted simply of arbitration, but over time negotiators developed more complex and efficient systems that featured a series of steps.

A typical labor grievance procedure might consist of the following three steps:

1. An initial conference between the grievant employee, a union steward, and an employer representative;
2. A second conference attended by an officer or representative of the employer and the union shop committee or a union representative;
3. Binding arbitration.

The unionized sector of the American economy has shrunk, and most Americans now work in a nonunion environment. At the same time, there has been an enormous growth in legislation to protect the rights of individual workers: civil rights statutes that bar job discrimination on the basis of race, disability, and other factors, as well as individual laws that provide medical benefits, family leave, and other protections. Not surprisingly, employees began to file legal claims against employers with unprecedented frequency. Employment law disputes constitute a significant segment of state and federal court dockets today.

Some of these new lawsuits addressed serious problems in the workplace, but others did not. Regardless of their intrinsic merit, the rapid increase in employee lawsuits imposed serious costs on American companies and their shareholders. In 2000, for example, the estimated average cost of defending an individual employment lawsuit was $92,000, and the cost of defending a class action was $496,000 (Stallworth et al., 2001).

There are also significant costs and related barriers for employees seeking legal redress. One survey of employee advocates determined that responding lawyers accepted only 5 percent of the employment discrimination cases of prospective clients seeking representation. The lawyers required, on average, minimum provable damages of $60,000 to $65,000, a retainer of $3,000 to $3,500, and a 35 percent contingency fee (Howard, 1995).

In an effort to respond to employee grievances and avoid the cost, disruption, and risk inherent in court litigation, many American companies have adopted dispute resolution systems for their employees.

Although these programs vary widely in detail, they include some of the most advanced applications of the systems approach advocated by Goldberg, Brett, and Ury. Some also benefited from the implementation strategies advocated by Costantino and Sickles Merchant. The most successful employment conflict resolution programs do more than just resolve individual disputes; they are important, integrated components of an organization's entire personnel policy and operations. Well implemented, these systems set the tone for employee-employer relations and the company's commitment to its employees.

At the same time, concerns about fairness and transparency require that such programs be designed and implemented with care. Where employees' access to the courts and/or to class actions are affected (as by provisions for binding arbitration that are established as a condition of employment), due process and other issues discussed at length in Chapter 19 are implicated.

Keep these issues in mind as you read the following excerpt, which summarizes the goals underlying the evolution of employment conflict management systems from a management perspective and compares several different employment programs.

❖ **Peter Phillips,** *HOW COMPANIES MANAGE EMPLOYMENT DISPUTES*

CPR Institute for Dispute Resolution (2003)

The case for establishing an employment dispute management program is, by this time, broadly recognized. Employment dispute resolution programs lend consistency and therefore manageability to the handling of employment workplace disputes. When neutrally applied and administered, they enhance employee confidence and morale.... Approached systematically, the interests of the employee and employer predominate over the individual employee's or supervisor's concern that his or her conduct be vindicated.

A systematic, managerial approach to employment disputes also encourages early assessment of conflicts in the workplace to determine at an early juncture such important issues as the extent of company legal exposure, the likelihood that the employee complaint is well-grounded, and ways in which company procedures or supervisory skills might be improved....

There are, of course, employment disputes to which ADR may be inappropriate or precluded. Certain employee claims, such as those involving workers compensation, pension benefits or unemployment insurance, often are expressly excluded from an ADR program by statute. Employers frequently want to reserve access to judicial process in order to prevent the immediate harm that can flow from breaches of non-compete agreements or unauthorized use of trade secrets or other proprietary information.... [Recall that employees may also have strong reasons for wanting to preserve the right to go to court to vindicate their rights. See Chapter 19.]

Because quantification of system performance is vital to the management of any system, one should consider what "benchmarks" might be useful to measure system success. These may include:

Cycle Time:　How many days, or person-hours, elapse between the initiation of the employment dispute process and the resolution of the issue? ...

Legal Costs: Over a period of time, how much money was spent on legal fees to address employee disputes?

Rate of Litigation: Has the number of private and governmental charges been reduced? ...

EEOC [Equal Employment Opportunity Commission] Charges: Has the rate of charges brought before state and federal employment agencies changed?

Utilization: Over a period of time, have more or fewer employees availed themselves of the program?

Rate of Resolution at Various Levels: Over a period of time, have issues been resolved more frequently at lower (i.e., less expensive) levels of management? ...

User Satisfaction: Are employees and other stakeholders satisfied by the process and the outcome of disputes taken through the program? Would they recommend that their peers use it?

[The author explains that institutional employment conflict management systems often include (1) internal efforts at resolution through discussion, negotiation, peer review, ombuds facilities or other advisory and facilitative techniques; (2) intervention by a third-party neutral using non-adjudicative tools such as voluntary mediation or neutral merits evaluation; and (3) adjudication in the form of binding arbitration. These elements vary considerably in detail, however, as the following examples reveal.]

ALCOA offers a program for disputes that cannot be resolved informally and directly that is a classic three-step structure: a review of the problem by senior management; then non-binding mediation; and finally binding arbitration. The program is voluntary — employees may choose to ignore the program and sue if they wish — and is offered to employees after a dispute has arisen rather than as a condition of employment. But an employee who chooses the dispute resolution program waives access to [the courts.] ...

Johnson & Johnson's "Common Ground" Program is mandatory but does not culminate in arbitration. The three parts of the program are "Open Door," "Facilitation," and "Mediation." "Open Door" encourages employees to discuss problems with their supervisor, their supervisor's boss, human resources personnel, or with "whatever level of management is necessary to resolve the issue." Although no documentation is needed to commence this stage, "Open Door" must be attempted before moving on to the next stage. "Facilitation" involves a designated individual who will ensure that all options of communication have been exhausted. "Mediation" introduces a trained neutral to assist the parties in reaching a mutually acceptable resolution. Employees are notified that, "if none of these steps resolves your dispute with the Company, you are free to pursue legal action in court." ...

CIGNA offers employees a mandatory program that comprises an "internal" and an "external" component. The employee must choose between two internal processes: the "Speak Easy Process" and the "Peer Review Process" — either, but not both. The Speak Easy Process consists of Phase I — where an employee discusses the problem with a manager/supervisor — and Phase II — a review of issues with an Employee Relations Speak Easy Consultant. The Peer Review Process has three steps: Step I with the supervisor/manager, Step II with the next higher level of management, and Step III with either the head of the division or a Peer Review Panel of five trained specialists including supervisors and exempt and nonexempt employees. Decisions of the Peer Review Board are binding on the company. Complainants dissatisfied with these processes are required to request arbitration, if the issue would otherwise be heard in court. Employees seeking arbitration may request mediation first, which the company may agree to at its discretion. . . .

The U.S. Air Force offers a wide variety of ADR tools, including facilitation, mediation, early neutral evaluation, and access to ombuds, in its Employment ADR Program for nonmilitary employees. As a federal agency the Air Force is prohibited from engaging in binding arbitration unless it is agreed to as part of a negotiated grievance procedure in a collective bargaining agreement. Facilitation, the most used technique, is offered on an ad hoc basis in various nationwide installations, with central guidance in the form of "best practices." Air Force personnel are trained in interest-based negotiation for this purpose. Mediation, the second most-used technique, is conducted pursuant to standard practices for intake, ethical standards, and treatment of settlement agreements, by a uniformly trained corps of practitioners. Notwithstanding a requirement that all Air Force installations have a champion and system for resolution of workplace disputes, and that the Air Force has a number of agreements with labor unions that provide for the use of ADR as an option prior to undertaking other dispute resolution procedures, the agency takes the position that all ADR use is voluntary. . . .

In Shell's "RESOLVE" program, employees are first offered "Early Workplace Resolution," which may involve a meeting with the person complained of, assistance from a supervisor, or intervention by Human Resources or upper management. Next, employees are offered a toll-free hotline to the "Shell Ombuds," who can "confidentially answer questions, offer support and advice, or refer [the complainant] to internal or external processes and resources, as needed." The third step is mandatory mediation, and the fourth step is optional, voluntary arbitration. Thus there is no waiver of any legal right by employees.

Under the program, "External Mediation" (that is, involving a neutral from outside the company) of an employee's claim is required before proceeding to arbitration (at the unilateral election of the employee), or to litigation on either an individual or class basis. If the conflict is not satisfactorily resolved through External Mediation and the conflict involves a legally protected right, an employee may request arbitration or proceed to litigation. . . .

[Further insights into the goals and evolution of the RESOLVE program are provided by an interview conducted by the author with the ombudsperson who administered the program.[1]]

QUESTION: Did any particular event or concern give rise to the decision to go ahead and do this program?

ANSWER: [T]here were at least two precipitating events, one internal and one external. [The new president of the company] brought a vision to bring to Shell a new way of doing business, with a heavy emphasis on employees. And how we resolved conflicts was a part of that. The issue was kind of on the periphery and never came into play until a race discrimination suit was filed by Texaco employees . . . that made national headlines. . . . So Shell, heeding the warning of what happened at Texaco, decided that now was the time to go forward with this . . . dispute resolution system which eventually became known as RESOLVE. . . .

Q: What were the metrics that the program was designed to address?

A: There were none. The orders did not include anything like, "You must reduce the number of lawsuits or EEO claims by 'x' factor." There were none. The president at the time . . . would probably say he was looking for something kind of immeasurable.

. . . *Shell* was a traditional command-and-control culture. [The president] wanted to change that. This was a conflict-averse culture. People raised issues at their own peril. [He] wanted to change that. He felt that knowing what was on people's minds, knowing what conflicts they dealt with, would help the business. Not only their workplace problems, but problems they face in doing their jobs — if we knew what those are, if we can figure them out and let people have the tools to solve their own problems, this can only help the business. . . .

Q: One consequence of that, I guess, might be lower turnover?

A: Absolutely. We have made investments in these employees and they have all this valuable information; and if they feel that they can't solve their own problems, they'll look for a workplace where they can. And there are many corporations that are developing that model. . . . We do a report from time to time about what's going on in the program, usually what kind of issues come forward — and, by the way, the number of lawsuits is down substantially. We kind of say that as an aside, but I know that to many people in the company, that's what they're looking for. Now with the changing economic situation [*Note:* The interview was conducted during a recession], the pendulum has swung back more to a concern for the business proposition: What is the bottom line here? . . . And clearly our business proposition is that we do save the company money.

We're getting these things earlier in the process, when the emotions haven't ratcheted up. Big lawsuits drag on and on and people perceive that the company is resisting and holding out and they become more and more angry, so the price of resolving it goes higher and higher. . . .

Q: What about the legal assistance plan? What did you accomplish by it?

A: We gained another incentive to solve problems early. If the employees could have access to good legal advice of their own choosing, paid for by the company, that would give the company a heads-up in terms of solving the problem. Now the counterargument was that people would just abuse this. The first thing that they would do would be to get a lawyer. We would have lawsuits on our hands. But the reality has been nothing near that. Very few employees have used this legal assistance program, and those

---

1. Interview with Wilbur Hicks, Shell Oil Company, Jan. 14, 2002.

that do so, do it after they're in the process. Where there has been an issue and a lawyer has raised that to the company's attention, the company has paid serious attention. . . . By the same token, where there has *not* been an issue, better that the person's own lawyer say that, than the company. It really worked out to the benefit of everybody. I know we haven't spent much at all on this legal assistance program over five years. And the benefits have just been enormous. That has been the experience across the board with all the companies with legal assistance programs.

Questions

6. Does it appear that Shell adhered to the basic principles espoused by Goldberg, Brett, and Ury in creating and implementing the RESOLVE Program?

7. In Chapter 19, we analyzed the concerns over provisions requiring employees to submit to mandatory binding arbitration of employment-related claims as a condition of employment and proposed solutions. In what ways did Shell and other companies described above try to address concerns associated with mandatory, predispute ADR clauses? Did they succeed?

8. The Director of Maryland-based Giant Food's Fair Employment Practices Program reports that the company mediates most EEOC claims and cases filed in the courts. Beforehand, her office uses various approaches to respond to and resolve workplace disputes early. Of 800 internal workplace complaints filed in 2002, only 20 resulted in formal complaints; of the latter, 90 percent were resolved through settlement. See *The Use of Alternative Dispute Resolution (ADR) in Maryland Business: A Benchmarking Study* by the Maryland Mediation and Conflict Resolution Office (2004). Do you think this should be taken as a sign of success? Why or why not?

9. Some well-known institutional employment mediation programs make use of mediators who are themselves employees of the institution. Is it possible to have a workable, reliable mediation program under such circumstances? What concerns must be addressed, and how?

10. Even where litigation is imminent and numerous parties are involved, ADR may provide an avenue to constructive resolution of the issues. For example, in *Kosen v. American Express Financial Advisors, Inc.* (Civ. Action No. 1: 02CV0082 (D.D.C. 2002)), a group of 15 women who worked as financial advisors for American Express filed a class action lawsuit against the latter alleging a systematic practice of denying equal employment opportunities to women. The next day they filed a proposed consent decree.

> Before filing the complaint and consent decree, plaintiffs and defendants retained a private mediator who facilitated negotiations leading to the consent decree. During the period of mediation, defendants turned over to plaintiffs data and other information about the makeup of and practices in their workplace, and counsel for the plaintiffs retained a consultant to conduct a statistical analysis of the data. The consent decree, approved by the court on June 16, 2002, provided for a settlement fund of $31 million. Class counsel together received $10.85 million, or 35 percent of the total amount. The decree also provided for various injunctive relief measures, including the creation of a central database for distribution of leads and client accounts, establishment of objective criteria for assignment of client accounts, and implementation of a diversity training program. At the parties' request, the court appointed a private attorney as special master to oversee implementation of the decree (Green, 2003).

In Chapter 19, we saw that the California Supreme Court rejected as highly problematic the binding, predispute arbitration process used by Kaiser Permanente for medical malpractice claims. *Engalla v. Permanente Medical Group, Inc.*, 64 Cal. Rptr. 2d 843 (Cal. 1997). Subsequently, Kaiser faced questions from legislators and needed to revamp its ADR system quickly. Kaiser funded a "Blue Ribbon Panel" of outside experts to suggest improvements. Professors Martinez and Smith have recently analyzed the Panel's recommendations, the changes implemented by Kaiser, and their effectiveness in addressing the cost and delay concerns found by the *Engalla* Court, finding some significant improvements as well as a work-in-progress. Lawyers considering dispute resolution design may be particularly interested in the Kaiser Panel's recommendations for reforming the mandatory predispute arbitration system:

- Appointment of an Independent Administrator to manage the Kaiser arbitration process;
- A permanent stakeholder advisory committee;
- A clear statement of goals and communication of those goals to stakeholders;
- A more expedited and efficient process, including calendar benchmarks for completion of cases;
- Encouragement of early settlement discussions;
- Expansion of the pool of arbitrators;
- External audits and evaluation of the new process:
- Written, reasoned decisions by arbitrators; and

- Making information about the arbitrators and their prior rulings available to all parties at the time of arbitrator selection.

(Smith and Martinez, 2009).

Questions

11. In what ways does this address the concerns of the health system's subscribers like the Engallas?
12. How are the health provider's interests protected?
13. Do you think this process would satisfy unconscionability and due process concerns in most states? Would you have included any other recommendations if you served on the Blue Ribbon Panel?
14. Consider how this system would fare if the Arbitration Fairness Act (discussed in Chapter 19) applied.

---

c. Mass Claims Programs

No discussion of the evolution of conflict management systems is complete without reference to the development of ADR programs to handle multitudes of individual claims pursuant to court settlements of class actions or mass claims. Often, such systems were put in place quickly — as a rapid response to great tragedies such as airline crashes, massive fires, and other large, single incidents. Creative judges, parties, counsel, and neutral settlement experts fueled responses designed to address human grief, legal uncertainty, a huge number of claimants, and, sometimes, multiple potentially responsible parties and insurers. Over several decades, the systems have evolved to address mass torts occurring not in a single incident, but over many years and in many places (e.g., toxic environmental leakages, medical devices and pharmaceutical claims, product and warranty litigation). The wide range of incidents and range of parties involved in mass torts (from governmental systems to private insurers) can yield a variety of processes designed to fit specific tragedies.

Prior to being appointed the Special Master charged with designing and implementing the program for resolution of claims by September 11 victims and their families, Ken Feinberg wrote the following about the nature and utility of mass claim ADR mechanisms.

❖ **Kenneth R. Feinberg,** ONE-STOP SHOPPING: USING ADR TO RESOLVE
DISPUTES AND IMPLEMENT A SETTLEMENT

19 Alternatives 59 (January 2001)

One curious feature of ADR is how often it is associated only with the resolution of an underlying dispute. Once mediation or some other form of ADR is effective in settling the dispute among the parties, it often disappears from the radar screen. When it comes to ADR, the visibility of any particular technique often begins and ends with news concerning its effectiveness in settling a major source of disagreement among the parties. What is usually ignored is the role of ADR after the underlying dispute is resolved; all too often there is little or no followup when it comes to the role ADR plays in implementing a settlement, in making sure that the terms and conditions of the settlement are satisfied in an efficient and fair manner.

The role of ADR in post-settlement implementation is most apparent in large class actions involving mass torts, major insurance policy settlements and consumer litigation. In these and other similar complex and protracted litigations, a comprehensive settlement involves literally thousands of individual plaintiff claimants, all demanding their fair share of allocated settlement proceeds. To the public and many ADR commentators, an aggregate settlement has in fact been achieved. But fundamental questions remain: Which claimants will receive the benefits of the comprehensive settlement? How much they will receive and based upon what terms and conditions? It is in resolving these questions that ADR plays an additional creative and important role.

First, the ADR neutral may play an important role after a settlement is reached by fashioning an allocation formula for distribution of proceeds to eligible claimants. Plaintiff's lawyers may welcome such an initiative, thereby avoiding potential conflict of interest problems in the allocation of limited funds among their various clients. The defendants also may support this initiative, eager to make sure that the settlement is successful and fair when it comes to eligibility criteria and the distribution of monies to the population of plaintiff claimants. In mass tort cases such as Agent Orange and silicone breast implants, as well as asbestos and DES litigation, and in some "vanishing premium" insurance settlements, the role of the neutral in fashioning and implementing settlement terms and conditions loomed large in the ultimate success of the settlement initiative.

Second, even in those cases where comprehensive settlement terms and conditions are negotiated up front by the litigating parties themselves, ADR may still play a critically important role in the settlement's implementation. Mediation or arbitration may become available to those individual claimants who challenge their allocated share of the aggregate award. Convinced that they are entitled to more of the proceeds, or that they have been unfairly placed on the wrong level of an allocation matrix, individual claimants may avail themselves of mediation or arbitration in an effort to improve their respective award.

In the mass tort heart valve and Dalkon Shield settlements, for example, the availability of ADR processes to assist individual claimants who honestly believed that they were wronged by their allocated award, went a long way in convincing the courts (and the claimants themselves) of the ultimate fairness of the settlement. At the same time, the availability of such ADR processes at the "back end" implementation stage of a comprehensive mass settlement, helps minimize the likelihood that individual claimants will opt-out of the deal and decide to litigate (thus threatening the comprehensiveness of the settlement itself).

All too often, the public and consumers of ADR services fail to recognize the value of alternative dispute resolution in providing "one-stop shopping" for the litigants themselves. Not only can ADR be used effectively to help resolve the underlying dispute among the parties, but it also can become a valuable tool in assuring effective implementation of a settlement, maximizing the likelihood that all parties will comply with the deal and will view the settlement as fair, just, and equitable.

Notes and Questions

15. *The 9/11 Compensation Fund.* After the terrorist attacks of September 11, 2001, Ken Feinberg was appointed special master of the federal compensation fund for victims and their families. The fund distributed over $7 billion to 5,562 people during three years (Feinberg, 2005). Robert Ackerman describes the process used in allocating the funds below (Ackerman, 2005). As you read, consider the process chosen. Would you suggest any other elements or procedures to help ensure just, speedy, cost-effective resolution of these claims?

> Procedurally, the regulations allowed claimants to choose one of two tracks for consideration of their claims. If a claimant chose Track A, a Claims Evaluator would determine eligibility and the claimant's presumed award in accordance with the regulations within 45 days of filing; thereafter the claimant could either accept the award or request a hearing before the Special Master or his designee. Under Track B, the Claims Evaluator would determine eligibility (again within 45 days); thereafter, eligible claimants would proceed directly to hearing. 28 C.F.R. 104.33 spelled out the procedures to be used at the hearing. Consistent with the statute, claimants could be represented by counsel, present evidence (orally or in writing), and present witnesses (including experts); the Special Master or his designee would be permitted to question witnesses. In short, "the objective of hearings shall be to permit the claimant to present information or evidence that the claimant believes is necessary to a full understanding of the claim." Hearings would, "to the extent practicable, be scheduled at times and in locations convenient to the claimant or his or her representative" and "limited in length to a time period determined by the Special Master or his

designee." The Special Master was required to notify the claimant in writing of the amount of the award, but was not obliged to "create or provide any written record of the deliberations that resulted in that determination." Again, consistent with the statute, there would be "no further review or appeal of the Special Master's determination." The process was designed to take no more than 120 days, consistent with 405(b)(3) of the Act.

The process would thereby resemble that which is used in final, binding arbitration, except that there would be no party opposing the claim. It featured flexibility, ease-of-use (although some would be daunted by the thirty-three-page claims form), and quick turnaround. A procedure was established under the regulations to provide advance benefits to survivors and injured claimants to alleviate financial hardship. The Special Master established a website and several Claim Assistance sites to help guide claimants through the process; ATLA established Trial Lawyers Care, through which experienced trial lawyers would provide free legal assistance to people making claims on the Fund. (Many claimants nevertheless availed themselves of lawyers charging fees, which were sometimes below the normal billing rate.)

Media commentators described the scheme for the Fund as "about as fair as it could possibly be," "a good start on the road to recovery," "eminently fair," and "offering speedy and rational compensation."

16. *The Hokie Spirit Memorial Fund.* This fund was created in response to thousands of spontaneous donations that came to the university in the aftermath of the April 16, 2007, Virginia Tech tragedy when a student killed 33 persons (including himself) and injured at least 21 others. Approximately $8 million of those funds were distributed to those most profoundly affected in accordance with protocols developed in conjunction with Kenneth Feinberg, administrator of the Hokie Spirit Memorial Fund (HSMF). The HSMF was initially closed December 31, 2007, and reopened in June 2008. What suggestions would you give Virginia Tech leaders about distribution of future funds? How much of the donations should go toward fund administration and how much to affected persons? Should any of the funds go toward amounts other than to compensation of victims and their families? As counsel for the university, how would one go about starting to design a fair and cost-effective memorial fund system? See *http://www.vt.edu/fund/index.html*.

17. As you can see from this section, special masters and ADR experts can be used in many creative ways to deal with mass tragedies or complex disputes. Counsel for parties often work closely with courts and private neutrals to design these processes. The drafting material below gives you a glimpse of the role lawyers can play in creating effective stepped processes. At the close of this chapter, the Springfield Power Problem gives you an opportunity to synthesize the concepts you have studied in this chapter and draw on your own creativity to design with your client an effective conflict management system.

3. Drafting a Multistep Clause

As more and more attorneys have acquired experience with multistep dispute resolution systems, it has reinforced a growing awareness that reliance on standard contract boilerplate, like that offered by many institutional providers of dispute resolution services, may not result in a conflict resolution approach that is most appropriate for a particular transaction or dispute. One former corporate house counsel warns, "The dispute resolution process . . . imposed on a client by using a boilerplate clause may permanently sour them on ADR when they experience just as many — or worse — problems than they did in the courts. In fact, they may be subjected to the worst of both worlds and end up spending inordinate time in court and in ADR and unhappy with the lawyer that suggested ADR" (Trantina, 2001). Attorneys are encouraged to take a proactive role in tailoring a dispute resolution process to a client's particular needs and goals. One checklist of drafting considerations includes the following:

- Take time to understand the client's needs, including the nature of probable or potentially significant disputes, the nature of underlying business relationships, and the client's concerns and expectations regarding conflict resolution [*cf.* Goldberg, Brett, and Ury].
- Be aware of the changing legal environment surrounding ADR, and consider drafting choices to avoid pitfalls and address key issues.
- Beware of standard templates or provisions that were designed for different situations.
- Develop and use an up-to-date "drafting issues checklist" — perhaps initially relying on a published checklist and revising it.
- Understand the differences between institutional procedures before deciding which to incorporate.

Given the importance of this preparation, it is a matter of concern that as the pivotal players in the development of approaches to resolving conflict, lawyers have often failed to move beyond traditional "liti-gotiation" approaches. As observed in a recent study, "[W]hile attorneys may be trained in representing parties in disputes, most have not been specifically trained in ADR techniques and processes" (Maryland Mediation and Conflict Resolution Office, 2004). Of particular concern is the relative ignorance of ADR and conflict management options among those who have the responsibility to negotiate and draft contracts. While "trial lawyers" have often had experience with mediation and other approaches, corporate transactional counsel tend to have little or no experience with these choices — and are reluctant or unable to incorporate discussions about dispute resolution in commercial contract negotiations. As one senior lawyer at a leading Boston law firm fretted,

> As an advocate who is a member of a good-sized law firm, I found one of the problems was that many of these ADR issues were addressed by my transactional corporate partners, who didn't like me tinkering with the ADR provisions at the end of the deals so they couldn't close the transaction. Unfortunately, the clauses they used were often taken out of form books and not really discussed between the parties.

(Stipanowich and Kaskell, 2001). Thus, opportunities to incorporate lessons learned from a company's or department's negotiation, mediation, or arbitration experiences are often foregone. Among other things, our investigations into corporate disputing must help us to understand how to effectively channel feedback into the negotiating and drafting process. The CPR Institute recently made an effort to inform and educate corporate counsel and business persons by assembling guidelines for drafters (Scanlon, 2003).

Problem

You are working with the general counsel of the Springfield Power Association (SPA), a regional utility that is finalizing a five-year contract with NatLee Coal Company (NatLee) to furnish SPA's requirements of coal for power generation. SPA's general counsel suggests she would prefer a multistep dispute resolution clause, and sends you "a great provision" that was furnished by a speaker at a recent meeting of the Springfield Bar Association's ADR Committee:

DISPUTE RESOLUTION
Before submitting any dispute between the parties to binding arbitration, they will first follow the informal and escalating procedures set forth as stated herein:

(A)   The complaining party's representative will notify the other party's representative in writing of the problem, and both parties will exercise good faith efforts to resolve the matter as quickly as possible.

(B)   In the event the matter is not resolved ten days after the delivery of the written notice, the complaining party must request a meeting between the senior representatives of each party to resolve the controversy. The meeting shall take place within five days.

(C)   In the event the meeting between the senior representatives does not resolve the issue in a timely fashion, they shall mediate in good faith before a mutually acceptable mediator within 10 days.

(D)   If the parties are unable to resolve the dispute through these procedures, they may ask the mediator to submit a non-binding award in order to promote settlement.

> BINDING ARBITRATION
>
> If none of the steps above are successful in resolving the dispute, the parties shall submit the matter to binding arbitration <u>within two weeks</u>. Each party shall select an arbitrator, and these two appointed arbitrators shall pick a third.

She realizes this provision is "rather rough" and would like you to critique it and offer suggestions. She warns you that it may be necessary for her company to obtain relief rather quickly in some cases — perhaps through a temporary injunction. She added the language that would require the institution of arbitration within two weeks after other options were exhausted. She also wants to keep the costs of dispute resolution down if possible. The situation is complicated because the requirements contract is a long-distance transaction; NatLee's operations are 750 miles away. She welcomes any pertinent questions that might assist in finalizing the arrangement.

Conclusion

As the foregoing reveals, much time and thought has been given to the development of appropriate conflict resolution processes for specific situations, including multistepped or multifaceted programs. As we look ahead to the final chapter, we examine an emerging variety of roles facing lawyers and neutrals in modern conflict management as well as foreshadow some fascinating new developments in the field, including the Internet's impact on ADR processes.

CHAPTER
22

Looking Ahead: Opportunities and Challenges in ADR and Conflict Management

We conclude these materials with a look at important opportunities and challenges confronting lawyers as problem solvers today and in the future. After more than a quarter-century of diverse and proliferating efforts aimed at developing and employing different, hopefully more appropriate and effective ways of managing conflict, we have a much better understanding of the dynamics of conflict and a much broader variety of tools to bring to bear in different settings.

Legal counselors now have the opportunity to approach the litigation experience in a wholly new way, with more satisfactory results for those they represent. As advisors to organizations, they are ideally poised to bring about a wholesale change in the culture of disputing. Whether they are representing individual clients expressly (and only) to achieve settlement, as in the emerging area of collaborative law, or they are designing systems for clients to manage conflict, lawyers are counselors on dispute resolution strategy. Understanding the role and value of mediators or other neutrals in enhancing relationships and facilitating the resolution of active conflict, lawyers may pioneer applications of interventions "upstream," such as the mediation of deals and the facilitation of long-term relationships. With the Internet and other modern technologies, problem-solving lawyers have unprecedented tools for realizing the goals of efficiency and economy in resolving disputes, even in long-distance transactions. And as citizens, they are equipped to play a leading role in creating a society transformed by the same principles that we have learned to apply in the resolution of individual disputes.

A. Changing Roles, Changing Cultures

1. Changing Views of Lawyering in the Litigation Landscape

Throughout this book, we have underlined the primary role played by judges in reordering the landscape of litigation. One of these leaders, Judge Dorothy Nelson of the U.S. Court of Appeals for the Ninth Circuit, has said,

> Lawyers and other ADR providers can expand the parties' tools for dealing with the psychological, social and economic dynamics that accompany and sometimes drive litigation. Their roles should be that of constructive problem solvers and peacemakers rather than zealous advocates. The approach in each case should be tailored to the context in which it evolves with particular attention to the cultural forces that are at work.

(Nelson, 2001). Another creative force in the judicial ranks is Wayne Brazil, who as U.S. magistrate judge in California's Northern District since 1984 pioneered one of the nation's most innovative multifaceted court-connected ADR programs. Here, Judge Brazil considers the ways in which, with a different mind-set, today's attorneys may dramatically alter the litigation experience for the benefit of those they represent.

❖ Hon. Wayne Brazil, *ADR in A Civil Action: What Could Have Been*
Dispute Resolution Magazine 25 (Summer 2007)

While there may be a dearth of ADR portrayed in recent fiction and nonfiction, it is not hard to imagine scenarios in which ADR could have drastically altered the stories we read. Jonathan Harr's book *A Civil Action* is just one example where wise counsel grounded in problem-solving approaches may have made for a happier ending for everyone involved. . . .

The litigation pitted 33 individual plaintiffs against large corporations. The plaintiffs alleged that by contaminating the local public water supply the defendants were responsible for the deaths of five children and for serious injuries and illnesses suffered by many other people.

After following a notoriously tortured course that included enormously expensive discovery and motion work, and a fractured, frustrating, highly publicized trial that was followed by visits to the court of appeals, the matter slid over a period of years toward a settlement that satisfied no one and did no real good. . . .

Many of the plaintiffs in *A Civil Action* had suffered in the most severe of ways, physically and emotionally. They felt both afraid and angry. They wanted answers. They wanted help dealing with the consequences of their tragedies. They wanted restoration of their community.

Lawyers with insufficient vision would have said that the plaintiffs were naive to think that they could achieve these kinds of ends through the legal system. Certainly the system as it was used in this litigation delivered precious little toward these ends. The transaction costs, not counting a dime of the settlement money that eventually was paid, appear to have been well above $15 million. But that huge investment of money and the eight years of the parties' time that the case consumed yielded a judgment and a settlement that brought no answers to the biggest questions, no emotional healing, no restoration of community, and no repair of severely damaged good will.

Instead of compounding the real-world tragedy with a litigation tragedy, a truly wise counselor would have helped the defendants understand, shortly after the severity of the harms became clear, that the circumstances presented an opportunity to build — to use ADR to create new, long-range value of great significance. Even if the only value that really mattered to defendants was profit, a good lawyer would have advised them to move in a very different direction, and to use ADR to do so. What could such a lawyer have helped his clients see?

Defendants knew that the Environmental Protection Agency had designated the area as a Superfund site and had been investigating the extent and sources of the obvious contamination for some time before the lawsuit was filed. Defendants knew that they were required by law to cooperate fully with the EPA investigation. Defendants knew that there was a substantial possibility that the EPA would order them to contribute toward the cost of clean up. The defendants knew that the U.S. Geological Survey also was studying contamination in the area. And defendants knew that if they were not truthful with federal authorities, the Department of Justice might well intervene. In fact, the justice department ultimately indicted one of the corporate defendants for just such untruthfulness, and that defendant ultimately pleaded guilty.

Defendants also could foresee that a case like this would generate a great deal of press coverage and that the defendants would not be favored in the sympathy slant; 77 percent of people polled in surveys taken as the trial date approached believed that the corporate defendants were responsible for the deaths of the children. Moreover, two of the three companies that ended up being pulled into the case knew they would remain in the community, employing local workers, working with local politicians, and needing local services.

Given these circumstances, a good lawyer would have counseled his client to use an ADR process early in the pretrial period, well before most of the litigation transaction costs were incurred and before the litigation process further alienated the plaintiffs and rigidified their positions. The goal would be to use ADR to explore what was most important to the plaintiffs themselves, as opposed to their lawyers, to un-demonize the defendants, and to reach out to the plaintiffs in a constructive and civic spirit that might make it possible to work out a settlement that would simultaneously save the defendants some money and yield potentially huge public relations benefits.

A good lawyer would have urged each corporate defendant to send its chairman or its CEO as its principal representative to the ADR session to demonstrate graphically that the company understood the gravity of the losses that plaintiffs had suffered. Direct participation by the highest level corporate officers was fully justified by financial considerations alone and could have considerably improved the odds that the companies' proposals would elicit favorable responses from the plaintiffs.

Good lawyers would have advised their companies' representatives to listen actively to the plaintiffs before making any statements of their own. After listening, each CEO or chairman would seek an opportunity to speak directly to the plaintiffs in the presence of their lawyers and the neutral. He or she would communicate, with compassion and concern, the following messages and proposals.

The company's representative would begin by telling the plaintiffs how sorry he or she and the company were about what had happened to them. The representative would acknowledge, directly and without qualification, that the plaintiffs had suffered severe losses, and that he or she was not about to claim that he or she could fully understand the pain they had experienced. Then, the speaker would say that he or she doesn't understand what the causes were of these tragedies, but he or she really wants to. The representative would explain that the scientists who advise him or her do not think that chemicals associated with the company's operations reached the wells or caused the illnesses, and he or she would emphasize that the company never would have permitted the operations to proceed if they had known that such tragic consequences would ensue. But he or she would concede that no one knows enough about the sources of these kinds of illnesses to be completely sure, so one of the representative's goals will be to support the effort to learn from these tragedies.

The representative would propose doing that in two ways. First, by cooperating fully with the EPA and all other governmental agencies who are investigating these matters. He or she would promise that his company would open its records and provide the authorities promptly with all the information and other forms of assistance they might seek. The second way his company, along with the other defendants, would support the search for answers would be to contribute several million dollars directly to support independent research into the possibility that there are environmental causes of leukemia.

In making these proposals, the spokesman for the company would emphasize that many of his or her valued and long-time employees live here, so it is partly on their behalf that she wants to help find out why this happened. But the representative also would emphasize that the company wants to be a responsible and valued member of this community and thus wants to identify with certainty any aspects of its operations that might cause harm to any other members of the community.

Next, the CEO or chairman would commit the company to contribute its full fair share to the cost of cleaning up the contaminated area. He or she would say that even though it is not clear that the contamination that has been found caused the cancer, it is clear that the contamination is a legitimate source of concern and must be removed. So the company, he or she would say, stands ready to pay toward the cost of the clean-up whatever share the government scientists conclude is appropriate. The representative also would say that the company would do everything it can to speed up the process of making that determination and to press for completion of the cleanup work on as fast a timetable as possible.

To evidence his or her good faith, the representative then would say that none of the commitments just described are contingent on the case settling. The company intends to go forward with them, including the commitment to support the cancer research, even if the parties cannot reach an agreement that would end the litigation.

Finally, on behalf of all defendants, the representative would offer money to help the plaintiffs meet the needs that the situation has created. He or she would start by acknowledging that no amount of money could adequately compensate for the personal losses that have been suffered. But he or she would also emphasize that the tragedies have had real and damaging consequences that require resources. The defendants collectively would like to provide some of those resources, and toward that end they would like to offer the plaintiffs, as a group, $10 million.

Making a package of proposals like this early in the pretrial period would have encouraged a perception that defendants were sincerely sorry about the plaintiffs' losses and wanted to act as responsible and engaged members of a shared community. The likelihood that the plaintiffs would not have responded positively to such an offer is small. With acceptance of this offer, defendants would have saved considerable money. They also would have generated considerable positive press and good will and avoided the years of bad press, to say nothing of the criminal indictment, that accompanied the protracted litigation. Moreover, they would have distinguished themselves from their competitors, encouraging investors to perceive them as possessing especially acute business judgment and thus being worthy of investment confidence.

There is a real chance that a scenario like the one just described could have occurred. That real possibility demonstrates that breadth of "solution-vision" can be an essential tool even in pursuing client interests that are limited to money. A lawyer who cannot help her client explore problem-solving solutions simply cannot be considered a wise counselor.

Question

1. Do you think Judge Brazil's advice is realistic? What barriers might there be — on the defendants' side, the plaintiffs' side, or elsewhere — to successfully executing the scenario he contemplates?

---

2.   Changing the Corporate Culture

Cathy Constantino and Christina Merchant have observed that organizations historically have failed to view the management of conflict systematically. "Rather, conflict in organizations is viewed and managed in a piecemeal, ad hoc fashion as isolated events, which are sometimes grouped by category if the risk exposure is great enough but that are rarely examined in the aggregate to reveal patterns and systemic issues. In a sense, most organizations regard disputes as 'local' events" (Constantino and Merchant, 1996). In Chapter 21, we introduced how lawyers can design and improve systems for preventing conflict and resolving disputes. This burgeoning area of "dispute resolution design" envisions a process of bringing about cultural changes in organizations. Increasingly, corporations, government entities, universities and other types of organizations — with the help of creative lawyers — are moving beyond piecemeal approaches, including ad hoc applications of ADR, to embrace a new way of managing conflict.

In a groundbreaking study, Professor Craig McEwen closely examined the way six large companies managed business-to-business disputes and concluded that whether or not a company employs mediation may be less important than the extent to which mediation is employed in the context of a systematic approach to the "management of disputing." Interviews with business leaders and senior corporate counsel and a study of roughly 170 disputes led McEwen to identify four major factors preventing faster and less costly resolution of disputes: contentious and competitive corporate cultures, the personal emotional investment of business managers in disputes, "misaligned incentives" such as hourly billing arrangements for outside counsel, and the professional legal culture that expects full information (and thus, discovery) before deciding how to dispose of the case (McEwen, 1998).

While several of the companies used mediation (some quite often), and all were concerned about litigation costs and had tried to address such concerns, one company (which he designated "MOD") distinguished itself by embracing an overall strategy for achieving corporate goals through thoughtful dispute management. Motivated by a company-wide effort to define efficiency and quality management in measurable ways, MOD's general counsel and several other key attorneys moved beyond the traditional "case-by-case client service role" and assumed the role of managers of the disputing process. The MOD legal division developed a clear organizational mission — "to maximize prompt and favorable settlements," measured by the shortness of dispute resolution, "favorable outcomes, cost savings, and client satisfaction." The program that evolved from these initial determinations included:

- redesign of the dispute resolution approach, including early case evaluation by inside and outside counsel to achieve earlier and less costly settlement in "Stage 1" (prior to discovery);
- examination of "patterns of disputing" in different business units, and efforts to train business managers about how to achieve the objectives of earlier settlements and fewer lawsuits;
- the use of "wise advisors" — high-level individuals without personal involvement in disputes who could promote reasonable outcomes;
- changed billing practices, including billing business units directly for outside counsel fees;

- encouraging lawyers and business people to learn about, understand, and apply the principles underlying mediation and interest-based negotiation;
- periodic measurements of favorable outcomes and other benchmarks of success.

Thus, "the lawyers at MOD went well beyond the more typical, reactive and case-centered roles of other corporate counsel by taking on leadership as managers of the disputing process" and achieved a greater level of success in altering the cost and timing of disputes as well as the quality of outcomes. In other words, instead of incorporating mediation into the traditional "litigotiation" culture of their company, the MOD legal department set about changing the whole culture of conflict management — employing mediation in the context of a systemic approach built on a clearly defined corporate objective aimed at speedy and low-cost resolution through settlement and preserved business relationships. The principles underlying mediation, including active listening and understanding and responding to interests were integrated into the evaluative and negotiating efforts of lawyers and business persons.

Questions

2. How does the approach undertaken by "MOD" lawyers in their organization compare with the role(s) implicitly described in your law school courses and casebooks?
3. A recent review of empirical studies on corporate conflict management suggests that MOD's proactive approach remains exceptional. Why do you suppose that is the case?

B. Dynamic Conflict Management: New Roles for Lawyers and Neutrals in Public and Private Settings

You now understand, as many practicing lawyers do, the potentially significant role that a neutral can play in resolving disputes, enhancing communication, and even transforming relationships. In Chapter 21, you saw that some lawyers work with clients to design ongoing conflict management systems, calling regularly on the use of mediators or ADR experts, either because they can anticipate disputes in long-term relationships and want to put an effective process in place early to minimize work disruption or because they are called in to address a flawed process needs revision. Sometimes courts appoint neutrals to help manage conflict over a long period in mass torts or other complex matters or to resolve pretrial discovery disputes.

Sometimes lawyers try to fulfill the role of conflict managers themselves for clients as they negotiate transactions or set up a dispute resolution system in connection with settlement of claims. In other emerging areas of law, collaborative or cooperative or preventive law, lawyers may specifically choose to act on behalf of their clients for settlement — but not litigation — purposes.

1.   The Creative Role of Magistrates, Special Masters, and Government ADR Experts

Many courts have taken the lead in appointing neutrals to offer assistance with conflict resolution. As discussed in Chapter 20, Professor Frank Sander's vision of the "multidoor courthouse" rested on three elements: flexibility, choice of various processes for parties, and a rational pairing of problem and process (Sander, 1976). While Sander's template for a "multidoor courthouse," with a clerk directing entrants to different "doors," has not been widely embraced in the form he envisioned, the three elements underlying his original proposal have been well served by many magistrates, who play a key case management role in many federal district court programs. Among other things, many federal magistrate judges explore a range of conflict resolution strategies, tailor methods to the issues at hand, and respond dynamically to the circumstances of the case and the needs of the parties. As compared to Sander's "screening clerk," magistrates may bring into play greater preparation, broader discretion and coercive authority, and a greater understanding of the circumstances of the case and the requirements of the parties.

Special masters and other court-appointed neutrals may also perform tasks that transcend their more traditional focus on fact-finding and evaluating or facilitating resolution of substantive issues. Some courts now utilize special masters for all aspects of pretrial case management, usually with the deliberate intention of preparing a case for mediation or other intervention. Like magistrate judges, court-appointed neutrals often function as "process architects." (See *Appointing Special Masters and Other Judicial Adjuncts: A Handbook for Judges,* Academy of Court-Appointed Masters, 2006.)

Court-annexed ADR programs are not well equipped to provide the long-term ADR assistance needed to move complex public policy consensus building forward, at least in some areas like environmental disputes, where issues involve more than allocation of pollution cleanup costs (Kloppenberg, 2003). Increasingly, government agencies such as the Environmental Protection Agency are employing neutrals to assist with conflict resolution, spending significant sums for ADR expertise. For example, environmental cases involving multiple public and private parties, complex scientific issues, and future resource claims are a ripe area for ADR investment. Just identifying all the federal entities with an interest in a particular environmental matter can be a complex task but ADR processes had proved so promising that Congress created a new federal agency in 1998, the U.S. Institute for Environmental Conflict Resolution, to address environmental disputes, sort the various intergovernmental interests, and provide conflict resolution expertise (Emerson et al., 2003).

As explored in Chapter 21, courts and governments sometimes appoint special masters for ongoing work to help resolve complex, multiparty problems and avoid or streamline litigation. Ken Feinberg speaks of the value of providing "one-stop shopping" for resolution of mass tort disputes (Feinberg, 2001). Pursuant to federal legislation, he was later appointed by the U.S. Attorney General as special master for the federal September 11 victim and families compensation fund (Feinberg, 2005). Although the legislation mandated certain matters (e.g., who could receive compensation from the fund), the special master had great discretion to design and implement the dispute resolution process.

2. *The Dispute Resolution Adviser*

While much has been done to enhance the ability of government agencies or courts to dynamically respond to the dispute resolution requirements of individual cases, there is even more room for innovation in the realm of private contracts in long-term relationships (Stipanowich, 1998). Long-term relationships involving significant financial stakes may justify more deliberate conflict management efforts that go beyond traditional ADR. For example, many public and private owners of major construction projects have found it advantageous to reduce the likelihood of major disputes by establishing a good working relationship at the outset, and set the pattern for more successful interaction throughout the project. They often employ "partnering" — a program of facilitated, structured workshops involving specific relational objectives — with contractors, design professionals, and other persons involved in the project before work begins and as it goes forward. See *Dispute Prevention Through Partnering*, CPR Institute For Dispute Resolution MAPP Series (1998).

Most discussions of partnering at the project level focus on a facilitated workshop conducted at the beginning of a construction project. Participants include representatives of the owner, the contractor, and other "stakeholders" — individuals closely affiliated with the project as well as key decision makers higher in the organization, including legal counsel for the project. A typical multiday partnering session might begin with training and exercises focusing on interpersonal communication, "disputing" styles, and management of conflict. The agenda also includes discussion of the project mission, the specific performance objectives and expectations of companies and individuals, and, in some cases, the development of a specific dispute resolution process for handling conflict on the project. The initial partnering session often concludes with the signing of a project charter setting forth the team's mission and specific goals — a document that may be displayed prominently at the project site.

To be effective, partnering must involve far more than a discrete event in the life of a project; it must permeate and become an integral part of project relationships. Although the inaugural workshop is often described as the "centerpiece" of partnering, it must reflect a commitment of the highest levels of management that is transmitted through the ranks to the level of field personnel. It must also amount to something more than a simplistic drill — a feel-good exercise that results in collective intonation of general platitudes — and business as usual during performance of the contract. It is essential that the workshop treat real project planning issues, allowing project participants to state their respective requirements in frank and specific terms, and to model the behaviors that will sustain those ends in the long term.

The initial partnering conference is also the ideal platform for exploration of a structure for long-term governance of the relationship, including a variegated conflict resolution scheme. The result might be a conflict resolution system that places initial emphasis on informal, face-to-face problem solving, and integrative bargaining, followed by settlement-oriented interventions (mediation, non-binding evaluation, dispute review boards) and, ultimately, adjudication (often some form of binding arbitration). As the following demonstrates, a major construction project successfully used a partnering system with a Dispute Resolution Adviser to help manage ongoing conflicts.

Example: A system put in place on a Hong Kong construction project represented a quantum leap in the evolution of contractual dispute systems. The contract for the renovation of Queen Mary Hospital, a venerable 56-year-old edifice, required performing intricate demolition and construction services while keeping the hospital and operating theatres operational — a complex and challenging theme likely to prove a hotbed of conflict. The project owner, the Hong Kong Government's Architectural Services Department (ASD), desirous of strict budget control, required a system that would identify and resolve disputes in the shortest possible time and prior to the completion of the project. ASD retained the services of an international team of consultants to develop an appropriate dispute resolution system for the project.

The result was a report setting forth specific recommendations for project organization and administration aimed at avoiding or minimizing areas of dispute. These included tight time frames for job site decision making and handling of claims, and the establishment of a flexible, dynamic dispute resolution system centered on the figure of a Dispute Resolution Adviser (DRA). The resulting agreement called for joint appointment of a neutral, a construction expert possessing dispute resolution skills, as the DRA at the time the construction contract commenced. A default mechanism was established for independent appointment of a DRA should the parties fail to agree on an appointee. The DRA's fees were to be shared equally between the owner and the general contractor.

The DRA's first function was to meet with job participants to explain and build support for a cooperative approach to problem solving on the project. Among other things, the DRA was to discuss basic rules of communication and attitudinal changes necessary to avoid adversarial positions. Thereafter, the DRA was to make monthly visits to the site for the purpose of consulting with project participants on the status of the job and facilitating discussions respecting any conflicts. The DRA was given considerable flexibility in managing such discussions. In the event of a formal challenge to a project decision, the parties were given four weeks to negotiate pertinent issues (with or without the assistance of the DRA). In the event the problem remained unresolved, a party's written notice of dispute would trigger a more formal stage of dispute resolution in which the DRA had freedom to employ any of several methods of dispute resolution.

If assisted site-level negotiations failed, the DRA was to prepare a report identifying the key issues in dispute, the positions of the parties, and the perceived barriers to settlement and making either a recommendation for settlement or a non-binding evaluation of the dispute. The report would be used by senior off-site representatives of the parties to further negotiations, perhaps assisted by the DRA. Should matters not be resolved within 14 days of the issuance of the DRA's report, the DRA would set into motion a short-form arbitration procedure or other mutually acceptable means recommended by the DRA. The arbitrator would be appointed by the parties; failing their agreement, the DRA would make the selection.

The DRA procedure worked well. Despite the usual problems and several hundred owner-directed changes [to the construction project], no disputes reached the stage of non-binding evaluation. The DRA system has since been applied on at least one other hospital project for the same owner.

The planners of Queen Mary Hospital and their able consultants came to recognize that in the relational sphere, conflict resolution is properly approached not as an event or set-piece intervention, but as a process inextricably intertwined with the relationships that evolve along with the physical design, procurement, and construction of the building. Their solution embraces a number of the following elements that might be the hallmarks of a contractual conflict management system:

1. a comprehensive *program* that commences with the contractual relationship(s) and extends throughout the life of the relationship(s);
2. the *active involvement of key contract participants* in "partnering," in initial program design and, ultimately, in the resolution of conflict;
3. the establishment of a *variegated conflict resolution scheme* that incorporates a series or selection of strategies consistent with the parties' goals; and
4. an *independent adviser* who, either alone or as part of a larger team or organization, advises, models, teaches, facilitates, and provides the human backbone for the entire program.

As the Queen Mary Hospital example demonstrates, partnering approaches have been combined with truly innovative efforts aimed at providing parties with a highly tailored yet flexible and dynamic conflict management process — moving beyond the confines of contractual dispute resolution provisions to address particular, unanticipated needs and changing circumstances. Partnering concepts are readily adaptable to other commercial arenas involving long-term performance and a high potential for disputes, such as joint ventures involving technology sharing or development. Effective partnering permits parties to clarify and prioritize goals and expectations, anticipate critical performance problems, enhance communications among key personnel, and establish a blueprint for resolving conflict at the earliest possible time.

3.   *Collaborative Law: Lawyers Working with Clients to Avoid Litigation*

The role of counsel in collaborative lawyering is very different from the traditional role of a zealous advocate within the adversarial litigation system. In Chapter 7, we described how a collaborative lawyer offers his or her services expressly to help clients resolve a dispute without resorting to litigation. In collaborative law, lawyers employ problem-solving negotiation techniques, acting like settlement counsel for a defined divorce and custody matter. Additionally, mediators, both lawyers and non-lawyers, are also commonly used in divorce and custody disputes. In collaborative law, role definition is critical. What are the limits on the lawyers' roles? Have they provided enough information about their limited roles so that clients can make informed choices (Lande, 2007)? As lawyers, family law judges and academics ponder the difficult issues and begin to write rules shaping the behavior of lawyers in less traditional and more cooperative roles, the interest in this phenomenon and related areas for use of collaborative, cooperative, or preventive law increases. For example, a drafting committee on Collaborative Law was appointed by the National Conference of Commissioners on Uniform State Laws in 2007.

Notes and Questions

4.   How does the Dispute Resolution Adviser concept differ from traditional ADR approaches you have encountered in this book? When, if ever, might you consider counseling a client to adopt this approach?

5.   Why do you suppose relatively few lawyers have participated in, let alone proposed, partnering processes? Should proposing partnering or deal mediation be within a lawyer's role as counselor to a client who is getting ready to enter into a long-term contractual relationship? Why or why not?

6.   Can you envision any areas other than family law cases in which collaborative lawyering might hold promise? Are there other types of family disputes or areas involving ongoing relationships that could benefit from the collaborative approach? What are the challenges to greater collaborative lawyering in areas outside domestic relations cases (Hoffman, 2004)?

C.   A New Frontier for Lawyers and Neutrals: Online Dispute Resolution

Many court systems have implemented electronic filing, video conferencing, and other new technologies to enhance the speed of dispute resolution and reduce the cost of litigation. ADR providers have also used technology to improve dispute resolution. Additionally, the Internet affords extraordinary opportunities for resolving disputes over long distances efficiently and at minimal cost, and it is only a matter of time before the new electronic media revolutionize our approaches to resolving disputes, along with most other aspects of modern life (Katsh and Rivkin, 2001). The advent of online dispute resolution, however, has not overtaken face-to-face ADR processes as quickly as some proponents predicted.

Online dispute resolution is still in its infancy, but will continue to emerge as new generations of lawyers and potential users accustom themselves to performing all kinds of tasks online and as global transactions increase. Ultimately, the concept of interaction in a virtual reality will likely transform many of our concepts of negotiating and adjudication, and even our notions of "in-court" and "out-of-court" processes.

❖ **Colin Rule,** *Online Dispute Resolution*
_____

**Adapted from Online Dispute Resolution for Business:
B2B, Ecommerce, Consumer, Employment, Insurance, and Other
Commercial Conflicts (2002)**

Dispute resolution and information technology have combined into an important new tool, a new system, a new way of doing business which is more efficient, more cost effective, and much more flexible than traditional approaches. The tool is called Online Dispute Resolution, and it combines the efficiency of alternative dispute resolution with the power of the Internet to save businesses money, time, and frustration.

Online dispute resolution is not tied to geography, so disputants can reach resolution even if they are located on different continents. ODR can move to resolve matters before they escalate, so that disputants can quickly resolve the matter and get back to business. ODR is not tied to particular bodies of law, so there is no need for each side to retain expensive legal counsel to learn the legal structure of the other side's country. ODR can be priced much more reasonably than legal options, and even less than the cost of a single plane ticket. ODR can also leverage expertise from skilled neutrals around the world, ensuring that the participants will get a fair hearing, from someone who has knowledge and experience in the matter at hand. ODR enables businesses, governments, and consumers to achieve the best resolution possible in the shortest amount of time.

These advantages apply to all kinds of disputes. Intellectual property disputes, insurance claims, and B2B and B2C e-commerce matters are all good fits with the power of ODR. Some disputes are over more abstract issues not related to monetary payments, like privacy or workplace conflict. For example, ICANN (the Internet Corporation for Assigned Names and Numbers) faced monumental problems when they decided to build a global process to handle domain name disputes. What courts should govern the matter? What laws should apply? No one country has the jurisdiction over domain names, it is a truly international system. ICANN solved the problem by creating a global domain name dispute resolution process, the UDRP, administered by a variety of ODR providers. Over the past three years this process has resolved thousands of disputes all over the world, none of which have ever been appealed in a courtroom. Soon similar ODR systems will be created for a wide variety of areas, such as insurance, commerce, privacy, government, workplace, and finance.

[T]he rapid growth in online-only disputes has cast the shortcomings of court litigation in even starker contrast. Legal systems are tied to geography almost by definition. In the U.S., lawyers are only admitted to the bar on a state-by-state basis, facing penalties if they even offer legal advice to clients in other states. Enforcement of court decisions involves jails and policemen that also only operate in a particular geographic area.

It is obvious that transaction partners who meet on the web can take little comfort from the redress options provided in the face-to-face world. You can't merely re-create offline judicial mechanisms online and expect them to work, with e-judges making e-rulings enforced by e-police running e-jails. The model doesn't work, on a fundamental level, when participants in the system can change their identity as easily as they change their email address. It might work to hunt down the odd international criminal who shuts down the stock exchange with a virus, but there's no way law enforcement is going to be able to get every fraudulent seller on eBay, especially when they may be on the other side of the planet.

The delays of face-to-face processes also hamper their applicability to online transactions. Over the web, consumers and businesses expect that any service they need should be available online, 24 hours a day. Courts, in contrast, have long been designed to involve delays, ornate filing requirements, and strict procedural rules, to deter potential users from being cavalier in their decision to file new cases. If two businesses engage in a transboundary transaction that goes awry they have no interest in waiting months for an offline dispute resolution body to initiate a process to resolve the dispute. They want to get the matter resolved as quickly as possible so that they can get back to doing business.

Simply put, offline courts do not work for online disputes. Courts can operate as an effective safety net for those cases that involve criminal wrongdoing, or where the parties are unwilling to use a non-public forum, or when they put the highest priority on due process and precedent. But for a huge number of cases that are cropping up online, where the value under dispute is less than likely legal bills, or where both parties truly participated in the transaction in good faith, online dispute resolution is the best solution.

In response to these conclusions, the consensus behind online dispute resolution is growing rapidly. International organizations (The OECD, The Hague Conference on Private International Law, the European Union), consumer groups, governmental bodies, professional associations and business organizations have all issued recommendations calling for online dispute resolution. While there is some debate about how to ensure that online dispute resolution services are fair to consumers, or how best to over-see online dispute resolution service providers, there is no debate over whether or not online dispute resolution is the best option for providing redress on the Internet.

Online dispute resolution is the future. Businesses that integrate it into the way they do business will reap rewards in the form of greater efficiency, cost savings, happier employees, protection from liability, and more loyal customers. Those businesses that ignore it will continue to be drawn into expensive and inefficient legal proceedings that breed ill will and sap competitive strength.

Notes and Questions

7. When might online ADR be particularly useful? When might you recommend "face-to-face" dispute resolution methods?
8. Will technological changes affect the way that people communicate? What impact will this have on counsel, clients, and mediators (Larson, 2006)?

D. Challenges Facing Lawyers as Neutrals

In recent years, many lawyers have become increasingly active as mediators and arbitrators. Their activities are a natural outgrowth of the expanding use of ADR in the management of conflict in many different settings — trends that have fueled a growing debate over the need for credentialing mechanisms for those offering ADR services in public and private contexts. In the following excerpt, Linda Singer, a longtime leader in the ADR field, offers her personal reflections on trends and challenges facing lawyer-neutrals.

❖ **Linda R. Singer,** The Lawyer as Neutral
_____
19 Alternatives 40 (January 2001)

For lawyers, a refreshing outcome of the increased use of ADR is the diversity of roles now available. From the role of zealous advocate in negotiation or litigation have evolved the roles of settlement counsel and advocate in a variety of forums. But what has most captured the imagination and enthusiasm of many lawyers is the role of neutral dispute resolver.

In the 1960s and 1970s, lawyers serving as neutrals were a fairly new phenomenon, and those of us who did had to struggle for acceptance. Most lawyers and judges then did not even know the difference between mediation and arbitration. Gradually, we caught the attention of a few courts, legislatures and agencies that were brave enough to experiment with alternative processes. Now, primarily as mediators, but possibly as arbitrators or case evaluators, neutral lawyers are likely to be a permanent fixture of the legal landscape.

The increased popularity of this field, however, means that it has attracted a large number of unevenly qualified entrants. As a result, a number of experienced practitioners have become concerned about whether the increased number of persons calling themselves ADR professionals have the necessary training and experience to do the job well. Legislators worry about the dearth of standards to protect the public from inferior services. Legal academics and bar associations question whether mediation or case evaluation constitutes the practice of law and thus, by implication, should be engaged in only by lawyers. Ethicists raise questions about rules — or the lack of all but the most primitive guidelines — and practitioners worry about ensuring the quality of services into the 21st century.

As a result of these often competing pressures, over the next 20 years the field will receive greater emphasis on credentialing, regulation, specialization and commercialization. . . .

In addition to enhanced credibility, one positive effect of specialization is the neutral's ability to ask probing questions and assist in developing sophisticated solutions in disputes in his or her specialized field.

The negative effect is more subtle. Lost may be the freshness, the tendency to question broadly and the lack of attachment to any particular option that a generalist can bring to a particular dispute because of his or her distance and objectivity. There also is the concern that substantive experts' knowledge can overwhelm the parties' ability to make their own choices, a feature that always has been a source of enhanced public confidence in the ADR process. Despite these concerns, retired judges may be the only group of generalists that remains into the next generation. I, for one, would consider such a swing toward specialization a loss.

Another result of a maturing profession is bound to be greater commercialization. As with the legal profession as a whole, some dispute resolution practices are being run like the businesses they have become.

Advertisements and marketing seminars no longer are a rarity. For those of us who consider the profession a calling, this is a difficult adjustment. Although there still remain think tanks and nonprofits that are oriented toward community and public policy conflicts, the dominant mode of professional practice is likely to become a commercial enterprise. We must be on alert that a trend toward commercialization does not detract from the public's and institutions' confidence in the process.

Some lawyer-neutrals increasingly are applying their skills to streams of disputes, rather than to individual cases. Increasingly, our task is to design systems to resolve the multiple conflicts of large organizations and to resolve class actions by separating individual claims from issues of more general applicability and creating claims processes to negotiate mediate and/or arbitrate each claim when needed. . . . Some of us have begun to focus on the issues such processes raise, such as benchmarking, or creating settlement standards, while balancing the goal of efficiency (sometimes needing to resolve thousands of longstanding claims) against the goal of providing access to meaningful processes for people who are one-time players in a system in which everyone else (attorneys, institutional representatives, and mediators) is a repeat player.

From peace in the Middle East and Northern Ireland to huge class actions and the Microsoft Corp.'s antitrust suit, judges and politicians, as well as disputants, are growing ever more ready to consider settlement negotiations assisted by neutrals. This development, together with the teaching of conflict resolution in the schools, should lead to greater public awareness of what we do. . . .

Efficiency remains the value that accounts for much of the interest of advocates, the courts and the general public in our processes. At the same time the values of access, preserving relationships, individualizing processes and solutions, party participation, and the opportunities for us to apply our own creativity are what attracted most of us to neutral lawyering in the first place and what will keep our practices vibrant in the coming years.

Questions

9.   Can lawyers bring value to resolving tensions among peoples of different races, religions, cultures, and genders? What skills or knowledge might be useful before tackling such types of conflicts? Jay Rothman suggests that identity-based conflict is particularly delicate because people draw meaning, safety, and dignity from their identities (Rothman, 1997). Clearly, identity-based conflict is not something "resolved" once and for all with a peace treaty; it requires resources for continued dialogue and community building (Schneider, 2006).

10.   The South African Truth and Reconciliation Commission granted amnesty to certain offenders who acknowledged past crimes and allowed victims to confront their persecutors. If you were designing a post-war restorative justice system, what would your goals be? Would you try to promote accountability, punishment, healing, financial redress, community norm-affirmation, or other goals (Waldman, 2004)?

E.   Transforming the Community

The following excerpts discuss the promising roles lawyers can play in transforming society by serving their clients, profession, and community as peacemaking leaders. President Abraham Lincoln long ago urged his fellow lawyers to be peacemakers, telling them they could do good and still secure enough business if they made litigation the last resort. The first female Attorney General of the United States, Janet Reno, extolled below the value lawyers add to society when they serve as peacemakers and problem solvers in the broader community. Lawyers with ADR knowledge and skills have the ability to foster justice and peace, through their paid work for clients or in their pro bono outreach. From training peer mediators in local schools to designing post-war reconciliation processes, lawyers can work to transform their own communities and build a more peaceful world.

In the 1850s, President Lincoln wrote:

Discourage litigation. Persuade your neighbors to compromise whenever you can. Point out to them how the nominal winner is often a real loser, in fees, expenses, and waste of time. As a peacemaker the lawyer has a superior opportunity of being a good man. There will still be business enough.

One of the authors of this text often quotes this famous advice from President Lincoln during orientation for new law students. The following excerpt about Lincoln's practice of law, written by another of the authors, draws lessons from Lincoln's life and writings for modern lawyers (Stipanowich, 2009b).

A veteran of many years of rough-and-tumble advocacy around frontier Illinois' Eighth Judicial Circuit, Lincoln could be a formidable opponent in the courtroom. Besides having a way with a jury, he was comfortable wielding any and all procedural arguments or technical devices that might avail a client of victory or postpone or ameliorate defeat. His law partner William Herndon asserted that Lincoln was even better in a "set piece battle" before appellate judges, where his intense emphasis on preparation and well-developed logic came to the fore. And yet, time and again, Lincoln discouraged clients from pursuing litigation or strongly cautioned them about the costs and risks of vouchsafing their cause to a judge or jury. One who espoused such great faith in the power of reason and logic and himself exhibited great precision of mind must have keenly discerned the limitations of legal process: crowded circuit court dockets, with court sessions in most counties limited to a few days a year; the difficulties of procuring evidence and witnesses; the unpredictability of local tribunals and juries; and the difficulties of executing on a debt in the face of a determined recalcitrant debtor.

Lincoln was also aware in a very personal way of the reputational cost of being sued. He experienced extreme indignation and anguish when two surviving partners of his father-in-law's business brought what turned out to be an unjustified cause of action against Lincoln for withholding monies due the partnership that he had allegedly collected — in essence charging him with fraud. Furthermore, he lived in a society which depended less upon banks than upon personal credit evidenced by promissory notes, and individuals were accustomed to functioning both as creditors and debtors. In times of economic downturn — including nationwide panics in 1837 and 1857 — many a promissory note would remain unpaid by its due date, and for a variety of reasons the most rational solution for a creditor was usually to make appropriate accommodations rather than seek foreclosure. Lincoln favored such adjustments wherever possible — perhaps calling to mind his own years of toil to repay the obligations of a failed business that he ruefully labeled "the National Debt." In a letter to one Louisville wholesaler who had retained him to collect debts from central Illinois merchants, Lincoln explained, "We have been receiving promises from time to time of the payment of those notes, but which payment has not yet been made. Unless payment is soon made we shall commence suits, though this course we shall regret, for they are honest and honorable men, but they are hard pressed."

Not surprisingly, Lincoln reserved his greatest contempt for those who would "stir up litigation": "A worse man can scarcely be found than one who does this. Who can be more nearly a fiend than he who habitually overhauls the register of deeds in search of defects in titles, whereon to stir up strife, and put money in his pocket. A moral tone ought to be infused into the profession which should drive such men out of it."

While some circumstances and legal processes have changed since Lincoln's time, his admonition to use litigation as a last resort rings true with many judges and experienced advocates today. His moral indignation at lawyers who dishonor the profession by fostering litigation without exploring other options is a reminder to all lawyers that we also have a duty to promote peace and help our communities function more effectively.

❖ **Hon. Janet Reno,** *Promoting Problem Solving and Peacemaking as Enduring Values in Our Society*

19 Alternatives 16 (January 2001)

[T]here is an understandable sense of accomplishment and pride within the dispute resolution community. We have witnessed significant growth in the use of dispute resolution by courts, corporations, government bodies, schools and communities. There is much to celebrate. There is also vast, untapped potential for appropriate dispute resolution in so many aspects of society. There are so many ways that dispute resolution can help to improve society's response to conflict. We must all learn how to be effective dispute resolvers and peacemakers. Indeed, our challenge for the 21st century is to make certain that dispute resolution becomes an enduring, ingrained value that is promoted and endorsed in all aspects of our society.

We begin this task by shedding the notion that "cookie-cutter" justice is sufficient, that one size or one process fits all when we deal with disputes. It is neither possible nor appropriate for the courts to serve as the single mechanism for resolving the many kinds of disputes that arise in this complex, busy age. Instead, we need to establish a range of options and processes to resolve disputes.

[T]he Society of Professionals in Dispute Resolution [has] adopted guidelines for organizations wishing to design integrated conflict management systems. These guidelines emphasize two important points. First, effective integrated systems provide multiple options for addressing conflict, including some processes that are rights based and others that are interest-based. Second, the goal of these systems is to empower people by making them more competent to resolve their own disputes and to offer assistance, rather than decision-making, when direct negotiations are difficult.

I think we need to build on this splendid work by committing ourselves to create an integrated conflict management system for society as a whole. At one end of the spectrum, we must make sure that people have the skills to negotiate disputes one-on-one without intermediaries. In the middle, we need more skilled people to provide an entire spectrum of dispute resolution processes. Here, people can tailor the process to suit the dispute. Finally, we need to ensure that there is adequate access to courts and that our judiciary has the resources to resolve disputes that they are best suited to address. In a sense, this means that we must encourage all elements in our society to identify the best process to resolve their dispute, before moving to the substance of the dispute. This would allow us to be less adversarial at the outset. By using the techniques and skills of the mediator, we can be better listeners, more creative problem solvers and better able to have those difficult conversations with one another. In this manner, we can avoid some disputes and resolve others much earlier.

Our challenge, then, is to engage all sectors of the public in dispute resolution, and to obtain society's recognition that dispute resolution is a necessary life skill at which we should all be proficient, just like math, reading, and spelling. To reach this goal, there are several steps that we must take. First, we must begin with the formal, structured means for resolving conflict in our society, and make sure that the courts have programs to divert those cases into dispute resolution that can and should benefit from facilitated negotiation. We must make the Multidoor Courthouse a reality to ensure appropriate access for all and greater respect for our system of justice.

Second, governments, law firms, and frequent litigants should have programs in place to avoid litigation by using dispute resolution at the earliest possible time. . . . I hope that the efforts now being made by the federal government also will contribute to the growing recognition that dispute resolution is a vital skill every lawyer and senior manager must have.

Third, we need to do more with our law schools to promote problem solving in legal education. Our young lawyers need to be educated to recognize that even if the outcome of litigation is relatively certain, there is not always just one right answer to a problem. Our lawyers need to be educated in how not only to root out the facts of a problem, but to understand the context in which the problem arose. We should work with law schools to encourage curricula that include an expanded approach to traditional casebook study of appellate decisions, exposure to interdisciplinary insights, as well as academic courses and clinics that promote crosscutting skills such as negotiation, mediation, and collaborative practices.

Fourth, the use of these skills should not be limited to a select segment of our society. Our schools should teach our children skills in dispute resolution. Through such training, our children can participate in peer mediation programs and, we hope, carry these skills with them to use through later life. It is my vision that every teacher, every school administrator, and every community police officer who comes in contact with young people will be trained in mediation skills to deal with disputes that involve our youth. It is so exciting to see what is going on in schools all across the country when young people gain insight and confidence into genuine, nonviolent problem solving. It truly makes a difference in their lives.

Fifth, we should make use of dispute resolution concepts in creating community courts where justice is approached from a problem-solving perspective, and all relevant players participate in the resolution of a dispute. At the Midtown Community Court in Manhattan, the building contains not only courtrooms but also a social services center, a community service program with mediators, community probation officers, and other services. Local residents, community prosecutors, businesses, and social service providers collaborate with the criminal justice system to provide swift, visible justice that is augmented by drug treatment, health care, employment counseling, education, and other services. By holding defendants immediately accountable for their crimes while, at the same time, addressing the underlying problems that contribute to crime, we improve the community and free other courts to prosecute more serious crime.

Sixth, we must work hard at developing mechanisms that address the impact of technology in conflict resolution. We are communicating ever so rapidly; our economy is truly global, and the possibilities for new types of disputes have expanded exponentially. We must find ways to use these technologies to resolve conflict and to address those types of conflicts that would not have occurred in an earlier age. Each of these steps represents a formidable undertaking. But we know the way, because substantial progress has been made in every one of these areas. What is needed now is the commitment to see all of this as integrated and effective conflict management for our society, where dispute resolution skills for everyone — participants, neutrals, and bystanders — are valued because of their contribution to the overall health of our institutions, organizations, and communities.

Conclusion

As this final chapter has revealed, the revolution in the management of conflict that inspired the writing of this book continues apace. While the future remains uncertain, it is likely that it will become more important for lawyers to provide their clients with the full benefit of a wide and expanding range of tools for managing and resolving disputes — which requires a thorough appreciation of their appropriate uses as well as their limitations and drawbacks. This is true for attorneys who advise or advocate on behalf of businesses and government institutions as well as those representing domestic partners, employees, or consumers. The authors hope that this volume has provided you with the fundamental understanding of process choices essential to modern law practice. If we have not led you to all of the answers, we hope to have equipped you to ask the right questions.

TABLE OF CASES

Principal cases are indicated by italics.

INDEX